P9-CQD-194

ARCHAEOLOGY

ARCHAEOLOGY

SIXTH EDITION

Robert L. Kelly
UNIVERSITY OF WYOMING

David Hurst Thomas
AMERICAN MUSEUM OF NATURAL HISTORY

WADSWORTH
CENGAGE Learning™

Australia • Brazil • Japan • Korea • Mexico • Singapore • Spain • United Kingdom • United States

Archaeology, Sixth Edition
Robert L. Kelly and David Hurst Thomas

Acquiring Editor: Erin Mitchell

Developmental Editor: Lin Gaylord

Assistant Editor: John Chell

Editorial Assistant: Mallory Ortberg

Media Editor: Melanie Cregger

Program Manager: Tami Strang

Content Project Manager: Cheri Palmer

Design Director: Rob Hugel

Art Director: Caryl Gorska

Print Buyer: Judy Inouye

Rights Acquisitions Specialist: Don Schlotman

Production Service: Melanie Field, Strawberry Field Publishing

Text Designer: Gopa

Photo Researcher: Terri Wright

Text Researcher: Sue Howard

Copy Editor: Margaret C. Tropp

Cover Designer: Riezebos Holzbaur / Brieanna Hattey

Cover Images: *North Entrance to Palace of Knossos,* photo by Walter Bibikow/JAI/Corbis

Male death-mask known as the "Mask of Agamemnon," photo by Vanni/Art Resource

Compositor: PreMediaGlobal

© 2013, 2010 Wadsworth, Cengage Learning

ALL RIGHTS RESERVED. No part of this work covered by the copyright herein may be reproduced, transmitted, stored, or used in any form or by any means graphic, electronic, or mechanical, including but not limited to photocopying, recording, scanning, digitizing, taping, Web distribution, information networks, or information storage and retrieval systems, except as permitted under Section 107 or 108 of the 1976 United States Copyright Act, without the prior written permission of the publisher.

Unless otherwise noted, all content is © Cengage Learning 2013.

For product information and technology assistance, contact us at
Cengage Learning Customer & Sales Support, 1-800-354-9706

For permission to use material from this text or product, submit all requests online at **cengage.com/permissions**. Further permissions questions can be emailed to **permissionrequest@cengage.com**.

Library of Congress Control Number: 2011929146

ISBN-13: 978-1-111-82999-5

ISBN-10: 1-111-82999-3

Wadsworth
20 Davis Drive
Belmont, CA 94002-3098
USA

Cengage Learning is a leading provider of customized learning solutions with office locations around the globe, including Singapore, the United Kingdom, Australia, Mexico, Brazil, and Japan. Locate your local office at **www.cengage.com/global**.

Cengage Learning products are represented in Canada by Nelson Education, Ltd.

To learn more about Wadsworth, visit **www.cengage.com/wadsworth**.

Purchase any of our products at your local college store or at our preferred online store **www.cengagebrain.com**.

Printed in the United States of America
1 2 3 4 5 6 7 15 14 13 12 11

For Matt and Dycus, for their love of big piles of dirt.

—R.L.K.

For LSAP(T), colleague, companion, advocate, and mother of my son.

And, most significantly, still my very best friend.

—D.H.T.

BRIEF CONTENTS

CONTENTS

CHAPTER 4   DOING FIELDWORK: WHY ARCHAEOLOGISTS DIG SQUARE HOLES 75

CHAPTER 7   THE DIMENSIONS OF ARCHAEOLOGY: TIME, SPACE, AND FORM

CHAPTER 8   TAPHONOMY, EXPERIMENTAL ARCHAEOLOGY, AND ETHNOARCHAEOLOGY

CHAPTER 10   BIOARCHAEOLOGICAL APPROACHES TO THE PAST........ 227

CHAPTER 11   RECONSTRUCTING SOCIAL AND POLITICAL SYSTEMS OF THE PAST.................................... 249

CHAPTER 12 THE ARCHAEOLOGY OF THE MIND 277

FEATURE CONTENTS

LOOKING CLOSER

IN HIS/HER OWN WORDS

PROFILE OF AN ARCHAEOLOGIST

WHAT DOES IT MEAN TO ME?

PREFACE

ARCHAEOLOGY, Sixth Edition, is a user-friendly introduction to archaeology: what it is, who does it, and why we should care about it. This text addresses archaeological methods and theory, yet it departs in some important ways from the standard introductory textbook.

Students tell us that they sometimes don't bother reading the introductory textbooks they've purchased—whether the books are about archaeology, chemistry, or whatever. We've heard several reasons for this paradox: The instructor covers exactly the same material, using the same examples as the text—so why bother reading what you can get condensed in a lecture? Or their textbooks are deadly dull, written in arcane academic jargon that no one can enjoy reading. Still others tell us that they take an archaeology course just because it sounds like a fun way to fulfill a distribution requirement—but the text actually has nothing to say to them.

We want students to know that we've heard them.

PERSONAL EXAMPLES, HIGH-INTEREST TOPICS

In most archaeology texts, the approach is fairly encyclopedic and dispassionate. But we can't do it that way. To be sure, modern archaeology is a specialized and complicated academic discipline, with plenty of concepts, several bodies of theory, and a huge array of analytical methods—all things we'd like students to learn about. But we think that the best way for students to begin to understand archaeology (or any subject, for that matter) is through a few well-chosen, extended, personalized examples—stories that show how archaeologists have worked through actual problems in the field and in the lab. So that's the approach we take here.

Writing a textbook is not easy. We must provide a solid foundation for students who intend to become professional archaeologists. This requires a thorough review of the discipline, including all its major concepts and jargon. But we must also write for the many students who will *not* become professional archaeologists.

Accordingly, we picked many of the book's topics with these students in mind.

As it turns out, these are the very subjects that the budding career archaeologist should know. We don't shy away from some controversial subjects—in fact, the text begins with one in its Introduction—that touch upon sensitive issues that influence both the professional archaeologist and the public. Many archaeology texts avoid these sensitive issues, such as the excavation of the dead or what archaeology has to say about climate change. But we think that these are precisely the issues that matter most to students and to instructors, so we've not backed away from them.

In fact, instructors tell us they have used previous editions of this text precisely because their students will actually *read* it.

ABOUT THIS EDITION

The first edition of *Archaeology,* authored by Thomas, was published back in 1979, and each succeeding edition focused on retaining the coverage and writing style that users praised and ensuring that the book reflected up-to-the-minute changes in the discipline. By the time the fourth edition rolled around, David Thomas decided one person just couldn't adequately cover the field anymore, and he invited Robert Kelly to join in the project. The two first met more than 30 years ago, when Thomas was excavating Gatecliff Shelter in Nevada and Kelly was a gangly, enthusiastic high school kid. When the time came to expand the authorship, Thomas turned to Kelly as a coauthor. This partnership continues with the present sixth edition. We've further streamlined this edition, keeping the same number of chapters, but removing some material from a few that seemed too long. We've continued to update the examples, especially in the areas of remote sensing and genetic analyses, and the photos and graphics for a better visual presentation that enables students to see more clearly the key points of a concept or example.

Aids to Learning, Old and New

What Does It Mean to Me? Throughout the text, we address issues about archaeology that should resonate with students, such as buying artifacts from online auction houses, climate change, human alteration of the environment, and the excavation of human burials. We think that students will find these topics thought provoking (and these sidebars could easily form the basis of writing assignments or group discussions).

Looking Closer A popular feature from earlier editions, these sidebars cover ancillary topics in each chapter. In addition, some seek to be helpful to the budding archaeologist, suggesting equipment students will need for survey and excavation, or what courses they might take. Others look at the lighter side of archaeology, such as how sites get their names, or give personal glimpses into fieldwork—what it's like to do survey or ethnoarchaeology.

In His/Her Own Words In several places we found that others told their own first-person stories better than we could, so we've included their words to help personalize the text.

Profile of an Archaeologist We've kept these five sidebars from the fifth edition to emphasize the diversity of today's working archaeologists and to illustrate the varied ways in which archaeologists make a living.

To help students master this complex, fascinating discipline, we include a running glossary in each chapter (with glossary terms defined at the bottom of the page on which the term is introduced) plus an alphabetized Glossary at the end of the text. In addition, in the sixth edition we have included with each chapter's preview several questions that students should be thinking about while reading. At the end of each chapter, we've provided brief answers to those questions to help students review the chapter's key points. We have also retained and updated the chapter-by-chapter Bibliography that provides an easy way to find references and additional reading on each chapter's subjects. We have eschewed placing citations in the text, but students will still be able to locate material discussed in each chapter, as well as additional readings, in the chapter's bibliography. Page references for the few longer quotes that appear are noted in the relevant bibliographic entry.

A DISTINCTIVE APPROACH

The following strategies all contribute to a fuller, more up-to-date exploration of the field.

Discussions of Archaeological Objects in Context You'll notice that we eschew an encyclopedic approach, which tends to encourage students to simply memorize a laundry list of techniques without context. Instead, we've embedded and contextualized discussions of things like stone tools and ceramics in substantive examples. For example, we talk about pottery—its manufacture and basic constituents—in Chapter 11, which deals with using petrographic analysis to track down trade networks. This presentation ensures that students learn about these basic archaeological objects in ways that carry significance for them—so that they see why, for instance, it might be useful to know where a sherd's temper comes from.

Balanced Coverage: Depth, Breadth, Theory The text is not encyclopedic, but it does cover the field in a comprehensive manner. Given the background knowledge that a first- or second-year college student brings to an introductory course, this text strikes a balance among the different directions that archaeologists take. While this text is one of the most readable available, it is not dumbed down, and places the thought process of archaeology in a wider field. Students learn about science and challenges to it, the Enlightenment, and evolutionary thought.

Expanded Geographic Coverage Many of the examples used in this text are drawn from the archaeology of western North America. Between us, we've spent nearly eight decades working there and, frankly, it's what we know best. But we've continued the expanded geographic coverage of the fifth edition, drawing upon work in the eastern United States, Central and South America, Egypt and the Near East, Madagascar, France, Australia, Micronesia, and other places. Although the text is focused, it is not provincial—and should inspire classroom discussions of research projects from around the world.

All in all, we think you'll find this text is one that both instructors and students will appreciate.

ORGANIZATION OF THE TEXT

We constructed this text so that various ideas build upon one another. We know that each archaeologist teaches his or her introductory course differently, but you should know that many chapters cross-reference material discussed in other chapters. We note each instance within the text.

The text begins with an Introduction that focuses on the Kennewick Man case—a purposeful selection because it shows both the potential of what archaeology can learn about the past and the ethical issues that confront archaeology in doing so.

Chapter 1 addresses the history of archaeology, with an emphasis on several individual archaeologists who have defined the field. In Chapter 2, we relate archaeology to the rest of anthropology and wrestle with the two major theoretical paradigms of contemporary archaeology. We discuss the intellectual process of archaeology in terms of low-, middle-, and high-level theory. This somewhat simplified presentation provides an entry into the diversity of contemporary archaeology. And rather than come down on the side of processual or postprocessual archaeology, we take a centrist position that we believe characterizes the majority of working archaeologists today.

Chapters 3 and 4 provide the nuts and bolts of archaeology, explaining how archaeologists go about doing surface survey, using remote sensing equipment, and excavating sites. In these chapters we try to give students some sense of how much fun fieldwork can be.

Chapter 5 covers geoarchaeology, emphasizing formation processes, but also archaeological stratigraphy, showing students how a site's stratigraphy can be "read" to provide a context for the artifacts contained there. Chapter 6 covers dating methods used in prehistoric and historic archaeology. The range of dating technology increases annually, and we had to make some tough choices about what to include. The major purpose of this chapter is not to write an encyclopedia of available methods, but to provide enough information about key techniques so that students can relate dating technology to ancient human behavior. Chapter 7 discusses various archaeological concepts—types, cultures, and phases—that help construct large-scale patterns in space and time. Our goal is to help the student see the world as an archaeologist views it, as an ever-changing spatial and temporal mosaic of material culture.

Chapters 8 through 12 show how archaeologists go about breathing some anthropological life into this spatial and temporal mosaic—how we infer human behavior from material remains. Chapter 8 covers middle-level theory—how it differs from standard analogy and how archaeologists construct it through taphonomic, experimental, and ethnoarchaeological research. Our goal here is to convince students that archaeologists don't just make stuff up, but instead give plenty of thought to how they infer ancient behavior from material objects and their contexts. Chapter 9 recounts how archaeologists reconstruct diet from faunal and floral remains and even how they can infer

symbolic meanings attributed to the natural world by ancient peoples. In Chapter 10 we consider what we can learn—about diet, disease, and workload—from human skeletal remains; this chapter also explores the field of molecular archaeology. Chapter 11 shows how archaeologists reconstruct social and political systems of the past and looks at gender, kinship, and social hierarchies. Chapter 12 presents how archaeologists address the symbolic meanings once attached to material remains; here, we look at the nature of symbols and what archaeologists can realistically hope to learn about them.

After describing (and rejecting) evolutionary unilineal thinking, Chapter 13 addresses two major transitions in human history: the origins of agriculture and the origins of the state. Chapter 14 explores historical archaeology, especially those aspects that set the field apart from prehistoric archaeology—the ability to uncover "hidden history," to provide a forensic analysis of historical events, and to present alternative perspectives on written history. Chapter 15 examines the legal structure of modern archaeology, emphasizing the field of cultural resource management (how it came to be and the critical role it plays in archaeology today). This chapter also covers international laws on antiquities and the subjects of reburial and repatriation in some detail. Finally, Chapter 16 looks at the future of archaeology, especially the ways in which archaeologists apply their knowledge to contemporary problems. We conclude by discussing the increased involvement of indigenous peoples in the archaeology of themselves and asking whether we are on the brink of another revolution—one that might produce a newer "new" archaeology.

SUPPLEMENTAL MATERIALS

This text also comes with a strong supplements program to help instructors use their class time most effectively and to aid students in mastering the material. (Each item is followed by its ISBN number.)

Online Instructor's Manual with Test Bank (9781111940768):

The instructor's manual offers chapter outlines, learning objectives, key terms and concepts, and lecture suggestions. The test bank consists of 40–60 test questions per chapter, including multiple-choice, true/false, and essay questions.

Doing Fieldwork: Archaeological Demonstrations CD-ROM, Version 2.0 (9780495604242):

Granted that students can learn field techniques only from actually participating, this CD shows professional archaeologists involved in various digs (many of which are referenced in the text), illustrates field techniques, gives students perspective about what they're learning, reinforces concepts and techniques through live examples, and encourages students to participate in a dig themselves. The presentation is organized by the main techniques that one uses on a dig. Users are taken through each step automatically or can navigate to any point via the navigation bar. Students review illustrations and video clips of each technique. After reviewing a step in the dig process, students are taken to "Check points," which are concept questions about each step of the dig. Students can see the answers, receive their score, and e-mail the score to the instructor.

PowerLecture™ *with ExamView*® *for Archaeology,* Sixth Edition (9781111987718):
A complete all-in-one reference for instructors, the PowerLecture CD contains Microsoft® PowerPoint® slides of images from the text, zoomable art, image library, PowerPoint lecture slides that outline the main points of each chapter, Microsoft® Word files of the Test Bank and Instructor's Manual, and ExamView testing software that allows instructors to create, deliver, and customize tests and study guides (both print and online) in minutes.

Anthropology CourseMate (www.cengagebrain.com): Cengage Learning's Anthropology CourseMate brings course concepts to life with interactive learning, study, and exam preparation tools that support the printed textbook. Watch student comprehension soar as your class works with the printed textbook and the textbook-specific website. Anthropology CourseMate goes beyond the book to deliver what you need!

Anthropology WebTutor™ *with ebook for Blackboard*® *and WebCT*®:
Jumpstart your course with customizable, rich, text-specific content within your Course Management System.

▶ Jumpstart – Simply load a WebTutor cartridge into your Course Management System.
▶ Customizable – Easily blend, add, edit, reorganize, or delete content.
▶ Content – Rich, text-specific content, media assets, quizzing, web links, discussion topics, interactive games and exercises, and more.

Case Studies in Archaeology, edited by Jeffrey Quilter: Enrich your students' study of archaeology with the many contemporary case studies in this acclaimed series. Students will learn how archaeologists study human behavior through analysis of material remains. They will learn about new interpretations and developments within the field—and the importance of the archaeological perspective in understanding how the past informs our experience of the present. These engaging accounts of cutting-edge archaeological techniques, issues, and solutions—as well as studies discussing the collection of material remains—range from site-specific excavations to types of archaeology practiced. Visit www.cengage.com/anthropology and see "Anthropology and Archaeology Case Studies" for complete information on all case study titles available.

WHO HELPED OUT?

Despite the personal flavor of these pages, this text was created by more than four hands. Many people helped out, and we'd like to thank them here.

The overall presentation was vastly improved by a contingent of top-notch colleagues and friends who provided advice and critical reviews of the manuscript. We are particularly grateful to several anonymous reviewers who provided comments on the fifth edition. We are most grateful for their advice and suggestions.

Paul E. Langenwalter II (Biola University)
Elizabeth A. Mancz (University of Akron)
Kenneth W. Mohney (Monroe County Community College)
Elizabeth L. Pintar (Austin Community College)

Many others commented on portions of chapters or entire chapters, answered questions, provided photographs or text for sidebars, and checked facts for us. We gratefully acknowledge timely and sometimes detailed assistance on this and previous editions from

Anna Agbe-Davies (University of North Carolina)
David Anderson (University of Tennessee)
Roger Anyon (Pima County, Arizona)
Bettina Arnold (University of Wisconsin, Milwaukee)
George Bagwell (Colorado Mountain College)
Doug Bamforth (University of Colorado)
Pat Barker (retired)
Ofer Bar-Yosef (Harvard University)
Mary C. Beaudry (Boston University)
Jeffrey Behm (University of Wisconsin, Oshkosh)
The late Lewis Binford
Michael Blakey (College of William and Mary)
Colonel Matthew Bogdanos (U.S. Marine Corps)
Charles A. Bollong (University of Arizona)

The late Rob Bonnichsen

Bruce Bradley (Exeter University, UK)

Steven Brandt (University of Florida)

Robert Brooks (Oklahoma State Archaeologist)

Peter Brosius (University of Georgia)

Jack Broughton (University of Utah)

Margaret Sabom Bruchz (Blinn College)

Jane Buikstra (Arizona State University)

Richard Burger (Yale University)

Virginia Butler (Portland State University)

Catherine Cameron (University of Colorado)

Robert Carneiro (American Museum of Natural History)

Philip J. Carr (University of South Alabama)

Beverly Chiarulli (Indiana University of Pennsylvania)

Cheryl Claassen (Appalachian State University)

C. William Clewlow (Ancient Enterprises)

Margaret Conkey (University of California, Berkeley)

John Cornelison (National Park Service)

The late Don Crabtree

George Crothers (University of Kentucky)

Jay Custer (University of Delaware)

Hester Davis (formerly Arkansas State Archaeologist)

William Davis (formerly University of California, Davis)

Kathleen Deagan (Florida State Museum of Natural History)

Jeffrey Dean (University of Arizona)

Rob DeSalle (American Museum of Natural History)

Christophe Descantes (University of Missouri)

Phil DiBlasi (University of Louisville)

William Dickinson (University of Arizona)

Tom Dillehay (Vanderbilt University)

Diana DiZerega-Wall (City College of New York)

William Doelle (Desert Archaeology, Inc.)

Kurt Dongoske (Zuni Cultural Resource Enterprises)

Sam Drucker (Bureau of Land Management, Wyoming)

Robert Elston (retired)

James Enloe (University of Iowa)

Clark Erickson (University of Pennsylvania)

George Esber (Miami University)

T. J. Ferguson (Anthropological Research, Tucson)

Terry Fifield (U.S. Forest Service, Alaska)

Ben Fitzhugh (University of Washington)

Kent V. Flannery (University of Michigan)

Don Fowler (formerly University of Nevada, Reno)

Anne Fox (University of Texas, San Antonio)

Richard Fox (formerly University of South Dakota)

Julie Francis (Wyoming Department of Transportation)

George Frison (University of Wyoming)

Robert Gargett (San Jose State University)

Ervan Garrison (University of Georgia)

Joan Gero (American University)

Diane Gifford-Gonzalez (University of California, Santa Cruz)

Dean Goodman (University of Miami, Japan Division)

Martha Graham (TRC Solutions, Albuquerque)

Donald K. Grayson (University of Washington)

David Grimaldi (American Museum of Natural History)

Donny Hamilton (Texas A&M University)

The late Marvin Harris

Charles Hastings (Central Michigan University)

Christine Hastorf (University of California, Berkeley)

Eugene Hattori (Nevada State Museum)

William Haviland (University of Vermont)

Brian Hayden (Simon Fraser University)

Michelle Hegmon (Arizona State University)

Kim Hill (Arizona State University)

Matthew G. Hill (Iowa State University)

Robert Hitchcock (Michigan State University)

Richard Holmer (Idaho State University)

Andrea A. Hunter (Northern Arizona University)

Tony Hynes (Danville Area Community College)

The late Cynthia Irwin-Williams

Steve Jackson (University of Wyoming)

Gregory Johnson (Hunter College of CUNY)

Kevin Johnston (Ohio State University)

Rosemary Joyce (University of California, Berkeley)

John Kantner (School of Advanced Research)

Barry D. Kass (Orange County Community College, SUNY)

William Kelso (Jamestown Rediscovery Archaeological Project)

Thomas King (National Park Service)

Keith Kintigh (Arizona State University)

Vernon James Knight, Jr. (University of Alabama)

Clea Koff (independent scholar)

Stephen Kowalewski (University of Georgia)

Steve Kuhn (University of Arizona)

Chapurukha Kusimba (Field Museum, Chicago)

The late Charles Lange

Clark Spencer Larsen (Ohio State University)

Mark Leone (University of Maryland)

Janet Levy (University of North Carolina, Charlotte)

Barry Lewis (University of Illinois, Champaign–Urbana)

David Lewis-Williams (University of Witwatersrand)

William Lipe (Washington State University)

Dorothy Lippert (Smithsonian Institution)

Sharon Long (Wyoming State Historic Preservation Office)

Diana Loren (Peabody Museum, Harvard)

Karen Lupo (Washington State University)

The late Scotty MacNeish

David B. Madsen (retired)
Joyce Marcus (University of Michigan)
Fiona Marshall (Washington University)
Patrick E. Martin (Michigan Technological University)
Patricia McAnany (University of North Carolina)
Heather McInnis (University of Oregon)
Heather McKillop (Louisiana State University)
Justine McKnight (independent archaeobotanical consultant)
Frank McManamon (National Park Service)
Shannon McPherron (Max Planck Institute, Germany)
David J. Meltzer (Southern Methodist University)
George Miller (California State University, Hayward)
Barbara Mills (University of Arizona)
Paul Minnis (University of Oklahoma)
Paula Molloy (National Park Service)
The late Craig Morris
Juliet E. Morrow (Arkansas State University)
Cheryl Munson (Indiana University)
Melissa Murphy (University of Wyoming)
Fraser Neiman (Monticello Archaeology Program)
Margaret Nelson (University of Arizona)
Michael J. O'Brien (University of Missouri)
James O'Connell (University of Utah)
John Olsen (University of Arizona)
Tim Pauketat (University of Illinois)
Christopher Peebles (University of Indiana)
Stephen Plog (University of Virginia)
Robert Preucel (University of Pennsylvania)
William Rathje (Stanford University)
Elizabeth Reitz (University of Georgia)
David Rhode (Desert Research Institute)
John Rick (Stanford University)
Anibal Rodriguez (American Museum of Natural History)
Nan Rothschild (Columbia University)
Irwin Rovner (North Carolina State University)
Ralph Rowlett (University of Missouri)
Ken Sassaman (University of Florida)
Verne Scarborough (University of Cincinnati)
Michael Schiffer (University of Arizona)
Enid Schildkrout (American Museum of Natural History)
Lynne Sebastian (SRI Foundation)
Payson Sheets (University of Colorado)
Stephen Silliman (University of Massachusetts, Boston)
Steve Simms (Utah State University)
Theresa Singleton (Syracuse University)
Jeff Sommer (University of Michigan)

Stanley South (University of South Carolina)
Charles Spencer (American Museum of Natural History)
Charles Stanish (University of California, Los Angeles)
Amy Steffian (Alutiiq Museum)
Vin Steponaitis (University of North Carolina)
Simon Stoddart (Cambridge University)
Elizabeth Stone (State University of New York, Stonybrook)
Todd Surovell (University of Wyoming)
The late William Tallbull
Ian Tattersall (American Museum of Natural History)
Anya Taylor (John Jay College of CUNY)
Mark Taylor (Manhattan College)
The late W. W. Taylor
Lawrence Todd (retired)
The late Bruce Trigger
Ruth Tringham (University of California, Berkeley)
Bram Tucker (University of Georgia)
Donald Tuohy (retired)
Christy Turner (Arizona State University)
Mary Vermilion (St. Louis University)
Nicole Waguespack (University of Wyoming)
Danny Walker (Wyoming State Archaeologist Office)
Mike Waters (Texas A&M University)
Patty Jo Watson (Washington University)
Gloria Cranmer Webster (U'mista Cultural Center)
Kathryn Weedman (University of South Florida)
John Weymouth (University of Nebraska)
The late Joe Ben Wheat
Mary Whelan (University of Iowa)
Nancy Wilkie (Carleton University)
Chip Wills (University of New Mexico)
Al Woods (Florida Museum of Natural History)
James Woods (College of Southern Idaho)
John Yellen (National Science Foundation)
Amy Young (University of Southern Mississippi)

Each contributed worthwhile suggestions, which we often followed. We alone, however, are responsible for any errors of commission or omission.

Thomas also wishes to thank others in the American Museum of Natural History, especially Lorann S. A. Pendleton, Matt Sanger, Anna Semon, and Molly Trauten, each of whom cheerfully helped out with dozens of details, as well as Ginessa Mahar, Elliot Blair, and Diana Rosenthal.

Kelly is grateful to his colleagues at the University of Wyoming, many of whom supplied photographs, answered innumerable questions about archaeological and anthropological trivia, and generally provided support. He is especially grateful to Lin Poyer and her unbounded patience and thoughtfulness.

We are also grateful to the crew at Wadsworth: Acquiring Sponsoring Editor Erin Mitchell, Content Project Manager Cheri Palmer, Associate Media Editor Melanie Cregger, Assistant Editor John Chell, Editorial Assistant Mallory Ortberg, and Program Manager Tami Strang. We thank the production team: production editor Melanie Field of Strawberry Field Publishing, copy editor Peggy Tropp, and photo researcher Terri Wright. We also gratefully acknowledge Dennis O'Brien, who created many of the illustrations used in this edition, as well as the contributions of the illustrators Diana Salles and the late Nicholas Amorosi, both of the American Museum of Natural History.

KEEPING IN TOUCH WITH YOUR AUTHORS

We see this textbook as an opportunity to become more available to both instructors and students. With e-mail, we can all have casual conversations with people around the globe, in more or less real time. We want to know what you think about this text and about archaeology—what you like and what you don't care for—so we can improve future editions. We encourage you to write us at the e-mail addresses below. Provided that we're not off on some remote dig

somewhere, we'll get back to you right away. Drop us a line—we'd enjoy hearing from you.

R. L. K.   D. H. T.
Laramie, Wyoming   New York, New York
RLKELLY@uwyo.edu   thomasd@amnh.org
                           July 2011

A Note about Human Remains

In several instances, this book discusses important new frontiers of bioarchaeological research. But we also recognize the need to deal with human remains in a respectful and sensitive manner. Several Native American elders have requested that we refrain from publishing photographs or other depictions of American Indian human remains. Although we know that not all Native Americans feel this way, no images of Native American skeletal remains appear in this book. Should other groups express similar concerns, their requests will be addressed in succeeding editions as appropriate.

About the Petroglyphs

Sidebars used throughout this text are highlighted with several rock art symbols. To the best of our knowledge, they do not infringe on anyone's intellectual property rights. They are not intended to suggest a cultural or religious connotation.

ABOUT THE AUTHORS

© Matt Stirn

ROBERT KELLY began collecting arrowheads in farmers' fields when he was 10 years old and has participated in archaeological research since 1973 when he was a high school sophomore. He has worked on excavations in North and South America and conducted ethnographic research in Madagascar. He is currently conducting research into the paleoindian archaeology of Wyoming's Bighorn Mountains. A former president of the Society for American Archaeology and a past secretary of the Archaeology Division of the American Anthropological Association, Kelly has published more than 100 articles and books, including the 1996 Choice Magazine Outstanding Academic Book *The Foraging Spectrum: Diversity in Hunting and Gathering Societies.* He has been a professor of anthropology at the University of Wyoming since 1997.

DAVID THOMAS has served since 1972 as Curator of Anthropology at the American Museum of Natural History in New York City. A specialist in Native American archaeology, Thomas discovered both Gatecliff Shelter (Nevada) and the lost sixteenth/seventeenth-century Franciscan mission Santa Catalina de Guale on St. Catherines Island, Georgia. Since 1998, he has led the excavation of Mission San Marcos near Santa Fe, New Mexico. A founding trustee of the National Museum of the American Indian at the Smithsonian since 1989, he has published extensively, including 100 papers and 30 books—most recently, the best-selling *Skull Wars: Kennewick Man, Archaeology, and the Battle for Native American Identity.* As an archaeologist, Thomas likes "old stuff," including his 1961 Corvette, his 120-year-old house, and the Oakland Raiders.

INTRODUCTION

JULY 1996: The two college students never intended to make a federal case out of the day's fun. They never meant to rock the ethical foundations of American archaeology, either. All they wanted was to see hydroplane boat races for free.

The month of July in the city of Kennewick (Washington) is a series of festivals topped off by hydroplane races on the Columbia River. To avoid paying admission to the races, two young men snuck through a brushy area of riverbank where they could get a good view, even if it meant getting wet. Trudging along the river's edge, they spied a smooth white object. One of them picked it up and jokingly pronounced it a skull. Imagine his surprise when he saw two dark eye sockets staring back at him. It *was* a skull.

After the races, the students reported their find to police, who called in the coroner to see if the remains were those of a murder victim. The coroner eventually called in archaeologist James Chatters. Although there was no evidence of a burial pit, the skull's near-pristine condition suggested that it had eroded from the riverside only days earlier; in fact, Chatters eventually found much of the skeleton in the shallow water.

WHO WAS "KENNEWICK MAN"?

The analyses that followed showed that the individual was male and roughly 45 years old when he died. He stood about 5 feet 9 inches tall. Laboratory analysis showed that two-thirds of his protein probably came from fish and that he ate limited amounts of starchy foods. In his time, the man might have been considered healthy, but today we would call him a "survivor." He suffered from severe disease or malnutrition when he was about 5 years old. He had minor arthritis in his knees, elbows, lower back, and neck from a lifetime of daily, intense physical activity. As a young adult, he had damaged the nerves to his left arm. He'd also suffered a serious chest injury, a blow to the head, and an injury to his right arm and shoulder in his youth. And,

as if that weren't enough, he had a stone spear point embedded in his hip. He had survived this injury, too.

Chatters knew that spear points like the one in the skeleton's hip were manufactured thousands of years ago, but he was still surprised when a radiocarbon date indicated that the man had died 9400 years ago. "Kennewick Man" was one of the oldest human skeletons ever found in the Americas.

Even more intriguing was that the skull did not look like other Native American skulls; some people even thought it might be European! It's not, but that suggestion titillated the media, which created sensationalist stories of how Europeans, rather than the ancestors of American Indians, first colonized the Americas. One group, the Asatru Folk Assembly, which says it practices an ancient Celtic religion, even claimed that Kennewick Man was their ancestor.

WHO CONTROLS HUMAN REMAINS?

Many laws govern archaeology in the United States (we'll examine some of these in Chapter 15). One such law, the 1990 Native American Graves Protection and Repatriation Act (NAGPRA), provides for the repatriation of Native American human remains to their culturally affiliated tribes. Several tribes from the Kennewick area claimed the new find to be their ancestor and requested that the remains be turned over to them under this law. Kennewick Man had been discovered on lands administered by the U.S. Army Corps of Engineers, and that agency quickly agreed to halt all scientific studies and return the skeleton to the tribes.

But a group of eight archaeologists and biological anthropologists filed a lawsuit, arguing that handing over the remains would actually violate NAGPRA—because, they argued, the skeleton was not affiliated with the modern tribes, it might not be Native American, and doing so would violate their First Amendment rights.

Eventually, the Ninth District Circuit Court heard the case, which presented the judge with uncharted legal waters: Was this 9400-year-old man a Native American or not? And if so, was he culturally affiliated with the modern tribes who claimed him as an ancestor? These are tough questions, both legally and scientifically. And the answers could potentially change forever the direction of American archaeology.

Five years after the boys found the skull, the judge ruled that Kennewick Man was not Native American. And even if he were, the judge ruled, the bones could not be culturally affiliated with any modern tribe. In February 2004, the appeals court upheld the district court's ruling: Kennewick, the courts said, is not Native American.

WHAT DOES IT MEAN TO YOU?

The Kennewick decision shows two facets of archaeology. It shows how much archaeologists can reconstruct about the past from remarkably limited material remains. We know what Kennewick Man ate, when he died, how old he was, what his life was like. But Kennewick also shows the difficult ethical issues that confront archaeology: What gives archaeologists the right to study the dead? Who owns the past, anyway? And who gets to decide? This is also what archaeologists do: They make difficult ethical and moral decisions about the past (and the present).

These sorts of questions should matter to you. Archaeologists often say that we study the past in order to help chart the future. But Kennewick points to a dilemma buried in this aphorism. By claiming the skeletal remains as their own, the Indian tribes asserted that scientists should conduct no studies. The tribes believed that they already knew their past and resented attempts by non-Indians to probe the remains of their ancestors. Although not all Native Americans agree with this position, many do, and this dispute underscores the important point that archaeology is not just about the dead; it is also about the living—you. How can we "study the past to create a better tomorrow" if scientific study is curtailed? Yet how can we pursue this laudable goal if the very act of conducting research offends the living descendants of the ancient people being studied? Archaeologists have to deal with these difficult ethical issues.

We don't expect every reader of this book to become a professional archaeologist. Many of you are probably taking this course to fulfill a distributional requirement, and because archaeology interests you. But throughout this text we will demonstrate that *the past matters to you*. We will do this through text boxes labeled, appropriately enough, "What Does It Mean to Me?" Sometimes these ask you to confront ethical issues, such as the excavation of burials or the buying and selling of artifacts. And sometimes they show you how knowledge of the past is crucial to planning for the future. After we learn something more about the practice of archaeology, we will return to the case of Kennewick Man to explore its implications for the future of archaeology.

ARCHAEOLOGY

1 MEET SOME REAL ARCHAEOLOGISTS

LEARNING OBJECTIVES

AFTER READING THIS CHAPTER YOU SHOULD BE ABLE TO ANSWER THESE QUESTIONS:

1. What makes an archaeologist an archaeologist?

2. Why is the study of the past controversial?

3. How was the rise of archaeology connected to the discovery of humanity's "deep" antiquity?

4. Who were the antiquarians, and why include them in a history of archaeology?

5. What trends have characterized archaeology over the last century?

Christie's Images/CORBIS

"Excavation of the Sphinx" by Ernst Koerner, 1883. The Sphinx was built about 2500 BC and is the largest monolith statue in the world. It was not fully excavated until 1936.

PREVIEW

 **THIS BOOK IS** about what archaeologists want to learn, how they go about learning it, and what they do with that knowledge. These tasks require archaeologists to piece together a picture of the past from scraps of bone, rock, pottery, architecture, and other remains that are hundreds, thousands, or tens of thousands of years old. To further complicate this already difficult process, the very nature of archaeology carries with it some serious ethical dilemmas.

In this book, we will also look at some of the different perspectives that characterize today's archaeology. Sometimes these approaches coexist; sometimes they clash. As we discuss these various archaeological perspectives, you should keep a couple of things in mind: First, no archaeologist fits perfectly into any of these named categories, and second, there is more than one way to do good archaeology.

 DOING FIELDWORK CD-ROM:
ARCHAEOLOGICAL DEMONSTRATIONS 2.0

See the "What Is the Question?" section of the CD-ROM to learn about topics covered in this chapter.

INTRODUCTION

Who is an archaeologist? Is it Indiana Jones, fighting Nazis and grabbing gold statues from curse-laden catacombs? Is it Laura Croft, battling all manner of beasts to retrieve some ancient treasure that holds the secret of time? Sydney Fox on *Relic Hunter*? Or is it Josh Bernstein or Hunter Ellis, on the History Channel program *Digging for the Truth*?

Of course, these are not real archaeologists. The media play up the physically thrilling side of archaeology, the mystery of discovery and the potential threats. Archaeology is indeed exciting, even if we don't do our research with whips and guns, have a camera crew trailing behind us, or battle ancient beasts. Closer to the mark is *Time Team America*, the recent science reality series on PBS that sends archaeologists on a race against time to excavate historic sites around the nation. But even with urgency, we certainly don't just grab the good stuff and dash out of the temple. We work with notebooks and pencils, measuring tapes, calipers, graph paper, and some high-tech tools like laser transits and proton magnetometers (more on those in later chapters). We document everything we find—*everything*—with a precision that we admit is often mind-numbing. But the results can be equally mind-blowing. We can extract blood from stone tools. We can determine the age of remains that are millions of years old. We can reconstruct ancient social and political organizations. We can analyze skeletal remains to tell if a person ate much plant food or meat. This kind of work takes years of careful, precise analysis. But from it comes an understanding of a realm of humanity that otherwise would remain lost to us, the realm of the past. While archaeological field research is exciting, the knowledge that comes from fieldwork provides the reason we do archaeology.

We think that the best way to introduce you to archaeology is through its history. Archaeology is a young field that has changed dramatically over the past century. As a relatively young discipline, archaeology is still experiencing some growing pains. What does not change, however, is that archaeology is about ancient objects—the **artifacts** we retrieve from sites are the primary source of our information. To borrow a phrase from archaeologist-philosopher Alison Wylie (University of Washington), archaeologists "think from things." The history of archaeology

artifact Any movable object that has been used, modified, or manufactured by humans; artifacts include stone, bone, and metal tools; beads and other ornaments; pottery; artwork; religious and sacred items.

LOOKING CLOSER

AD/BC/BP ... ARCHAEOLOGY'S ALPHABET SOUP

In anything written by archaeologists, you'll encounter a blizzard of acronyms that refer to age. Let's clear the air with some concise definitions of the most common abbreviations:

BC ("before Christ"): For instance, 3200 BC; note that the letters follow the date.

AD ("anno Domini"): Meaning "in the year of the Lord," indicates a year that falls within the Christian era (that is, after the birth of Christ). Given the English translation of the phrase, archaeologists place the "AD" before the numerical age—we say the Norman Invasion occurred in "AD 1066" rather than "1066 AD." The earliest AD date is AD 1; there is no AD 0 because this year is denoted by 0 BC and double numbering is not allowed.

CE ("Common Era"): Basically the same as AD, except that it is intended to avoid religious connotations or privilege.

BCE ("Before Common Era"): The same as BC, but as with CE, it avoids the religious connotation.

BP ("Before Present"): Most archaeologists feel more comfortable avoiding the AD/BC split altogether, substituting a single "before present" age estimate (with AD 1950 arbitrarily selected as the zero point; we'll explain why in Chapter 6). By this convention, an artifact from, say, the Hastings battlefield would be dated 884 BP (AD 1950 − AD 1066 = 884 BP). We will primarily use this system in the text, or we will use the more colloquial "years ago."

reflects a changing relationship to those things: from a fascination with objects themselves, to a concern with objects' ages, to what they tell us about the lives of ancient peoples, to a recognition of their power and ethical treatment.

Who Was the First Archaeologist?

Many historians ascribe the honor of "first archaeologist" to Nabonidus (who died in 538 BC), the last king of the neo-Babylonian Empire (see "Looking Closer: AD/BC/BP . . . Archaeology's Alphabet Soup"). A pious man, Nabonidus's zealous worship of his gods compelled him to rebuild the ruined temples of ancient Babylon and to search among their foundations for the inscriptions of earlier kings. We are indebted to the research of Nabonidus's scribes and the excavations by his subjects for much of our modern picture of the Babylonian Empire. Though nobody would call Nabonidus an "archaeologist" in the modern sense, he remains an important figure for one simple reason: *Nabonidus looked to the physical residues of antiquity—things—to answer questions about the past.* This may seem like a simple step, but it contrasted sharply

with the beliefs of his contemporaries, who regarded tradition, legend, and myth as the only admissible clues to the past.

For archaeology to become an intellectual field, scholars first had to grasp the idea of "the past." Through the Middle Ages, Europeans recognized only a remote past, which they reified through myth and legend. This remote past was accessed largely through the Bible, as well as Roman and Greek texts. During the Renaissance (circa AD 1300 to 1700), however, scholars such as Francesco Petrarch (1304–1374) saw a stark difference between the present and the past. To Petrarch, the "father of humanism," the remote past was an ideal of perfection, and he looked to antiquity for moral philosophy. Of course, to imitate classical antiquity, one must first study it. This led to a rediscovery of the past by those in the Western European intellectual tradition, and Petrarch and his contemporaries began to collect ancient texts and to make systematic observations on archaeological monuments.

It remained for the fifteenth-century Italian scholar Ciriaco de' Pizzicolli (1391–1455) to establish the modern discipline of archaeology. Upon translating the Latin inscription on the triumphal arch of Trajan in

Ancona, Italy, he was inspired to devote the remainder of his life to studying ancient monuments. His travels took him into Syria and Egypt, throughout the islands of the Aegean, and to Athens. When asked his business, Ciriaco is said to have replied, "Restoring the dead to life"—which today remains a fair definition of the everyday business of archaeology.

Archaeology Can Be Controversial

But not everyone wants the dead to be restored. Ever since Petrarch looked to ancient texts to provide moral philosophy (and probably even before), people have used the past to justify their actions in the present. For example, in 1572 Matthew Parker, Queen Elizabeth's archbishop of Canterbury, formed the Society (or College) of Antiquaries, devoted to the study of Anglo-Saxon law and writings. At the same time, Parliament upheld English Common Law, said to have been granted by William the Conqueror upon his conquest of England in 1066. English Common Law was based on the laws and customs of the Anglo-Saxons. Unfortunately, British kings had persistently claimed that their authority to rule—the "divine right of kings"—originated in their descent from the legendary King Arthur (who probably lived about AD 500, but no one really knows). King James therefore asserted that Common Law did not apply to the Anglican Church or the King because it originated with William rather than with Arthur. But the Society of Antiquaries used ancient documents to demonstrate that William the Conqueror did not actually create English Common Law—instead he had simply allowed it to stand and to be fused with his own ideas of justice. This was a problem for King James, for in English Common Law people had the right to rebel against an unlawful and unjust king. King James saw that meddling with this particular piece of the past had the potential for starting riots in the streets, so he ordered the dissolution of the Society of Antiquaries in 1614. The study of the past is often controversial.

But the die was cast, and the Society for Antiquaries (re-formed in 1707) was only the first of many British scholarly associations interested in the relevance of the past to the present. Of course, many private collectors were concerned only with filling their curio cabinets with *objets d'art*, but the overall goal of British antiquarianism was to map, record, and preserve national treasures. By the late eighteenth century, members of Europe's leisure classes considered an interest in classical antiquities to be an important ingredient in the "cultivation of taste."

THE DISCOVERY OF DEEP TIME

Archaeological research until the eighteenth century proceeded mostly within the tradition of Petrarch—that is, concerned primarily with clarifying the picture of classical civilizations of the Mediterranean. This lore was readily digested by the eighteenth-and early nineteenth-century mind because nothing in it challenged the Bible as an authoritative account of the origin of the world and humanity.

But a problem arose when very crude stone tools like that shown in Figure 1-1 were discovered in England and continental Europe. About 1836 a French customs official and naturalist, Jacques Boucher de Crèvecoeur de Perthes (1788–1868), found ancient axe heads in the gravels of the Somme River. Along with those tools, he also found the bones of long-extinct mammals. To Boucher de Perthes (as he is more commonly known), the implication was obvious: "In spite of their imperfection, these rude stones prove the existence of [very ancient] man as surely as a whole Louvre would have done."

Few contemporaries believed him. Why? Some 200 years before Boucher de Perthes's discoveries, several scholars had figured the age of the earth as no more than about 6000 years. The most meticulous of these calculations were those of James Ussher (1581–1656), Archbishop of Armagh, Primate of All Ireland, and

© American Museum of Natural History

Figure 1-1 Boucher de Perthes found Paleolithic handaxes like this in the Somme River gravels.

Vice-Chancellor of Trinity College in Dublin. Using biblical genealogies and correlations of Mediterranean and Middle Eastern histories, Ussher concluded that Creation began at sunset on Saturday, October 22, 4004 BC. His effort was so convincing that the date 4004 BC appeared as a marginal note in most Bibles published after AD 1700. (The precision of his date sounds silly today, but though Ussher was wrong, he followed very careful reasoning.)

This reckoning, of course, allowed no chance of an extensive human antiquity; there simply wasn't enough time. Therefore, the thinking went, Boucher de Perthes must be mistaken—his rude implements must be something other than human handiwork. Some suggested that the "tools" were really meteorites; others said they were produced by lightning, elves, or fairies. One seventeenth-century scholar suggested that the chipped flints were "generated in the sky by a fulgurous exhalation conglobed in a cloud by the circumposed humour," whatever that means.

But customs officials have never been known for their reserve, and Boucher de Perthes stuck to his guns. More finds were made in the French gravel pits at St. Acheul (near Abbeville), and similar discoveries turned up across the Channel in southern England. The issue was finally resolved when the respected British paleontologist Hugh Falconer visited Abbeville to examine the disputed evidence. A procession of esteemed scholars followed Falconer's lead and declared their support in 1859; the idea that humans had lived with now-extinct animals in the far distant past was finally enshrined in Charles Lyell's 1863 book *The Geological Evidences of the Antiquity of Man.*

The year 1859 was a banner year in the history of human thought: Not only was the remote antiquity of humankind accepted by the scientific establishment, but Charles Darwin published his influential *On the Origin of Species.* Although Darwin mentioned humans only once in that book (on nearly the last page he wrote, "Much light will be thrown on the origin of man and his history"), he had suggested the process by which modern people could have arisen from ancient primate ancestors. In the beginning, though, Darwin's theory (which had to do with the transformation of species) was unconnected to the antiquity of humanity (which was a simple question of age). We'll come back to Darwin's contributions in Chapter 13.

Nonetheless, the discovery of deep time—the recognition that life was far more ancient than recognized by biblical scholars and that human culture had evolved over time—opened the floodgates. British archaeology soon billowed out across two rather divergent courses. One direction became involved

with the problems of remote geological time and the demonstration of long-term human evolution. The other continued the tradition of Petrarch and focused on classical studies, particularly the archaeology of ancient Greece and Rome, a field now known as **classical archaeology.** This philosophical split has continued into modern times, although some signs suggest that these fields are coming back together.

Archaeology and Native Americans

Across the Atlantic, American archaeology faced its own vexing issues of time and cultural development. How, nineteenth-century scholars wondered, could regions such as the Valley of Mexico and Peru have hosted the civilizations of the Aztecs and the Inkas while people in many other places—such as the North American West—seemed impoverished, even primitive? When did people first arrive in the New World? Where had these migrants come from, and how did they get here?

Speculation arose immediately. One idea held that Native Americans were one of the Lost Tribes of Israel. Another suggested that Indians came from Atlantis. Others said they were voyaging Egyptians, Vikings, Chinese, or Phoenicians.

Gradually, investigators came to recognize considerable continuities between the unknown prehistoric past and the Native American population of the historic period. As such knowledge accumulated, the profound differences between European and American archaeology became more apparent. While Europeans wrestled with their ancient flints—without apparent modern correlates—American scholars saw that living Native Americans were relevant to the interpretation of archaeological remains. In the crass terms of the time, many Europeans saw Native Americans as "living fossils," relics of times long past.

New World archaeology thus became inextricably wed to the study of living Native American people. Whereas Old World archaeologists began from a baseline of geological time or classical antiquity, their American counterparts developed within an anthropological understanding of Native Americans. The study of American Indians became an important domain of Western scholarship in its own right, and North American archaeology became linked with anthropology through their mutual interest in Native

---

classical archaeology The branch of archaeology that studies the "classical" civilizations of the Mediterranean, such as Greece and Rome, and the Near East.

LOOKING CLOSER

AMERICAN INDIAN OR NATIVE AMERICAN?

Some years ago, as Thomas was telling his son's third grade class what it's like to be an archaeologist, a small (but adamant) voice of protest came from the back of the room.

"How come you keep saying 'Indians'? Don't you know they want to be called 'Native Americans'?" a girl asked.

She had a good point. Many people are confused about these terms. In fact, our Native American colleagues tell us that people often correct them when they say "Indian," as if the term has become a dirty word.

Names are important because they are power; the people who name things are generally the people who control them. The word "Indian," of course, is a legacy from fifteenth-century European sailors, who mistakenly believed they'd landed in India. "Native American" arose among Indians in the 1960s and 1970s, during the civil rights movement. But many Indians point out the ambiguity in this term. Although your authors are not American Indians, both are native Americans (because we were born in the United States).

Most indigenous people of North America today simply accept the imprecision of today's terms and use American Indian, Canadian Native, First Nations, Native American (or Native Hawaiian), Indian, and Native interchangeably; we follow this lead.

Of greater concern to most Indian people is the tribal name. Many Navajo people, for instance, wish to be known as Diné (a traditional name meaning "The People"). When discussing particular tribes, we attempt to use the term preferred by the tribe in question.

American culture (see "Looking Closer: American Indian or Native American?").

We must stress an important point here: As Europeans refined the archaeology of Europe, they were studying their own ancestors (Anglo-Saxons, Celts, Slavs, Franks, and so forth). But New World archaeology involved Euro-Americans digging up Native Americans' ancestors. This has led to some fundamental issues in the ethical treatment of archaeological remains in the New World compared to Europe. We will return to some of these issues in later chapters.

A BRIEF HISTORY OF ARCHAEOLOGY

The history of archaeology is illustrated here by a few individuals whose lives and careers typify archaeology of their time. These individuals were by no means

the only ones practicing archaeology over the last 200 years. However, their stories demonstrate stages in the growth of archaeology and show how goals and perspectives have changed. At their heart, though, lies an abiding interest in ancient objects as the source of information about the past.

Giovanni Battista Belzoni: Circus Strongman—and Early Archaeologist

The earliest archaeologists are like the crazy uncle that no one wants to talk about. In fact, we don't call them archaeologists at all, but refer to them as **antiquarians,** people who were fascinated by ancient objects but who rarely used those objects to reconstruct the past.

Giovanni Battista Belzoni (1778–1823) was one of the earliest antiquarians. Though Figure 1-2 suggests Belzoni was a native of the Near East, he was actually born in Italy. The son of a barber, Belzoni came to archaeology by a circuitous route. He left home at 16 to join a monastic order and study hydraulics in Rome. But with Napoleon's entry into Italy, Belzoni found his opportunities curtailed and he left, eventually settling in England in 1802. More than six and a half feet tall,

---

antiquarian Originally, someone who studied antiquities (that is, ancient objects) largely for the sake of the objects themselves, not to understand the people or culture that produced them.

© Topham/The Image Works

Figure 1-2
Giovanni Battista Belzoni, dressed in Middle Eastern garb, was an antiquarian from Italy.

with a broad, powerful torso, his physique earned him employment as a circus strongman. Billed as the "Patagonian Sampson," he traveled England and Ireland lifting heavy weights, carrying a dozen men nightly around the stage, and, using his engineering knowledge, creating stage shows featuring jets of flame and water. In 1812, Belzoni took his show on the road, leaving England to perform in Portugal, Spain, Sicily, and eventually the island of Malta.

In Malta he met an agent of Mohammed Ali Pasha, Egypt's ruler. Though Mohammed Ali was Albanian, he rose to power in Egypt after a British-Ottoman force defeated Napoleon's army and left a power vacuum that Ali, a member of the conquering force, managed to fill. He immediately set about industrializing Egypt, especially the production of cotton that British textile factories were eager to buy. To do so, he needed to irrigate Egypt's deserts, and to do that, he needed someone, the agent told Belzoni, who knew hydraulics. Tired of his career as a circus performer, Belzoni saw his chance. In 1815, he traveled to Egypt and after a year demonstrated an oxen-driven waterwheel to the pasha. Though it worked splendidly, an unfortunate accident led the pasha to reject it and throw Belzoni out of the palace. Penniless, he was stuck in Egypt, with no prospects in sight.

But the past provided his future. Several European nations were looting Egypt of its antiquities to stock their museums, and the British consul in Egypt had promised associates at the British Museum that he would send antiquities for display. Many of these antiquities were huge statues, and the British consul saw how to put Belzoni's knowledge and strength to work. With Britain's financial backing, Belzoni soon became one of the best of the pillagers. His first task was to move the 8-ton head and torso of a statue of Ramesses II from Thebes. This effort required not only his great physical strength but also his engineering ingenuity, for the statue fragment had to be placed on a sledge and rolled, inch by inch, for two weeks to the Nile River, where it was loaded on a boat and floated north. It also required considerable negotiating skills, for Belzoni had to convince local leaders to provide him with the workmen needed for the effort. Sometimes this required bribery, and sometimes he simply picked up an obstinate tribal leader and "shook him like a rat." The statue of Ramesses II is still on display at the British Museum.

In only three years, Belzoni "recovered" numerous statues, mummies, and carvings. He was the first European to enter the temple at Abu Simbel, and the first European to enter the pyramids on the Giza plateau outside Cairo. He removed the 6-ton granite obelisk from Philae, and discovered five tombs in the Valley of the Kings (where 100 years later the tomb of King Tutankhamen would be found). It was Belzoni's spoils, in fact, that inspired Shelley's famous poem "Ozymandias."

Looters from various countries vied for the spoils (the French took the obelisk from Belzoni at gunpoint). Belzoni soon tired of the fighting and in 1819 he returned to England, where he received considerable acclaim for his accomplishments (and booty). An inveterate wanderer, he left again in 1823 to seek the origin of the Nile, but was felled by dysentery, and died in Benin.

Why do we remember Belzoni, and not his rivals in what is now known as "the rape of the Nile"? Belzoni's methods were destructive enough to make modern archaeologists cringe. Once, crawling nearly naked through a mummy-filled cave, Belzoni tried to sit, but "when my weight bore on the body of an Egyptian, it crushed it like a band-box. . . . I sank altogether among the broken mummies, with a crash of bones, rags, and wooden cases." Valuable information was lost by such carelessness. And no archaeologist today would so thoughtlessly remove another country's cultural heritage. But Belzoni stands out because he bothered to take notes and to make illustrations and observations of the places he visited. To be sure, the antiquities were first on his mind, but he, and some other antiquarians, were also interested in what those things had to tell us. There was no professional archaeology at the time; there were no excavation manuals, no national laws protecting antiquities, and no idea that crucial knowledge was being lost. Nonetheless, it is from such humble (and humiliating) beginnings that the science of archaeology arose.

Jens Jacob Asmussen Worsaae: The First Professional Archaeologist

Many of the early antiquarians felt no shame in trashing ordinary mummies or less spectacular sites because they knew little of the potential for ancient objects to tell us something about the past. These men thought they already knew the past, or they simply didn't care. They thought *about* things, but they didn't think *from* things. This began to change in the mid-nineteenth century.

With hindsight, we can see that the antiquarians' role in the development of archaeology was to create collections of objects from which patterns eventually emerged, patterns that suggested ancient cultures were not static, but had changed over time. Trying to get a handle on the chronology of these changes, then, was the first order of business, and this is what the world's first professional archaeologist set out to do.

Jens J. A. Worsaae (1821–1885) was a toddler when Belzoni passed away (Figure 1-3). Born in Denmark, he was fascinated as a child by artifacts and even dug into a few mounds and barrows. Worsaae intended to study law, but before he was 20 he was volunteering for Christian Thomsen (1788–1865), who was organizing the archaeological collections at what is now the National Museum of Denmark (Thomsen had devised the now well-known typological scheme of the Stone, Bronze, and Iron Ages). Thus, Worsaae was the first person to receive training, albeit informal, in archaeology.

Courtesy National Museum of Denmark

Figure 1-3 Jens Jacob Asmussen Worsaae, the first professional archaeologist.

midden Refuse deposit resulting from human activities, generally consisting of sediment; food remains such as charred seeds, animal bone, and shell; and discarded artifacts.

potsherd Fragment of pottery.

Through connections, Worsaae received financial support from the king of Denmark to write his first book, *Primeval Antiquities of Denmark*, published in 1843, when he was only 22. Later he was appointed Denmark's first Inspector for the Conservation of Antiquarian Monuments and, at age 34, became the first professor of archaeology at the University of Copenhagen.

We recognize Worsaae as the first archaeologist because, unlike antiquarians, who excavated to find things, Worsaae *excavated to answer questions.* He was interested in what artifacts tell us about the lives of ancient people; Worsaae was *thinking from things.* Moreover, he was not content with studying artifacts found by farmers or pillagers. He argued that "antiquities have a value with reference to the spot in which they are found" and that it was "necessary to examine and compare with care the places in which antiquities are usually found." In other words, he knew that an artifact's archaeological *context* was as important as the artifact itself. We'll return to the idea of context in Chapter 4.

Here's an example. Large piles of shells once lay all along the Danish shore, and during the mid-nineteenth century some geologists argued that these piles were created by wave action. But Worsaae's excavations demonstrated that these were **middens,** trash heaps created by people. In one of his notebooks he wrote that the "heaps were the places where the people of the neighborhood, in that far-off time, took their meals, as witness, for example, the **potsherds,** charcoal, bones of animals and stone implements." He also excavated sites to test Thomsen's Three-Age system, showing that the Stone, Bronze, and Iron Ages were real chronological phases, as Thomsen had hypothesized. In sum, Worsaae demonstrated two important attributes of an archaeologist: He excavated to answer questions, not just to find things; and he knew that an artifact's context was as important as the artifact itself.

Alfred Vincent Kidder: Founder of Anthropological Archaeology

Professional archaeology developed a bit later across the Atlantic, and one of its early figures was Alfred Vincent Kidder (1885–1963), shown in Figure 1-4. Kidder was born in Michigan, and his father, a mining engineer, made sure that his son received the best education available. First enrolled in a private school in Cambridge, Massachusetts, Kidder then attended the prestigious La Villa in Ouchy, Switzerland, and then registered at Harvard. Kidder joined an archaeological expedition to northeastern Arizona, exploring

© Faith Kidder Fuller

Figure 1-4 Alfred V. Kidder (right), conducting a survey with Jesse Nusbaum at Mesa Verde, Colorado, in 1907.

territory then largely unknown to the Anglo world. The southwestern adventure sealed his fate.

When Kidder returned to Harvard, he enrolled in the anthropology program and in 1914 was awarded the sixth American PhD specializing in archaeology—and the first with a focus on North America. Kidder's dissertation examined prehistoric Southwestern ceramics, assessing their value in reconstructing culture history. Relying on scientific procedures, Kidder demonstrated ways of deciphering meaning from one of archaeology's most ubiquitous items, the potsherd. Urging accurate description of ceramic decoration, he explained how such apparent minutiae could help determine cultural relationships among various prehistoric groups. Kidder argued that only through controlled excavation and analysis could researchers draw inferences about such anthropological subjects as acculturation, social organizations, and prehistoric religious customs.

In 1915, the Department of Archaeology at the Phillips Academy in Andover, Massachusetts, was seeking a site of sufficient merit to justify a multiyear archaeological project. Largely because of his anthropological training, Kidder was selected to direct the excavations. After evaluating the possibilities, he decided on Pecos Pueblo, a massive prehistoric and historic period ruin located southeast of Santa Fe, New Mexico. Kidder was impressed by the great diversity of potsherds scattered about the ruins and felt certain that Pecos contained enough stratified debris to span several centuries. He dug at Pecos for ten summers.

The Pecos excavations were consequential for several reasons. Kidder followed and separated particu-

lar strata, distinctive layers of earth, to construct a cultural chronology. He also went beyond the pottery to make sense of the artifact and architectural styles preserved at Pecos. His intensive artifact analysis, done before the advent of radiocarbon dating or tree-ring chronology (methods that we discuss in Chapter 6), established the framework of Southwestern prehistory, which remains intact today.

After joining the Carnegie Institution of Washington, DC, as director of the Division of Historical Research, Kidder launched an ambitious archaeological program to probe the Maya ruins of Central America. He directed the Carnegie's Maya campaigns for two decades, arguing that a true understanding of Maya culture would require a broad plan of action with many interrelated areas of research. Relegating himself to the role of administrator, Kidder amassed a staff of qualified scientists with the broadest possible scope of interests. His plan was a sea change in archaeological research, enlarging traditional archaeological objectives to embrace the wider realms of anthropology and allied disciplines. Under Kidder's direction, the Carnegie program supported research by ethnographers, botanists, geographers, physical anthropologists, geologists, meteorologists, and, of course, archaeologists. With the help of Charles Lindbergh, Kidder even employed aerial reconnaissance to discover new ruins and map the boundaries of various types of vegetation. Today the interdisciplinary complexion of archaeology is a fact of life, but when Kidder proposed the concept in the 1920s, it was revolutionary.

Through his research in the Maya region and in the American Southwest, Kidder helped shift archaeology toward more properly anthropological purposes. Kidder maintained that archaeology should be viewed as "that branch of anthropology which deals with prehistoric peoples," and that archaeologists were merely a "mouldier variety of anthropologist." Although archaeologists continue to immerse themselves in the nuances of potsherd detail and architectural specifics, the ultimate objective of archaeology is to move from *things* to *people*.

Courtesy The Principal and Fellows, Newnham College, Cambridge

Figure 1-5
Gertrude Caton-Thompson, one of the pioneers of modern excavation in Egypt.

Gertrude Caton-Thompson: Looking Beyond Tombs

Born in England to a wealthy family, Gertrude Caton-Thompson (1888–1985) had the physical and intellectual grit required in archaeology (Figure 1-5). Several trips to Egypt, Greece, Palestine, and Malta as a youth generated a deep interest in prehistory, but initially she led the sort of carefree existence typical of the wealthy around the turn of the century. This changed during World War I, when she volunteered for various offices and eventually attended the Paris peace talks in 1919 as a personal assistant. Here she met T. E. Lawrence ("Lawrence of Arabia"), who had done some archaeology, as well as Gertrude Bell, an archaeologist and student of Arabia (she helped found the Baghdad Museum and create the modern national borders of Iraq). Her encounter with Lawrence and Bell encouraged Caton-Thompson to return to her childhood passion, and she began studying archaeology formally in 1921. Recognizing, like Kidder, that archaeology requires a knowledge of many fields, she studied geology, zoology, paleontology, Arabic, and, of course, anthropology.

A quick learner, she soon found herself in Egypt working with Sir Flinders Petrie, an important figure in archaeology. Working in remote parts of Egypt or other parts of Africa was and still is difficult, but Caton-Thompson was up to the task. On one trip, she slept in an empty stone tomb—apparently with two cobras—with a revolver under her pillow for protection against hyenas. On another, she had to hike across the desert one night to find help for a crew that

was running out of water. And in southern Africa, she tangled with a leopard on the edge of a cliff.

More important, she advanced archaeology intellectually. At the time, most archaeologists in Egypt focused their attention on tombs and temples, but Caton-Thompson thought that they were missing something by not excavating settlements. In the 1920s, she became the first archaeologist to excavate a village site in Egypt, using the same careful methods that she had learned under Petrie. A few years later she undertook a survey of the northern Fayum Desert in Egypt. This was a groundbreaking project because it was interdisciplinary: Caton-Thompson worked with a geologist to reconstruct the sequence of settlements and their relationships to ancient lake levels preserved in sediments and landforms.

Caton-Thompson continued to work in Egypt, as well as elsewhere, but her work in Zimbabwe (then Southern Rhodesia) shows an important element of modern archaeology. For decades, the colonial powers had known of the massive ruins of a site known as Great Zimbabwe (from which the modern nation took its name after independence). Sitting atop a hill, the site contains massive stone walls and buildings (Figure 1-6). Several investigators (whose methods were those of the worst of the antiquarians) argued that the site was Ophir (the location of King Solomon's mines) or the palace of the Queen of Sheba. None wanted to believe that indigenous African people were capable of creating such a structure. They asserted that the Phoenicians had built the site, and used its alleged biblical connections to justify European colonization and control of southern Africa.

In 1929, the British government invited Caton-Thompson to resolve the controversy. Reasoning that previous efforts failed because they had ignored the site's **stratigraphy** (we'll discuss this concept in Chapter 6), she approached the problem with two straightforward questions: How old is the site, and was it built by Africans? Caton-Thompson carefully excavated deep trenches to bedrock in several places, and even tunneled under a massive solid stone conical tower. Studying glass trade beads, she eventually demonstrated that the site had been inhabited in the thirteenth and fourteenth centuries—far too late for its alleged biblical associations. She also found that the pottery and other implements, as well as the architecture, were little different from those of later known African peoples. By thinking from things, Caton-Thompson concluded that Great Zimbabwe was African in origin. She took considerable flak for this conclusion because it did not support colonial rule of southern Africa. The past is often used to justify the

---

stratigraphy A site's physical structure produced by the deposition of geological and/or cultural sediments into layers, or strata.

© Robert Harding World Imagery/Corbis

Figure 1-6 Great Zimbabwe, a medieval-age ruin in Zimbabwe, Africa. Caton-Thompson disproved hypotheses that it was built by European or Asian peoples.

Caton-Thompson received more formal training, much of it hands-on. American archaeologists were also well versed in the broader field of anthropology, although this was less true for European archaeologists.

Archaeologists by mid-century wanted to transcend mere cultural chronology, but classifying artifacts and sorting out their patterns in space and time left little time for more anthropological objectives, such as reconstructing society. Most archaeologists by the middle of the twentieth century were practicing what is called **culture history,** documenting how material culture changed over time and space. Their main goal was to track the migrations and development of particular prehistoric cultures. Some archaeologists tried to explain changes by relating them to climatic change, for example, or to vague ideas about cultural evolution. But for the most part, archaeologists attributed differences in artifact frequencies between sites to the presence of different cultures or ideas. Changes in artifact frequencies over time, such as the types of pottery found in different layers of earth at a site, were attributed to the diffusion of ideas from other cultures or the replacement of one culture by another. Worsaae, for example, thought that the Stone, Bronze, and Iron Ages marked the diffusion of new ideas or the migration of new people into Denmark, rather than a technological evolutionary sequence.

By the 1950s, the basic prehistory of many world regions was sufficiently well understood that some archaeologists could move beyond simple documentation to more in-depth reconstructions of prehistory. Worsaae wanted to paint a picture of life alongside the growing shell middens of Denmark. Caton-Thompson excavated village sites because she knew that she could not draw a complete picture of life in ancient Egypt

present—and archaeologists are often called upon to judge these claims. This is one of the realities of archaeology that we will touch upon in later chapters.

Archaeology at Mid-Twentieth Century

Archaeology began as a pastime of the rich, but developed into a professional scientific discipline. Most professional archaeologists were affiliated with major museums and universities; others joined the private sector, working to protect and conserve America's cultural heritage. This institutional support not only encouraged a sense of professionalism and fostered public funding, but also mandated that public repositories care for the archaeological artifacts recovered. The twentieth-century archaeologist was not a collector of personal treasure: All finds belonged in the public domain, available for exhibit and study.

We can also see a distinct progression toward specialization in our target archaeologists. Scholars accumulated knowledge of the past so rapidly that by the early twentieth century, archaeologists specialized in particular regions. It is difficult today to find someone like Caton-Thompson doing seminal work in Egypt while simultaneously tackling challenging issues in southern Africa. Possibly the greatest change, however, has been the quality of archaeologists' training. Worsaae was more or less self-taught, but Kidder and

culture history The kind of archaeology practiced mainly in the early to mid-twentieth century; it "explains" differences or changes over time in artifact frequencies by positing the diffusion of ideas between neighboring cultures or the migration of a people who had different mental templates for artifact styles.

by excavating tombs alone. But only later, as methods and basic cultural chronologies developed, could archaeologists move on to more anthropological goals and seek explanations for the prehistory they were reconstructing.

H. Marie Wormington: Ancient Man in North America

Born in Denver, Colorado, H. Marie Wormington (1914–1994) was part of the generation that began to take archaeology further (Figure 1-7). Like many archaeologists before her, she had originally intended to pursue another career—zoology or medicine, in her case. But while taking an archaeology class at the University of Denver, she discovered her passion. "Once I discovered there was such a thing as archaeology," she later said, "I just never looked back." Wormington continued her education in France, working on a cave excavation in the Dordogne in 1935, then joined the staff at what is now the Denver Museum of History and Science. She left temporarily to obtain her doctorate from Radcliffe, but remained employed at the museum until 1968, when she left to occupy several teaching positions. She was among the first American anthropologists to enter the former Soviet Union, as well as the People's Republic of China.

This vignette exposes some of archaeology's dirty laundry. The many women involved in the earliest days of archaeology faced a difficult time and hard decisions because women were often considered unsuited for the

© Denver Museum of Nature and Science

Figure 1-7 Marie Wormington, a female pioneer in American archaeology.

rigors of archaeology. Some, such as Caton-Thompson, sacrificed marriage and family. Marie Wormington once had to sit in the corridor because, as a woman, she was prohibited from entering the lecture hall at Harvard. She signed her work "H. M. Wormington," concealing her gender because the director of the Denver museum feared that no one would read a book on archaeology by a woman. Into the late 1960s, many male archaeologists refused to take women on their field crews.

Times have changed—fully half of the several thousand archaeologists in the United States today are female—but in the 1930s, women like Marie Wormington were in the vanguard. She was only the second woman admitted to study in Harvard's anthropology department, and was the first female president of the Society for American Archaeology. Though remembered as eminently polite and diplomatic, she was no shrinking violet: She once told the dangerous Nicaraguan dictator Anastasio Somoza Debayle that a site in Nicaragua was not as old as he hoped.

Wormington worked in many places and on various research topics, but her first love was "paleoindian" archaeology—the archaeology of pre-8000-year-old North America. In 1939, at the age of 25, she published *Ancient Man in North America*, which went through four editions, the last published in 1957. These editions demonstrate how archaeology matured over time. In 1939, the American scientific community was only able to estimate how long people had lived in the New World; by 1957, radiocarbon dating gave certainty to those estimates. The last edition contains discussions of genetic data (blood typing), geology, skeletal data, and comparisons to archaeological material in South America and Siberia. Importantly, Wormington wrote *Ancient Man* (as well as *Prehistoric Indians of the Southwest*, 1947) for the general public, anticipating the present-day concern that the results of archaeology be accessible to the public that supports the field.

The various editions of *Ancient Man* chronicle not only the astonishing growth in the amount of information available, but also the progress in interpreting archaeological data in terms of technology, subsistence, migratory routes, and age. The book evolved from a straightforward catalog of sites and finds to a discussion of what those finds *mean* in terms of the lives of the ancient people who left them behind. That is, the various editions of *Ancient Man* demonstrate the shift from a concern with *things* to a concern with *thinking from things*. "Artifacts themselves are not important," Wormington once said, "it's the information they can provide about cultures and about people." She closed *Ancient Man in North America* with a clear statement of why modern archaeology abandoned the misguided confidence of the antiquarians in favor of a more rigorous concern for methods and techniques:

> To the casual observer the growing list of unanswered questions regarding the ancient inhabitants of North America may seem appalling; actually it should be regarded as encouraging. With a new subject the tendency is to oversimplify through lack of knowledge. Only with increased knowledge comes the realization of the complexity of the problem, for with each solution which is reached new fields are opened and new perplexities arise. To find an answer one must first have sufficient knowledge to formulate the question.

As the knowledge of prehistory accumulated, the methods and objectives of archaeology changed, as demonstrated by archaeologists who were trained in the 1960s.

Lewis R. Binford: Archaeology's Angry Young Man

If archaeology has ever had an "angry young man," it was Lewis R. Binford (1931–2011; Figure 1-8). After a period of military service, Binford enrolled in 1954 at the University of North Carolina, wanting to become an ethnographer. But by the time he entered the graduate program at the University of Michigan, Binford was a confirmed archaeologist.

The 1960s were a watershed time for American college campuses. Baby-boom demographics and the GI Bill inflated enrollments. Campuses became the focal point for the waves of social and political confrontation that roiled the nation. Clashes over the war in

Vietnam and civil rights created a revolutionary atmosphere. Archaeology was firmly embedded in this intellectual climate. Everyone, including archaeologists, braced for the change.

Binford thrived in this cultural climate. He could lecture, sometimes for hours, with the force and enthusiasm of an old-time southern preacher, and he rapidly assumed the role of archaeological messiah. His students became disciples spreading the word: As the study of cultural change, archaeology has obvious relevance to modern problems. To fulfill this role, Binford argued, archaeology must transcend potsherds and spear points to address larger issues, such as cultural evolution, ecology, and social organization. Archaeology must take full advantage of modern technology by using scientific methods and sophisticated, quantitative techniques. Archaeology must study the remaining preindustrial peoples to scrutinize firsthand the operation of disappearing cultural adaptations. And archaeology must be concerned with methods for reconstructing the past. In the 1960s, this became known as the **new archaeology** (see "In His Own Words: The Challenge of Archaeology" by Lewis R. Binford). Archaeology had, in Marie Wormington's words, sufficient knowledge to start asking more complex and difficult questions.

The new archaeology (a now-antiquated term for us all, and especially to today's student) emphasized a new way of studying the past and a new agenda for doing archaeology. The master plan was set forth in a series of articles published through the 1960s and early 1970s, many by Binford and his students.

Binford asked why archaeology had contributed so little to general anthropological theory. His answer was that, in past studies, material culture had been simplistically interpreted. Too much attention had been lavished on artifacts as passive traits that "blend," "influence," or "stimulate" one another. Binford proposed that artifacts be examined in their cultural contexts and interpreted instead as reflections of technology, society, and belief systems. That is, Binford underscored the need to change from thinking *about* things to thinking *from* things.

Binford also emphasized the importance of precise, unambiguous scientific methods. Archaeologists, he argued, must stop waiting for artifacts to speak up. They must formulate hypotheses and test these on the

Courtesy of Lewis R. Binford, photo by Grant Spearman

Figure 1-8 Lewis R. Binford (right) at Tulugak Lake in Alaska in 1999 with a Nunamiut friend, Johnny Rulland. Binford helped develop the "new archaeology" of the 1960s.

new archaeology An approach to archaeology that arose in the 1960s, emphasizing the understanding of underlying cultural processes and the use of the scientific method; today's version of the "new archaeology" is sometimes called processual archaeology.

IN HIS OWN WORDS

THE CHALLENGE OF ARCHAEOLOGY

by Lewis R. Binford

As I was riding on the bus not long ago, an elderly gentleman asked me what I did. I told him I was an archaeologist. He replied: "That must be wonderful, for the only thing you have to be to succeed is lucky." It took some time to convince him that his view of archaeology was not quite mine. He had the idea that the archaeologist "digs up the past," that the successful archaeologist is one who discovers something not seen before, that all archaeologists spend their lives running about trying to make discoveries of this kind. This is a conception of science perhaps appropriate to the nineteenth century, but, at least in the terms in which I myself view archaeology, it does not describe the nature of archaeology as it is practiced today. I believe archaeologists are more than simply discoverers....

Archaeology cannot grow without striking a balance between theoretical and practical con-

cerns. Archaeologists need to be continuously self-critical; that is why the field is such a lively one and why archaeologists are forever arguing among themselves about who is right on certain issues. Self-criticism leads to change, but is itself a challenge—one which archaeology perhaps shares only with palaeontology and a few other fields whose ultimate concern is making inferences about the past on the basis of contemporary things. So archaeology is not a field that can study the past directly, nor can it be one that merely involves discovery, as the man on the bus suggested. On the contrary, it is a field wholly dependent upon inference to the past from things found in the contemporary world. Archaeological data, unfortunately, do not carry self-evident meanings. How much easier our work would be if they did!

---

remains of the past. Binford argued that, because archaeologists always work from samples, they should acquire data that make the samples amenable to statistical analysis. He urged archaeologists to stretch their horizons beyond the individual site to the scale of the region; in this way, an entire cultural system could be reconstructed (as we discuss in Chapter 3). Such regional samples must be generated from research designs based on the principles of probability sampling. Random sampling is commonplace in other social sciences, and Binford insisted that archaeologists apply these scientific procedures to their own research problems.

Binford's ideas about methodology fostered projects designed to demonstrate how this approach can help comprehend cultural processes. Intricate statistical techniques were applied to a variety of subjects, from the nature of Mousterian (some 150,000 years old) stone tools to the archaeology of historic forts. He proposed new ideas, rooted in the field of human ecology, to explain the origins of plant domestication. These investigations were critical because they

embroiled Binford in factual, substantive debate. Not only did he advocate different goals and new methods, but Binford also gained credibility among field archaeologists because he was arguing about specifics, not just theory. Binford conducted his own ethnographic fieldwork among the Nunamiut Eskimo, the Navajo, and the Australian aborigines, testing the utility of archaeological concepts and methods on the trash of living peoples.

Binford and his students set off a firestorm that quickly spread throughout the archaeological community. A 1970s generation of graduate students and young professionals was greeted with the inquisition, "Are you a new archaeologist, an old archaeologist, or what? Make up your mind!"

The "new archaeology" of the 1960s has today evolved into so-called processual archaeology. In subsequent chapters, we explore the tenets of this position and also examine how yet another wave of archaeological criticism—postprocessual archaeology—finds fault with Binford's approach and suggests some alternative directions.

ARCHAEOLOGY IN THE TWENTY-FIRST CENTURY

So, what about today? Who is a mover and shaker of the twenty-first century?

Perhaps in another 50 years or so, hindsight will suggest one person who truly captures the spirit of these times. But right now, we do not detect a single, defining trend that dominates archaeology; instead, the discipline has several branches, each growing and intersecting with the others in interesting ways.

Many of these diverse approaches result from new techniques and perspectives; others arise from the nature of employment in archaeology. Archaeologists still work in museums and universities, but most today are employed by federal agencies and especially private "cultural resource management" firms (companies that arose in response to federal legislation passed in the 1960s designed to protect the nation's archaeological resources—more about these in Chapter 15). Before the 1970s, most American archaeologists were white and male; today the archaeological profession comprises equal numbers of men and women, and more minorities, including Native Americans, are actively involved in the field. Throughout these pages, we will meet some archaeologists who exemplify those trends (in boxes labeled "Profile of an Archaeologist"). For now, we'll present just one more archaeologist as a way to introduce modern archaeology.

Kathleen A. Deagan: Archaeology Comes of Age

Kathleen Deagan (b. 1948) helped fulfill Binford's call for a better archaeology (Figure 1-9). Deagan received her doctorate in anthropology from the University of Florida in 1974. Still a curator at the Florida Museum of Natural History, she specializes in Spanish colonial studies. She has pushed the frontiers of historical archaeology (see Chapter 14), especially the archaeological investigation of disenfranchised groups, and remains actively involved in bringing archaeology to the public. She is concerned with the people and culture behind the artifact and with explaining the social and cultural behaviors that she reconstructs from archaeology—that is, she thinks from things.

Deagan is perhaps best known for her long-term excavations at St. Augustine (Florida). Continuously occupied since its founding by Pedro Menéndez in 1565, St. Augustine is the oldest European enclave in the

Figure 1-9 Kathleen Deagan, a contemporary archaeologist, excavating at St. Augustine, Florida.

United States (see "In Her Own Words: The Potential of Historical Archaeology" by Kathleen Deagan).

Deagan addressed the processes and results of Spanish–Indian intermarriage and descent, a topic dear to the hearts of many anthropologists and ethnohistorians. The fact that mestizos, people of Spanish/Indian descent, constitute nearly the entire population of Latin America brought this issue to the forefront long ago. Similar processes took place in Spanish Florida, but the Hispanic occupation left no apparent mestizo population in La Florida, what Deagan called "America's first melting pot." Accordingly, when she began her doctoral research, we knew virtually nothing about early race relations in North America.

Deagan hypothesized how the mestizo population fit into this colonial setting. Given the nature of the unfortunate interactions that characterized eighteenth-century Florida, she expected the burdens of acculturation to have fallen most heavily on the Indian women living in Spanish or mestizo households. Because no mestizo people survive here, the tests for her hypothesis were necessarily archaeological. If her hypothesis is true, then acculturation should affect mostly the Native American women's activities visible in archaeological sites (food preparation techniques, equipment, household activities, basic food resources, child-related activities, and primarily female crafts such as pottery manufacture). Conversely, male-related activities (house construction technology and design, military and political affairs, and hunting weapons) should show less evidence of Spanish infusion.

To explore these processes, Deagan began in 1973 a series of archaeological field schools at St. Augustine. This long-term, diversified enterprise excavated sites whose inhabitants represented a broad range of

IN HER OWN WORDS

THE POTENTIAL OF HISTORICAL ARCHAEOLOGY

by Kathleen Deagan

From its emergence as a recognized area of research in the 1930s, historical archaeology has advanced from providing supplemental data for other disciplines, through an anthropological tool for the reconstruction of past lifeways, to a means of discovering predictable relationships between human adaptive strategies, ideology, and patterned variability in the archaeological record.

Because it can compare written accounts about what people said they did, what observers said people did, and what the archaeological record said people did, historical archaeology can make contributions not possible through any other discipline. Inconsistencies and inaccuracies in the written records may be detected and ultimately predicted. Insights into conditions provided by such written sources may be compared to the more objective archaeological record of actual conditions in the past in order to provide insight into cognitive processes.

The simultaneous access to varied sources of information allows the historical archaeologist to match the archaeological patterning of a given site against the documented social, economic, and ideological attributes of the same site to arrive at a better understanding of how the archaeological record reflects human behavior.

The unique potential of historical archaeology lies not only in its ability to answer questions of archaeological and anthropological interest, but also in its ability to provide historical data not available through documentation or any other source. Correcting the inadequate treatment of disenfranchised groups in America's past, excluded from historical sources because of race, religion, isolation, or poverty, is an important function of contemporary historical archaeology and one that cannot be ignored.

---

incomes, occupations, and ethnic affiliations. Hundreds of students have learned their first archaeology at St. Augustine, where a saloon long sported a placard celebrating the years of "Digging with Deagan."

It was not long before her explorations into Hispanic–Native American interactions led Deagan to the Caribbean, where she headed interdisciplinary excavations at Puerto Real, the fourth-oldest European New World city (established in 1503). As she steadily moved back in time, Deagan's research eventually led her literally to the doorstep of Christopher Columbus.

In northern Haiti, Deagan discovered La Navidad, the earliest well-documented point of contact between Spanish and Native American people. On Christmas Eve, 1492—following two nights of partying with local Taino Arawak Indians—Columbus's flagship *Santa Maria* ran aground. He abandoned ship, moved to the *Nina*, and appealed to the local Native Americans for

help. This disaster left the explorers one boat short. When Columbus sailed home with his world-shattering news, he left 39 unfortunate compatriots behind, protected by a small stockade built from the timbers of the wrecked *Santa Maria*. Returning a year later, Columbus found the settlement burned, his men killed and mutilated.

Columbus soon established the more permanent settlements of La Isabela and Puerto Real—sites of the first sustained contact between Europeans and Native Americans—and Deagan has also conducted important field excavations there. With a population of nearly 1500 people, La Isabela was home to soldiers, priests, stonecutters, masons, carpenters, and nobles. Although this first Columbian town lasted only four years, several critical events took place here: the first intentional introduction of European plants and animals; the first expedition into the interior; and the first Hispanic installation of urban necessities, such as canals, mills, roads, gardens, plazas, ports, ramparts, and hospitals.

The biological aftermath of the Columbian exchange soon overtook La Isabela. European and Native American alike suffered from dietary deficiencies, an excessive workload, and contagious disease. Influenza struck during the first week, affecting one-third of the population. When Columbus ordered the settlement abandoned in 1496, fewer than 300 inhabitants were left. Deagan extended her research to investigate daily life in the initial colonial period, including the ways in which European colonists coped with their new and largely unknown New World environment.

Beyond new directions in historical archaeology, Deagan's research demonstrates the degree to which contemporary archaeology is played out in the public arena. Her work creates headlines, and she was featured in consecutive years in *National Geographic* magazine. She has recently published, with Venezuelan archaeologist José María Cruxent, two books on La Isabela—one a data-laden professional monograph, the other a readable volume for the public. Deagan knows that archaeologists cannot afford to isolate themselves in ivory towers or archaeology labs. One way or another—whether through federal grants, state-supported projects, tax laws, or private benefaction—archaeology depends on public support for its livelihood. Consequently, it owes something back to that public.

Decades ago, Margaret Mead (1901–1978), one of the nation's first anthropologists, recognized the importance of taking the work of anthropologists to the public. Mead kept anthropology alive in the print and electronic media. Today archaeology enjoys unprecedented press coverage, and archaeologists like Deagan know that without such publicity, archaeology has no future.

CONCLUSION: ARCHAEOLOGY'S FUTURE

Archaeology does indeed have a future, however, and it's a lively and vibrant one. Archaeology enjoys enormous public interest, as shown by the popularity of places such as Mesa Verde National Park, expanding television programming, and popular college courses. This level of public support suggests that more, not less, archaeology will be needed in the future.

Archaeology has evolved from a pastime of the wealthy to an established scientific discipline. But with these changes has come the realization that studying the human past raises numerous ethical issues. Nobody can practice archaeology in a political or cultural vacuum. We argue that archaeology remains a science that insists on high standards of evidence and must continue to examine how we make inferences from evidence. Science in this sense is self-correcting, making it essential to most inquiry (including archaeology). But we also recognize that scientific inquiry is susceptible to cultural biases. We think that archaeologists must continue to work closely with indigenous peoples and descendant communities, attempting to recognize and correct cultural biases (as in Figure 1-10, which shows a working example of this compromise). We'll return to this matter in the text's final chapter.

© David H. Thomas

Figure 1-10 Archaeology today confronts both scientific and ethical challenges. Yet there are many signs that archaeology need not be antagonistic to indigenous peoples. Here, Bryceson Pinnecoose (Hopi/Cheyenne, on right) and Ron Winters use a power sifter to screen archaeological deposits at Mission San Marcos, New Mexico.

SUMMARY

1. What makes an archaeologist an archaeologist?

- Archaeologists reconstruct and explain the past by "thinking from things," using their analyses of material remains as the basis for knowledge of the past.

2. Why is the study of the past controversial?

- People typically use their vision of the past to justify their actions in the present. The assumption that Great Zimbabwe was built by Europeans justified Europeans' taking southern Africa. The archaeologist can (and should) question such mistaken beliefs.
- New World prehistory is largely studied by people of European descent, setting up inevitable and important disagreements about the past and its use in the present.

3. How was the rise of archaeology connected to the discovery of humanity's "deep" antiquity?

- Studying the past depends on *recognizing* a past.
- Although many early scholars were aware of the classical civilizations, the discovery in France of human artifacts with extinct animals made evident the need to study that past in great detail, without ancient documents as a guide.

4. Who were the antiquarians, and why include them in a history of archaeology?

- For better or worse, these looters helped spark an interest in the ancient world. They built museum collections that inspired later generations to create the profession of archaeology (which would reject the methods and attitudes of antiquarians).

5. What trends have characterized archaeology over the last century?

- The evolution from antiquarianism to professional archaeology has involved the movement from thinking *about* things to thinking *from* things.
- Archaeologists have always sought to build cultural chronologies, reconstruct ancient societies, and explain why cultures change over time. Today we can see they were initially successful with the first objective, then the second, and eventually the third. Along the way, archaeologists have increasingly borrowed information and techniques from many fields—geology, zoology, mathematical statistics, astronomy, climatology, and others—as they develop ways of making solid inferences from material remains using solid scientific methods.
- Archaeology is today a diverse field that covers both prehistoric and historical eras. Archaeology is concerned with bringing knowledge to a broader public, with making research relevant to contemporary society, and with understanding the opinions and needs of indigenous and descendant communities.

MEDIA RESOURCES

Doing Fieldwork:
Archaeological Demonstrations CD-ROM 2.0
This CD, developed by the authors, shows professional archaeologists involved in various digs, many of which are referenced in the text. The presentation is organized by the main techniques used on an archaeological dig, reinforcing concepts and techniques via live examples. The CD takes you through each step automatically, or you can navigate to any point via the navigation bar. After reviewing a step in the dig process, you are taken to Check Points, which are concept questions about each step of the dig. Then you can see the answers, receive your score, and even send your scores to your instructor.

The Companion Website for *Archaeology,*
Sixth Edition
www.cengagebrain.com
Supplement your review of this chapter by going to the companion website to take one of the practice quizzes, use the flash cards to master key terms, and check out the many other study aids that are designed to help you succeed in your introductory archaeology course.

2 THE STRUCTURE OF ARCHAEOLOGICAL INQUIRY

LEARNING OBJECTIVES

**AFTER READING THIS CHAPTER
YOU SHOULD BE ABLE TO ANSWER THESE QUESTIONS:**

1. What is an anthropological approach?

2. What two paradigms do anthropologists use to study culture, and how are these different ways of thinking reflected in archaeology?

3. What is science and how does it explain things?

4. What three levels of theory does a scientific approach in archaeology entail? How do these relate to paradigms?

Courtesy of the Southeast Archaeological Center, National Park Service, photo by David G. Anderson.

Excavation of a 500-year-old Mississippian Mound at Shiloh National Military Park.

PREVIEW

IN THIS CHAPTER we consider how archaeologists relate to the broader field of anthropology and how archaeologists go about trying to reconstruct the past. The concept of culture is crucial to anthropology, and archaeologists study it in different ways. We'll also see how scientific approaches work in archaeology.

Archaeologists use theories at all levels of their research; we are especially concerned with the concept of *paradigms*, the overarching frameworks used to help us understand the human condition. Finally, we'll examine the cyclical structure of archaeological inquiry.

 DOING FIELDWORK CD-ROM:
ARCHAEOLOGICAL DEMONSTRATIONS 2.0

See the "What Is the Question?" section of the CD-ROM to learn more about topics covered in this chapter.

INTRODUCTION

More than 50 years ago, archaeologist Philip Phillips (1900–1994) declared that "Archaeology is anthropology or it is nothing." Especially within the United States, archaeology remains a subfield of anthropology. Although both of us are archaeologists, our multiple degrees are all in anthropology, and we both work in departments of anthropology. In fact, there are few U.S. departments of archaeology (the most prominent is at Boston University). Outside the United States, however, archaeology is often more closely aligned with the humanities, such as history, classics, or art history (and it sometimes appears in these departments at U.S. universities). But the boundaries between these various archaeologies and these former alliances are crumbling. Archaeology will always change, but we believe that good archaeology will always be closely aligned with an anthropological approach.

anthropology The study of all aspects of humankind—biological, cultural, and linguistic; extant and extinct—employing a holistic, comparative approach and the concept of culture.

WHAT'S AN ANTHROPOLOGICAL APPROACH?

Everyone knows what anthropologists do: They study native people and fossils and chimpanzees. They grin from the pages of *National Geographic* magazine and show up on the Discovery Channel. But few people know everything that anthropologists actually do, or even what makes them anthropologists at all. **Anthropology** is tough to pin down because anthropologists do so many different things.

So, what makes an anthropologist an anthropologist? The answer is surprisingly simple: All anthropologists believe that the best understanding of the human condition arises from a global, comparative, and holistic approach. It's not enough to look at a single group of Americans, Chinese, or Bushmen to find the keys to human existence. Neither is it enough to look at just one part of the human condition, as do economists, historians, political scientists, and psychologists. Because looking at part of the picture gives you just that—only part of the picture.

What holds anthropology together is its insistence that every aspect of every human society, extant or extinct, counts. This broad-based approach qualifies anthropology as uniquely capable of understanding what makes humankind distinct from the rest of the animal world. This isn't to say that all anthropologists study everything. The Renaissance anthropologist—the individual who does everything—has faded into folklore. Today, nobody can hope to do everything well.

So, anthropologists specialize. Archaeologists are anthropologists who specialize in ancient societies.

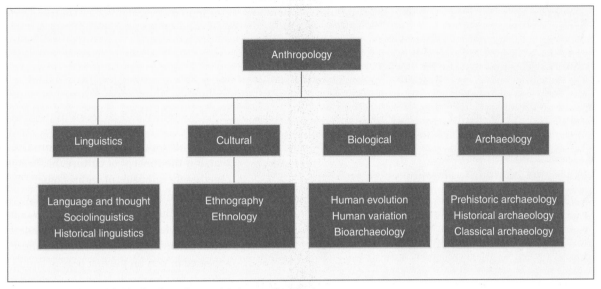

Figure 2-1 The four subfields of anthropology and their areas of study.

But archaeologists still draw upon each of the other subfields of anthropology (and several other sciences). Before examining how modern archaeology articulates with the rest of anthropology, let's first see how anthropologists carve up the pie of human existence.

Kinds of Anthropologists

Anthropology embraces four primary fields of study: **biological anthropology, cultural anthropology, linguistic anthropology,** and **archaeology** (all shown in Figure 2-1).

Biological Anthropology Biological (or physical) anthropologists study humans as biological organisms. Some work with human fossils to reconstruct the biological evolution of humans. Others study modern human biological (genetic) variability or work in forensic anthropology (featured in TV programs such as *CSI* and *Bones*); others study the biology and behavior of nonhuman primates, such as chimpanzees; still others are bioarchaeologists, who study the past via human skeletal remains. Archaeologists overlap with biological anthropologists because they often encounter human skeletons, and biological anthropologists are essential in the recovery and analysis of these remains. (We return to bioarchaeology in Chapter 10.)

Cultural Anthropology Cultural anthropologists describe and analyze the culture of modern human groups. Cultural anthropologists commonly employ the method of **participant observation,** gathering data by personally questioning and observing people

by actually living in their society. Anthropologists study rituals, kinship, religion, politics, art, oral histories, medical practices—anything and everything that people in contemporary societies do, say, or think. Archaeology overlaps with cultural anthropology in that some archaeologists conduct research with living peoples to understand the relationships between behavior and material remains (see Chapter 8). And all archaeologists look to ethnographic research for ideas about how to interpret the things they find in sites.

Linguistic Anthropology Anthropological linguists evaluate language: how sounds are made, how sounds create languages, the relationship between language and thought, how linguistic systems change through time, the basic structure of language, and the role of language in the development of culture. Anthropological linguists also use language to chart historical relationships and track ancient migrations between

biological anthropology A subdiscipline of anthropology that views humans as biological organisms; also known as physical anthropology.

cultural anthropology A subdiscipline of anthropology that emphasizes nonbiological aspects: the learned social, linguistic, technological, and familial behaviors of humans.

linguistic anthropology A subdiscipline of anthropology that focuses on human language: its diversity in grammar, syntax, and lexicon; its historical development; and its relation to a culture's perception of the world.

archaeology The study of the past through the systematic recovery and analysis of material remains.

participant observation The primary strategy of cultural anthropology, in which data are gathered by questioning and observing people while the observer lives in their society.

Figure 2-2 Hayonim Cave in Israel, where careful excavation has allowed archaeologists to make important discoveries in human evolution.

now separate, but linguistically related, populations. Many modern linguists study how people acquire second languages and work with native peoples to revive dying languages. Archaeology overlaps with linguistics when language helps reconstruct when and from where modern populations migrated.

Archaeology Archaeologists study human culture as well, but their technology and field methods differ from those of cultural anthropologists. Lacking living, breathing informants, archaeologists acquire their data through the recovery of material remains—stone tools, broken bones, potsherds, pollen, plant parts, and so on—commonly by meticulous excavation (Figure 2-2). They analyze these material remains with a powerful array of techniques. As we will see, these methods produce information and insights that living, breathing informants probably never would (or could) provide.

Today archaeology is a major component in many graduate programs in anthropology. Undergraduates often tell us that archaeology is the liveliest and most exciting program within anthropology. Cultural resource management (see Chapter 15) is the most employable kind of archaeology, even for undergraduates (it's a good way to make a living). In later chapters, we explore the dazzling assortment of new ways to understand and re-create the past. Look for archaeology to

continue making significant contributions to the overall mission of anthropology.

The Culture Concept

We have said that a global, comparative, and holistic perspective unites the diversity within anthropology. But even more than that, it is the concept of **culture** that brings together the subfields of anthropology. The classic definition of culture was offered by Sir Edward Burnett Tylor (1832–1917), whom many consider to be the founder of modern anthropology. Tylor's definition of "culture" appeared in 1871 on the first page of anthropology's first textbook: "Culture . . . taken in its wide ethnographic sense is that complex whole which includes knowledge, belief, art, morals, law, custom, and any other capabilities and habits acquired by man as a member of society."

Culture in Tylor's sense is *learned*—from parents, peers, teachers, leaders, and others. Note that culture is not biological or genetic; any person can acquire any culture. And under this anthropological definition, all peoples have the same amount of culture. Somebody who can recite Shakespeare and listens to Beethoven is no more "cultural" than one who reads *People* magazine and prefers Lady Gaga. If a baby born to European parents were raised in China, that individual's appearance would come from its genes (as moderated by environmental factors), but he or she would speak Mandarin or Cantonese, and act and think as other Chinese do.

Culture creates our different conceptions of life, about what is proper and what is not. Tribal people in New Guinea think it laughable that American women wear earrings, but believe it's normal to wear bone or shell nose ornaments for ceremonies. Cultures change over time; material factors (such as nutrition) and historical factors (such as contact with other peoples) affect this process. Because archaeology is concerned with how cultures change over time, the concept of learned culture is essential to archaeology.

Culture is also *shared*. Although everyone is an individual with his/her own values and understandings, members of a human group share some basic ideas about the world and their place in it. Anthropology focuses on such shared ideas, rather than on individual variations of those ideas. Many Euro-American homes, for instance, are divided into multiple rooms, including a living room, a smallish kitchen, a family room, and bedrooms. This pattern is considered normal and comfortable by most Euro-Americans. But,

culture An integrated system of beliefs, traditions, and customs that govern or influence a person's behavior. Culture is learned, shared by members of a group, and based on the ability to think in terms of symbols.

according to George Esber (Miami University), when Apache people were given the chance to design their own homes, they preferred a single large living area that included the kitchen, with only the bedrooms and baths separate. The central living area was to accommodate large social gatherings. In order to cook for those gatherings, Apaches also preferred kitchens with an almost industrial capacity, including large cabinets to hold large cooking pots. Clearly, shared ideas about life are reflected in shared social behaviors that in turn result in patterned sets of material remains—the sort of things that archaeologists recover.

Finally, culture is *symbolic*. Consider the symbolism involved in language: There is no reason that the word "dog" in English means "a household pet," any more than does "chien," "perro," or "alika" (French, Spanish, and Malagasy). What's more, dogs are not inherently pets. Indeed, in many places, such as Micronesia and Southeast Asia, dogs are feast foods. Though this disturbs many Americans, the idea of "pet" is not inherent in a dog—it is a socially constructed, symbolic meaning that a culture gives to dogs. Symbolic meanings of behavior condition what we do—for example, what we eat—which in turn affects the material traces of those behaviors, such as which bones wind up in ancient middens.

So, culture is learned, shared, and symbolic. Culture provides you with a way to interpret human behavior and the world around you; and it plays a key role in structuring the material record of human behavior—which archaeologists recover.

How Do Anthropologists Study Culture?

To oversimplify a bit, anthropologists study culture in two basic ways. An **ideational perspective** focuses on ideas, symbols, and mental structures as driving forces in shaping human behavior. Alternatively, an **adaptive perspective** emphasizes technology, ecology, demography, and economics as the key factors defining human behavior. Let's examine each of these.

Culture as Ideas The ideational perspective holds that culture is a complex set of conceptual designs and shared understandings that govern the way people act. This perspective on culture emphasizes ideas, thoughts, and shared knowledge and sees symbols and their meanings as crucial to shaping human behavior. It encompasses material culture insofar as material things manifest symbolic ideas.

The ideational theorist insists on "getting inside a person's head" to seek out the shared meanings of a society. According to the ideational view of culture, one cannot comprehend human behavior without understanding the symbolic code for that behavior.

Culture as Adaptation An adaptive perspective privileges "culture as a system." Social and cultural differences are viewed not as reflections of symbolic meanings, but rather as responses to the material parameters of life, such as food, shelter, and reproduction. Human behaviors are also seen as linked together systemically, meaning that change in one area, say technology, will result in change in another area, such as social organization. It is the cultural system—technology, modes of economic organization, settlement patterns, forms of social grouping, and political institutions—that articulates the material needs of human communities with their ecological settings.

In the adaptive perspective, culture keeps societies in equilibrium with their ecosystems. Change results from those elements of technology, subsistence economy, and social or political organization most closely tied to life's material needs. Archaeologists working with the adaptive perspective link cultural behaviors largely to the environment, demography, subsistence, or technology.

Let's look at an example of how these two perspectives produce different (but complementary) understandings of cultural behavior.

An Example: The Kwakwaka'wakw Potlatch

The Kwakwaka'wakw (pronounced KWAK-WAK-A-WAK, meaning "speakers of Kwak'wala") are a Native American tribe living on the coast of British Columbia. Prior to European contact, they lived primarily by fishing for salmon and halibut, hunting sea mammals, and gathering shellfish. They particularly depended on fall salmon runs to provide most of their food for the long winter. Kwakwaka'wakw once lived in villages that consisted of many large decorated cedar-plank houses and that often housed several related families. They had a social hierarchy in which some families claimed a higher rank than other families; slaves were occasionally

ideational perspective A research perspective that focuses on ideas, symbols, and mental structures as driving forces in shaping human behavior.

adaptive perspective A research perspective that emphasizes technology, ecology, demography, and economics as the key factors in defining human behavior.

Figure 2-3 Artist's rendering of a late-nineteenth-century Kwakwa̠ka'wakw potlatch ceremony (painting by Will Taylor).

taken in raids between villages. Many Kwakwa̠ka'wakw still live in their original territory, and although some are commercial fishermen, others are carpenters, computer programmers, lawyers, and teachers.

The **potlatch** is an element of Kwakwa̠ka'wakw life that has fascinated anthropologists for more than a century (Figure 2-3 shows a contemporary artist's rendering). The potlatch is an example of competitive feasts, a social custom found in many societies. The term comes from Chinook, a Northwest Coast **trade language,** and means "to give." Potlatches varied in size, from small affairs between families to huge feasts between villages—the kind the Kwakwa̠ka'wakw called "doing a great thing."

Potlatches accompanied high-ranking marriages between villages, funerals, and the raising of totem poles. Each potlatch involved ambitious, status-hungry men who battled one another for social prestige by hosting massive, opulent feasts that proceeded according to culturally dictated rules. The host parceled out gifts of varying value to his guests from another village: boxes of candlefish oil, baskets of berries, stacks of blankets, animal skins. As the chief presented

potlatch Among nineteenth-century Northwest Coast Native Americans, a ceremony involving the giving away or destruction of property in order to acquire prestige.

trade language A language that develops among speakers of different languages to permit economic exchanges.

each gift, the guests responded with (culturally prescribed) dissatisfaction, careful not to imply that their host was being generous.

Potlatches involved bonfires, magic tricks, and singing, with ranking families displaying valuable family heirlooms such as carved dishes. There were elaborate dances, such as the cannibal dance, in which members of the audience might be bitten, and others in which birds and whales were portrayed by wooden masks whose hinged mouths would dramatically open wide to reveal a human face peering up from the throat.

And there was food, lots and lots of food. Men drank fish oil from shovel-sized spoons. Guests stuffed themselves and crawled groaning into the forest, to vomit and return for more. The more food one gave away, the greater one's prestige.

The feasting extended beyond simple gluttony. A high-ranking member of the host village would give away blankets, slaves, canoes, and other goods to a high-ranking man from a rival village. One particularly important item was "coppers"—hammered, shield-like sheets of European copper, often with designs embossed or painted on their surfaces. These copper sheets had names, such as "Killer Whale," "Beaver Face," and "All Other Coppers Are Ashamed to Look at It." Late-nineteenth-century potlatching sometimes culminated in the outright destruction of property— hosts threw coppers into the sea and burned food, clothing, money, and canoes.

There was a cultural logic behind this conspicuous consumption: The more goods given away or destroyed, the greater the host's prestige. The guest chief would belittle the host's efforts, but to regain prestige he would eventually have to give an even grander feast.

The Potlatch as Ideational Message So, what was the potlatch all about? What was the symbolic message of the feasts? How did the participants understand it?

For the person giving the feast, the objective was prestige. Hosts obtained the dispersed goods through hard work, but also by giving smaller potlatches within their own villages. Traditionally, the value of goods given in those potlatches had to eventually be returned (not the exact same gifts, but their equivalents) plus a little bit more. This was investment banking. By giving away all the collected goods to a visitor or by destroying them, a host insulted his guests by symbolically saying "This is how powerful I am. I can give all this away and it does me no harm. You can't do this." And through association with this man, village members also gained prestige. For them, a successful potlatch truly was "doing a great thing."

To the non-Kwakwaka'wakw, the images of killer whales, huge spoons, bears, and boxes of candlefish oil seemed bizarre and chaotic. Indeed, the Canadian government found potlatches to be barbaric and wasteful and banned them in 1885 (a ban not lifted until 1951). Euro-Canadians did not share in Kwakwaka'wakw culture. They did not know the stories and legends that "made sense" of the masks and symbols. Failing to comprehend the "purpose" of potlatching, Euro-Canadians saw only chaos and waste that stood in the way of converting the Kwakwaka'wakw to Christianity and a system of Western values.

But suppose a nineteenth-century Kwakwaka'wakw person could view an American football game. Huge costumed, helmeted men smash into one another. Observers in the stands scream, some literally calling for blood; many have painted their faces and bodies in garish colors or wear horned helmets. Observers often drink to excess, and fights may break out in the bleachers. Would a Kwakwaka'wakw person have understood? Or would he/she have thought this was sheer madness?

The Potlatch as Adaptive Strategy An adaptive perspective seeks different interpretations for the potlatch. How could the loss of so much personal property serve useful ecological, technological, or economic purposes?

Recall that the Kwakwaka'wakw depended on salmon for their winter food supply. Some villages were located on streams with large, reliable salmon runs; others were on streams of smaller, less reliable runs. These less fortunate villages tried to ally themselves with the larger, more fortunate villages—villages they could count on for assistance in years of poor salmon runs. Through alliances cemented by potlatching, the large villages also forestalled the possibility that smaller villages might, under desperate conditions, try to attack them. They fought wars of "property" in addition to (or instead of) wars of "blood." Through the potlatch system, the less fortunate villages were invited to potlatches hosted by their more prosperous neighbors. Although visitors were required to endure seemingly endless barbs and slights, they departed with full bellies—and, more important, with a powerful ally.

What if some villages sustained a continued subsistence catastrophe? Some research suggests that the potlatch helped shift population from less productive to more productive villages. Economically prosperous villages could boast of (and demonstrate) their affluence at the potlatch ceremonies, thereby inducing guests to leave their impoverished situations and join the wealthier, more ecologically stable village. More people meant more laborers and bigger, more elaborate feasts that would allow a chief to outcompete his rivals. In other words, the drive for individual prestige held a material significance for the rank-and-file villagers.

Which Perspective Is Better? In a word, neither. Each perspective sees the world differently, privileging some aspects and downplaying others. An adaptive perspective recognizes that humans must respond to the material conditions of their environments; it helps account for why the potlatch occurred where and when it did. An ideational perspective shows how humans respond through particular, symbolically charged behaviors; it helps account for the particular ways in which the potlatch was conducted. We need both perspectives to understand human diversity and history. Both perspectives fall within an overarching scientific approach.

WHAT'S A SCIENTIFIC APPROACH?

Science (from the Latin "to know") refers, in its broadest sense, to a systematic body of knowledge about any field. Although the beginnings of modern science are generally traced to the European Renaissance and, earlier, to Islamic scholars, the origins of scientific thinking extend far back in human history. Archaeological sites preserve examples of early scientific reasoning: astronomical observations, treatment of disease, and calendrical systems. Cave paintings and carvings in bone or stone are often cited as early instances of systematizing knowledge.

Science as a distinct intellectual endeavor began in the seventeenth century, when Sir Francis Bacon codified the scientific method in his book *Novum Organum* (1620). Today, pure science is divided primarily into the physical sciences (including physics, chemistry, and geology), the biological sciences (such as botany and zoology), and the social sciences (such as anthropology). These are very different fields, and just as culture unifies the diversity of anthropology, it is a scientific approach that unifies the sciences. Anthropologist Lawrence Kuznar (Indiana-Purdue University at Fort Wayne) provides several characteristics of a scientific approach:

science The search for answers through a process that is objective, systematic, logical, predictive, self-critical, and public.

▶ **Science is empirical, or objective.** Science is concerned with the observable, measurable world. Questions are scientific (a) if they are concerned with the detectable properties of things and (b) if the result of observations designed to answer a question cannot be predetermined by the biases of the observer.

▶ **Science is systematic and explicit.** Scientists try to collect data relevant to solving a problem, and they try to specify their procedures, so that any trained observer under the same conditions would make the same observations.

▶ **Science is logical.** Scientists work not only with data, but also with the ideas that link data to interpretations, and with the ideas that link the ideas together. These linkages must be grounded in previ-

WHAT DOES IT MEAN TO ME?

DOES ARCHAEOLOGY PUT NATIVE AMERICANS ON TRIAL?

Many American Indians do not trust anthropologists, including archaeologists. This seems odd because anthropologists have long been the champions of Native American legal and cultural rights. Many anthropologists, for example, testified on behalf of tribes in the 1950s and 1960s when Indian land claims were decided in courts, and many work to maintain Indian rights and languages today.

One problem is that anthropologists often take a scientific perspective toward American Indian culture, and many Native Americans see a "scientific" approach to understanding their history as denigrating their own indigenous versions of history. This disconnect is particularly evident in the research regarding American Indian origins—one of the major questions in American archaeology. As early as 1589, the Jesuit missionary José de Acosta wrote in *Historia Natural y Moral de las Indias* that Indians had walked to the New World via a land route that connected the New World with Asia. He was prescient: genetic data demonstrate that the ancestors of Native Americans indeed migrated from Asia at least 13,500 years ago.

This position contrasts with most Native American origin stories. In many of these, the first people emerged from a hole in the earth, having traveled up from successive layers of worlds that lie below this one. Traditional Hopi beliefs, for example, hold that the modern world is the fourth world (with more to come).

No Native American religion explicitly states that "people came from Asia," and many American Indians see this suggestion as insulting, an affront to their religious beliefs (just as the idea of evolution is insulting to fundamentalist Christians). Some scholars agree, suggesting that archaeologists have no right to ask questions that put Native American religion on trial.

We disagree with this implied censorship; no one can deny another the right to ask questions. But more to the point, asking questions about Native American origins does not challenge American Indian (or any other) religion. Science evaluates claims about the *material* world, and religion is fundamentally about the *nonmaterial* world. Religions do sometimes make claims about the material world: How old is the earth? Where did people come from? What's the relationship between humans and animals? Because these are claims about the material world, we can subject them to scientific scrutiny.

So, what does it mean that scientific archaeology holds that the ancestors of Native American people came from Asia? Does this prove that Native American religions are wrong?

Absolutely not. Nobody can prove or disprove claims of the nonmaterial world using a method that evaluates claims about the material world. Archaeologists can prove only that a religious claim about the material world cannot be taken at face value. Some might think this means that the religion is false; but it might also mean that a religion's claim about the material world, even if unsubstantiated by science, holds deeper truths. From such a perspective, science encourages one to look deeper into religious beliefs, to find a significance that goes beyond issues of mere space and time.

ously demonstrated principles; otherwise an argument is a house of cards.

▶ **Science is explanatory and, consequently, predictive.** Science is concerned with causes. It seeks theories—explanatory statements that not only predict *what* will happen under a specified set of conditions, but also explain *why* it will happen.

▶ **Science is self-critical and based on testing.** Many people think that science is about white lab coats, supercomputers, and complex equations. Although science may involve such things, it's really about honesty. Scientists propose hypotheses, then they say, "Here is my idea; here is the evidence that will prove it wrong; and here is my attempt to collect that evidence." Scientists acquire understanding *not* by proving that an idea is right, but by showing that competing ideas are wrong. The best scientists are professional skeptics, always asking themselves: *How do I know that I know something?* Science, in this sense, becomes the right to be wrong.

▶ **Science is public.** Scientific methods, the observations, and the arguments linking observations with conclusions are explicit and available for scrutiny by the public. The origin or political implications of ideas are irrelevant. What matters in science is that ideas can be tested by objective methods.

Taken together, these characteristics of science produce scientific methods, elegant and powerful ways to understand the workings of the material world. Archaeologists have been doing scientific research for a long time. The public, however, frequently misunderstands science (see "What Does It Mean to Me? Does Archaeology Put Native Americans on Trial?"). To understand how the scientific method works, let's see how it was used to solve the "mystery" of the Moundbuilders.

How Science Explains Things: The Moundbuilder Myth

Sixteenth-century Europeans arriving on the North American continent confronted a serious intellectual challenge: Who were the people already living here? This was an important question because its answer begged another, more practical one: Did Europeans have the right to take the land?

Colonial Americans justified the taking of Native American lands in several ways, and one involved archaeology. Colonists settling the eastern woodlands encountered thousands of mounds and earthworks, especially in the Ohio and Mississippi River valleys. Some mounds were modest, only a few meters in diameter, but others were enormous: Monk's Mound at the site of Cahokia (just across the Mississippi River from St. Louis) stands nearly 70 feet tall, with a footprint larger than the largest pyramid in Egypt. Some mounds were conical in shape; others were truncated pyramids. Some were "effigy mounds," fashioned in the shape of animals such as serpents and birds (Figure 2-4 shows an example); others were precise geometric embankments enclosing many acres.

Colonial farmers plowed many of the mounds, finding curious things inside. Many contained human skeletal remains, but some mounds produced remarkable, eye-catching artworks such as copper and antler headdresses and stone pipes crafted into birds and other animals. They also found sheets of intricately shaped mica, carved shells, massive log tombs, spear points, incised pottery, copper ornaments, and polished stone disks (Figure 2-5). Today, we understand that some mounds were constructed as early as 5500 years ago in the southern Mississippi River valley and by 3000 years ago the practice was widespread across the eastern United States.

Ohio Historical Society

Figure 2-4 Aerial photo of Serpent Mound, an effigy mound in Ohio.

Courtesy of the Peabody Museum of Archaeology and Ethnology, Harvard University 96-11-10/48122

Figure 2-5 An etched slate from Moundville, Alabama. Artifacts such as these convinced nineteenth-century scholars that the Moundbuilders were a superior culture.

Inspired by such finds, colonial scholars dreamed up several ideas to explain who built the mounds. The favored interpretation held that the Moundbuilders were a superior race wiped out by Indians. Some thought this pioneering race was Viking; others nominated the Egyptians, Israelites, Chinese, Greeks, Polynesians, Phoenicians, Norwegians, Belgians, Tartars, Saxons, Hindus, Africans, Welsh, or residents of the lost continent of Atlantis. An Ohio minister even suggested that God had created the Serpent Mound in southern Ohio to mark the site of Eden.

The Moundbuilders, it seemed, might have been anyone—except the ancestors of American Indians. Nineteenth-century scholars saw the Indians as late-arriving marauders, destroyers of a magnificent civilization. After all, weren't the mounds full of human bones, evidence of past battles? Thus arose the myth of a Moundbuilder civilization.

This view of history provided colonists with a sense of innate superiority and the right to avenge the Moundbuilders by dispossessing Native Americans of their land. Handy history—but was it true?

A President's Attention From the start, Moundbuilder myths attracted scrutiny at the highest levels of American society—including that of Thomas Jefferson (1743–1826), author of the Declaration of Independence and third president of the United States. Jefferson was also an expert musician (the violin being his favorite instrument), an inventor, a connoisseur of French cooking, an avid chess player, an accomplished

horticulturalist, scientist, architect—and the first scientific archaeologist in America.

Jefferson's contribution to archaeology shows up in his only book, a response to questions sent to him by French scholars. *Notes on the State of Virginia* (1787) dealt, in part, with the aborigines of Virginia, their origin, and the question of the mounds. Jefferson listed the various Virginia tribes, related their histories since the settlement of Jamestown in 1607, and incorporated a census of Virginia's current Native American population. He argued that Native Americans were the intellectual and physical equals of Europeans and wholly capable of constructing the prehistoric earthworks of the United States.

Jefferson took another critical step by proceeding to excavate a burial mound located on his property. Today this step seems obvious, but Jefferson's contemporaries vastly preferred rummaging through libraries and archives rather than soiling their hands with bones, stones, and dirt to answer intellectual questions.

Jefferson's account described his method of excavation, the different layers of earth, and the artifacts and human bones that he encountered. He then tested the idea that the bones resulted from warfare. Noting the absence of traumatic wounds (such as those made by arrows) and the presence of children, Jefferson rejected the idea that the bones were those of fallen soldiers. Instead, he surmised that the burials had accumulated through repeated use. Overall, Jefferson saw no reason to doubt that the ancestors of Native Americans had built the mounds. Few archaeologists today would modify Jefferson's conclusions.

Still, Jefferson did not take sides in the Moundbuilder debate because he thought that more information was needed. As president of the American Philosophical Society in 1799, he distributed a pamphlet calling for the systematic collection of information on the mounds. Jefferson's suggestion finally bore fruit in 1848, thanks to the joint efforts of two very different men.

The Surveyor and the Doctor Ephraim Squier (1821–1888) was a Connecticut civil engineer, surveyor, journalist, and later in life, a politician intent on making a name for himself (advocating the radical idea of building a canal across Central America). Like many educated people of the time, Squier had wide-ranging interests, but the Moundbuilders held a special fascination for him.

Edwin Davis (1811–1888), an Ohio physician, was also intrigued by the mounds, especially those near his hometown of Chillicothe. But unlike Squier, Davis pursued a calm, anonymous life with his family near his hometown.

With Squier's ambition and Davis's money, the two gentlemen formed an alliance to study the mounds. Although the two came to dislike each other intensely, their names will forever be wed in American archaeology because of their 1848 monograph, *Ancient Monuments of the Mississippi Valley*—the first publication by the newly formed Smithsonian Institution.

Squier and Davis claimed that they did not seek to "sustain" any particular hypothesis, only "to arrive at truth" and to avoid "speculation." True to this intent, they devoted the first 300 pages of their book to meticulous description of mounds and earthworks. They based their work on others' reports as well as on their own investigation of some 200 sites, primarily in the Ohio River valley. They illustrated many artifacts, mound cross-sections, and maps of earthworks (e.g., Figure 2-6).

Only in the final pages did Squier and Davis allow themselves to speculate. The Moundbuilder population, they wrote, "was numerous and widely spread," as was "evident from the number and magnitude of the ancient monuments and the extensive range of their occurrence." It was also homogeneous in customs and habits, as was "sustained by the great uniformity which the ancient remains display." They described the Moundbuilders as agricultural peoples because agriculture, they assumed, was necessary to a "large population, to fixedness of institutions, and to any considerable advance in the economical or ennobling arts."

Squier and Davis emphasized the differences between the Moundbuilders and American Indians. The mounds contain art objects that were "immeasurably beyond anything which the North American Indians are known to produce." They saw differences in burial practices, skull form, warfare, defensive structures, and subsistence, arguing that the Moundbuilders were agriculturalists and the Indians only hunters (an odd thing to say since Indians had taught maize horticulture to the colonists!).

In the end, Squier and Davis supported the Moundbuilder hypothesis, suggesting that the Moundbuilders were related to the "semi-civilized" nations of Mexico and Central America (such as the Aztecs). By 1873, the president of the Chicago Academy of Sciences thought it "preposterous" that Indians could have built the mounds. And in his 1872 book, *Ancient America*, J. D. Baldwin considered any relationship between the Moundbuilders and Indians to be "absurd."

The Explorer and the Entomologist During the Civil War battle at Shiloh, a young Union captain raised his right arm to give an order to fire and a Confederate minié ball took it off at the elbow. Unwilling to accept a setback, John Wesley Powell (1834–1902) went on to explore the West, mount the first expedition down the Colorado River through the Grand Canyon, and hold several important posts in the federal government.

Powell's western explorations brought him into close contact with many Native Americans, who fascinated him, and he found himself in a position to pursue the Moundbuilder issue when, in 1879, he became head of the newly formed Bureau of Ethnology (which was later placed within the Smithsonian Institution). Because the Moundbuilder issue captivated public interest, Congress insisted that the Bureau spend a fifth of its budget on mound exploration. Searching for someone to head up the bureau's new division of mound studies, Powell settled on Cyrus Thomas.

Born in Tennessee, Thomas (1825–1910) spent his early career as a lawyer and merchant, but then shifted his attention—to bugs. Entomology may seem an odd background for an archaeologist, but since archaeology did not exist as a profession, Thomas was as qualified as any of his contemporaries.

Thomas's study took a dozen years and amassed data from 2000 sites in 21 states. He published a 700-page final report in 1894 that began with an explicit question: "Were the mounds built by the Indians?"

Initially a proponent of the Moundbuilder hypothesis, Thomas tried to evaluate objectively each piece of relevant evidence, asking, for instance, Did the Indians have the knowledge of mound building?

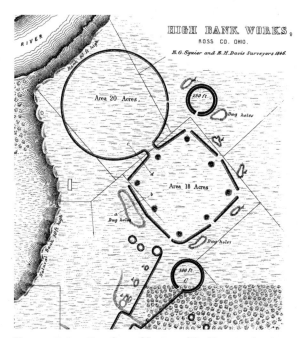

Figure 2-6 A portion of one of Squier and Davis's maps, showing a mound group in Ohio. *From © Squier, Ephraim G. and Edwin H. Davis, 1848. Ancient Monuments of The Mississippi Valley, edited by David J. Meltzer, 51. Washington D.C.: Smithsonian Institution Press, 1998. Image in the public domain.*

Figure 2-7 Mounds in use among southeastern Indians, as illustrated in the account of Jacques Le Moyne, a sixteenth-century French explorer. *Courtesy The Florida Center for Instructional Technology, University of South Florida, Special Collections.*

Thomas pointed out that earlier scholars had overlooked Spanish and French explorers' reports that described mound construction and use in the southeastern United States (see Figure 2-7). He also studied the copper objects found in the mounds. Indians had no smelting technology, but Thomas concluded (correctly) that the copper occurring naturally in the Great Lakes region did not need to be smelted. Mining and shaping such native copper required little more than a stone hammer.

Thomas concluded, modestly, that "the author believes the theory which attributes these works [the mounds] to the Indians to be the correct one." The implications carried far beyond the Smithsonian Institution: There was no lost race of Moundbuilders. Native Americans had not destroyed them. There was no justification for Europeans to seek revenge. The myth that helped perpetuate a racist attitude toward Native Americans was simply that—a myth. But sadly, by 1894, the truth about the Moundbuilders was too late. The Indian Wars were officially over, and virtually all Native Americans were confined to reservations.

scientific method Accepted principles and procedures for the systematic pursuit of secure knowledge. Established scientific procedures involve the following steps: (1) define a relevant problem; (2) establish one or more hypotheses; (3) determine the empirical implications of the hypotheses; (4) collect appropriate data through observation and/or experimentation; (5) compare these data with the expected implications; and (6) revise and/or retest hypotheses as necessary.

hypothesis A proposition proposed as an explanation of some phenomenon.

inductive reasoning Working from specific observations to more general hypotheses.

The Scientific Method

The history of the Moundbuilder myth provides a simple example of some characteristics of the **scientific method,** which we can reduce to six steps:

1. Define a relevant problem.
2. Establish one or more hypotheses.
3. Determine the empirical implications of the hypotheses.
4. Collect appropriate data through observation and/or experimentation.
5. Test the hypothesis by comparing these data with the expected implications.
6. Reject, revise, and/or retest hypotheses as necessary.

This is an idealized summary, and scientific research does not always progress neatly through each of these steps. Nonetheless, this framework remains the goal of modern science.

The Role of Inductive Reasoning The first two tasks (Steps 1 and 2) define a relevant question and translate it into an appropriate **hypothesis.** The idea is simply to describe the known facts and create a hypothesis to account for them. Such hypotheses are generated through **inductive reasoning,** working from specific facts or observations to general conclusions. The known facts serve as premises in this case, meaning that hypotheses should not only account for the known facts but should also predict unobserved phenomena.

No rules exist for induction (just as there are no rules for thinking up good ideas). Some hypotheses are derived by enumerating the data, isolating common features, and generalizing to unobserved cases that share these features. Archaeologists also turn to analogies, relatively well understood ethnographies that are relevant to poorly understood archaeological cases. Judgment, imagination, past experience, and even guesswork all have their place in science. It's irrelevant where or how one derives the hypothesis. What matters is how well the hypothesis accounts for unobserved phenomena.

The Moundbuilder hypothesis arose from both facts and cultural biases: Nineteenth-century scholars had trouble reconciling what they found in mounds with their views of Native American culture. Squier and Davis (as well as Jefferson) were scientists in the tradition of Francis Bacon. They believed that when a sufficiently large number of facts were collected—when 200 mound sites were mapped and probed for artifacts—the meaning of those facts would become apparent. This is why Jefferson promoted more systematic collection of data.

Jefferson, Squier, and Davis worked in the inductive phase (Steps 1 and 2) of Moundbuilder research. Because so little was known about the mounds, the first priority became gathering some relevant facts: How many mounds were there? How much variability was there among the mounds? Were there different kinds of mounds? How old were they? What were they made of? Based on available data, Squier and Davis inductively derived a conclusion: The living Indians of the United States were not descendants of the Moundbuilders.

Science Is Self-Correcting Squier and Davis, as it turned out, were completely wrong. But the beauty of the scientific method is that it's self-correcting. Scientists always ask: *Do we really know what we think we know?* Squier and Davis thought they were at Step 6 in the process, but we can now see that they had only inductively formulated a hypothesis. It was left to others to test this idea. Science sometimes proceeds this way, by backtracking and rethinking things that others thought were over and done with. Although Thomas didn't use the rhetoric of science, he was indeed testing the hypothesis that Indians were the descendants of the Moundbuilders.

So, how does one test this hypothesis (Steps 4 and 5)? The hypothesis must first be translated into testable form. Ironically, *hypotheses can never be tested directly* because they are abstract statements. The truth is that scientists don't actually verify hypotheses—rather, they test the logical material consequences of their hypotheses (the empirical implications established in Step 3).

Deductive reasoning is required to define these logical outcomes. Deductive arguments hold that the conclusions must be true if the premises are true, typically expressed as "if . . . then" statements: *If* the hypothesis is true, *then* we expect to observe the following outcomes. The tricky part is bridging the gap between the *if* and the *then*.

It's easy to see the simple deductive reasoning Thomas employed for Step 5. *If* American Indians did not know about mound building, *then* there should be no explorer accounts of mound building by Indians. *If* the mounds were built by a long-vanished race, *then* they should be considerably older than the known age of Indian culture. *If* the metal artifacts in mounds were signs of a "superior" Moundbuilder culture, *then* the manufacturing technology associated with them should be absent from later Indian culture. This is how Thomas laid out the criteria whereby he could claim the Moundbuilder hypothesis to be false.

"Testing" for Thomas meant collecting, analyzing, and publishing data, evaluated openly against competing hypotheses. The **testability** of a hypothesis is critical. An idea is testable if the implications of the hypothesis can be measured in some fashion *with the same results obtained by different observers.* This means that how the observation is made must be independent of who's doing the observing. We have to know that you would make the same observations that we would make.

Science Is Reiterative The scientific method is really more of a cycle. Step 6 (testing, rejecting, or revising the hypothesis) normally leads back to Step 1 (redefining the problem at hand). Scientific cycles commence in the world of facts. Through the process of induction, these facts are probed, and hypotheses are devised to account for what is already known. But because hypotheses are general declarations, they cannot be tested against further facts until they are translated into their logical consequences.

The scientific cycle thus begins and ends with facts. Newly discovered facts will suggest new hypotheses, and once again inductive reasoning will lead from the world of facts to the world of abstraction, initiating a new cycle of investigation.

Scientific thinking in archaeology applies at many different levels, from questions such as "What's this red stain in the soil?" or "What was this stone tool used for?" to questions such as "Why did humans switch from hunting and gathering to agriculture?" or "What is human nature?" Sometimes the cycle is played out over the course of a day, sometimes over the course of many lifetimes (as in the Moundbuilder controversy).

Science Is Not Infallible As a human venture, science is subject to false starts, dead ends, preconceived notions, and cultural biases. The Moundbuilder hypothesis was not drawn directly and inductively from sterile archaeological facts. Even in the absence of much data, the idea (myth) was widespread because it conveniently facilitated and justified what colonists wanted all along—to seize Indian land. Science will be forever embedded in the cultural biases of the scientist. Beyond question, the social, cultural, and political context of archaeology influences its theories. Scientific approaches do not always deliver the right answer on the first try, or even the second or third.

deductive reasoning Reasoning from theory to predict specific observational or experimental results.

testability The degree to which one's observations and experiments can be reproduced.

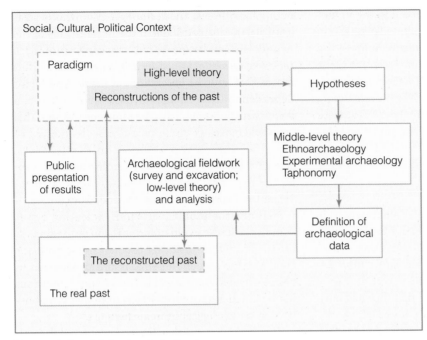

Social, Cultural, Political Context

Paradigm

High-level theory

Reconstructions of the past

Hypotheses

Public presentation of results

Archaeological fieldwork (survey and excavation; low-level theory) and analysis

Middle-level theory
Ethnoarchaeology
Experimental archaeology
Taphonomy

Definition of archaeological data

The reconstructed past

The real past

Figure 2-8 A model of archaeological inquiry.

Sometimes the truth is only evident in hindsight. But we generally find, in the end, that we've learned something. And that is what science is all about.

With this background, let's consider the application of scientific methods to the archaeological enterprise.

THE STRUCTURE OF ARCHAEOLOGICAL INQUIRY

Figure 2-8 translates the generic scientific cycle into a format specific to archaeology. You'll see that the term **theory** crops up three times. In science, "theory" refers

theory An explanation for observed, empirical phenomena. It seeks to explain the relationships between variables; it is an answer to a "why" question.

low-level theory The observations and interpretations that emerge from hands-on archaeological field and lab work.

data Relevant observations made on objects that then serve as the basis for study and discussion.

rockshelter A common type of archaeological site, consisting of a rock overhang that is deep enough to provide shelter but not deep enough to be called a cave (technically speaking, a cave must have an area of perpetual darkness).

ecofact Plant or animal remains found at an archaeological site.

feature Nonportable archaeological evidence such as fire hearths, architectural elements, artifact clusters, garbage pits, and soil stains.

to statements that purport to explain observed, empirical phenomena. In this sense, theories answer the "why" questions, which occur at a low level, a middle level, and a high level. We distinguish the different levels not by complexity or difficulty, but by their place in the process of archaeological inquiry.

Low-Level Theory

Low-level theory begins with archaeological objects and generates relevant facts or data about those objects. Some data are physical observations. For example, "Artifact 20.2/4683 is (a) made of obsidian, (b) 21.5 mm long, and (c) weighs 2.1 grams." This statement contains three observations made on an archaeological object (the number 20.2/4683 is the item's unique catalog number—more on that in a later chapter). Other observations might be contextual: "Artifact 20.2/4683 was found in excavation unit B-5, 56 cm below the surface."

Before going further, we need to consider another term, **data.** You might consider "data" to be a straightforward concept, but it's actually much more complex.

Gatecliff Shelter is a Nevada **rockshelter** where people camped, now and then, beneath a shallow overhang over a period of some 7000 years (Figure 2-9). Thomas found Gatecliff in 1970 and excavated the site's deposits with an interdisciplinary team throughout the 1970s.

Gatecliff is nearly 40 feet deep, with cultural deposits stacked up within a floor area of about 300 ft². Thousands of artifacts were buried inside Gatecliff Shelter: stone projectile points, bone awls, willow basketry, grinding stones, small pieces of slate incised with enigmatic geometric designs, woven sagebrush bark mats, stone scrapers, shells and turquoise used as ornaments. Gatecliff also contained objects not made by humans—**ecofacts,** which are items relating to the natural environment, such as bighorn sheep bones, charcoal, piñon nut hulls, and pollen. We also encountered **features**—pits, hearths, rodent burrows—which are nonportable cultural and noncultural things that archaeologists measure, draw, photograph, and sample.

© American Museum of Natural History, photo by Dennis O'Brien

Figure 2-9 Gatecliff Shelter, late in the excavation: removing deposits through a bucket brigade method.

The point here is simple but important: After nearly a decade of excavating at Gatecliff, Thomas excavated no data at all. So why, you might ask, would an archaeologist waste a decade digging holes that produce no data? The simple truth is that data don't lie out there waiting for somebody to pick them up, like Easter eggs on the lawn. *Data depend on theory*, much as *theory depends on data*.

Thomas found no data at Gatecliff because archaeologists don't excavate data. Archaeologists excavate objects; data are *observations* made on those objects. Those observations enable archaeologists to make *interpretations* of the objects: Is this grubby little black thing a piece of pottery? To answer that simple question, we need to ask if it contains the characteristics of pottery: Does it contain clay and temper (material added to the clay to give it strength)? Does it look as though it had been fired (heated)? If the answers are yes, then we "interpret" the grubby little black thing to be a piece of pottery.

Data, then, become the observations that allow us to make interpretations. Data tell us *why* something is what we think it is. This means that the observations we make on objects, as well as the interpretations of

those observations, are all *theory-driven*. This is what low-level theory is all about.

Why are these observations that create data theoretical statements? Because each is based on a "why" question: Why do we know that something is obsidian? Because the stone has certain characteristics that fit a definition of obsidian (a dark volcanic glass), and this knowledge derives from a theoretical understanding of how rocks form. Why do we know the length, weight, and provenience? Because these measurements were made using digital instruments whose ability to measure things reliably is based on theories from physics.

Here's another example: While excavating, a student comes upon a curving red band in the sediment. On the concave side of the red band are some black flecks that turn out to be charcoal. The student calls to her crew chief, "I've got a hearth over here!" How does she know it is a hearth—and not a filled-in rodent burrow, an ancient posthole, or something else?

The charcoal was a clue, but archaeological sites often contain scattered charcoal. She also observed the feature's properties (its diameter, depth, and fill), and interpreted those. Apparently, she knows that heat has a predictable effect on sediments with high iron content: The iron is oxidized (bonded with oxygen) and turns red. Our student may be unaware of the theory that accounts for the oxidation and color change, but her interpretation is still based on that theory.

This kind of archaeology is "low-level" theory, not because it is simple or unimportant, but because archaeologists normally give little thought to the theories that stand behind their basic observations in the field or lab. We record that we found something—a hearth or bison femur or potsherd—without presenting the geochemical, evolutionary, or other theory that gives us the ability to identify something as a hearth or a bison bone.

We can make an infinite number of observations on any single archaeological object. Many of these are made on the object itself: length, width, thickness, weight, angle measurements, material, color, curvature, chemical composition, manufacturing techniques, and so forth. Others might be observations on the object's context—that is, where it was found in a site. Overall, the important dimensions of low-level theory are the classical ones in archaeology: form and context.

Low-level theory remains critical because it allows archaeologists to know that their data are comparable. However, these basic observations can become the focus of scrutiny if, for instance, archaeologists try to determine when humans began to use fire intentionally (perhaps some hundreds of thousands of years ago). In this case, what constitutes an *intentional* hearth becomes of more than passing interest. The same is true when archaeologists try to determine whether some chipped stones are tools or simply rocks that Mother Nature has broken in fortuitous ways (more than one archaeologist has been fooled). When archaeologists give this sort of attention to inferences made from observations, they move into the realm of middle-level theory.

Middle-Level Theory

Middle-level theory links some specific set of archaeological data with the human behavior or natural processes that produced them. At this middle level, we make a critical transition, moving from the archaeologically observable (the low-level theoretical facts) to the archaeologically invisible (relevant human behaviors or natural processes of the past). How does this transition actually take place?

Keep in mind that the archaeological record is the *contemporary* evidence left by people of the past. Strictly speaking, the archaeological record is composed only of static objects—the artifacts, ecofacts, and features that have survived the passage of time. Those objects are the products of both human behavior and natural processes. Our job is to infer the long-gone behavior and natural processes from the static results—the objects we recover from archaeological sites. Figure 2-10, for example, shows a large scatter of bison bone at a site in Wyoming. All that the archaeologist can record is the kind of bones that are present and their arrangement and condition. But how does the archaeologist infer from these observations whether people killed and butchered these bison?

Archaeologists conducting middle-level research seek situations in which they can observe (1) ongoing human behavior or natural processes and (2) the material results of that behavior or those processes. This requires that archaeologists step out of their excavation trenches and turn to experimental archaeology, ethnoarchaeology, or taphonomy. We'll discuss these fields in detail in Chapter 8. For now, it's only important to remember that middle-level theory is necessary to infer human behavior and natural processes from archaeological data. Middle-level theory allows archaeologists to create the "if . . . then" statements in Step 3 of the scientific method discussed earlier. This can take the form of experimenting with the manufacture of stone

Figure 2-10 The Horner site in Wyoming. The bones are those of dozens of bison. How would we know if these animals had been hunted?

© University of Wyoming, Frison Institute

tools or pottery to determine the material results—the things that might be left behind. It could also entail studying living populations to see how their behaviors are translated into material remains. Or it might require the study of natural processes to see, for example, how carnivores break bones of their kills, or how rivers move bones and artifacts in patterned ways.

High-Level Theory

High-level theory is archaeology's ultimate objective; low- and middle-level research are necessary steps to attain this goal. High-level theory goes beyond the archaeological specifics to address the "big questions" of concern to many social and historical sciences. High-level theory applies to all intellectual inquiry about the human condition, raising questions such as: Why did we humans become cultural animals? Why did hunter-gatherers become agriculturalists? Why did social stratification arise? Why did human history take the particular course it did in the New World as opposed to the Old World? Why did aboriginal hunter-gatherers in California not take up agriculture? Why did large civilizations develop in some parts of the world and not in others?

Some general theories stress environmental adaptation, some emphasize biological factors, and some involve only cultural causality; others try to combine these. Chapter 13 will explore some of the general theories that archaeologists have offered as answers to some big questions.

middle-level theory Hypothesis that links archaeological observations with the human behavior or natural processes that produced them.

high-level theory Theory that seeks to answer large "why" questions.

Paradigms

Paradigms provide the overarching framework for understanding "how the world works" that each researcher brings to a particular question or problem. This is the most abstract and yet the most important of our concepts.

Paradigms are a lot like culture—both are learned, shared, and symbolic. Archaeologists sharing the same paradigm can converse with one another and leave a lot unstated; an archaeologist following another paradigm might have to ask many questions, seeking definitions of basic concepts and terms. Like culture, your paradigm influences how you frame your research questions, and how you interpret the answers. Paradigms contain some *a priori* notions of which variables are relevant and which are not. And, like culture, a paradigm can give you both correct and incorrect answers. Paradigms are not open to direct empirical verification or rejection; they just turn out to be useful or not.

Just as all humans participate in a culture, all archaeologists operate within a paradigm, whether they are aware of it or not. Without a paradigm, nothing would make sense. So, although a paradigm can give you an inaccurate bias, the goal isn't to become paradigm-free. Rather, we simply must be aware of the paradigm we're using.

The two basic paradigms in modern archaeology—the processual and the postprocessual paradigms—closely mirror the adaptive and ideational approaches previously discussed. We will deliberately simplify our presentation of these paradigms because the history of any intellectual field resembles more a braided stream than a simple river of thought. No archaeologist today, for example, falls neatly into either category, and we intend to give you only the basic differences between these two ways of thinking (summarized in Table 2-1) in order to show the range of ways in which archaeologists think about the past.

Processual Archaeology The **processual paradigm** includes the new archaeology of Lewis Binford and his generation (see Chapter 1) and extends to the evolutionary approaches practiced today. Processual archaeology takes its name from its concern with "process"—that is, with the ways that cultures change over time. Processual archaeologists search for a "grand narrative" about how culture changes.

The processual paradigm has several key characteristics. First, *processual archaeology emphasizes evolutionary generalizations, not historical specifics, and often downplays the importance of the individual.* In

TABLE 2-1 Some Contrasts between Processual and Postprocessual Archaeology

PROCESSUAL ARCHAEOLOGY	POSTPROCESSUAL ARCHAEOLOGY
Emphasizes evolutionary generalizations and regularities, not historical specifics; downplays the importance of the individual.	Rejects the search for universal laws and regularities.
Views culture from a systemic perspective and defines culture as adaptation.	Rejects the systemic view of culture and focuses on an ideational perspective.
Explanation is explicitly scientific and objective.	Less enthusiastic about scientific methods and denies possibility of objectivity.
Attempts to remain ethically neutral; claims to be explicitly nonpolitical.	Argues that all archaeology is unavoidably political.

the early days of the processual paradigm, archaeologists viewed history as the opposite of science, as description rather than explanation. The processual paradigm claims to be scientific, not historical. It focuses on regularities, correlations, and patterns among different historical cases to point to causal variables. An interest in developing cultural (as opposed to biological) evolutionary theory directed the processual paradigm away from ideology and history and toward environmental change, population growth, food production, trade, and conflict over limited resources as the forces driving cultural evolution.

Processual archaeology saw particular historical sequences as individual "experiments" from which one could construct theory and law-like generalizations. Early on, processual archaeologists did not consider culture history by itself to be important.

Reflecting the processual paradigm's focus on historical regularities and correlations, Binford and others rejected "great man" explanations of history—explanations that attribute major changes in economy or social or political organization to a single person who had a "great idea." Archaeologists, for instance, once thought that the origin of agriculture was one of these great ideas, a hypothesis that has since been disproven.

paradigm The overarching framework, often unstated, for understanding a research problem. It is a researcher's "culture."

processual paradigm The paradigm that explains social, economic, and cultural change as primarily the result of adaptation to material conditions. External conditions (for example, the environment) are assumed to take causal priority over ideational factors in explaining change.

Second, *processual archaeology views culture from a systemic perspective and takes an adaptive approach to the study of human culture.* Because culture provides the nonbiological system through which people adapt to their environment, processual archaeology could (and briefly, did) tap into a much larger body of established external theory, often called **general systems theory.** The theoretical premise is that various complex entities—thermostats, computers, glaciers, living organisms, and even human societies—are most profitably viewed as systems composed of multiple parts that interact in a number of predictable ways. Depending on the application, the rules governing all systems (such as positive feedback, negative feedback, and equilibrium) could explain the behavior of the major parts of any system—regardless of its specifics. (Although many processual archaeologists today view human societies as systems, they no longer explain them in the sterile terms of general systems theory.)

Processual archaeology focuses attention on technology, ecology, and economy and takes an adaptive rather than ideational perspective on culture. Consequently, processual archaeology focuses on behavior rather than on the cultural ideas that stand behind that behavior. Religion and ideology are seen as "epiphenomena"—cultural add-ons with little long-term explanatory value.

Third, *explanation in processual archaeology is explicitly scientific.* Procedures in processual archaeology depend on deductive models grounded in the hard sciences (math, chemistry, physics) and emphasize the importance of being objective. By objective, we mean that processual archaeologists believe that they can see the world "as it really is," not through a filter that colors their perception of the world.

The processual paradigm initially championed the view that predicting events (even those in the past) is equivalent to explaining them. More recent approaches, however, stress the interplay between induction and deduction, the *relative* objectivity of observations, and the probabilistic nature of explanation in the social sciences.

general systems theory An effort to describe the properties by which all systems, including human societies, allegedly operate. Popular in processual archaeology of the late 1960s and 1970s.

postprocessual paradigm A paradigm that focuses on humanistic approaches and rejects scientific objectivity. It sees archaeology as inherently political and is more concerned with interpreting the past than with testing hypotheses. It sees change as arising largely from interactions between individuals operating within a symbolic and/or competitive system.

Fourth, *processual archaeology attempts to remain ethically neutral and claims to be explicitly nonpolitical.* Processual archaeology tries to generate evidence about the past that is deliberately disconnected from the present. Politics of the present, processual archaeologists argue, should have nothing to do with the study of the ancient past. Archaeology should avoid subjectivity, and its conclusions should not be influenced by modern politics. Processual archaeology is not interested in passing moral judgments on people of the past.

Processual archaeology does wish to be relevant to the modern world and to provide an understanding of cultural evolution that is useful in directing the world's future. Archaeology should influence politics, the thinking goes, but politics is not to influence archaeology.

Perhaps half of archaeologists today pursue the processual paradigm in one form or another (although many of them also agree with some tenets of the postprocessual paradigm, as discussed below). Why does processualism hold such appeal for archaeologists? One reason is that it emphasizes technology, economy, environment, and demography—those aspects of human existence that leave the clearest traces in the archaeological record. Processualism may also be popular because it suggests that the world and cultural change result from orderly processes—an idea challenged by the postprocessual paradigm.

Postprocessual Archaeology The **postprocessual paradigm** is embedded within the larger arena of postmodernism. It arose in archaeology largely in Great Britain and Europe, nurtured by archaeologists such as Ian Hodder (Stanford University), but adherents today can be found on both sides of the Atlantic. We will characterize postprocessual archaeology in contrast to the points we just made about processual archaeology.

First, *postprocessual archaeology rejects the processual search for universal laws and emphasizes the role of the individual.* The postprocessual paradigm holds that universals of human behavior do not exist (or that they are banal) and that scientific explanations are inadequate because they downplay historical circumstances in their search for universals. Processual archaeology saw the particulars of history—such as a certain culture's ideas about men and women or specific religious beliefs—as playing no significant role in the grand scheme of history. Postprocessual archaeologists see the grand scheme, if it exists at all, as uninteresting; instead, they see the trajectory of particular societies as heavily influenced by that society's particular cultural ideas, so much so that the search for a grand narrative is rendered meaningless. Some postprocessual archaeologists think archaeology should be more closely allied with history than with anthropology.

In fact, postprocessual archaeology often emphasizes the role of the individual in human society. We do not mean that postprocessual archaeology aims to see particular individuals in archaeology—for example, to find the name of the person who made a particular pot. Instead, postprocessual archaeology argues that large social change results from individuals going about their daily lives. In this view, societies are not animated strictly by change from the "outside" (such as environmental change). More specifically, postprocessual archaeology tends to see social tension—for example, competition between men and women, elites and nonelites, or regional groups—as especially important in generating (or negotiating) social change. Postprocessual archaeology is keenly interested in how cultural change results from the process of individuals' negotiating their daily lives around issues of power.

Second, *postprocessual archaeology rejects the systemic view of culture and focuses more on the ideational approach to culture.* Postprocessual archaeology discredits the systems approach as a "robotic view of humans." Postmodernism in general distrusts any deterministic perspective that reduces individual humans to the status of a historical droid, not significantly different from conditioned laboratory rats.

Postprocessualists argue that the systemic view of human society suggests a coordinated, uniform organism responding only to outside pressures, mainly the environment and demography. But recall that postprocessual archaeologists see society as composed of conflicting individuals, groups, genders, and classes, whose goals are not necessarily identical and whose interests and actions are often in conflict with the adaptive success and functional needs of the cultural system as a whole. How can we reconcile a vision of society as a well-oiled adaptive machine with the fact that specific individuals, such as dictators, whose interests are maladaptive for others, often control a society?

Postprocessualists tend to look at artifacts differently than do processual archaeologists. Processual archaeologists generally see things, such as the pot shown in Figure 2-11, in terms of functions: Was the pot used for cooking? Food or water storage? Is it a serving vessel? But postprocessual archaeologists remind us that things also carry symbolic meanings: Did this pot "stand for" women, or hospitality, or the Raven

© Melissa Murphy

Figure 2-11 An Inca-style aribalos vessel from the site of Puruchuco-Huaquerones. Processual archaeology focuses on its function, postprocessual archaeology on its meaning.

clan? Thus, postprocessualists argue that we cannot understand what artifacts mean simply by looking for their functions; we must also consider their symbolic meanings.

Third, *postprocessual archaeology sees knowledge as "historically situated," and not as objective as processual archaeologists argue.* By "historically situated," postmodernists emphasize the degree to which our understanding of the world reflects the specific time and place in which we live. This is demonstrated through the method of deconstruction. Coined by French philosopher Jacques Derrida (1930–2004), **deconstruction** refers to efforts to expose the assumptions behind the allegedly scientific search for knowledge.

Anthropologist Richard Wilk (Indiana University), for instance, has shown that explanations for the demise of Maya civilization are linked to the larger cultural and political context of archaeologists. The Maya civilization flourished in portions of Central America and Mexico, reaching a zenith about 1300 years ago. The Maya constructed magnificent centers with stone pyramids, surrounded by thousands of households. These complexes were the center of a rich ceremonial life, places where kings recorded their exploits in hieroglyphs on stone monuments called **stelae** (Figure 2-12). The society ran according to a set of complex calendars and supported its agriculture with water storage systems (see Chapter 13).

deconstruction Efforts to expose the assumptions behind the alleged objective and systematic search for knowledge. A primary tool of postmodernism.

stelae Stone monuments erected by Maya rulers to record their history in rich images and hieroglyphic symbols. These symbols can be read and dated.

© Charles & Josette Lenars/CORBIS

Figure 2-12 Stela B at Copán, Honduras. Erected in AD 731, it depicts the ruler, 18-Rabbit.

But the Maya civilization collapsed about 1100 years ago (although the Maya people never disappeared, of course, because they are still there today). People abandoned the ceremonial centers, which were gradually consumed by the jungle. Why?

Processual archaeologists proposed many explanations for the collapse of Maya civilization, especially war, environmental degradation, and the abuse of power by political elites. Wilk argues that these explanations waxed and waned in popularity in relation to major U.S. political events. Warfare as an explanation began in 1962, the beginning of the Vietnam War, and grew in popularity until the end of that war. During the ecology movement of the mid-1970s, explanations tended to focus on environmental degradation. And after 1974, in the aftermath of the Watergate fiasco and historic resignation of Richard Nixon, abuse of government power was a favored explanation in the professional literature.

By deconstructing archaeological thinking about the Maya collapse, Wilk demonstrated the degree to which modern events can influence our understanding of the past. There is nothing new in suggesting that

archaeologists are products of their own culture; scientists (like Wilk) have always tried to discover biases, remove their effects, and move on. Although some postmodernists argue that objectivity is impossible and that truth is subjective, most postmodernists adhere to a weaker version of this thesis, seeing the effects of cultural biases as difficult but not impossible to remove. Deconstruction helps achieve that goal.

Fourth, *postprocessual archaeology argues that all archaeology is political.* Processual archaeologists wanted to be "relevant" to modern society but politically neutral. But postprocessual archaeology argues that all research is inescapably political. The Moundbuilder researcher Ephraim Squier, for example, was a confirmed polygenist—meaning that he believed that humankind included several "races," each having separate instances of creation and separate capacities for progress. Squier did not believe that Indians originated in the same act of creation as did people of European ancestry, and this belief probably clouded his interpretation of the archaeological evidence. Likewise, postprocessualism argues that the evolutionary approaches favored by processual archaeologists are based on Western notions of progress and hence are potentially (some would say fundamentally) racist.

Processual-Plus Is there a middle road? Absolutely. Intellectual change occurs through the process of "thesis–antithesis–synthesis." The clock is a useful analogy here. One paradigm pulls the clock's pendulum far to one side and in response another paradigm pulls it the opposite way. Eventually, the pendulum will come to rest in the middle. In recent years many (perhaps most) archaeologists have listened to debates and settled on the compromise that Michelle Hegmon (Arizona State University) calls "processual-plus."

Most archaeologists today adhere to some form of scientific inquiry as a way to evaluate ideas about what happened in the past; few subscribe to the extreme postmodern idea that we cannot know anything true about the past. And most still believe that material factors such as technology, subsistence, and environment play critical roles in how human societies have changed. But few seek universals; instead, many seek generalities, patterns that point to how material factors may constrain or channel, but not determine, cultural change.

We also recognize the importance of other factors. All archaeologists know that artifacts carried symbolic meanings for people in the past and that humans respond to situations through their cultural understandings of the world. And all archaeologists view history as the combined result of the actions of individuals,

individuals who actively made decisions grounded in material concerns and cultural ideas simultaneously. Especially important has been a trend to look at gender, at the roles that men and women played in ancient societies (we'll return to this topic in Chapter 11). Most modern archaeologists also recognize the linkage between politics and research. Although few approach their research for purely political purposes, archaeologists today are taught to understand the political context and implications of their research.

Those, in a nutshell, are the important components of archaeological inquiry. How might these different elements work together in a research project? How would you start thinking like an archaeologist?

HOW ARCHAEOLOGICAL INQUIRY WORKS

Take another look at Figure 2-8 on page 32. Notice first that the entire process of archaeological inquiry takes place within a box labeled "Social, Cultural, Political Context." The idea here is that scientists can't step outside their culture; if we tried to do that, we'd cease being human, and lose our ability to analyze and understand the world. We can never ignore how our personal cultural context affects our understanding of the past. By constantly checking ourselves, over time we should be able to distinguish between what is cultural bias and what is actually true.

The dotted line defining the "Paradigm" box symbolizes this interplay between one's research agenda and cultural context. Both paradigm and culture provide (often vague) understandings of the world, and each points the researcher toward a question's answer. These biases are not necessarily wrong. Richard Wilk's analysis, for instance, suggests that Vietnam War–era experiences encouraged 1960s researchers to privilege war as the primary cause of the Maya civilization's collapse. Although these contexts are relevant, they do *not* mean that war did *not* cause the Maya collapse.

Paradigms provide specific guidelines for high-level theory—general statements such as "Agriculture occurs when a human population grows to the point where it exceeds the natural carrying capacity of the local environment." Paradigms also generate more specific claims about a region's prehistory, such as "In the Mimbres Valley of southern New Mexico, there was a change in social organization as evidenced by a shift from pithouse to pueblo villages about 1000 years ago." Both statements are linked to the overarching paradigm by directing researchers to measure some variables (such as demography and changing social organization) and to set other variables (such as religion) aside. Such propositions tend to occur to archaeologists operating within a processual paradigm.

By contrast, an archaeologist operating within a postprocessual paradigm might suggest "Agriculture originated from the need to create goods to give away at competitive feasts" or "In the Mimbres Valley, a new symbolic order appeared about 1000 years ago, as evidenced by an art style involving painted naturalistic designs on bowls that are ritually 'killed' and placed in human burials."

Testing Ideas

In either case, hypotheses must be constructed to test the competing propositions. For each hypothesis, we can frame one or more "if . . . then" statements that build upon the research proposition and predict some presently unknown aspect of the archaeological record. Figure 2-8 shows this as "Hypotheses" resulting from high-level theory.

Take, for example, the question relating population growth and agriculture. Suppose we already know that an agricultural economy began about 4000 years ago in our research area. We might hypothesize: If our proposition is true—that is, if population is the driving force behind agriculture—then signs of population growth and subsequent pressure on the food base should appear prior to 4000 years ago.

Here is where hypotheses lead to middle-level theory (as shown in Figure 2-8). Testing this proposition requires some way of inferring population numbers from archaeological data. Because we can't measure population directly—the people in question died a long time ago—a bridging argument is required to infer changes in population over time from archaeological variables. Perhaps we need to survey existing ethnographic data or conduct original ethnoarchaeological research to find correlates between population size and things that an archaeologist could record, such as house, cemetery, or village size.

Likewise, how do we measure "stress" on the food base? Maybe we can find ethnographic evidence that people use foods under conditions of stress which are more difficult to harvest. We might then have to conduct experiments, gathering foods with aboriginal technologies and measure the efficiency with which they are collected. Such research might tell us that very small seeds are less efficiently harvested than large seeds, and their use might signal subsistence stress.

PROFILE OF AN ARCHAEOLOGIST

AN ACADEMIC ARCHAEOLOGIST

Michelle Hegmon is a professor of anthropology at Arizona State University.

Michelle Hegmon.

Two tenets are key to my brand of archaeology, processual-plus. The first is open-mindedness, a willingness to set theoretical egos aside, and the second is recognition of the power of theory, words, and labels to shape our understanding of the past.

I work in the Mimbres region of New Mexico, a place that is famous for its pottery, but it was analysis rather than artifacts that originally drew me to archaeology. I don't remember my first piece of pottery, but I definitely remember the Introduction to Archaeology class in which Steve Plog described how ceramic designs could tell us about the social lives of people 1000 years ago. That's what caught my interest: solving puzzles and learning from artifacts.

I began graduate school in 1981 at the University of Michigan—renowned for its processual approach—and in 1982 postprocessualism appeared. Those were heady days for me and my fellow students (including Kelly). Born too late to be a real hippie, I tried to rebel intellectually. No ecology or evolution for me, I was going to be a real postprocessualist. I cringe when I think back on my young theoretical ego, passionately identifying with labels, and now appreciate the patience of my teachers (especially Henry Wright and Richard Ford). By the time I finished my dissertation, which returned me to my early interest in pottery design, I had developed much of what I now call processual-plus: a melding of postprocessual interest in symbols and meaning with processual concerns regarding systematic generalizations.

At the conclusion of my PhD defense, my committee stood to congratulate me. I stood, and (I am only 5'3") literally looked up at the tall men surrounding me. Until then, I

With adequate middle-level theory, we can define what constitutes relevant archaeological data (shown at lower right in Figure 2-8). If house size is a good measure of population, then we should measure a sample of houses from sites that date to time periods before and after 4000 years ago to see if there is evidence of population growth *before* the appearance of an agricultural economy. And if decreasing seed size is a good way to monitor stress on the food base, then let's recover and measure seeds from the appropriate archaeological sites.

Having done this background work, we can state the general hypothesis in a more specific way: If agriculture appears because population exceeds carrying capacity, then (1) house size should increase before 4000 years ago, and (2) seeds found in trash associated with those houses should become smaller over time.

Here's the fun part: the archaeological fieldwork required to collect the data necessary to test our hypothesis (shown in the center of Figure 2-8). As archaeologists, we must design fieldwork to generate adequate samples of house floors and seeds from the right time periods. Low-level theory is required to identify house floors (through the presence of postholes, packed clay floors, hearths, and so forth) and to identify seeds (we'll discuss fieldwork much more in the following chapters).

Reconstructing the Past

Hypothesis testing requires that we reconstruct the past, that we figure out what actually happened back in time (as shown at the lower left in Figure 2-8). Perhaps we will find that houses became larger over time

had paid little attention to gender. My mother, a physicist and feminist, had fought those battles for me; her generation made it possible for women in mine to move ahead with relative ease. For me, Southwest archaeology was a supportive environment. At a seminar on engendering Southwest archaeology, I joined a group of colleagues who pushed the intellectual envelope. As my mother's daughter, I assumed prehistoric women's domestic labor (such as corn-grinding) was drudgery, but others assumed it was highly respected. This disagreement made clear the importance of labels and of prior experience. Gender research—a key component of processual-plus—also taught me that feminism still has much to do.

I've done most of my professional research as part of the Eastern Mimbres Archaeological Project (EMAP), which Peggy Nelson and I began in 1993. The rich floodplain of the Mimbres River of southwest New Mexico is known for its Classic Mimbres villages, many of which were depopulated at a time of low rainfall around 870 BP. Unfortunately, looters have destroyed many of those sites, searching for pottery. In contrast, the eastern Mimbres region is drier but more remote. Landowners (including Ted Turner) have protected sites and supported our research. One of EMAP's most important conclusions is that the eastern area sustained a more continuous occupation than the Mimbres Valley. We documented a post-870 BP

regional reorganization, when people changed their lifestyle and their pottery but remained in their homeland.

EMAP is, above all, a collaboration, and becoming part of it is one of the best things I have ever done. Peggy Nelson's specialties include lithic technology and ecology, while mine are ceramic style and social theory, but rather than dividing these realms we have brought our perspectives together to delve into issues such as socioecology and the technology of style. Together we also have more fun. For many years we have run a large field school, in which we teach our students the importance of collaboration and the many skills—ranging from tire-changing to soils analysis—that are part of archaeological research. We also prepare a generation of young scholars to move ahead in a world of both women and men. Finally, our collaboration has taught me the importance of relinquishing some degree of control, trusting that Peggy and our students know what they are doing.

This lesson is key to a new direction in our research. Together with our colleagues at Arizona State University, we are embarking on several interdisciplinary projects that, by their very nature, draw on data and theory more vast than any of us can master single-handedly. These projects must be collaborations in which we set our theoretical egos aside.

(or maybe not); perhaps we learn that seeds became smaller through time (or maybe not). Notice that in Figure 2-8, the dotted line enclosing "The reconstructed past" is itself inside a larger box labeled the "The real past." We did this to emphasize that we cannot hope to reconstruct the complete past. Although we're getting better at recovering and extracting information from material remains, a complete picture of the past will always elude us.

As the postprocessual critique makes clear, our experiences in the present heavily color our vision of the past. Our sample hypothesis looks to demography (rather than religion or social change) to explain a change in subsistence. The implication from this hypothesis is that to reconstruct the past, some issues are important and others can be downplayed. Had we hypothesized a religious cause to agricultural origins,

then we would have generated very different data during our fieldwork. We might have looked, for example, for evidence of how plants were used in different rituals, and we would probably have excavated religious structures instead of houses.

Back to the Beginning

Let's return to the original propositions to see whether we confirmed or falsified them: Did the fieldwork and ensuing analyses find evidence of population growth and resource stress prior to 4000 years ago, or did it not?

At this point, the archaeological narrative goes public. This presentation necessarily begins with scientific monographs or papers that other archaeologists will scrutinize. But modern archaeologists know that results need to be conveyed to a broader public through books or magazine articles written in lay terms, public lectures, television presentations, or museum exhibitions. This is how the public can learn from and comment on the research. This professional and public feedback might require the archaeologist to revisit the research propositions and maybe even start the process all over again. Sometimes, through this recursive process (shown at left in Figure 2-8), archaeologists recognize a poor fit between their ideas and the archaeological record—maybe it's time to discard one paradigm for another, and begin anew.

Conclusion

Archaeology is firmly embedded in anthropology, drawing upon the methods and approaches of the other subfields of anthropology. The differing perspectives of anthropologists on culture are reflected in archaeological research as well. Although archaeologists can approach their subject in many different ways (which we've characterized as processual and postprocessual paradigms), most archaeologists believe that they conduct scientific research as we've described it: Define a specific problem, then conduct objective research to test the hypotheses.

Few archaeologists can do every step in the process of archaeological inquiry; almost everyone specializes. Some emphasize middle-level theory, doing experimental or ethnoarchaeological research. Others concentrate on the public side, presenting their research and that of others to a broader audience. Others work mostly with theory or critiques of paradigms, and still others spend most of their time doing fieldwork. But however archaeologists spend their time, it's critical that each understand the role that he or she plays in the overall process of archaeological inquiry.

SUMMARY

1. What is an anthropological approach?

⚙ Anthropologists believe that a true understanding of humankind can arise only from a perspective that is comparative, global, and holistic. Anthropology includes four subfields: biological, cultural, and linguistic anthropology, and archaeology. The concept of culture unites these diverse fields. Culture is a learned, shared, and symbolically based system of knowledge that includes traditions, kinship, language, religion, customs, and beliefs.

2. What two paradigms do anthropologists use to study culture, and how are these different ways of thinking reflected in archaeology?

⚙ There are two major approaches to the study of human culture. The ideational perspective deals with mentalistic, symbolic, cognitive culture; it sees culture as an instrument to create meaning and order in one's world. The adaptive perspective emphasizes those aspects of culture that most closely articulate with the environment, technology, and economics, and sees culture as the way in which humans adapt to their natural and social environment.

⚙ These approaches are reflected in the two major paradigms of modern archaeology: processual and postprocessual archaeology. The former takes a scientific approach and focuses on the material factors of life; the latter emphasizes symbolic meanings, power relationships, individual actions, and gender.

3. What is science and how does it explain things?

⚙ Science is a search for answers through a process that is objective, systematic, logical, predictive, self-critical, and public. It works through a cyclical process that entails constructing hypotheses, determining their empirical implications, and testing those hypotheses with empirical data. For more than a century, archaeology has been firmly grounded in a scientific perspective, which provides an elegant and powerful way of allowing people to understand the workings of the visible world.

4. What three levels of theory does a scientific approach in archaeology entail? How do these relate to paradigms?

⚙ Low-level theory involves the observations that emerge from archaeological fieldwork; this is how archaeologists get their "data," their "facts."

- Middle-level theory links archaeological data with human behavior or natural processes; it is produced through experimental archaeology, taphonomy (the study of natural processes on archaeological sites), and ethnoarchaeology (the study of living peoples to see links between behavior and material remains).

- High-level theory provides answers to larger "why" questions.
- Paradigms are frameworks for thinking that interrelate concepts and provide research strategies. They apply to intellectual inquiry in general and are not specific to archaeology.

MEDIA RESOURCES

Doing Fieldwork:
Archaeological Demonstrations CD-ROM 2.0
This CD, developed by the authors, shows professional archaeologists involved in various digs, many of which are referenced in the text. The presentation is organized by the main techniques used on an archaeological dig, reinforcing concepts and techniques via live examples. The CD takes you through each step automatically, or you can navigate to any point via the navigation bar. After reviewing a step in the dig process, you are taken to Check Points, which are concept questions about each step of the dig. Then you can see the answers, receive your score, and even send your scores to your instructor.

The Companion Website for *Archaeology,*
Sixth Edition
www.cengagebrain.com
Supplement your review of this chapter by going to the companion website to take one of the practice quizzes, use the flash cards to master key terms, and check out the many other study aids that are designed to help you succeed in your introductory archaeology course.

3 DOING FIELDWORK: SURVEYING FOR ARCHAEOLOGICAL SITES

LEARNING OBJECTIVES

**AFTER READING THIS CHAPTER
YOU SHOULD BE ABLE TO ANSWER THESE QUESTIONS:**

1. Why do archaeologists "survey"?

2. What is the main principle of survey? Why does this matter?

3. What limits surface survey? What are the basic remote sensing techniques and their benefits?

4. What is "landscape archaeology"?

© IRA BLOCK/National Geographic Stock

Chaco Canyon, in northwestern New Mexico, contains several massive pueblos that were occupied in the eleventh century, including Pueblo Bonito (lower right); many smaller sites were revealed by surface survey, and a road system by remote sensing.

PREVIEW

 **NOW THE FUN BEGINS!** The next two chapters will show you what it's like to do real archaeology. For many in the discipline—ourselves included—fieldwork is why we became archaeologists in the first place. That said, we must begin this introduction to archaeological field techniques with two important warnings:

▶ There is no one "right" way to find and excavate sites (but there are plenty of wrong ways).

▶ Nobody ever learned how to do proper archaeological fieldwork from a book (including this one).

Despite recent advances, archaeological fieldwork remains as much art as science. All we can do here is examine some common techniques, list some archaeological standards and principles, and give you a sense of what it feels like to participate in an archaeological exploration.

 DOING FIELDWORK CD-ROM: ARCHAEOLGICAL DEMONSTRATIONS 2.0

See the "Remote Sensing" and "Beginning to Excavate" sections of the CD-ROM to learn more about topics covered in this chapter.

INTRODUCTION

Every archaeologist is eventually asked the same question: "How do you know where to dig?"

There are many answers. Some **archaeological sites,** such as Egypt's pyramids, have been known for centuries—they were never lost. The locations of other sites have been handed down through the generations, preserved in oral and written traditions. Sites are sometimes deliberately discovered in large-scale systematic surveys, during which large regions are scanned for the remains of previous habitation. And some of the most important archaeological sites in the world were found by accident, hard work, and luck.

archaeological site   Any place where material evidence exists about the human past. Usually, "site" refers to a concentration of such evidence.

GOOD OLD GUMSHOE SURVEY

In Chapter 2 we mentioned Gatecliff Shelter in Nevada, where both of us excavated in the 1970s. But before we could dig at Gatecliff, the site had to be found. How did that happen?

Gatecliff was found by a fortunate combination of happenstance, hard work, and luck, a process that James O'Connell (University of Utah) calls old-fashioned "gumshoe survey."

In the summer of 1970, Thomas was in central Nevada's Reese River Valley conducting a systematic archaeological survey (a technique we discuss later in this chapter). Basically, this fieldwork entails mapping and collecting archaeological materials found on the ground. The survey went well, but it could not answer all the questions. Thomas needed to know, for example, something about prehistoric subsistence and the chronology of different artifact types. Such information is best understood from buried sites, where food remains (bones and seeds) might be preserved and where artifacts can be dated. Rockshelters and caves often contain the necessary buried deposits, but despite the Reese River crew's best efforts, they could not locate even one.

At the end of the first field session in Reese River, Thomas assembled the crew for steak dinners in the town of Austin, about an hour's dusty ride away. Austin is a pocket-sized Nevada mining town with fewer than 250 citizens, a picturesque little desert dive. Writer Oscar Lewis described it as "the town that died laughing," and William Least Heat Moon called it "a living ghost town: 40 percent living, 50 percent ghost and 10 percent not yet decided."

When two dozen grubby archaeologists come to such a town for steaks and beverages, word gets around quickly. Thomas soon found himself talking with the waitress's husband, Gale Peer, a mining geologist who had prospected central Nevada for 40 years. There are few places Gale Peer had not been, so Thomas asked if he knew of any caves or rockshelters.

Indeed, Mr. Peer did know of a cave—in Monitor Valley, about 20 kilometers east of Austin. He had not been there in years, but the details were fresh in his mind.

"You take the main dirt road south in Monitor Valley, then turn west, up one of the side canyons. I don't remember which one. As you drive along, oh, let's see, maybe 10 or 15 miles, there's a large black chert cliff. At the bottom of the cliff is a cave. Sometime, a long time ago, the Indians painted the inside of the cave. There are pictures of people and animals, plus a lot of writing I don't understand. Top of the shelter's caved in. Maybe in an earthquake. There's not much of the cave left. Drive out there when you get a chance. I'd like to know what's in that cave." He sketched a map on his business card.

The next summer Thomas and his crew returned, hoping to find the cave that Mr. Peer had described. They knew that the rockshelter was several miles up a canyon, on the north side—but there were 15 such canyons.

Beginning at the southern end of Monitor Valley, the crew drove up and down each side canyon, working their way northward. They were hampered by spring snow and washed-out roads—typical fieldwork conditions in central Nevada.

Each of the canyons had potential. The crew would see something, stop the truck, and skitter up the hillside. But each time, the "something" turned out to be a shadow, an abandoned mine shaft, or just a jumble of boulders.

After a week, Thomas came to Mill Canyon, just another one on the list, with no greater potential than the ten canyons they had already combed. The road was a little worse than most and, even in four-wheel drive, the truck lurched down a steep ridge into the rocky canyon. Finally, as the crew moved up the flat canyon bottom, a black cliff loomed ahead, riddled with small caves and rockshelters.

As usual, the shelters seemed empty, unless you count coyote scats and pack rat nests. Finally, the crew spied a dim shadow where the black dolomite formation was swallowed up beneath the Mill Canyon bottomland.

The paintings were invisible until you stood right in the mouth of the shelter. But there they were, just as Mr. Peer had said: small human figures, painted in red and yellow. On the other wall were cryptic motifs in white and black. And, yes, the roof had caved in years before. One boulder dwarfed the pickup.

There was nothing "archaeological" on the surface, but a small test pit turned up telltale signs that people had once lived in the shelter: several pieces of broken bone, a few of them charred, and a dozen stone flakes (probably debris from resharpening stone knives or **projectile points**).

Across the campfire that night, the crew assayed the finds. The rock art was intriguing; only two similar sites were known in central Nevada. The stones and bones were suggestive, but the shelter seemed hardly the deep site they were seeking. Thomas named the site after the rock formation, Gatecliff, in which they found it (see "Looking Closer: How Do Archaeological Sites Get Their Names?").

On the strength of this meager evidence, they decided to dig some—a good decision, it turned out, because the deposits inside Gatecliff Shelter proved to be 10 meters deep, making it one of the deepest rockshelters in the Americas. And the strata were spectacularly layered. In fact, Gatecliff had what textbooks—including this one—describe as "layer-cake stratigraphy." Sandwiched between layers of flash-flood deposited silts was a wonderful 7000-year record of human activity and environmental change in Monitor Valley. And it was found only because a waitress's husband in Austin, Nevada, remembered an interesting place from years before.

Many important sites have been found by ranchers, cowboys, sheepherders, farmers, geologists, and amateur archaeologists—anyone who spends a lot of time wandering about outdoors (see "What Does It Mean to Me? I'm Not a Professional Archaeologist, but Can I Still Play a Role?"). This is the essence of gumshoe survey—hanging out in coffee shops, bars, and gas stations, listening to those who know more about the landscape than you do.

projectile points   Arrowheads, dart points, or spear points.

LOOKING CLOSER

HOW DO ARCHAEOLOGICAL SITES GET THEIR NAMES?

It's long been an archaeologist's prerogative to name new sites. Many are named after a prominent topographic feature, such as the canyon in which the site is located, or a nearby mountain, river, or town—or a rock formation, as in the case of Gatecliff Shelter.

Sites on private land are commonly named after the landowners; some become the namesakes of the amateur archaeologists who find them. And sometimes the archaeologist can have fun with a site's name. Robert Bettinger (University of California, Davis) named one California cave site Gimme Shelter (after a Rolling Stones tune).

Some names have stories attached to them. Danger Cave, on the edge of Utah's Great Salt Lake, for example, was originally called Hands and Knees Caves by locals, to describe how it was entered. But during Elmer Smith's 1941 excavation, a huge piece of the lip broke off and crashed into the excavation, narrowly missing several crew members and, according to legend, landing right where some had just finished lunch. This incident resulted in a permanent name change. During Jesse Jennings's excavations there in the 1950s, the students elected to change the name to Lamus Cave, after Blair Lamus, a superintendent of the potash plant in nearby Wendover, to recognize the help he had given to the project (which apparently included small amounts of dynamite). Jennings apparently nixed the suggestion.

Today, as many archaeologists are working more closely with native consultants, American Indians' names are often applied to newly recorded sites.

So, sites acquire their names in many different ways. There is, in fact, only one cultural rule to follow: The archaeologist can *never* name a site after him- or herself.

THE FALLACY OF THE "TYPICAL" SITE

Sometimes archaeologists survey to find good places to dig; this is why Thomas was looking for Gatecliff Shelter. But archaeology is more than just digging individual sites. Archaeological survey is a way to generate archaeological data on a regional scale.

Survey is important because of the problem of representation. Suppose you spend seven years digging a site like Gatecliff (as we did). You recover plenty of artifacts from the stratified and well-dated sediments. But what do all these ancient things mean in human terms?

Nobody lives in just one place—not now and not millennia ago. To understand the past, we need to examine the range of places where ancient peoples lived. Look at the map of the **seasonal round** of the Western Shoshone people of the central Great Basin

(Figure 3-1). Produced by anthropologist Julian Steward (1902–1972), this map charts the cultural landscape of the Shoshone, a people who survived by hunting antelope and bighorn sheep and by collecting various plant foods.

This ecological adaptation depended on a knowledgeable exploitation of Great Basin environments. The prehistoric Shoshone were nomadic hunter-gatherers, and because of their intimate relationship with the natural environment, they worked out a seasonal round during which they traveled from one habitat to another to harvest local wild foods as they became available.

The numbered triangles on the map are winter villages in the Toiyabe and Shoshone mountain ranges, where people lived seasonally to hunt bighorn sheep and to collect the piñon pine nuts that grow there. These nutritious nuts ripened in the late summer and early autumn and were stored for the winter, along with buffalo berries and currants available in the low foothills. Other kinds of sites (denoted by letters) occur at lower elevations and along the Reese River, where the Shoshone lived during the summer, gathering ricegrass seeds and roots, catching rabbits, and hunting

seasonal round Hunter-gatherers' pattern of movement between different places on the landscape, timed to the seasonal availability of food and other resources.

WHAT DOES IT MEAN TO ME?

I'M NOT A PROFESSIONAL ARCHAEOLOGIST, BUT CAN I STILL PLAY A ROLE?

There are thousands of avocational archaeologists in the United States—individuals who are interested in archaeology but have no academic credentials. Many of these people collect artifacts on their own. They are often important sources of information for gumshoe survey. Some professionals love them, others begrudgingly tolerate them, and others won't deal with them at all because they feel that any association with collectors condones looting.

Most archaeologists differentiate between the weekend collector of surface artifacts and those who dig for profit. They condemn the latter, but find relationships with avocationals to be productive. George Frison, professor emeritus at the University of Wyoming, a member of the National Academy of Sciences, and past president of the Society for American Archaeology, says, "I think you gain a hell of a lot more by cooperating with amateurs . . . than if you deride them and chase them underground. Then they'll really do you some damage."

As an avocational archaeologist, is there a role for you in professional archaeology? According to Hester Davis, retired state archaeologist, Archaeological Survey, Fayetteville, Arkansas, the answer is yes:

The greatest potential for site protection is through statewide avocational groups. The secret weapon held by these organizations is their ability to influence their own members, politicians, landowners, teachers, schoolchildren, and even pothunters (looters). By their very numbers and the fact of their organization, avocational archaeological societies should be the real advocates for site protection.

Avocational archaeological groups have the greatest potential for making a real difference in which sites and how many sites are protected in the future. All archaeologists, in my use of the term, must coordinate, communicate, organize nationally, and become pro-protection. Legislation protecting unmarked graves must hit hard on the looters and vandals; ordinances at the local level must become commonplace. The names and faces of archaeological organizations speaking for less wanton destruction must be on educational television and the evening news.

There are probably four or five times as many avocational archaeologists as there are professional ones, and dozens more avocational archaeological organizations than professional ones. Since their interests are supposed to be the same, they must all become strong active advocates for site protection, from the individual site where the shopping center is going in, to the national historic landmarks still in private ownership.

---

pronghorn antelope. In upland areas they gathered berries, tubers, and hunted bighorn sheep. They did other things at other places on the landscape for ceremonial purposes or in pursuit of specific foods.

Steward based this reconstruction on what Shoshone people told him in 1935 and 1936. Because most of the mapped sites were abandoned in the nineteenth century, Steward's native consultants were often recalling events of 50 years or more before. Even though Steward's consultants could not recall everything, the map still demonstrates the native peoples' intricate and complex seasonal round. This seasonal round also provides an example of what archaeologists call a **settlement pattern**—the distribution of sites across a landscape—and a **settlement system,** which describes the movements and activities inferred from the sites that make up the settlement pattern (a seasonal round is one type of settlement system).

> **settlement pattern** The distribution of archaeological sites across a region.
>
> **settlement system** The movements and activities reconstructed from a settlement pattern.

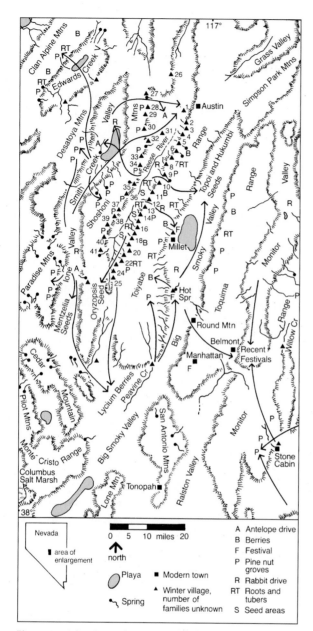

Figure 3-1 Julian Steward's reconstruction of the seasonal round of the Western Shoshone and Northern Paiute people (Nevada), projected for the mid-nineteenth-century period. *After Steward 1938, Figure 8.*

sandals, snares, and pieces of bows, arrows, food bones, seeds, and fire-making apparatus. But these small shelters represent only a minor portion of the overall Western Shoshone pattern. Women were probably not included in small hunting parties, and men conducted only a limited range of activities there.

The difficulty is clear: No matter which site you select, you'll miss a great deal, and will likely come away with a biased reconstruction because *no site is typical of the entire settlement system.* And this isn't just a problem for archaeologists who study nomadic foragers. Agricultural peoples do not live their lives in one location. They create residences in one place, field houses near outlying crops, check dams in the arroyos, hunting camps in the mountains, and maybe ritual centers elsewhere. Trying to reconstruct someone's life, including your own, from just a single place will create a very biased view.

The goal of archaeological survey, then, is not just to find deep sites full of interesting artifacts. Instead, the goal is to document the range of archaeological remains across a landscape, to avoid creating a biased image of the lives of ancient peoples. Archaeological surveys do this by looking—systematically—at how sites are distributed across a region.

Surface sites provide unique data regarding past human–land relationships. In the next section, we consider the surface archaeology of the Carson Desert in western Nevada to illustrate how archaeologists implement this regional perspective (see "Looking Closer: The Surveyor's Toolkit").

SURFACE ARCHAEOLOGY IN THE CARSON DESERT

The Great Basin is best known for vast stretches of sagebrush and arid mountain ranges, but it also contains several substantial wetlands. Julian Steward's Depression-era research documented the lives of those Shoshone and Paiute people who lived in areas *without* wetlands. So, without much ethnographic data, archaeologists in the 1970s debated how the wetlands were incorporated into the seasonal round of the region's native peoples.

One hypothesis held that the wetlands provided abundant, high-quality foods and consequently a permanent, sedentary home; this hypothesis assumed that foragers became sedentary whenever the opportunity presented itself. An opposing hypothesis was that the wetlands served as only one element of a broader seasonal round; this hypothesis assumed

This map also illustrates the fallacy of the "typical" site. Suppose you had a chance to locate and excavate just one of these Western Shoshone sites. Which one should you choose? Winter village sites represent the lengthiest occupation and probably contain remains of a great variety of activities. But winter village sites are typically located on windswept ridges (where the wind blows the snow away), and all that is preserved are stone tools and ceramics.

Or would it be better to seek out one of the small upland shelters where hunters briefly camped while pursuing bighorn sheep? The preservation in such shelters is often excellent, and the chances are good for finding

LOOKING CLOSER

THE SURVEYOR'S TOOLKIT

If you are thinking of doing archaeology, your first job will likely be site survey. To prepare yourself, you'll need many of the following items in addition to the normal things you would carry on a long day hike (water, food bar, first aid kit, matches, rain gear, sunscreen, etc.).

▶ A GPS instrument (Garmin and DeLorme make good models)

▶ A two-way radio (with at least a 2-mile capacity), unless you're in cell phone range

▶ A good but cheap watch (we've crushed several climbing over rocks)

▶ A good compass (Brunton's pocket transit or Finland's Suunto)

▶ A surveyor's K1E field notebook (college bookstores carry them)

▶ Mechanical or regular pencils (wrap them with duct tape; use the duct tape to protect blisters)

▶ Ziploc bags of different sizes (these can be purchased inexpensively online)

▶ A black Sharpie marker

▶ A trowel (for quick test pits)

▶ A tape measure (metric only!)

▶ Graph paper for site maps (crew chiefs often carry this and other paperwork in an aluminum clipboard box)

▶ A small flashlight (useful when investigating caves and rockshelters)

▶ In some places, a snake bite kit (although we have yet to use one), shin guards (to protect against snakes in more densely vegetated areas), mosquito repellent, or pepper spray (in bear country; archaeologists in grizzly territory often carry guns)

---

that foragers only became sedentary when population growth forced them to do so. Put simply, the research hypotheses were: Did prehistoric peoples settle down and focus exclusively on the wetlands, or did they incorporate the mountains' resources into a more diversified seasonal round?

One of the Great Basin's wetlands lies in the Carson Desert, about 100 kilometers east of Reno, Nevada. A large basin filled with sand dunes and alkali flats (Figure 3-2), the Carson Desert is the terminus of several large rivers that create a vast wetland. This wetland hosted many species of plants and animals that provided

Figure 3-2 Students conducting a site survey in the Carson Desert; Stillwater Mountains are in the background.

Figure 3-3 Archaeologists excavating inside Hidden Cave (Nevada). Without the 500-watt quartz-halogen landing lights (evident on the left), the excavation area would be pitch black. Note also the respirators and hard hats—often required equipment for working inside such enclosed cave environments.

ancient peoples with food and raw material for clothing, houses, and tools: cattail, bulrush, and other plants; fish, muskrats and other animals. Piñon pine nuts grow in the forest of the Stillwater Mountains that form the eastern edge of the Carson Desert, and foragers could find tubers, seeds, bighorn sheep, and other game there as well. Previous research suggested that people had lived in this region for more than 9000 years.

In the late 1970s, we both were excavating Hidden Cave, a site located at the south end of the Stillwater range, which overlooks the Carson Desert (Figure 3-3). The site was used primarily between 5000 and 1500 years ago as a place to cache hunting gear and as a cool escape from the desert's extreme summer heat. Hidden Cave is an intriguing site, but remember the fallacy of the typical site: Because we knew that people had lived in the Carson Desert for at least 9000 years, we figured that Hidden Cave documented only a portion of the region's prehistory. Furthermore, a specialized cache cave obviously provides only limited insight into the lives of the people who lived in this area—like trying to reconstruct someone's life by looking only at his or her safe deposit box. (We'll have more to say about Hidden Cave in Chapter 9.)

mano   A fist-sized, round, flat, handheld stone used with a metate for grinding foods.

metate   A large, flat stone used as a stationary surface upon which seeds, tubers, and nuts are ground with a mano.

To understand ancient life in the Carson Desert, we needed to explore the regional archaeological record. Kelly hypothesized that if the wetland was exploited by a sedentary population, then there should be evidence of large, year-round populations living near the marsh. There should be little evidence of use of the mountains, except perhaps by hunting parties seeking bighorn sheep. People should have made far less use of the dunes and alkali flats surrounding the wetland because their economic potentials are low compared with that of the wetland. If, on the other hand, the wetlands were just one stop on a broad-scale seasonal round, then we should find evidence of more transient use of the wetlands and more intensive use of the mountains.

With these alternative hypotheses in mind, Kelly generated some archaeological expectations for each. Forced to rely strictly on surface archaeology, where organic remains are not preserved, he focused on stone tools (pottery is rare in this region) and the waste flakes from their manufacture and resharpening. We'll talk more about these kinds of artifacts in Chapter 8.

The point is this: Long before taking to the field, archaeologists need a good idea of what should be found if one hypothesis is correct and the other is incorrect. For example, if a sedentary population had used the wetlands, then we expected to find dense scatters of waste flakes and broken tools (the remains of villages occupied for years at a time) in the wetland. In the uplands, we expected to find only evidence of hunting activities, small campsites containing broken projectile points. If, instead, the second hypothesis was correct, then we should find small settlements on the valley floor and, in the mountains, evidence not only of hunting but also of tuber, seed, and piñon gathering, as shown by the **manos** and **metates** (grinding stones) used for processing seeds and nuts.

Some Sampling Considerations

You can see that the fieldwork appropriate to test our hypotheses must explore the character of archaeological evidence across a large region. But what should that region be? And did we need to search every square inch of it? Given the practicalities of desert archaeology, it was obvious that we could not look everywhere. We must *sample*, but capricious and biased sampling methods can lead the archaeologist astray. What if we looked only in places where we thought sites would be located? Not being Great Basin hunter-gatherers, we don't see the landscape as past foragers did. We would undoubtedly overestimate the importance of some places and overlook others, generating a biased image of the region's archaeology.

The best way to ensure unbiased results is through a **systematic regional survey** that makes use of statistical sampling. We'll cover only the basic principles of this large and complex subject here. (But note that any student contemplating a career in archaeology will need several statistics courses because statistical analysis is as indispensable to archaeologists as their trowels.)

To acquire a statistical sample, you must first define the **statistical population** that you wish to characterize. In this case, that population is the observations we could make on the stone artifacts and waste flakes found in the archaeological sites of the Carson Desert and Stillwater Mountains.

Statistical sampling also requires that we define a relevant **sample universe,** the archaeological sites that will provide the sample that will characterize the statistical population. Because the research questions concerned the relationships between sites on the valley floor (in particular, those in the wetland) and sites in the mountains, our sample universe had to contain both of these regions.

The result was a sample universe—a survey area—of some 1700 square kilometers that looks like the head of a barking dog (shown in Figure 3-4). The size and shape of a survey area comes from the research question and practical considerations. In this case, the survey area needed to encompass the various lowland environments—wetland, dunes, and alkali flats—as

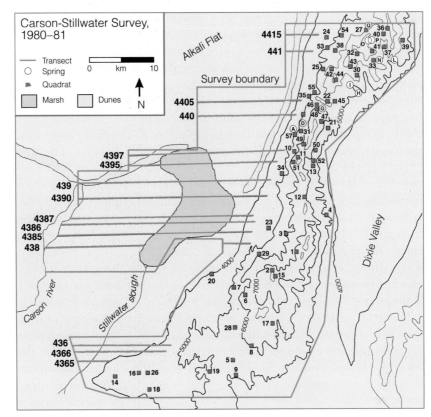

Figure 3-4 Map of the Carson Desert and Stillwater Mountains (Nevada), showing the locations of survey transects, quadrats, and spring surveys. *Robert Kelly, "Prehistory of the Carson Desert and Stillwater Mountains," University of Utah Anthropological Papers, No. 123, 2001. Used by permission.*

well as the Stillwater Mountains. But we also needed to avoid (1) the town of Fallon, (2) a large wildlife refuge that lies in the dog's "mouth," and (3) in front of the dog's "ear," a large naval bombing range that contained unexploded ordnance. (Fallon is home to one of the U.S. Navy's elite fighter pilot schools. Watch the film *Top Gun*, and you'll catch some glimpses of our survey area beneath the screaming F-14s.)

Because soil formation in deserts is often slow and vegetation is sparse, many archaeological remains still lie on the surface, where people dropped or discarded them hundreds or even thousands of years ago. Doing surface archaeology in such places means that you

systematic regional survey A set of strategies for arriving at accurate descriptions of the range of archaeological material across a landscape.

statistical population A set of counts, measurements, or characteristics about which relevant inquiries are to be made. Scientists use the term "statistical population" in a specialized way (quite different from "population" in the ordinary sense).

sample universe The region that contains the statistical population and that will be sampled. Its size and shape are determined by the research question and practical considerations.

simply spot an artifact, plot its location in your field notes, pick it up, and label it—no digging!

But who could survey all 1700 square kilometers? That could take a lifetime! This is where statistical sampling helps out, providing a way to characterize a population without having to record data on every site within that huge area. We draw upon the same methods and theory that pollsters use to take the nation's political pulse by interviewing only a thousand people.

You begin by selecting a **random sample** of the site population. The word "random" here is critical, for it specifically means that *each site has an equal chance of being included in the sample.* If there were 100 sites, say, then each site must have a 1/100 = 1 percent chance of being included in the sample. If the sample is not selected in a random manner, then some sites may be overrepresented and others underrepresented in the sample. And that could bias the final results.

Randomly selecting the samples permits us to analyze the results statistically. Because statistical analysis generally requires a random sample, archaeologists who use a biased sampling design will never know if their results are meaningful or not.

Getting the Sample

Once we have decided on the sample universe, the next task is to select the sample. The first step is to decide on the **sample fraction.** What portion of the sample population will be included—1 percent of the sites? 5 percent, 10 percent, 50 percent? Archaeologists are somewhat hampered in this regard because the size of the sample depends on characteristics of the population being sampled. For example, if there is a lot of variation, say, in the number of projectile points in sites (some have few, others have many), then we would need a larger sample than if there were only a small amount of variation. The problem is that archaeologists rarely know much about the populations they are sampling; this is especially true when undertaking survey in a new region.

One solution is to start with a small uniform sample across the region and then use the findings to decide whether some regions need more intensive sampling. So, Kelly began in 1980 with a 1 percent sample of the entire region and then increased the sample fraction in particular areas the following summer.

The second step is more pragmatic: How do you actually acquire the sample? Ideally, we could take all the sites in the sample universe, give each one a number, and then randomly select some portion of those numbers and examine those sites. But we didn't know how many sites there were in the survey area, let alone their locations. This means that to sample the sites, we had to sample the landscape.

You could just go out and start walking across the land, but it would be hard to keep track of how much land you covered and hence difficult to compute the sample fraction. And you would almost certainly bias the sample by avoiding areas that were hard to reach or unpleasant to walk across.

Kelly solved this problem by using randomly selected **sample units.** Sample units can be many different shapes, although squares, circles, and transects (long, narrow rectangles) are the most commonly used; all three were employed in this survey. The choice of which to use depends somewhat on the research questions, but also on practical considerations.

In the mountains, we used 500 × 500 meter squares (we called them quadrats) as the sample unit. Previous experience suggested they were a manageable size, given the exigencies of survey in the mountains and the number of crew members at hand.

We located these squares randomly using the **UTM** (Universal Transverse Mercator) grid. What is the UTM grid? Simply put, mapmakers divide the world into a grid of 1 × 1 meter squares; each intersection in that grid has north and east coordinates. Look at a standard USGS topographic map, and you will see these coordinates written in small black numbers along the map's margins. These numbers provide a handy, preexisting way to sample a landscape.

Kelly randomly selected sets of north and east coordinates (by putting the UTM coordinates in a hat—nothing fancy here!). Each set of north and east coordinates defined the northwest corner of a 500 × 500 meter sample square; for example, the coordinates of Quadrat 36 were 4416000 North, 407500 East. We then located these squares on the appropriate topographic map and drew them in. We selected a number of units from predefined portions of the mountains to ensure that survey units were spread throughout the extent of the Stillwater Mountains.

random sample A sample drawn from a statistical population such that every member of the population has an equal chance of being included in the sample.

sample fraction The percentage of the sample universe that is surveyed. Areas with a lot of variability in archaeological remains require larger sample fractions than do areas of low variability.

sample units Survey units of a standard size and shape, determined by the research question and practical considerations, used to obtain the sample.

UTM Universal Transverse Mercator, a grid system in which north and east coordinates provide a location anywhere in the world, precise to 1 meter.

We also drew 500-meter radius circles around all the active springs in the northern mountains. Water is critical for hunter-gatherers living in a desert environment. In the Stillwater Mountains, water is mostly present as springs that create a small seep or a short creek. Other Nevada surveys had found that sites tended to occur within about 450 meters of a water source, so Kelly chose to survey a 500-meter radius around a sample of the springs.

On the valley floor we used 100-meter-wide transects (instead of 500-meter squares) as the sample unit. We chose this width because we had 10–12 students working on the project, and this meant that they could be spaced about 10 meters apart—an interval that previous experience told us was the maximum distance surveyors could be apart and still find small sites. We located the transects by randomly selecting UTM north coordinates and using that to define the middle of the transects (that is, the transect extended 50 meters north and 50 meters south of the random UTM north coordinate).

Why didn't we use 500 × 500 quadrats on the valley floor? Quadrats are fairly easy to locate on the ground in areas with topographic relief. Plotted on the map, we could see that the southeast corner of Quadrat 36, for example, could be reached by walking up a particular canyon, then, where the canyon makes a turn to the south, by going north up a small draw to the ridge top.

But the Carson Desert is flat, with only 1 to 2 meters of elevation over vast stretches. We could have spent hours just trying to locate the corner of a survey unit (this was before GPS units were available—more on those later). We used transects because we could locate them on the ground where they crossed a road (using the truck's mileage gauge from some known point, such as an irrigation canal or a permanent USGS marker). Once we located the transect the survey team only needed a compass to keep itself on track.

Doing the Work

Kelly's team completed the Carson-Stillwater survey in two summers. The first summer's 1 percent sample of the entire sample universe found that archaeological remains were most dense and variable in the piñon-juniper forest of the mountains and less so in the unwooded portion of the mountains.

So, during the second summer, we pursued a **stratified random sample,** which takes the sample universe and stratifies it into sub-universes. We eventually divided the sample universe into five strata: the wetland, the dune area west of the wetland, the

south valley, the northern Stillwater Mountains, and the southern Stillwater Mountains. Drawing upon the first summer's survey sample, we sampled some of these areas more intensively than the others.

The first summer's survey team consisted of 10–12 student archaeologists and volunteers (see "Looking Closer: Archaeological Survey in the Carson Desert"). When surveying the transects, surveyors walked at 8- to 10-meter intervals, winding their way through the sagebrush and greasewood. A similar procedure was used in the quadrat survey, but because these units were 500 × 500 meters, we made five 100-meter-wide passes across them; we used the same procedure for the spring surveys.

When someone found a site, each crew member marked his or her place on the line (so they'd know where to resume surveying) and then all of us gathered together. We located the site on a sketch map of the quadrat and then sketched a map of the site itself (today we would use a GPS instrument to locate the site). Most sites were unglamorous scatters of flakes, but occasionally we found rock art on scattered boulders and once a standing **wickiup** (a conical log structure) that had been built sometime in the early twentieth century, judging from the enamel pot hanging in a tree and the metal axe cuts on the logs.

For each site, we filled out a form that asked for a variety of information: the site's location and topographic setting; distance to water; type and density of surrounding vegetation; evidence of disturbance by people or erosion; potential for buried deposits; estimates of site age and size; outcrops of stone suitable for making tools; structures or features such as hearths; slope; and general comments. The team photographed each site and collected a large sample of the stone tools and waste flakes.

Each site received a field number, but eventually was assigned a permanent **Smithsonian number**—a cataloging system that most states use to keep track of their sites. For example, one site found in the survey acquired the number 26CH798: The 26 stands for Nevada because it is the twenty-sixth state alphabetically (excluding Alaska and Hawaii, which became states after this system was in place; they are now 49 and 50).

stratified random sample A survey universe divided into several sub-universes that are then sampled at potentially different sample fractions.

wickiup A conical structure made of poles or logs laid against one another that served as a fall or winter home among the prehistoric Shoshone and Paiute.

Smithsonian number A unique catalog number given to each site; it consists of a number (the state's position alphabetically), a letter abbreviation for the county, and the site's sequential number within the county.

LOOKING CLOSER

ARCHAEOLOGICAL SURVEY IN THE CARSON DESERT

Part of the joy of fieldwork is living outdoors. In the Carson Desert, we camped at line cabins, in an abandoned one-room schoolhouse, at miners' camps, and alongside many dirt roads.

Our day began at 4 AM. Depending on whose turn it was to cook, breakfast might be eggs and bacon or just a bag of granola and a carton of milk on the table. Someone else checked the vehicles' fluid levels and tires and made sure there was emergency food and water in the trucks.

When surveying the valley floor, we dropped a truck off in the afternoon where the transect to be surveyed the next day crossed a dirt road. We also left a cooler full of water underneath the truck. The next morning, we left camp before sunup, parking at the opposite end of the transect. We spread out over the 100-meter width, sat down, and waited for the sun to come up. At sunrise we'd start our slow trek to the truck at the opposite end of the transect. We tried to finish the day's work by 2 PM, but sometimes we arrived at the truck closer to sundown, our packs full of labeled bags of artifacts. There's nothing like carrying a pack full of rocks across the desert to get you in shape.

Lunch was oranges, cookies, and peanut butter and jelly sandwiches—affectionately known as "death wads" (a survey tip: Put peanut butter on both halves so the jelly doesn't soak through). We often ate beneath a couple of bedsheets draped over greasewood for shade. The sun's reflection off the alkali flats sometimes burned the *bottom* of our chins, and we welcomed the chance to wade across an irrigation ditch or through a stretch of wetland. Occasionally, a dust devil would blow up, and the crew would call out bets as to who would get hit!

In the mountains, we drove as close as we could to the day's quadrat—but even with a four-wheel drive, this still meant walking many kilometers just to reach the survey area. Once we hiked until lunchtime to reach a unit high in the mountains. The crew was so tired that *everyone* fell asleep after eating—and did not wake up until 4 PM. We finished the job, but returned to camp that night about 10 PM—hiking by flashlight. After finishing a unit in the mountains, we drove as close as possible to the next unit, camped by the truck, and then got up the next morning to start again.

Living in close quarters for weeks on end can create tensions, and crews solved this problem the same way small hunting and gathering bands do—through humor. It was not unusual to see someone jump on the hood of the truck and dance to Steppenwolf's *Born to Be Wild* at 5 AM. Conversations along the survey line and at mealtimes were running jokes and embarrassing, but good-natured, stories. "Oranges are better than sex!" announced one crew member on an especially hot day at lunch. This began days of suggestions involving conjugal relations and fruit. Cow-chip fights and rock-throwing contests were also popular.

The CH stands for Churchill County, and 798 means it was the 798th site recorded in that county.

After two summers, Kelly's team had surveyed 57 quadrats, 8 springs, and 260 kilometers of transects—about 47 square kilometers, or a sample fraction of the total survey universe of about 3 percent. But some strata were sampled more intensively than others; Table 3-1 shows how the sample was distributed across the five strata. We recorded 160 sites and collected some 10,400 stone tools and more than 70,000 manufacturing and resharpening waste flakes. Kelly analyzed these over the next several years.

So, What's a Site?

Archaeologists speak all the time about sites, but many are hard-pressed to define what "site" actually means. In the Carson Desert, Kelly defined a site as five pieces of cultural material—such as waste flakes from the manufacture of a stone tool—within approximately

TABLE 3-1 Sampling Fractions of the Survey Strata and Predicted Site Densities

REGION	SIZE (km²)	QUADRATS	SPRINGS	TRANSECTS (km)	SAMPLE FRACTION	SITES	SITE DENSITY (sites/km²)
Piñon-juniper forest	150	23	5	—	6.5	41	4.2
Unforested mountains	820	34	3	—	1.3	12	1.1
Wetlands	305	—	—	133	3.4	30	2.9
Dunes	243	—	—	93	3.8	57	6.1
South valley	53	—	—	346	4	20	5.9
Total	1571	57	8	260	2.7*	160	3.4*

SOURCE: Kelly 2001, Table 6-1.

Note: Some areas of survey, such as the alluvial fans, are excluded from this table; areas covered by open water are excluded from the wetland total; * indicates values calculated from the entire survey region.

50 square meters. Often geography places a boundary on a site's edges, such as a riverbank or a steep slope. But sometimes artifact scatters are more or less continuous, and the archaeologist has to make a judgment call. For example, Figure 3-5 is a map of Quadrat 36 in the Stillwater Mountains. We recorded ten sites in this quadrat; but it's possible that another archaeologist might have recorded eight, or five, or just one big site.

The problem becomes even more complex when we factor in geology. In the Carson Desert, many of the

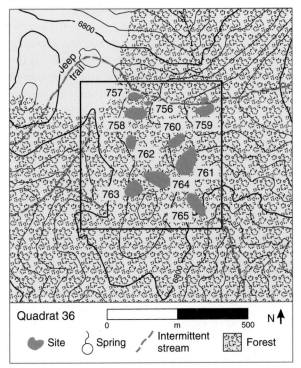

Figure 3-5 Topographic map of Quadrat 36 in the Stillwater Mountain survey. Sites are shown as numbered patches. Is there one site here, or ten? *Robert Kelly, "Prehistory of the Carson Desert and Stillwater Mountains," University of Utah Anthropological Papers, No. 123, 2001. Used by permission.*

"sites" on the valley floor were actually conglomerates of unrelated material produced through **deflation,** the geologic process whereby fine sediment is blown away by the wind and larger items—mostly stone artifacts in this case—are left behind. As a result of this process, archaeological remains that originally might have been discarded at different times throughout an accumulating dune are eventually left together on the same surface after the sand has blown away. This process produces a dense scatter of debris that is not a site in the traditional sense of the term, but a number of isolated items brought together through a geologic process. Many of the sites we recorded in the Carson Desert were, in fact, such geologic aggregates of cultural material.

Finally, even if we could define sites "correctly," what would they be? We tend to think of sites as discrete behavioral entities. But sites, especially surface sites, are not necessarily the archaeological equivalent of the ethnographer's village, hamlet, or foraging camp (although sometimes they are). Sites can result from multiple occupations over decades, or even hundreds or thousands of years, and archaeologists have to be wary of all the natural processes that go into the formation of a site (we'll discuss more of these in Chapter 5).

Is there a solution? Yes, it's known as **non-site archaeology.** This approach focuses not on the artifacts collected from a single site, but on *regional* patterns in artifacts.

In the Carson Desert, Kelly never even tried to reconstruct the daily activities that transpired at a specific site because he assumed that the sites were merely

deflation A geologic process whereby fine sediment is blown away by the wind and larger items—including artifacts—are lowered onto a common surface and thus become recognizable as a site.

non-site archaeology Analysis of archaeological patterns manifested on a scale of kilometers or hectares, rather than of patterns within a single site.

different-sized samples of a more or less continuous distribution of archaeological debris. Thus, he grouped the data in terms of the five sample strata, comparing, for example, what he found in the piñon-juniper forest *as a whole* to what we found in the other four strata. With this approach, it didn't matter if Quadrat 36 contained ten sites or only one—he added the artifacts from this quadrat's sites to everything else found in the piñon-juniper zone for analysis. In this way, he looked for large-scale patterns in artifact distribution that were more meaningful, in terms of the research questions, and more reliable than a fine-grained interpretation of any single site.

Archaeologists will never completely dispense with the notion of "site" because the concept is critical from an administrative point of view. All state archaeological databases record archaeology in terms of sites, and researchers receive permits to work on particular sites. But archaeologists today have a realistic and sober understanding that, under many conditions, sites are *samples* and are rarely equivalent to something that might make intuitive sense to us, such as a "village" or "camp."

What We Learned

Kelly's research in the Carson Sink involved two different hypotheses about the role of wetlands in the ancient hunter-gatherer seasonal round. The first hypothesis held that wetlands had been the focus of a sedentary settlement system, predicting that the highest site density should be in the wetland. But our survey found that the highest site densities occurred in the dunes, the south valley region, and the northern forested portion of the mountains.

The first hypothesis also predicted that sites in the wetlands should contain evidence of long-term habitation. But the archaeological survey recovered stone tools and evidence of stone tool manufacturing techniques suggesting that wetland sites were short-term camps. This evidence is more in line with the second hypothesis, which argued that the wetland was but one stop on a complex seasonal round (and, in fact, the sites in the dune region contained tools and waste flakes that suggested even more transient stays than those in the wetland).

But the second hypothesis also suggested that the piñon forests should have seen use for a variety of subsistence pursuits. Although Kelly's crew found evidence of hunting there, evidence for plant collecting, in the form of grinding stones, was almost nonexistent.

In sum, neither hypothesis seems to provide an adequate reconstruction of ancient life in the Carson Desert and Stillwater Mountains. We have come full circle in the research cycle and are now back at the beginning, proposing new hypotheses that take into account what we have learned.

GPS Technology and Modern Surveys

Surveys today are assisted by **global positioning system (GPS)** technology. This system did not exist when Kelly surveyed the Carson Desert, but he certainly wished that it did. The survey team had to use compass triangulation and pacing to locate sites—and all of that took time. Additionally, we've since discovered that, in the heat of the day, you can make a lot of mistakes.

GPS technology has changed all that. The GPS consists of 27 satellites (24 active ones and 3 spares) that circle the earth in 12-hour evenly distributed orbits at an altitude of about 14,000 kilometers. These orbits repeat the same ground track (because the earth turns beneath them) twice each day. Each satellite carries a computer and very accurate atomic clocks. This technology is commonplace in many new cars.

Handheld GPS units operate by picking up the continuously broadcast signals from at least four satellites. The GPS receiver triangulates a position fix using the interval between the transmission and reception of the satellite signal. Even inexpensive units ($150) will give 5-meter accuracy within seconds, and expensive devices can give sub-centimeter accuracy. GPS technology has made fieldwork easier, and no archaeologist today would take to the field without a GPS unit.

LOOKING BELOW THE GROUND

The archaeological surveys that we've discussed so far recorded only evidence that is visible with a pedestrian survey. In places like the Carson Desert, important archaeological remains can lie on a stable desert surface for millennia. But elsewhere artifacts can be washed away or deeply buried (as at Gatecliff Shelter).

This issue cropped up in the Carson Desert after we finished our survey in 1981. Two years later, and about 300 kilometers away, torrential rains and heavy snows began falling across the headwaters of the Humboldt

global positioning system (GPS) Handheld devices that use triangulation from radio waves received from satellites to determine your current position in terms of either the UTM grid or latitude and longitude.

Figure 3-6 An archaeological crew excavating a semi-subterranean house pit in the Stillwater Marsh (Nevada). Surface survey missed dozens of sites like this because they were not visible beneath sand and saltgrass.

River, which eventually drains into the Carson Desert. The heavy precipitation kept up until the Carson Desert—that barren basin of sand dunes and alkali flats—became a 40-mile-wide lake.

During the summer of 1986, as floodwaters receded, they stripped away the tops of dunes and exposed hundreds of human burials and archaeological sites containing shallow houses (Figure 3-6 shows an example), storage pits, bones, stone tools, beads, and grinding stones (we discuss these sites and burials in Chapters 9 and 10). After the U.S. Fish and Wildlife Service (the agency that manages the Carson Desert's wetland) plotted the newly exposed finds, we saw that our survey crews had literally walked right over some of these sites. Kelly's crew missed them because there was no surface indication of what lay buried below.

Surface archaeology documents only what lies on or near the ground surface. Although you can never be absolutely certain about what lies below, there are ways to get a pretty good idea. Archaeologists working in the eastern United States, Europe, and elsewhere confront this problem all the time, because these areas witness considerable soil buildup and artifacts rarely lie on the undisturbed ground surface. In agricultural regions, archaeologists do **plow zone** archaeol-

ogy, walking through plowed fields after spring tilling (especially after a rain) because the plow will turn up shallowly buried archaeological remains.

In other areas, archaeologists use **shovel testing.** Survey crews carry small shovels and sometimes a backpacked screen with them. As the crew moves across a survey unit, each member stops at a predetermined interval, digs a narrow hole, and screens the dirt, looking for evidence of buried archaeological remains. It's slow going, and it cannot locate remains that are more than about a meter deep.

Looking for more deeply buried remains, some archaeologists use backhoe trenches or hand or mechanical soil augers, but the former can be very expensive (as well as destructive) and the latter very slow. We normally use them in areas that previous research suggests are good places to prospect for buried remains. In other cases, archaeologists use natural exposures,

plow zone The upper portion of a soil profile that has been disturbed by repeated plowing or other agricultural activity.

shovel testing A sample survey method used in regions where rapid soil buildup obscures buried archaeological remains; it entails digging shallow, systematic pits across the survey unit.

© Robert Kelly

such as arroyos or riverbanks, which sometimes expose deeply buried deposits.

Archaeologists also can use some pretty high-tech ways to "see" below ground. Next, we will consider how surface survey was combined with some of this new technology to find and explore Mission Santa Catalina, a Spanish Franciscan mission lost in Georgia's Sea Islands for more than 300 years.

HOW TO FIND A LOST SPANISH MISSION

At its seventeenth-century zenith, Spanish Florida had three dozen Franciscan missions, satellite settlements each heavily dependent on the colonial capital at St. Augustine. To the west lived the Timucuan, Apalachee, and Apalachicola Indians; to the north, toward St. Catherines Island, lay the province of the Mocamo and the Guale. Although a dozen sixteenth- and seventeenth-century missions once existed in the present state of Georgia, archaeologists and historians had not identified a single one when Thomas began his search for Santa Catalina.

Historians and archaeologists have long thought that the lost mission of Santa Catalina lay along the western margin of St. Catherines Island, a 1400-acre tract 80 kilometers south of Savannah. Unlike the other so-called Golden Isles, St. Catherines Island hasn't been subdivided and developed. The Georgia-based, not-for-profit St. Catherines Island Foundation owns the island and sponsored a comprehensive program of research and conservation. This land management policy ensured that Mission Santa Catalina was not destroyed beneath the crush of condos and fast-food joints that typify so many southern barrier islands.

Surface Survey

In 1974, when Thomas first visited St. Catherines Island, the combined French, English, and Spanish historic documentation supplied only vague geographic clues, and although several first-rate archaeologists had previously worked on the island, none had successfully located this important mission site.

Virtually uninhabited, St. Catherines Island is today blanketed with dense forest, briar patches, and almost impenetrable palmetto thicket. When Thomas began his search for Santa Catalina, he was overwhelmed by the vastness of the area involved. So little was known about the landscape that he could not overlook any portion of the island.

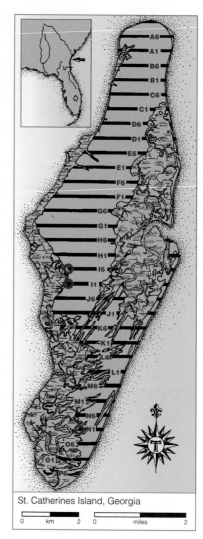

St. Catherines Island, Georgia

0 km 2   0 miles 2

Figure 3-7 Systematic transect research design used to derive a 20 percent regional randomized sample on St. Catherines Island (Georgia). All surveyed transects (the darker stripes) have a letter 1 number designation. Occurrences of sixteenth- and seventeenth-century Spanish ceramics have been circled. *From the American Museum of Natural History.*

Archaeological fieldwork is slow and tedious—and nobody could (or should) excavate an entire island—so Thomas began by random sampling. He calculated that 30 east-west transects, each 100 meters wide, would provide a 20 percent sample of the island (Figure 3-7). This sample allowed him to characterize the island's archaeology and help search for the lost mission of Santa Catalina de Guale. But random sampling, even with a relatively large 20 percent sample, is not good at finding rare sites—and there was only one Santa Catalina de Guale.

In systematic archaeological surveys, the idea is to walk the straightest line possible, climbing over rocks and deadfalls, skirting along the sides of steep ridges—looking even in places where you don't expect to find anything. In Nevada's wide-open spaces, it's fairly easy to keep your bearing even without a compass: Just keep walking toward that peak, mesa, or other landmark in the distance. But on densely vegetated St. Catherines Island, it was impossible to see past the palmetto bush directly in front of you (Figure 3-8). The field crew was

Figure 3-8 Systematic archaeological survey on St. Catherines Island (Georgia).

experienced in desert survey and carried compasses, but even then, some veered off their paths as they wound their way through bushes and briars. Palm-sized orb spiders hung down from Spanish moss–draped oaks; an occasional scream told others that someone had taken one in the face. Orb spiders are not dangerous; but cottonmouths and canebrake rattlesnakes are, and the crew quickly learned about tides and alligators.

In Nevada we could see sites on the ground surface—but on St. Catherines, the sites are almost always buried. We searched for them partly by using probes—meter-long sharpened steel rods. We would push the probe down into the ground every few steps and see if we hit something. This was effective because St. Catherines Island is one huge sand dune—there is no natural stone on the island. Eventually, we learned to tell the difference between the feel of a tree root and rock or shell—the last two suggesting a buried archaeological site. We recorded 135 sites, ranging from massive shell middens to isolated shell scatters. We investigated each site with several 1-meter square test units (see Chapter 4); we excavated more than 400 such test pits.

Subsurface Testing

The surface survey and testing told us that sixteenth- and seventeenth-century Spanish ceramics occurred only at 5 of the 135 archaeological sites, all but one along the western perimeter of the island. The ruins of Mission Santa Catalina almost certainly lay buried in a target area the size of 30 football fields along the southwestern margin of the island.

But 30 football fields is a huge area to dig with dental pick and camel hair brush. Moreover, although our confidence was growing, we had to admit almost complete ignorance of what we were looking for. Did Santa Catalina survive merely as heaps of sixteenth- and seventeenth-century garbage? Or could we realistically hope to find buried evidence of buildings as well? Clearly, it was time to scratch the surface.

Looking around for better ways to find the needle hidden in this haystack, Thomas learned about Kathleen Deagan and her successful search for sixteenth-century St. Augustine. Deagan and her students used a gasoline-powered posthole digger and excavated hundreds of round holes on a grid system. Following her lead, Thomas did the same on St. Catherines Island for the area that the survey had identified as most likely to contain the mission. With the noisy, nasty auger, two people could dig a 3-foot-deep hole in less than a minute. The power auger threw up a neat doughnut of dirt that was hand-sifted for artifacts. We dug hundreds of such holes.

Once the field testing was complete, we identified all materials recovered and plotted the distribution in a series of simple maps. The power auger allowed us to focus further field evaluation on a single 100 × 100 meter square in the overall sampling grid where diagnostic mission-period artifacts were found.

Although this area contained absolutely no surface evidence to distinguish it from the surroundings, judicious use of surface and subsurface sampling had narrowed the search from an entire island to a relatively small area. And this is indeed where we eventually discovered the remarkably well preserved ruins of Mission Santa Catalina de Guale.

But where to dig? In the past we might have excavated a trench across the 10,000 m² and hoped for the best. But just as medical science can use CAT scans and ultrasound to see inside your body, archaeologists today can see below the ground, map subsurface features in detail, and execute pinpoint excavations, minimizing damage to the rest of the site.

Remote Sensing

Remote sensing refers to an array of photographic and geophysical techniques that rely on some form of electromagnetic energy—it might be raw electricity, light, heat, or radio waves—to detect and measure characteristics of an archaeological target. This greatly enhances our ability to see, quite literally, given that the human eye can detect less than 1 ten-millionth of the entire electromagnetic spectrum. We'll say more about photographic techniques later; here we consider how other kinds of remote sensing helped find Mission Santa Catalina on St. Catherines Island.

Thomas used transect survey and power auger testing to narrow down the location of the mission to a 1-hectare (2.6-acre) area. One of the survey units in this area, Quad IV, was an undistinguished piece of real estate covered by scrub palmetto and live oak forest. The only evidence of human occupation was a little-used field road for island research vehicles. Although we could see aboriginal shell midden scatters here and there, Quad IV betrayed absolutely no surface clues as to what lay below. We'd driven over it dozens of time. At this point, Thomas shifted the field strategy from preliminary subsurface testing to noninvasive, nondestructive remote sensing.

Choosing the right method depends on what you expect to find. So what, exactly, were we looking for? For more than a century, Santa Catalina had been the northernmost Spanish outpost on the eastern seaboard, and this historical fact implied considerable size and permanence. The seventeenth-century mission must have had a fortified church and some buildings to house soldiers and priests, plus enough granaries, storehouses, and dwellings for hundreds of Guale Indian neophytes.

We figured that the mission buildings were built of wattle and daub (Figure 3-9). Freshly cut timbers were probably set vertically along the walls and reinforced with cane woven horizontally between the uprights. This sturdy wattlework was then plastered (daubed) with a mixture of marsh mud, sand, and plant fibers (probably Spanish moss). Roofs were thatched with palmetto.

So constructed, wattle-and-daub buildings are totally biodegradable. The thatch roof will eventually rot and blow away. And once directly exposed to the

Figure 3-9 Artist's reconstruction of the wattle-and-daub technique used to build Mission Santa Catalina. The upright wattlework is being daubed (plastered) with a mixture of marsh mud and organic fibers. *Boyd, Mark F., H. G. Smith, and J. W. Griffin. 1951. Here They Once Stood: The Tragic End of the Apalachee Missions. Gainesville: University of Florida Press.*

weather, mud and twig walls will simply wash away. Archaeologists seeking such a dissolved mission would soon be out of business.

But thatched roofs often burn, and if that happened at Santa Catalina, the heat would have fired and hardened the daub walls, like a pot baking in a kiln. Fired daub, nearly as indestructible as the ubiquitous potsherd, thus became a key in our search for the mission.

So, how do you find chunks of burned mud buried beneath a foot of sand without excavating thousands of square meters?

The Proton Magnetometer

The marsh mud used in daub plaster contains microscopic iron particles. Normally, these are randomly oriented to all points of the compass. But when intensely heated, the particles orient toward magnetic north—like a million tiny compass needles. To pinpoint these magnetically anomalous orientations, we relied upon a **proton precession magnetometer.** The theory behind this device is complicated, but the principle is simple: Magnetometers measure the strength of magnetism between the earth's magnetic core and

---

remote sensing The use of some form of electromagnetic energy to detect and measure characteristics of an archaeological target.

proton precession magnetometer A remote sensing technique that measures the strength of magnetism between the earth's magnetic core and a sensor controlled by the archaeologist. Magnetic anomalies can indicate the presence of buried walls or features.

a sensor controlled by the archaeologist. If hundreds of these readings are taken across a systematic grid, we can generate a magnetic contour map reflecting both the shape and the intensity of buried magnetic anomalies.

Many subsurface anomalies are archaeologically irrelevant magnetic "noise"—interference from underlying rocks, AC power lines, or hidden iron debris. The earth's magnetic field fluctuates so wildly on some days that the readings are meaningless, and electrical storms can hopelessly scramble magnetometer readings. Even minor interference, such as the operator's wristwatch or eyeglasses, can drive a magnetometer crazy.

But when everything works just right, the magnetometer provides the equivalent of an MRI, tipping off archaeologists to what's going on beneath the earth's surface. Many archaeological features have characteristic magnetic signatures—telltale clues that hint at the size, shape, depth, and composition of the archaeological objects hidden far below. Shallow graves, for instance, have a magnetic profile vastly different from, say, a buried fire pit or a wattle-and-daub wall.

Working with Ervan Garrison (University of Georgia) and a team from Texas A&M University, we conducted a magnetometer survey of Quad IV. As they were packing up their field equipment to work up the data in their lab, they shared a couple of hunches, based strictly on their raw magnetometer readings: "If we were y'all, we'd dig in three places: here, over yonder, and especially right here." We took their advice and explored all three magnetic anomalies in the few days remaining in our May field season. One anomaly—"especially right here"—turned out to be a sixteenth-century iron barrel ring. Excavating further, we came upon another ring, and more below that. At about 3 meters down, we hit the water table. Digging underwater, we encountered a well-preserved oak well casing.

Archaeologists love wells because, like privies, they can be magnificent artifact traps. After removing the bones of an unfortunate fawn (which had long ago drowned), we found an array of distinctive Hispanic and Guale Indian potsherds and a metal dinner plate dropped (or tossed) into the well. All artifacts were typical of the sixteenth and seventeenth centuries. We had indeed found Mission Santa Catalina, and we pressed on to see what else the magnetometer might have turned up.

Our second magnetic anomaly—the one "here"—was a small mound. After removing the overburden, we came across a burned daub wall that, as it fell, had crushed dozens of Spanish and Guale domestic artifacts: imported tin-enameled glazed cups, painted ceramic dishes, a kitchen knife, and at least two enor-

mous pots for cooking or storage. Charred deer and chicken bones littered the floor, and dozens of tiny corncobs lay scattered about. This time, the magnetometer had led us to the kitchen (in Spanish, *cocina*) used by seventeenth-century Franciscan friars at Santa Catalina.

Finally, we began digging the "over yonder" anomaly, which proved to be a linear daub concentration more than 12 meters long—obviously the downed wall of yet another, much larger mission building. Here excavations turned up none of the everyday implements and debris so common in the scorched *cocina*. Instead, we found a complete buried sixteenth-century mission church.

The search was over. We had discovered the paramount house of worship at Santa Catalina de Guale. Our magnetometer survey provided trustworthy directions to the buried daub walls and iron barrel hoops. Even lacking computer processing, the magnetometer took us to the very heart of Mission Santa Catalina.

We spent two decades excavating the church ruins. The lateral church walls were constructed of wattle and daub that, when encountered archaeologically, consisted of a densely packed linear rubble scatter; this is what the magnetometer "saw" in Quad IV. It's among the very oldest Christian churches in North America.

Geomagnetic survey has progressed considerably since we searched for Mission Santa Catalina de Guale. Today we use an instrument called a fluxgate gradiometer to monitor magnetism in buried deposits (see Figure 3-10). The new instruments are quicker to use, more accurate, and less expensive, but the basic principles remain unchanged. As we discuss in the next section, we have recently conducted extensive geomagnetic surveys at several sites on St. Catherines Island, including Mission Santa Catalina de Guale and the McQueen Shell Ring site, combining the gradiometer results with another technique known as soil resistivity.

Soil Resistivity

Proton magnetometry was just one of the techniques used to locate and define Santa Catalina de Guale. **Soil resistivity survey** monitors the electrical resistance of soils in a restricted volume near the surface of an

---

soil resistivity survey A remote sensing technique that monitors the electrical resistance of soils in a restricted volume near the surface of an archaeological site; changes in the amount of resistance registered by the resistivity meter can indicate buried walls or features.

© American Museum of Natural History, photo by Ginessa Mahar

Figure 3-10 Christina Friberg and Rachel Cajigas performing an FM 256 fluxgate gradiometer survey at the McQueen Shell Ring, a 5000-year-old archaeological construction on St. Catherines Island. Rachel is walking a survey transect with the gradiometer and Christina is recording significant magnetic readings. The data generated in this survey are mapped in Figure 3-12.

© American Museum of Natural History, graphics by Elliot Blair

Figure 3-11 This aerial view of Mission Santa Catalina de Guale has been enhanced with the results of both geophysical prospection and archaeological excavation. The light square (lower right) is a one hectare (100 m × 100 m) clear-cut around the mission church and outlying buildings (outlined in black). The multicolored inset shows projected outlines of shell middens (in red) and of buildings (in black) erected in the Pueblo part of the mission complex; these outlines are conjectural, based on the results of noninvasive soil resistivity surveys.

archaeological site. In part due to its relatively low cost, soil resistivity survey has become a popular technique of geophysical prospecting over the past four decades.

The degree of soil resistance depends on several factors, the most important of which is the amount of water retained in the soil—the more water, the less resistance to electrical currents. Compaction such as occurs in house floors, walls, paths, and roads tends to reduce pore sizes and hence the potential to retain water; this registers as high resistance. When electricity is sent through the soil, buried features can often be detected and defined by the differential resistance to electrical charge caused by their differential retention of groundwater.

The aggregation of fill in pits, ditches, and middens also alters resistivity. Foundations or walls, particularly those in historic-period sites, generally have *greater* resistivity than surrounding soil, whereas the generation of humus by occupation activity increases the ion content of the soil, *reducing* resistivity.

After the initial discovery of the mission and a pilot resistivity survey, Mark Williams and the late Gary Shapiro returned to St. Catherines Island to help us conduct a more comprehensive study. We measured soil resistance by setting four probes in line at 1-meter intervals, each probe inserted to a depth of 20 centimeters. We conducted one of the preliminary resistivity surveys in a 15 × 15 meter area that straddled a test excavation of Structure 2 at Santa Catalina, initially located by the proton magnetometer survey. From our test excavations, we suspected that this building was probably the kitchen, but we had no idea of the building's configuration. The resistivity diagrams clearly identified the margins of the unexcavated building. Later excavations confirmed the accuracy of the soil resistivity diagram.

Today, resistivity survey has been streamlined with new instruments and sophisticated ways to analyze the data. The earliest resistivity survey at Mission Santa Catalina took two days; we can now conduct the same survey in two hours. Figure 3-11 shows the results of modern resistivity surveying at Mission Santa Catalina, remote sensing results that disclose the presence of several still-buried buildings constructed around the mission core.

Figure 3-12 combines the results of geomagnetic and resistance surveys at the McQueen Shell Ring, another archaeological site on St. Catherines Island. The McQueen ring is a circular construction made entirely of marine shell (clam, oyster, mussel, and the like). It stands about 1 meter high and forms a perfect circle 70 meters across. The inside is perfectly clean, and large enough to play a full-court game of basketball—but it is completely buried; virtually no trace remains on the surface. The McQueen shell midden dates between 4000 and 5000 years old, and contains hundreds of pieces of fiber-tempered ceramics (the oldest pottery complex known in North America). As shown in Figure 3-10, we conducted a gradiometer survey across the entire surface, with a follow-up resistivity survey as well. Figure 3-12 combines the results of both remote sensing surveys, providing a detailed roadmap of what lies there. For the past three years, we have used these geophysical surveys to guide our pinpoint testing of this important site.

Ground-Penetrating Radar

Yet another method of geophysical prospecting is **ground-penetrating radar (GPR).** Although this method tends to be expensive, its cost is offset to some degree by its speed. But neither operating the radar equipment nor interpreting the results is simple, and the assistance of trained specialists is required.

GPR was first developed in 1910, but a significant peak in interest coincided with the *Apollo 17* lunar sounding experiment in the early 1970s. Today, environmental engineering firms commonly employ GPR techniques to find buried rock or deep swamp deposits or to search for caverns.

In GPR, radar pulses directed into the ground reflect back to the surface when they strike targets or

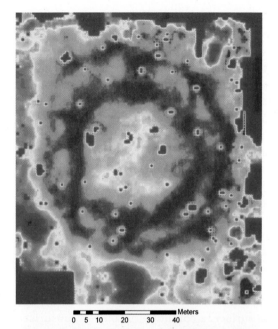

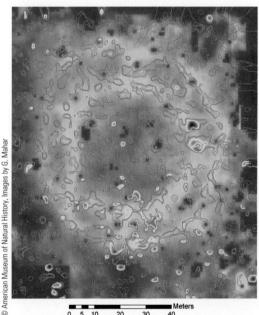

© American Museum of Natural History. Images by G. Mahar

Figure 3-12 Remote sensing data can be arrayed in several ways. Top: a soil resistance map of the McQueen Shell Ring (St. Catherines Island), coded with high resistance indicated by purple and low resistance by dark orange. Bottom: Also the McQueen Shell Ring, but the resistivity data are arrayed in grayscale and gradiometry results (generated in Figure 3-10) are rendered as an overlay contour. Magnetic anomalies with a weaker signature are shown here as warm colored contours, while stronger anomalies are shown as steep contour arrangements of warm and cool colors.

ground-penetrating radar (GPR) A remote sensing technique in which radar pulses directed into the ground reflect back to the surface when they strike features or interfaces within the ground, showing the presence and depth of possible buried features.

interfaces within the ground (such as a change in the density of dirt, groundwater, buried objects, voids, or an interface between soil and rock). As these pulses are reflected, their speed to the target and the nature of their return are measured. The signal's reflection provides information about the depth and three-dimensional shape of buried objects.

With transducers (devices that convert electrical energy to electromagnetic waves) of various dimensions, a researcher applying GPR can direct the greatest degree of resolution to the depth of specific interest. A pulsating electric current is passed through an antenna, inducing electromagnetic waves that radiate toward the target and return in a fraction of a microsecond to be recorded. The dimensions of the transducer influence the depth and detail that are desired in any specific archaeological application. As the antenna is dragged across the ground surface, a continuous profile of subsurface electromagnetic conditions is printed on a graphic recorder. The location and depth of subsurface targets can be inferred from, and tested against, this graphic record (Figure 3-13).

Groundwater is a problem for GPR studies because it changes the relative permeability of most sediments. Soils are good reflectors when they are associated with steep changes in water content, as occurs in coarse materials. Unsorted sediments, such as glacial till, will have a broad and varying capillary zone, and thus no clear reflection. GPR is generally ineffective over saltwater, in penetrating some clays, and at depths of more than about 30 meters below the surface. The maximum depth of penetration depends on the conductivity of the overlying deposit.

GPR works best when the soil resistivity is high, as in well-drained soils and those with low clay content. Subsurface wells, foundations, cellars, voids, cavities, and well-defined compacted zones, such as house floors, can provide clear radar echoes.

Why did we begin using GPR at Santa Catalina? Historical documents suggested that the Spanish had fortified the mission as a precaution against British attack, perhaps by building a stockade and moat complex to protect the buildings immediately adjacent to the central plaza. Yet, after three years of magnetometer and resistivity surveys and limited test excavations, we had failed to locate any trace of defensive fortifications, such as palisades, bastions, or moats encircling the central mission zone. Given that these features might not have burned, and because they could be as saturated with water as the surrounding sediment, they might have eluded the magnetometer and resistivity instruments. However, these features might have differed from the background sediment in terms of their compaction, and that suggested to us that GPR might help locate them.

We ran a number of systematic north-south transects at 20-meter intervals, followed by a series of east-west transects. Obvious anomalies were hand-plotted on the grayscale computer output, and additional transects were run across these target areas. We located significant anomalies on the ground by means of pin flags. We then ran a third set of transects at a 45° angle, to intercept buried anomalies at a different angle.

These preliminary radar profiles led us directly to the palisade and bastion complex encircling the central buildings and plaza at Santa Catalina. Although this defensive network could surely have been located by extensive test trenching, the radar approach proved to be considerably more cost-effective and less destructive than conventional archaeological exploration.

© American Museum of Natural History, photo by Samantha Williams

Figure 3-13 David Hurst Thomas (right) and Lawrence Conyers (University of Denver) conduct a ground-penetrating radar survey on the site of San Marcos, a Spanish mission and pueblo site in New Mexico.

THE BENEFITS OF NONINVASIVE ARCHAEOLOGY

It is clear from these examples that remote sensing can help archaeology in very significant ways. One drawback has been that remote sensing techniques are expensive, but the cost has been going down as the machinery becomes more widely available. And remote sensing can pay for itself, given that the alternative—hand excavation—is also costly. By targeting excavation efforts, remote sensing can actually reduce a project's cost.

Some form of remote sensing can work almost anyplace, though not everywhere (at least not yet). Where there is a lot of background noise—such as a high groundwater table, considerable background rock, or natural subsurface features—it is often difficult for the geophysical devices to pick out which anomalies are worth investigating. But with increasing refinements to the technology, remote sensing has become an indispensable tool facilitating both archaeological survey and excavation.

The advances in geophysics have implications that reach to the core of archaeological thinking. For years, archaeologists analyzed only those artifacts that they could hold in their hands or excavated archaeological features that they could see with their eyes. Remote sensing has changed that focus, allowing us to construct robust linkages between the larger things that archaeologists find—walls, structures, and features—and the way that they are remotely perceived by the sensors of geophysical machinery and remote imagery.

In effect, remote sensing allows modern archaeologists to transcend an "archaeology by capture" approach—the only real truth is the artifact in your hand—opening the door to a more noninvasive, conservation-oriented archaeology of the future.

GEOGRAPHIC INFORMATION SYSTEMS

Archaeological data are inherently spatial, and archaeologists map things all the time. Maps show where things are and, more important, how they relate to each other. Archaeologists use maps to plot the results of remote sensing, such as artifact distributions within a site and distributions of sites across a region, a state, or even a continent.

But in their traditional form, maps are difficult to update with new information, and the resulting distributions are often unwieldy to analyze.

This all changed in the late 1980s with the advent of **geographic information systems (GIS),** computer programs designed to store, retrieve, analyze, and display cartographic data. GIS lets you view information—any geographically related information—visually. The most common programs in use today are ArcView and ArcInfo.

Every GIS consists of three primary components: a powerful computer graphics program used to draw a map, one or more external databases that are linked to the objects shown on the map, and a set of analytical tools that can graphically interpret or statistically analyze the stored data. Most of the United States is in the process of putting all their archaeological site records into a GIS. Clearly, GIS is a basic skill that any student contemplating a career in archaeology should learn.

In true GIS format, the earth's various features are not depicted visually—as they would be on standard two-dimensional maps—but as digital information. Virtually every standard USGS topographic map is now available digitally (some high-end GPS units contain them already). Data stored digitally, of course, can be manipulated and displayed in numerous ways.

In GIS, a database is composed of several themes, or layers. Envision a base topographic map—that's one theme. Now envision laying a clear sheet of plastic over that map (this is how we used to do it!). You plot on the sheet all the archaeological sites you just found in a survey. This layer is another theme. Over the first sheet, you lay another on which you draw in all the water sources; this is a third theme. On yet another sheet, you draw the distribution of different vegetation communities. On another, you plot the results of high-altitude imagery; on still another, the region's different soils . . . you get the picture.

Mapping like this with physical plastic sheets is unwieldy, and the resulting patterns are difficult to analyze statistically. However, by inputting all these different data digitally into a single **georeferenced** database, we can call up one or more of the layers and analyze the distributions. "Georeferenced" means that data are input using a common mapping reference, such as the UTM grid system mentioned previously. Because the data are digital, we can do spatial analyses in minutes that previously might have taken

geographic information system (GIS) A computer program for storing, retrieving, analyzing, and displaying cartographic data.

georeferenced Data that are input to a GIS database using a common mapping reference—for example, the UTM grid—so that all data can be spatially analyzed.

Figure 3-14 Pueblo Bonito, photo by Charles Lindbergh, 1929.

© Charles A. Lindbergh, Courtesy Palace of the Governors Photo Archives (NMHM/DCA), neg.# 130198

LANDSCAPE ARCHAEOLOGY

GIS is a tool that opens up new ways to analyze spatial data. Partly because of this new ability, archaeologists have developed a new approach called **landscape archaeology.** Although the word "landscape" has a colloquial meaning, Carole Crumley (University of North Carolina) defines "landscape" as "the material manifestation of the relation between humans and their environments."

In a sense, landscape archaeology has been around since the 1940s, when Gordon Willey (1913–2002) conducted the first archaeological settlement pattern study in Peru's Virú Valley. In this regard, landscape archaeology is similar to the settlement pattern archaeology we discussed earlier, but it adds a concern with how people use and modify their environment. The case of the "Chacoan roads" shows how GIS, combined with remote sensing, can help test hypotheses about how ancient peoples used a landscape.

weeks or longer. Each of the data points is linked to a database, which can include complete information on that point. A site record, for example, might contain information on a site's artifacts—how many projectile points or potsherds were found there—plus other data such as its size, its slope, and the kind of architecture that was present.

We can ask myriad questions of this database. For example, we might ask, "How far away from water sources are pueblo sites found?" With a GIS database, we can quickly *buffer* springs and streams at some standard distance, say 1-kilometer intervals. Think of this as drawing concentric circles around the springs with radii of 1 kilometer, 2 kilometers, 3 kilometers, and so on. Likewise, we would trace out land areas within 1, 2, and 3 kilometers of rivers and streams. We could then ask the program to tell us how many pueblo sites versus other kinds of sites are in the various buffers. We could also see if sites are more frequently associated with a particular kind of vegetation community or soil type—in fact, with any data set that has a spatial dimension to it.

The Chacoan Roads: Discovery

Chaco Canyon was the center of a vast social and political network between 950 and 850 years ago, when two distinct kinds of sites appeared in the region. Throughout the Four Corners area, numerous smaller pueblo sites dotted the landscape. But huge sites—the Great Houses such as Pueblo Bonito (Figure 3-14, and the chapter's opening photo)—appeared in Chaco Canyon and a few other places on the Colorado Plateau. The Great Houses were centrally located amid a cluster of smaller sites, defining a "community." By 900 years ago, the Great Houses had developed into large, formal ancestral Pueblo towns.

In 1970–1971, archaeologist R. Gwinn Vivian (Arizona State Museum) was mapping what he thought was a series of ancient canals in Chaco Canyon. As he began excavating, Vivian realized that the linear fea-

landscape archaeology The study of ancient human modification of the environment.

tures were like no canals he'd ever seen. Instead of having a U-shaped cross-section, the Chaco "canal" appeared to be a deliberately flattened and carefully engineered *roadway*.

Vivian described his curious find to Thomas Lyons, a geologist hired to experiment with remote sensing possibilities in Chaco Canyon. Together, Vivian and Lyons started looking at the available aerial photographs of the area. Some of these photographs dated to the 1960s, but others had been taken in the 1930s by Charles Lindbergh (1902–1974), the famous American aviator-explorer, before grazing was permitted at Chaco.

Looking carefully at these black-and-white photos, Vivian and Lyons saw unmistakable traces of a prehistoric road network. They commissioned new flights, and road segments were field-checked against the aerial photographs. By 1973, Gwinn and Lyons had identified more than 300 kilometers of prehistoric roads (diagrammed in Figure 3-15). Amazingly, Lindbergh's photographs actually showed the famous Chacoan roads—but nobody recognized them as such until 1971, when archaeologists had a clue of what to look for. (Actually, Navajos living in Chaco Canyon knew about portions of the roads more than a century ago, although they, too, were unaware of their extent.)

Aerial photography traces its origins to 1857, when photographs were taken from a balloon suspended over Paris. Not long afterward, a few archaeologists were taking aerial photos of their sites, primarily with cameras attached to crewless balloons.

But these photos were simply to record a site and its excavations. During World War I, airplanes developed into a reliable technology and archaeologists began to rely on aerial photography to find buried sites. British archaeologist O. G. S. Crawford (1886–1957) first saw

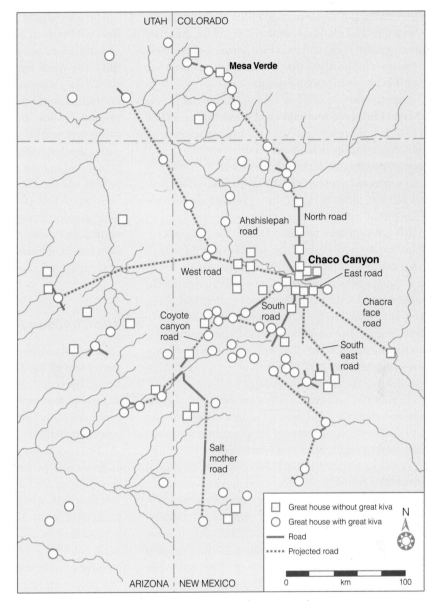

Figure 3-15 A diagram of Chaco road system as it may have appeared 950 years ago.

the potential in aerial photography when he analyzed photographs of German military units and saw signs of buried archaeological ruins. Taken with sunlight at an oblique angle, black-and-white photographs show shadows alongside slight undulations in the ground surface that point to shallowly buried walls not discernible on the ground. Soon after World War I, Crawford used aerial photography to locate Roman settlements in Britain.

Aerial photography has come a long way from black-and-white photos taken while hanging off the side of a biplane. Archaeologists have since employed everything from balloons and airplanes to the Space Shuttle and satellites to use photography to detect buried remains. Early photographic techniques were restricted to the visible portion of the electromagnetic spectrum, and cloud cover was a problem. But new photographic techniques capture portions of the electromagnetic spectrum that the naked eye cannot see and that are unaffected by cloud cover.

One technique used at Chaco in the 1980s was **thermal infrared multispectral scanning, or TIMS.** TIMS measures infrared thermal radiation given off by the ground; it is sensitive to differences as small as 0.1° centigrade. Although we've had the ability to make infrared photographs for some time—the Landsat satellite did it in the 1970s—TIMS produces photographs of higher quality.

All photographs consist of pixels, and an instrument cannot record anything smaller than the size of a particular technique's pixel. In early satellite imagery, the pixels were 30 meters on a side, so these techniques could not record anything smaller than about 900 square meters. Such photos were of limited use to archaeology. The resolution of TIMS images depends on the altitude at which the photos are taken, but photos with a resolution of 8 meters, or even 1–2 meters, can be quite useful to archaeology.

TIMS images require a very complex kind of camera, and the data—the sensed infrared radiation—are transformed via a computer program into so-called false-color images. False-color images map the ground in terms of infrared radiation—rendering terrain in garish colors such as red, blue, and purple.

Because the Chacoan roads are more compacted than the surrounding matrix (even if their compacted surface is buried), they reflect more radiation than the surrounding sand. In false-color images, the roads appear as clear, tan lines against a backdrop of red sand. The Chaco experiment proved that TIMS can detect features such as buried road systems, even if they are invisible to an archaeologist standing on top of them.

Today, analysis of aerial and high-altitude photographs has revealed possibly as many as 600 kilometers of ancient roadways around Chaco Canyon. These roads are only 5 to 10 centimeters deep, yet sometimes 7 to 10 meters wide. Often they turn suddenly in doglegs, and they are occasionally edged by low rock berms. Sometimes they are littered with potsherds. Some are cut into the earth, and others were made by simply clearing away the surface rock and vegetation.

thermal infrared multispectral scanning (TIMS) A remote sensing technique that uses equipment mounted on aircraft or satellites to measure infrared thermal radiation given off by the ground. Sensitive to differences as small as 0.1° centigrade, it can locate subsurface structures by tracking how they affect surface thermal radiation.

The longest and best-defined roads, probably constructed between 925 and 860 years ago, extend some 50 kilometers outward from Chaco Canyon. Sometimes the roads are just short segments, and it is unclear if they were intended to be segments, if they were unfinished, or if portions of the road have disappeared through erosion. In places, the Chacoans constructed causeways, and elsewhere they cut stairways into sheer cliffs. The generally straight bearings suggest that the people laid out the roads prior to construction.

Why did the Chaco people build these roads across the desert? This elaborate road system covered more than 250,000 square kilometers; yet these ancestors of modern Pueblo peoples had no wheeled vehicles or even beasts of burden. Why are the roads so wide and so straight? What were they used for?

The Chacoan Roads: Interpretation

One hypothesis is that the Chacoan roads facilitated movement of food and other goods across the landscape. The roads radiate outward from Chaco Canyon, so perhaps they were a way to provision the inhabitants of the canyon's Great Houses with maize, timber, and other supplies.

But landscapes carry symbolic meanings as well as economic potential. Perhaps the roads were not economic at all, but instead served some ceremonial function with symbolic meanings. In fact, because the roads tend to cut straight across hills, rather than skirt around their bases, and make inexplicable sharp turns in the middle of the desert, many archaeologists favor a noneconomic interpretation. To hypothesize what this purpose might be, we can look to the descendants of Chaco.

Among the likely descendants of the people who inhabited Chaco Canyon are the Keres, the Puebloan peoples who live along the northern Rio Grande in New Mexico in the pueblos of Cochiti, San Felipe, Santa Ana, Santo Domingo, and Zia. In traditional Pueblo theology, the world consists of several nested layers, surrounded at the edges by four sacred mountains. As James Snead (George Mason University) and Robert Preucel (University of Pennsylvania) describe them, these nested layers center on a village, and different directions are associated with different powers, societies, and supernatural beings, as well as with maleness and femaleness (Figure 3-16). Direction is important in this view of the world.

This symbolic landscape is physically manifested by different kinds of shrines. The shrine on Mount Taylor, for example, the west mountain shrine for

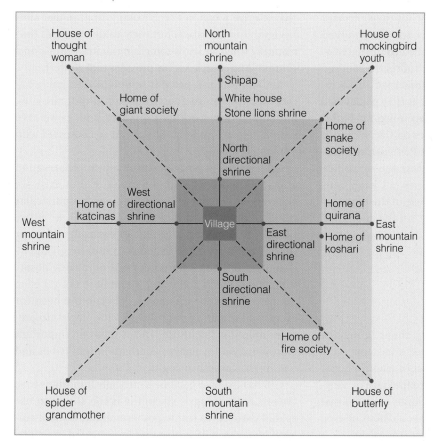

Figure 3-16 A schematic representation of the Keres symbolic landscape. *From J. Snead and R. Preucel, "The Ideology of Settlement: Ancestral Keres Landscapes in the Northern Rio Grande." In W. Ashmore and A. B. Knapp (Eds.),* Archaeologies of Landscape: Contemporary Perspectives *(pp. 169–197). Oxford: Blackwell Publishers. Used by permission.*

Laguna Pueblo, is a shallow pit where people still come to pray. Directional shrines may be located closer to the villages and are often found in caves or near springs. One important directional shrine is two mountain lions carved from bedrock and surrounded by a circle of stones. Closer to the village are directional shrines that mark a village's boundaries. Located in the four cardinal directions, they are often keyhole-shaped stone structures with openings to the north or east. Other shrines are found within the village itself, especially in plazas where important dance rituals take place.

So, it is clear that landscape has both economic and symbolic meanings in the Puebloan world. Direction, in particular, seems to hold special symbolic significance in Pueblo religion. Although the ancient Chacoans probably did not share the Keres worldview exactly, they may have had a similar one, or at least one in which shrines marked significant places and directions on the landscape.

Working just south of Chaco Canyon, John Kantner (School of Advanced Research) used GIS to test whether the roads were linked to the economic or symbolic aspects of the desert landscape. He reasoned that if the roads were for purely economic purposes, then they should follow the path of least resistance between Pueblo villages; if they did not, then perhaps the roads fulfilled a more religious purpose that was driven by the ancient peoples' symbolic interpretation of the landscape.

Using a digital elevation model, Kantner asked GIS to perform a straightforward task: find the easiest walking route between settlements that are connected by roads. The easiest walking route would be the one on which a person gained the least amount of elevation in walking from one village to another. Although it would take an archaeologist many days to walk out the possibilities in the field or even to trace them out on topographic maps, GIS could quickly calculate the "path of least resistance" for someone walking from one settlement to another.

Kantner found that GIS did *not* predict the locations of the roads. In fact, some of the roads crossed terrain that is substantially different from that predicted by GIS. The Chacoan roads do not follow the path of least resistance. We assume that anyone as familiar with their landscape as the Chacoans were would know the easiest way to walk from one settlement to another. But perhaps this assumption was wrong—perhaps people did *not* know or did *not* use the easiest paths between settlements. To test this hypothesis, Kantner asked whether there were any archaeological remains associated with GIS-predicted paths.

In fact, he found that small stone shrines occur along the predicted footpaths; it appears that someone was using the predicted paths, probably on a regular basis. In contrast, large circular stone shrines, ones that required more effort to construct, were almost always found with the roads, not the predicted footpaths.

From this, Kantner concluded that the roads did not serve simply as part of the Chacoan economy. Although food and other goods may have been moved along the roads, this was probably not their primary purpose. Instead, people probably routinely moved food and goods along trails that followed the paths of least resistance between villages, footpaths marked by small shrines today. But the formal roads' association with large shrines suggests that they performed some other role. Perhaps they were religious paths; some, in fact, lead directly to places on the landscape that figure prominently in modern Puebloan religion. Or perhaps they helped to integrate the small far-flung pueblos with the Great Houses in Chaco Canyon. We still don't know the purpose of the roads for sure, but GIS clearly casts doubt on the economic hypothesis.

Conclusion

We began this chapter by talking about "gumshoe survey"—looking around for a good site to excavate by talking with lots of people, most of whom are not archaeologists. This is a good way to find rare or spectacular sites because those are the kinds of places that nonarchaeologists remember. Few would note, or even notice, small scatters of potsherds or stone flakes.

But archaeologists are interested in more than the big, spectacular sites. They are trying to understand the whole range of human settlement—from the showy, spectacular pueblos to the small scatter of a single broken pot. Systematic surveys arose in the 1960s not as a way to find sites, but as an unbiased means to characterize a region's archaeology. Spectacular sites are always informative, but their value increases dramatically when we know something about their regional context. And sample survey provides that context.

A complete, 100 percent sample is preferable because it alone can guarantee the discovery of rare sites. But complete surveys are expensive, and, as we have shown here, research questions can be addressed with a far smaller sample.

Archaeology is also constrained by a conservation ethic. Because only a finite number of sites exist, we excavate only what we must to answer a particular research question, saving portions of sites, or entire sites, for future researchers. Remote sensing will never replace excavation (nor should it). But by giving archaeologists a cost-effective means of making observations on objects and features that have not yet been excavated, remote sensing can obviate the need for excessive excavation and permit archaeologists to preserve more for the future. This is today an important consideration for many American Indian tribes and for any ethical archaeologist.

GIS has likewise become a critically important tool. One of archaeology's strengths is the ability to use spatial patterns to test hypotheses about ancient cultural behavior. GIS is also extremely useful to federal and state agencies that must manage the archaeological sites on their properties. For these reasons, it is likely that GIS will become as indispensable to archaeologists as their trowels. However, these methods will never replace our need to excavate sites. And this realization brings us to the next chapter.

SUMMARY

1. Why do archaeologists "survey"?

⊕ We do survey because no single site reveals everything about an ancient society.

2. What is the main principle of survey? Why does this matter?

⊕ The main principle of archaeological survey is to generate a representative sample of a landscape; sometimes a survey is randomized to ensure that every site has an equal chance of being included in the sample.

⊕ This matters because if we only look in the "logical" places, we will almost certainly bias the sample and our reconstruction of the past.

3. What limits surface survey? What are the basic remote sensing techniques and their benefits?

⊕ Survey can only find what lies on the ground; remote sensing helps us understand what lies below the ground.

was "How long have Native Americans been here?" As we saw in the Moundbuilder controversy, many scholars believed that American Indians arrived in the Western Hemisphere only shortly before European colonists. This matter was important politically because if archaeology showed that American Indians were longtime inhabitants of the New World, then their claim to the land was strengthened. But if Indian people were only recent immigrants, their rights to the land could be minimized in favor of the Europeans.

So, from the earliest colonial times, scholars debated the antiquity of humanity in the New World (and they still do). Some claimed that the discovery of apparently crude stone tools demonstrated that humans had been in the New World for thousands of years, since the last phase of the Ice Age, but others showed that these crude artifacts could be mere quarry rejects, unfinished pieces that the artisans deemed too flawed to complete, and had nothing to say about how long Indians had lived in the New World.

The argument over the antiquity of humanity in the New World came down to animals. Nineteenth- and early-twentieth-century archaeologists couldn't tell how old a site was. But they knew that the world had experienced a great Ice Age in the distant past. And they reasoned (quite accurately, it turns out) that this Ice Age, more properly called the **Pleistocene,** had ended about 10,000 years ago. Scholars also knew that different kinds of animals lived in North America during the Pleistocene—including mammoths, mastodons, a large species of bison, giant bears, ground sloths, horses, and camels. Anybody who found artifacts in undisputed association with the bones of such extinct fauna would prove that humans had been in North America for at least 10,000 years. Thus, the quest relied heavily on context: seeking ancient artifacts in unquestionable association with the bones of extinct fauna.

In the last chapter, we mentioned that some of the most important archaeological sites are found by nonarchaeologists. A hard-rock miner found Gatecliff Shelter, and an ex-slave named George McJunkin (1851–1922) found the Folsom site—the place that proved the extent of human antiquity in the Americas (Figure 4-1).

The Black Cowboy Born into slavery, McJunkin acquired his freedom at age 14, "borrowed" a mule from his former owner, and left his home on a Texas plantation in search of work. By 1868 he was breaking horses for a Texas rancher; later he held down a string of ranch jobs in Colorado and New Mexico. He became an expert cowboy and knew just about all there was to know about horses and cattle.

Figure 4-1 The Folsom site in 1998. A bison skull is uncovered in the excavation unit.

McJunkin also learned a lot about many other things. Although he never received a formal education, he taught himself to read and to play the fiddle. He was curious about everything, especially natural history; one of his prize possessions was a wooden box filled with rocks, bones, fossils, and arrowheads. McJunkin never married and lived most of his life as the only African American in his community.

Early in the 1890s, McJunkin's talents were recognized by the owner of the Crowfoot Ranch in northeastern New Mexico, near the town of Folsom. Soon McJunkin was ranch foreman and proved himself an able cowpuncher, wrangler, and leader.

One day in August 1908, torrential rains fell, creating a flash flood that destroyed much of Folsom. (Many people were killed, but more would have died had not the local telephone operator, Sarah Rooke, remained at her post, calling people to warn them until the floodwaters claimed her life.) After helping to search for the dead, McJunkin began checking the Crowfoot's fences. Up Wild Horse Arroyo, he found a line that dangled across a now deep, muddy gully. Pondering how to fix

Pleistocene A geologic period from 1.8 million to 10,000 years ago, which was characterized by multiple periods of extensive glaciation.

Figure 4-2 A fluted Folsom spear point lying between the ribs of an extinct species of bison at the Folsom site.

it, he spotted bones protruding from the walls of the arroyo, some 15 feet down the embankment.

McJunkin had seen plenty of cow bones in his day, and these were definitely not cow. The bones seemed too large even for bison. McJunkin returned to the site over the years to collect bones that he then stacked on his mantle at home. He would talk to anyone about them and showed the site to several interested townsfolk.

A Spear Point between the Ribs The find eventually came to the attention of Jesse Figgins, director of the Colorado Museum of Natural History (now the Denver Museum of Nature and Science), who was looking for skeletons of the extinct Pleistocene bison, *Bison antiquus*, for a museum display. Sadly, McJunkin had died a few years before Figgins's arrival, so he did not live to see his site make archaeological history.

Some of the townsfolk who had visited the site with McJunkin had occasionally found an artifact or two among the bones (now identified as ancient bison), but they did not document their finds, meaning that the *context* of these artifacts was unknown. In 1926, Figgins's crew found a beautifully made spear point with a distinct central groove or channel (what we now call a "flute"). But, unfortunately, they could not tell whether the artifact was found with the bison skeletons or had

fallen from a later, higher level—the newest find also lacked the necessary *context*.

Figgins telegraphed the crew to leave any artifacts exactly where they were discovered so that he could personally observe them in place. So, when excavators located similar spear points the following summer, they left the artifacts **in situ** (in place) so that their context could be recorded. One of these points lay between the ribs of a bison (Figure 4-2). Figgins sent telegrams to prominent members of the archaeological community, including the skeptical A. V. Kidder (see Chapter 1), who was excavating at Pecos only 100 miles away.

After joining other archaeologists at the excavation site, Kidder solemnly pronounced that the association between the spear points and the extinct bison remains was solid. There was no evidence that rodents had burrowed into the deposit, carrying later artifacts from higher in the ground down to the bison skeletons. There was no indication that streams had redeposited the artifacts on top of the remains. Everyone present saw undeniable evidence of a spear that had been thrust between the ribs of a bison.

For the first time, scientists had confirmed the association between extinct fauna and human artifacts: People had been in the Americas since at least the end of the Pleistocene, some 10,000 years ago. Today, we know McJunkin's site as the Folsom site, and the distinctive spear points found there are called Folsom points—both named after the nearby town that had been devastated by the flood that exposed the site.

As you can see, *context* was everything at the Folsom site. And this is true for any site. In fact, other than "When's lunch?" what you'll hear most frequently on any archaeological dig is "Show me exactly where that came from."

EXCAVATION: WHAT DETERMINES PRESERVATION?

The exact procedures used to record context in any excavation depend on several factors, beginning with the kinds of materials that have survived the passage

in situ From Latin, meaning "in position"; the place where an artifact, ecofact, or feature was found during survey or excavation.

© National Museum of the American Indian, Smithsonian Institution (13/4516) photo by Scott Klettes

Figure 4-3 A 2000-year-old duck decoy from Lovelock Cave, Nevada. *Courtesy Nevada State Museum, Carson City, Nevada Department of Cultural Affairs, and National Museum of the American Indian, Smithsonian Institution 13/4512. Photo by Scott Klettes.*

of time. Some sites preserve organic materials wonderfully, including basketry, leather, and wood; in other sites, only ceramics, stones, and bones survive; and in the earliest archaeological sites, only stone tools remain. Here are some examples that demonstrate the various conditions under which organic remains are preserved.

The Duck Decoys of Lovelock Cave

Lovelock Cave (Nevada) sits on a barren hillside just north of the Carson Desert, described in the last chapter. But thousands of years ago, anybody sitting in the cave's mouth would have looked out upon a vast wetland just a few kilometers away. Lovelock Cave was first excavated in 1912 by Lewellyn Loud, a museum security guard at the University of California sent there by anthropologist Alfred Kroeber to gather museum specimens, and again in 1924 by Mark Harrington of New York's Museum of the American Indian. Like Hidden Cave (see Chapter 3), the dry and dusty interior of Lovelock Cave was used more for storage than for habitation.

Loud and Harrington found several caches of gear. One, Pit 11, held a buried basket that contained 11 duck decoys. Cleverly crafted from tule reeds twisted to simulate the body and head of a duck, some decoys had plain tule reed bodies and others were adorned with paint and feathers. As artifacts, the decoys are striking (Figure 4-3). Even *Sports Illustrated* extolled the creativity and craftsmanship of these prehistoric duck hunters.

Someone buried this basket of decoys (in fact, they were interred beneath the pit's false bottom), evidently

intending to use them on a later hunt. Although the person who buried the decoys never retrieved them, it was wise to cache them inside Lovelock Cave because they were perfectly preserved; they are usable even today. And we know from radiocarbon dating (discussed in Chapter 6) that these decoys were made about 2000 years ago.

The Houses of Ozette

Equally remarkable, yet strikingly different, preservation is seen at the site of Ozette on Washington's Olympic Peninsula (Figure 4-4). Ozette was a major beachside village once occupied by the ancestors of the Makah people. In fact, some Makahs remained at Ozette into the 1920s, and their oral traditions helped lead Richard Daugherty (then at Washington State University) to the site in the first place.

Ozette was once a lively village stretching for a mile along the Pacific Coast, home to perhaps 800 people who lived in massive split-plank cedar houses. They hunted, gathered berries in the forest, collected shellfish along the coast, and fished for halibut, salmon, and other species. They even hunted killer whales.

Part of Ozette village lay along the bottom of a steep hill. Some 300 years ago, during an especially heavy rain (or possibly a tsunami), the hillside above the village became saturated, and an enormous mudslide descended on the village, shearing the tops off

© Ruth Kirk

Figure 4-4 The archaeological site of Ozette on the coast of Washington.

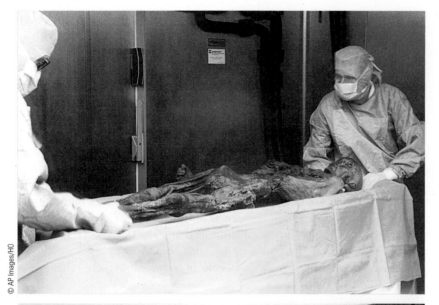

© AP Images/HO

© South Tyrol Museum of Archaeology/www.iceman.it

Figure 4-5 Ötzi, the "Ice Man" (above), and portions of some of his tools (below).

The Ice Man of the Alps

Our third example demonstrates yet a different kind of archaeological preservation. In 1991, two skiers in the Alps came upon the body of a man lying in a pool of icy glacial water at 10,000 feet. The body was so well preserved that the authorities thought at first he might be a mountaineer who had perished in a blizzard a few years earlier. But today, we know this man as Ötzi, the "Ice Man," who died some 5300 years ago. His body was remarkably well preserved—even tattoos are clearly visible on his skin—because he froze shortly after he died and a small glacier then sealed his body in the shallow depression where it had come to rest. Here he freeze-dried and lay undisturbed until the warmth of recent decades caused the glacier to recede, exposing his remains.

Realizing the significance of the Ice Man, archaeologists scoured the site and recovered portions of his clothing— a belt to hold up a leather breechcloth and leggings, a coat of deerskin, a cape of woven grass, a leather fur-lined cap, and calfskin shoes filled with grass. They also recovered tools, including a hafted copper axe, a bow and a quiver of arrows, bone points, extra bowstrings, a wooden pack frame, birch bark containers, a stone scraper, a hafted knife, and a net (Figure 4-5).

By analyzing the contents of the Ice Man's stomach and intestine, scientists determined that he had not eaten for at least 8 hours before his death and that his final meal had been barley, wheat, deer, and wild goat. Pollen contained in his intestine suggests that he died in the spring, and the mixture of plant pollen suggests that he had just climbed to the summit from the valley floor, probably in one day.

Why did this 30-year-old man die at such a high elevation, far from any village or camp? An arrow point that penetrated past his shoulder blade suggests that

five houses and burying their interiors. Some people escaped, but others were caught inside. Because the coast of Washington is so wet, the destroyed portion of Ozette remained waterlogged and was capped by the mudslide with a thick layer of clay.

The saturated dirt and the clay cap preserved entire houses with all their furnishings and gear. During the 1970s, Richard Daugherty excavated the houses, recovering some 42,000 artifacts, including baskets, mats, hats, halibut hooks, bowls, clubs, combs—even an entire cedar canoe. The archaeological team worked closely with the Makah people, and many of the artifacts from Ozette village are now on display at the Makah Cultural and Research Center in Neah Bay, Washington. These displays highlight the remarkable degree of preservation at this waterlogged site.

he had been attacked. One of his hands also bears unhealed cuts, as though he had warded off an assailant armed with a knife. One hypothesis is that he was fleeing, stopped to rest in a depression away from the wind, and quietly passed away from his wounds.

The Preservation Equation

Why were the Lovelock duck decoys, the houses of Ozette, and the Ice Man so well preserved?

Decomposition is carried out by microorganisms that require warmth, oxygen, and water to survive. In each of the three cases, one of these was lacking: Lovelock Cave lacked moisture, the wet deposits beneath the clay cap at Ozette were anaerobic (without oxygen), and the Ice Man's glacial environment lacked warmth.

These different preservation conditions present the archaeologist with both opportunities and challenges. At Ozette, the waterlogged archaeological deposits were a muddy gumbo that was almost impossible to trowel or shovel. And because the wooden artifacts were saturated with water, a misplaced shovel stroke could slice them like a knife through butter. To cope with these conditions, Daugherty assembled a complex system of pressurized hoses to wash the mud away. By adjusting the water pressure, they could use fire hoses to clean off the massive house posts and wall planks, switching to a fine misting spray when exposing delicate basketry.

Likewise, sites such as Lovelock Cave offer a wealth of artifacts not normally found, but such sites tend to be extremely complex. They are favorite places for rodents and carnivores, whose actions can move artifacts up and down, making it difficult to sort out context. This means that they require especially slow and careful excavation.

And although the Ice Man contributed enormously to our knowledge of the past, his preservation now requires a sophisticated storage chamber (at Italy's South Tyrol Museum), where museum personnel control the temperature and humidity.

Preservation, of course, is only one factor conditioning how we excavate a site; other factors include the site's depth, time and financial constraints, accessibility, and perhaps most important, the research questions being pursued. We have excavated with backhoes, shovels, trowels, dental tools, and garden hoses (see "Looking Closer: The Excavator's Toolkit"). We even used a jackhammer to remove rooffall in Gatecliff Shelter.

Archaeologists try to use the latest technologies, but sometimes financial constraints or remote conditions require the use of less elegant methods. Archaeologists excavate ancient pueblo sites in New Mexico that contain well-defined room clusters very differently from high-altitude caves in Peru. Peeling off sequential levels of a Maya temple in Guatemala differs radically from excavating through seemingly homogeneous shell middens in Georgia. Submerged sites, such as ancient shipwrecks, require their own special brand of archaeology (see "Looking Closer: Underwater Excavation").

There are many ways to excavate a site, and each is appropriate if it allows the archaeologist to achieve the project's research goals within the constraints of time, funding, and technology. The important thing is that *the excavation techniques must record an artifact's context as precisely as possible.*

PRINCIPLES OF ARCHAEOLOGICAL EXCAVATION

The key to maintaining information about an artifact's context is to record its provenience. Provenience means an artifact's location, but location is both hierarchical and relative.

Location is hierarchical because an artifact's provenience is simultaneously a particular country, a particular state in that country, a particular county in that state, a particular site in that county, a particular excavation unit in that site, a particular vertical level in that unit, and a particular position and orientation in that level. Obviously, recording an artifact's provenience to the finest levels in this hierarchy provides more information than recording only general location. Figgins's excavators found some spear points at the Folsom site, but it was not until they found them in situ, lying between the bison's ribs, that their provenience became meaningful to a particular question.

Location is relative because we measure an artifact's position relative to a spatial system. We could use the UTM grid (mentioned in Chapter 3), or we could use a site-specific format. The key is to use a procedure that will allow a future archaeologist to reconstruct, in great detail, where you found things in the site.

How do we go about excavating a site so that we recover an artifact's provenience? Let's return to Gatecliff Shelter to see how this is done.

Test Excavations

From day one, Thomas wanted to learn two things: How long had people used Gatecliff Shelter? Could the buried deposits tell us about how human life and

LOOKING CLOSER

THE EXCAVATOR'S TOOLKIT

In Chapter 3, we presented a list of equipment that the modern archaeological surveyor should carry. Here we list things that the well-equipped excavator should carry in his or her excavation toolbox.

▶ A 5- to 6-inch trowel (Marshalltown brand only, accept no substitute! Sharpen the edges and cut a V-notch in one of the back edges—it's useful for cutting roots. It's also useful to have both a pointed- and a square-ended kind—the latter is especially helpful when cleaning stratigraphic profiles.)

▶ A metal file (for sharpening that Marshalltown)

▶ A 2-meter and a 25-meter tape measure (metric only)

▶ Work gloves

▶ A builder's line level and string (nylon, yellow)

▶ A builder's angle finder (to take artifact inclinations)

▶ A compass (to take artifact orientations)

▶ Pencils (regular and mechanical), pencil sharpener, and Sharpie pens

▶ Spoon (a very useful excavation tool and handy at lunchtime)

▶ Jackknife (One blade with a serrated edge is useful against larger roots.)

▶ Nails (to hold a level string for drawing a stratigraphy)

▶ Straight-edge 12-inch ruler with metric markings

▶ Torpedo level (to maintain good vertical profiles)

▶ Root clippers

© Nicole Waguespack and Todd Surovell

Excavators at the Barger Gulch site, Colorado, showing some of the tools every excavator needs.

▶ Small wire cutters (to cut root hairs to prepare a stratigraphic profile for photos)

▶ Empty film canisters (for various sorts of samples)

▶ A variety of small Ziploc bags (as in your survey kit)

▶ Toilet paper (for wrapping delicate artifacts)

▶ Dental tools (Dentists discard them when worn.)

▶ Brushes (whisk broom and 1- to 2-inch paintbrushes)

▶ Bamboo slices (whittle the ends to a rounded tip; essential for excavating bone)

▶ Aluminum foil (for radiocarbon and other samples)

▶ Toothpicks (useful for temporarily marking artifact locations or strata in a profile)

---

environments had changed over time in this part of the Great Basin? The initial goal, then, was to decide if Gatecliff could help answer these questions. This meant that Thomas had to know what kind of

test excavation A small initial excavation to determine a site's potential for answering a research question.

historical record Gatecliff preserved. Was it a short or a long record? Was it nicely stratified or a jumbled mess?

This is why the initial **test excavation** strategy was vertical, designed to supply, as expediently as possible, a stratified sequence of artifacts and ecofacts associated with potentially datable materials. Consequently, Thomas "tested" Gatecliff with two test pits. Like most archaeologists, we dig metrically, typically in 1-meter

LOOKING CLOSER

UNDERWATER EXCAVATION

Underwater archaeology is a specialized subfield of archaeology. It entails the excavation of shipwrecks—the oldest of which so far found is 3300 years old and lies off the coast of Turkey—but also of submerged settlements. Underwater archaeologists work in both salt and fresh water, excavating ancient Phoenician wrecks in the Mediterranean, World War II ships in Pacific lagoons, nineteenth-century wrecks in the rivers of the Yukon, and historic settlements that earthquakes slipped beneath the waves, such as Port Royal, Jamaica. These sites are found by combing through historic records, using remote sensing equipment, and luck.

Though it shares the same goals and principles of excavation as terrestrial archaeology, underwater archaeology operates under unique constraints. Depth and water temperature dictate how long excavators can work, and strong currents may limit excavation to periods of ebb tides. Underwater archaeology is often very expensive, especially if it requires a research vessel.

Working underwater, you can't simply trowel and screen the sediments as you do at a terrestrial site. Excavators of shipwrecks often use a vacuum-like device to suck up sediment to the research vessel above; here the sediments are run through screens to recover small objects. Artifacts are hoisted aboard the research vessel using baskets, nets, and winches; some larger items are floated to the surface using balloons filled below water. Researchers take notes using waterproof pencils and paper, while a suspended grid system maintains provenience and lets excavators draw scale maps. Digital photography has been a boon for recording underwater sites.

Nautical archaeology is an exciting and growing field. For a student interested in pursuing a career in this field, the first task is to become a certified diver.

A diver records excavation notes of an eleventh-century merchant shipwreck near Serçe Limanı, off the coast of Turkey.

© Institute of Nautical Archaeology

---

squares for practical as well as scientific reasons: Squares much smaller would squeeze out the archaeologist, and larger units might not allow sufficient accuracy and would remove more of the site than necessary to answer the initial questions.

Test pits are somewhat quick and dirty because we must excavate them "blind"—that is, without knowing exactly what lies below (Figure 4-6). But even when digging test pits, archaeologists maintain three-dimensional control of the finds, recording the x and y axes (the horizontal coordinates) and the z axis (the vertical coordinate) for each one. This is one reason why archaeologists dig square holes. Provided the pit sidewalls are kept sufficiently straight and perpendicular, excavators can use the dirt itself to maintain horizontal control on the x and y axes by measuring directly from the sidewalls. Here the horizontal provenience is relative to the sidewalls of the

Figure 4-6 Russian archaeologist Katya Gavrilova standing in a test pit in a rockshelter in Paint Rock Canyon, Wyoming. The unit's temporary datum stake is to the left of the test pit.

pit. (But you have to be careful: as test pits deepen, their sidewalls can slope inward, creating a "bathtub" effect that throws off the measurements.)

What about vertical control? At Gatecliff, Thomas dug the test pits in arbitrary 10-centimeter levels. Everything of interest—artifacts, ecofacts, soil samples, and so forth—was kept in separate level bags, one for each 10-centimeter level. The z dimension for each level was usually designated according to distance below the ground surface: Level 1 (surface to 10 centimeters below), Level 2 (10 to 20 centimeters below), and so forth. Thus, excavators measured vertical provenience relative to the ground surface. This also can be a problem, given that the ground surface can change over time and make it potentially difficult for future archaeologists to correlate their levels with those of a previous archaeologist. But every project requires trade-offs, and there is no point in investing

much effort in a site before knowing if it will provide the necessary information. This is why test pits often record only minimal levels of provenience.

Expanding the Test Excavation

The test pits at Gatecliff told Thomas that the site warranted taking a closer look, and he returned the next year to do just that. He first divided the site into a 1-meter grid system, oriented along the long axis of the shelter. The exact compass orientation of this grid was recorded (many archaeologists today routinely orient their grids to magnetic or true north, but sometimes pragmatics dictate otherwise). He assigned consecutive letters to each north-south division and numbered the east-west divisions (see Figure 4-7). By this method, each excavation square could be designated by a unique alphanumeric name (just like Bingo—A-7, B-5, and the ever popular K-9). Other archaeologists use different systems, some numbering each unit according to the x and y coordinates of the unit's southwest (or some other) corner. In this system, a unit with the designation North 34 East 45 (or N34 E45) means that its southwest corner is 34 meters north and 45 meters east of the site's N0 E0 point.

At Gatecliff, the east wall of the "7-trench" (so named because it contained units B-7 through I-7) defined a major profile that exposed the site's stratigraphy. Stratigraphy, a term we first introduced in Chapter 1, is the structure produced by the deposition of geological and/or cultural sediments into layers, or strata (we'll talk about this in more detail in the next chapter). The master stratigraphy is a vertical section against which the archaeologist plots all artifacts, features, soil and pollen samples, and radiocarbon dates. (Some archaeologists use the term "stratification" to refer to the physical layers in a site, reserving "stratigraphy" for the analytical interpretation of the temporal and depositional evidence.)

A vertical datum was established at the rear of the shelter. For all on-site operations, this **datum point** was arbitrarily assigned an elevation of zero. All site elevations were then plotted as "x centimeters below datum," rather than below surface (given that the surface almost never has the same elevation across any given site). Using an altimeter and a U.S. Geological Survey topographic map, Thomas also determined the elevation of this datum point to be 2319 meters (7607 feet) above sea level. All archaeological features—fire hearths, artifact concentrations, sleeping areas, and the like—were plotted on a master site map, and individual artifacts found in situ were plotted in three

datum point The zero point, a fixed reference used to keep control over the locations of artifacts, features, etc., on a dig; usually controls both the vertical and horizontal dimensions of provenience.

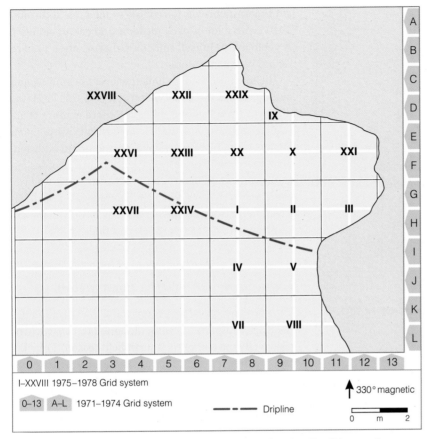

Figure 4-7 Plan view of the two grid systems used at Gatecliff Shelter. The alphanumeric system (consisting of letters and numbers) defined 1-meter excavation squares used in the first four seasons. Roman numerals designate the 2-meter squares used later, when large horizontal exposures were excavated. *After Thomas et al. 1983b, Figure 8. Courtesy American Museum of Natural History.*

horizontal excavation units just described in **natural levels** and **arbitrary levels.** Natural levels are the site's **strata** (singular **stratum**), which are more or less homogeneous or gradational material, visually separable from other levels by a change in texture, color, or rock or organic content, or by a sharp break in depositional character (or any combination of these).

Archaeologists excavate in natural levels wherever possible. Figure 4-8 shows the main reason for this practice. In this hypothetical profile are four natural strata—A, B, C, and D—each containing a particular kind of artifact (denoted by the different symbols). If you imagine that each of these strata represents some unit of time, then you can see that there was a clear change in the kind of artifacts left behind at this site over the four time periods. But note that these strata slope. If we excavated them blindly using arbitrary levels—denoted by the solid lines and numbers 1, 2, 3, and 4—those levels would crosscut the various strata. Arbitrary Level 1 contains artifacts from only Stratum A; but Level 2 contains artifacts from three different time periods (Strata A, B, and C); Level 3 contains artifacts from all four strata; and Level 4, artifacts from Strata C and D. If we assumed that the arbitrary levels correlate to time, then the results of this method of excavation would suggest a very different—and erroneous—image of artifact change over time than that suggested by the natural strata.

dimensions—their x and y coordinates based on the map, and their z coordinates (that is, their elevation) based on the datum point.

This is how we did things in the 1970s. Today, we would have placed the datum many meters off the site in an area that would remain undisturbed by construction, natural processes, or future excavation. The datum would be an aluminum or brass cap marked with the site's Smithsonian or other identifying number, set in concrete or on top of a long piece of reinforcement bar driven into the ground. Today, we would also use a GPS instrument to determine the datum's elevation and UTM location. Once the datum is tied into the UTM grid, a future archaeologist can re-create its location even if the marker is destroyed.

How Archaeologists Dig

Despite what action-hero characters like Indiana Jones or Lara Croft might lead you to believe, archaeologists do not dash in, grab the goodies, and then run for their lives. Instead, we meticulously excavate within the

natural level A vertical subdivision of an excavation square that is based on natural breaks in the sediments (in terms of color, grain size, texture, hardness, or other characteristics).

arbitrary level The basic vertical subdivision of an excavation square; used only when easily recognizable "natural" strata are lacking or when natural strata are more than 10 centimeters thick.

strata (singular **stratum**) More or less homogeneous or gradational material, visually separable from other levels by a discrete change in the character of the material—texture, compactness, color, rock, organic content—and/or by a sharp break in the nature of deposition.

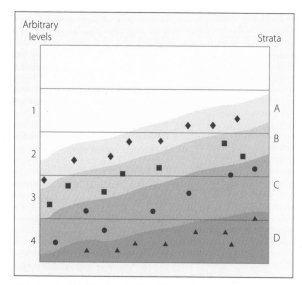

Figure 4-8 Hypothetical relationship between natural (A through D) and arbitrary (1 through 4) levels showing how arbitrary levels can potentially jumble together artifacts that come from different natural strata.

Excavators at Gatecliff—most of them college students—excavated by natural levels wherever possible. Where these natural levels were thicker than 10 centimeters, they excavated in arbitrary levels no more than 10 centimeters in thickness within the natural levels. Today, when many archaeologists excavate in arbitrary levels, they excavate ones only 5 centimeters deep to maintain even greater control over provenience.

Excavators carefully troweled the deposit, then passed the deposit outside the cave for screening (we'll say more about this later); artifacts and ecofacts found in the screen were bagged by level. Individual excavators kept field notes at this stage in bound graph-paper notebooks. Good field notes record everything, whether or not it seems important at the time. Remember, the excavator's goal is to capture the detail that will allow a future archaeologist to "see" what the excavator saw as he or she was digging. Today, field notes employ standardized forms (unique to each excavation) so that excavators record the same detailed information for each level (Figure 4-9). Depending on how much he or she finds, it might take the excavator a week to complete this one form (but usually it is less than a day). This information will include the date, the excavator's name, a map of the unit showing where artifacts and features were found, and a detailed description of the sediments ("rock-hard clay,

living floor A distinct buried surface on which people lived.

grading from brown to reddish-orange" or "loose and dusty, with a lot of pack rat feces and cactus spines"). A geologist's Munsell soil color chart is often used to record sediment colors.

The form will also include the level's beginning and ending elevations, observations on how this level was different from the one above it ("there is more charcoal in this level"), whether any samples were taken (soil, carbon, plant materials), and so on. In addition, we take copious photographs of all unit profiles, all significant finds in situ, and all features. Nowadays, some archaeologists make a video recording of all excavation units at the end of each day or during the excavation of important features and finds.

Expanding Gatecliff's Excavation

The vertical excavation strategy at Gatecliff was a deliberately simplified scheme designed to clarify chronology. By the end of the fourth field season, Trench 7 had reached a depth of 9 meters (nearly 30 feet) below the ground surface. We had learned a good deal about the cultural sequence of Gatecliff Shelter, but our vertical excavation strategy had also left us with a series of extremely steep and hazardous sidewalls. Even though the excavation was stair-stepped to minimize the height of these sidewalls (see the terraces in Figure 2-9 on page 33), they were still dangerous. Today, deep excavation trenches are heavily shored. Unshored walls higher than 4 feet are a violation of federal OSHA—Occupational Safety and Health Administration—regulations. And with good reason: More than one archaeologist has been nearly killed by collapsing profiles. Clearly, a change was in order for safety reasons.

Change was required for conceptual reasons as well. The early excavations demonstrated that Gatecliff could contribute much more than mere chronology. The vertical excavation showed us that Gatecliff had witnessed something unique. Periodically, flash floods filled the shelter with thick beds of silt. Eventually, the shelter dried out, and people used it once again. The result was that layers of sterile silt neatly separated **living floors,** occupational surfaces, inside the overhang. This was a remarkable opportunity to study discrete living surfaces within a rockshelter environment.

Few archaeologists have such a chance, so we shifted away from the initial chronological objectives to concentrate on recording the spatial distributions of artifacts and features on the living floors. The goal now was to reconstruct what activities took place in the shelter, as indicated by the distribution of artifacts

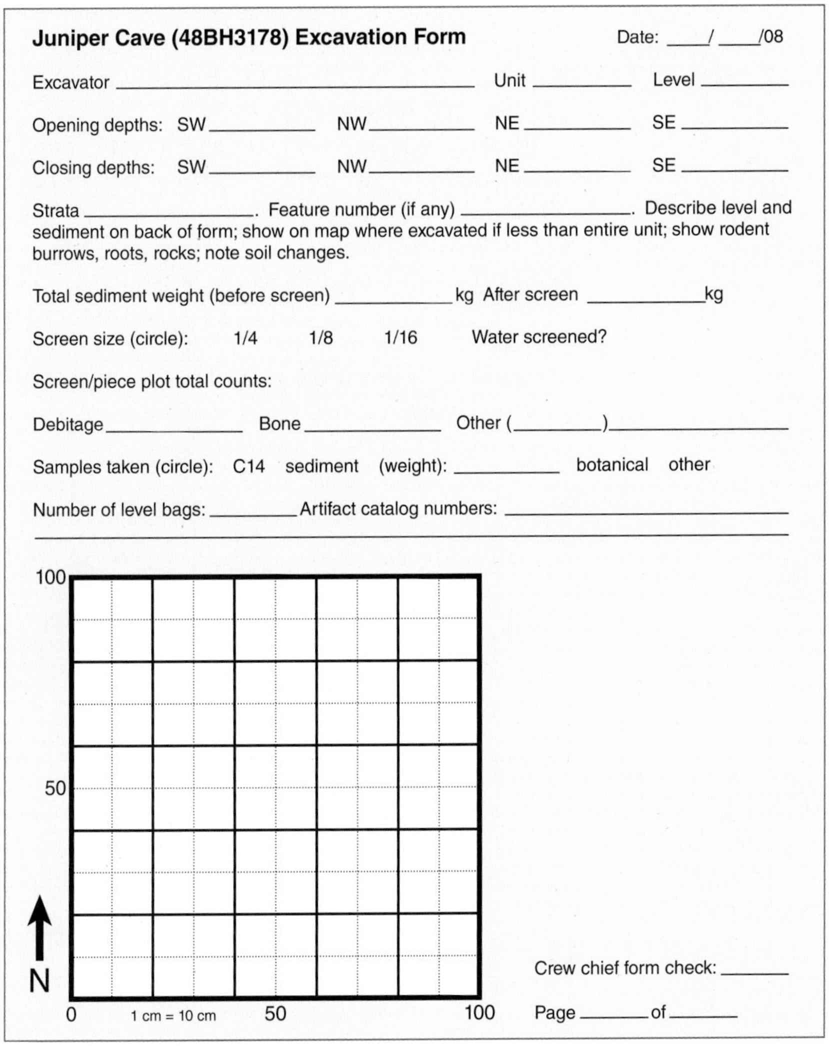

Juniper Cave (48BH3178) Excavation Form   Date: ____/ ____/08

Excavator _____ Unit _____ Level _____

Opening depths: SW_____ NW_____ NE_____ SE _____

Closing depths: SW_____ NW_____ NE_____ SE _____

Strata _____. Feature number (if any) _____. Describe level and sediment on back of form; show on map where excavated if less than entire unit; show rodent burrows, roots, rocks; note soil changes.

Total sediment weight (before screen) _____ kg After screen _____ kg

Screen size (circle):   1/4   1/8   1/16   Water screened?

Screen/piece plot total counts:

Debitage_____ Bone _____ Other (_____)_____

Samples taken (circle): C14 sediment (weight): _____ botanical other

Number of level bags: _____ Artifact catalog numbers: _____

Crew chief form check: _____

Page _____ of _____

N

0   1 cm = 10 cm   50   100

Figure 4-9 A typical excavation form.

across the living floors sandwiched between the silt layers. With the stratigraphy suitably defined, extensive vertical sections were no longer necessary, and we concentrated on opening entire (horizontal) living surfaces.

We switched to 2 × 2 meter units, but excavated the living floors more slowly than in the previous vertical excavations, and excavators tried to recover and map all artifacts in situ. We excavated and screened features such as hearths separately, and soil samples were retained for laboratory processing. We plotted artifacts, scatters of waste flakes from stone tool manufacture, concentrations of bone—anything found in situ—on master living floor maps.

This horizontal strategy required significantly more control within contemporary layers. A single excavator carefully worked each 2-meter square, attempting to find as many artifacts as possible in situ. All artifacts, features, and large ecofacts were plotted onto the

large-scale living floor maps for each surface. The result was a set of living floor maps that are rare among rockshelter excavations in the world (Figure 4-10).

PRECISION EXCAVATION

This description of the Gatecliff excavation provides a general sense of what goes on at archaeological sites. But Thomas excavated Gatecliff in the 1970s, and excavation has become an even more exact science since then. Given the importance of an artifact's context, archaeologists continue to devise ways to record provenience for more objects with greater precision.

For example, at Gatecliff we first used string line levels tied to the datum and tape measures to determine an artifact's vertical provenience (its depth below datum); we later switched to a more precise builder's level and measuring rod. We recorded horizontal provenience by measuring distances from two of a unit's sidewalls. But today, many archaeologists, ourselves included, use **total stations** to record provenience. These new instruments are pricey, but they are necessary for state-of-the-art excavation.

How does a total station work? The device is set up on a tripod over the site's datum. After excavators input the correct data, the total station "knows" where it is on the grid system and which direction it is pointing. When an artifact is found, a glass prism is held on the artifact's location, and the total station is turned and aimed at the prism. Push a button, and the station shoots a beam of infrared light. By measuring the time it takes the light to bounce back from the prism, and by knowing its location and angle, the total

total station A device that uses a beam of light bounced off a prism to determine an artifact's provenience; it is accurate to millimeters.

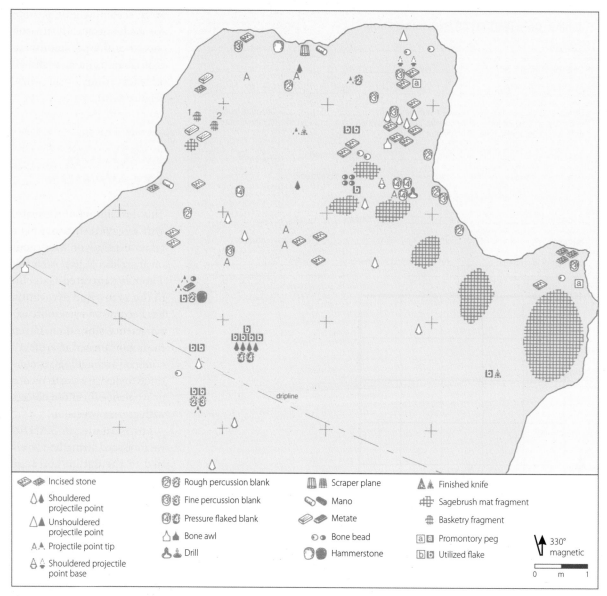

Figure 4-10 A living floor map showing the distribution of artifacts and hearths on Horizon 2 (deposited about AD 1300) at Gatecliff. *Courtesy American Museum of Natural History.*

station calculates and records the artifact's *x*, *y*, and *z* coordinates—its provenience. This information is later downloaded to a database for mapping and analysis. Total stations take only a second or two to make measurements that are accurate to *millimeters*. These instruments can be used at distances of hundreds of meters, so that a site may need only one, rather than the several datums that other measurement systems may require (Figure 4-11).

Some archaeologists record the provenience of virtually every item found in situ (a practice sometimes called piece-plotting). Others set a cutoff, recording provenience on everything found in situ that is larger than, say, 3 centimeters (about an inch) in any dimension. As we said before, there are always trade-offs.

Recording the provenience of every item found in situ provides the archaeologist with a very accurate record of where he or she found things, but it takes much more time—meaning that less gets excavated (this is a special problem if the site is threatened with destruction). How much you piece-plot depends on how much time you have for the excavation and the questions you need the data to answer.

Is that all there is to it? No, there is more to recording provenience than simply location. Today, archaeologists sometimes record not only an artifact's *x*, *y*, and *z* coordinates, but also which side of the artifact was "up" when it was found, the compass orientation of its long axis, and its slope or inclination (recorded with a builder's angle finder or clinometer). We would also

Figure 4-11 Harold Dibble (center) and Shannon McPherron (right) record data on-site while excavating Pech de L'Azé IV in France; the student at the far left is using a total station.

note if the artifact is burned, has calcium carbonate or a particular kind of sediment adhering to it, or possesses other characteristics. Although this can make excavation mind-numbing, we will see in Chapter 5 that the resulting information is critical to understanding how a site was formed and, consequently, for inferring what people did there in the past.

SIFTING THE EVIDENCE

Digging is just the beginning of excavation. No matter how carefully you excavate, it is impossible to see, map, and recover everything of archaeological interest; this is why we use sifters to find things that hand excavation misses. This is also the second reason why we excavate in square units—sometimes only .5 × .5 meter in size. If the excavator misses something, the sifting process can at least tie its provenience down to a particular level in a particular unit—a very small area of the site.

At Gatecliff, excavators removed deposit with a trowel and whisk broom or paintbrush, carefully sweeping it into a dustpan. When excavators found an artifact in situ, they recorded the artifact's provenience; sometimes it was photographed in place and a sketch drawn in the field notes before the artifact was placed in a separate bag and labeled with an identifying number.

The dustpan of dirt was then poured into a bucket and tagged with a label identifying the unit and level. When the bucket was full, the day's "gopher" took it

to the screening area, outside the shelter in the hot sun (the gopher is the person whose daily assignment is to "go for" this and "go for" that). Here the bucket was poured onto a screen with ⅛-inch mesh (to give you some idea of the size, standard window screen is ¹⁄₁₆-inch mesh), where workers sifted and carefully checked for any artifacts missed by the excavators, including stone tool manufacturing waste flakes, fragments of bone, and anything else of importance.

Although archaeologists agree that Marshalltown makes the only trowel worth owning, there are many opinions on screens. Many archaeologists manufacture their own, so the design and workmanship of screens varies from dig to dig (a few are shown in Figure 4-12). Some are suspended from tripods, some are mounted on rollers, and others are driven by gas engines to speed things up. When Thomas dug Alta Toquima, a village located at 11,000 feet in the mountains of central Nevada, he invented a "backpacker" design for the screens. At Gatecliff, we used the most common kind—a shaker screen mounted on two pivoting legs.

Exactly what kind of screen you use is far less important than the mesh. Many archaeologists prefer ⅛-inch hardware cloth, but the choice of mesh size varies with the circumstances. The important point is that *screen size affects what you recover and how fast you can recover it.* Use ¼-inch mesh and you can process dirt fast, but you will lose a surprising number of important objects. Use ¹⁄₁₆-inch mesh and the recovery rate goes up—but so does the time to process the dirt.

Thomas once experimented to see how different screen sizes might affect the recovery of animal bones in archaeological sites. He built a three-decker screen with superimposed layers of ¼-inch over ⅛-inch over ¹⁄₁₆-inch mesh screens, and then ran a set of faunal remains recovered from a site through the screens.

As you might guess, he found that ¼-inch mesh was fine for recovering bones of large animals such as bighorn or bison. But he also found that significant numbers of bones of medium-sized animals, such as rabbits and rodents, were lost. The ⅛-inch mesh screen was better for recovering the bones of these small mammals. But, significant numbers of small

Figure 4-12 A few of the innumerable sifter designs used by archaeologists.

mammal bones are even lost through ⅛-inch screens! One needs ¹⁄₁₆-inch mesh (or flotation; see below) to recover the remains of animals the size of, say, pack rats, small birds, and especially fish.

Water-Screening and Matrix-Sorting

Archaeologists sometimes use **water-screening,** especially when the artifacts and ecofacts are expected to be very small. As the name suggests, water-screening requires that plenty of water be available. The dirt is simply poured onto a screen (usually ⅛- or ¹⁄₁₆-inch mesh) and sprayed with a garden hose until all the sediment is washed through. The screen is then set aside and, once dry, searched. Kelly used water-screening at a site in the Stillwater Marsh in the Carson Desert (Figure 4-13). Because the site was located on a clay dune that

water-screening A sieving process in which deposit is placed on a screen and the matrix washed away with hoses; essential where artifacts are expected to be small and/or difficult to find without washing.

matrix-sorting The hand sorting of processed bulk soil samples for minute artifacts and ecofacts.

contained no natural rock, he simply water-screened the deposits through ¹⁄₁₆-inch mesh, dried what was left, and bagged it all. He saved literally everything—flakes from the manufacture of stone tools, burned pieces of mud, fish and bird bones, and shell fragments—and sorted it later in the field camp.

You should always use the finest mesh screen possible. But using very fine mesh during the excavation can slow everything down to the point where you do not excavate a sufficient sample of the site to say anything worthwhile. Dense clay deposits, for example, can clog even a ¼-inch screen quickly. For this reason, many archaeologists use a larger screen mesh in the field, but take bulk sediment samples from each level. These are processed in the lab and provide a sample of those items missed by the ¼-inch screens. If the deposit has low clay content, the sediment samples may simply be fine-screened. If they have a high clay content, they may be deflocculated (have the clay removed) by soaking the sediments in a solution of dishwasher detergent. After the clays are broken down, the slurry is poured through a fine screen (or often a set of screens), dried, and sorted by hand to separate stone from small stone tool waste flakes, shells, bits of ceramics, and bones. This is known as **matrix-sorting,** and, along with writing catalog numbers on artifacts, it is often one of the first tasks a novice may be assigned in a lab.

Ideally, as with piece-plotted artifacts, we wish to record data from the screening process that will allow us to reconstruct the site in the most detail possible. Running

Figure 4-13 Water-screening in the Stillwater Marsh, Nevada.

dirt through a screen, believe it or not, is *not* enough. In some sites, we also weigh it. We record how much each bucket of deposit weighs, keeping a running tally on the level's excavation form. After screening a bucket, we return the material remaining in the screen to the bucket and weigh it again. (In most cases, the material that goes back into the bucket is unmodified rock.) By recording the before- and after-screening bucket weights, we record the frequency of rock in the deposits and determine the different densities of artifacts and ecofacts among a site's strata. These data help us understand how a site formed (more on that in the next chapter) as well as changes in the intensity of site use over time.

© Justine W. McKnight, photo by Jonathan McKnight

Figure 4-14 Archeobotanist Justine McKnight operating a Flot-Tech flotation tank outside her lab in Severna Park, Maryland.

Flotation

In some archaeological sites, like the upper parts of Gatecliff Shelter, the deposits are sufficiently protected from moisture that plant remains simply dry up and can be recovered by screening. But in other kinds of deposits, plant remains may be preserved only if they were burned and carbonized. These remains are often quite small and nearly impossible to collect by hand in the field. Even in dry caves, the carbonized plant remains in hearths would be impossible to collect through simple matrix-sorting.

The most common method of recovering such plant remains is **flotation,** a technique that is standard at most excavations (Figure 4-14). Several procedures exist for floating archaeological samples, but all are based on the same principle: Dirt doesn't float, but carbonized plant remains do (as well as things like insect body parts and fish scales). With this technique, archaeologists can float most burned plant remains out of samples of archaeologically recovered dirt. Today, we "float" a large portion of features such as hearths (if not the entire hearth), as well as samples of the sediments themselves.

In one of the earliest applications, Stuart Struever (retired, former president of the Crow Canyon Archaeological Center) floated soil samples from 200 features attributable to the Middle Woodland component at the Apple Creek site, Illinois (we'll explain the term "component" in Chapter 7). The samples were hauled to nearby Apple Creek, where they were placed in mesh-bottomed buckets and then water-separated by students who worked midstream. More than 40,000 charred nutshell fragments, 2000 carbonized seeds, and some 15,000 identifiable fish bones were collected in this manner. Standard dry screening techniques would have missed most of these.

While excavating at Salts Cave in Kentucky, Patty Jo Watson (Washington University) and her associates were not blessed with a nearby stream, so they improvised. The sediments to be floated were placed in double plastic bags and carried outside the cave. They first spread the samples (weighing a total of 1500 pounds) in the shade to dry. They then filled two 55-gallon drums with water, placed the dry samples in metal buckets whose bottoms had been replaced with window screen, and submerged the buckets in the 55-gallon drums.

After a few seconds, the investigator skimmed off the charcoal and carbonized plant remains that had floated to the surface, using a small scoop made from a brass carburetor screen (cloth diapers work well, too). They spread the debris that floated to the top

flotation The use of fluid suspension to recover tiny burned plant remains and bone fragments from archaeological sites.

(called the light fraction) and the material that sank (the heavy fraction) on labeled newsprint to dry again. These flotation samples yielded carbonized remains of hickory nuts and acorns, seeds from berries, grains, sumpweed, chenopods, maygrass, and amaranth.

Flotation is not an expensive or even a particularly time-consuming process. Flotation techniques can (and should) be fitted to the local requirements. At Mission Santa Catalina, Thomas also used a converted 55-gallon drum, and one person could process dozens of samples each day. Some elaborate power-driven machines are equipped with aeration devices and use deflocculants or chemicals to remove sediment that might adhere to and sink carbonized plant remains. The technology is available to fit any budget.

The issue is not technology, but accuracy. For a long time archaeologists saved only bone (and even then, just the large, identifiable pieces) and ignored plant remains. This frequently led archaeologists to overemphasize hunting and herding, thereby de-emphasizing the plant component of the economy. After flotation techniques came into their own, we discovered new things about the past. For example, from those seemingly innocuous burned seeds of sumpweed, chenopods, maygrass, and amaranth that Patty Jo Watson and others collected through flotation, archaeologists made the important discovery that Native Americans had domesticated some indigenous plants of North America's eastern woodlands some 4000 years ago—more than 1000 years before maize appeared on the scene. Those tiny bits of burned plant material floating on the water turned out to be very important.

Cataloging the Finds

Excavating objects is just the beginning; in fact, excavation is only about 15 percent of a project—most of our time is spent in the lab analyzing the finds. And before the artifacts and field data can be analyzed, the objects must be cataloged. In many cases, the archaeologist assigns artifacts their catalog numbers in the field as they are excavated. We do this by printing up sheets of sequential catalog numbers on peel-off return address forms (some use the format 48BH3178/xxxx, where the 48BH3178 is the site's Smithsonian number and the xxxx is a sequential number, but others use more complex systems). When an artifact is found, it is piece-plotted and placed in a small Ziploc bag. The excavator peels a catalog number off the sheet (ensuring that there can be no duplicate numbers) and places it inside the bag (in case the label peels off, it will still be in the bag with the artifact). A crew member then records the number in the total station's data log and on the excavation form.

Back in the lab, the archaeologist catalogs the artifacts. Most archaeologists are fanatical about cataloging their finds because it's easy for one distracted lab worker to mess up an artifact's record of provenience. The catalogers work through the field bags, writing the catalog number onto the artifact itself with an archival pen, and sealing the number with clear fingernail polish; numbered tags are sometimes tied to some artifacts, such as small beads. Some archaeologists preprint the catalog numbers on minute labels and glue them to artifacts with archivally stable glue. Even those items that were not found in situ or otherwise assigned a catalog number in the field will be given a number in the lab. The catalog number is what ties a particular artifact back to observations made in the field. Thus, although cataloging can often take hundreds of person-hours, it is necessary to ensure that an artifact's original provenience, and consequently its context, is never lost.

Lab workers then enter the cataloged artifacts' information into a computer database, usually including rudimentary observations (such as weight, condition, color), collection date, its provenience (for example, unit, level, x, y, z coordinates), and contextual data (for instance, stratum, inclination, orientation). A digital photo may be attached to the data record. Copies are then made of the database so that the artifacts' all-important contextual information will not be lost. Later, all the artifacts, sediment samples, and documentary information will be stored in an archaeological repository (see "Looking Closer: What Happens to All That Stuff after the Excavation?")

Conclusion

Archaeologists have traditionally protected their excavations against vandals and pothunters. Excavation often draws unwanted attention, and vandals have been known to attack sites at night, even during a field season. On Thomas's first job in archaeology, a 24-hour guard (armed, appropriately enough, with bow and arrow) was posted to protect the open excavation units from looters. At Gatecliff, we tediously backfilled the site by hand every year to protect the archaeology from the curious public, and to protect the public from the dangers of open-pit archaeology.

On St. Catherines Island, the problem is somewhat different. The only visitors are scientists, who realize the research value of archaeological sites and leave the excavations untouched. It is thus possible to open a

LOOKING CLOSER

WHAT HAPPENS TO ALL THAT STUFF AFTER THE EXCAVATION?

Archaeologists hate to throw anything away, and many consider it unethical to dispose of *anything* found in an excavation. But archaeologists personally own nothing that they find—not one bone, not one sherd. So what happens to all the stuff? After the analysis is completed, the report is written, and the monograph is published, all those labeled bags and cataloged artifacts go where they will be cared for and where future researchers can study them in perpetuity. Where is this?

In the United States, archaeologists usually curate artifacts in a federally approved archaeological repository; in fact, we must do this to obtain a permit or research grant. Most states have several such repositories; the cost of maintaining these facilities is borne by you, the taxpayer.

But we're running out of room. No one knows for sure how many objects are currently held in these repositories, but a good guess is between 100 and 500 *million*. And more items come in every day. As a result, some repositories have literally shut their doors. Others cannot afford to meet recommended federal guidelines and house their artifacts under substandard conditions where artifact provenience can be lost through neglect, mold, and leaking roofs. With inadequate funds to catch up on inventories, some repositories cannot loan materials to researchers, so research on the collections comes to a halt. That, of course, contradicts the very purpose of repositories.

It will cost millions of taxpayer dollars to bring repositories up to code and to expand their capabilities. Some wonder if the cost is worth it. Do we really need all those soil samples? Or another box of sherds from a Pueblo site? Maybe not, but every archaeologist can tell how he or she wished that some past archaeologist had kept *all* the animal bones and not just the clearly identifiable ones, or all the charcoal, or all the stone tool waste flakes. We have to make a trade-off here—between our realistic abilities as taxpayers to support archaeological repositories that cannot expand infinitely and the need to keep materials for future questions and new techniques. Although the problem is clear, the answer is not.

---

few test units on several sites, process the finds, and then return next year to the more promising sites for more intensive excavation.

On strictly research projects—like our work at Mission Santa Catalina—where sites are not threatened by outside incursions, one must adopt a conservative excavation strategy. *Archaeologists usually only excavate as much of a site as is needed to answer their research questions*; extensive excavations are undertaken only in the case of sites threatened by development or erosion. We leave as much of a site intact as possible for later investigators, who undoubtedly will have different questions and better techniques. As we saw in the last chapter, remote sensing technology and archaeological survey techniques sometimes provide archaeologists with ways to learn without digging at all.

Regardless of whether we use high-tech instruments or old-fashioned elbow grease, our personal responsibility for site conservation remains unchanged and fundamental. Archaeology is a destructive science. We said it at the beginning of this chapter and it is worth repeating: Sites can be excavated only once, so it is imperative we do things right. Sometimes those sites have remarkable preservation and many, many kinds of materials are preserved; other times, only stone artifacts remain. This affects the kind of excavation techniques we use and how quickly the excavation can proceed. But how much or how little is found in a site does not change our fundamental responsibility to obtain and record provenience for virtually every artifact, ecofact, and feature encountered. We excavate in controlled units, sometimes as small as .5 × .5 meter, using a systematic grid system; we excavate in natural levels where possible and, even if natural strata are present, in levels no more than 10 or even 5 centimeters thick. We record everything we can about an item before we pull it from the ground, and we assign catalog numbers to everything found so that each item can be related back to information gathered on its context. Once we have this information in hand, we are prepared to move on to the next chore of archaeology: making sense of everything we have found.

SUMMARY

1. Why does context matter? How is it recorded?

- Context matters because information comes from what artifacts are associated with each other, with features, and with particular strata. It's not enough to know that an artifact came from a particular site; we need to know how it relates to everything else found at the site.
- Context is recorded by recording the provenience of artifacts, features, and ecofacts.

2. What determines preservation?

- Preservation is enhanced in continuously dry, continuously wet, and/or very cold environments—anyplace where conditions prevent the existence of the microorganisms that promote decay.
- Diverse excavation strategies respond in part to different preservation conditions, constraints, and objectives in order to record provenience. From test pit to full-scale excavation, archaeologists maintain records of the three-dimensional provenience of the objects being recovered. Archaeological records

record an excavation in such a way that another archaeologist can "see" what the original excavator saw.

3. What is the difference between arbitrary and natural levels? Why do these matter?

- Natural levels follow the site's geologic stratigraphy; arbitrary levels are normally 5 or 10 cm thick and are based on depth below the datum point. Arbitrary levels are normally used only in test pits when the natural stratigraphy is unknown or when natural layers are more than 10 cm thick.
- Arbitrary levels could mix artifacts from different natural levels, of different geologic contexts.

4. How do archaeologists recover the smallest artifacts and ecofacts?

- We use screening, flotation, and bulk matrix processing to recover extremely small artifacts and ecofacts.

MEDIA RESOURCES

Doing Fieldwork: Archaeological Demonstrations CD-ROM 2.0

This CD, developed by the authors, shows professional archaeologists involved in various digs, many of which are referenced in the text. The presentation is organized by the main techniques used on an archaeological dig, reinforcing concepts and techniques via live examples. The CD takes you through each step automatically, or you can navigate to any point via the navigation bar. After reviewing a step in the dig process, you are taken to Check Points, which are concept questions about each step of the dig. Then you can see

the answers, receive your score, and even send your scores to your instructor.

The Companion Website for *Archaeology*, Sixth Edition

www.cengagebrain.com

Supplement your review of this chapter by going to the companion website to take one of the practice quizzes, use the flash cards to master key terms, and check out the many other study aids that are designed to help you succeed in your introductory archaeology course.

5 GEOARCHAEOLOGY AND SITE FORMATION PROCESSES

LEARNING OBJECTIVES

**AFTER READING THIS CHAPTER
YOU SHOULD BE ABLE TO ANSWER THESE QUESTIONS:**

1. What is geoarchaeology?

2. What is the law of superposition? How can it be violated?

3. What is the difference between systemic and archaeological contexts?

4. Why does this difference matter?

© Mario Modesto Mata

Students excavating the 300,000-year-old level at the site of Gran Dolina, Spain, in 2008.

PREVIEW

EVERY ARCHAEOLOGICAL SITE is unique. Some sites are remarkably well preserved; others are not. Some sites lie on the surface, some are deeply buried, and others lie underwater. Some are frozen; others are dry. Each site that we have personally worked on has presented new challenges. But they all had one thing in common: dirt.

Although archaeology is firmly embedded in anthropology, it has a foot securely in geology as well. In fact, we can't do archaeology without also doing geology. Archaeological sites are created by human activities, but they also build up through many natural processes, including those that are commonly studied by geologists (and, especially, geomorphologists). The study of the dirt in and around archaeological sites has become an important subfield of archaeology, known as geoarchaeology.

Geologists first pulled together the major principles of stratigraphy. This chapter introduces the important concept of superposition, the simple operating principle behind the interpretation of archaeological sediments. We then discuss how geoarchaeologists contribute to our understanding and interpretation of archaeological sites, focusing on natural and cultural site formation processes. Our point here is simple: Archaeological stratigraphy is complex, but it can be understood.

DOING FIELDWORK CD-ROM:
ARCHAEOLOGICAL DEMONSTRATIONS 2.0

See the "Stratigraphy" section of the CD-ROM to learn more about topics covered in this chapter.

INTRODUCTION

Michael Waters (Texas A&M University) defines **geoarchaeology** as "the field of study that applies the concepts and methods of the geosciences to archaeological research." In his opinion, geoarchaeology has two objectives. The first is to place sites (and the artifacts found in them) in a "relative and absolute temporal context through the application of stratigraphic principles and absolute dating techniques." We'll focus on stratigraphic principles in this chapter and discuss dating techniques in the next.

For Waters, the second objective of geoarchaeology is "to understand the natural processes of **site formation**," which includes all the human and natural actions that work together to create an archaeological site. In the past, many archaeologists worked with geologists to fulfill this need. But as important as these collaborations were, it became clear that archaeology needs geologists who are not only trained in **geomorphology,** the geological study of landforms and landscapes (rivers, sand dunes, deltas, marshes, glacial and coastal environments, and so on), but who also understand the special brand of geology that applies specifically to archaeological sites. Rockshelter sediments—like those that filled Gatecliff Shelter— are often foreign to traditionally trained geologists, as are the sediments that fill a collapsed pueblo room. Traditional geologists may also look at sediments on a broader temporal scale than is required for understanding the formation of archaeological sites.

Despite their different emphases, however, geological and geoarchaeological analyses share a common foundation, beginning with the law of superposition.

geoarchaeology The field of study that applies the concepts and methods of the geosciences to archaeological research.

site formation The human and natural actions that work together to create an archaeological site.

geomorphology The geological study of landforms and landscapes, including soils, rivers, hills, sand dunes, deltas, glacial deposits, and marshes.

THE LAW OF SUPERPOSITION

Nicolaus Steno (1638–1686) is generally acknowledged as having formulated the **law of superposition,** which says that in any pile of **sedimentary rocks** undisturbed by folding or overturning, the strata on the bottom were deposited first, those above them were deposited second, those above them third, and so on. Today, this principle seems preposterously simple, but it was a critical breakthrough in the seventeenth century. Why?

Steno was an anatomist (a curious background for one who would make a major contribution to geology). In dissecting a shark, he noticed that the teeth looked exactly like things occasionally found in rocks, what Steno's colleagues called "tongue stones." The tongue stones were, of course, fossil shark teeth, but scholars of Steno's day commonly believed that fossils were stones that had fallen from the moon or had grown inside rocks; a contemporary of Steno attributed them to "lapidifying virtue diffused through the whole body of the geocosm," whatever that means.

Others, including Steno, held the then radical notion that these odd "stones" were actually ancient shark teeth. Left unsolved, however, was the perplexing question of how one solid, a shark's tooth, came to be inside another solid, a rock. Steno pondered this question in his *Preliminary Discourse to a Dissertation on a Solid Body Naturally Contained Within a Solid* (1669), concluding that at some point in time, one of them must not have been solid. But which one? Believing that all rock began as liquid, Steno postulated that rocks must have been laid down horizontally (a concept he termed the "principle of original horizontality"); any departure from the horizontal, Steno reasoned, must have resulted from later disturbance. He then reasoned that if a thing were already a solid when the liquid rock was laid down, it would force that liquid to mold itself around the existing solid. So Steno argued that fossils came to be inside solid rock because they were older, and because the rock was originally laid down as a liquid. Conversely, if a solid formed after the rock had hardened, it would conform to voids and fissures already in the rock (thus crystals and mineral-filled veins conform to voids in the rock that contains them).

Working from these observations, Steno postulated that if rock were originally deposited horizontally as a liquid, then the oldest layer should be the deepest and progressively younger layers should lie above it. Although formulated as an aside, Steno's law of superposition became the foundation of all stratigraphic interpretation—whether we are talking about the Grand Canyon, Kidder's excavations at Pecos Pueblo, or the world's oldest footprints.

Fossil Footprints at Laetoli: The Law of Superposition in Action

Mary Leakey (1913–1996) was one of the world's most famous fossil finders. With her esteemed husband, Louis Leakey (1903–1972), she scoured East Africa, seeking archaeological evidence of the earliest human ancestors who once lived there. In 1959, the Leakeys electrified the world with finds that included the celebrated *Zinjanthropus* skull (now known as *Australopithecus boisei* or *Paranthropus boisei*) from Olduvai Gorge in northwestern Tanzania. To many, Mary Leakey's discovery of the "Zinj" cranium heralded a new age, the beginning of modern paleoanthropological research in East Africa.

Two decades later, as she stood staring at the ground in a place called Laetoli (lay-*toe*-lee, a Masai name for a red lily that grows throughout the area), it was Mary Leakey's turn to be shocked. Just below the surface of the Serengeti Plain, her research team found animal footprints—hundreds of them—as clear as if they had been cast in fresh concrete.

Why were these footprints preserved? Sometime in the remote past, the nearby Sadiman volcano had erupted, blanketing the landscape around Laetoli with a lens of very fine volcanic ash. Then a light rain moistened the ash layer without washing it away, turning it into a thin slurry. Animals meandered across this wet surface, apparently on the way to a nearby water hole: spring hares, birds, buffaloes, pigs, a saber-tooth tiger, and baboons—each leaving dozens of footprints in the gooey ash. Fortuitously, the ash was carbonatite, which quickly solidifies to a concrete-like hardness after being wet, in this case capturing the footprints in an enduring land surface.

Not only birds and four-legged mammals walked across there. At one point, at least two **hominins,** early human ancestors, also strolled across the ash (Figure 5-1). More than five dozen individual human footprints clearly demonstrate a human-like gait— fully bipedal with a stride and balance similar to our own. Across a distance of about 25 meters, two of our

---

law of superposition The geological principle that in any pile of sedimentary rocks that have not been disturbed by folding or overturning, each bed is older than the layers above and younger than the layers below; also known as Steno's law.

sedimentary rock Rock formed when the weathered products of preexisting rocks have been transported by and deposited in water and are turned once again to stone.

hominins Members of the evolutionary line that contains humans and our early bipedal ancestors.

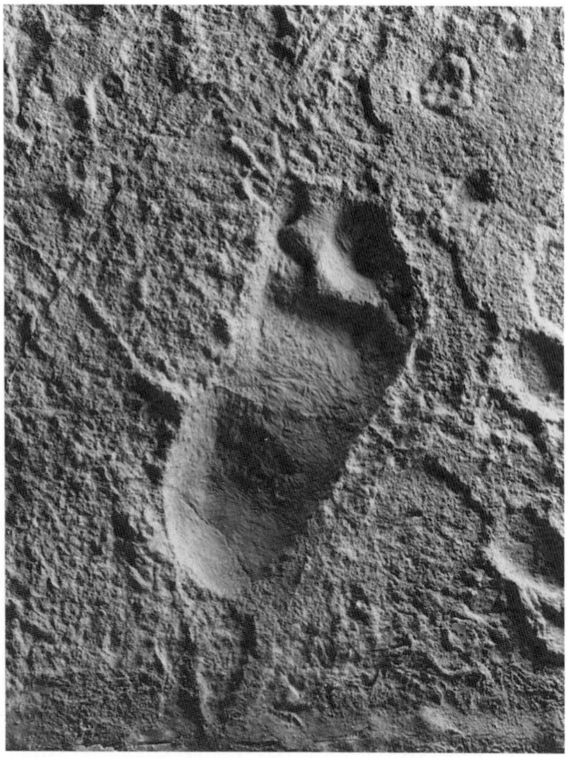
© American Museum of Natural History

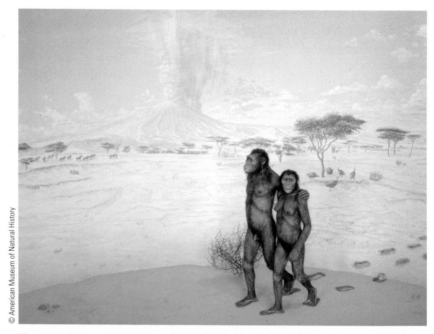

Figure 5-1 One of the famous hominin footprints at Laetoli (Tanzania, Africa).

ancestors, one larger than the other, walked side by side, close enough to touch each another. The tracks of the smaller of the two suggest that he or she may have been burdened with extra weight on one hip—perhaps carrying an infant (Figure 5-2)? Some analyses of the tracks even suggest that a third, still smaller, individual followed close behind, stepping in the footprints of the largest hominin.

Assuming that this evidence could be trusted—and assuming that the ancient age could be firmly established—Mary Leakey realized that these footprints could test a major hypothesis of paleoanthropology. For decades, specialists in human evolution had argued that bipedalism (walking upright on two feet), a preeminent human characteristic, must have arisen in response to tool use. After all, if you're going to make and use stone tools, having your hands free would come in handy. This hypothesis thus predicted that stone tools are older than bipedalism. At the time, the world's oldest stone tools were about 1.3 million years old (today the earliest known stone tools, found in Ethiopia, are between 2.5 and 2.6 million years old).

Based on her knowledge of the region's geology, Leakey guessed that the age of the footprints was more than a million years older than 1.3 million years. If so, then the world's most ancient human footprints implied that our human ancestors walked upright long before the appearance of the oldest stone tools in the area. And if that's true, then the hypothesis that tool use led to bipedalism must be wrong.

The Geologic Background The fossil footprints were contained in the upper portion of the so-called Laetolil beds, within a geological subunit known as Tuff 7 ("tuff" being hardened volcanic ash). Leakey found the actual footprints near the bottom of the Tuff 7 formation in what she called, appropriately enough, the Footprint tuff. But to determine the age of the footprints, it was necessary to place this key geological stratum within its appropriate stratigraphic context.

Richard Hay (1929–2006) spearheaded the geological investigation of the site's stratigraphy. Over a period of 6 years, Hay worked out the complicated geological sequence at Laetoli, summarized in

© American Museum of Natural History

Figure 5-2 Reconstruction of the early hominins (*Australopithecus afarensis*) who made the 3.5-million-year-old footprints at Laetoli. Although the fossil-based proportions are accurate, many of the details (such as hair density and distribution, sex, skin color, form of the nose and lips, and so on) are conjectural.

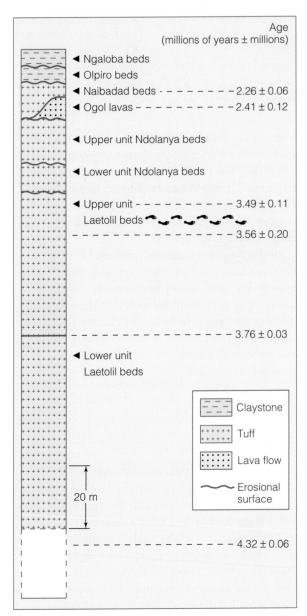

Figure 5-3 The major stratigraphic profile at Laetoli.

19–23 meters thick; apparently windblown sediments

Laetolil beds   The basal stratigraphic unit, consisting of a series of eight tuffs (divided into upper and lower beds) reflecting eight periods of major volcanic ash deposition, in places more than 150 meters thick (*Note:* The name of the site is spelled "Laetoli"; the basal formation is called the *Laetolil* beds.)

These are the geological "facts." But what do they tell us about the footprints?

From evidence preserved on the surface of the Footprint tuff, it was clear the ash buried the footprints rapidly, soon after they formed. This accounts for their extraordinary state of preservation. Geologists could also infer the season in which the hominins had taken their walk. Because there was no evidence of grasses at the base of the ash lens, the grass must have been grazed off, suggesting that the eruptions took place during the dry season. But toward the middle of the Footprint tuff is evidence that this surface was gently rained upon—actual raindrop impressions occur along with the footprints. Then, toward the upper part, there was widespread erosion, which Hay attributed to rainy season downpours.

Therefore, the research team concluded, the Footprint tuff was deposited over a short span of time, probably only a few weeks, beginning near the end of the dry season and lasting into the rainy season. This amazingly detailed reconstruction is based strictly on the available geological evidence.

How Old Are the Footprints? Because the footprints themselves cannot be directly dated, we have to rely on the geology. Here the law of superposition comes to our aid. Steno's law holds that, all else being equal, older layers lie at the base of the stratified geologic sequence.

So we work from the bottom up. The Laetolil beds lie beneath the Ndolanya beds; this is a geological fact. The law of superposition applied to this stratigraphic fact *suggests* that the Laetolil beds *should be* older than the Ndolanya beds; this is geological interpretation. Similarly, because the Ogol lavas lie above both the Laetolil beds and Ndolanya beds, these lavas should be younger still. Because they lie uppermost in the stratigraphic column at Laetoli, the Ngaloba beds should be the most recent of all. The law of superposition provides the interpretive key to unlock the *relative* stratigraphic sequence at Laetoli.

Figure 5-3 and as follows (with, of course, the youngest layer on top):

Ngaloba beds	Sheetwash and mudflow sediments containing volcanic ash, pebbles, and cobbles
Olpiro beds	Volcanic tuff layers, maximum thickness about 6 meters
Naibadad beds	Volcanic tuff layers, generally 11–15 meters thick
Ogol lavas	A series of distinctive lava flows and ash sediments; in places, 230 meters deep
Ndolanya beds	Upper and lower units of sedimentary layers, generally

LOOKING CLOSER

WHAT HAPPENED TO THE LAETOLI FOOTPRINTS?

The Laetoli footprints were one of the world's most important archaeological discoveries. *Did the archaeologists just leave them there?* When Leakey completed her work with the footprints, she did what most archaeologists do when completing an excavation: She backfilled the site to preserve it. After putting about 2 feet of soil on top of the footprints, Leakey covered the site with large basalt boulders to prevent elephants from walking on the tracks.

Unfortunately, the soil was rich and loose, and the shade from the boulders helped this garden-like soil hold moisture. After a few years, acacia trees began to grow on the spot, and some archaeologists worried that the roots would destroy the footprints.

So, in 1995 (when Leakey was in her 80s), Fiona Marshall (Washington University), an archaeologist with years of experience in African archaeology, returned with a team from the Getty Conservation Institute. Marshall's team carefully excavated the site again, but this time the goal was to carefully unearth the trees' roots without disturbing the tracks. Fortunately, they discovered that the roots had not yet done significant damage.

Although various ideas were proposed as to how the footprints could be safely removed, the Getty team finally decided that the footprints were best preserved in the ground, for now, with periodic removal of the trees. In 100 years, the footprints will be uncovered again to check on their condition, and if new technology permits, the footprints will be safely removed to a museum.

The potassium-argon dating technique pinned down the date of the Laetoli footprints. (In Chapter 6 we will describe how archaeologists use this technique and its modern descendant, argon-argon dating, to date strata and artifacts.) Leakey worked with geologists Robert Drake and Garness Curtis (retired, University of California, Berkeley), who processed a series of potassium-argon dates on samples from the major stratified layers recognized in the Laetoli area. The bottom of the upper Laetolil beds dated to about 3.76 million years. The Naibadad stratum, lying near the top of the stratified layer, dated to 2.26 million years. Dates of intermediate age (between 3.56 and 2.41 million years) occur from tuffs sandwiched in the middle of the stratigraphic column. Note particularly how the suite of dates follows in stratigraphic order, from most ancient at the bottom to most recent at the top. In this case, absolute dating technology confirmed the relative stratigraphic sequence inferred from the law of superposition.

The base of the Footprint tuff—recall that it was located near the bottom of Tuff 7—dated to about 3.56 million years; the base of the tuff above, Tuff 8, dated to 3.49 million years. Finally, we can answer the single most important question at Laetoli: *The fossil hominin footprints are between 3.49 and 3.56 million years old.* Given that the footprints are closer to the bottom of Tuff 7 than to its top, they are probably closer to 3.56 than 3.49 million years old. (See "Looking Closer: What Happened to the Laetoli Footprints?")

With the dating of the Laetoli footprints, Leakey showed that humans were bipedal long before they made stone tools. Therefore, the hypothesis that stone tool use led to bipedalism must be incorrect (unless there are still older stone tools yet to be found).

READING GATECLIFF'S DIRT

The law of superposition gives us the first geoarchaeological tool for reading a site's stratigraphy. With it, we know that the story begins at the bottom, with succeeding "chapters" lying above. With a few more tools, we can fill in some more of a site's geologic history. Gatecliff Shelter, with a 40-foot stratigraphic profile covering more than 7000 years, again provides an example (Figure 5-4).

The Gatecliff sediments, like those of all archaeological sites, resulted from both natural processes and human behavior. The first question we need to ask is, "What are all the possible ways in which the materials

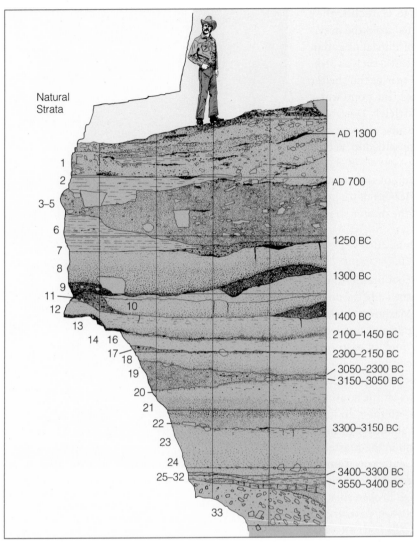

Natural
Strata

AD 1300

AD 700

1250 BC

1300 BC

1400 BC

2100–1450 BC

2300–2150 BC

3050–2300 BC
3150–3050 BC

3300–3150 BC

3400–3300 BC
3550–3400 BC

Figure 5-4 The master stratigraphic profile from Gatecliff Shelter. The standing figure is exactly 6 feet tall, and the grid system shows 1-meter squares. Only the upper 33 of the 56 stratigraphic units show in this particular profile. © *American Museum of Natural History; from Thomas 1983b, Figure 22.*

surfaces. Altogether there are 16 such surfaces, each of which resulted largely from human activities. These surfaces contain fire hearths, charcoal, broken stone tools, grinding slabs, flakes, food remains, and occasional fragments of basketry and cordage. (Although not true for Gatecliff, in many other sites people might very well have built walls, houses, or floors, dug deep pits or wells, and in general contributed much more to a site's stratigraphic record.) Because the living surfaces are so vividly separated by the sterile flood layers, we can see clearly what was brought into the cave by (or during) human activity.

Most of the strata in Gatecliff Shelter are of purely geological origin—the rock, silt, and dirt entered the shelter via nonhuman processes. Thomas divided the Gatecliff profile into a sequence of 56 strata: layers of more or less homogeneous material, visually separated from adjacent layers by a distinct change in the character of the material deposited. Some layers, such as Stratum 8, consisted of coarser **alluvial** (water-carried) **sediments,** grading from gravels at the bottom to fine sand silts at the top. Sometimes, during extreme storm events, the ephemeral stream that flows occasionally in front of Gatecliff diverted into the shelter itself. Water from such flash floods would first deposit coarse sediments, as pea-sized gravels. As the water's velocity diminished, its carrying capacity decreased, and smaller particles were deposited. Finally, when the water slowed, the tiniest silt particles would cap the stream sediments. Such floods occurred several times throughout the 7000 years of deposition at Gatecliff, and each time they buried the existing occupation surface.

in Gatecliff—artifacts, bones, rock, and dirt—could have entered the shelter?"

We know that the artifacts and a good portion of the animal bones entered Gatecliff through human behavior, but natural processes were also at work. Many of the bones are of animals that lived (and died) in the site, or whose bodies were brought in by carnivores, raptors, or human hunters. And, of course, there is a lot of rock and dirt. The geoarchaeologist must consider both human and natural factors in reading a stratigraphy.

Gatecliff's Stratigraphy

In Gatecliff's master stratigraphy, the thin dark levels (such as those numbered 9, 11, and 13) are living

alluvial sediments Sediments transported by flowing water.

When the inhabitants returned to Gatecliff, they stepped onto a new "floor," separated from the previous one by nearly a meter of sterile alluvial or **eolian** (wind-blown) **sediments.** In some cases, such as Stratum 2, small ponds formed at the rear of the shelter after one of the flash flood episodes. The pond water acted as a trap for eolian dust particles. Dust blew into the shelter (as it did the whole time we excavated there), landed in the pond, and then settled to its bottom as finely laminated silts.

Thomas described in detail each of the 56 such strata stacked up inside Gatecliff. Here's a description of one stratum near the bottom of the master stratigraphy, shown in Figure 5-5:

> Stratum 22, Rubble:
> Angular limestone clasts, charcoal firepit, and baked area at top, somewhat churned into the underlying silty top of Stratum 23. Maximum thickness 50 cm. on the southwest pile and formed continuous layer up to 15 cm. thick in eastern parts of excavation, but was discontinuous elsewhere. Almost as voluminous as Stratum 17, the top was ~4.85 m. [below datum] on the southwestern pile and ranged from ~5.50 to ~5.30 m. elsewhere, and its bottom was about ~5.30 m. in the southwest corner, ~5.35 m. in the Master Profile, and ~5.32 m. in the present excavation. . . . Stratum 22 was created by gradual accumulation of roof fall and talus [loose, broken rock] tumbling over the shelter lip between 5,250 and 5,100 years ago. Stratum 22 was called GU 6R-74 in the field and contained [living floor] 14.

Note the detail involved here. Exact depths are given relative to the site datum. When paired with the horizontal grid system, these arbitrary elevations document the exact configuration of each geological stratum.

Each geological term is sufficiently well defined so that geologists who have never visited Gatecliff can understand what Stratum 22 looked like. Note also how Thomas separated such descriptions from interpretation. This way, others can use his data to make their own assessments.

© American Museum of Natural History, photo by Susan L. Bierwirth

Figure 5-5 An exposure of the bottom half of the stratigraphic column at Gatecliff Shelter. At the very bottom is Stratum 55 (about 7000 years old). Rob Rowan and Dennis O'Brien are standing on Stratum 39 (comprised of sand and fine silt and dating about 6200 years old). They are pointing to Stratum 26 (a rubble unit that is about 5500 years old). Incidentally, an exposure such as this today would be extensively shored.

You can also see the dates we found for Stratum 22. Of the 47 radiocarbon dates (we'll describe this dating method in the next chapter) processed on materials from Gatecliff, four came from this particular stratum. This information, combined with the added radiocarbon evidence from strata above and below Stratum 22, allowed us to estimate that the stratum was laid down between 5250 and 5100 years ago.

Marker Beds

Most of the Gatecliff strata are unique to this site; they are found nowhere else. But sometimes, archaeologists encounter distinctive strata that turn up in other sites in the same region. If these so-called **marker beds** have been dated in other sites, they can provide clues to the age of sediments in a new site.

eolian sediments Materials transported and accumulated by wind (for example, dunes).

marker bed An easily identified geologic layer whose age has been independently confirmed at numerous locations and whose presence can therefore be used to date archaeological and geological sediments.

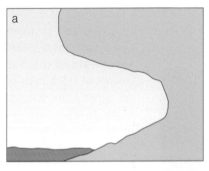
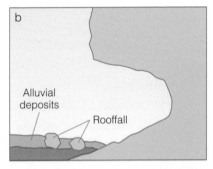
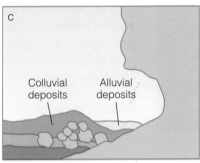
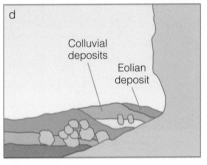

Figure 5-6 A hypothetical rockshelter, filling with colluvial and eolian sediments, as well as rooffall, over time.

Gatecliff as a Geologic Deposit

What can we learn from Gatecliff's stratigraphic profile? For any archaeological site, the archaeologist must consider the ways in which that site formed *as a geologic deposit*.

Sediments enter rockshelters like Gatecliff in three primary ways (Figure 5-6). Rocks fall from the ceiling and the shelter's front lip (known as the dripline). As the front part of the shelter erodes, the habitable space inside moves toward the back wall; this, incidentally, means that earlier habitations might be found outside the modern dripline. Large blocks falling from the roof may also reduce the habitable space. This happened at Gatecliff, when a pickup truck–sized piece of the roof broke off the ceiling about 1000 years ago, covering the eastern side of the shelter and reducing the floor space by almost half. Such changes in a shelter's floor plan can alter the way people use it (or can cause them to abandon it altogether). Eventually, a shelter may erode back so far that it will be no more than a cliff face (and archaeologists may not even recognize it as a potential site).

Rocks also enter a shelter as **colluvial sediments** from the surrounding hillside. Colluvial sediments are rock and dirt that move downslope through gravity or during rainstorms or snowmelt. These sediments fall over a shelter's dripline, or they may creep, roll, or wash in around the sides. As a result, rockshelters sometimes have a berm of earth along the front, and another one at either or both sides.

Fine eolian dust blows into the shelter (sometimes from a source near the shelter, sometimes from distant sources), and alluvial sediments may accumulate if a stream runs into the shelter, carrying with it rocks of various sizes, depending on the stream's force, as well as silt and clay. A fast-moving stream, on the other hand, may remove sediments from a shelter.

Gatecliff contained one of these marker beds. Stratum 55, near the very bottom of the site, contained an inch-thick lens of sand-sized volcanic ash, or tephra, which consisted of fragments of crystal, glass, and rock once ejected into the air by a volcanic eruption. Not discovered until the last week of the last field season, the tephra was indistinct, mixed with the cobbles and rubble of Stratum 55. In the laboratory, Jonathan Davis (1948–1990), a leading expert on the volcanic ashes of the American West, confirmed that this was ash from the eruption of Mount Mazama. When this mountain (in the Oregon Cascades) blew up 6900 years ago, it spewed out 11 *cubic miles* of pumice and related materials, forming a caldera that today contains Crater Lake (500 miles to the northwest of Gatecliff). The prevailing winds, coupled with the force of the explosion itself, carried Mazama ash across eight western states and three Canadian provinces.

Wherever the ash settled, it created a marker bed— a geologic layer that geoarchaeologists can identify and whose age has been independently confirmed at numerous locations. Archaeologists can use it, therefore, as a check on age estimates. The Mazama ash is dated at numerous locations to 6900 years old. Wherever the Mazama ash appears—and it appears in many archaeological sites in the western United States—it tells the archaeologist that everything above the ash is less than 6900 years old, and everything below it is more than 6900 years old.

colluvial sediments Sediments deposited primarily through the action of gravity on geological material lying on hillsides.

The mode of deposition changed between 6500 and 4250 years ago. Strata of this age consist of thick beds of silt (giving the stratigraphy its layer-cake appearance) interspersed with thin layers of angular rock. Davis interpreted these sediments as indicating an increase in summer precipitation and perhaps overall drier conditions. Summer precipitation tends to fall as torrential thunderstorms, producing mud and debris flows or flash floods that can rapidly (that is, in a single storm) deposit massive amounts of silt and/or rock to the shelter. Moreover, with less overall precipitation, there was less vegetation to hold sediments back when downpours did occur.

© Todd Surovell

Figure 5-7 A buried A horizon (< 10,000 years old) exposed in an arroyo near the Barger Gulch site in Colorado.

With this information, what do the sediments at Gatecliff tell us about how this particular site formed? Let's begin with Stratum 55, where Jonathan Davis found the Mazama ash marker bed. This stratum was composed of angular rubble, with bedding planes that conformed to the sloping surface of the site, and no alluvial sediments. Davis argued that slow, downslope colluvial action and debris falling from the shelter's lip and ceiling created this stratum. He also suggested that this stratum tells us that precipitation fell primarily in the winter. Why did he say this?

Winter precipitation falls as snow, but during the day it melts and seeps into cracks in the shelter's ceiling. There it will freeze at night, expand, and break off chunks of the ceiling that fall to the shelter's floor (producing that angular rubble in Stratum 55). In addition, winter snow normally melts slowly and does not produce the energy needed to move much sediment and rock downslope. Hence, it does not move much colluvium into the shelter (resulting in the bedding planes seen in Stratum 55).

Then, about 5100 years ago, a **soil** developed in the shelter's sediments. Why would this happen?

A Word about Soils

Soils are not depositional units. They are developmental sequences—distinctive layers that develop in place. You've seen these as dark bands in road cuts or pipeline trenches. The **A horizon** is the topsoil—the dark, humus layer where organic material and rock undergo chemical and mechanical decomposition (Figure 5-7). The **B horizon** lies below this and is where clays accumulate as rainfall and snowmelt transport them downward from the A horizon. Still deeper lies the **C horizon,** a mineral horizon that consists of the sediment's parent material. Below the C horizon is bedrock. (This is only a basic soil description; soils are often more complex with subdivisions of each of these horizons.)

The fact that a soil developed inside Gatecliff tells us that about 5100 years ago, sediments accumulated more slowly; at this time, in fact, sediments entered the shelter primarily around its edges as colluvium, with lesser amounts of rooffall and eolian sediments. This pattern continued for the rest of the shelter's history. These sediments suggest fluctuations between wet and dry intervals, and winter and summer precipitation.

soil Sediments that have undergone in situ chemical and mechanical alteration.

A horizon The upper part of a soil, where active organic and mechanical decomposition of geological and organic material occurs.

B horizon A layer found below the A horizon, where clays accumulate that are transported downward by water.

C horizon A layer found below the B horizon that consists of the unaltered or slightly altered parent material; below the C horizon is bedrock.

WHAT DOES IT MEAN TO ME?

RECONSTRUCTING CLIMATE CHANGE: GLOBAL WARMING

We can't talk about global warming unless we know how earth's current mean temperature relates to past temperatures—and that means reconstructing climate change from the sorts of data that archaeologists rely on.

The evidence for global warming comes from data sets. The "instrumental records"—data from thermometers and the like—provide information for the last century or so. For earlier times we rely on "proxy" measures, variables that are indirectly linked to temperature changes. These proxy measures include data from ice cores.

Greenland and Antarctica are the major sources of ice cores. In Antarctica, the ice sheets average 2400 meters (8000 feet) thick; in Greenland researchers have retrieved ice cores some 3 kilometers (2 miles) long. In Antarctica, the record goes back almost 800,000 years; in Greenland, some 110,000 years. The layers of ice in the cores provide an annual record of climate change. As snow builds up, the deeper layers become compacted and recrystallize, trapping various gases, including oxygen.

Oxygen comes in several isotopes; the two relevant ones here are ^{18}O and ^{16}O. Precipitation that falls under warmer conditions has higher amounts of ^{18}O than ^{16}O because ^{16}O, being lighter, evaporates before ^{18}O. Scientists can therefore translate the ratios of these two isotopes into temperature. This is a primary record of global temperature change.

What do these ice core records tell us? First, they tell us that the last 10,000 years has been the warmest time on earth of the last 100,000 years. Second, they tell us that although the earth has witnessed significant and *rapid* climate "reversals" every 5000 years, the last 10,000 years have been surprisingly stable.

Finally, if we look closely at the last millennium, we see something disturbing. The accompanying figure shows the so-called "hockey-stick" graph that synthesizes several sources of data, including instrumental records, tree rings, and ice cores spanning the last 1000 years. Although some scientists have critiqued the graph's data and analysis, it shows that global temperature has increased significantly in the last 100 years. To date, no one has provided a better explanation than an increase in the greenhouse gases produced by the burning of fossil fuels. The question now is whether the warming trend will continue or if a long-overdue rapid climate reversal will occur.

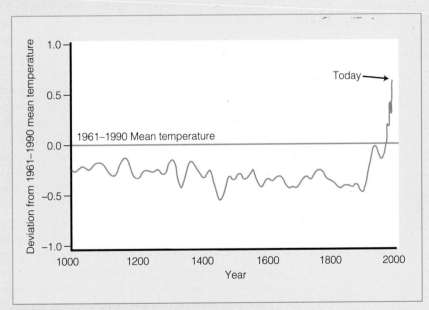

The so-called "hockey-stick" graph showing a significant increase in global temperature over the last century. *Redrawn from Mann et al. 1998.*

So it is that the dirt and rock at Gatecliff have as much of a story to tell about the shelter's history as do the artifacts themselves. In this case, the geoarchaeology provided important clues about the changing environments to which the ancient hunter-gatherers who used Gatecliff had to adapt. (See "What Does It Mean to Me? Reconstructing Climate Change: Global Warming.")

Is Stratigraphy Really That Easy?

Unfortunately, no. Gatecliff has textbook stratigraphy because it makes for nice photographs and is relatively easy to understand. Some sites are like this. For example, much like the site of Pompeii in Italy, the Maya village site of Cerén in El Salvador was caught by volcanic activity about 1400 years ago and buried so quickly beneath 5 meters of ash that little happened to it until its discovery. The adobe walls, flooring, and thatched roof of the houses were perfectly preserved. When archaeologist Payson Sheets (University of Colorado, Boulder) and his crew excavated this site, they found all artifacts left in place. The site was a moment "frozen" in time.

But many archaeological sites can be geological nightmares. Human and natural processes churn the sediments, moving things up or down. In Figure 5-8 you see a hypothetical scenario that makes this point. Hunter-gatherers first lived in a temporary camp beside a stream about 5000 years ago, leaving behind some artifacts on the surface, along with a hearth and some postholes from a windbreak that they built. The river overflowed and deposited layers of silt over the camp. So far, so good.

But about 200 years later, people built **pithouses**—semi-subterranean homes with log roofs covered with sod. They dug into the previous campsite and threw the charcoal from the hearth of the earlier camp up onto the current land surface—thereby moving older material (the charcoal) upward in the stratigraphic sequence. At the same time, their houses cut down into the previous living surface, introducing younger artifacts to older layers of earth. You can see that the law of superposition, blindly applied, would lead us astray here.

pithouse A semi-subterranean structure with a heavy log roof covered with sod.

Now suppose that about 1200 years ago the nearby river was diverted, cutting an arroyo next to the pithouse. The hillside slumped, pushing part of the pithouse and its contents into the arroyo. Then people built a pueblo, like those in Chaco Canyon. A new hearth appeared outside the walls, and a trash pit too. Once again, later materials moved downward in the stratigraphic sequence.

Many years pass. The pueblo is abandoned, its roofs and walls collapse, and the rooms accumulate eolian deposits. A nineteenth-century farmer scavenges posts from the long-abandoned pueblo to build a fence. The river returns and cuts through the buried pithouse and pueblo trash pit. The river then dries up. Any archaeologist walking along this gully would see pithouse occupation debris on one side and, at the same elevation, pueblo trash on the other. The law of superposition might suggest that they were of the same age, yet clearly they are not.

Most archaeological sites are similarly complex. Let's turn to an archaeological example that shows how the law of superposition can mislead us if we do not consider the human behavior that goes into the formation of a site.

Reverse Stratigraphy at Chetro Ketl

Florence Hawley Ellis (1906–1991) was a pioneer of Southwestern archaeology. Beginning in the 1920s, she embarked on a long-term research program in Chaco Canyon, focusing on the site of Chetro Ketl (*chee*-tro *ket*-tle), along the northern wall of the canyon. This three- to five-story pueblo contained more than 500 rooms, although it was located only about a quarter-mile from the equally large Pueblo Bonito. On the cliffs behind Chetro Ketl are near-vertical steps cut into the rock face that lead to one of the Chacoan roads (mentioned in Chapter 3). While excavating there, Hawley figured out that Chetro Ketl had been built in four major construction periods, beginning in 1055 BP and continuing until 884 BP (see "In Her Own Words: Fieldwork 1920s-Style at Chetro Ketl," by Florence Hawley Ellis).

But Hawley was less successful in creating a ceramic chronology, a record of how pottery styles had changed over time (more on this in Chapter 6). She kept returning to the site, excavating the huge refuse heap to the east of Chetro Ketl. The archaeological sediments reached nearly 6 meters deep in places.

Hawley recognized that two kinds of strata were present. Beginning at the bottom, she defined Strata 1 and 3 as household debris: daily sweepings contain-

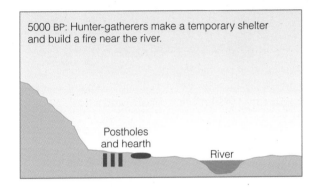

5000 BP: Hunter-gatherers make a temporary shelter and build a fire near the river.

Postholes and hearth

River

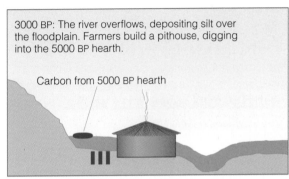

3000 BP: The river overflows, depositing silt over the floodplain. Farmers build a pithouse, digging into the 5000 BP hearth.

Carbon from 5000 BP hearth

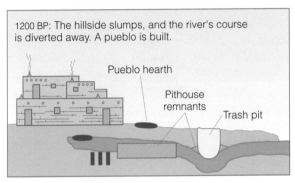

1200 BP: The hillside slumps, and the river's course is diverted away. A pueblo is built.

Pueblo hearth

Pithouse remnants

Trash pit

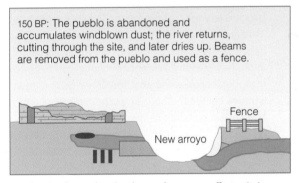

150 BP: The pueblo is abandoned and accumulates windblown dust; the river returns, cutting through the site, and later dries up. Beams are removed from the pueblo and used as a fence.

Fence

New arroyo

Figure 5-8 The development of a hypothetical archaeological site over time, showing how cultural and natural processes affect a site's formation.

ing ash, charcoal, and potsherds heaped in small, overlapping mounds. After examining comparable dumps in modern pueblos, Hawley decided that these sediments must have accumulated basketful by basketful, as trash was thrown out of individual homes daily.

By contrast, Strata 2 and 4 consisted of a mass of refuse, with a generalized gray color signaling a mixing of ash and charcoal throughout. Although these strata also consisted of stone, ash, and charcoal debris, they lacked the laminations and outlines of small basketloads.

But the kind of pottery contained in these strata seemed wrong. What Hawley knew to be the more recent pottery turned up near the base of the trash mound. This material seemed to have been removed in bulk from some abandoned section of the pueblo, perhaps to make way for a new building to be constructed on the site of a previous dumping area.

In other words, part of the dump appeared to be upside down. Hawley stewed about this interpretation: "The suggestion looked far-fetched, however, for this would place *half the mound* as re-dumped material." But eventually, tree-ring dating (which we will discuss in the next chapter) confirmed that yes, indeed, the lower sediments were *younger* than the upper sediments. The stratigraphy violated the law of superposition: It was reversed.

Why was it "upside down"? Decades later, archaeologist Steven Lekson (University of Colorado) and others found out that the midden Hawley excavated at Chetro Ketl was actually a deliberately constructed *architectural* feature. The strata were layers of trash deliberately hauled in for building purposes. When the ancient Chacoans looked around for easily excavated fill sediments, they turned to their own trash. Naturally, then, the first material they scooped up in baskets was the material on top of the trash mounds—material that had been thrown out the most recently. That recent material was the first to be placed down for the mound's base. As they dug deeper into the trash mound, they removed progressively older sediments and piled these on top of the younger trash.

In a way, the law of superposition was still correct— the material at the bottom had been deposited first, the material above that second, and so on. But because the ages of the artifacts in the layers of fill are in reverse order, archaeologists refer to this situation as **reverse stratigraphy.**

reverse stratigraphy The result when sediment is unearthed by human or natural actions and moved elsewhere in such a way that the latest material is deposited on the bottom of the new sediment and progressively earlier material is deposited higher and higher in the stratigraphy.

IN HER OWN WORDS

FIELDWORK 1920s-STYLE AT CHETRO KETL

by Florence Hawley Ellis

It was 1928. [Ellis was 22 years old.] At Chetro Ketl we were 60 miles from the railroad; mail came only when our truck went for provisions. If summer storms struck, everyone gathered along the steep-sided but usually dry Chaco arroyo to watch the return of the heavy vehicle through a tumbling torrent. Pushing might be necessary. Telephone connections between the little Chaco trading post and Crownpoint (administrative center and boarding school for the Eastern Navajo Reservation) finally were put in, the line being on the top wire of 40 miles of ranch fencing. When a cow leaned against that fence, the phone went out.

A canvas bag of water was delivered to each occupant of the two-party tents every morning. Those who could not scrub teeth, underwear, and their persons in the single gallon must carry their own water. On weekends we washed our hair and then our jeans in a scant bucket of well water and finally used what remained to settle the sand of the tent floor. Then, virtuously clean, we could drop in to the post to watch the trader dicker for rugs, still sold by the pound, from Navajo women who with equal care took out their credit in flour, lard, sugar, Arbuckle's coffee, sometimes a small bag of hard candy, and perhaps a payment on some item of pawn hung back in the closet. If we were hungry we could do as the Navajo did: buy a can of tomatoes and a box of soda crackers. The trader opened the can and fur-

nished the spoon; the consumer perched on the high counter to swing his heel and enjoy the treat.

Courtesy Palace of the Governors Photo Archives (NMHM/DCA), neg. # 29747

Florence Hawley Ellis (right) supervising University of New Mexico's 1964 field school at Chaco Canyon (New Mexico).

SITE FORMATION PROCESSES: HOW GOOD SITES GO BAD

The casual observer may think of the ground as stable and unchanging, but every archaeologist knows better. Sites are complex, and things can move around after they are buried. It's the job of the archaeologist to draw inferences about human behavior from sites, but to do that we have to know how a site formed over time.

Always bear in mind that *the archaeological record is only the contemporary evidence left over from past behavior.* Artifacts are the static remains of past dy-namic behavior. Because both natural and cultural factors impinge on these remains to such a degree, the archaeological record is rarely a *direct* reflection of past behavior.

The archaeological record is a contemporary phe-nomenon. Although the objects and their contexts may have existed for centuries or millennia, observa-tions and knowledge about those objects and contexts are as contemporary as the archaeologists who do the observing. In the words of Robert Gargett (San Jose State University), archaeological strata are "leaky"— artifacts can move around quite a bit from where they were originally deposited.

To help interpret the archaeological record more accurately, Michael Schiffer (University of Arizona) distinguishes between **systemic** and **archaeological contexts.** Artifacts, features, and residues were once part of an ongoing, dynamic behavioral system. Arrowheads were manufactured, used for specific tasks, broken, repaired, and then lost or discarded. Potsherds were once part of whole pots which had been manufactured and decorated according to prescribed cultural criteria. People used the pots for cooking or storage or ceremonies. The pots broke or were intentionally broken or discarded, perhaps as part of a ritual. Food bones and plant remains are the organic residues of a succession of activities—hunting or gathering or farming, butchering or processing, cooking, and eating. While these materials were being manufactured and used, they existed in their systemic context. These items were part of a living behavioral system.

But by the time such materials reach the archaeologist's hands, they have long since fallen out of this behavioral system. The artifacts, features, and residues encountered by archaeologists are recovered from their archaeological context, where they may continue to be affected by human action, but where they are also affected by the natural environment.

Formation Processes in the Systemic Context

Using Schiffer's distinction between systemic and archaeological context, we can discuss **formation processes**—how artifacts enter the archaeological record and how they are modified once they are there (summarized in Table 5-1). We will distinguish among four major processes in the systemic context that influence the creation of archaeological sites: cultural deposition, reclamation, disturbance, and reuse.

TABLE 5-1 Site Formation Process Summary	
SYSTEMIC CONTEXT	**ARCHAEOLOGICAL CONTEXT**
Cultural Deposition	Floralturbation (plants)
Discard	Faunalturbation (animals)
Loss	Cryoturbation (freezing)
Caching	Argilliturbation (wet-dry cycles)
Ritual interment	Graviturbation (hillslopes)
Reclamation	
Cultural Disturbance	
Reuse	

Cultural Depositional Processes Four major **cultural depositional processes** control how artifacts enter the archaeological record:

Discard   Tools, clothing, structures—everything eventually breaks or wears out and is discarded. When this happens, the object ceases to function in the behavioral system and becomes part of the archaeological context.

Loss   Other things are inadvertently lost, such as an arrow that misses its target or a necklace or pot left at an abandoned camp. In this case, the items are most likely small and still in usable condition.

Caching   Still others are intentionally cached. The duck decoys we mentioned in Chapter 4 were intentionally buried in Lovelock Cave (for later use). They remained part of the archaeological record because the person who cached them never returned.

Ritual Interment   Burials and their associated grave goods are the most obvious example of ritual interment, but other examples include offerings left at a shrine or, alternatively, deliberate destruction and burial of a shrine or religious site.

Reclamation Processes Part of the archaeologist's job is to figure out whether the artifacts entered the archaeological record through discard, loss, caching, or ritual interment. This task is made difficult because artifacts sometimes move back and forth between systemic and archaeological contexts. Artifacts can be *reclaimed,* for instance. Archaeologists frequently find artifacts that were scavenged by later peoples. Pueblo peoples, for example, believed that ancient stone arrow and spear points contained power. If they happened to encounter a point while out working, they might keep it and later make a ritual offering of it. In this case, the arrowhead has moved from a context where it was (perhaps) lost to one in which it was intentionally interred. It has also moved from the context of an earlier time period to a later one, and from a context that reflects its original everyday function to one reflecting another culture's ritual.

systemic context A living behavioral system in which artifacts are part of an ongoing system of manufacture, use, reuse, and discard.

archaeological context Once artifacts enter the ground, they become part of the archaeological context, where they can continue to be affected by human action but are also affected by natural processes.

formation processes The ways in which human behaviors and natural actions operate to produce the archaeological record.

cultural depositional processes Human behaviors by which artifacts enter the archaeological record, including discard, loss, caching, and ritual interment.

Whenever a discarded projectile point is resharpened, a potsherd picked up and used to scrape hides, or an old brick reused in a new fireplace, a **reclamation process** has occurred. The farmer who used posts from an abandoned pueblo to build a fence in our previous hypothetical scenario was reclaiming older materials.

All archaeologists must also cope with the fact that nonprofessionals (amateur archaeologists and looters) often collect artifacts from sites. If we ignore this fact, we run the risk of misinterpreting archaeological data. In the Carson Desert, for example, we knew that local people had collected projectile points from sites in the wetland for decades. One man had more than 25,000 projectile points in his collection. The walls of his dining room were covered with picture frames full of artifacts, and he lined his driveway with large stone mortars and metates. The fact that our survey recovered relatively few projectile points from sites in the marsh probably reflected this reclamation process—otherwise known as looting—and not necessarily a lack of hunting.

Cultural Disturbance Processes Reclamation processes transfer materials from the archaeological to the systemic context. But the archaeological record is also heavily conditioned by transformations *within* archaeological contexts. **Cultural disturbance processes** change the contexts of materials within an archaeological site itself. Examples include dam building, farming, and construction of houses, pits, hearths, and so on. In the previous hypothetical example, movement of charcoal from the early hunter-gatherer hearth upward in the stratigraphic sequence was an instance of cultural disturbance.

Reuse Processes In **reuse processes,** an object moves through a series of different behavioral settings before it enters the archaeological record. Sometimes objects are recycled. Potsherds, for example, are sometimes ground up and used as temper in manufacturing new vessels. Broken arrowheads are sometimes re-chipped into drills and scrapers. Beams from one building are sometimes pulled out and reused in another. Clearly, an object can be created for one purpose, but later

modified and deposited in an entirely different context from similar objects that are not reused.

The difference between reuse and reclamation depends on the archaeological context involved. If beams are taken from a currently occupied building, it is an instance of reuse; if they are taken from a building long abandoned, then it is reclamation. The distinction seems trivial, but it tells us something about potential differences in the age of items being reused. Something reclaimed is probably moving from an archaeological context considerably older than the systemic context being entered; reused items, on the other hand, are probably moving between systemic contexts that are much closer in age.

This brief review of cultural formation processes shows why archaeologists must be aware that human activities frequently move things from their original depositional provenience to another. This can make archaeological sites very complicated and difficult to interpret. Natural processes can complicate matters even further.

Formation Processes in the Archaeological Context

Once an object enters an archaeological context, a host of natural formation processes kick in, determining not only whether organic material will be preserved (as we discussed in Chapter 4) but also where the object will be found. In the previous hypothetical example, a river and a landslide played major roles in creating the archaeological record. Here, we will briefly introduce a few natural site formation processes (Figure 5-9) to help you conceptualize just how complex an archaeological site can be. We also emphasize how natural processes can both disrupt patterns that would otherwise tell us something about human behavior and, at the same time, create their own patterns, which could be misinterpreted as the result of human behavior. The point is that *there is no simple correspondence between the distribution of artifacts in a site and human behavior*. We provide an example of how important an understanding of site formation processes can be (and revisit this critical aspect of archaeology in Chapter 8).

Floralturbation Walking down almost any sidewalk, you see how tree roots can dislocate concrete slabs. Roots do the same to buried ancient walls, by loosening soil and promoting the downward movement of artifacts from their original stratigraphic context. Roots can also move artifacts upward. When a large tree falls over, its roots pull up large amounts of

---

reclamation processes Human behaviors that result in moving artifacts from the archaeological context back to the systemic context, as in scavenging beams from an abandoned structure to use them in a new one.

cultural disturbance processes Human behaviors that modify artifacts in their archaeological context, as in the digging of pits, hearths, canals, and houses.

reuse processes Human behaviors that recycle and reuse artifacts before they enter an archaeological context.

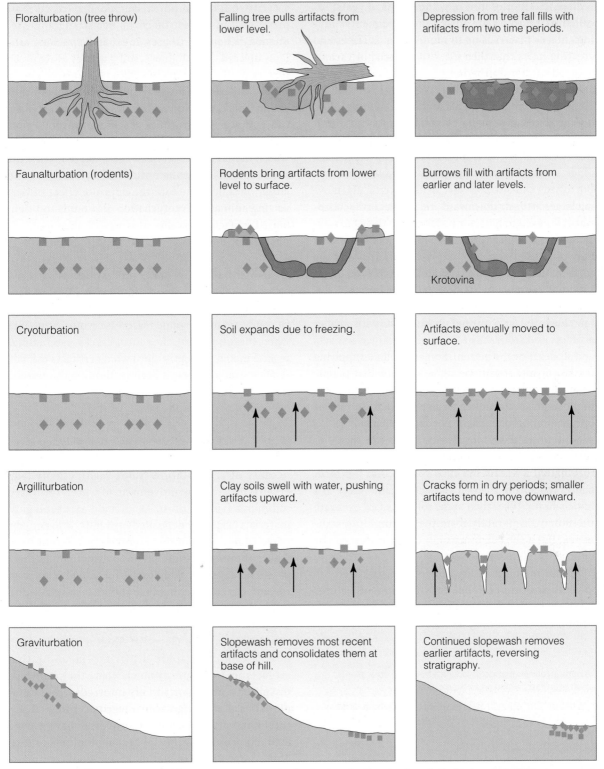

Figure 5-9 The effects of some natural formation processes on the distribution of artifacts in a hypothetical archaeological site.

sediment. After hundreds or thousands of years, so-called tree throw can churn a site's sediments, pulling ancient materials up to more recent surfaces and creating holes that then fill with material of various ages. This is **floralturbation.**

Faunalturbation Rodents and other animals often dig into sites, producing two major types of **faunalturbation.** First, burrowing rodents can push artifacts from lower layers up to the surface, effectively placing older artifacts into a younger stratigraphic context. Burrowing can also size-sort artifacts vertically, moving larger artifacts downward and smaller artifacts upward. Pocket gophers, for instance, dig their burrows around any object larger than about 5 centimeters; they push smaller objects out of their burrows to the surface. The larger artifacts and rocks left behind might eventually tumble to the bottom of the burrows. Repeat this process over hundreds or thousands of years (and burrows), and you end up with a site with smaller artifacts and stones near the top, and larger artifacts and stones near the bottom. Someone blindly applying the law of superposition might conclude that people changed from using large to small tools over time. But that conclusion would be wrong: The pattern tells us only about pocket gophers, not about people.

Sometimes these burrows are filled with rock and earth washed or blown in from above, forming a feature called a **krotovina** (kro-toe-*vee*-na; the term comes to us from Russian soil science and refers to a mole's hole). If so, then archaeologists can excavate the burrow separately from the surrounding sediments. But if the burrows simply collapse, they can be difficult or impossible to see.

Burrowing animals are only one factor. Even the lowly earthworm can obliterate the edges of features like burials, pits, and hearths, making them more difficult for the archaeologist to see and record.

floralturbation A natural formation process in which trees and other plants affect the distribution of artifacts within an archaeological site.

faunalturbation A natural formation process in which animals, from large game to earthworms, affect the distribution of material within an archaeological site.

krotovina A filled-in animal burrow.

cryoturbation A natural formation process in which freeze/thaw activity in a soil selectively pushes larger artifacts to the surface of a site.

argilliturbation A natural formation process in which wet/dry cycles in clay-rich soils push artifacts upward as the sediment swells and then moves them down as cracks form during dry cycles.

graviturbation A natural formation process in which artifacts are moved downslope by gravity, sometimes assisted by precipitation runoff.

Cryoturbation In northern climates, freeze/thaw processes can move artifacts up in a stratigraphic sequence. When soil freezes, it expands, pushing artifacts upward. As soil thaws, soil particles move down first, partially or completely filling the void below artifacts, ensuring that the artifacts cannot move back down. This is why freeze/thaw cycles move large artifacts upward (sometimes at a rate of several centimeters per year). **Cryoturbation** can create a site in which artifacts are vertically size-sorted, with the smallest artifacts at the bottom of the sediment and larger ones near the top (the opposite effect of burrowing animals). Cryoturbation also tends to orient buried artifacts vertically—that is, with their long axis pointing up and down.

Argilliturbation A similar process happens in clay-rich soils that undergo wet/dry cycles. When these soils become wet, they expand and push larger artifacts upward for the same reason as cryoturbation. But when these soils dry, they form cracks—sometimes several meters in depth—into which artifacts can fall. A site's stratigraphy can become thoroughly churned if this **argilliturbation** process takes place over and over for hundreds or thousands of years.

Graviturbation Archaeological materials deposited on hillsides eventually move downslope. This occurs because of precipitation (slopewash), gravity (soil creep), or the slow movement of water-saturated sediments (solifluction). As a result, archaeological materials originally deposited on a hillside eventually come to rest in a context completely different from where they were originally lost, discarded, cached, or ritually interred. **Graviturbation** can also result in reverse stratigraphy because the material closest to the surface will be the first to slide or tumble down the slope.

Some sites (like Gatecliff Shelter) have a high degree of stratigraphic integrity—meaning that artifacts are found pretty much where they were lost, discarded, cached, or ritually interred. Other complex sites lack stratigraphic integrity; a range of cultural and natural formation processes have moved artifacts from their initial archaeological context. This complexity does *not* make archaeology impossible, but it does mean that archaeologists must first establish just how the artifacts got to where they were found. Although how we do this is different for each site, the following case study shows how understanding a site's geologic context is essential to knowing what the site can, or cannot, tell us about ancient human behavior.

An Ancient Living Floor at Cagny-l'Epinette?

The site of Cagny-l'Epinette (Figure 5-10) sits on a gently sloping terrace in a broad river valley in northern France. French archaeologist Alain Tuffreau and his team had slowly and carefully excavated its 3 meters of sediments for many years. In the lower levels, in sediments that were some 200,000 to 300,000 years old, Tuffreau found artifacts as well as the bones of various large game animals. He interpreted Stratum I1 as a living floor, a surface like those sandwiched between the thick silt layers at Gatecliff Shelter, where our ancient human ancestors lived, made tools, and butchered animals. Tuffreau carefully mapped the locations of artifacts across Stratum I1 to look for clusters that could reconstruct where different activities took place and create a fuller picture of the past.

But Level I1 at Cagny-l'Epinette had a few troubling aspects. Unlike Gatecliff, where the living floors were only a few centimeters thick, the artifacts found in Stratum I1 were separated by 11 to 64 centimeters of sediments. This could mean that instead of one living floor, Level I1 at Cagny-l'Epinette preserved multiple floors; or perhaps the artifacts had been deposited on one living floor, but were later moved up and down by burrowing rodents. Or maybe the artifacts were deposited at widely different times through different formation processes.

Also troubling was the fact that the sediments of Stratum I1 were fluvial sands, deposited by a river. Because the deposit was mostly sand, it would seem that the river was usually slow moving. But the presence of some larger rocks indicated periods of higher river energy. This could mean nothing more than that the river occasionally flowed over the terrace and created a pleasant sandy surface on which people later camped, made tools, and ate the game they killed along the river's banks. But many of the stone tools bore breaks that suggested they had been treated roughly, as if they had rolled along in a stream bed and been struck by other cobbles. Could the artifacts have been left by the same river that deposited the sand, and not by people?

Animal bones presented a third problem. In Chapter 9, we will learn about the distinctive breaks created when fresh limb bones are broken open for their calorie-rich marrow. We will also see how distinctive cut-marks result when stone knives nick bone as an animal is butchered. Oddly, the bones recovered at Cagny-l'Epinette bore very few such telltale signs. Perhaps these were the remains of animal carcasses that had floated downstream and not the remains of game hunted by people. How could the excavators know for certain?

Determining the Effect of Formation Processes

All archaeologists dream of finding an undisturbed site. By this, they usually mean a site that Mother Nature has not thoroughly mixed up or that looters have not destroyed. But deep down, archaeologists know that *there is no such thing as an undisturbed site.* Even a site such as Pompeii is not as pristine as it may first seem. As you learned in this chapter, a lot can happen between the time an artifact is deposited in the ground and when an archaeologist excavates it. Formation processes affect all archaeological sites to one extent or another. Our task is to figure out how these processes have affected a site in order to know what analytical use the site has.

Late in the excavation of Cagny-l'Epinette, Tuffreau was joined by Harold Dibble, Philip Chase (University of Pennsylvania), and Shannon McPherron (Max Planck Institute). The recovery strategy changed somewhat in order to collect data relevant to determining the kind and effect of formation processes on the site.

Recall from Chapter 4 that archaeologists sometime record an in situ artifact's inclination (the angle at which it is lying in the ground) and its orientation (the compass bearing of its long axis). Archaeologists did this during later seasons at Cagny-l'Epinette, not only for artifacts and bones, but also on all unmodified stones found in situ. This information is important both for understanding the site as a geological deposit and also for seeing the same site as an archaeological deposit. What did these observations tell the archaeologists?

After compiling the data, Dibble and his colleagues discovered that the artifacts were oriented largely along two axes, perpendicular to one another. One axis was the same as the ancient stream that ran over the site. The other followed the slope of the terrace. And it was not only the artifacts that fit this pattern;

Figure 5-10 The site of Cagny-l'Epinette, showing the distribution of artifacts and rock on a portion of Stratum I1.

unmodified rock and bone did, too. The inclination data were also intriguing. Artifacts, bone, and unmodified rock lay nearly, but not quite, flat—those that pointed in the same direction as the ancient stream had their "downstream" ends raised slightly above their "upstream" ends. What do these patterns mean?

For one thing, that the artifacts, bones, and unmodified rock all fit the same orientation and inclination patterns suggested that the same process was responsible for their deposition. Experimental studies also showed that when a river washes an object along, those objects eventually come to rest with their long axis pointing along the direction of the river's flow (Figure 5-11). This was true at Cagny-l'Epinette, where a river probably deposited the rocks, bones, and artifacts. Some of these artifacts were apparently left exposed on the terrace's surface as the river's channel shifted. While they were exposed, rainfall washed over them and, as a result of slopewash, they came to point downslope—perpendicular to the direction of the river's previous flow. When the river shifted to flow over the terrace again, these artifacts were sufficiently buried that their orientations were preserved and not affected by the river.

Fluvial geologists also know that stones on river bottoms tend to lie nearly, but not entirely, flat. After removing sediment from the upstream ends of stones, the river then redeposits it beneath the downstream end. This leaves stones lying with their upstream ends slightly lower than their downstream ends, often with the downstream end of one stone overlapping the upstream end of another (a process called imbrication).

These patterns strongly suggested that the artifacts in Stratum I1 were probably washed out of a site located some unknown distance upstream and then redeposited at Cagny-l'Epinette. This means that Level I1 is not the pristine living floor that archaeologists originally thought it was.

But neither is it completely useless. Cagny-l'Epinette still contains a record of what ancient humans did in northern France more than 200,000 years ago. That record is not as detailed as originally thought, but we now know what analytical utility this stratum in the site has. The distribution of artifacts within the site is probably meaningless; it does not reflect activity areas but only fluvial action and slopewash. But the site is still useful for making comparisons between the I1 artifact assemblage as a whole and those from other strata at the site, or from other sites. Likewise, the data from Stratum I1 could serve as a control, a background against which to compare data from other strata at the site to demonstrate that those other strata do indeed contain living floors.

CONCLUSION

The important point of this chapter is that understanding the effects of site formation processes is the first step in knowing what information an archaeologist can realistically extract from a site. Archaeologists need to keep in mind all the processes that affect how artifacts and ecofacts enter the ground—and everything that can happen to them once they are there. In so doing, the archaeologist must appreciate that a site records not only human behavior, but also a range of natural processes. This is why sites have both geological and archaeological records. Increasingly, archaeologists find that they need meticulous data, such as the orientation and inclination of plain old rocks as well as of artifacts, to accomplish this goal. Realizing the critical importance of formation processes influences how we go about excavating archaeological sites.

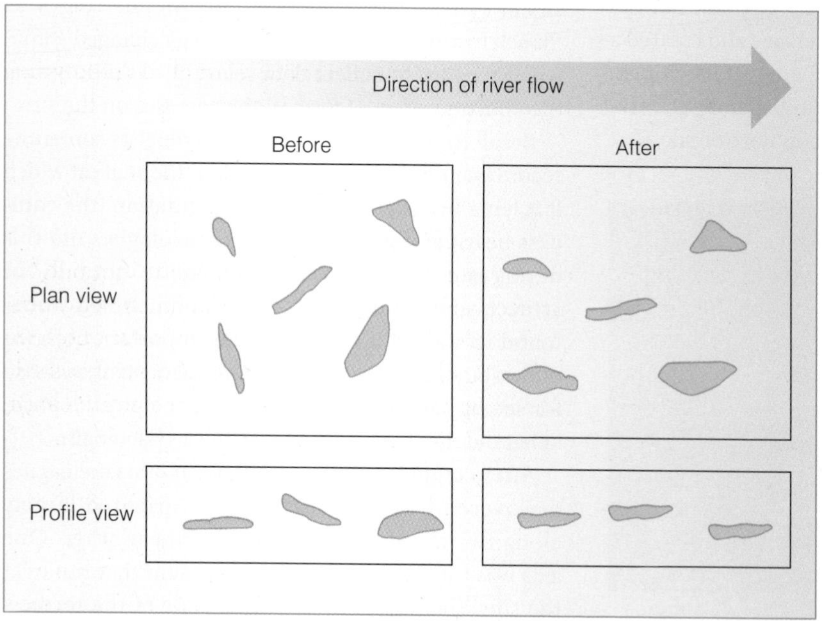

Figure 5-11 How artifacts become oriented to the direction of river flow.

SUMMARY

1. What is geoarchaeology?

- Geoarchaeology applies the concepts and methods of the geosciences to archaeological research to assist in determining a site's age and its formation, including all the human and natural processes that work together to create an archaeological site.

2. What is the law of superposition? How can it be violated?

- The law of superposition holds that (all else being equal) older geological strata tend to be buried beneath younger strata.
- The law of superposition is only an organizing principle; in some instances, reverse stratigraphy can occur, as for example, when people excavate sediments to create a mound.

3. What is the difference between systemic and archaeological contexts?

- The systemic context refers to artifacts as they are being used or manipulated by people; the archaeological context refers to natural processes that act on artifacts and features once they are deposited in the ground.
- Artifacts leave the systemic context (and enter the archaeological context) through cultural depositional processes, including loss, discard, caching, and ritual interment.
- Once in the archaeological context, artifacts can continue to be moved and altered by a variety of natural site formation processes, including landslides, burrowing animals, earthworms, tree throw, and the actions of water and climate.

4. Why does this difference matter?

- In most sites, stratigraphy results from a complex interplay between natural and cultural processes.
- Archaeologists must understand the difference between an artifact's systemic and archaeological contexts in order to know how an artifact in the ground relates to the human behavior that is their ultimate interest.

MEDIA RESOURCES

Doing Fieldwork:
Archaeological Demonstrations CD-ROM 2.0
This CD, developed by the authors, shows professional archaeologists involved in various digs, many of which are referenced in the text. The presentation is organized by the main techniques used on an archaeological dig, reinforcing concepts and techniques via live examples. The CD takes you through each step automatically, or you can navigate to any point via the navigation bar. After reviewing a step in the dig process, you are taken to Check Points, which are concept questions about each step of the dig. Then you can see the answers, receive your score, and even send your scores to your instructor.

The Companion Website for *Archaeology,*
Sixth Edition
www.cengagebrain.com
Supplement your review of this chapter by going to the companion website to take one of the practice quizzes, use the flash cards to master key terms, and check out the many other study aids that are designed to help you succeed in your introductory archaeology course.

6 CHRONOLOGY BUILDING: HOW TO GET A DATE

LEARNING OBJECTIVES

**AFTER READING THIS CHAPTER
YOU SHOULD BE ABLE TO ANSWER THESE QUESTIONS:**

1. What is the difference between relative and absolute dating?

2. What are the major dating techniques, what materials do they date, and what is their time range?

3. What are the major dating techniques of historic sites?

4. What do archaeological dates date?

© George H.H. Huey/Corbis

The site of Betatakin, a 13th century cliff dwelling in the Navajo National Monument in northern Arizona.

PREVIEW

THIS CHAPTER IS about dating archaeological sites—how archaeologists get a grasp on time. Here you'll find a broad range of dating techniques: tree-ring dating, radiocarbon dating, thermoluminescence dating, and others that allow us to date organic material, rocks—even dirt. The chemical and physical underpinnings of these techniques can be mind-boggling, but you need to have at least a basic grasp of them to know when you can and cannot use a particular technique.

You also need to understand the basis of these techniques to appreciate just what the "date" is actually telling you, because *dates in and of themselves mean nothing*. Demonstrating the *validity of association* between dates and human behavior is a key issue in archaeological dating.

DOING FIELDWORK CD-ROM:
ARCHAEOLOGICAL DEMONSTRATIONS 2.0

See the "Dating" section of the CD-ROM to learn more about topics covered in this chapter.

INTRODUCTION

The Fourth Egyptian Dynasty lasted from 2613 to 2494 BC. The Roman Coliseum was constructed between AD 70 and 80. The Battle of the Little Big Horn took place on June 25, 1876. Each date represents the most familiar way of expressing chronological control—the **absolute date** (in terms of the Gregorian calendar). Such dates are expressed in specific units of scientific measurement—days, years, centuries, or millennia—but no matter what the measure, all such absolute determinations attempt to pinpoint a specific year or a specific range of years.

In the early days, archaeologists did not have absolute dating methods. Before the 1950s, most dates were instead **relative dates** involving unspecified segments of time, expressed as relationships or comparisons: The stepped pyramid at Saqqara in Egypt is *earlier* than Khufu's pyramid; the historic settlement of Williamsburg is *later* than the pueblos of Chaco Canyon; Folsom spear points are *earlier* than Chupadero Black-on-white pottery. Relative dates are obviously not as precise as absolute dates, but prior to the 1950s, they were the best that archaeology had. The advent of absolute dating helped revolutionize archaeology in the 1960s.

RELATIVE DATING

The keys to relative dating are the law of superposition (introduced in Chapter 5) and the **index fossil concept.**

Developed in the early nineteenth century, the index fossil concept is often attributed to British geologist William "Strata" Smith (1769–1839). Geologists of Smith's day wrestled with the problem of how to correlate the ages of widely separated exposures of rock. Smith observed that forms of life change over time, with different fossils characterizing different rock strata. Thus, widely separated strata could be correlated and assigned to the same time period if they contained the same fossils. This simple idea allowed Smith and others to make the first geological maps, and these

---

absolute date A date expressed in specific units of scientific measurement, such as days, years, centuries, or millennia; absolute determinations attempting to pinpoint a discrete, known interval in time.

relative dates Dates expressed relative to one another (for instance, earlier, later, more recent) instead of in absolute terms.

index fossil concept The idea that strata containing similar fossil assemblages are of similar age. This concept enables archaeologists to characterize and date strata within sites using distinctive artifact forms that research shows to be diagnostic of a particular period of time.

radically altered the way that geologists conceived of the landscape. For the first time, they could see broad patterns that told a story of ancient seas, mountain building, and ice ages.

The Index Fossil Concept in Archaeology

Archaeology faced a similar problem. The law of superposition suggested which artifact types or styles were older than other forms in particular sites. But how did the individual site chronologies become correlated with one another? The index fossil concept provided the answer, except that in archaeology, artifacts replaced fossils. This meant that strata in widely separated sites containing the same distinctive artifact forms—called **time-markers** in archaeology—are assumed to be of similar age.

The index fossil concept was introduced to archaeology by Swedish archaeologist Oscar Montelius (1843–1921). Trained in the natural sciences, Montelius switched to archaeology and became interested in Europe's Stone, Bronze, and Iron Ages (which, you will recall from Chapter 1, were the "ages" created by Christian Tomsen and tested by Jens Jenssen). Working for the State Historical Museum in Stockholm, Montelius traveled over Europe examining collections from various sites, paying special attention to objects in unmixed contexts, such as those from burials, hoards, and individual rooms.

Based on this evidence, Montelius divided the Stone, Bronze, and Iron Ages into chronological subdivisions, each with its own set of distinctive artifacts or artifact styles, such as particular kinds of axe heads, swords, or brooches. In some cases, Montelius had stratigraphic controls to help decide which artifact styles were earlier or later, and sometimes the artifacts appeared in contexts such as Egyptian tombs, where documentary sources provided the age. In this way, Montelius advanced archaeology by developing a way to create a chronology of artifact time-markers for Europe.

Time-Markers in the American Southwest

What Montelius could have really used, though, was a master sequence—a site with a deep stratigraphic profile that would permit the law of superposition to demonstrate the changing sequence of artifact types and styles. Early-twentieth-century archaeologist Nels Nelson (1875–1964) searched for just such a master sequence for the American Southwest during his excavation at Pueblo San Cristobal in New Mexico. Nelson knew that there were deep deposits at San Cristobal, and he hoped that a carefully controlled excavation would show whether certain artifacts could act as time-markers (Figure 6-1).

Selecting an area of minimal disturbance, Nelson isolated a block of debris measuring 3 feet by 6 feet wide and nearly 10 feet deep. Clearly, the midden had accumulated over a long interval, and several distinctive kinds of pottery were buried there. Because the dusty black midden lacked sharp stratigraphic divisions, Nelson personally excavated the block in 1-foot arbitrary levels, cataloging the potsherds recovered by level. Imposing arbitrary levels on an undifferentiated stratigraphy seems almost pedestrian today, but in 1914, Nelson's stratigraphic method was revolutionary. New World archaeologists immediately put the idea into practice as a fundamental excavation technique (for the record, however, Nelson got the idea from his European colleagues).

Nelson then applied the law of superposition to define culture change within the midden column. All else being equal, the oldest trash should lie at the bottom, capped by more recent accumulations. Even though the dense midden lacked tangible stratigraphy, Nelson searched for time-markers in the form of distinctive pottery types.

This is how Nelson applied the index fossil concept to the prehistoric ceramics of San Cristobal. Just as geologists learned to distinguish certain extinct life forms as characteristic of various rock strata, so too could archaeologists use distinctive artifact forms to characterize and correlate strata between archaeological sites. Pottery was a natural choice because potsherds were common cultural debris and Nelson knew that ceramic styles varied considerably across the American Southwest.

More than 2000 potsherds turned up in the 10-foot test section at San Cristobal. Nelson first grouped them into obvious types, then plotted their distribution according to depth below the surface (we'll discuss the principles of creating artifact types in Chapter 7). Table 6-1 summarizes his results. Column 1 is the frequency of corrugated pottery, the most common everyday cooking ware. Because the relative frequency

---

time-markers Similar to index fossils in geology; artifact forms that research shows to be diagnostic of a particular period of time.

Figure 6-1 General view across Nels Nelson's excavations at San Cristobal (New Mexico). The 700-year-old walls of this huge pueblo are clearly evident. Note also that no screens appear anywhere; sifting of archaeological deposits did not become standard practice until almost 50 years after this picture was taken.

© American Museum of Natural History

of corrugated potsherds remained more or less constant throughout the occupation of San Cristobal, Nelson rejected Column 1 as a potential time-marker. For the same reason, he also rejected biscuit ware, a dull whitish-yellow pottery (Column 2).

Nelson then turned to the three remaining kinds of pottery—which he termed Types I, II, and III—and discovered that specific forms were associated with specific stratigraphic levels (Figure 6-2). The most ancient levels at San Cristobal contained a predominance of Type I painted pottery, black designs on a white background. Type I potsherds were most numerous at and below the 8-foot mark and only rarely recovered above 7 feet. Type II pottery—

TABLE 6-1 Potsherd Frequencies from Pueblo San Cristobal, New Mexico

DEPTH BELOW SURFACE Column number	CORRUGATED WARE 1	BISCUIT WARE 2	TYPE I: BLACK-ON-WHITE WARE 3	TYPE II: TWO-COLOR GLAZE 4	TYPE III: THREE-COLOR GLAZE 5	TOTAL
1st foot	57 (36.7)	10 (6.5)	2 (1.3)	81 (52.2)	5 (3.2)	155
2nd foot	116 (31.3)	17 (4.6)	2 (.01)	230 (62)	6 (1.6)	371
3rd foot	27 (15.3)	2 (1.1)	10 (5.7)	134 (76.1)	3 (1.7)	176
4th foot	28 (21.3)	4 (3)	6 (4.5)	93 (70.9)	0 (0)	131
5th foot	60 (17.3)	15 (4.3)	2 (.01)	268 (77.6)	0 (0)	345
6th foot	75 (18.6)	21 (5.2)	8 (1.9)	297 (73.8)	1? (.01)	402
7th foot	53 (23.1)	10 (4.3)	40 (17.5)	126 (55)	0 (0)	229
8th foot	56 (24.6)	2 (.01)	118 (51.9)	51 (22.4)	0 (0)	227
9th foot	93 (45.4)	1? (.01)	107 (52.5)	3 (1.4)	0 (0)	204
10th foot	84 (54.4)	1? (.01)	69 (44.8)	0 (0)	0 (0)	154
Total	649	83	364	1,283	15	2,394

Figures in parentheses are row-wise percentages.

SOURCE: Nelson 1916.

The Next Step: Seriation

The index fossil concept was essential to the archaeology of the early twentieth century. The law of superposition permitted archaeologists to produce a chronology of cultural change at a particular site, and the index fossil concept allowed them to date sites *relative* to one another. With established ceramic time-markers, archaeologists could date other Southwestern Pueblo sites based on the type of pottery found in them. A site with predominantly black-on-white pottery is older than one that contained red glazed pottery. Archaeologists did not know *how much* older the first site was than the second, but they could at least place sites into a relative chronological sequence. This was a tremendous advance for the time.

This advance became the basis of **seriation,** a relative dating technique that was crucial to archaeology in the mid-twentieth century. Developed by European archaeologists in the late nineteenth century, the technique was introduced to the New World by Alfred Kroeber (1876–1960). Seriation is grounded in the same observation that guided Oscar Montelius: Styles change, and new technologies arise over time. In ancient times, just as now, most new ideas are slow to catch on, with only a few pioneers participating in the fad. Eventually, a new idea may become chic and replace earlier vogues, only to fall gradually into disuse and to be replaced by the next "new thing."

The index fossil concept relied primarily on the presence or absence of distinctive kinds of artifacts. Seriation refined this concept by using changes in the *frequencies* of artifacts or styles to date sites relative to one another (paleontologists, by the way, do the same thing with fossils).

To get a sense of how seriation works, look at Figure 6-3, which shows changes in lighting technologies in late-nineteenth-century Pennsylvania. At mid-century, most houses were illuminated by candles and oil lamps; only a few households had gas lamps. But over the next 50 years, families increasingly switched to gas lamps. Those who could not afford such installations used kerosene lamps (made possible by the growing petroleum industry in Pennsylvania and elsewhere). By 1900, however, electric lights were replacing gas lamps and, by 1940, gas lamps had all but disappeared. By that year, virtually everyone used incandescent

© American Museum of Natural History, photo by Craig Chesek

Figure 6-2
Examples of Nels Nelson's Types I (bottom), II (middle), and III (top) pottery from San Cristobal Pueblo.

red, yellow, and gray potsherds ornamented with a dark glaze—occurred most commonly at and above the 7-foot mark. In other words, Type I potsherds characterized the lower strata, and the Type II potsherds dominated the upper deposits. Type III pottery, three-colored glazed ware, was rare at San Cristobal, appearing in only the uppermost levels of Nelson's column. Given that Pueblo peoples were making three-colored wares when the Spaniards arrived in New Mexico in the sixteenth century, this made sense.

Nelson's arbitrary levels made possible the definition of three important ceramic time-markers. Not only did he document specific ceramic changes at San Cristobal, but more important, his controlled stratigraphic excavation provided a master sequence with which to place other sites, strata, or features in the region into a relative chronological sequence.

seriation A relative dating method that orders artifacts based on the assumption that one cultural style slowly replaces an earlier style over time; with a master seriation diagram, sites can be dated based on their frequencies of several artifact (for instance, ceramic) styles.

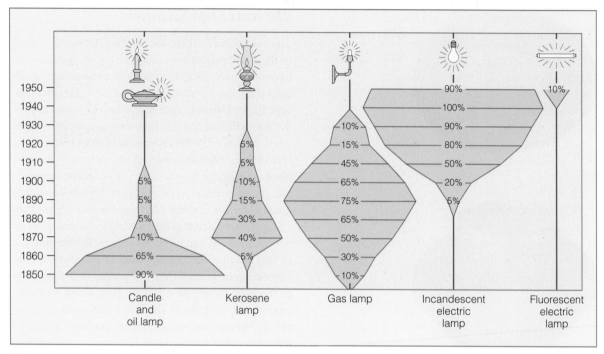

Figure 6-3 Seriation diagram showing how methods of artificial illumination changed in Pennsylvania between 1850 and 1950. *Redrawn from Mayer-Oakes 1955, Figure 15.*

lightbulbs—which by 1950 were already being replaced by fluorescent lamps.

The shape of such popularity curves, which archaeologist James Ford (1911–1968) termed "battleship-shaped curves" because they often look like a battleship's silhouette from above, is the basis for seriation. By arranging the proportions of temporal types into lozenge-shaped curves, one can determine a relative chronological sequence.

This phenomenon is evident in Nelson's potsherd counts from San Cristobal Pueblo; Figure 6-4 translates the frequencies from Table 6-1 into a seriation diagram. As we've already noted, when San Cristobal was first built, ceramics were most commonly decorated with black designs painted on a white background; corrugated ware was also fairly abundant. Moving up Nelson's stratigraphic column, two-color glaze rapidly takes over, with black-on-white pottery fading out. In the top half of the column, three-color pottery comes into use. The midden at San Cristo-

bal faithfully preserved these changes in ceramic "fashion."

Sometimes these changes reflect mere changes in style (such as pottery types), and sometimes they reflect changes in technology and economy (e.g., the lighting example above). But for the time being what matters is the empirical pattern, and the fact that shifts in the frequency of a particular artifact or style can help date sites.

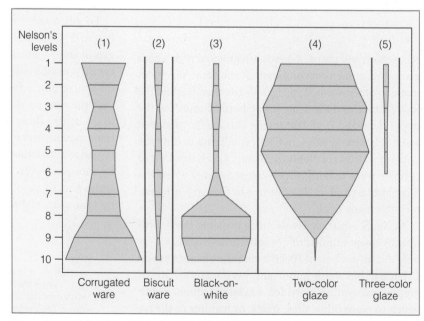

Figure 6-4 Seriation diagram based on Nelson's San Cristobal potsherd frequencies.

For example, the sequence of pottery frequencies at San Cristobal helps date other sites in the American Southwest. Instead of just using the presence or absence of a particular artifact type, we use frequencies of those different artifacts to place sites into a finer chronological sequence. For example, sites with high percentages of black-on-white ceramics should be older than sites with high percentages of two-color glaze and small percentages of black-on-white pottery. These sites, in turn, would be older than sites with high percentages of two-color glaze, small percentages of corrugated ware, and only trace amounts of black-on-white pottery.

And these sites would be older than sites dominated by two-color glaze with trace amounts of three-color glaze. Pottery has long been used to date archaeological sites, and it will in the future. (Unfortunately, pottery is also a primary target of thieves and looting; see "What Does It Mean to Me? What's Wrong with Buying Antiquities?")

We can use the seriation method based on a single master stratigraphy, or we can compile one analytically by linking several overlapping stratigraphies at different stratified sites. Thus, seriation refines the index fossil concept to create a more fine-grained relative sequence. Nonetheless, seriation still cannot tell us *how old* a site or stratum is, only whether it is older or younger than another.

Seriation was a common technique in the mid-twentieth century, and while the concept still remains central to archaeological thinking, today the technique is used mostly where absolute dating methods cannot be employed or are not sufficiently specific. Archaeologists still use the index fossil concept, too, but often just implicitly. For instance, we know from numerous excavations that Folsom spear points, like those found at the Folsom site mentioned in Chapter 4, date to around 12,300 to 12,900 years ago. If we excavated a site with Folsom points in it—or even just found several Folsom points lying together on the surface—we would gleefully tell our colleagues that "we had a Folsom site." And all of us would know that the site probably dated between 12,300 and 12,900 years. But we would *always* try to refine that estimate by using an absolute dating technique.

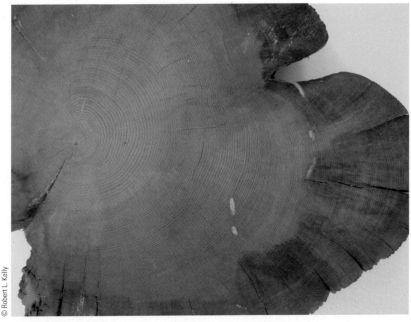

© Robert L. Kelly

Figure 6-5 Cross section of a ponderosa pine showing a detailed record of the tree's lifespan. Each year is represented by a light (summer) and a dark (winter) ring.

ABSOLUTE DATING

Absolute dating gave archaeology some incredibly powerful tools, helping to define the science that it is today. In this chapter, we will highlight only the most commonly used methods among the many techniques available. We emphasize radiocarbon dating in order to demonstrate the issues that archaeologists must consider when determining what an absolute date actually means.

Tree-Ring Dating

Tree-ring dating, also called **dendrochronology,** was developed by Andrew E. Douglass (1867–1962), an astronomer studying the effect of sunspots on the earth's climate. Douglass knew that trees growing in temperate and arctic areas remain dormant during the winter and then burst into activity in the spring. This results in the formation of the familiar concentric growth rings. Trees have alternating dark and light rings (Figure 6-5). The light rings are a year's spring/summer growth, and the dark rings are that year's late summer/fall growth (the darkness comes from the cell walls; when growth slows down in winter, the cell

tree-ring dating (dendrochronology) The use of annual growth rings in trees to assign calendar ages to ancient wood samples.

WHAT DOES IT MEAN TO ME?

WHAT'S WRONG WITH BUYING ANTIQUITIES?

Many people collect artifacts. They pick them up while walking through plowed fields or hiking in the mountains. Perhaps they place them on their mantle or mount them in a picture frame. It seems harmless enough. Is it?

Often, yes. But not when there's money to be made. Cruise any online auction house and you'll find artifacts for sale. These houses usually have policies prohibiting the sale of unethically or illegally obtained materials. For example, e-Bay prohibits the sale of items from Native American or Native Hawaiian grave sites, including funerary objects, grave markers, and human remains. Likewise prohibited are sacred items such as ceremonial masks and prayer sticks, or any artifacts taken from federal, state, or Native American lands, or battlefields.

But it's hard to police these sites, and the sale of artifacts encourages the destruction of archaeological sites. For example, on the day we wrote this, e-Bay listed two Mimbres black-on-white pots, and a number of pot fragments, with a total value of $5200.

Mimbres pottery is special. It was manufactured only between 1000 and 850 years ago in New Mexico's Mimbres Valley. The bowls contain naturalistic designs that are rare in Southwestern pottery: depictions of rabbits, bighorn sheep, birds, and people. Even more important, these bowls are often found in graves. Usually, they were ritually "killed" by punching a small hole in the bowl's center and then placed over the deceased's head. One of the bowls on auction at e-Bay was clearly ritually killed; both had probably been taken from graves—a violation of e-Bay's policy.

The selling of artifacts promotes their unauthorized and destructive collection. *There is not a single Mimbres pueblo that has not been extensively looted*; some were flattened by bulldozers in a search for the graves that lie beneath the pueblos' floors (see

A classic Mimbres bowl.

Chapter 15). Looters are arrested when they can be caught, but no amount of money can replace what they have destroyed. And for every looter arrested, a dozen evade the law.

Mimbres sites are not the only ones hit hard. Dry caves that preserve organic remains such as baskets are targets, as are Maya, Inka, and Egyptian sites—almost any site, in fact.

You can be sure that in gathering Mimbres bowls, plenty of other artifacts were disturbed and destroyed, to say nothing of the human remains. We will never know what information was lost from looted sites, but we can be sure that it was volumes.

Buying artifacts is like buying drugs: The buyer is the only reason the business exists. And the business is the reason that we are losing irreplaceable artifacts and information about the past every day.

And that's what's wrong with buying artifacts.

© Steven LeBlanc and the Mimbres Foundation

walls crowd together and take up a greater proportion of the ring's space). Because each ring represents a single year, it's a simple matter to determine the age of a newly felled tree: just count the rings.

For many tree species, ring width varies, and Douglass reasoned that tree rings might preserve information about past climates. Because climate affects all the trees in a forest, Douglass reasoned, year-by-year patterns of tree growth manifested as variable ring widths should produce a long-term chronological sequence.

Douglass began his research on living trees, mostly yellow pines in central Arizona. He studied recent stumps and cores taken from still-living trees, counted the rings, and recorded the pattern of light and dark ring widths. To extend this chronology backward in time, he searched for an overlap between the early portion of young trees with the final years of growth of an old tree or stump. This way, he created a master sequence of tree rings, but the stumps and living trees went back only about 500 years.

But Douglass worked in the American Southwest, where arid conditions enhance preservation. Sampling ancient beams in pueblo sites, he slowly built up a prehistoric "floating chronology" that spanned several centuries, and eventually linked it to the modern tree chronology, giving Southwestern archaeology a reliable, year-by-year dating tool (Figure 6-6).

Year-by-Year Chronology Becomes a Reality

In August 1927, Douglass visited Betatakin, an impressive cliff dwelling in northeastern Arizona (see this chapter's opening photo). He collected two dozen samples that bracketed the construction of Betatakin within a decade of AD 1270. Accuracy to this degree

was stunning back then—and still is, compared with every other technique.

But tree-ring dating can be even more accurate. Jeffrey Dean of the University of Arizona's Laboratory of Tree-Ring Research collected more samples at Betatakin in the 1960s. The total collection grew to 292 individual beams, allowing Dean to document the growth of Betatakin literally room by room; his findings are summarized in Figure 6-7. (By the way, we take samples using a hand or power drill equipped with a bit that removes only a quarter-inch diameter cylinder of wood; the technique does not harm living trees and is minimally destructive of archaeological materials.)

Dean found that Betatakin was first occupied about AD 1250 by a small group who built a few structures that were soon destroyed. This occupation was probably transient, with the rockshelter providing a seasonal camping spot for people traveling to plant fields at some distance from their home.

The actual village at Betatakin was founded in AD 1267, when three room clusters were constructed; a fourth cluster was added in AD 1268. The next year, a group of maybe 20 to 25 people felled several trees, cut them to standardized lengths, and stockpiled the lumber, presumably for future immigrants to the village. Inhabitants stockpiled additional beams in AD 1272, but they did not use them until AD 1275, which signaled the beginning of a 3-year immigration period during which more than ten room clusters and a kiva were added. Population growth at Betatakin slowed after AD 1277, reaching a peak of about 125 people in the mid-1280s. The village was abandoned sometime between AD 1286 and AD 1300 for unknown reasons. This is a remarkably precise reconstruction for a 700-year-old settlement.

Methodology of Tree-Ring Dating In practice, tree-ring dating works like this: An archaeologist digs up a sample of charcoal or wood of the appropriate species that bears at least 20 rings, then sends it to one of several labs around the world (with appropriate contextual data). There, an analyst cuts or sands the sample down so that the rings are easily visible, then measures the widths individually.

Then the hard work begins. Normally, an archaeologist will have some idea of

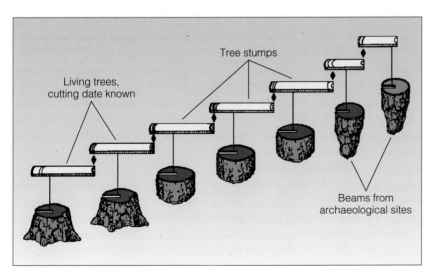

Figure 6-6 How a tree-ring chronology is built up by matching portions of tree-ring sequences from known-age living trees (lower left) to older archaeological samples; the diamonds indicate the portions of the sequences that overlap.

Living trees, cutting date known

Tree stumps

Beams from archaeological sites

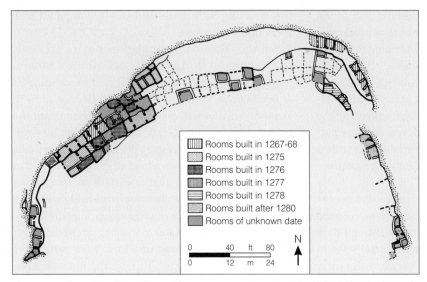

Figure 6-7 Floor plan of Betatakin and the construction sequence inferred by Jeffrey Dean from the tree-ring evidence. *Redrawn from Dean 1970, Figure 13.*

how old the site is—perhaps less than 500 years old, or between 750 and 1000 years old. With that information, a lab analyst tries to match the sample with the appropriate portion of the regional sequence. This can be a slow, laborious process because the analyst is looking for a segment of the master sequence that has the same order of variable-width rings as the archaeological sample. Computer programs can help, but exact matching often requires visual comparison because some samples have oddities, such as missing rings or partial rings, that only a trained technician can detect.

For tree-ring dating to work, the analyst must make several adjustments and weigh several variables. For example, young trees grow more quickly than old ones, so absolute tree-ring width is a function of both climate *and* a tree's age. By using the estimated curvature of the ring on a sample, dendrochronologists solve this problem using a mathematical function that converts a tree's ring diameter into a standardized index that takes the tree's age into account.

A sample's age is the age of the last (outermost) ring present on the piece. But if that outer ring is absent—if part of the outside of the sample was adzed off or burned away—we won't know what year the tree died. By looking for markings that are diagnostic of the outer edge of a tree—such as signs of bark or beetle activity—a trained analyst can determine whether the outermost ring on the sample was the tree's final ring. If so, then you have a so-called *cutting date;* if not, then your date is only a maximum age (that is, we know that a sample was cut down after, say, AD 1225, but we would not be able to say *how many* years after).

Finally, the sample sent to the lab must have at least 20 rings to increase the chance that the sample will match one and only one segment of the master sequence. Samples with fewer rings might match to several segments, leaving the archaeologist to guess which match is the correct one.

Tree-ring dating works on many species of trees, so long as that species reflects climatic change. The most commonly used are piñon pine, ponderosa pine, Douglas fir, juniper, and white fir. Limber pine, bristlecone pine, oak, red cedar, and the giant sequoia work sometimes. But some species are unsuitable. Cottonwood, for example, grows only near water sources and taps into a more continuous supply of groundwater. As a result, cottonwood rings do not reflect local climate very well, and without climatically induced variation in ring width, we cannot link individual samples and build a chronology.

Additionally, because climate varies from region to region, tree-ring sequences are workable only for an immediate region. A tree-ring sequence from northern New Mexico, for example, tells little about the Mediterranean, or even southern New Mexico.

Dendrochronological sequences have been developed in many areas, including the American Southwest, the Arctic, the Great Plains, the American Midwest, the American Southeast, Germany, Great Britain, Ireland, New Zealand, Turkey, Japan, and Russia. In the American Southwest alone, more than 60,000 tree-ring dates exist for some 5000 sites. Here the logs used to make pueblo rooms and pithouses allow the tree-ring sequence to extend back some 2300 years; using oaks preserved in ancient bogs, one sequence in Germany extends back almost 10,000 years.

Tree Rings and Climate Dendrochronology also provides climatic data. Because tree-ring width is controlled by precipitation as well as temperature, trees preserve a record of past environmental conditions. Although tree metabolism is complex, analysts have made great progress in such ecological reconstructions. In the American Southwest, detailed models tell us how much rain fell in, say, northwestern New Mexico, year by year, even season by season. For example, these data tell us that devastating droughts occurred there in the mid-1100s, and catastrophic floods occurred in AD 1358. These detailed climatic reconstructions provide archaeologists with fine-grained paleoenvironmental chronologies—provided an appropriate dendrochronological sequence is available locally.

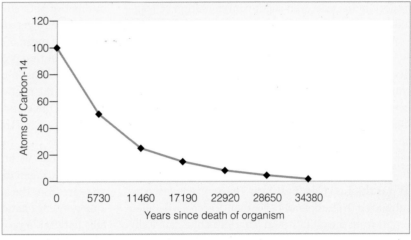

Figure 6-8 The amount of ^{14}C in the remains of an organism is reduced by half every 5730 years, radiocarbon's so-called half-life.

Radiocarbon Dating: Archaeology's Workhorse

In 1949, physical chemist Willard F. Libby (1908–1980) announced to the world that he had discovered a revolutionary new dating technique: radiocarbon dating. For his efforts, Libby deservedly received the Nobel Prize in Chemistry in 1960. Although dendrochronology is a more precise technique, radiocarbon dating is more widely applicable and has become today the workhorse in archaeology's stable of dating methods.

How It Works There are three principal isotopes of carbon—^{12}C, ^{13}C, and ^{14}C. The isotope ^{14}C (read this as "carbon-14") matters here, even though it is the rarest: only one ^{14}C atom exists for every *trillion* atoms of ^{12}C in living material. ^{14}C is produced in the upper atmosphere, where cosmic radiation creates neutrons that replace one of nitrogen's (^{14}N) protons to create ^{14}C. This ^{14}C is oxidized to form carbon dioxide, then dispersed throughout the atmosphere by stratospheric winds. About 98 percent of all ^{14}C enters the oceans; plants take up much of the rest through photosynthesis. From plants, radioactive carbon enters herbivores and carnivores—and you.

All radioactive isotopes are unstable and break down, or "decay," over time. ^{14}C decays through beta emissions (the emission of a negatively charged electron) back into ^{14}N. The amount a living organism loses through decay is replaced from the environment; so, as long as an organism is alive, its ^{14}C remains in equilibrium with the atmosphere. Once dead, the organism no longer takes in ^{14}C, and the amount of ^{14}C in its body decreases through decay.

But not very quickly. The **half-life** of ^{14}C is 5730 years; this means that half the amount of ^{14}C pres-

ent in a sample will convert to ^{14}N every 5730 years. Imagine a piece of wood that contained 100 atoms of ^{14}C when it died (actually, it would contain plenty more, but let's keep it simple). After 5730 years, 50 of these atoms (more or less) would have decayed into ^{14}N. After another 5730 years, half of those 50 ^{14}C atoms (that is, 25 atoms, again, more or less) would have converted to ^{14}N, leaving only 25 ^{14}C atoms. After another 5730 years (a total of 17,190 years), this amount would be halved again to about 12 ^{14}C atoms. After a long time, very few ^{14}C atoms remain (Figure 6-8). Theoretically, radiocarbon dating could extend far back in time, but current technology places a practical limit on it: *Radiocarbon dating is good only for organic remains that are younger than about 45,000 years.*

Radiocarbon dates can be run on anything organic, but some materials are better than others. Carbon, as charcoal, is perhaps the most common material dated. The wood species is identified, and root hairs or other obvious organic contaminants are removed. The archaeologist then sends the sample to one of the world's 130 radiocarbon labs, along with appropriate contextual data.

The lab pretreats the carbon with one of several protocols to remove any other contaminants. The sample might be physically crushed, dispersed in de-ionized water, and then washed first with hot hydrochloric acid to remove carbonates and then with an alkali wash (NaOH) to remove organic acids. Such pretreatment is

half-life The time required for half of the carbon-14 available in an organic sample to decay; originally set at 5568 years, it was later changed to 5730 years.

important because even slight contamination can significantly alter the measured date of a sample.

After pretreatment, the lab counts the amount of ^{14}C in the sample by using a scintillation or ionization detector (think of them as very sophisticated Geiger counters), which counts the number of beta emissions over a measured interval of time. The emission rate is high for young samples, lower for older ones. By using an established equation, the lab converts the measured rate of beta emissions to an age.

What the Lab Can Tell You The archaeologist who submitted the sample will eventually receive a detailed report from the radiocarbon lab. Here's one date Kelly got on a carbon sample from the Pine Spring site in southwestern Wyoming:

Beta-122584   6510 ± 70 BP

The alphanumeric string records the laboratory and sample number: Beta Analytic (a radiocarbon lab in Florida), sample number 122584. The second part estimates the age of the sample in radiocarbon years BP (recall from Chapter 1 that this means "before present"). Therefore, the radiocarbon lab told us this about the Pine Spring sample: A plant died and burned about 6510 *radiocarbon years* before AD 1950.

Why "radiocarbon years"? Labs measure samples in radiocarbon years, not calendar years. As we will see, radiocarbon dating has some biases, and the raw laboratory date must be corrected to reflect actual calendar years. We'll return to this later.

Why 1950? In radiocarbon dating, the present is defined as AD 1950—the year Libby invented the method. The reason is that "the present" soon becomes the past, so we need a standard that keeps still. This means that a date of, say, 1000 BP obtained in the year 1960 is actually about 1060 years old in the year 2010 (add 60 years because 2010 is 60 years after AD 1950).

Can You Handle the Uncertainty? So far, so good. But remember that the lab report attached "± 70" to the age estimate. The decay process of ^{14}C is a statistical process, and the number of beta emissions is not constant over short periods, though it averages out over the half-life. For this reason, the lab measures the

number of beta emissions many time and then averages those to get an age. In Beta-122584, the number 6510 is the mean of the lab's measurements.

The counting process also produces a standard deviation, read as "plus or minus 70" in this case, which estimates the degree of consistency among the counting runs. The standard deviation expresses the range within which the true date falls. We know from statistical theory that there is a 68 percent chance that the true date falls within one standard deviation on either side of the mean date. So, by adding and subtracting 70 years from the age estimate, we know that there is a 68 percent chance that the true age of the carbon falls between 6440 (6510 − 70) and 6580 (6510 + 70) radiocarbon years BP. If you want to be even more certain, statistical theory tells us that there is a 95 percent chance that the actual age falls within *two* standard deviations of the mean date, which in this case means between 6370 and 6650 radiocarbon years BP.

The standard deviation must never be omitted from a radiocarbon date because without it one has no idea how precise the date is. If the standard deviation is very large, the date may be worthless (although it depends on the specific research question). Today, with appropriate field selection and preliminary processing, some radiocarbon laboratories can routinely produce dates with ± 20 year accuracy (unheard of even a few years ago).

Are All Organics Created Equal? The simple answer is no.

Bone, for example—and especially very old bone (>5000 years)—can create problems. Bone is chemically complex and contains nonorganic as well as organic components. In addition, it can be easily contaminated by younger carbon percolating in from surrounding sediments. For these reasons, bones can give dates that are older or younger than their actual ages. One way around this problem is to extract the amino acids chemically and date the carbon that is part of those organic molecules.

Plant remains are also tricky. All plants take in carbon through the process of photosynthesis, but different plant species do it differently, through one of three **photosynthetic pathways.** The first such pathway converts atmospheric carbon dioxide into a compound with three carbon atoms. This so-called C_3 pathway is characteristic of sugar beets, radishes, peas, wheat, and many hardwood trees. A second pathway converts carbon dioxide into a complex compound with four carbon atoms. This C_4 pathway typifies plants from arid and semiarid regions, including maize, sorghum, millet, yucca, and prickly pear. A third, the CAM

photosynthetic pathways The specific chemical process through which plants metabolize carbon. The three major pathways discriminate against carbon-13 in different ways; therefore, similarly aged plants that use different pathways can produce different radiocarbon ages.

pathway ("crassulacean acid metabolism") is found in succulents, such as cactus.

These different photosynthetic pathways are important because C_4 plants take in *more* ^{14}C relative to the other isotopes of carbon than do C_3 and CAM plants. Because Libby developed radiocarbon dating before this diversity in photosynthesis was known, his system uses the photosynthetic process of C_3 plants as the standard. This can create problems.

Imagine a maize plant growing next to an oak; the maize, being a C_4 plant, takes in more ^{14}C than the oak, a C_3 plant. If both die at the same time, and both are later dated by an archaeologist, the maize sample will appear to be *younger* than the oak tree by 200 to 300 years because the maize began the decay process with more radiocarbon than did the oak.

Fortunately, radiocarbon labs can correct this problem by measuring the ratio of ^{13}C to ^{12}C and normalizing the resulting date if a C_4 plant is being dated. This is why archaeologists always identify the kind of plant that they are dating.

The Reservoir Effect A second problem concerns the **reservoir effect.** Libby's method was based on the abundance of ^{14}C in the atmosphere, but some organisms obtain their carbon from sources whose carbon content may differ significantly from that of the atmosphere. Snails that live in lakes in areas of limestone will incorporate "dead" carbon (meaning the carbon source is so old that no discernible ^{14}C remains) by incorporating the limestone's carbonate into their shells. If dated, a snail that died yesterday in such a situation can appear to be hundreds, or even thousands, of years old.

Marine organisms present a similar challenge. Fish and shellfish take in carbon from the water, not the atmosphere. The ocean is a huge carbon reservoir with more "old" carbon than the atmosphere. Because the radiocarbon method is based on an atmospheric standard, marine organisms tend to date older than they actually are—by something like 400 years (although the bias varies considerably both locally and regionally). There's a related problem in dating skeletal remains of organisms that ate a lot of seafood because their skeletons reflect the composition of the foods they ate—meaning they too appear to be older than they actually are. Again, archaeologists can help labs correct this problem with sufficient background information on the sample.

Tree Rings Refine Radiocarbon Dating Libby assumed that the amount of ^{14}C in the atmosphere remains constant over time, but we now know that this is not correct.

The first investigator to find fault with Libby's atmospheric assumption was Hessel de Vries of the Netherlands. In the 1950s, de Vries cut several beams from historic buildings and determined the age of the wood by counting the rings. When he dated the known-age specimens by radiocarbon assay, he found the ^{14}C dates to be 2 percent older than expected for the known-age wood. Scientists at the time generally dismissed the work because the errors de Vries discovered were relatively small—just barely outside the limits of expected error.

But the specter of larger errors finally inspired several radiocarbon labs to look more closely into the problem. In one landmark study, Hans Suess (University of California, San Diego) analyzed wood from bristlecone pine trees. Native to the western United States, bristlecones are the world's oldest living organisms (some living specimens are 4600 years old). Working from live trees to ancient stumps, investigators had already extended the bristlecone tree-ring sequence back nearly 8200 years. Suess radiocarbon-dated dozens of known-age samples and compared the results obtained by each method. When he did so, it became clear that significant fluctuations, now known as **de Vries effects,** occurred in the atmospheric ^{14}C concentrations. There were at least 17 such fluctuations over the past 10,000 years, produced, we believe, by pulses in sunspot activity.

This tree-ring research led to the discovery that the production of ^{14}C has not remained constant over time as Libby assumed. This is generally not a big problem for dates younger than about 3500 years, but it becomes progressively worse as we move further back in time. In fact, a piece of carbon that gives a radiocarbon date of around 10,000 years is actually closer to 12,000 calendar years old.

So, the bad news is that *radiocarbon years are not the same as calendar years*. The good news is that we can fix the problem through calibration.

The fluctuations in ^{14}C are worldwide because the earth's atmosphere is so well mixed; studies made during aboveground testing of atomic bombs show that material is more or less evenly distributed throughout the atmosphere in a few years. (We say "more or less" because southern hemisphere radiocarbon dates

reservoir effect Samples from organisms that took in carbon from a source that was depleted of or enriched in carbon-14 relative to the atmosphere may return ages that are considerably older or younger than they actually are.

de Vries effects Fluctuations in the calibration curve produced by variations in the atmosphere's carbon-14 content; these can cause radiocarbon dates to calibrate to more than one calendar age.

are 24 to 40 years "too old" compared with northern hemisphere dates; that is, a sample of carbon from South Africa will give a radiocarbon age that is 24 to 40 years older than a sample from, say, Germany that is actually the same age. The land-to-ocean ratio is smaller in the southern than in the northern hemisphere, and this means that the oceans deplete the southern hemisphere's atmosphere of ¹⁴C relative to the northern hemisphere. The 24- to 40-year error is minor, and we can correct for it before calibration.)

Using tree-ring chronologies from several places in the world, as well as other corroborative sources, researchers have created a calibration curve that covers the last 45,000 calendar years (although specialists debate the accuracy beyond 25,000 years). We can now convert radiocarbon dates into calendar dates through easy-to-use programs available online. And radiocarbon labs routinely provide the calibrated date along with the conventional radiocarbon age (see "Looking Closer: How to Calibrate Radiocarbon Dates").

LOOKING CLOSER

HOW TO CALIBRATE RADIOCARBON DATES

Let's calibrate the 6510 ± 70 BP radiocarbon date mentioned in the text. We could calculate the calendar age simply by subtracting AD 1950 from 6510, since BP means "before AD 1950." This gives an answer of 4560 BC. But recall that radiocarbon years are not the same as calendar years.

The calibration curve uses tree rings of known age, removed one by one and then radiocarbon-dated. A curve is then statistically fit to the resulting data points. We use this curve to convert a radiocarbon date to its calendar age. The figure shows a portion of the calibration curve with the radiocarbon age of 6510 ± 70 BP on the *y* axis, and the corresponding calendar age on the *x* axis. The dark bar is one standard deviation on either side of the mean date; the light bar is two standard deviations. To find the calibrated calendar age, draw a line from the mean date on the *y* axis horizontally to the calibration curve, then drop down and intersect the *x* axis. The radiocarbon date of 6510 BP converts to a calendar age of 5435 BC, a difference of *875 years* from the straightforward conversion. By following the same procedure for the standard deviations, we can say that there is a

68 percent chance that the actual date lies between 5465 and 5345 BC—a span of some 120 years. That may not seem terribly precise, but for something that's more than 7000 years old, it's about as good as it gets.

Some dates are difficult to calibrate. The de Vries effects can cause a radiocarbon date to calibrate to more than one calendar date. Nonetheless, these dates are still "absolute" in that they point to *a particular age range at a known level of probability*. Sometimes those age ranges are large; sometimes they are small. Whether they are useful depends on your research question.

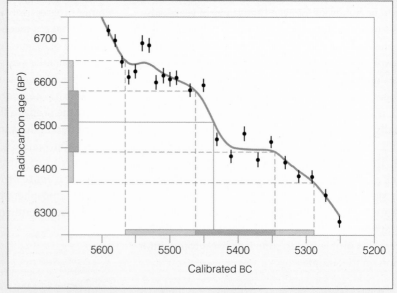

A portion of the calibration curve showing how the radiocarbon date of 6510 ± 70 BP is calibrated to a calendar age.

Calibration had an enormous effect in the Old World. In areas where writing was invented early, historical records provide a firm chronology over some 5000 years. Radiocarbon dates for the Near East and Egypt were corrected and supplemented by independent historical records. Western European chronologies, however, lacked historical evidence and were therefore arranged according to radiocarbon determinations alone. Over the years, archaeologists interpreted these data as indicating that the early traits of civilization, such as metallurgy and monumental funerary architecture, were originally developed in the Near East and later diffused into Europe, first appearing in the Mediterranean region. Near Eastern peoples appeared to be the inventors, and the "barbaric" Europeans the recipients. This, in fact, was the conclusion that Oscar Montelius reached after he used the index fossil concept to construct European chronologies. In his day, the Near East was considered the "cradle of civilization."

© Adam Woolfitt/Corbis

Figure 6-9 Stonehenge, in England. Calibrated radiocarbon dates showed that it is older than initially believed.

Radiocarbon calibration changed much of that. Colin Renfrew (Cambridge University) showed that calibration shifted most European chronologies several centuries *earlier*, altering the temporal relationships between developments in Europe and those of the Mediterranean and Near East. Archaeologists considered Stonehenge (Figure 6-9), for example, the work of Greek craftsmen who traveled to the British Isles in 1500 BC. But calibration shows that Stonehenge was actually under construction in 2750 BC and therefore predates even the Mycenaean civilization. Other calibrated dates show that monumental temples were built on the island of Malta before the pyramids of Egypt, and that the elaborate British megalithic tombs are 1000 years older than those in the eastern Mediterranean. These "corrected" radiocarbon dates suggest that western Europe was not simply a passive recipient of cultural advances from the Mediterranean, and that the Near East was not the sole "cradle of civilization."

Accelerator Dating: Taking Radiocarbon to the Limit

Some scholars see archaeology as an odd science because it progresses through unique and unrepeatable experiments. Digging remains our primary "experimental" method, and all archaeologists know that, as they dig, they are destroying data that no one has even yet thought of collecting. Before 1950, for example, archaeologists rarely saved charcoal—how could they have anticipated radiocarbon dating? This is why, today, we slowly excavate only that portion of a site necessary to answer a question, and it's why we compulsively save at least a sample of everything we find. We know that future technologies will allow us to learn things that we cannot even imagine now. New methods of radiocarbon dating demonstrate this principle.

Recall that labs obtain conventional radiocarbon dates by counting beta emissions, requiring a fairly large sample of carbon (see Table 6-2). Back in the 1970s, archaeologists were taught that you needed a "double handful" of carbon for a decent date. But often we find only small, isolated bits of carbon; we can't simply combine them because we'd then risk combining carbon of vastly different ages—which would produce an average date that would be meaningless.

The development of **accelerator mass spectrometry (AMS)** for radiocarbon dating in the 1980s alleviated this problem by drastically reducing the quantity of material required. Rather than count beta emissions, as conventional radiocarbon dating goes, accelerator technology uses an electrostatic tandem accelerator and mass spectrometry to count the *proportion* of

accelerator mass spectrometry (AMS) A method of radiocarbon dating that counts the proportion of carbon isotopes directly (rather than using the indirect Geiger counter method), thereby dramatically reducing the quantity of datable material required.

TABLE 6-2 Recommended Sample Sizes for Radiocarbon and AMS Dating

	CONVENTIONAL (grams)	AMS (milligrams)
Charcoal	10–30	20–50
Wood	15–100	20–100
Dung	10–30	20–100
Peat	10–30	30–100
Seeds	n/a	20–50
Organic sediments	200–2000	2–10 grams
Bone/antler	200	2–10 grams
Shell	20–100	50–100
Pollen	n/a	15
Water	n/a	1 liter

SOURCE: Beta Analytic Laboratory.

carbon isotopes in a sample. Because a single gram of modern organic material contains some 59 *billion* atoms of ^{14}C, a much smaller amount of material is required. AMS requires only a few milligrams of carbon—a sample about the size of a sesame seed!

This new radiocarbon method allows archaeologists to test old ideas by dating sites or objects that previously defied adequate dating. In some cases, AMS dating has corrected some significant errors. Here's one example.

How Old Is Egyptian Agriculture? In 1978, Fred Wendorf (retired, Southern Methodist University) and his research team made a remarkable discovery in southern Egypt, just west of the Nile River, in a series of small sites in Wadi Kubbaniya (a *wadi* is a dry stream drainage). The sites contained many stone tools, some large grinding stones, and the bones of fish, especially catfish and eel, and of waterfowl, wild cattle, hartebeest, and gazelle. They also found several hearths that yielded some 30 charcoal samples, dating the site between 17,000 and 18,300 years old.

Most of the food remains associated with the hearths pointed to a hunting-and-gathering population that fished, hunted, and gathered plants along what was then a sluggish stream.

What was surprising, however, were four small grains of domesticated barley and one grain of wheat. In 1978, archaeologists thought that agriculture had begun about 10,000 years ago, far to the east in places such as Iran and Iraq. But the new evidence from

Wadi Kubbaniya hinted that agriculture in the Near East was 7000 to 8000 years *older*, and in Egypt, not farther east. This was an important find.

Note that Wendorf did not directly date the few grains of wheat and barley; he could only determine their age based on their *association* with hearths containing charcoal that was dated using the conventional method. In Chapter 5, you learned that objects, especially small objects like seeds, can move around quite a bit in archaeological sites. So the question was: Were the seeds deposited at the same time that the hearths were used?

Wendorf saw no evidence that the seeds had been moved from a later level. But he knew that such movement is often hard to see. It would be vastly better to date the small wheat and barley seeds directly, but even if lumped together, the sample would be too small for the conventional radiocarbon method.

Wendorf is a cautious archaeologist, and he knew that his claim required further testing. In 1978, AMS dating was just under development, but Wendorf knew that it could provide a test of the conventional radiocarbon dates. So he submitted four barley seeds for analysis along with some charcoal from the hearths as a control; these were among some of the first archaeological samples dated with the new technique. As before, the charcoal dated between 17,500 and 19,000 years old, but all the barley seeds were *younger than 5000 years*. Obviously, the barley seeds (and presumably the lone wheat seed as well) were contaminants that had somehow worked their way down from a more recent level. Admirably, Wendorf quickly published a retraction of his earlier claim. Were it not for AMS dating, our understanding of the origins of agriculture might be quite different—and wrong.

Because AMS dating provides reliable dates on extremely small samples, archaeologists can now date objects previously held back due to ethical considerations (see "Looking Closer: Is the Shroud of Turin the Burial Cloth of Christ?").

But AMS dating is not a panacea. Archaeologists initially thought that AMS would push the radiocarbon barrier back to 100,000 or more years, but that hasn't happened—at least not yet. Although researchers keep trying, today AMS cannot reliably date anything that is older than about 45,000 years. To do this, we need other methods.

Trapped Charge Dating

Those other methods include three—thermoluminescence, optically stimulated luminescence, and electron spin resonance—that are jointly known as

LOOKING CLOSER

IS THE SHROUD OF TURIN THE BURIAL CLOTH OF CHRIST?

Accelerator dating has uses beyond its original one. Musicians, for instance, are turning to AMS technology to detect fakes, such as fraudulent Stradivarius violins.

AMS dating grabbed headlines when it was applied to the Shroud of Turin, thought by many to be the cloth in which Christ's crucified body had been wrapped. Although the Roman Catholic Church never officially proclaimed the shroud to be Christ's burial cloth, 3 million of the faithful filed past the shroud when it was displayed in the Cathedral of St. John the Baptist in 1978. Many believed they had looked into the face of Christ. What did they see?

The shroud itself is a simple linen cloth, about 14 feet long and a yard wide. On it appears a pale sepia-tone image of the front and back of a naked man about 6 feet tall. Pale stains of presumed blood mark wounds to the head, side, hands, and feet. Some believe the shroud to be a relic of Christ's Passion. But since the fourteenth century, others have said that the shroud is a cruel, if clever, hoax.

Over the years, scientists have examined the shroud in detail, photographing it under various lights, bombarding it with x-rays, peering at it microscopically. But they could not arrive at a clear conclusion. If the shroud was a fraud, it was a darned clever one.

Radiocarbon dating could help settle the issue, because for the shroud to even possibly be Jesus' burial cloth, it had to be about 2000 years old. If it were a fourteenth-century hoax, then it would be only some 600 years old. Conventional radiocarbon dating would have destroyed a handkerchief-sized piece of the shroud, and church authorities rejected all such requests. But because AMS requires only a minuscule sample, the Pontifical Academy of Sciences agreed in 1984 to such dating.

The face on the Shroud of Turin.

Postage-stamp-sized pieces of the shroud were sent to three different radiocarbon laboratories, along with control specimens of various known ages. Only British Museum officials, who coordinated the research, knew which specimen was which. When the owner of the shroud, Pope John Paul II, was informed of the outcome, his response was simple: "Publish it."

And so they did. In October 1988, a gathering of ecclesiastical and technological specialists solemnly announced that all three laboratories agreed that the flax plants from which the linen in the shroud was made had been grown in medieval times—between AD 1260 and 1390—long after the death of Jesus.

Mystery still surrounds the shroud, since nobody can explain how the image was created using medieval technology, but one thing is clear: Radiocarbon dating has resolved a controversy that spanned five centuries. The Shroud of Turin cannot possibly be the authentic burial cloth of Jesus.

trapped charge dating. Although rarely applied 20 years ago, trapped charged dating methods are increasingly common in archaeology today. Their ultimate age ranges are unknown, but they extend back at least 300,000 years.

trapped charge dating Forms of dating that rely on the fact that electrons become trapped in minerals' crystal lattices as a function of background radiation. The age of the specimen is the total radiation received divided by the annual dose of radiation.

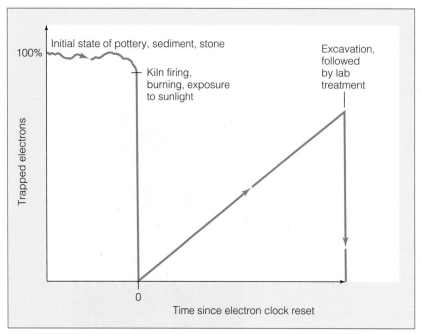

Figure 6-10 The process of setting an object's clock to zero in trapped charge dating. An object begins with some number of trapped electrons that is "reset" to zero when the object is heated or exposed to sunlight. The object then slowly gathers more trapped electrons through time due to background radiation. Its clock is again reset in the lab, where the number of trapped electrons is estimated to calculate the object's age.

The geochemical basis for these methods is complex, but we'll simplify. The same principle underlies all three techniques: Over time, background gamma radiation (generated primarily by uranium, thorium, and a radioactive isotope of potassium) in sediment causes some electrons of the atoms of certain minerals, notably quartz and feldspar, to move to a different energy state. When this happens, some electrons are "trapped" in atomic imperfections in the minerals' crystal lattices (Figure 6-10). As time passes, an increasing number of electrons are trapped in this way.

Assuming a constant radiation dose over time, electrons will be trapped at a constant rate. If we could somehow measure the number of electrons trapped in the crystal lattice, we could estimate the *total* radiation dose an archaeological object has received over time. If we then knew the *annual* background radiation dose, we could calculate a specimen's age simply by dividing

dosimeter A device to measure the amount of gamma radiation emitted by sediments. Often a short length of pure copper tubing filled with calcium sulfate, it is normally buried in a stratum for a year to record the annual dose of radiation.

thermoluminescence A trapped charge dating technique used on ceramics and burned stone artifacts—anything mineral that has been heated to more than 500° C.

the first measure by the second. How might we calculate these values?

We figure the annual dose by burying a radiation-measuring device, called a **dosimeter,** in an archaeological site and retrieving it a year later. The device records the amount of radiation exposure over a year's time.

To determine a specimen's total radiation dose, we need to measure the number of trapped electrons in that specimen. Obviously, we can't just count them, but several methods can achieve this. The three different techniques are partially distinguished by the methods used to determine the total radiation dose, as well as the kinds of material that they date. To understand *how* we can measure the total radiation dose, you must first understand *what* it is that trapped charge techniques measure.

Electrons that are moved *out* of their orbits (that is, trapped) by background radiation are *returned* to their orbits by heat (500° centigrade) or by exposure to even a few minutes of sunlight. By applying heat or light, we can reset a specimen's clock to zero, so to speak, and the slow trapping process will begin again. So, strictly speaking, *trapped charge dating identifies the last time a specimen had its electron traps emptied.* Knowing this tells us how to apply the different techniques.

Thermoluminescence (TL) measures the total radiation dose by heating a specimen rapidly to 500° centigrade. Trapped electrons in quartz and feldspar crystals slip free and move back to their orbits. When they do, they release energy in the form of light. The lab measures the amount of light released as the specimen is heated, thereby measuring the total radiation dose. Like radiocarbon dating, trapped charge dating generates a mean age estimate with a standard deviation.

Archaeologists use TL to date ceramics. Imagine a ceramic pot, consisting of clay with some sand added to give the pot strength. The sand contains quartz and feldspar that have been slowly accumulating trapped electrons. When that pot is fired, those traps are emptied, and the pot's clock is reset. Eventually, the pot breaks and its sherds are discarded. Once those sherds become buried, the quartz and feldspar are exposed to gamma radiation and begin to collect trapped charges again. When the sample is reheated under laboratory conditions (a small portion of the specimen has to be destroyed for analysis), the intensity of the light emission measures the number of electrons that were trapped between the two episodes of heating—in the original fire and in the lab. The time between when a pot was fired and its burial is usually unimportant. The method is also used to date burned stone artifacts because heat resets the TL clock of the minerals in the stone. After the stone cools and is buried, its minerals are subjected to background radiation and electrons begin to be trapped again.

The artifact's context is critical because the archaeologist cares about the age of the artifact, which may or may not coincide with the events that trapped charge methods date. If a stone tool was accidentally burned 1000 years after its manufacture, for instance, TL will date the age of the burning, not the age of the artifact's manufacture. Still, if we pay attention to context, trapped charge dating can potentially rewrite prehistory because it can date objects that radiocarbon cannot and because it can date objects that are beyond the range of radiocarbon.

Archaeologists Ofer Bar-Yosef (Harvard University) and Bernard Vandermeersch (University of Bordeaux) employed this technique to challenge our understanding of human evolution. The transition between **Neanderthals** and modern *Homo sapiens* was for many years based on the chronology of western Europe, where *Homo sapiens* replaced Neanderthals about 40,000 years ago. But for various reasons, Bar-Yosef suspected that "archaic *Homo sapiens*" (so-called because their skulls appear to be transitional between earlier hominins and biologically modern humans) had appeared earlier in the Near East. Excavating the site of Qafzeh in Israel (Figure 6-11), Bar-Yosef and Vandermeersch found strata containing skeletal remains of archaic *Homo sapiens* along with stone tools, some of which had burned in hearths. Tests showed that these strata were beyond the range of radiocarbon dating and hence must be at least 45,000 years old—older than their western European counterparts.

But how much older? TL dating provided the answer. Dating a series of the stone tools, Bar-Yosef found that the artifacts had burned some 92,000 ± 5000 years ago, much earlier than the European chronology. While the date's standard deviation may seem large, it's only 5 percent of the mean age estimate. Assuming that the tools were made by archaic *Homo sapiens*, this suggests that modern humans appeared much earlier in the Near East than in Europe.

© Ofer Bar-Yosef

Figure 6-11 The cave site of Qafzeh (Israel).

Optically Stimulated Luminescence Another trapped charge dating technique, **optically stimulated luminescence** (OSL), is finding a home in archaeology because it can date our most common material—dirt.

OSL dating relies on the fact that some of the trapped electrons are sensitive to sunlight as well as to heat. Sand grains of quartz and feldspar have their clocks reset (a process referred to as bleaching) in a matter of minutes as they are exposed to sunlight when they blow through the air; once buried, they begin accumulating trapped electrons again. *OSL therefore dates the time when the sands were buried.* Although OSL can be used on a variety of sediments, eolian sands are the best because they are more likely to have

Neanderthals (or Neandertals) Hominins who lived in Europe and the Near East about 300,000 to 30,000 years ago; biological anthropologists debate whether Neanderthals were in the direct evolutionary line leading to *Homo sapiens*.

optically stimulated luminescence A trapped charge dating technique used to date sediments; the age is the time elapsed between the last time a few moments' exposure to sunlight reset the clock to zero and the present.

been sufficiently bleached by sunlight (and thus have their clocks reset) than alluvial or colluvial sands.

Instead of measuring luminescence through the application of heat, OSL does this by passing light of a particular wavelength over the specimen. This causes light-sensitive electrons to emit their own light as they return to orbit, and it's the intensity of that light that measures the total radiation dose. This technique, by the way, requires some special handling because the archaeologist must take soil samples in such a way that the samples are not exposed to sunlight, usually by hammering a steel tube into sediments and capping it.

OSL offers enormous potential to archaeologists because it dates dirt itself, but we still must be careful about contamination. Archaeologists learned this lesson at Jinmium Rockshelter in Australia.

Named after a female character in an Aboriginal Dreamtime myth (who turned herself into stone to evade a lover), Jinmium Rockshelter is a lone block of sandstone that Native Australians used as a temporary shelter for thousands of years. While there, they painted its ceiling with pictures of kangaroos and other animals.

For years, available evidence suggested that people first occupied Australia about 40,000 years ago. So the archaeological community was shocked when thermoluminescence dates on Jinmium's sediments dated to 175,000 years. What's more, red ocher, a stone commonly used to make red pigment, appeared in Jinmium sediments that TL dated to 75,000 years. If true, Jinmium was the site of the world's oldest art!

But many archaeologists were skeptical. So a new team, headed by Richard Roberts (La Trobe University), decided to try the then new method of OSL on the shelter's sediments. Why? Simply put, some electrons have their clocks reset quickly, after only a few minutes' exposure to sunlight. Others require hours or even days of exposure. OSL measures the signal from the quick-bleaching electrons, and TL measures the signal from slow-bleaching electrons. This means that TL dates on sediments could be too old because they might measure the signal from electrons that were not fully bleached—whose clocks were not fully reset—before they were slowly buried by the winds that carried sands into the shelter.

This turned out to be a problem at Jinmium. As the wind blew, the sandstone block eroded, grain by grain.

Those grains had had their clocks reset millions of years ago. Deposited in the shelter's shade, the slow-bleaching electrons were not exposed to sufficient sunlight to have their clocks fully reset, and these contaminated the samples that the first team of archaeologists dated with TL. The problem is identical to combining carbon samples of different ages. Even if only 1 or 2 percent of the grains in a sample were from the sandstone block, TL would produce misleadingly early dates.

So Roberts's team redated the sediments *grain by grain* using OSL. The OSL technique guaranteed that they were dating the last time the grain had its clock fully reset, and dating each individual quartz grain allowed them to discover some anomalously early dates. Grain-by-grain dating is the standard today, and a single OSL date is actually the result of 1000 dates on quartz grains from a single sample. The redating of Jinmium's sediments, backed up by AMS radiocarbon dates, showed that human occupation at the site was less than 10,000 years old, and the site's claim to fame fell by the wayside.

Electron Spin Resonance Our final trapped charge dating method is **electron spin resonance** (ESR), whose primary archaeological application is the dating of tooth enamel.

Ninety-six percent of tooth enamel consists of the mineral hydroxyapatite, which contains no trapped charges when formed. But once the tooth is deposited in the ground, it accumulates charges from background radiation. To measure those trapped charges, part of the specimen is exposed to electromagnetic radiation, which resets the electrons. In this case, the total radiation dose is proportional to the amount of microwave energy absorbed by the specimen.

ESR dating has also challenged our understanding of human evolution. As we noted previously, the European chronology showed that modern humans rapidly replaced Neanderthals about 40,000 years ago. But when ESR was applied to tooth enamel of animals found in strata containing evidence of *Homo sapiens* and Neanderthals at Qafzeh in Israel, as well as at three nearby cave sites (Tabun, Skhul, and Kebara), the dates showed that *Homo sapiens* existed as early as 120,000 years ago, and Neanderthals as late as 60,000 years ago. This means that for a long period of time, perhaps as long as 60,000 years, modern humans and Neanderthals existed side by side—a different scenario than in western Europe, where they overlapped for much less time.

Trapped charge dating techniques can date objects that are beyond the range of radiocarbon dating. But we must remember that we are dating *the last time*

electron spin resonance A trapped charge technique used to date tooth enamel and burned stone tools; it can date teeth that are beyond the range of radiocarbon dating.

that the clock was reset—by light in the case of OSL and by heat in the case of TL (neither seems to affect ESR measurements). And like radiocarbon dating, these techniques date accurately to a range of years, not a single year.

Argon-Argon

Archaeologists use a host of other radiometric dating techniques that, like radiocarbon dating, are based on radioactive isotopic decay. Because these radioactive isotopes have extremely long half-lives, they are useful only for dating materials that are hundreds of thousands or millions of years old. This means that they are generally used to date rock. These dating methods are important for archaeologists who work in Africa and other places where early human remains are found that are hundreds of thousands, if not several million, years old. We'll limit ourselves to one of these methods, **argon-argon dating.**

To understand argon-argon dating, you first must know about its progenitor, potassium-argon dating. Many rocks, including volcanic ones, contain traces of potassium, which, like carbon, occurs naturally in several isotopic forms. One of these isotopes, potassium-40 (^{40}K), decays slowly, with a half-life of 1.31 *billion* years, into argon-40 (^{40}Ar), an inert, stable gas—hence the name potassium-argon dating. By comparing the relative proportions of these potassium and argon isotopes in a sample, we can determine its age. As with radiocarbon dating, the principle is simple: The more ^{40}Ar in a sample relative to ^{40}K, the older that sample is.

For potassium-argon dating to work, there must have been no argon trapped at the time of rock formation. As with trapped charge dating methods, a rock's argon-accumulating clock must have been reset to zero, so that all argon is the result of potassium decay. Fortunately, during major volcanic eruptions, high temperatures drive all gases—including ^{40}Ar—out of the microscopic rock crystals. Therefore, all ^{40}Ar present in an ash today must have accumulated since the ash was ejected from the volcano, as a result of the decay of ^{40}K. Accurate dating also requires that all argon be retained in the rock structure without loss to the atmosphere. Because some rocks "leak" argon, we must be careful in deciding which rock types to date using potassium-argon.

This is why volcanic ash deposits are so useful. If an archaeologist finds human fossils or stone tools just *below* a layer of volcanic ash, the law of superposition tells us that the potassium-argon method will provide

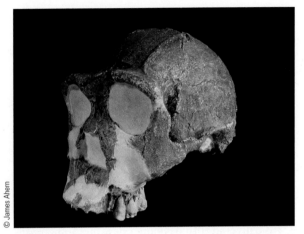

Figure 6-12 A 1.8-million-year-old *Homo erectus* skull (KNM-ER 3733, from Koobi Fora, Kenya).

© James Ahern

a *minimum* age estimate for the tools and fossils contained in the archaeological stratum below. Find fossils between two layers of volcanic ash deposits, and you bracket the age of the archaeological material (although you can't date the archaeological material itself). This is how archaeologists dated the Laetoli footprints that we discussed in Chapter 5.

The maximum age range of potassium-argon dating is theoretically the age of the earth—some 5 billion years. Although this method is not as precise as radiocarbon dating, its results are close enough for some critically important early sites in Africa and elsewhere.

For example, potassium-argon dating was used to estimate the age of ***Homo erectus,*** an early hominin, in southeast Asia. For decades, investigators believed that *Homo erectus* evolved exclusively in Africa, the earliest fossils being slightly less than 2 million years old (Figure 6-12). Then, sometime after 1.5 million years ago, *Homo erectus* expanded out of Africa, colonizing other parts of the Old World.

This is why human paleontologists were shocked in 1971 when Garniss Curtis (University of California, Berkeley) used potassium-argon to date the sediments associated with an infant *Homo erectus* skull from Mojokerto, Java. Because Java is a long way from Africa, most investigators thought that the Mojokerto skull should be much younger than a million years. But

argon-argon dating A high-precision method for estimating the relative quantities of argon-39 and argon-40 gas; used to date volcanic ashes that are between 500,000 and several million years old.

Homo erectus A hominin who lived in Africa, Asia, and Europe between 2 million and 500,000 years ago. These hominins walked upright, made simple stone tools, and may have used fire.

Curtis estimated that it was nearly twice that age—1.9 million years old. Most paleontologists rejected this extraordinarily ancient age because they were convinced that the only hominins in the world prior to 1 million years ago lived in Africa.

Both these early dates and the dating technique itself were criticized. Although potassium-argon dating had been around for decades, the laboratory methods were cumbersome, and the process required a large sample that increased the chance for contamination (in a manner analogous to Jinmium's initial TL dates).

So Curtis teamed up with Carl Swisher (Arizona State University) to develop a new method, argon-argon dating, that simplifies the lab process and avoids the contamination problem by using small samples. The method works by irradiating the volcanic crystals. When a neutron penetrates the potassium nucleus, it displaces a proton, converting the potassium into ^{39}Ar, an "artificial" isotope not found in nature. The minute quantities of artificially created argon and naturally occurring ^{40}Ar are then measured to estimate the ratio of potassium to ^{40}Ar. This high-precision method allows investigators to focus on single volcanic crystals, which can be dated one by one; thus, any older contaminants can be discarded.

In 1992, Curtis and Swisher used the argon-argon method to date volcanic pumice obtained from the matrix inside the braincase of the Mojokerto fossil.

The result was virtually the same as the "old-fashioned" potassium-argon date: 1.8 million ± 40,000 years. While these dates remain controversial, it is clear that dating techniques such as the argon-argon method will be increasingly important in evaluating fossil evidence in the years to come.

WHAT DO DATES MEAN?

These are just some of the ways that archaeologists can date sites—there are many others. It is important to keep in mind what materials the different techniques date, how far back in time they can extend, and what events the techniques actually date (summarized in Table 6-3) because these factors are necessary to answering the most important question of all: *What do the dates mean?*

We can never date archaeological sites by simple equivalences. The radiocarbon lab, for instance, takes a chunk of charcoal and tells you how long ago that tree died. By itself, this date says nothing important about your site. However, if we can show that the charcoal came from a tree used as a roof beam in a pueblo, then we have a date that matters.

In every case, you must demonstrate that the dated event is contemporaneous with a behavioral event of interest—such as building a house, cooking a meal,

TABLE 6-3 Summary of Absolute Dating Methods			
TECHNIQUE	**TARGET MATERIAL**	**RANGE OF ACCURACY**	**COMMENTS**
Dendrochronology	Wood, as carbon, roof beams, firewood	Depends on length of sequence; back to about 2000 years in the American Southwest	Useful only on particular species of trees. Sequence cannot be extended beyond the region it was developed in.
Carbon-14	Any organic material; carbon the most common	To 45,000 BP	Requires calibration; calibration curve reliable to only about 11,000 years. Accelerator mass spectrometry permits dating of minute samples.
Thermoluminescence	Ceramics, burned stone	Unknown, but perhaps back to 300,000 years	Dates the last time an object was heated to 500° centigrade.
Optically stimulated luminescence	Quartz, feldspars in eolian sands	Unknown, but perhaps back to 300,000 years	Dates the last time sand was exposed to sunlight sufficient to empty the electron traps. Samples must avoid sunlight; lab must date individual grains.
Electronic spin resonance	Tooth enamel, burned stone tools, corals, shells	10,000 to 300,000 or more years	Dates when a tooth was buried. Electron traps reset by exposure to electromagnetic radiation in the lab.
Argon-argon	Volcanic ash	200,000 to several million years	Dates the eruption that produced the ash. Needs small sample.

Figure 6-13 The pyramids at Giza.

© Charles & Josette Lenars/CORBIS

killing a deer, or making a pot. We can drive this point home by examining a common issue of radiocarbon dating: the **old wood problem.**

How Old Are the Pyramids?

When most people hear the word "archaeology," they think of Egypt's pyramids (Figure 6-13)—with good reason. They are impressive structures, especially the three that stand watch over modern Cairo on the Giza Plateau. One of these, the pyramid of Khnum-khuf ("the god Khnum is his protection"; often abbreviated to Khufu or, in Greek, *Cheops*) is the largest in Egypt. Made of some 2,300,000 blocks of stone, each weighing an average of two and a half tons, the pyramid measures 230 meters (756 feet) on a side and is oriented only 3 minutes and 6 seconds off true north. It contains several interior passageways and three chambers—one at the end of a tunnel cut into the bedrock deep below the structure. The burial chamber, in the center of the pyramid, has several roofs above it; the Egyptians specifically engineered this roof to distribute the weight of the overlying rock outward and prevent the chamber from being crushed. The pyramid's exterior was originally covered in polished white limestone, making it a landmark for miles

around (the limestone was scavenged by later pharaohs). At 146 meters (481 feet), Khufu's pyramid was the world's tallest permanent building until the Eiffel Tower was built in 1889! It is a remarkable piece of architectural engineering.

But how old is it? The ages of the pyramids are based on historical documents—the hieroglyphs that cover the insides of tombs and temples (and that are found on papyrus used to stuff the bulls, crocodiles, ibexes, and other animals that were mummified and buried in the pyramids and other structures). The hieroglyphs give us the dates of the reigns of kings and document their accomplishments. The Egyptian civilization is probably one of the best dated in the world, and the pyramids on the Giza Plateau outside Cairo are among the oldest in Egypt. From these hieroglyphs, we surmise that Khufu began building his tomb soon after his reign began in 2551 BC.

But some people speculate that the pyramids are actually thousands of years older, built by a civilization some 10,000 years ago. To check the ages based on historical documents, a consortium of archaeologists

old wood problem A potential problem with radiocarbon (or tree-ring) dating in which old wood has been scavenged and reused in a later archaeological site; the resulting date is not a true age of the associated human activity.

PROFILE OF AN ARCHAEOLOGIST

AN ACADEMIC ARCHAEOLOGIST

Chapurukha (Chap) M. Kusimba is Curator of African Archaeology and Ethnology at the Field Museum of Natural History (Chicago).

Chap Kusimba.

I became interested in the natural history of East Africa when, as a youth in Kenya, I learned of the discoveries of Louis and Mary Leakey at Olduvai Gorge in neighboring Tanzania. I was intrigued by claims that East Africa was the cradle of humankind and fascinated by the idea that all humankind ultimately traced its beginnings to Africa. The fact that there was so much to discover in my own backyard shaped the way I viewed my heritage and encouraged my interest in becoming a scientist.

From 1986 to 1996, I focused my attention on understanding how the communities of the East African Coast had developed into complex coastal chiefdoms and city states over the past 2000 years.

The study of social complexity has long been contentious in Africa. Assuming that Africans could not be innovative, previous scholars credited social complexity and "high culture" to immigrants from Southwest Asia. Today, African archaeologists reject this explanation, and look instead to the specific processes of development.

My research focuses on the role of technology, economy, and Indian Ocean trade in the development of chiefdoms and states in East Africa. I have conducted regional

in 1984, led by Shawki Nakhla and Zahi Hawass (the Egyptian Minister of Antiquities), decided to radiocarbon date the pyramids. But what could they date? The pyramids are made of stone, and the organic remains buried in them were often treated with tar and chemicals that make them unreliable for radiocarbon dates.

But Nakhla and Hawass knew of another source of carbon. Contrary to popular belief, the pyramids were put together with mortar. Workmen made this mortar by burning gypsum, apparently on the work platforms that were erected around the pyramid as it was being constructed. They mixed the resulting ash with water and sand and then slopped the mortar into the cracks between the massive blocks of stone. Pieces of carbon were caught in the mortar, and trapped there for eternity.

In 1984 and 1985, the Egyptian archaeological teams scrambled over the pyramids like ants on an anthill, looking for fingernail-sized bits of carbon. They found quite a few pieces, dated them using the AMS method, and then calibrated the dates.

They found not a shred of evidence that the pyramids were thousands of years older than the documentary sources indicate. But what they found still surprised them: The radiocarbon dates on Old King-

dom (4575–4134 BP) pyramids were from 100 to 400 years *older* than the documentary dates suggested. But later Middle Kingdom pyramids (4040–3640 BP) were not far off from their accepted ages. Why were the Old Kingdom dates "too old"?

The first explanation was the "old wood" problem: In desert (or high-altitude or arctic) environments, wood can lie around without decaying for a long time. In California's White Mountains, you can make a fire today from bristlecone wood, send a piece of the charcoal to a lab, and be told that your fire was 2000 years old. The wood *is* 2000 years old—but the fire that made the charcoal is not.

Egyptian archaeologists thought this "old wood" problem was unlikely. By Old Kingdom times, the Nile River valley had been occupied for millennia by a large population. Excavations near the pyramids reveal a community of stoneworkers, builders of the pyramids, that housed 20,000 people. All the Nile's people cooked over wood and used wood in house construction. And there is not much wood to begin with along the Nile; the floodplain is rich, but it's a narrow strip of green in a vast, treeless desert. For these reasons, archaeologists postulated that there could have been no old wood lying along the Nile.

archaeological surveys and problem-oriented excavations in key locales and sites in southeastern Kenya. Some of the results appear in my book, *The Rise and Fall of Swahili States*, a text on the archaeology of social complexity in Africa.

With a few exceptions, all sites on the Kenya coast are large urban centers with monumental structures composed of elite residences, chiefly courts, and mosques. This inevitably introduced significant biases in data collection and influenced the rendering of the regional history.

But we cannot ignore the relationship between urban areas and their trading partners in the hinterlands. And so, beginning in 1998, Dr. Sibel Barut Kusimba (Northern Illinois University) and I began to examine the role of trade in shaping East Africa's diverse ethnic identities. We did this by surveying areas in the Tsavo National Park and surrounding area, 150 kilometers from Kenya's eastern coast. We described more than 200 sites, from the Early Stone Age into the historic era, including hunter-gatherer rockshelter camps and residences, pastoral, agropastoral, and agrarian villages and chiefdom-level settlements, fortified stockades, market centers, and iron production areas.

An important pattern emerging from our research is the web of social interactions among peoples of diverse origins and languages practicing and inventing different ways of life. The Tsavo region was a mosaic of political and economic alliances, an example of regional systems that exist in many areas of the world but are not completely understood. Understanding the development of social complexity in Africa requires attention to such regional interactions. Indeed, the mosaic is important to us not just as grist for the archaeologist's mill, but as a reservoir for potentially understanding Africa's future because Africa's modern dynamics of ethnicity, social, and political power are rooted in these earlier interactions.

But perhaps Egyptians found another source of old wood. The Old Kingdom's construction projects at Giza were massive: three huge and several small pyramids, associated temples, boat docks on the Nile, the Sphinx, and the workers' quarters. These projects required massive amounts of wood—for construction; for ovens to bake bread for the workers; for levers, wedges, and sledges to move the stone blocks; for scaffolding; and for firewood to produce the mortar.

To get all the wood needed, it is likely that Khufu and other pharaohs raided older settlements or looted their predecessors' temples and tombs for wood—which Egypt's dry climate would preserve for hundreds, even thousands, of years. We know that pharaohs raided earlier temples and tombs for construction material and jewelry. Perhaps for these Old Kingdom projects, they also sought out firewood. This may account for the early dates on Old Kingdom pyramids.

But then, why were the Middle Kingdom radiocarbon dates not "too old"? By Middle Kingdom times, Nakhla and Hawass reasoned, earlier construction projects had depleted the sources of old wood, and Middle Kingdom builders had to make do with the wood at hand—which would not have been very old.

The old wood problem is a common one. At Betatakin, for example, Jeffrey Dean found that beams were scavenged from old rooms and incorporated into new rooms. In Alaska, archaeologists found that the driftwood used in some structures had apparently lain on the shore for a century before being used. In both cases, the dates (tree-ring or radiocarbon) would be older than the cultural behavior of interest.

The more general point here is important: Every absolute dating technique dates a particular event, but the archaeologist must decide how the date of that event relates to the age of human behavior.

THE CHECK, PLEASE

How an archaeologist excavates a site depends on several factors, one of them being cost. None of these dating methods is cheap. Right now, a standard radiocarbon date runs about $300, an AMS date costs about $600, and bone dates can run as high as $850. Tree-ring dates are cheaper—the University of Arizona's Tree-Ring Lab charges about $25 per sample. TL and OSL dates may cost $800 apiece. There are no commercial rates for the other trapped charge and radiometric dating methods, but they have hidden costs. Because so much background information is required for their successful implementation, it is often necessary to finance a visit to the site by the specialist and cover additional sediment studies.

Archaeologists try to get as many dates as they can for a site, but they always have to do so within budget limitations.

DATING IN HISTORICAL ARCHAEOLOGY

As we pointed out in Chapter 1, historical archaeology is a rapidly growing subfield of archaeology. Sometimes, historical archaeologists work on sites whose ages are well known; for example, there is no question about when Jefferson's home at Monticello was built and occupied. But often they work on sites that are not documented, and these sites need to be dated. Dendrochronology is sometimes used, but radiometric and trapped charge techniques are not. Even with small standard deviations, these methods are not sufficiently precise to be useful to historical archaeology. If we already know that a Spanish settlement in Florida was occupied sometime in the sixteenth century, a radiocarbon date on the site of AD 1550 ± 25 would tell us that there is a 96 percent chance that the site was occupied sometime between AD 1500 and 1600—and we already knew that.

For this reason, historical archaeologists employ their own dating methods. They use documented changes in technology and styles of material culture to make fine-grained use of the index fossil concept and seriation. For example, before 1830, the metal fibers in nails ran crosswise to the nail's axis; after that, the fibers ran lengthwise. Examine the nails in a site, and you can tell if it dates to before or after 1830. Likewise, nineteenth-century glass often had a purplish cast, caused by sunlight reacting with manganese in the glass, but after World War I, manufacturers stopped adding manganese. Purple glass is always older than about 1921.

Often this information is contained in industrial and other written documents, but sometimes the archaeologist has to get creative. Kathleen Deagan, for example, knew that green and clear glass bottle fragments littered sixteenth-century Hispanic sites in Florida and the Caribbean and that these artifacts could be used as time-markers. The problem was that not a single complete bottle from this period survived anywhere. Rather than give up, Deagan turned to paintings, because bottles, it turns out, are frequently depicted in sixteenth-century Spanish art. By studying these dated paintings, Deagan constructed a chronological sequence of bottle forms. By reconstructing bottle forms from the glass fragments present on sites, she could use this chronological sequence to date the sites.

Pipe Stem Dating

One clever way to date Colonial-period American sites was developed in the mid-twentieth century by J. C. "Pinky" Harrington (1901–1998). Clay tobacco pipes and broken fragments turn up by the hundreds in many Colonial-era archaeological sites. These clay pipes held great potential as time-markers because they generally broke within a year or so of their manufacture. And their shapes, decorations, stem lengths, and thicknesses changed markedly in the seventeenth and eighteenth centuries.

The difficulty in applying any of these observations to archaeological sites was that the fragile clay pipes rarely survived in a condition sufficiently complete to allow fruitful analysis. However, while working with the pipe collection from Jamestown, including some 50,000 small chunks of broken stems, Harrington observed that the early pipe stems had relatively large bores, which became smaller in the later specimens.

Measuring the stem hole diameters for 330 pipes of known age from Jamestown, Colonial Williamsburg (Virginia), and Fort Frederica (St. Simons Island, Georgia), Harrington confirmed that the inside diameter changed through time. His resulting pipe stem chronology ran from AD 1620 to 1800 and was divided into five cultural periods. Fifteen years later, Lewis Binford (see Chapter 1) reworked the original data to derive a statistical regression formula for estimating age from the size of pipe stem holes: $y = 1931.85 - 38.26x$, where x is the mean stem bore for a sample of pipe fragments and y is the projected mean date. By calculating the mean bore diameter of the pipe stems found in a site and plugging that value into the equation, we can come up with a pretty good estimate of the site's age.

Terminus Post Quem *Dating*

Dates in historical archaeology are generally of two types: Either they define a temporal cutoff point (the site cannot be any older than a particular year) or they estimate a central temporal tendency (the site's "average" age). Let us explain how each works.

Kathleen Deagan and Joan Koch excavated an important cemetery named Nuestra Señora de la Soledad

Figure 6-14
Ichtucknee Blue
on White plate,
AD 1600–1650.

© American Museum of Natural History

in downtown St. Augustine. They first classified the sherds into the various ceramic types commonly found in Spanish American sites. One such type, Ichtucknee Blue on White (Figure 6-14), is named for the surface decoration (blue designs on a white background) and the Ichtucknee River in north central Florida (where the type was first recognized). The estimated age of Ichtucknee Blue on White ceramics ranges between AD 1600 and 1650.

Deagan and Koch dated each grave pit according to the concept of ***terminus post quem*** ("limit after which") or **TPQ**, the date *after* which the object must have found its way into the ground. At Soledad, the TPQ indicates the first possible date that the latest-occurring artifact could have been deposited in that grave pit. So when a sherd of Ichtucknee Blue on White turned up in the grave fill at Soledad, excavators knew that this grave could not have been dug before AD 1600 (because Ichtucknee Blue on White did not exist before that date). Had the same grave pit contained a sherd of, say, San Luís Polychrome (with an associated age range from AD 1650 to 1750), then the TPQ date would be revised to 1650.

TPQ estimates the earliest possible date for the grave, based on the accuracy of the known date range for a particular artifact. When combined with the excavation data and documentary evidence about site usage, the TPQ estimates enabled Deagan and Koch to group the Soledad burials into three culture periods: seventeenth-century Spanish (TPQ: pre-1700), eighteenth-century Spanish (TPQ: pre-1762), and eighteenth-century British (TPQ: post-1762). Once this classification was established, they could look for cultural differences and similarities among burial assemblages. The Spanish-period burials, for example, were mostly shroud wrapped, whereas the British used coffins; the Spanish crossed the arms over the chest, whereas the British were interred with arms along the sides; Spanish burials were oriented toward the east, British toward the west; and so forth.

Mean Ceramic Dates

There is some disagreement about the utility of *terminus post quem* ceramic dating in historical archaeology. Many find the concept useful in providing a baseline for site chronology, but other archaeologists are less enthusiastic. They point to several complicating factors. For example, less is known about seventeenth-century Anglo-American ceramics, and status differences influence relative ceramic frequencies. In addition, there may be a considerable time lag between an artifact's date of manufacture and its date of deposition, making TPQ dating subject to gross error.

Stanley South (University of South Carolina) derived a provocative method to minimize these perceived problems. South's **mean ceramic date** approach emphasizes the mid-range or median age, rather than beginning and end dates for ceramic wares. Using Noël Hume's *A Guide to Artifacts in Colonial America*, South constructed a model based on selected ceramic types defined by attributes of form, decoration, surface finish, and hardness plus the temporal dates assigned by Noël Hume for each type.

South included 78 ceramic types in his formulation. Canton porcelain, for instance, was manufactured between AD 1800 and 1830. The median date for this type is thus (1800 + 1830)/2 = AD 1815. Bellarmine Brown, a salt-glazed stoneware decorated with a well-molded human face, ranges from AD 1550 through 1625; the median date is thus AD 1587. The mean ceramic date pools this information across a feature (such as a grave pit or house) or site to determine the median date of manufacture for each time-sensitive sherd and then averages these dates to arrive at the mean occupation date implied by the entire collection.

Table 6-4 shows how South calculated the mean ceramic date for sediments filling the cellar of the Hepburn-Reonalds Ruin in North Carolina. The median date of each ceramic type is weighted by multiplying each type's median date by the number of sherds found of that type. These products are then added and the total divided by the total number of sherds. South's mean ceramic date came out to be 1758.4. To test this conclusion, he compared it to available historic records. These records revealed that the building was standing in AD 1734 and burned in 1776; the median historic date is thus (1734 + 1776)/2 = AD 1755,

terminus post quem (TPQ) The date after which a stratum or feature must have been deposited or created.

mean ceramic date A statistical technique for combining the median age of manufacture for temporally significant pottery types to estimate the average age of a feature or site.

TABLE 6-4 Applying the Mean Ceramic Date Formula to the Brunswick Hepburn-Reonalds Ruin

CERAMIC TYPE	MEDIAN YEAR OF MANUFACTURE	×	SHERD COUNT	=	PRODUCT
22	1791		483		865,053
33	1767		25		44,175
34	1760		32		56,320
36	1755		55		96,525
37	1733		40		69,320
43	1758		327		574,866
49	1750		583		1,020,250
44	1738		40		69,520
47	1748		28		48,944
53, 54	1733		52		90,116
56	1733		286		495,638
29	1760		9		15,840
Totals			1960		3,446,567

$3{,}446{,}567 \div 1960 = 1758.4$

SOURCE: South 1977, Table 32. Used by permission of the author and Academic Press.

only 3½ years earlier than the median historic date. Moreover, the pipe stem date for this site is AD 1756, so substantial agreement exists among all three sources. In fact, South has found that mean ceramic dates seldom deviate beyond a range of ± 4 years from sites' known median historic dates. Such agreement is nothing short of remarkable.

The mean ceramic date relies on two assumptions: (1) that ceramic types are roughly contemporary at all sites where they occur and (2) that the mid-range date of manufacture approximates the modal date of popularity. These are, of course, some fairly large assumptions, but the method still seems to produce useful age estimates on historic-era sites.

CONCLUSION

In Chapter 1 we pointed out that archaeology underwent a revolution of sorts in the 1960s. Lewis Binford's generation brought about a transformation of the discipline. Binford, however, claimed it was the widespread availability of absolute dating methods, notably radiocarbon dating, that brought about the change in how we do archaeology. Why did he say this?

As you have seen, relative dating techniques helped to lift the fog of time that obscures the past. They were a significant advance because they helped to place objects and cultures into a historical sequence. Absolute dating techniques were an even more significant advance because they could assign artifacts to a particular year or a specific range of years. Absolute dating techniques allow us to see not only the order of events, but the rate of change as well. Why did this permit Binford's generation to change archaeology?

One reason is that absolute dating techniques freed archaeologists to do other things with their data. Instead of spending time on seriation diagrams, an archaeologist could simply send a piece of carbon to a lab for a radiocarbon date.

A more significant reason is that absolute dating techniques allowed archaeologists to control a major dimension of their data—time—in a more rigorous and absolute manner. Seriation was grounded in an often unspoken theory of culture change—material items appear, grow in popularity, then disappear. No one knew, or cared, why this happened; all that mattered was that the technique provided a way to build a chronology. But for archaeologists to transcend chronology, they needed to know more. They needed to know how rapidly an item became prevalent, or how rapidly another replaced it. They needed to know how long a piece of material culture was used—50 years, 500 years, 5000 years?

Relative dating methods could not answer these questions precisely; in fact, relative dating methods tended to carry their own answers to them. Archaeologists relying on seriation, for instance, tended to see innovations as having only one center and then spreading from there. They saw cultural change as gradual, rather than abrupt. Absolute dating methods permitted archaeologists to know when styles appeared, how quickly they spread, and whether there were multiple centers of innovation. These methods opened the door to questions about past lifeways instead of focusing simply on chronology. This is why absolute dating techniques had a large effect on archaeological paradigms.

In recent years, technology has afforded us increasingly sophisticated ways to date artifacts, sites, and strata, and these innovations show no sign of stopping (e.g., a new technique promises nondestructive radiocarbon dating). We can expect, then, that continual advances in dating methods will not only permit a greater understanding of the chronology of the past but also help create new paradigms, new ways of understanding the past.

SUMMARY

1. What is the difference between relative and absolute dating?

- Relative dating places sites, strata, features, and artifacts in relative order, without saying how much older or younger one site, stratum, feature, or artifact is than another.
- Absolute dating provides specific ages or specific age ranges. Absolute dating methods are absolute in the sense that they provide a particular age range at a known level of probability.

2. What are the major dating techniques, what materials do they date, and what is their time range?

- Tree-ring dating (dendrochronology) dates wood of particular species; it is limited to relatively small regions and usually cannot date samples that are more than 2000 years old.
- Radiocarbon dating dates any organic material using the known rate of decay of ^{14}C; it is useful for materials less than 45,000 years old.
- Trapped charge dating techniques—thermoluminescence (TL), optically stimulated luminescence (OSL), and electron spin resonance (ESR)—date ceramics or burned stone tools, eolian sediments, and tooth enamel, respectively. They date an object by calculating the amount of background radiation the object has been subjected to since the object's electron "clock" was last reset by heat (TL) or sunlight (OSL). These techniques can extend back several hundred thousand years.

- Argon-argon dates volcanic rock, especially ash. This technique can date volcanic layers that are millions of years old.

3. What are the major dating techniques of historic sites?

- Documentary evidence usually provides dates for historical sites.
- When such evidence is not available, known ages of particular artifact types are generated to create agerange or median ages for historical features or sites using TPQ and mean ceramic age dates.

4. What do archaeological dates date?

- Dating techniques tell us nothing *directly* about cultural activities. Radiocarbon dating, for example, tells us when a plant or an animal died—it is up to the archaeologist to relate the event being dated to a behavioral (cultural) event of interest.

MEDIA RESOURCES

Doing Fieldwork:
Archaeological Demonstrations CD-ROM 2.0
This CD, developed by the authors, shows professional archaeologists involved in various digs, many of which are referenced in the text. The presentation is organized by the main techniques used on an archaeological dig, reinforcing concepts and techniques via live examples. The CD takes you through each step automatically, or you can navigate to any point via the navigation bar. After reviewing a step in the dig process, you are taken to Check Points, which are concept questions about each step of the dig. Then you can see

the answers, receive your score, and even send your scores to your instructor.

The Companion Website for *Archaeology,* Sixth Edition
www.cengagebrain.com
Supplement your review of this chapter by going to the companion website to take one of the practice quizzes, use the flash cards to master key terms, and check out the many other study aids that are designed to help you succeed in your introductory archaeology course.

7 THE DIMENSIONS OF ARCHAEOLOGY: TIME, SPACE, AND FORM

LEARNING OBJECTIVES

AFTER READING THIS CHAPTER
YOU SHOULD BE ABLE TO ANSWER THESE QUESTIONS:

1. What are the principles of archaeological typology?

2. What is the strength of archaeology?

3. What role does typology play in archaeology's strength?

4. What are archaeological cultures, site components, and phases?

left, © Werner Forman/CORBIS; right, © Bowers Museum of Cultural Art/CORBIS; (four projectile points), center: © Art Resource, NY;
© (projectile point) center bottom: National Park Service, Chaco Culture National Historic Park

A collection of artifacts that can provide key time-markers in archaeology.

PREVIEW

IN THE NINETEENTH CENTURY, archaeological sites were viewed as little more than mines in which to prospect for artifacts. But professionally trained archaeologists, such as Kidder and Wormington, shifted their objectives to focus more on understanding the person behind the artifact rather than the artifact itself. And in the 1960s, archaeology further refined that focus, wishing not only to reconstruct what happened in the past, but to explain that past as well.

To achieve these objectives, archaeology analyzes how artifacts and features fall into changing patterns over space and time; this chapter shows how archaeologists identify those patterns. We first consider classification—the ways that archaeologists divide the many kinds of objects found into reasonable and useful artifact types. We then discuss the concepts of archaeological cultures, periods, phases, assemblages, and components—all of which are used to organize archaeological data into what is called *space-time systematics*.

  DOING FIELDWORK CD-ROM:
ARCHAEOLOGICAL DEMONSTRATIONS 2.0

See the "Stratigraphy" section of the CD-ROM to learn more about topics covered in this chapter.

INTRODUCTION

The title of this chapter comes from an article by archaeologist Albert Spaulding (1914–1990), who pointed out that archaeology is all about patterns in *form* (shape) of artifacts and features through *time* and across *space*. We divide the spatial and temporal continuum of reality into parcels of space and time based on differences in material culture. For example, the houses found in much of the American Southwest about 2000 years ago were semi-subterranean pithouses, usually round, covered with heavy log roofs and a layer of sod. They were warm in the winter and cool in the summer. At the same time, but in a different place—farther north in the Great Basin—houses were more ephemeral, consisting of simple windbreaks or shade structures for summer houses and conical log structures for the winter. Returning to the Southwest, we see a dramatic change in house form around 1300 years ago. At that

time, many people lived in square, aboveground masonry homes—the familiar pueblos—rather than pithouses. Back in the Great Basin, however, people continued to live in the same sort of houses that they occupied 2000 years ago. Archaeologists have spent the greater part of the last century documenting such patterns in how material culture changes through time and across space; these patterns reflect differences in human behavior and culture and therefore are what archaeologists seek to explain. How we organize these data into meaningful spatial and temporal patterns is the subject of this chapter.

This organization is vital to the field because *archaeology's major strength is its access to tremendous quantities of time and space.* Although many ethnologists study cultural evolution and culture change, they are restricted to short-term study if they deal exclusively with ethnographic evidence. Even if they include oral history or historical documents, ethnologists cannot go back in time more than a century or two. Archaeology, on the other hand, can address the entire history of humanity based on the things that people left behind, from 2.5-million-year-old stone tools in Africa to World War II destroyers on the bottom of Pacific lagoons. No other social science has so much time at its disposal.

Archaeologists also deal with worlds of "space." Many ethnologists can study a single society for years on end, but none can realistically employ the tools of ethnography to study an entire region such as the American Southwest, to say nothing of continents or hemispheres. So, what archaeology loses in detail it makes up by recording what the ethnologist cannot: patterns of human behavior as they were manifested over vast reaches of space, far beyond the confines of a single community.

The goal of archaeology is to reconstruct and explain the past: What did people do, and why did they do it? We achieve this goal through the material remains that people left behind. Therefore, our first goal is to gain a firm grasp on artifact patterning in time and space. We must know the when and the where in broader terms before contemplating the how, the who, the what, and especially the why. Defining a spatial and temporal framework requires that archaeologists date the physical remains, classify archaeological objects into useful categories, and explore their distribution across time and space. In previous chapters we've discussed the fieldwork of archaeology. In this and succeeding chapters, we move into the other half of archaeology: the part that goes on after the excavation.

AFTER THE EXCAVATION: CONSERVATION AND CATALOGING

Suppose that you've just completed a regional survey and have excavated a sample of the sites discovered. You did the survey and excavations by the book, dated the sites, studied the sites' formation processes, and so on. You've returned home with many, many carefully labeled bags full of bones, stone tools, ceramics, beads, and figurines. What happens to all this stuff now that the fieldwork is over?

The first step is to conserve the recovered materials. Once this meant little more than washing the artifacts off with water (except for things that water would obviously damage, such as basketry). But today, many archaeologists hesitate to wash some artifacts because even this simple operation might destroy some information. Stone and ceramic artifacts, for example, can contain pollen or residues of blood, plants, or other materials that can be identified and used to reconstruct tool use and diet—but not if a scrupulous lab worker has thoroughly scrubbed the piece. In general, though, a simple cleaning is in order.

Other artifacts may require more attention, especially organic or metal artifacts recovered from wet deposits. Conservation on wooden artifacts recovered from the Ozette site (see Chapter 4) began as soon as excavators removed them from the muddy matrix, because wet wooden artifacts quickly crumble as they dry out. Richard Daugherty preserved Ozette's wooden artifacts by soaking them in vats of Carbowax—polyethylene glycol—melted and diluted with water. He needed huge vats to soak the houses' cedar timbers. Some of the artifacts, especially those made of hardwoods (which have small pores and soak up liquid slowly), had to soak for years.

During an excavation near New York's Wall Street, archaeologists found several Revolutionary War–era cannons lying on the bottom of what was once the East River. The first task in preserving these artifacts was to replace the brackish water that had impregnated the metal with fresh water. Looking for watertight containers large enough to hold the bulky cannons, project directors Roselle Henn (U.S. Army Corps of Engineers) and Diana diZerega Wall (City College of New York) finally settled on metal coffins! The conservation of artifacts has become a significant specialty within archaeology (see "Looking Closer: Preserving the *Hunley*").

It may also be necessary to reconstruct broken pieces. This is frequently done with pottery because ceramics are often found in pieces, and reconstruction obviously tells us about vessel shape, size, and decoration. Piecing together a broken pot is like trying to put together a three-dimensional jigsaw puzzle with no picture on the box and some of the pieces missing. It requires a particular personality—somebody who can stay put for long hours—and a sculptor's eye. Some people can do this with ease; others are lucky if they get two pieces to fit.

The cataloging procedure, which starts at the excavation, continues in the lab after the field season is over. Every single item must be accounted for and its provenience retained through a catalog. The novice's first job in a lab is almost always cataloging: writing all those minute numbers on artifacts or labels and entering the information into a database. This can take a great deal of time. In fact, as a rule of thumb, for every week spent excavating, archaeologists spend 3 to 5 weeks or more cleaning, conserving, and cataloging the finds. Sometimes it seems mindless, but cataloging is essential because without the catalog provenience is lost, and without provenience an artifact's value to future researchers is greatly reduced.

LOOKING CLOSER

PRESERVING THE *HUNLEY*

In 1864, the Confederacy was losing the Civil War and needed to destroy the Union Navy whose blockades were strangling the South. The Confederacy thought it had the answer in a secret weapon: a small submarine designed to destroy Union vessels from beneath the waves.

The South had planned submarine warfare from the war's beginning. Funded by Horace Hunley, whose name would grace the third model, the subs were bold designs, but early versions had leakage and control problems. Even the *Hunley's* first voyages were catastrophes. It capsized on its first and second runs, losing half the first crew and the entire second crew, including Hunley himself. Nonetheless, the submarine was recovered, and a third crew stepped forward.

Crammed into a space 18 feet long and 4 feet wide, seven men propelled the *Hunley* by manually turning a crankshaft while the captain guided the sub and worked the ballast tanks that controlled depth. Two 15-inch manholes, fore and aft, were the only escape routes; a single candle lit the captain's depth gauge.

The tactic was to approach a Union ship, dive, and then ram a long, barbed spar equipped with a 90-pound explosive charge into the enemy's hull. As the sub backed away, a rope played out. At 150 feet, the rope tightened and detonated the charge.

This design worked perfectly on February 17, 1864, when the *Hunley* met the USS *Housatonic*. The Union's largest ship sank within minutes.

The *Hunley* surfaced, signaled shore, and started home. But she never made it. For reasons still unknown, she sank, killing all eight men aboard. A submarine did not sink a ship again until World War I.

The *Hunley's* location remained a mystery until persistent efforts by author Clive Cussler and archaeologists Ralph Wilbanks, Wes Hall, and Harry Pecorelli located her in 1995 (using a magnetometer towed behind a research vessel) only 30 feet below the surface. The submarine's hatches were unopened (only one viewport was broken) and the hull unbreached. Buried beneath 3 feet of silt, the sub was protected from the saltwater currents that normally destroy iron ships.

Once removed from the water, however, the ship would have quickly corroded. Chlorides from the seawater had infiltrated the iron hull; if they dried, they would form crystals that would expand and destroy the metal. To prevent this, the hull was sprayed with water from the moment it was raised until it was placed in a specially designed water-

ARCHAEOLOGICAL CLASSIFICATION

Cataloging and conservation are just the beginning, because at the end of those tasks you are faced with thousands of artifacts that differ in terms of function, style, raw material, provenience, and condition. This is where the really time-consuming part of archaeology begins.

Archaeologists get a handle on variability in material culture through **typology,** the classification of artifacts into types. Even before cataloging and conservation begin, we've already begun classifying the finds. Students will sort everything found into simple categories of stone, bone, shell, ceramic, organic, brick, cloth, wood, metal, or some other relevant category. When objects can't be identified and sorted in the field, the rule is always "When in doubt, send it to the lab."

In the lab, the cataloged artifacts are further separated into even finer categories. Stone tool analysts might sort the stone artifacts into waste flakes and tools, later sorting each into narrower categories. Ceramics may be sorted into decorated and undecorated sherds, or into rim sherds (those that preserve a bit of the vessel's rim or mouth) and body sherds. And so forth.

But then what? How should you deal with all this stuff?

Here's a clue: *The archaeologist's first responsibility is to simplify.* Generations of archaeologists have

typology The systematic arrangement of material culture into types.

filled tank. A lab now keeps the tank's fresh water at 10° C to prevent the growth of fungus and algae and to reduce the rate of corrosion. The lab also monitors the tank for pH, temperature, chlorides, conductivity, and oxygen.

After the vessel was stabilized, its interior, which had filled with silt, was excavated, and the human remains and personal effects removed (the human remains were buried in April 2004 in Charleston, South Carolina). The next question was how to preserve the *Hunley*.

Through microbial and electrochemical reactions, the vessel had developed a carbonate coating that prevented oxygen from reaching the sub's metallic surface. Without this carbonate coating, the sub would see more corrosion in six months than in the previous 136 years. Keeping this carbonate layer intact is thus critical to preservation of the vessel. But how do we preserve the *Hunley* indefinitely?

Metal artifacts are normally preserved through electrolysis—that is, by running an electric current through the water, which then removes oxygen. But this technique may not work on a long-term basis, and it may be ineffective for large objects, especially ones in which many surfaces are welded, bolted, or riveted together and made of different metals. One solution would be to dismantle

The *Hunley* submarine in drydock in Charleston, South Carolina, 1863. Oil painting by Conrad Wise Chapman (1842–1910).

the entire sub; but this option, understandably, does not excite the *Hunley*'s conservators.

An alternative is to anneal the sub through hydrogen reduction. This means baking the sub in a hydrogen furnace over a week or more, slowly raising the temperature to 1060° C. This, too, has its problems, the first being locating a furnace that is large enough and that can withstand the hydrochloric acid that is a by-product of this process. Clearly, the preservation of this important piece of American history will puzzle conservators for years to come.

found it unrealistic, even preposterous, to cope simultaneously with all the variability that turns up in a batch of archaeological objects. Anybody could write a detailed paragraph on each artifact found. While this might produce a wonderful descriptive catalog, we'd learn little. Meaning lies not in endless data, but in *patterns within those data*. And patterns appear only when you isolate some aspect of the variation and deliberately ignore the rest (for now).

So, to seek meaningful patterns, you simplify. Because archaeology's twin strengths have always been time and space, we must first develop the categories necessary to reveal patterns in material culture through time and space. Archaeologists call this **space-time systematics.** And our first step in that direction is identifying types of artifacts.

Types of Types

Archaeology's basic unit of classification is termed a **type.** Be careful here because "type," like "culture," is one of those everyday words appropriated by anthropology and reassigned a very specific, nonintuitive meaning.

Archaeologists can classify the same object in several different ways. Think about a familiar set of modern

space-time systematics The delineation of patterns in material culture through time and space. These patterns are what the archaeologist will eventually try to explain or account for.

type A class of archaeological artifacts defined by a consistent clustering of attributes.

artifacts—say, a workshop of woodworking tools. Carpenters classify their tools by function—hammers, saws, planes, files, drills, and spokeshaves. But when insuring a carpenter's workshop, the insurance agent uses another classification, sorting these same tools into new categories, such as flammable and nonflammable, or perhaps according to replacement value: "under $10," "between $10 and $25," and so on. Should the carpenter relocate, the furniture movers will group these same tools into another set of divisions, such as heavy or light, bulky or compact, or perhaps fragile or unbreakable.

There are two important points here. First, *types are abstractions* arbitrarily imposed by the archaeologist on a variable batch of artifacts. We saw in Chapter 2 how cultures classify the world differently. Dogs are considered food in some cultures, pets in others. There is nothing inherent in dogs that makes them "really" food or "really" pets. And there is nothing inherent in an artifact that makes it belong to one and only one type.

We've said before that your analysis (and the types you create) depends on your research question. Suppose, for instance, we're interested in learning whether everyone in an ancient society made pots, or if pots were made only by specialized potters. To figure this out, we find a way to classify ceramics into pots made by novices and pots made by experts, maybe by classifying the ceramics according to the quality of their construction or painting. On the other hand, if we want to know how various rooms functioned within a household, we might classify the ceramics into cooking vessels, water jars, serving vessels, and storage containers. You can classify the same object in plenty of ways.

But we do *not* necessarily try to classify things the way ancient peoples saw them. Archaeologists might divide stone scrapers into several types based on their shape (looking for useful time-markers), but people who used those same artifacts might have recognized only two kinds: stuff that's useful, and stuff that's used up. Both classifications are completely valid because each one works, depending on the interest.

There's a second point: We formulate classifications with specific purposes in mind. Archaeology has no general, all-purpose classification. Archaeologist

Irving Rouse (1913–2006) put it well: "Classification—for what?"

In Chapter 6, you saw one answer to this question: to create time-markers. At San Cristobal, Nelson was looking for distinctive types of pottery that he could use to assign strata or sites to a relative chronology. Nelson found various kinds of pottery, such as biscuitware and three-color glaze ware, but he didn't care about the pots' functions, or quality, or anything else; he just wanted to know if some types were earlier or later than others. Other researchers can (and do) have different questions, and they create different typologies.

But where do such types come from? To answer this question, let's look at three important types of types.

Morphological Types Modern observers exploring the range of material remains left by an extinct group run into many unfamiliar artifacts. To use these remains to make sense of the past, the first analytical step is to describe the artifacts carefully and accurately by grouping them into **morphological types.**

From Chapter 1, you'll recall Alfred Kidder and his early-twentieth-century excavations at Pecos Pueblo in New Mexico. Kidder dug up many different kinds of artifacts, including clay figurines. He classified these into four major types, two of which had several subdivisions. Here's how Kidder described type A-2 (Figure 7-1), called "flat bodied with protruding legs":

> The bodies are . . . broad and flat; the arms are either entirely ignored or suggested by very slight extensions of the square shoulders. The legs, however, are (to stretch the term) realistically modeled, being one-half to one-third as long as the body,

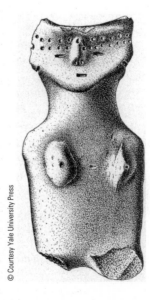

© Courtesy Yale University Press

Figure 7-1 A clay type A-2 figurine from Pecos Pueblo. *From Kidder 1932, p. 120, Figure 93a.*

morphological type A descriptive and abstract grouping of individual artifacts whose focus is on overall similarity rather than function or chronological significance.

and round in cross-section. The thighs set forward, there is a bend at the knee, and the lower leg, a mere stump with no attempt to depict the foot.

Note that Kidder did not speculate on how people used the figurines; he simply illustrated and described them in enough detail so that other archaeologists could visualize the artifacts without having to view them firsthand. Such bald description doesn't make for great reading, but it serves the primary function of a morphological type (sometimes termed a "class" in archaeological literature).

Morphological types have a second, basic property: They are abstract. This is an important point, because types are not the artifacts as such; they are instead composite descriptions of many similar artifacts. This means that every morphological type must encompass a certain range of variability: Several colors may have been applied; the quality of manufacture may vary; absolute size may fluctuate; and so forth.

Morphological types are purely descriptive. We ascribe no function to them at this point, and they don't necessarily have any chronological significance. No set rules exist for creating morphological types, although basic raw material (such as pottery, stone, shell, or bone) normally serves as the first criterion, followed by shape. Morphological types help communicate what the archaeologist found without describing every single specimen.

Temporal Types **Temporal types** are morphological types with demonstrable and specific chronological meaning within a particular region. They're time-markers, and that's good. If morphological Type B, for instance, occurs only in strata dating between 1500 and 1000 BP, then it can be elevated to the status of a temporal type. This promotion is important because when artifacts assigned to temporal Type B turn up in an otherwise undated context, the time span from 1500 to 1000 BP becomes the most plausible hypothesis for their age.

Functional Types **Functional types** reflect how objects were used in the past. Functional types often crosscut morphological types. A set of stone scrapers, for instance, might have had the same function, say hide preparation, so they are a functional type. But some are big and others are small; some are thin and others are thick; some are made of chert, but others are of quartzite and obsidian; some are sharpened on the ends of stone flakes, others along their sides. But they all have the same function. The remaining variability is (for now) irrelevant.

Functional types can also crosscut temporal types. Sometimes, pots are painted with distinctive designs for a limited period (like some of the pottery types that Nelson defined at San Cristobal; see Chapter 6). These distinctive styles of finish made the ceramics a temporal type. But all the differently decorated pots may be of the same functional type—they may all be cooking vessels, water jars, or seed storage pots.

Projectile Point Typology at Gatecliff

Let's recap. Good typologies possess two crucial characteristics:

1. Regardless of its final purpose, *a typology must minimize the differences within each created type and maximize the differences between types.* If types overlap or are ambiguous, they cannot reveal any significant or meaningful patterning.
2. *The typology must be objective and explicit.* This means that the result should be replicable by any trained observer. If somebody else can't replicate your results, then it's not science.

Once you've created a solid typology, you can focus on placing it in time and across space.

To show you how the abstract principles of typology work, let's walk step by step through Thomas's classification of the Gatecliff projectile points. By now, you know that the first question must be this: What was the goal of Thomas's classification?

Thomas asked several research questions at Gatecliff Shelter. One was whether the shelter would allow him to create and test a projectile point typology that would provide temporal types—time-markers. Once successfully defined, these temporal types could estimate the age of surface assemblages (where radiocarbon dates can't be processed). That was the goal—the research question—of the Gatecliff typology.

Choosing Criteria Great Basin archaeologists knew that projectile points were made of different types of stone, such as chert, quartzite, obsidian, and rhyolite. But experience showed that the raw material did not change over time in a systematic way, and most artifacts were made of locally available rocks. So a

temporal type A morphological type that has temporal significance; also known as a time-marker or index fossil.

functional type A class of artifacts that performed the same function; these may or may not be temporal and/or morphological types.

typology based on raw material doesn't help construct fine-grained temporal types.

But archaeologists who worked in the Great Basin also knew how much projectile point *shape* changed over time. Small points tended to cluster in upper (later) strata; larger points showed up in the lower (earlier) strata. And small points notched from the side seemed to occur stratigraphically above small points notched from the corners. These observations suggested that a typology based on shape and size could be used to construct temporal types.

The first step in applying your criteria can be informal, sometimes just separating superficially similar artifacts into piles on the laboratory table. We can ignore variables like stratigraphy, time depth, cultural affiliation, and even provenience (for now) because the idea is to reduce the complexity to our primary criteria—shape and size.

Look at the projectile points in Figure 7-2, just a few of the 400 recovered from Gatecliff Shelter. Even a casual glance shows some important similarities and differences. For one thing, the points at the top of the figure are smaller than those at the bottom. Some are notched from the side (specimens 7, 8, and 9), others from the base (artifacts 14 and 15), and some from the corner (16 and 24); some are not notched at all (1 and 3).

Defining Attributes Differences like size and notch position are called **attributes**—measurable or observable qualities of an object. We could make an infinite number of observations and take an infinite number of measurements on any of the projectile points shown in Figure 7-3. There are no rules governing the number of attributes to record, nor should there be; in general, we're trying to use the fewest steps necessary to accomplish our purpose.

In this case, two attributes (size and notching) are sufficient to create workable morphological types. But it's not enough simply to say "size" and "notch position." Defining adequate attributes requires that we explain precisely what's meant by the terms, so somebody else could make identical observations.

Take size. Everyone knows what size means, but it can be recorded in several ways. We could measure a point's length or width, or we could weigh it. Which size are we talking about?

attribute   An individual characteristic that distinguishes one artifact from another on the basis of its size, surface texture, form, material, method of manufacture, or design pattern.

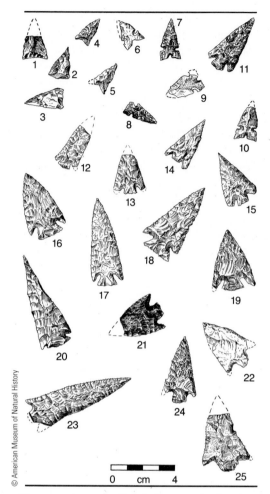

© American Museum of Natural History

Figure 7-2   An unsorted batch of stone projectile points recovered at Gatecliff Shelter (Nevada).

Weight is a good measure of projectile point size (although some error is introduced when we're required to estimate the original weight of broken specimens). Other attributes that measure size (such as length, width, and thickness) all correlate with weight: As a point gets longer, wider, and/or thicker, it also becomes heavier. But weight is the easiest to measure, and so it was one of the first attributes Thomas used to define morphological types. The lightest point in the Gatecliff sample weighs only 0.4 gram (about the weight of a paper clip) and the heaviest, more than 5 grams (about the same as a nickel). The weights for the 25 Gatecliff Shelter points in Figure 7-2 are presented in Table 7-1.

You can see that these weights are patterned, with certain natural breaks defining three projectile point sizes in this collection (this is even clearer when you look at the data on all 400-plus points):

Small points: Weight less than 1.0 gram
Medium points: Weight between 1.0 and 2.5 grams
Large points: Weight over 2.5 grams

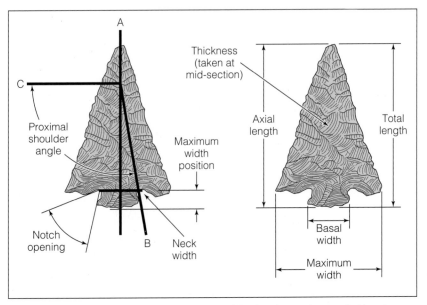

Figure 7-3 A Great Basin projectile point and some of the data that can be recorded from it. These observations are only a few of all that could be made on a projectile point.

can be reshaped into usable points—but this makes them smaller than the maker initially intended (this can have an effect on typology; see "Looking Closer: The Frison Effect"). But for each of the three weight categories, the point's maker had an idea (a "mental template") of what the "proper" point's size should be. By and large, the three size categories reflect natural breaks in the distribution of weights.

The second attribute is notch position. Some of the small points (Points 1 to 10 in Figure 7-2) have notches and others do not. So two categories are apparent: small, unnotched points and small, side-notched points. Thomas was hardly the first archaeologist to notice this distinction, and the literature of Great Basin archaeology refers to these two morphological types in this way:

These projectile point weights are variable because flintknappers cannot erase their mistakes; they must work around errors, creating some variation in the finished products. Points also break when they are used. If they are not too severely broken, they

TABLE 7-1 Attributes for Gatecliff Shelter Projectile Points					
SPECIMEN NUMBER	WEIGHT IN GRAMS	PROXIMAL SHOULDER ANGLE	SPECIMEN NUMBER	WEIGHT IN GRAMS	PROXIMAL SHOULDER ANGLE
1	(0.9)	—	14	1.5	85
2	0.8	—	15	2.5	80
3	0.9	—	16	4.1	110
4	0.4	—	17	3.5	120
5	(0.9)	—	18	3.9	130
6	(0.4)	200	19	3.5	120
7	0.8	180	20	(4.2)	150
8	(0.6)	180	21	(2.8)	80
9	0.7	180	22	(3.4)	85
10	(0.8)	190	23	(5.5)	80
11	2.3	100	24	2.7	100
12	(1.5)	100	25	(5.5)	60
13	(1.4)	95			

Note: Weights in parentheses are estimates on broken points.

LOOKING CLOSER

THE FRISON EFFECT

Stone tools are important because they are ubiquitous in prehistoric sites. But as they are used, stone tools are resharpened and, as a result, become smaller and change shape. This can affect tool typologies.

François Bordes (1919–1981) was a well-known French archaeologist whose groundbreaking research on stone tools influenced many archaeologists. (A member of the French underground during World War II, Bordes also wrote science fiction novels under the pen name Francis Carsac.)

The stone tools found in Neanderthal cave sites intrigued Bordes. These assemblages, dating from 130,000 to 35,000 years ago, are referred to as **Mousterian,** after Le Moustier, the site where they were first found. Bordes divided these stone tools into 63 types, including a variety of points, scrapers, knives, handaxes, and denticulates (flakes with crenulated edges). He created these types simply by laying assemblages out and then sorting them visually into morphological categories. Tabletop typology was common in Bordes's day, though statistical analysis later supported his findings.

Bordes then looked at Mousterian sites and found something interesting: The 63 tool types co-occurred in set frequencies, creating four major types of assemblages. For example, the Mousterian of Acheulean Tradition contained many handaxes, denticulates, and "backed" knives, but only moderate numbers of scrapers; the Typical Mousterian contained few handaxes and backed knives.

Bordes found that the four assemblages often alternated with one another throughout a site's strata. From this, he argued that the four assemblages reflected different cultural groups of Neanderthals, just as different car and architecture styles reflected different groups of Europeans. Bordes's typology was successful because it allowed him to see a higher level of patterning.

His interpretation of this patterning assumed that the stone tools were in their final intended form. Different scrapers, he thought, had different shapes because their makers had different ideas about what a "proper" scraper should look like. But scrapers wear out, and are rejuvenated by removing a few flakes along their edges. In the 1960s, George Frison (University of Wyoming) pointed out that a stone artifact's original shape can change considerably through such resharpening.

Harold Dibble (University of Pennsylvania) investigated whether the "Frison effect" was responsible for at least some of the variation in Bordes's Mousterian scraper types. Undertaking some experimental and archaeological studies, he eventually concluded that resharpening accounts for some of Bordes's scraper types. For example, "single edge scrapers" turn into "transverse scrapers" simply by resharpening.

Does this mean that Bordes was wrong? Absolutely not. He saw and categorized morphological variation, and that process allowed him to see patterning. His interpretation of the patterning may be wrong or incomplete because some differences in tool form reflect only how heavily some tools were used. Assemblages with many transverse scrapers, for example, were probably produced by longer occupations than assemblages dominated by single edge scrapers. Archaeologists proceed in exactly this way—they sort through variability, removing those parts explained by humdrum factors so that they can determine the more intriguing parts. Classification is an important step in that process.

Mousterian A culture from the Middle Paleolithic ("Middle Old Stone Age") period that appeared throughout Europe after 250,000 and before 30,000 years ago. Mousterian artifacts are frequently associated with Neanderthal human remains.

Cottonwood Triangular (Points 1–5)
 Weight: less than 1.0 gram
 Notching: absent
Desert Side-notched (Points 6–10)
 Weight: less than 1.0 gram
 Notching: present (from the side)

So, the smallest points—Points 1 through 10—belong to already recognized morphological types.

Points 11 through 15 are medium sized (weighing between 1.0 and 2.5 grams) and have notches creating a small base (or stem). Thomas described them as follows:

> Rosegate series (Points 11–15)
>   Weight: between 1.0 and 2.5 grams
>   Notching: present

Archaeologists get to name the point types they define. The first name generally refers to the site or region where they were first distinguished. The last name describes some morphological characteristic. Thomas's term "Rosegate" is a combination of "Rose Spring," a site in southeastern California, and "Eastgate," a small overhang near Eastgate, Nevada. These two point types were originally defined separately, each named after one site. But because Thomas didn't see any important difference between the two, he combined them. (In this case, he modified the naming convention somewhat: The first term still denotes the places of discovery, but because "Rosegate" combines two former types, it is termed a "series"—a higher-order category.) Points 11 through 15 have now been "typed."

The larger points are more complicated. Numbers 16 through 25 weigh more than 2.5 grams. Some have expanding bases (that is, the neck is narrower than the base), and others have contracting bases. But "expanding" and "contracting" are ambiguous terms, and archaeologists often disagree about just which stems expand and which contract. Look at Point 24: We call this stem contracting, but you might think that it is expanding. Who's right? Neither, because we have yet to define the attribute—a necessary step toward replicability.

The stem is created by the notches—the two slits added so that the point can be tied more securely to a shaft. The lower edge of this notch forms an angle with the major longitudinal axis of the point, and angles are useful because they can be measured.

To measure the angle, draw an imaginary line along the long axis of the point (Line A in Figure 7-3). Now draw another line (Line B) along the bottom of the point's notch, extending it to where it intersects the line you drew down the axis. Finally, draw a line perpendicular to that point of intersection on the opposite side of the point (Line C) and measure the angle between Line C and Line B.

Thomas called this attribute the "proximal shoulder angle" (PSA) because this side of the notch is nearest ("proximal to") the point shaft. Table 7-1 lists the proximal shoulder angles for the ten large points (Points 16 through 25) from Gatecliff Shelter. Now the difference between expanding and contracting stems is apparent:

Points 16 through 20 have PSAs greater than 110°, and Points 21 through 25 have PSAs smaller than that. On this basis, Thomas separated them into the following morphological types:

> Elko Corner-notched (Points 16–20)
>   Weight: Greater than 2.5 grams
>   PSA: 110°–150°
> Gatecliff Contracting Stem (Points 21–25)
>   Weight: Greater than 2.5 grams
>   PSA: ≤100°

Elko points were initially recognized at sites in Elko County, Nevada, and Thomas defined Gatecliff points based on artifacts recovered at Gatecliff Shelter. As morphological types, they differ only in basal form, as described by the PSA measurements.

We have now classified all 25 points. This example is purposely simplified, but it demonstrates the first step in projectile point classification. Although a number of additional attributes were necessary to deal with the more than 400 points found at Gatecliff, the fundamental procedures are the same.

Memorizing endless type names may seem meaningless, but remembering these five descriptive names is vastly better than coping with 25 individual artifacts—to say nothing of the 400 individual points at Gatecliff, or the thousands we've studied from across the Great Basin. And that is the function of morphological types.

What Did the Typology Do? Our typology has now organized the jumble of projectile points into groups based on measurable characteristics. But before we think about broader issues—those crucial dimensions of time and space—we must first ask if we've satisfied the two necessary goals of a good typology.

Consider the first characteristic: *Minimize the differences within each type and maximize the differences between types.*

In the past, archaeologists did this simply by placing artifacts on a table and sorting them into piles. But most modern typologies use statistical analyses to analyze a set of attributes and generate an objective measure of how well a typology accomplishes its goal. We've avoided the statistical detail of the Gatecliff typology, but you can get a sense of how this works by looking at Figure 7-4. Here, we plotted the 20 notched points in terms of their weight and PSA. Desert Side-notched, Elko Corner-notched, and Rosegate points are clearly different from one another in terms of both weight and notching. Rosegate and Gatecliff Contracting Stem points are less easily distinguished. They are similar in terms of PSA, and their difference in weight is less clear. However, Gate-

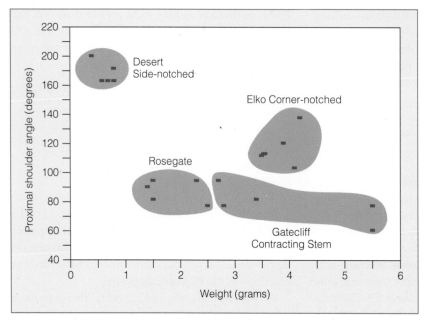

Figure 7-4 The relationship between the attributes of weight and proximal shoulder angle for the 20 notched projectile points in Figure 7-2.

cliff points are more frequently resharpened than are Rosegate points—making them smaller than they were originally. This is a subtle difference, and a larger sample would separate these two point types more clearly in terms of weight. Therefore, the typology meets the first criterion: It minimizes the differences within groups and maximizes the differences between groups.

The second characteristic was: *The typology must be objective and explicit.* Thomas's typology actually used more attributes than simply weight and proximal shoulder angle, and he defined more than the four projectile point types discussed here. By examining patterning in attributes, Thomas organized the resulting Great Basin projectile point types into a flowchart, shown in Figure 7-5. To see if this typology is objective and explicit, let's take an "unknown" projectile point and classify it according to the Gatecliff criteria.

Figure 7-3 (page 155) illustrates artifact 20.4/2010, a projectile point recovered during Kelly's survey of the Carson Desert. Projectile point 20.4/2010 has the following attributes:

Total length: 37.5 mm
Axial length: 37.5 mm
Basal indentation ratio: 1
Maximum width: 18 mm
Maximum width position: 4 mm
Basal width: 7 mm
Neck width: 7 mm
Proximal shoulder angle: 100°
Notch opening: 40°
Weight: 1.6 grams

To type this point, we need definitions of Thomas's other attributes.

Total length is obvious; axial length, however, is the length from the point's tip to the basal concavity. Artifact 20.4/2010 has no basal concavity, so the axial length equals the total length. (If this point had a concave base, the axial length would be somewhat shorter than the total length.) The utility of this measurement is that, by dividing the axial length by the total length, we have a measure of how concave the base is, what Thomas called the "basal indentation ratio." A high ratio means a shallow concavity; a low ratio means a deep one.

Maximum width position is simply the distance from the point's base to the point's greatest width. Dividing the maximum width position by the total length generates a measure of the point's shape. A high ratio indicates a more triangular point (like 20.4/2010); a lower ratio indicates a more leaf-shaped point.

With these attributes, we can now use the flowchart to classify artifact 20.4/2010. Let's start with the question: Is the point notched? The answer is yes, so we follow the arrow down to the next box. Is the point side-notched? No, so we move on to the corner-notched box. Now, there's a third question: Is its basal width (BW) less than or equal to 10 mm? Yes, it is. Is its PSA between 90° and 130°? Also, yes. Is the neck width (NW) less than the basal width plus .5 mm? Yes.

If any of these questions had been answered no, then we'd have moved to the box below. But since all questions came up yes, the point is typed as a Rosegate. With this key, any trained student would classify this point as accurately as the most seasoned archaeologist. By using an explicit and objective typology, archaeologists know that when they talk about a "Desert Side-notched" or "Rosegate" or some other type of point, all of them are talking about the same thing. We have created attributes that are objective and explicit. And that is what "replicability" is all about.

So, this typology fulfills both of the essential characteristics: It sorts things using objective and explicit criteria into categories that minimize the

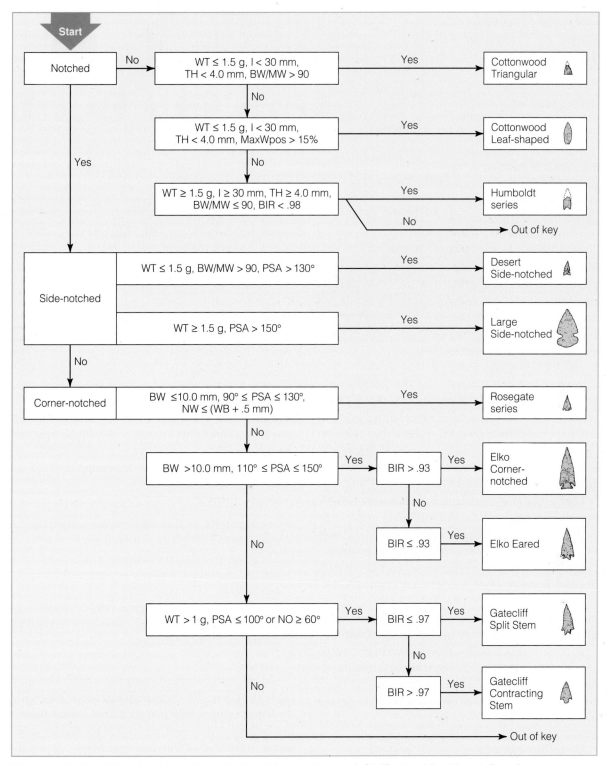

Figure 7-5 The Central Great Basin projectile point key. *From Thomas, 1981, Journal of California and Great Basin Anthropology 3:7–43, p. 25, a Malki Museum Press Publication. Used by permission. The Journal is available by subscription. Malki Museum, 11–795 Fields Road, P.O. Box 578, Banning, CA 92220, www.malkimuseum.org.*

differences within them and maximize the differences between them.

So far we've only been talking about morphological types, but remember that the goal of this typology was to create temporal types, or time-markers. Now that we've identified the types occurring at Gatecliff, we can see if they have any temporal significance.

Gatecliff Projectile Points as Temporal Types

As the name implies, temporal types help archaeologists monitor time; they provide us with index fossils that allow archaeologists to date surface sites and strata within buried sites.

In Chapter 5, we compared the stratigraphy of Gatecliff Shelter to a giant layer cake, stacked 40 feet high. Geology's law of superposition tells us that, all else being equal, the oldest artifacts lie at the bottom, with later artifacts showing up in progressively higher strata. The Gatecliff deposits thus provide extraordinary temporal control over the past 7000 years. Plotting the vertical distribution of the 400+ classifiable projectile points from Gatecliff Shelter creates the distribution shown in Figure 7-6. (This figure includes all the types used to classify the entire Gatecliff collection.)

Look at the sharp stratigraphic differences (which, you should note, exhibit the battleship curves like those in the seriation diagrams of Chapter 6). Desert Side-notched and Cottonwood Triangular points occurred mostly in the very uppermost part of Gatecliff Shelter. These replaced Rosegate series points, confined to slightly older strata. These, in turn, had replaced Elko points, found in lower, still older strata. Elko points replaced more ancient Gatecliff points.

At the time, 47 radiocarbon dates were available to date the geological sequence at Gatecliff (we have more now), and Thomas assigned the following time ranges to the projectile point types discussed previously:

Desert Side-notched	post-700 BP
Cottonwood Triangular	post-700 BP
Rosegate series	1500–700 BP
Elko Corner-notched	3500–1500 BP
Gatecliff Contracting Stem	4500–1500 BP

With this critical step, several of our morphological types have become temporal types. Whenever

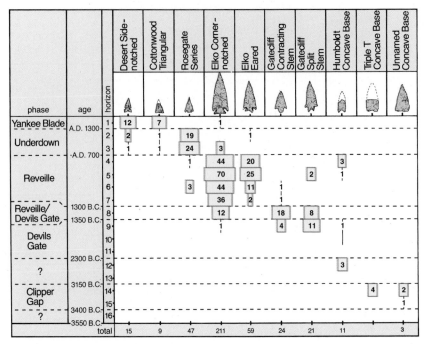

Figure 7-6 Relative proportions of selected projectile point types across the stratigraphic units of Gatecliff Shelter. Note that one or two extremely abundant temporal types seem to dominate most strata. *After Thomas 1983b, Figure 66. Courtesy American Museum of Natural History.*

similar points are found in undated contexts, we now have a clue (a hypothesis, really) to their time of manufacture.

Note what has happened in this example:

1. Individual artifacts were first grouped strictly on formal criteria; all that mattered for morphological types was that the artifacts looked alike.
2. These morphological categories were then tested against independent evidence—specifically, the layer-cake stratigraphy and Gatecliff's 47 radiocarbon dates.
3. Because all five morphological categories were significantly restricted in time, they were elevated to the status of temporal types.

Not all morphological point types from Gatecliff made the grade. The frequencies of some (especially the larger, concave base points) did not change significantly through time, so they flunked the test for graduating to the level of temporal type. Maybe somebody will eventually demonstrate that concave base points are indeed time-markers in the Great Basin; but for now, these types remain merely "morphological," without temporal significance.

We began with the simplifying assumption that change through time reflects shifts in ancient peoples' "mental templates" for an idealized projectile point shape. Never mind what the artifacts meant to the makers, whether they were spear or arrow points, or how they were made. At this stage, we care only about whether some cluster of measurable attributes (grouped into "types") changed through time.

The seriation-like diagram for Gatecliff projectile points shows what changes over time and what does not, begging some more interesting questions. For instance, although we now know that Desert Side-notched and Cottonwood Triangular points both postdate 700 BP, we are clueless as to *why* two morphological types should exist simultaneously. Did two social groups live at Gatecliff after 700 BP? Were Desert Side-notched points designed for hunting bighorn, whereas Cottonwood points were for rabbits? Were Cottonwood points for "war arrows" left unnotched so that they remain embedded if the shaft is pulled out? Or perhaps the difference was technological: Maybe Cottonwood Triangular points weren't finished, but were still to be notched (thereby becoming Desert Side-notched points)? Notching is often the last thing done to a point, and if done incorrectly, it can ruin the point. Were Cottonwood Triangular points made by novices who were not adept at notching points? All these guesses are hypotheses at present untested—and they would have been impossible without first creating projectile point temporal types.

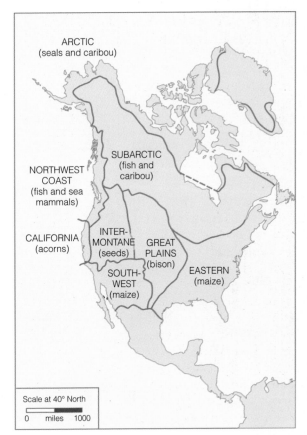

Figure 7-7 North American culture areas. Such areas were important to nineteenth-century anthropology, but are less so today.

SPACE-TIME SYSTEMATICS

So far we have been talking only about the temporal dimension of archaeology, changing artifacts over time. We now shift and consider the spatial dimension of these temporal changes.

Archaeology has adopted a relatively standardized framework for integrating the kind of chronological information just discussed into a regional framework. Gordon Willey (1913–2002) and Philip Phillips (1900–1993) initially set out this regional infrastructure in their influential book *Method and Theory in American Archaeology* (1958). Since then, the nomenclature has varied somewhat from region to region, some terms have been discarded because they reflect outdated theoretical paradigms, and others do not have quite the significance that they once carried. Nonetheless, the 50-year-old Willey-Phillips framework remains the most generally accepted system in North America.

Archaeological Cultures: Dividing Space

Let's begin by going back to an era before Willey and Phillips, to the early-twentieth-century concept of *culture areas*. Long before anthropology became a discipline in America, scholars recognized that not all nineteenth-century Native American societies were alike. Some people were nomadic; others lived in large pueblos. Some hunted bison; others were maize farmers. Those in California relied heavily on acorns for their food; Northwest Coast peoples fished and hunted sea mammals. By the late nineteenth century, American anthropology had formalized these observations into culture areas (Figure 7-7), large regions defined primarily in terms of what people ate. The theory that attempted to explain these geographic patterns is no longer important to anthropology, but the culture areas left a legacy in that archaeologists who study the prehistory of North America tend to focus on one of these culture areas. They work on the Plains, or in the southeastern United States, California, or the Southwest.

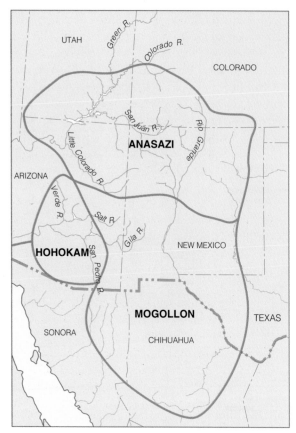

Figure 7-8 Southwestern archaeological cultures, or traditions. The theory that lay behind these areas is outdated today, but the patterns that stand behind these traditions still demand explanation. *From L. Cordell,* Prehistory of the Southwest, *1984, p. 15. Reprinted by permission of Elsevier.*

Working with the prehistory of one of these regions, archaeologists quickly saw "subculture areas"—regions within a culture area whose material culture (such as house styles, settlement patterns, ceramics, or subsistence) differed from one another. These subdivisions of culture areas are called "traditions" or **archaeological cultures.** Figure 7-8 shows the location of the three major archaeological cultures of the Southwest culture area: the Hohokam, Mogollon (*muh*-ghee-own), and Anasazi. These three regions are distinguished from one another in terms of pottery and architectural styles.

But these archaeological cultures are *not* ethnographic cultures. If we could go back in time

archaeological culture A regional manifestation within a culture area marked by a particular set of material culture traits.

period A length of time distinguished by particular items of material culture, such as house form, pottery, or subsistence.

in, say, the Mogollon region and travel around, we would probably encounter several different languages, as well as different customs in different villages. In all likelihood, people in a village at the southern end of the Mogollon region considered themselves different from those who lived at the northern end. By drawing lines around areas on a map and labeling them archaeological cultures, we are simply drawing attention to spatial differences in the kinds of artifacts that are found in those regions. The *meaning* of these differences is another matter.

Periods: Dividing Time

As archaeologists began to investigate the prehistory of regions, they also discovered that the Native American culture that ethnographers documented (and that formed the basis for maps of culture areas) had not always been there. People living in the American Southwest some 5000 years ago, for example, were nomadic hunter-gatherers who never knew maize or built pueblos. As the chronologies of different culture areas were worked out, prehistory was organized into slices of time that were given different names.

Archaeologists divided prehistory into **periods** based on gross changes in easily observable archaeological remains, such as subsistence or house forms. The concept of periods is still used to organize archaeological thinking about time. For example, pick up a text on Southwestern archaeology and an early chapter will be on the "Paleo-Indian Period" (from 13,000 to 7500 BP), a period of time in which the distinctive Pueblo archaeological cultures, such as the Mogollon, did not exist, and people were nomadic hunters of large game and gatherers of wild plant foods. The next chapter might be on the "Archaic Period" (from 7500 to 1900 BP). This is a time when people made heavier use of plant foods, began to develop distinctive regional traditions in material culture, and, toward the end of the period, experimented with agricultural crops, most notably maize. This may be followed by chapters that describe "Early Village" and "Pueblo" periods.

The concepts of archaeological cultures and periods helped map out major spatial and temporal patterns in material culture. Periods record change over time, archaeological cultures record change over space. Knowing *how* and *when* material culture changed over time and space is an obvious first step toward explaining *why* those changes occurred.

Phases: Combining Space and Time

As archaeologists became increasingly familiar with the time-markers of a region, they found that different regions in a culture area did not all change in lockstep with one another. Pottery, for example, may first appear at different times in different areas; likewise, from a common base, pottery styles may differentiate over time at different rates and in different ways in different regions. In other words, there are temporal and spatial changes in material culture of which periods were just a first approximation.

A **phase** is a block of time that is characterized by one or more distinctive artifact types—a particular kind of pottery, housing style, and/or projectile point, for example. The phase has become the practicable and intelligible unit of archaeological study, defined by Willey and Phillips as "an archaeological unit possessing traits sufficiently characteristic to distinguish it from all other units similarly conceived . . . [and] spatially limited to the order of magnitude of a locality or region and chronologically limited to a relatively brief interval of time."

How do we construct phases? Phases are defined by temporal types (like our Gatecliff points), items of material culture that show patterned changes over time. We have already seen how to derive temporal types: You group individual artifacts into morphological types, then test them against independent data (such as a dated site stratigraphy, correlation with other known sites, or direct dating of the artifacts themselves). We recognize those types of artifacts that change systematically and observably through time as time-markers.

The next analytical step is to see how the time-markers themselves cluster to reflect site chronology. Here we have to define a few other terms that archaeologists commonly use.

Archaeological sites consist of **assemblages**, collections of artifacts recovered from some unit of provenience. We could talk about a site's stone tool or ceramic or projectile point assemblage. In this case, the provenience might be the site itself. We could also talk about the assemblage of a particular stratum—say, the stone tool assemblage of Stratum 22 at Gatecliff. In a well-stratified and carefully excavated site like Gatecliff, there could be many assemblages.

We might then analytically cluster these assemblages into **components**. A component is considered a culturally homogeneous unit within a single site. By "culturally homogeneous" we mean that, whereas the assemblages that make up a component might have been deposited during different years and by different individuals, they were probably left by people sharing the same culture. Some small archaeological sites may contain only one assemblage representing a single component; some could contain multiple assemblages that nonetheless still represent one component. Others may contain multiple assemblages representing several components. And some sites may be too badly mixed to sort out assemblages or to define components at all.

Defining archaeological components involves the intangible factor of cultural homogeneity, so there are no firm rules for their construction. But it helps if the strata are obvious from the stratigraphic profile, as at Gatecliff, where numerous strata of non-artifact-bearing silts separated the deposits into discrete living floors. During analysis, we could keep the floors distinct (as individual assemblages) or group them together on the basis of shared similarities. Although Gatecliff contained many living surfaces, Thomas concluded there were only five distinct cultural components, each incorporating the assemblages from one to six living surfaces. Components are truly site-specific—a given component is, by definition, from a single site.

Each component at Gatecliff is defined by its associated array of dates and its particular set of characteristic artifacts, including projectile points and artifacts such as incised slates and carved wooden pegs (used to construct snares to trap small mammals).

How do these observations help create phases? By comparing Gatecliff's components with those of other nearby sites, we define the spatial and temporal range of particular artifact types, and from this comparison archaeologists construct a regional chronology of phases. Briefly, assemblages (all items of one kind from one stratum or location) are grouped into site-specific components (differentiated in culture and in time). Components from nearby sites are grouped into phases. These building blocks therefore identify similarities across space and time.

---

phase An archaeological construct possessing traits sufficiently characteristic to distinguish it from other units similarly conceived; spatially limited to roughly a locality or region and chronologically limited to the briefest interval of time possible.

assemblage A collection of artifacts of one or several classes of materials (stone tools, ceramics, bones) that comes from a defined context, such as a site, feature, or stratum.

component An archaeological construct consisting of a stratum or set of strata that are presumed to be culturally homogeneous. A set of components from various sites in a region will make up a phase.

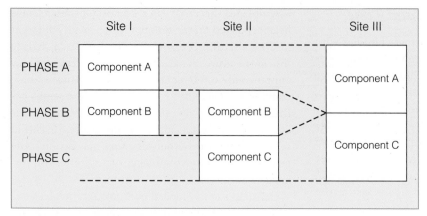

Figure 7-9 Relationship of archaeological sites to the analytical concepts of component and phase.

each composed of different kinds of artifacts (primarily projectile points) and spanning other episodes of time.

Phases: The Basic Units of Space-Time Systematics

The phase is archaeology's basic unit of space-time systematics, combining both spatial and temporal patterns in the material culture we dig up. Phases are defined by time, but also by space. There is no Yankee Blade phase in Georgia, or New Mexico, or even Utah because the nature and tempo of change in material culture in those places differed from that of the Great Basin. Even within the Great Basin, phases are not synchronous. Figure 7-10 shows some of the phase names used in the western and central Great Basin. Time and periods appear at left, along the vertical axis; space appears along the horizontal axis. This diagram is one result of archaeologists' efforts to create space-time systematics. Each phase, or block, in this figure—Cowhorn, Early Lovelock, Grass Valley—is defined by particular artifact types that have particular temporal ranges in their particular regions.

So that's how the temporal boundaries work within the central Great Basin. But where are the geographic "edges" of this chronology? At the town of Austin, in central Nevada? Or 100 miles east at Fallon in the Carson Desert? It's hard to say. Phases are a lot like pieces of a three-dimensional jigsaw puzzle with very fuzzy

To see how this works, consider the three hypothetical archaeological sites in Figure 7-9, all located in the same geographic region. They have been carefully excavated and analyzed and, as is often the case, no single site contains the complete cultural sequence. The first site has Components A and B; the second site contains Component B plus a new component called C; and the third site has Components A and C but lacks Component B. By analyzing the temporal types shared among the components and comparing the absolute dates, a regional sequence of phases can be constructed from evidence at these three sites.

To give a more concrete example, archaeologists working in the central Great Basin divide the last 5500–6000 years into five phases, each defined by one or more temporal projectile point types (as well as other artifact types). Figure 7-6 (page 160) shows how different morphological point types at Gatecliff sort out in time. These phases were defined by analyzing assemblages from many stratified sites, teasing out consistent associations between particular morphological artifact types and particular spans of time.

The latest of these, the Yankee Blade phase (named after a nineteenth-century silver mine in the town of Austin) is typified by ceramics and Desert Side-notched and Cottonwood Triangular points. This phase began about 700 years ago and lasted until Euro-American contact, about 1850 in central Nevada. The other phases were similarly defined,

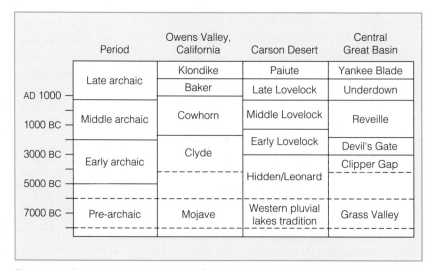

Period		Owens Valley, California	Carson Desert	Central Great Basin
AD 1000	Late archaic	Klondike	Paiute	Yankee Blade
		Baker	Late Lovelock	Underdown
1000 BC	Middle archaic	Cowhorn	Middle Lovelock	Reveille
3000 BC	Early archaic	Clyde	Early Lovelock	Devil's Gate
				Clipper Gap
5000 BC			Hidden/Leonard	
7000 BC	Pre-archaic	Mojave	Western pluvial lakes tradition	Grass Valley

Figure 7-10 Time-space systematics: Some of the phases used in three regions of the Great Basin, with period names. Dashed lines indicate phase boundaries that are not well dated.

edges. Neighboring regions may have different phases because they experienced histories and progressions of change in material culture through time.

Constructing phases lets the archaeologist synthesize reams of data into (admittedly simplistic) time-slices which, in turn, can be compared and contrasted with similar schemes from neighboring areas. They allow us to see, in a rough way, differences and similarities in the spatial and temporal scale of artifact change over time. Because we presume that artifacts reflect culture and behavior, phases help track spatial and temporal change in human cultural behavior. Phases are the first step toward developing ideas about regional patterns and trends—ideas that can be tested, refined, and expanded.

The phases can last a few generations or thousands of years. This depends in part on the kind of archaeological remains involved and on our contemporary knowledge of those remains. If pottery styles changed rapidly, then we can, with sufficient study of tightly controlled and well-dated stratigraphic excavations, develop short phases using seriation. Chronological control tends to be better for younger material, so young phases tend to be shorter than old phases. One phase that precedes the 550-year-long Yankee Blade phase is the Reveille phase, from 3300 to 1300 years ago—some 2000 years. The Reveille phase is longer because the material remains used for its definition (including Elko series projectile points) lasted longer than the artifacts used to define the Yankee Blade phase (Desert Side-notched points, Cottonwood Triangular points, and pottery). Phases covering the most recent prehistory of the American Southwest may be only 25 to 50 years long.

The phase concept is vague, and deliberately so. Archaeology needs to impose a set of minimal units on time. The phase is that minimal unit. Phases allow archaeologists to provisionally define time, which is actually a continuous variable, as if it were a discrete set of temporally ordered points. When we discuss the Yankee Blade phase, we treat the interval from 700 to 150 years ago as if it were an instant. By definition, two components of the Yankee Blade phase are simultaneous, provided that "simultaneous" is understood to last 550 years.

Keep in mind that phases are always defined *provisionally*. As

knowledge of the Yankee Blade phase expands, we may be able to recognize divisions within the phase—for instance, to distinguish an early Yankee Blade component from a late Yankee Blade component. When this happens, the initial phase is divided into *subphases*. These finer criteria reflect the amount of research accomplished on each phase and underscore how much our knowledge of the archaeological record will always be a contemporary phenomenon. We must keep the concept of phase vague to accommodate new findings and help us learn more, rather than place blinders on our ability to see new patterns in prehistory.

CONCLUSION

We began this chapter with the simple observation that patterning in archaeology falls along three dimensions: space, time, and form (of artifacts). The construction of space-time systematics requires a simplification of the enormous variation in material culture over time and space into some meaningful patterns, and you now appreciate how we go about doing that. But building space-time systematics is not the goal of archaeology; it's the means to an end. Since the goals of archaeology are to reconstruct and explain the past, it's fair to ask how space-time systematics help achieve this goal.

To answer this question, let's look at the case of Shoshone pottery (Figure 7-11). Shoshone ceramics

© Donald R. Tuohy/Nevada State Museum

Figure 7-11 Shoshone ceramic vessel.

appear suddenly in many parts of the Desert West about 700 years ago, and the Shoshone people made similar pottery until about 150 years ago. Shoshone pottery thus implies certain limits: time (such as the Yankee Blade phase in the central Great Basin, from 150 to 700 years ago) and space (the Desert West).

With its temporal parameters estimated, Shoshone pottery becomes a useful time-marker. Sites containing these potsherds in the Desert West can be provisionally assigned to the 700–150 BP interval.

But we're not nearly finished. We've just begun because as a time-marker, the concept "Shoshone pottery" leaves many questions unanswered. Was this pottery introduced by migrating Shoshone-speaking peoples? Or did the idea of pottery simply spread across the Desert West? Did the various peoples of the Desert West independently invent the idea of pottery? Or were the vessels traded in from elsewhere?

Each of these is a research question that could inspire years of investigation: Can we document a population movement across the Desert West 700 years ago? If so, where did these newcomers come from? And what happened to the pre-700 BP inhabitants of the Desert West? Are there signs of trading activity or warfare beginning 700 years ago?

Questions like these can pile up without end. True, we cannot reconstruct what happened in the past just by looking at time-markers—but we don't even know the right questions to ask or hypotheses to test until we've sorted out the when and the where of the past.

And reconstructing *what* happened in the past is itself but one step in the process. As we pointed out in Chapter 1, archaeologists today are equally interested in *why* prehistory took the particular courses that it did; we are interested in explaining the past as well as in reconstructing it. Shoshone pottery, as a time-marker, tells us that distinctive potsherds occur in archaeological deposits dating from 700 to 150 years ago across the Desert West. But (again, as a time-marker), Shoshone pottery

tells us nothing about *why* pottery was introduced 700 years ago. For some reason, one segment of the Desert West cultural system changed, and people began manufacturing pottery. This complex issue can be studied only by pursuing related shifts in the lifeway, drawing evidence from the settlement pattern and demography, cultural ecology, social organization, and religion.

Let's just say, for instance, that research eventually leads us to conclude that the pottery was introduced by a migrating Shoshone population. The next question would then be: Why did this population migrate in? What gave it the ability to replace the existing (pre-700 BP) population? Did climate change render the pre-700 BP adaptation untenable, thereby enabling the Shoshone to invade the Desert West? Did the ecological adaptation change to make ceramic vessels more efficient after 700 BP? Did population growth drive the migration, or was it warfare, or some environmental calamity?

By definition, we select time-markers based on certain aspects of shared culture, and deliberately ignore much cultural behavior. Obviously, questions such as diffusion, migration, invention, and adaptation are complex, reflecting changes in the underlying cultural systems. Time-markers, grounded only in shared behavior, are patently inadequate for unraveling the mechanics of cultural systems.

In many respects, the basics of space-time systematics of archaeology have been worked out, especially for North American archaeology, and they no longer preoccupy archaeologists as they did during the first half of the twentieth century. Still, space-time systematics were and are a crucial first step in the archaeological process, and some of us are still working out the details. Only after documenting temporal and spatial change in selected artifacts can we hope to reconstruct what people actually did in the past. In the following chapters, we will discuss how archaeologists go about doing exactly that.

SUMMARY

1. What are the principles of archaeological typology?
⚙ We create groups (based on one or more attributes of form) that minimize the differences within each group and maximize the differences between groups.

⚙ We construct these groups through an objective, explicit, and replicable process.

⚙ We recognize that there is no single "correct" typology. A typology's usefulness is judged relative to the question it is used to answer.

2. What is the strength of archaeology?

- Although surrendering some of the detail available to ethnographers, archaeologists can focus on mega-patterns spanning vast reaches of space and time—across continents and millennia.

3. What role does typology play in archaeology's strength?

- Seeking changes across space and time—so-called space-time systematics—archaeologists can find important patterns in the form of material culture. Because this can't be done by focusing on artifacts individually, archaeologists address "types" of material culture—projectile points, pottery, architecture, and so on—across spans of space and time.
- By testing morphological types against solidly dated contexts, archaeologists define temporal types, the backbone for building cultural chronologies.

4. What are archaeological cultures, site components, and phases?

- Spatial patterning in material culture defines archaeological cultures, but these are not the same as ethnographic cultures.
- By seeking out clusters of temporal types, we construct site components, which are culturally homogeneous units within a single site that can be synthesized into phases—archaeological units of cultural homogeneity that are limited in both time and space.
- Phases are the basic archaeological building blocks for regional synthesis, capturing temporal and spatial similarity in material culture.

MEDIA RESOURCES

Doing Fieldwork:
Archaeological Demonstrations CD-ROM 2.0
This CD, developed by the authors, shows professional archaeologists involved in various digs, many of which are referenced in the text. The presentation is organized by the main techniques used on an archaeological dig, reinforcing concepts and techniques via live examples. The CD takes you through each step automatically, or you can navigate to any point via the navigation bar. After reviewing a step in the dig process, you are taken to Check Points, which are concept questions about each step of the dig. Then you can see the answers, receive your score, and even send your scores to your instructor.

The Companion Website for *Archaeology*, Sixth Edition
www.cengagebrain.com
Supplement your review of this chapter by going to the companion website to take one of the practice quizzes, use the flash cards to master key terms, and check out the many other study aids that are designed to help you succeed in your introductory archaeology course.

8 TAPHONOMY, EXPERIMENTAL ARCHAEOLOGY, AND ETHNOARCHAEOLOGY

LEARNING OBJECTIVES

AFTER READING THIS CHAPTER
YOU SHOULD BE ABLE TO ANSWER THESE QUESTIONS:

1. What is the difference between analogy and middle-level theory?

2. What is the principle of uniformitarianism?

3. What do taphonomy, experimental archaeology, and ethnoarchaeology study?

© Robert Kelly

Mikea women pounding maize in southwestern Madagascar (and watching the anthropologists).

PREVIEW

YOU NOW KNOW how archaeologists locate and excavate sites, how they date those sites, and how they construct cultural chronologies. Now it is time to move up the theoretical ladder and see how archaeologists actually go about reconstructing the past. To do so, it's critical to understand the role of middle-level research in modern archaeology.

We have already discussed the various natural and cultural processes that combine to create the archaeological record. Low-level theory enables us to generate data from this record. Now, we can apply theory developed in middle-level research to relate these data to past human behaviors. If you flip back to the model of archaeological inquiry in Figure 2-8 (page 32), you'll recall that archaeologists sometimes put down their trowels, climb out of their trenches, and conduct research designed to generate the tools necessary to interpret the data at hand. In this chapter, we concentrate on three areas of middle-level research introduced in Chapter 2:

▶ Taphonomy studies the role that natural processes play in creating the archaeological record.

▶ Experimental archaeology uses controlled experiments to replicate the past under different conditions, looking for significant links between human behavior and its archaeological consequences.

▶ Ethnoarchaeology studies living societies to see how behavior can literally translate into the archaeological record.

INTRODUCTION

Archaeologists are often compared to detectives, a comparison that is both appropriate and instructive. Both want to know what happened in the past, and both make inferences about the past based on material remains. Ideally, detectives work on crime scenes that are quickly discovered and immediately sealed off. Imagine if they were confronted by a crime scene that is several thousand years old, in which nothing organic survives and where burrowing rodents have jumbled the evidence. Even Sherlock Holmes would have a hard time making his conclusions stand up in court. Yet this is what archaeologists deal with every day.

Archaeologists also face the complication that, unlike detectives, they commonly recover objects with unknown functions and meanings. Imagine if our detectives first had to figure out that the metallic cylinder lying on the floor was a spent cartridge (and not a piece of jewelry, a child's toy, or some ritual object). Detectives routinely use "common sense"—knowledge of their own culture, actually—to decide if something "doesn't look right" at a crime scene. Think of how much more slowly investigations would proceed if detectives first had to decide if a chair lying on its side or dishes strewn about the floor were culturally normal or an aberration.

It is important to realize that archaeological sites are contemporary phenomena. Many of you might think that archaeological sites are like Pompeii, the Roman city covered by volcanic ash in AD 79 which seemingly preserved a moment in time (horrific as it was). But the truth is that all sites, even Pompeii, are the complex result of natural and cultural processes that make each site unique. Interpreting archaeological evidence is *never* straightforward because low-level facts cannot explain themselves. Middle-level research aims to provide archaeology with the crucial tools needed to infer behavior from the contemporary archaeological record.

MIDDLE-LEVEL RESEARCH: WHAT IS IT?

Archaeologists develop such tools by observing behavior and its material correlates simultaneously, yet independent of one another. Archaeological sites contain only material remains. Behavior must be inferred from those remains; it cannot be observed independent of them. So where do archaeologists get the means to make these inferences?

Let's consider how archaeology's sibling discipline, geology, solved this problem. Like the archaeological record, the geological record consists of two things: objects and the relationships among them. A "geological fact" is a contemporary observation made by a geologist on objects from the geological record. Rocks do not speak, so how do geologists go from contemporary observations to meaningful inferences of the remote geological past?

Geologists addressed this question in the eighteenth century. A Scottish doctor and farmer, James Hutton (1726–1797) was also intrigued by geology. He formulated a simple principle that provides one of the cornerstones of modern geology. The so-called **principle of uniformitarianism** asserts that the processes now operating to modify the earth's surface are the same processes of the geological past. It's that simple: Geological processes, past and present, are assumed to be *identical*.

We know from modern observations, for instance, that as glaciers move, their massive weight leaves striations—scratches—on bedrock deposits. They also deposit rock and earth at their fronts and sides, often forming distinctive moraines. Study of modern glaciers demonstrates that moraines and striations are formed only through glacial action.

Now suppose a geologist finds moraines and striated rocks in New England, where no glaciers exist today. Armed with knowledge of contemporary glacial processes, a geologist can confidently interpret those features as evidence of past glaciers.

The same logic applies to archaeology. Archaeologists recover the material remains of past human behavior. And, like geologists, archaeologists must look to the contemporary world for hypotheses that account for the formation and deposition of these physical remains. This is an important point: Observing the contemporary world provides the information necessary to infer past human behavior and natural processes from observations on archaeological objects.

Some Bones of Contention

Perhaps you are thinking that, sure, this makes sense—but shouldn't the meaning of some remains still be relatively obvious?

Consider a simple problem in the interpretation of animal bones (also known as **faunal** remains) from archaeological sites. As we will discuss in Chapter 9, archaeologists study animal bones to learn about past diets, hunting and butchering practices, how animals

were domesticated, the season in which the hunt occurred, and other related issues.

Most of these faunal studies begin by determining the relative frequencies of animal bones in a site. When analyzing the bones from Suberde, an 8500-year-old Neolithic village in Turkey, Dexter Perkins and Patricia Daly observed that the upper limb bones of wild oxen were usually missing. Perkins and Daly suggested that the frequencies of the different bones resulted from how people had butchered the oxen. People must have first skinned the animals, stripped the meat from the forequarters and hindquarters, and then thrown away the defleshed upper limb bones. Perkins and Daly presumed that the meat was piled on the skin and that the lower limb bones were used to drag the hide bearing the meat back home. Calling this the "schlep effect," they believed their interpretation explained why only lower limb bones were discarded at the habitation site.

Now jump across Europe to England, where R. E. Chaplin analyzed the bones recovered from a late-ninth-century Saxon farm. The facts in this case also included a shortage of upper limb bones, this time of sheep and cattle, but Chaplin suggested that these bones disappeared because the carcasses were dressed and exported to market.

Across the Atlantic, archaeologists working on American Plains Indian sites also discovered that the upper limb bones of food animals were often missing. Theodore White decided that the bones must have been destroyed during the manufacture of bone grease. Relying on ethnographies of Plains Indians, White argued that the limb bones were pulverized and boiled to render their grease to make pemmican (a mixture of dried meat, fat, and berries), which was stored for the winter.

We could cite other examples, but the point should be clear: Three different teams made three different inferences from exactly the same archaeological facts—the lack of upper limb bones in habitation sites. Archaeologists face such problems daily: Several competing hypotheses account for the same body of facts. And most of the hypotheses are entirely reasonable.

Scientific protocol stipulates how to select among the competing hypotheses (for the present, we will restrict our attention to the three target hypotheses).

---

principle of uniformitarianism The principle asserting that the processes now operating to modify the earth's surface are the same processes that operated long ago in the geological past.

faunal In archaeology, animal bones in archaeological sites.

Each one is a generalized statement about human behavior. But a contemporary archaeologist can never observe a Neolithic villager butchering a wild ox, and none of us will ever watch nineteenth-century American Plains Indians making bone grease. Archaeologists must therefore concentrate on finding the material *consequences* of activities like butchering Neolithic oxen or making bison bone grease.

We do this by constructing a series of logical "if . . . then" statements: *If* bone grease were manufactured from bison bones, *then* we should find artifacts X, Y, and Z and physical residues M, N, and O; bones should be distributed in patterns C, D, and E; and bone elements J, K, and L should be missing. Similarly, to test the second hypothesis, we must generate some "if . . . then" statements regarding the trading of meat and bones. Before we can do that, we need answers to some very specific questions: Which are the best cuts to trade? How far can meat be transported before it spoils? Is meat marketed only in the winter months? Are carcasses butchered in special ways so that certain cuts can be traded? Then we can create arguments like "*If* these carcasses were being dressed for market, *then* we should see marks A and B on bones X and Y, and the site should include features G or H and implements K and L."

These "if . . . then" statements are critical bridging arguments that translate hypotheses into specific expectations that can be tested using archaeological evidence. These bridging arguments are essential to testing ideas with archaeological evidence, and their construction is one of the most difficult things that archaeologists do.

But—we hope you are wondering—how do we know these things? Why do archaeologists surmise that making bone grease requires artifacts X, Y, and Z? And how do we know which bone elements are destroyed in the process? This is the tough part, and hypothesis testing is only as robust as these "if . . . then" bridging arguments. If we generate incorrect implications, then our hypothesis testing will be worse than useless because it will lead us to specious or erroneous conclusions. For instance, if we assume that the lack of limb bones *always* means that people were rendering grease from bones, we would make a completely incorrect inference if the lack of limb bones in a particular site was really the result of the schlep effect.

Here is where the notion of middle-level research comes into play. Since facts never speak for themselves, archaeologists must provide bridging arguments that breathe behavioral life into the objects of the past. Properly formulated, middle-level theory links human behavior to empirical data that are archaeologically observable. Although it has been an important aspect of archaeological inquiry for more than a century, Lewis Binford's call for middle-level research in the 1960s and 1970s focused additional attention on this neglected area of archaeology.

To create relevant bridging arguments, archaeologists must observe the workings of a culture in its systemic context, much as geologists defined their processes through observation of the contemporary world. Geologists interested in glacial processes cannot study firsthand the massive continental glaciers that once covered portions of the Northern Hemisphere. But they can examine the effects that mountain glaciers today have on the landscape and use those observations to infer the past from geological traces.

Archaeologists do the same: They study modern analogies in order to understand the processes that created the archaeological record.

Analogy versus Middle-Level Theory

We used the term "analogy" in the previous paragraph, and you may be wondering how that differs from middle-level theory. The answer is that *middle-level theory is a particularly rigorous analogy*.

To see why this is so, let's first consider what a simple analogy is. An **analogy** notes similarities between two entities—for example, an archaeological feature and an ethnographic description of a similar feature—and infers from those facts that an *additional* attribute of one (the ethnographic feature) is also true of the other (the archaeological feature). Following Nicholas David (University of Calgary) and Carol Kramer (1943–2002), simple analogies take the following form:

▶ An archaeological object is characterized by attributes A, B, C, and D.
▶ The ethnographic analogy is also characterized by A, B, C, and D and has the function or property E.
▶ Therefore, the archaeological object also has the function or property E.

Archaeologists, for instance, who excavate ancient pueblo ruins in the American Southwest, often

analogy Noting similarities between two entities and inferring from that similarity that an *additional* attribute of one (the ethnographic case) is also true of the other (the archaeological case).

uncover **kivas** in the settlements. Kivas are religious structures where native peoples of the American Southwest hold various rituals. They are usually round and semi-subterranean, with massive log roofs that are covered by dirt. People enter via a ladder placed in a central opening in the roof that also serves as a smokehole.

Many archaeological kivas share certain features: an exterior, stone-lined vertical shaft that opens near the kiva floor, a central fireplace, and an upright stone slab (or a small masonry wall) between the fireplace and the shaft's opening. These features (shown in Figure 8-1) are probably functional. The fireplace provided light and warmth. The shaft provided ventilation, and the upright stone deflected wind blowing down the shaft and prevented smoke and embers from disturbing the ritual.

Along the wall opposite the ventilator shaft, archaeologists usually find a very small pit or simply a depression called the **sipapu** (a Hopi term meaning "place of emergence"). Unlike the fireplace, ventilator shaft, and deflector stone, the sipapu has no apparent material function. To interpret this recurrent feature, archaeologists turned to living Pueblo societies, such as the Hopi, who use kivas today for rituals.

Hopi kivas also contain this small, innocuous pit, and its size belies its cultural significance, for the sipapu symbolizes the place where the Hopi emerged from the underworld. In traditional Pueblo theology, the world consists of several levels, and oral histories recount stories of people moving from one level to the next by crawling through a small opening. The current world, the Hopi say, is the fourth world, with more worlds above it. The kiva's sipapu is a reminder of these stories, and a portal through which the natural and supernatural worlds communicate. Archaeologists commonly infer that sipapus in archaeological kivas had the same function as they do in modern kivas.

Does this inference fit the definition of an analogy? Let's put it into the David and Kramer definition:

▶ Archaeological kivas are semi-subterranean with entry through the smokehole; they have a central fireplace, a ventilator shaft, a deflector stone, and a small pit opposite the ventilator shaft.

▶ Hopi kivas are semi-subterranean with entry through the smokehole; they have a central fireplace, a ventilator shaft, a deflector stone, and a small pit (the sipapu) opposite the ventilator shaft. The sipapu represents the hole where the Hopi emerged into the current world; it allows communication between the natural and supernatural worlds.

▶ Therefore, the small pits in archaeological kivas are sipapus, and represent the place where ancient peoples say they emerged from a previous underworld, and where the natural and supernatural worlds communicate.

This seems straightforward enough, but such analogies must be used cautiously. Why? Because just as we enumerated the similarities between the Hopi and the archaeological kivas, we can also list the *differences* between them: Hopi kivas are often square,

© Robert Kelly

Figure 8-1 Looking down into an unroofed kiva at Mesa Verde National Park; note the square opening for the ventilation shaft (at the top of the photo), the upright stone between the ventilation shaft and the central hearth, and the sipapu—the small hole near the bottom of the photo.

kiva A Pueblo ceremonial structure that is usually round (but may be square or rectangular) and semi-subterranean. They appear in early Pueblo sites and perhaps even in the earlier (pre–AD 700) pithouse villages.

sipapu A Hopi word that loosely translates as "place of emergence." The original sipapu is the place where the Hopi are said to have emerged into this world from the underworld. Sipapus are also small pits in kivas through which communication with the supernatural world takes place.

not round; they are often placed in open plazas or streets between room blocks, rather than incorporated into blocks of residential rooms as they were at many prehistoric pueblos. We could list the similarities between Hopi and archaeological kivas and stack those up against the differences. But how similar do ethnographic and archaeological cases have to be for the analogy to hold true?

Formal and Relational Analogies To answer this question, we must consider two major kinds of analogy, which Alison Wylie (University of Washington) terms **formal** and **relational analogies.** Formal analogies rely on similarities in *form*—hence "formal" attributes—between the archaeological and ethnographic cases, regardless of whether the analogies come from the same culture. For example, we infer that stone projectile points, such as those you saw in Chapter 7, are in fact projectile points because they are so similar to the stone tips found on the spears and arrows of many ethnographically known peoples the world over. Formal analogies are strengthened (1) if many ethnographic cases demonstrate the same pattern and/or (2) if the archaeological and ethnographic cases have many attributes in common. But no rules tell us *how many* ethnographic cases make a strong analogy, or *how many* similarities between the archaeological and ethnographic cases are needed to justify an analogy. We only know that more of each is better.

Relational analogies entail formal similarities, but the archaeological and ethnographic cases must be related in some fashion. By "related," we mean that they both come from societies with similar settlement systems, economies, or environments; for instance, they may both be desert-adapted hunting-and-gathering societies, or the ethnographic society that serves as an analogy may be a cultural descendant of the archaeological case. In addition, relational analogies may entail "natural" relations—that is, a causal and hence *necessary* link between the attributes of an object or a feature and their interpretation. We'll come back to this aspect of relational analogies in a moment.

The kiva example involves elements of both formal and relational analogies because (a) there are formal similarities between the archaeological and contemporary Hopi kivas, and (b) modern Hopi culture is clearly related to ancient Pueblo culture. Analogies such as this have been and always will be important to archaeological inference.

But analogy entails certain risks. Suppose, for instance, you are studying a prehistoric horticultural and pastoral society in the deserts of Kenya. In the site you've excavated are many stone scrapers. You are interested in inferring who used these tools, men or women. As we will see in Chapter 11, inferring gender-specific activities from archaeological data is an extremely difficult task. Analogy is one option for making the inference.

Knowing that analogies are safer the closer they are in time and space to the archaeological case, you might look around Africa for a contemporary society that is roughly comparable to the archaeological one— one that lives in a similar environment with a similar economy and a similar culture. Doing this, you would encounter the ethnographic research of Steven Brandt (University of Florida) and Kathryn Weedman (University of South Florida) with several Ethiopian peoples. Among these people today are individuals who work cattle skins to manufacture bedding and bags; about a third of these hide-workers use stone tools.

This would seem to have terrific potential for building an analogy, but which Ethiopian group should you use? If you pick the Gamo, you'll find that men do all the hide working and tool manufacture. The Gamo analogy would imply that men also did all the hide working in your archaeological society. But among the Konso, *women* do virtually all the stone tool manufacture and hide working (Figure 8-2), so the Konso analogy would generate a very different conclusion.

Like dynamite and backhoes, analogies belong in the archaeologist's toolkit, but they must be used with caution.

One solution to this problem is to determine the relative strength of the analogy. By increasing the number of formal similarities between an ethnographic and an archaeological case, we increase the probability that the formal analogy is correct. Still, we don't know if an analogy that relies on ten attributes is twice as good as one with only five. Even the best analogy is no more than a probability—and there's always a chance that you're wrong.

Drawing the analogy from an ethnographic case that is culturally related to the archaeological one improves the analogy, but what if recent events have caused cultural discontinuity between the past and the present? And what happens with archaeological cases that have no clear ethnographic referent, such as the 10,000-year-old Folsom site mentioned in Chapter 4?

formal analogies Analogies justified by similarities in the formal attributes of archaeological and ethnographic objects and features.

relational analogies Analogies justified on the basis of close cultural continuity between the archaeological and ethnographic cases or similarity in general cultural form.

Figure 8-2 Sokati Chirayo, a Konso woman in Ethiopia, working a hide with a stone scraper mounted in a wooden handle.

theories through taphonomy, experimental archaeology, and ethnoarchaeology.

TAPHONOMY

The word **taphonomy** (from the Greek meaning "the laws of burial") was coined by the Russian paleontologist I. A. Efremov in the 1940s; it refers to the study of how organisms become part of the fossil record. Archaeologists expanded the term to refer to the study of how natural processes contribute to the formation of archaeological sites. In Chapter 5, we discussed site formation processes—how human behavior and natural processes affect the creation of the archaeological record. Taphonomy is an important aspect of the study of site formation processes because it considers how human behavior and natural processes incorporate bones and plants into sites.

Taphonomists study bizarre stuff. One might record how large animal carcasses decompose on an African savanna (Figure 8-3). How long does it take the carcass to disarticulate? Which bones separate first? Which ones are carried away by carnivores? Is decomposition in the rainy season the same as in the dry season? Others might examine lion kills and ask what telltale markings lions leave behind. How do these differ from the evidence that human hunters leave behind?

Another might climb to raptor nests along a cliff to collect their feces or pellets (actually dried up vomit; many raptors eat prey whole and then regurgitate the bones and hair). What do rodent bones look like after they have passed through a raptor? Or what do fish bones look like after passing through a dog? How about through a human? Depending on your perspective, taphonomic research is either gross or really cool.

Middle-Level Theory as Powerful Analogy As noted previously, relational analogies can rely not just on cultural continuity but also on "natural" relationships, by which Wylie means causal linkages between attributes of a thing and the inference being made.

Analogies based on such causal linkages are considered middle-level theory. Middle-level theory is a special kind of analogy simply because it *is* theory. As you will recall from Chapter 2, theories explain things; they answer "why" questions. Middle-level theory tries to make an analogy more certain by explaining *why* a *necessary* relationship exists between an object's or feature's attributes and an inference made from those attributes. Relying on the principle of uniformitarianism, middle-level theory attempts to explain why an inference must be true.

This isn't easy. In fact, establishing such *necessary* relationships might be the archaeologist's most difficult chore. Consider the previous example in which the archaeologist wanted to know whether men or women used stone scrapers. What theory can *necessarily* link some observable attribute of a scraper—such as length, width, thickness, raw material, or context—to the gender of its user? It's hard to imagine.

Absolute certainty will forever elude archaeological inference, but archaeologists have been able to make increasingly secure inferences from archaeological remains by constructing their middle-level

taphonomy The study of how organisms become part of the fossil record; in archaeology, it primarily refers to the study of how natural processes produce patterning in archaeological data.

© Steven Brandt/Kathryn Weedman

Figure 8-3 Diane Gifford-Gonzales collecting data in 1973 for a taphonomic study in Africa.

© Diane Gifford-Gonzalez, photo by Michael J. Mehlman

How many ways do seeds, leaves, twigs, and pollen enter archaeological sites? Here you might study the feces of various herbivores, the plant-collecting behavior of pack rats (more on them in Chapter 9), or the way that wind or water carries leaves, pollen, and sediments.

Recall that taphonomy tries mostly to understand the natural processes that contribute to a site's formation. Although still difficult, it's easier to infer natural processes from artifacts and ecofacts than it is to infer human behavior because natural processes are more mechanistic (and hence more predictable) than human behavior. This observation is useful to archaeology for two reasons: Remember first that data are *observations* on objects and that archaeologists seek *patterns* in their data. So one strategy for understanding an archaeological site is first to *remove all the patterns resulting from natural processes*. This leaves us with the remaining patterns that must be explained in terms of human behavior. We saw this approach in action at the site of Cagny-l'Epinette (discussed in Chapter 5).

Second, knowing how a site formed is crucial to understanding not just the human behavior that took place there, but also the *environmental context* of that behavior. This information can tell us if the climate was temperate or tropical, if a landscape was eroding away or aggrading, if streams were running or were dry, if forest fires were prevalent, and so on.

Archaeologists use taphonomic research to develop bridging arguments by simultaneously (yet independently) observing natural processes in action and their material results. By trying to explain *why* those natural processes produce the particular material results that they do, you move from simple analogies into middle-level theory. The Hudson-Meng bison **bonebed** provides an example of taphonomic research in archaeology.

Taphonomy at the Hudson-Meng Bison Bonebed

The Hudson-Meng site lies in a low swale in windswept northwest Nebraska, where the remains of at least 500 bison were discovered crowded into an area of 1000 square meters (Figure 8-4). Twenty-one spear points (or point fragments) were found among the remains. AMS dates indicate that the site is about 9500 radiocarbon years old.

Paleontologist Larry Agenbroad (Northern Arizona University) was the first to dig at Hudson-Meng, in the 1970s. Using the standard conventions of the day, he inferred human behavior from *patterns* he observed in the faunal remains. It was striking that the tops of the crania were missing. Mandibles were present along with some cranial fragments, but the top of nearly every single skull was missing. Agenbroad knew that modern Plains Indians often broke bison skulls open to remove the brains for tanning hides. Using this analogy, he reasoned that the skull tops at Hudson-Meng were missing for the same reason and, therefore, that humans must have killed the animals.

Agenbroad then made several more inferences. How could hunters on foot, armed only with spears, have killed 500 bison? Horseless hunters, Agenbroad reasoned, could not control such a large herd. So he inferred that there must be a low cliff nearby that is

bonebed Archaeological and paleontological sites consisting of the remains of a large number of animals, often of the same species, and often representing a single moment in time—a mass kill or mass death.

© Lawrence C. Todd

Figure 8-4 Students excavating a small portion of the Hudson-Meng site, Nebraska. A weather-port covers this excavation.

now buried beneath the sand that blows daily across western Nebraska. The hunters must have driven the bison over the cliff and then dragged 500 carcasses to a processing area. Calculating that 500 bison could produce nearly 10,000 kilograms of dried meat, Agenbroad further inferred that the ancient hunters were a large group, with a sophisticated way to store meat.

So, Agenbroad had made inferences about (1) the presence of humans, (2) hunting strategy, (3) group size, and (4) food storage, all based on the patterning—the missing skull tops—evident in the skeletal assemblage. Each inference was based on an analogy with historically known Plains Indians, with elements of both formal and relational analogies:

▶ This was formal analogy because it relied on the similarity in bison skull form (the missing top of the cranium), and parallels between the site and ethnographically documented butchering practices.

▶ This was relational analogy because it extrapolated known behaviors of Plains Indians back in time to Plains Indian ancestors.

But this was not middle-level theory because Agenbroad did not draw upon Plains Indian butchery practices to explain the appearance of the bison skulls at Hudson-Meng. The necessary bridging argument was assumed, not demonstrated. From a taphonomic perspective, archaeologists look at the foundation of Agenbroad's inferences—the missing crania—and

wonder: Could any natural processes create the same pattern?

Hudson-Meng has always presented some troubling facts. For example, comparing it with similar bison kill sites, we might expect something closer to 150 points and point fragments, not just 21. And why are there no cut marks on the bones? In the process of butchering 500 bison, isn't it likely that a stone knife would occasionally have cut to bone as it sliced through tendons and meat? Archaeologists have encountered thousands of such telltale nicks at other kill/butchery sites, but only carnivore tooth marks appear on the bones at Hudson-Meng. Finally, many of the skeletal remains were discovered in anatomical position, lying in the ground as if the bison had simply died there and were buried undisturbed. If ancient hunters had butchered these animals, wouldn't they have removed at least some of the meaty portions of the body, such as the upper rear leg (containing the femur)?

Lawrence Todd (retired) and David Rapson (Wyoming State Historic Preservation Office) were bothered by these questions, so they excavated a portion of the Hudson-Meng site using a battery of high-precision excavation techniques. They also applied the perspective of taphonomy by asking a very simple question: How do bison fall apart?

For years, taphonomists have studied the carcasses of large animals as they lay decomposing on North America's high plains, Africa's Serengeti, and elsewhere. Some of these animals had been shot; others had frozen to death or simply died of old age. Some were ravaged by carnivores; others were undisturbed. Some died on hillsides, others in gullies. Some died in the winter (wet season), others in the summer (dry season). Sometimes the hide dried to form an armor-like case, holding the bones together years after death; sometimes the rotting carcass burst from the maggots within. In other words, taphonomists had documented what actually happens to a large animal carcass under a variety of natural circumstances.

Are there any patterns in how these large animal skeletons fall apart? Absolutely. Andrew Hill

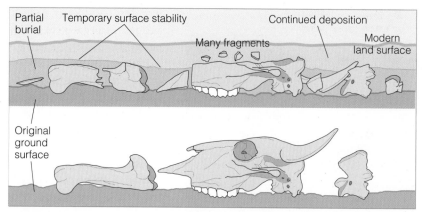

Figure 8-5 Todd and Rapson's reconstruction of how taphonomic processes, rather than human butchering, created the pattern of incomplete crania at the Hudson-Meng site. The animal dies and decomposes; as the body collapses into a pile of bone (bottom), it continues to trap sediment until it is mostly buried, although the skull's top remains exposed. The cranium weathers (top), and the small bone fragments that flake off are blown away by the wind.

(Yale University) and Anna Behrensmeyer (Smithsonian Institution) found that the first joint to disarticulate is where the scapula attaches to the vertebral column, allowing the entire front limb to drop away. Then the caudal (tail) vertebrae-to-sacrum joint goes, followed by the scapula-humerus joint, and then the "elbow," where the humerus articulates with the radius and ulna. The vertebrae tend to be the last joints to disarticulate. Such documented sequences of natural disarticulation provide a baseline against which to judge the distinctiveness of human butchering practices.

A decomposing bison carcass will eventually collapse into a flat pile of bones (Figure 8-5). The skull often ends up resting on its mandibles (the lower jaw). Carnivores may drag some limb bones away and, eventually, the entire skeleton lies flat on the ground—with the skull poking up above all the other bones.

This bone pile effectively becomes a sediment trap, catching the blowing dust and sand. It takes 10 to 15 centimeters of sediment to cover the now collapsed limb bones and rib cage, but 30 to 40 centimeters to cover the skull. This means that much of the skull is left sticking up above the ground surface after the rest of the bones are buried. And once leg bones, vertebrae, and ribs are buried—thus covering most of the irregular surface that traps blowing sand—sediment accumulates less quickly, leaving the top of the skull exposed for a longer period of time than the rest of the skeleton.

Then the sun goes to work. Sunlight is quite destructive of bone, and the exposed top of the skull quickly flakes away. Eventually, the top of the skull is destroyed and the rest is buried.

Taphonomy and Uniformitarianism

So the incomplete crania, the basis of Agenbroad's analogy, can readily be explained by natural processes, not human behavior. This is more than simple analogy—it is middle-level theory because we understand *why* bison bones disarticulate, become buried, and weather the way that they do. But this understanding is based on observations of modern animals. Can we trust these observations to explain archaeological remains?

The principle of uniformitarianism applies here because ancient animals, like the bison that died at Hudson-Meng, had the same anatomy as the animals observed in taphonomic studies. Bison skeleton disarticulation is governed by the amount of cartilage and tendons holding bones together and the amount of muscle tissue around them. The more cartilage, tendon, and muscle in a joint, the more that joint resists disarticulation. If skeletal disarticulation is largely a product of anatomy, and if bison anatomy has not changed over the past 10,000 years (and it hasn't), then modern observations are relevant to the interpretation of archaeological data.

Likewise, the effects of the sun reflect the nature of both bone and sunlight. Given that neither sunlight nor bone composition has changed over time, we have gone beyond analogy to explain *why* particular natural factors have particular predictable effects on bone.

This is middle-level theory. And the implication is that humans played little role, if any, in the deaths of the 500 bison at Hudson-Meng. But if humans did not kill them, what happened? Todd and Rapson hypothesize that a summer storm sparked a massive prairie fire that drove the bison herd into the swale for protection (many of the bison lie with their heads to the southeast, which, using analogy with modern bison behavior, suggests that they were responding to a northwest wind). None of the bones are burned, so these animals were not burned to death. But the fire could have jumped the swale and asphyxiated the bison by sucking up all the oxygen for a few critical minutes. This hypothesis remains to be tested.

And what of the 21 projectile points found there? As you have seen in previous chapters, archaeological sites are often reoccupied. In their careful excavations, Todd and Rapson found several thin soils containing a few archaeological remains *above* the bison. And Agenbroad actually found fewer than 10 points *among* the bones. The spear points, then, were probably discarded or lost long after the bison had died, decomposed, and become buried, and a few points moved downward into the bonebed through the sorts of post-depositional processes we discussed in Chapter 5.

EXPERIMENTAL ARCHAEOLOGY

Taphonomy uses observations of modern processes to help make inferences from archaeological data. But what if this is impossible? What if we want to know the material effects of behaviors *that no longer exist*? This is especially relevant to human behaviors because people did things in the past that they no longer do today. Understanding the material remains of these behaviors requires **experimental archaeology.**

Experimental archaeology is not new. Nearly a century ago, for example, Saxton Pope, a surgeon at San Francisco's University of California Medical Center, began experimenting with archery methods. The poignant story began in 1911, when a starving, defeated Indian was found crouching in a slaughterhouse corral near Oroville, California. His family may have been murdered, or perhaps they starved to death. Ishi (circa 1860–1916) himself may have lost his will to live. He could neither speak nor understand English. The local sheriff locked him in the jail because "wild" Indians were not allowed to roam about freely in those days.

Alfred Kroeber (1876–1960), a young anthropologist at the University of California, was brought to the jail; he recognized the Indian's language as Yahi, a native language of California. Kroeber named the man Ishi ("human" in Yahi) and brought him to San Francisco, where he stayed at the university museum, worked as an assistant janitor, and demonstrated arrow making and fire starting for museum visitors. Kroeber and his staff taught Ishi their culture, and the Indian shared many of his survival skills.

But Ishi soon developed a tubercular cough—which later cost him his life—and he was treated daily by Dr. Pope. Over their short association, Pope and Ishi found a common interest in archery. An odd combination: Pope, the urbane scholar paired with the Yahi Indian, hair singed in tribal custom, together shooting arrows through the parks of downtown San Francisco. Pope was a good student and, after Ishi's death (see "Looking Closer: What Happened to Ishi?"), the doctor continued his research, studying bows and arrows in museum collections and often test-shooting the ancient specimens.

Pope wrote *Hunting With the Bow and Arrow* in 1923, describing his experiments in archery. The book provided baseline information for interpreting ancient finds and quickly became the bible of the bow-hunting fraternity (in fact, it is credited with reviving the sport of bow hunting in America).

From early studies such as Pope's, experimental archaeology expanded dramatically and has become an important way for archaeologists to reconstruct the past.

How Were Stone Tools Made?

Many prehistoric techniques died with their practitioners, and experimental archaeologists have been forced to rediscover them. Making stone tools is one such technique, and many archaeologists have experimented by manufacturing their own stone tools.

To make a stone tool, you must first locate and collect the appropriate raw materials—rocks that break with a glassy fracture such as obsidian, quartzite, or chert. This may require excavating into bedrock because frost fracturing and sunlight can ruin surface specimens. Some ancient peoples excavated major quarries into bedrock using only fire and wooden wedges.

If the stone is chert or quartzite, you might improve it by **heat treatment**—burying large **flakes** or small **cores** in about 5 centimeters of sand, then burning a fire on top for a day or so. Ancient flintknappers learned that they could more easily chip and shape

experimental archaeology Experiments designed to determine the archaeological correlates of ancient behavior; may overlap with both ethnoarchaeology and taphonomy.

heat treatment A process whereby the flintknapping properties of stone tool raw material are improved by subjecting the material to heat.

flake A thin, sharp sliver of stone removed from a core during the knapping process.

core A piece of stone that is worked ("knapped"). Cores sometimes serve merely as sources for raw materials; they also can serve as functional tools.

LOOKING CLOSER

WHAT HAPPENED TO ISHI?

Ishi was well cared for in his modest quarters at the University of California's museum in San Francisco. But the museum was located next to the university's medical center, where physicians performed autopsies on the bodies of the poor. Ishi always expressed trepidation about these practices, and he asked Kroeber that no autopsy be performed when his time came.

When Kroeber left for an extended stay on the East Coast in 1916, he suspected that Ishi was ill, so he kept in close contact with museum authorities. When Pope informed Kroeber of Ishi's impending death, Kroeber demanded that Ishi not be autopsied and that his remains be cremated, in accordance with what Kroeber believed to be Yahi custom. Kroeber must have feared that his orders would be ignored, for he wrote to a colleague, "If there is any talk about the interests of science, say for me that science can go to hell."

But Kroeber's directions were ignored, and the hospital staff autopsied Ishi. Eventually, his remains were cremated and his ashes placed in a Pueblo Indian jar at Mount Olive Cemetery. But Ishi's brain was preserved in a jar of formaldehyde and presented to Kroeber upon his return to Berkeley.

Given Kroeber's passionate feelings toward Ishi, it is odd that he quickly wrote to renowned biological anthropologist Alés Hrdlička at the Smithsonian Institution, asking him if the institution wished to have Ishi's brain, given that "There is no one here who can put it to scientific use." Hrdlička agreed, and Ishi's brain eventually was stored in a warehouse in Maryland. And there it sat for nearly 85 years (alongside the brain of John Wesley Powell; see Chapter 2).

In 1997, members of the Pit River tribe requested that the University of California turn over Ishi's remains for proper burial. The ashes were located, but the university denied that the brain had been removed, and the Smithsonian denied that it had it. But these denials were impossible to maintain after Orin Starn (Duke University) found Kroeber's correspondence and tracked down Ishi's brain at the warehouse. On August 8, 2000, Ishi's ashes and his brain were returned to the Pit River tribe, who buried the remains in a secret place.

Why did Kroeber act this way? Why did he send Ishi's brain away rather than cremate or bury it? We don't really know because Kroeber never spoke publicly about Ishi. Perhaps he simply saw the autopsy as a *fait accompli*

stone treated in this way. The problem is that, over the millennia, plenty has been forgotten about the detailed technology required to make good stone tools from a pile of rocks.

Fortunately, a school of experimentalists—many of them dedicated amateur archaeologists—has rediscovered some of this technology. One of the best known, Don Crabtree (1912–1980) spent a lifetime experimenting with stone tool manufacturing methods (Figure 8-6). One of his projects was to rediscover the techniques used to fabricate Folsom spear points.

Remember from Chapter 4 that Folsom points, including those found at the Folsom site in New Mexico, date to 10,200–10,900 radiocarbon years ago. These exquisite points turn up in many sites on the Great Plains and in the Rocky Mountains where, mounted on spears or darts, they brought down game, including bison. Although the points are often only about 6 to

© James Woods

Figure 8-6
Accomplished flintknapper Don Crabtree uses a hammerstone to percussion-flake a block of obsidian.

and decided that some good might as well come out of it (although the Smithsonian never used Ishi's brain for study). Others see in Kroeber's actions a fundamental, if unconscious, racism. With a century of hindsight, it is easy to criticize.

But anthropologist Nancy Scheper-Hughes (University of California, Berkeley) suggests another interpretation. Scheper-Hughes studies violence—physical and psychological—and she understands the myriad ways that people respond to the grief that comes with the loss of loved ones. She interprets Kroeber's actions as evidence of "disordered mourning." Kroeber had lost his first wife—also to tuberculosis—only 2 years before Ishi's death. Indeed, Kroeber was depressed and melancholic from 1915 to 1922 (because of these losses and the effects of Ménière's disease). Scheper-Hughes sees Kroeber's actions as a way to conceal deep feelings of loss—over Ishi and his first wife— that were too difficult to confront. So perhaps we should not be so quick to pass judgment on Kroeber.

© American Museum of Natural History

Ishi, a Yana-Yahi man.

8 centimeters (2½ to 3 inches) long, Crabtree counted more than 150 minute sharpening flakes removed from their surface.

The most distinctive property of Folsom artifacts is the **flute**—the wide, shallow, longitudinal grooves on each face of the point (Figure 8-7). Flutes are made by removing **channel flakes** from the point's base on both sides. Nobody is sure why these artifacts were thinned this way, but everybody agrees that fluting is an extraordinary feat of flintknapping.

The technical quality of Folsom points intrigued Crabtree. With enough practice, you can learn to quickly fashion many kinds of projectile points. But making Folsom points must have required hours, assuming that you understood how to do it in the first place. And in the twentieth century, nobody did.

Archaeologists have long speculated how ancient peoples removed the channel flakes. And for 40 years,

Crabtree tried every way he could think of to manufacture Folsom replicas. He eventually described 11 different methods he had tried to remove channel flakes. Most simply didn't work: Either the technique was impossible with primitive tools or the resulting flute was different from those on the Folsom points. One method succeeded only in driving a copper punch through his left hand.

Crabtree eventually concluded that channel flakes could be removed in only two ways. In one experiment, he placed an antler shaft, known as a "punch,"

flute Distinctive channel on the faces of Folsom and Clovis projectile points formed by removal of one or more flakes from the point's base.

channel flake The longitudinal flake removed from the faces of Folsom and Clovis projectile points to create the flute.

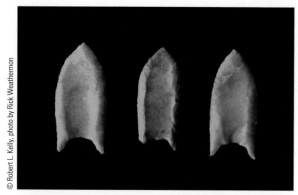

Figure 8-7 Experimental Folsom spear points manufactured by Eugene Gryba. Note the large "fluting" flakes that were removed from surfaces of the points. Points are about 5 cm long.

on the bottom of the unfinished artifact and then struck the punch with a sharp upward blow. Because placing the antler punch was critical, this technique required two workers. A second technique was based on the seventeenth-century observations of Juan de Torquemada, a Spanish Franciscan friar who traveled through the Central American jungles in 1615. This method used a chest crutch to drive flakes off a core, and Crabtree wondered if it could also remove channel flakes off a Folsom point.

So Crabtree manufactured a chest crutch following Torquemada's description, padding one end and equipping the other with the end of an antler (Figure 8-8). He tied an unfinished experimental Folsom point into

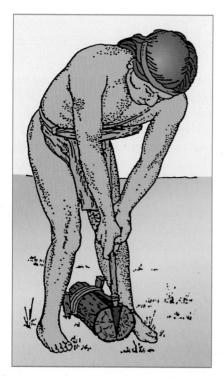

Figure 8-8 Conjectural reconstruction of the use of a chest crutch to drive off the central flute from a Folsom point.

a wood-and-thong vise, which he gripped between his feet. Bracing the crutch against his chest and pressing downward, he successfully detached perfect channel flakes, time after time. The resulting artifacts were almost identical to prehistoric Folsom points.

Crabtree's research unleashed an avalanche of experimentation in the fluting problem (it also had some unintended practical consequences; see "Looking Closer: Obsidian Blade Technology: Modern Surgery's Newest Ancient Frontier"). Today, we know that some ten different methods can successfully remove channel flakes and produce the distinctive flutes of Folsom points.

Experimental Archaeology and Uniformitarianism

Archaeologists have used replicative experiments in several ways. Some have experimented with methods of moving enormous blocks of stone, such as the huge statues on Easter Island in the Pacific Ocean or the large blocks of Stonehenge. They have experimented with all sorts of manufacturing techniques to make what is found in archaeological sites—stone tools, pottery, basketry, metal tools, houses, and so on. Some have even built structures and then burned them down to see how destruction translates into archaeology.

But what do these experiments actually prove? Researchers have found many ways to remove channel flakes from Folsom points, but which method was actually used in Folsom times? Where's the element of uniformitarianism?

Sometimes, a variety of methods will work successfully. Crabtree demonstrated that it was *not impossible* to use a chest crutch to replicate Folsom points. But experiments show that other methods were also possible. None of the experimental flintknappers demonstrated conclusively how Folsom points were *actually made*. Replicative experiments often only demonstrate that a given technique *could have* been used in the past—that it was *not impossible*.

Determining which method (or methods) Folsom flintknappers actually used requires more research, experiments comparing the characteristics of ancient Folsom points and the waste flakes from their manufacture with experimentally produced Folsom points and their corresponding waste flakes. Because we know that stone breaks according to certain principles of fracture mechanics, studying the characteristics of flakes produced in modern experiments can help us infer what techniques were used in the past.

LOOKING CLOSER

OBSIDIAN BLADE TECHNOLOGY: MODERN SURGERY'S NEWEST ANCIENT FRONTIER

Should you try your hand at flintknapping, it won't be long until you cut yourself. In his 50 years of flintknapping, Don Crabtree slashed himself in every conceivable way—across his fingers, through his palm, through a fingernail; one flake zipped right through his shoe.

Examining his cuts one day, Crabtree noticed that, although he still had scars from jagged-edged flint flakes, the wounds caused by obsidian had healed quickly and were almost invisible. He wondered about that.

Then Crabtree saw a friend slice himself while handling some newly made obsidian artifacts. The gash bled profusely, and a physician was summoned. But by the time the doctor arrived, some 20 minutes later, the wound had already begun to heal.

Curious, Crabtree used an electron microscope to compare some fresh obsidian flakes with new razor blades. Interestingly, he found that the fresh flakes were many times sharper than the best razor blades.

Crabtree recognized the potential of such super sharp instruments for surgical applications, but worried that "the surgeon who pioneers the use of such blades may be accused of reverting to caveman tactics." Then, in 1975, when Crabtree himself faced major surgery, he managed to convince his surgeon, Dr. Bruce A. Buck, to use obsidian blades Crabtree himself had fashioned.

The first surgery was when I had a rib removed and a lung section. The cut goes from right under the breast there, clear around back under the shoulder blade. So it's about an 18" cut. And you know I hardly have a scar.... And then I've had abdominal surgery four times, from my sternum down to the pelvis.... Then I had bilateral femur arteries of woven dacron tubing put in.... And there was no problem with sterilization. A fresh blade comes off sterile.

Not long thereafter, more assessments cropped up in medical journals reporting on successful experimental surgeries and speculating about additional applications. Everyone was impressed with the "exquisitely sharp" obsidian edge. It turns out that obsidian blades are as sharp as the newest diamond scalpels, are 100 to 300 times sharper than steel scalpels, and leave a smaller cut with much clearer edges—meaning that obsidian blade incisions are quicker to heal and less likely to leave a scar than incisions made with a steel blade.

Several archaeologists now produce obsidian blades commercially for surgery. These blades have been used in eye surgery, breast biopsies, bilateral vasectomies, facial plastic surgery, and nerve microsurgery.

But even lacking these findings, experimental archaeology has already taught us three important things about Folsom spear point manufacture. First, regardless of which technique is used, it's difficult to flute points; it takes much practice. Second, fluting results in a rather high breakage rate near the end of the manufacturing sequence, regardless of the technique. And third, fluting appears to have no specific function. In fact, after Folsom times, similar but unfluted spear points were made for another thousand years. Presumably, these were as effective as Folsom points.

The uniformitarian element of experimental archaeology often comes in the guise of telling us what *could* or *could not* have happened in the past. Although this may not pinpoint the precise technique that was actually used, it can provide powerful tests of hypotheses. Here's an example.

Building the Pyramids

Swiss author Erich von Däniken long argued that aliens from outer space had built the world's prehistoric wonders, including the pyramids. Von Däniken looked at those engineering marvels (see Chapter 2) and asked: How is it possible that a primitive people working with the simplest of tools could have built structures of such astounding size and sophistication? How could the

Egyptians have even moved the large stones and statues without the aid of advanced technology? Since Von Däniken assumed these were impossible feats for ancients, why not attribute them to aliens?

Von Däniken's hypothesis can be tested using experimental archaeology: Can stones weighing several tons be moved using only the tools and materials that the ancient Egyptians had available to them? If not, then perhaps his hypothesis has some merit. But if such stones *can* be moved with Egyptian technology, his hypothesis is undermined.

Had von Däniken done his homework, he would have learned about the paintings within Egyptian tombs that showed men hauling stones and statues. One shows 172 men pulling a statue of Djehutihotep (a Middle Kingdom noble), estimated to weigh some 58 tons (thus, each man is pulling about 650 pounds). The statue rides on a wooden sledge accompanied by a man who pours a liquid onto the runway in front of the sledge—perhaps oil to cut down the friction and thereby lighten the workmen's burden.

But does this method really work? Can people haul stone up ramps hundreds of feet long? Maybe the Egyptian tomb painters just made it up.

More than a decade ago, experimental archaeology answered this question. Archaeologist Mark Lehner (Oriental Institute of the University of Chicago and Harvard Semitic Museum) and stonemason Roger Hopkins staged an experiment to see whether they could move large blocks of stone this way. Working with Egyptian quarrymen and masons, they built a pyramid 20 feet high using ancient Egyptian technology (Figure 8-9). A TV crew from the series *NOVA* filmed the experiment, so they had to complete the pyramid on a tight schedule—3 weeks.

Lehner experimented with several possible techniques to move and lift stone. One used the method depicted in Djehutihotep's tomb, but with the loaded sledge resting on wooden rollers. As the sledge was pulled, the workmen would pick up the rollers behind the sledge and move them to the front. Although this idea seemed sound, Lehner's experiment showed that if the rollers were not placed perfectly, the sledge would veer off course. The same error happened if the rollers were not perfectly lathed. Lehner concluded that moving large stones over long distances with this method might have been more trouble than it was worth.

Another idea was using wooden levers to lift the stones up high. In this method, one side of the block is levered up, and planks are placed beneath it. Then the block's opposite side is levered up, and planks are placed below that side. The workers then repeated

Figure 8-9 Twenty men easily pull a 2-ton block on a sledge along lubricated transport tracks for the *NOVA* pyramid-building experiment.

the process until they raised the stone to the desired height. This idea worked for small rises but, as the block rose higher, levering became difficult and the stone's balance became precarious.

Lehner then turned to ramps. Archaeologists have found remnants of ramps at several Egyptian sites, including the stone quarry beside the Giza Plateau. These ramps consist of two parallel retaining walls, the area between them filled with rubble and topped with sand or crushed gypsum. In this top layer, the Egyptians set planed logs, perpendicular to the retaining walls, about 50 centimeters apart.

Egyptologists speculate on the kinds of ramps used by the ancient Egyptians. Some suggest a straight ramp—although, by the time the pyramid reached its peak, the ramp would have been hundreds of meters long. Other suggestions include ramps that formed a spiral up the sides of the pyramid or multiple ramps built at different levels during construction.

Lehner built his ramp with a 7 percent incline and found that a 2-ton stone resting on a sledge could easily be hauled up by 20 men. Once the stone was on top of the pyramid, 4 or 5 men using levers could roll it. With this method, Lehner built his pyramid within the 3 weeks allotted for the task.

As in the Folsom fluting experiments, researchers found many ways to build a ramp, and perhaps the

© Mark Lehner/Ancient Egypt Research Associates

Egyptians used all of them. But the precise technique does not matter in this case. The principles involved in simple machines like levers and wedges have not changed from the days of the pharaohs; their capabilities today are the same as they were in the past. This is the important element of uniformitarianism that allows Lehner's experiments to test von Däniken's hypothesis. With no more than dirt ramps, wooden sledges, rope, and plenty of strong backs, the ancient Egyptians were well equipped to move the stones necessary to build their pyramids and temples. Aliens from outer space were not required.

What Were Stone Tools Used For?

Experimental archaeology can also help establish the unambiguous signatures of past human activities and contribute to archaeology's bridging arguments. Returning to stone tools, one direction of experimental study is determining the function of prehistoric stone implements.

As stone tools are used, the edges become damaged and dulled. Compare the edges of used and unused stone tools under a microscope, and you will see **microwear** consisting of minute striations, polish, pitting, and/or microflaking—all of which can reveal something about how the tool was used and what it was used on.

Because so few modern people use stone tools in their daily lives, we must turn to experimental research. Microwear research was begun by the late Russian archaeologist Sergei Semenov, whose major work, *Prehistoric Technology*, was published in the Soviet Union in 1957. Many archaeologists have followed his lead and conducted hundreds of experiments to find out what kinds of microwear result from a specific use. Some of the variables include the type of motion (cutting, scraping, boring), the length of time a tool is used, the material being worked (for example, meat, antler, bone, wood, hide), and the stone tool's raw material (such as chert, basalt, or obsidian).

Ruth Tringham (University of California, Berkeley) studied with Semenov and was one of the first to follow up his research. She reproduced tools from British flint and used each in different ways on antler, bone, wood, skin, flesh, and plant fiber, carefully maintaining constant direction of force and counting the number of strokes. Some of the tools were handheld, and others were hafted to handles.

Tringham then examined and photographed the experimental tools under a low-power (40X to 60X) stereoscopic microscope. She concentrated on the microflaking that occurs as stone tools are used and found that different kinds of use produce different kinds of microflakes on different parts of the tools. Cutting, for instance, produced a series of tiny uneven flake scars along both sides of the working edge. Scraping, however, produced flake scars only on the surface opposite that in direct contact with the worked material. Boring produced distinct trapezoidal flake scars, especially on the sides of the tool.

In addition, Tringham found that edge damage varied with the type of materials being worked. Soft materials such as skin and flesh produced only scalar-shaped scars, whereas hard materials such as antler and bone slowly crushed the edges, eventually dulling the tool so that it would no longer cut at all.

Tringham's experiments established the value of functional analysis with low-power microscopy, and numerous investigators have followed her, taking advantage of the relatively inexpensive equipment and rapid rate of analysis.

Lawrence Keeley (University of Illinois) pioneered an alternative approach. He used high-power microscopy (up to 400X) and focused on micropolishes rather than microflaking. He found that different worked materials produce different kinds of polish. Some polishes were pitted, some were not; some were extensive, others were present only on the high points of a tool's microtopography (Figure 8-10).

M. H. Newcomer (University of London) was skeptical of Keeley's ability to determine tool use from microwear analysis, and Keeley agreed to a series of blind experiments to test his method's accuracy. Newcomer manufactured 15 tools of fine-grained black English flint. He then worked on a series of materials, such as pine wood, ox hide, and lamb meat, and replicated a range of simple activities, such as scraping, slicing, and boring.

Newcomer then turned the artifacts over to Keeley. The implements were cleaned using detergent, warm water, some chemicals, and an ultrasonic cleaning tank (this is now fairly standard in microwear studies because it removes even fingerprints and organic deposits from tool surfaces). Keeley then studied each piece microscopically, looking at (1) general tool size and shape, (2) type and placement of damage, (3) distribution and orientation of microscopic scratches, and (4) location and extent of polish.

microwear Minute, often microscopic, evidence of use damage on the surface and working edge of a flake or artifact; can include striations, pitting, microflaking, and polish.

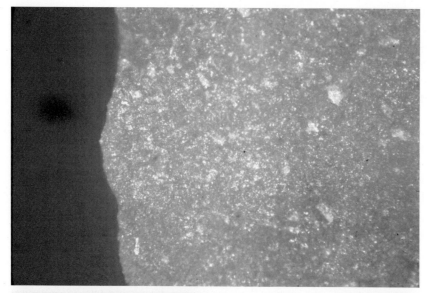

© Doug Bamforth

Figure 8-10 Comparison of tool use wear polishes. On the top is a photo taken of a tool's edge before use; on the bottom, the same tool edge after using it to scrape the inside of a hide (both photos taken at 200X).

worked (63% correct), but look at some of the "misses": In conducting his butchering experiments, Newcomer had used a wooden cutting board, and Keeley felt that the wood and meat polishes confounded the interpretation of Tool 12. Similarly, Keeley misread the polish on Tool 7 as bone polish and that on Tool 11 as antler polish. But as it turned out, Newcomer had used extremely well-seasoned wood in both cases, at least 10 years old. Such hard wood would mimic the effects of antler.

All in all, these results established the validity of Keeley's high-power microwear method, which has become an important method in the analysis of ancient stone tools.

Others have conducted more experiments to refine Keeley's method. Experimental research, for instance, shows that tools used for only a few minutes do not develop distinctive microwear (this may be why Keeley got the material worked by Tool 15 wrong—that tool was only used for 11 minutes, not enough time to develop the polish distinctive of bone).

So, only microwear on heavily used tools can be fruitfully studied. Others have found that some microwears are difficult to distinguish, such as those produced by working hard wood versus bone (as Keeley found). And different kinds of stone—chert, quartzite, and so on—produce different kinds of polishes. In addition, archaeological objects may have seen multiple uses, with the latest form of wear masking an earlier form. And if people resharpened stone tools when they became dull, edges that bore traces of previous use would have been removed, leaving only evidence of the tool's last use. Tools were also dropped, trampled, and affected by geological processes—all of which can mask microwear traces. Because archaeological tools almost always go through

How well did Keeley's method do? In 14 of 16 interpretations (because the right and left edges of Tool 14 seemed different, they were scored independently), he correctly identified the business end of the tool. Keeley admits to "simple human error" in the case of Tool 10, but contends that the lone mistake should not be held against him. There is no doubt in Keeley's mind that, had he looked at the right area of the implement's edge, he would have made the correct interpretation of its function. And Tool 5, used to scrape pig hide for 31 minutes, had no apparent wear, as fat will not damage flint.

Keeley's success fell off slightly when he reconstructed tool use (75% correct), but it wasn't bad. His accuracy fell more when identifying the material being

more confusing life histories than Newcomer's experimental tools, Keeley's success rate is probably the best that the archaeologist should expect.

This experimental research is important, but it is still not quite middle-level theory because it does not tell us *why* microchipping and polish develop in the ways that they do. For example, what is it about chert that results in one type of polish when working meat and another when working antler? Answering this question would allow archaeologists to invoke the principle of uniformitarianism and assume that processes observed in the present can be expected to be true of the past as well. As such research develops, experimental studies of use-wear will have an increasingly more secure footing and play an even more important role in archaeological inference.

Taphonomy is good for understanding the role that natural processes play in creating patterns in data at archaeological sites. And experimental archaeology is useful for establishing how things might have been made in the past or for discovering "mechanical" relationships between behavior and material remains, such as tool use and microwear. But how do we develop middle-level theory to study larger behavioral patterns of human behavior?

ETHNOARCHAEOLOGY

What if we want to know about ancient kinship, social, or political organizations that no longer exist? These are the kinds of questions that archaeologists in the 1960s tried to answer; unfortunately, the answers require a type of behavioral inference that archaeologists at the time had no ability to make.

Binford Takes Off for Points North

In the 1960s, the ways to infer social behavior from archaeological remains were little more than simple rules of thumb that were often culturally biased. Archaeologists began to test them through **ethnoarchaeology**, with the understanding that if generalizations cannot cover *contemporary* behavior, then they cannot be used to interpret the evidence of *ancient* behavior.

Binford was concerned with this inferential problem and he helped solve it by conducting ethnoarchaeological research in the 1970s among the Nunamiut Eskimo of Alaska. Binford's real interest lay in the Middle Paleolithic archaeology of Europe, especially France (see "In His Own Words: Why I Began Doing Ethnoarchaeology" by Lewis R. Binford). Why would he study living Eskimos in Alaska if he was interested in the Middle Paleolithic archaeology of France?

Recall from Chapter 7 ("Looking Closer: The Frison Effect," page 156) that the French archaeologist François Bordes argued that different stone tool Mousterian assemblages were a product of different Neanderthal cultures. These assemblages often alternated throughout the strata of some key French sites, and Bordes argued that this meant that the caves were used alternately by different "tribes" of Neanderthals.

Binford saw things differently. He suspected that the different assemblages were the by-products of different activities, not different tribes. He argued that Bordes's inference (different tool assemblages = different Neanderthal tribes) needed to be evaluated. But we cannot evaluate an inferential argument using archaeological data because the behavior cannot be observed independently of the archaeological data. Binford had to find a place where he could observe living hunting peoples and see what remains their activities left behind—where he could record human behavior and its material consequences without having to infer the former from the latter. The Nunamiut's Arctic environment was somewhat analogous to the French Middle Paleolithic environment, and the Nunamiut hunted large game (caribou and sheep), as had the Neanderthals. But Binford was not as interested in animal bones or the Nunamiut as he was in evaluating the concepts that archaeologists of the time employed to understand the past.

Binford accompanied Nunamiut hunters on their hunting trips, recording what they did at each locality and what debris was left behind. In so doing, he demonstrated that the same people—the same individuals, in fact—left different kinds of tools and bones at different locations on a landscape depending on what they were doing. What Nunamiut hunters left behind was a product not just of their culture, but also of the season of the year, the distance back to camp, the availability of transportation, the amount of food already in camp, the weather, and other factors. Although culture plays a significant role in determining what kinds of artifacts are left behind, Binford demonstrated that archaeologists couldn't uncritically *assume* that a difference in artifact types or frequencies reflects *only* a difference in culture. Other hypotheses, such as site function, have to be

ethnoarchaeology The study of contemporary peoples to determine how human behavior is translated into the archaeological record.

IN HIS OWN WORDS

WHY I BEGAN DOING ETHNOARCHAEOLOGY

by Lewis R. Binford

In 1967 I received funds to go to Europe for a year to work more closely with François Bordes in Bordeaux. My program for research was the following. If we could not study the chipped stone directly, perhaps we could study faunal remains and the horizontal distributions, on excavated archaeological floors, of both fauna and chipped stone. Then it might be possible to relate variability in the lithics to these other properties of the archaeological sites in question. I worked for a year in France, identifying and plotting all the stone tools and animal bones by anatomical part and by breakage pattern.

Thus began a series of disillusionments. I performed one correlation study after another—so many, in fact, that I needed a great steel trunk in order to carry all the papers back to the United States. I could tell you cross-correlations between any pair of Mousterian tool types, between tools and bones, between bones and the drip-lines in cave sites, between almost any type of data you care to name. What I found, of course, was many new facts that

nobody had seen before. But none of these new facts spoke for themselves.

My metal trunk was so big and heavy that I decided to return home by boat and that 5-day trip from Le Havre to New York gave me an opportunity for some disconsolate self-reflection. The whole project was obviously a total failure. What had I done wrong? What had I not done that I should have done? Could it really be that archaeologists simply cannot learn anything about the past? Where was I missing the real problem?

By the time we steamed into New York City, just before the New Year of 1969, some of the answers to these problems were suggested, at least in my thoughts. I prepared a research proposal to go to the Arctic in the spring of 1969 to live with a group of Eskimo hunters. My reasons for going there were little more specific at that stage than that it could hardly fail to be a good educational experience. If I was ever to be able to make accurate inferences from archaeological facts, I was convinced that I had to understand the dynamics of living systems and study their static consequences.

---

tested and discarded before inferring that different tool assemblages in a site's strata indicate use of the site by different cultures.

Ethnoarchaeologists have frequently provided such cautionary tales. But ethnoarchaeology can also be a powerful tool for creating middle-level theory. It can do so (1) if it focuses on aspects of ethnographic data that are archaeologically observable and (2) if it attempts to explain why a relationship between behavior and archaeologically observable remains should necessarily hold true. As we will see, however, the principle of uniformitarianism is harder to implement in ethnoarchaeology than in taphonomy or experimental archaeology.

Ethnoarchaeologists have researched pottery and stone tool production, hunting and butchering, plant gathering, architecture, trash disposal, trade, and burial rituals in many kinds of societies all over the world. All these studies help archaeologists create better ways

of inferring human behavior from archaeological remains. Here we describe one such project conducted by Kelly in Madagascar.

Ethnoarchaeology in Madagascar

Kelly was trained as an archaeologist of western North America. He was particularly interested in how nomadism factored into people's lives. In some cultures, especially hunting-and-gathering societies, people are highly nomadic, moving as often as every week. In others, especially part-time farming cultures, people change their residence less frequently, perhaps only once or twice a year. Some people return seasonally to a settlement for several years in a row, and some stay year-round in sedentary villages.

Kelly wanted to discern different levels of nomadism archaeologically, so he looked for an ethnographic

© Robert Kelly

Figure 8-11 Mikea habitations. Clockwise from upper left: A family sits around a hearth outside a lean-to in a temporary forest camp; a wattle-and-daub house in a permanent village (note the lack of trash); a house with shade structure in a forest hamlet; and a set of less well-made houses in a seasonal hamlet.

situation where he could see variation in nomadism and study its material consequences. He finally learned of the Mikea, a little-known people in the forest of southwestern Madagascar who grow maize and manioc, raise cattle, and do some hunting and gathering.

If you know anything about Madagascar, it's probably lemurs leaping through a tropical forest, but such forests actually make up only a small part of Madagascar. The southwest part of the island, where the Mikea live, is drier and more open. It has distinct wet and dry seasons, and the wet season is blisteringly hot. The forest contains dense vine-covered thickets, stands of 5-meter-high cacti, and baobab trees. There are no rivers in the Mikea Forest and only a few wells. Bordering the forest on one side is the Mozambique Channel and on the other, a vast savanna.

Mikea live in four major kinds of settlements, each occupied for different lengths of time (Figure 8-11). Many have houses in large, permanent villages of 1000 people or more located on the edge of the forest. Here they grow manioc and other crops and raise cattle, pigs, and chickens. These villages frequently host weekly markets that people attend from many miles around.

Other Mikea live most of the year in forest hamlets, kin-related groups of about 40 people. Most people who live in these hamlets also have a house in the larger villages. Around the forest hamlets are **slash-and-burn** maize fields. As the arable land around the settlement becomes exhausted, the hamlet is moved, about every 3 to 10 years.

Some Mikea who live in the villages also occupy seasonal hamlets in the forest during the growing season so that they can tend to their maize fields. These are much like forest hamlets, but they differ in that they are occupied for a much shorter period of time—only during the growing season.

Finally, most families in the forest hamlets, and some who live in the villages, move from their homes into the forest during the dry season. Here they live in foraging camps of a few families, staying in a camp

slash-and-burn A horticultural method used frequently in the tropics wherein a section of forest is cut, dried, and then burned, thus returning nutrients to the ground. This permits a plot of land to be farmed for a limited number of years.

IN HIS OWN WORDS

DOING ETHNOARCHAEOLOGY IN MADAGASCAR

by Robert Kelly

I conducted ethnographic work in Madagascar with my wife, Lin Poyer, a cultural anthropologist. On our first trip we flew to Washington, DC, then to Paris, Cairo, Nairobi, and finally to the capital of Madagascar, Antananarivo. The entire trip took nearly 48 hours. Once in the capital, we introduced ourselves to the necessary officials and ensured that our permits were in order. We then flew to the provincial capital of Toliara, where we met our Malagasy colleagues, Jean-François Rabedimy and Jaovola Tombo.

You do archaeology with a trowel and ethnography with a pencil and notebook, but that is just the beginning of the differences between the two. Because Madagascar was a French colony, all educated people speak French, and few speak English. And the Mikea spoke only their dialect of Malagasy. So for weeks, our daily language was a mixture of French, Malagasy (as we learned the dialect), and English.

There's also no schedule—an ethnographer is always "on the job." One time we arranged to leave for another village "early in the morning." Our guide arrived at 3 AM—

so we got up and left. Another time, the men in the village, armed with spears, went off to catch cattle rustlers—at midnight. So, we stayed up all night to learn the result.

We spent several weeks, on and off, in the bush, living in Mikea hamlets and foraging camps. We were there in the dry season, so we either walked many kilometers to the nearest well or we did what the Mikea do: dig up *babo* (a wonderful water-engorged tuber) and eat it. Meals were tubers, white rice with a dollop of peanut butter, and the occasional scrawny chicken or dried fish.

The Mikea asked us for virtually everything that we owned, especially clothing (which is hard for them to come by). We avoided such dunning by carrying no spare clothing. We freely handed out tobacco, however (a standard gift among the Mikea); occasionally, we gave gifts of food, money, and clothing; and, when possible, we provided medical assistance.

The Mikea were both curious and suspicious about why we were there. They couldn't believe that foreigners would come such a long way just to measure house posts, draw maps, and weigh tubers. One man asked if we were

for a week or so. While in these camps, people collect tubers and honey and search tree hollows for estivating hedgehogs.

Mikea Settlements from an Archaeological Perspective Kelly asked, "Are the different lengths of stay reflected in the material remains left behind at these sites?" To answer this question, remember that ethnoarchaeology's objective is to relate behavior to *archaeologically observable phenomena*. Over time, all that might remain of Mikea camps and settlements are features such as postholes, hearths, and pits, as well as scattered trash, such as burnt maize, bone fragments, and broken tools.

Accordingly, Kelly and his associates collected data on houses, features, and the distribution of trash in some 30 settlements; for some, they recorded data

over a 3-year period (see "In His Own Words: Doing Ethnoarchaeology in Madagascar" by Robert Kelly and "In His Own Words: The Ethics of Doing Ethnoarchaeology" by Bram Tucker). They also counted the number of posts in houses and measured their diameters—an activity that amused their Mikea hosts (and once sparked an accusation of witchcraft). They mapped the settlements, showing the locations of houses and features, as well as the placement of trash deposits. Through interviews, Mikea told the history of each settlement, how it was used, why it was abandoned, and other information. What did Kelly find out?

Trash Disposal Ethnoarchaeologists often begin by observing what people do with their trash because, after all, that's mostly what archaeologists study—

looking for gold. They were remarkably patient with us.

Ethnographers try to immerse themselves in another culture and to participate in it as much as possible. We witnessed trance dances, spirit possession ceremonies, and a goat sacrifice. Like the Mikea, we traveled on foot or by oxcart, often in the cool of the night. We dug tubers, hunted hedgehogs, ate honey from a hive while bees buzzed about, and slept on the ground around the fire.

But I found that the largest difference between archaeology and ethnography is that although you return from an archaeological excavation pretty much the same person you were when you left, that is never the case with ethnography. It's an extreme growth experience; you learn as much about your

© Robert Kelly, photo by Jim Yount

Kelly (in middle) interviewing a Mikea man.

limits and prejudices as you do about another culture. It's also a special growth experience for an archaeologist because you quickly learn the difficulty of interpreting human behavior from static material remains.

trash. In foraging camps, people unceremoniously tossed ash from fires and other trash into bushes only 1 to 2 meters away from the family hearth. In the forest and seasonal hamlets, however, Mikea disposed of their trash in an arc some 3 to 9 meters in front of the house door. Unlike the foraging camps, hamlets were periodically swept clean. This meant that larger items would end up in the trash arc, whereas smaller pieces missed by the broom were trampled into the sand.

As people occupied their hamlets for longer periods of time, they deposited their trash farther away from the house door. For example, Kelly visited one settlement the year it was established and found that trash was deposited some 3 to 4 meters from the house. A year later, trash was deposited some 8 meters away. Why? Early in a settlement's life, bushes grow near

the house, and they are a convenient place to toss trash. Eventually, however, the bushes are destroyed (for firewood, by children playing, and by goats and cattle foraging). As bushes disappear, trash is swept into bushes farther from the house. In hamlets occupied for several years, in fact, periodic cleanings create a second trash deposit, this time as a ring around the entire settlement.

The permanent villages exhibit a major change in the disposal of trash. Here one cannot simply sweep trash to the side of one's house because this would mean sweeping trash into a neighbor's space. Consequently, people throw trash into pits next to the houses (the pits were excavated to make mud for the wattle-and-daub house), or they collect trash in baskets inside the houses and periodically dump it at the edge of the settlement, as much as 30 or 40 meters away.

IN HIS OWN WORDS

THE ETHICS OF DOING ETHNOARCHAEOLOGY

by Bram Tucker

Ethnoarchaeology entails working with the living, and cultural anthropologists have thought quite a bit about the ethics of such fieldwork—in fact, the first line of the American Anthropological Association's Statement on Ethics reads: "Anthropologists' paramount responsibility is to those they study."

Anthropologists involve the host population in the project, and seek approval first. For every house he measured, every settlement that he mapped, every photo that he took, Kelly explained his goals and asked permission. Often, however, conflict arises between research goals and human decency. One cannot stand idly by while people are harmed, but an anthropologist also has a responsibility to the research and to the organization that sponsored it. Bram Tucker (University of Georgia) confronted such a problem during his research with the Mikea.

In July 1998, I was living in Behisatse, a hamlet of six houses in the Mikea Forest, studying how the Mikea make a living in an unpredictable environment. Rainfall, the main source of water for wild and domestic plants and animals, varies unpredictably from 100 mm to 1500 mm each year. Mikea deal with this unpredictability by diversifying their economy, combining foraging with farming, herding, and producing hard goods for market. They forage in different microenvironments. They plant crops that do well in rainy years and those that do well in dry years.

Some years, even the best economic strategies are ineffective, and the food supply is inadequate. This was the case in 1998. The maize crop germinated late because of insufficient rainfall, and then in February grasshoppers ate the withered stalks. Thieves ransacked manioc fields in the night. By March, the families at Behisatse were relying almost entirely on wild ovy tubers (*Dioscorea acuminata*). Ovy is an excellent food, but is prone to overharvesting. As the ovy patches near camp were depleted, foragers traveled increasing distances to find food, returning to camp each evening with barely enough to see them through the night.

I was faced with an ethical dilemma. The curious scientist in me wanted to know how Mikea households cope with food shortage. But as their friend and honorary kinsman, I couldn't just watch them go hungry!

My field assistant and I informed the camp elder that we planned to do something to help. The next day we visited a farmer friend in a distant village. I purchased 100

By the way, this doesn't imply that Mikea settlements are filthy or reeking of rotting garbage. Much of the trash, in fact, is maize husks and other dry plant material. Any wet garbage—including almost all bones—is eaten by ever-hungry dogs and pigs.

House Posts After trash, the next thing an ethnoarchaeologist might notice is the houses. Not surprisingly, the amount of labor and care that people invest in a house is related to the amount of time they expect to inhabit it. But how is that investment reflected archaeologically?

In the villages, Mikea often build wattle-and-daub houses about 10 square meters in size. They first set posts upright in the ground, 75 centimeters deep (the length of an adult's arm), and then weave smaller saplings horizontally between these posts. They pack this lattice with coarse mud, smoothing the surface. The house has a door made of planks, usually with a lock, and one or two windows, with wooden shutters. The floors are packed clay. Most of these houses have thatch roofs that extend beyond the walls, forming a narrow veranda around the house. A wattle-and-daub house takes a month or more to build but, if the owner maintains the roof, will last 25 years or more.

In the forest hamlets, Mikea have more modest homes. About half the size of village houses, they are made of thinner posts not so deeply set and have roofs of baobab bark slabs and walls of bark, grass, or reeds. A cold wind blows nightly in the dry season, so the door is on the north wall, and the south wall is woven tightly. There is a hearth just inside, to

Bram Tucker (in middle) surrounded by his Mikea hosts.

manioc. During the following week at Behisatse, the adults continued to forage for ovy all day, leaving the children back at camp hungry. So, at each meal we prepared twice as much food as normal and invited the children to join us. Eventually, our manioc gift arrived. Our friends continued to work hard and forage frequently, but they could now afford to rest a little without worry.

I still learned a lot about how Mikea cope with food shortage. By the time our gift arrived, people were starting several alternative strategies, including planned movements to other locations and recalling debts from more prosperous acquaintances. But as field researchers, we become part of the communities we study. As such, we have a responsibility to help out when we can.

Kg of manioc, enough to feed everyone in Behisatse for a month and a half, for 40,000 Malagasy francs, about $7. The farmer said it would take a week to finish drying the

one side of the door. Two to three meters outside the door is another hearth, covered by a flat shade structure, the top of which serves to store dried corn and tools. These forest hamlet houses can be built in a week and need repair every year or so. Some are used for only a year.

The houses in seasonal hamlets look similar to those in forest hamlets, but they appear to a westerner's eye to be shabbier. They are often shorter and have few shade structures outside the front door.

Because foraging camps are used in the dry season and it rarely rains at that time of the year, houses are rare in foraging camps; when they are present, they are no more than lean-tos or simple boxlike structures, fashioned from whatever wood is handy, and built in an hour or two.

The amount of labor involved in each of these houses is reflected in the roof and walls, but these things disappear. However, labor is also reflected in the postholes. And these features are familiar to most archaeologists because they are often all that remain of ancient houses. What can they tell us?

Plenty, and all of it is pretty commonsense. Although some of the wattle-and-daub houses are large, many of the reed or grass houses are about the same size. However, the long wall of village houses contains *twice* as many posts as does the same wall in houses in seasonal hamlets; houses in forest hamlets fall between these two. In addition, the posts used in seasonal hamlets (those settlements used the least amount of time) have more variable diameters than the posts used in the more permanent settlements—especially the

TABLE 8-1 Summary of Differences in Mikea Settlements

SETTLEMENT TYPE	HOUSE SIZE	POST VARIABILITY	SECONDARY POSTS	DISTANCE TO TRASH (meters)	FEATURE DIVERSITY
Villages	Various, but can be large	Low	Many, closely spaced	10–40	High
Forest hamlets	Small	Low–Medium	Fewer, farther apart	4–9	Medium
Seasonal hamlets	Small	High	Fewer, farther apart	3–4	Medium–Low
Foraging camps	Lean-tos or "boxes," if present at all	n/a	n/a	1–2	Low

n/a = not applicable

wattle-and-daub houses. In seasonal hamlets, people use whatever wood is handy, often scavenging poles from abandoned houses. Post diameters as well as *consistency* in post diameters reflect the fact that people are more selective about the wood they use when building houses that are more permanent.

Features Outside Houses Recall from Chapter 2 that features are artifacts that can't be removed from a site—things like hearths, houses, pits, and postholes. In Mikea settlements, these features include fenced compounds, animal corrals, wash areas, cookhouses, troughs, drying racks, wells, ceremonial enclosures, maize threshers, blacksmith bellows, and storage bins and racks. The particular kinds of features found in a settlement are linked to the particular kinds of activities that take place in Mikea settlements and are not so useful to the development of middle-level theory. But differences in the range of diversity of features among the different settlement types are useful.

The more permanent a Mikea settlement, the greater the range of features it contains. When people intend to stay in one place for years or plan to return to a settlement seasonally for several years, they invest more time in features that have a single purpose, rather than "making do" with temporary facilities. Washhouses, for example, are never found in foraging camps or seasonal hamlets: People are basically "camping" at both, and water is a rare commodity in dry season forest camps. People bathe back at the forest hamlet or village. Washhouses are also rarely found in forest hamlets—where the small, related community means that people can expect privacy without bothering to build a separate facility. However, washhouses are common in the densely populated villages, where privacy is more difficult, and where investment in a facility is worthwhile.

Table 8-1 summarizes these differences among Mikea settlements. In this table we have related some archaeologically recoverable variables (trash distribution, postholes, features) to human behavior (the length of occupation). Simply by recording the way trash is distributed, the range of features present, the number of postholes per house, and the variation in posthole diameter, we could place a new settlement into one of the four categories with a high degree of accuracy. This fulfills the first criterion of a middle-level study—it focuses on aspects of ethnographic data that are archaeologically observable. But does it explain why the relationship between behavior and archaeologically observable remains is necessarily true? What do such ethnoarchaeological studies do for archaeology?

Ethnoarchaeology and Uniformitarianism

As we have pointed out, middle-level theory tries to *explain* patterning between behavior and material remains. Such explanations depend on the principle of uniformitarianism. It is relatively easy to see how this principle applies in both taphonomy and experimental archaeology because both study natural processes and mechanical relationships.

But the principle of uniformitarianism is tougher to apply in ethnoarchaeology because human behavior is anything but mechanical. We conducted our study of the Mikea within a theoretical framework known as human behavioral ecology. One tenet of this framework is that because people have many demands on their time, they make choices that maximize the utility of their decisions. Choices about what kind of house to build reflect this principle. Why would someone in a forest hamlet invest more than a month in building a wattle-and-daub house when one built in less than a week will suffice for the time that the hamlet will be occupied? The "extra" three or four weeks can be used for clearing another maize field, building a ceremonial enclosure, or some other task. Similarly, why take time to select just the right poles for a house in a seasonal hamlet that will be occupied for only a few months of the year? From the perspective of behavioral ecology, the time would be better spent in some other task. Indeed, the Mikea themselves said that the longer they intended to remain in a settlement, the more care they put into constructing houses and facilities such as maize-threshing bins and outhouses. They also said they would be more selective in their building material, choosing poles of a particular diameter for posts and even searching out certain species of wood, such as ones known to resist destruction by insects.

These seem like logical choices, and several ethnoarchaeological studies have found similar patterns in trash disposal, house form, and feature diversity in other societies in the world. Combined with these other studies, the Mikea research helps form a strong formal analogy; combined with the theoretical framework of human behavior ecology, it also contains elements of middle-level theory.

What about Culture? But the issue of culture can make ethnographic analogies, even ones strong enough to qualify as middle-level theory, problematic. We have discussed, for instance, the disposal of trash among the Mikea as being simply a function of how long a settlement is occupied. The longer it is occupied, the farther away from a house trash is removed. But cultural ideas about trash could also come into play.

Ian Hodder, a postprocessual archaeologist, conducted ethnoarchaeological research with the Moro and Mesakin in Sudan. Both groups raise various grains, as well as pigs, cattle, and goats. In both, families live in household compounds. But the Moro's compounds are relatively free of trash, whereas the Mesakin's are messier; in particular, the Moro keep pig bones out of the compounds.

Hodder argues that this difference results from different ideas about women. Moro men see contact with women as potentially "polluting" their strength and authority. And because Moro women take care of pigs, they are associated with these animals (men are associated with cattle). As a result, Moro men consider pig remains to be foul, and Moro women take care to remove pig bones from the trash and dispose of them separately. The Mesakin do not share the Moro's beliefs about women, and they treat pig bones the same as any other animal remains. Thus, Hodder argues that archaeologists need to consider the symbolic meanings of material culture in order to appreciate how it will be treated as trash.

But the "cultural" component is very difficult to study archaeologically. And this means that the principle of uniformitarianism will remain difficult to implement in ethnoarchaeology. For some archaeologists, this means that ethnoarchaeology can provide us only with strong analogies, not middle-level theory.

For others, ethnoarchaeological studies conducted across a spectrum of societies provide archaeology with analogies that, taken together, suggest some important principles of human behavior. These principles could *provisionally* be taken as uniform for the purpose of creating and testing hypotheses, and allow ethnoarchaeology to act as middle-level theory to support archaeological inferences. Let's see how this might work.

Settlement Pattern Change in the Mimbres Valley The Mikea case shows that more labor is invested in more permanent houses than in more transient ones. This could be reflected archaeologically in the use of more substantial building materials (such as wattle-and-daub or stone masonry rather than poles and thatch), a larger number of posts, and more standardized posts. This information can be used to make archaeological interpretations.

Michelle Hegmon and Margaret Nelson (Arizona State University) have surveyed and excavated in the eastern Mimbres region of southern New Mexico for a number of years. (This is the homeland of Mimbres pottery, mentioned in Chapter 6.) The Mimbres region is far removed from Madagascar, but exhibits some similarities: Both regions are arid, and both are or were occupied by maize horticulturalists who also hunted and gathered wild resources.

Nelson and Hegmon's survey found sites that contained two components, one dated to the Classic Mimbres phase (1000–850 BP), and the other to the Post Classic phase (850–700 BP). Nelson and Hegmon were interested in understanding the abandonment of regions. Although many archaeologists had previously argued that people abandoned the Mimbres region after 850 BP, Nelson and Hegmon believed that the region was still occupied but that the settlement pattern had changed in such a way that it gave the region the *appearance* of having been abandoned.

Figure 8-12 Margaret Nelson (right) standing inside a Mimbres pueblo room; some postholes are visible on the floor.

Nelson and Hegmon found that during the Classic Mimbres phase, people lived in large pueblo villages. The houses were built of stone masonry, with roofs of heavy beams (Figure 8-12). Radiocarbon and tree-ring dating indicated that many of these villages were, indeed, no longer occupied after 850 BP.

But another kind of settlement was also in use during the Classic Mimbres phase. Although people lived in large pueblo villages, they also used what Nelson and Hegmon term "farmsteads." These were small sites, consisting of only one or a few structures, usually open on one side and lightly constructed of a few small posts, with few interior features. Nelson and Hegmon argue that a few members of the family occupied these sites during the growing season to care for the young maize plants. Located some distance from the villages, the field houses contained only minimal shelter requirements.

Nelson and Hegmon's careful excavation and extensive dating showed that, on some of these sites, someone modified the flimsy Classic phase structures into farmsteads during the following Post Classic phase. Added to the lightly constructed buildings were larger and more numerous posts, masonry walls, and more substantial roofs. Eventually, they formed small pueblos of some 6 to 12 rooms. Inside these small pueblo structures was also a greater diversity of features than was found in the Classic phase field houses. From these data, Nelson and Hegmon argue that the Mimbres region was not abandoned. Instead, during the Post Classic phase, people moved out of the large pueblos into smaller, dispersed communities and turned their field houses into permanent residences.

Nelson and Hegmon's Classic phase field houses are analogous to Mikea seasonal hamlets, and their Post Classic phase modifications are analogous to Mikea village house construction. Taken by itself, the Mikea case is only analogy—and a weak one at that, given that no cultural link exists between the Mikea and the prehistoric peoples of the American Southwest.

However, the Mikea study does highlight some necessary links between house size and construction elements—for example, large houses require larger support posts. Coupled with other ethnoarchaeological studies that reach similar conclusions, the Mikea data provide a solid warrant for treating Nelson and Hegmon's interpretation as a viable hypothesis for further testing.

In this way, ethnoarchaeology will continue to play an important role in future archaeological inference.

CONCLUSION

Archaeology is all about making inferences from artifacts, ecofacts, features, and their contexts. Middle-level theory is what allows archaeologists to know that they really do know something about the past. It lies at the heart of archaeology. As you have seen in this chapter, archaeologists go about constructing middle-level theory through taphonomy, experimental archaeology, and ethnoarchaeology. It requires that archaeologists step out of their excavation trenches and conduct a different kind of research. Some archaeologists, in fact, have permanently hung up their trowels and devoted their careers to the development of middle-level theory. And this is good, because without middle-level theory, our inferences from archaeology would be little more than just-so stories, with no more credence behind them than silly ideas like aliens building pyramids. In the following chapters, we will see how archaeologists have put studies in taphonomy, experimental archaeology, and ethnoarchaeology to use in reconstructing the past.

SUMMARY

1. What is the difference between analogy and middle-level theory?

☺ Analogy and middle-level theory both seek to make inferences about human behavior from archaeological remains.

☺ Analogy is one way to reconstruct the past but is limited to societies that have very close geographic and cultural counterparts (preferably ones with a historical connection) or to fairly low-level inferences. The greater the number of similarities, the greater the probability that the analogy is correct.

☺ Middle-level theory uses modern data from taphonomy, experimental archaeology, and ethnoarchaeology to explain why particular natural processes or human behaviors can be inferred from particular material remains. Middle-level theory relies on the principle of uniformitarianism.

2. What is the principle of uniformitarianism?

☺ The "facts" of archaeology are incapable of speaking for themselves; therefore, archaeology follows geology's principle of uniformitarianism, studying ongoing processes and their material consequences to develop ways of making inferences from archaeological data.

☺ The principle of uniformitarianism does not assume that the past and the present are the same; it does assume that the processes of the past and the present are the same. This is why we can use modern observations, such as the material effect of sunlight on bone, or the relationship between house posts and house permanence, to help us interpret the archaeological record.

3. What do taphonomy, experimental archaeology, and ethnoarchaeology study?

☺ Taphonomy studies the natural processes that help produce archaeological sites.

☺ Experimental archaeology re-creates behaviors that no longer exist today, such as stone tool manufacture, or replicates behaviors, events, or processes that need controlled observation.

☺ Ethnoarchaeology studies living peoples in order to see how human behavior is translated into material remains.

MEDIA RESOURCES

Doing Fieldwork:
Archaeological Demonstrations CD-ROM 2.0
This CD, developed by the authors, shows professional archaeologists involved in various digs, many of which are referenced in the text. The presentation is organized by the main techniques used on an archaeological dig, reinforcing concepts and techniques via live examples. The CD takes you through each step automatically, or you can navigate to any point via the navigation bar. After reviewing a step in the dig process, you are taken to Check Points, which are concept questions about each step of the dig. Then you can see the answers, receive your score, and even send your scores to your instructor.

The Companion Website for *Archaeology,*
Sixth Edition
www.cengagebrain.com
Supplement your review of this chapter by going to the companion website to take one of the practice quizzes, use the flash cards to master key terms, and check out the many other study aids that are designed to help you succeed in your introductory archaeology course.

9 PEOPLE, PLANTS, AND ANIMALS IN THE PAST

LEARNING OBJECTIVES

**AFTER READING THIS CHAPTER
YOU SHOULD BE ABLE TO ANSWER THESE QUESTIONS:**

1. What does a zooarchaeological study involve?

2. How do animal bones and plants help establish a site's season of occupation?

3. How do plants help to reconstruct ancient diets?

4. How can pollen help reconstruct past environments?

© AP Images/Ermindo Armino

An archaeologist uncovers the skeletons of horses in the Netherlands, casualties of a 17th-century battle.

PREVIEW

ARCHAEOLOGISTS HAVE PLENTY of methods and techniques for reconstructing how people made a living in the past, and in this chapter, we discuss a few of them. We begin with faunal analysis, the identification and interpretation of animal remains recovered in archaeological contexts. Animal bones not only enable the archaeologist to study ancient hunting methods and diet, but they also assist in reconstructing past environments. Of course, getting at the meaning behind the bones is neither easy nor straightforward. This chapter provides you with the basics for understanding what archaeologists can do with a bunch of animal bones.

Plant remains are also valuable to archaeology. We have already seen how the study of tree rings provides archaeologists with a trustworthy way to date specific events of the past—when a certain Pueblo dwelling was built, for example. We learned also that tree-ring analysis indicates something about past climates, environments, and the local history of forest fires. Archaeological plant remains—pollen, seeds, charcoal, and phytoliths—also tell us about what wild plants people collected, the crops they grew, the fuels they burned, and even the roles played by plants in rituals. Plant and animal remains can also indicate what season of the year people occupied a site.

DOING FIELDWORK CD-ROM:
ARCHAEOLOGICAL DEMONSTRATIONS 2.0

See the "Reconstructing the Past" section of the CD-ROM to learn more about topics covered in this chapter.

INTRODUCTION

So far, we have talked mostly about artifacts and features—objects created by humans and left behind. Archaeological sites also contain ecofacts—plant and animal remains; some of these are food refuse left by humans, but sometimes similar remains enter sites through natural processes (as when plants and animals die on a site). Remember how taphonomic studies figure out how plant and animal remains accumulate in archaeological sites? Here, we're more concerned with what plant parts and animal bones can tell us about human behavior.

Formation processes are critical to inferences based on plant and animal remains. As you read the next few chapters, keep asking yourself: How do archaeologists know to interpret their data in one way rather than another? What middle-level research stands behind the inferences that archaeologists make? Could there be other interpretations? If so, how can we test those alternatives?

Archaeologists use so many methods to recover and interpret animal and plant remains, we can present only a few here. Rather than blanket the field, we will introduce some of the major categories of data and provide a sense of how archaeologists go about interpreting them. We begin with the skeletal remains of animals.

STUDYING ANIMAL REMAINS FROM ARCHAEOLOGICAL SITES

A **faunal assemblage** consists of the animal bones recovered from an archaeological site. Faunal assemblages differ from paleontological assemblages because we assume that humans played some role in their formation. We find animal bones at **kill sites,**

faunal assemblage   The animal remains recovered from an archaeological site.

kill sites   Places where animals were killed in the past.

Figure 9-1 The Agate Basin site, showing the Folsom level under excavation in 1978.

where bones may lie more or less the way they were when the hunters left, affected by carnivore scavenging, weathering, and other natural processes. We also find them in camps and villages, where people butchered game and/or domesticated animals.

Sometimes a site might contain tens of thousands of bones, including those of animals killed on site, some transported from kill sites elsewhere, and many noncultural remains, bones of animals that simply died at the site or that carnivores or raptors brought in after people abandoned a camp.

After recovering a faunal assemblage, a **zooarchaeologist** commonly performs a **faunal analysis,** studying and interpreting the animal remains. To see how this is done, look at how one zooarchaeologist analyzed the faunal assemblage of the Folsom component at Wyoming's Agate Basin site.

The Agate Basin Site

Sometime around 1916, rancher William Spencer was riding across the broken terrain of his ranch in eastern Wyoming. Visiting a spring, he noticed some large bones protruding from the edge of an arroyo (just as George McJunkin did at the Folsom site in New Mexico). His curiosity piqued, he returned to the spring several times, eventually collecting a number of large, beautiful spear points as well as bison bones.

Years later, in 1941, Spencer met Robert Frison, a state game warden, at an informal gathering of history buffs under some cottonwood trees on the Cheyenne River, a short distance north of the Agate Basin site.

Frison's job took him outdoors a lot, and he had visited many sites and developed quite an interest in artifacts. The following year, the men visited the site together and found more bison bones and spear points. Frison thought the points were old, so he sent one to Frank H. H. Roberts (1897–1966) at the Smithsonian Institution.

The points intrigued Roberts, and he excavated at Agate Basin that summer and in the following years. Later, in the 1970s, Robert Frison's nephew, archaeologist George Frison (see Chapter 7), and Dennis Stanford (Smithsonian Institution) worked there together (Figure 9-1).

Frison and Stanford published a thorough report on their research, but there is always more that we can do with archaeological collections. This is why Matt Hill (Iowa State University) decided to take another look at Agate Basin's Folsom component faunal assemblage.

Let's begin with Hill's conclusions. About 10,780 radiocarbon years ago, a small group of Folsom hunters camped by the Agate Basin site in late March or early April. They killed at least 11 bison (*Bison antiquus*) and five pronghorn antelope (*Antilocapra americana*), probably not too far away from their camp. They partially butchered the bison at the kill site and, for the most part, brought entire limbs back to camp. The antelope were field-dressed at the kill site, and the nearly intact carcasses were carried back to the camp. Despite their success, the hunters may have had a hard time making ends meet. Unlike later hunter-gatherers on the Plains, these Folsom hunters seem not to have relied heavily on meat storage.

How did Hill extract all this information from a bunch of broken bones?

Identifying Bones Hill first identified bones from the Folsom component, working through the cataloged collection, piece by piece, and assigning each bone or bone fragment to a species, if possible.

zooarchaeologist An archaeologist who specializes in the study of the animal remains recovered from archaeological sites.

faunal analysis Identification and interpretation of animal remains from an archaeological site.

© University of Wyoming, Frison Institute

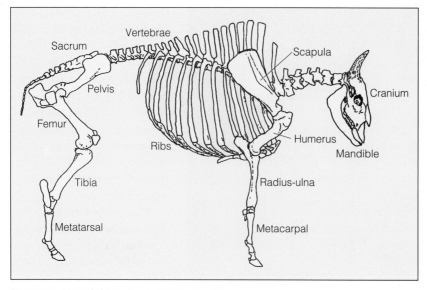

Figure 9-2 Bison skeleton showing major elements.

"Identifying the bones" is more complicated than it might sound. Field archaeologists know, at least in a rough way, what mammal, bird, reptile, and fish bones look like, but we need more detailed information for faunal analysis. The first step is to assign each specimen to **element** (the anatomical part of the body). Is this bone a rib splinter, part of the pelvis, or a skull fragment? A femur, tibia, or calcaneus (the heel bone)? Identifying elements requires a solid working knowledge of comparative anatomy (Figure 9-2).

But conventional comparative anatomy classes are insufficient because they deal with whole bones—not the dirty fragments that archaeologists confront. Classroom experience helps, but you really learn faunal analysis by handling a lot of bones yourself.

The next step is to identify the specimens to **taxon** (kind of animal). Success here depends on the condition of the specimen and the expertise of the analyst. The aim is to identify each bone to a species, but sometimes the bones are so fragmentary that you can only identify them to higher-order groups, such as family or class. One can rarely determine, for instance, whether a long bone fragment (that is, a small piece of one of the long limb bones, such as a femur) came from a deer or a bighorn sheep—but anyone can see that it's not a mouse bone. In this case, the analyst might only be able to identify the fragment to the order Artiodactyla (because deer and sheep are in different families, the next broader level of classification is used). So identification to taxon often means "narrowing down the possibilities" rather than identifying the exact species—although that is always preferred.

Sometimes, a specimen might be so difficult to identify that you can only assign it to one of five standard animal **size classes.** Rodent- and rabbit-size animals are in size class 1; wolf- and pronghorn antelope–size animals are in class 2; animals the size of mule deer and bighorn sheep are in class 3; bison- and elk-size animals are in class 4; and in class 5 are large animals such as giraffes, hippos, and elephants.

So, how did Hill know whether a scrap of bone was a piece of a bison femur, pronghorn radius, flat-headed peccary tibia, or striped skunk skull? The zooarchaeologist makes these identifications through a **comparative collection.** The standard zooarchaeology lab commonly contains box after box of modern animal skeletons—everything from elephants to deer mice. Each box is labeled with the species, the individual's approximate age at death, its sex, and where and when it was collected. A comparative collection contains examples of young and old, as well as male and female, members of a species. These collections are built by hunting or trapping animals, picking up road kills (you need a license to do these things in most states), or acquiring carcasses from a state fish and game office (sometimes confiscated from poachers).

This is stinky business because once collected the specimens must be defleshed and cleaned. Sometimes the remains are buried and nature is allowed to take its course. Other methods include simmering the bones in a solution of detergent or placing the greasy bones in a colony of dermestid beetles, which, over a few weeks' time, will literally pick the bones clean of all tissue.

Using a comparative collection, Hill identified the archaeological bones to taxon. Measurements taken on some adult bones helped determine if the bone was from a male or female.

element In faunal analysis, a specific skeletal part of the body—for example, humerus or sternum.

taxon In faunal analysis, the classification of a skeletal element to a taxonomic category—species, genus, family, or order.

size classes A categorization of faunal remains, not to taxon, but to one of five categories based on body size.

comparative collection A skeletal collection of modern fauna of both sexes and different ages used to make identifications of archaeofaunas.

Eventually, Hill found that most of the Agate Basin bones were bison or pronghorn. Other species included wolf, striped skunk, and frog, but because there were only a few bones from most of these species, Hill focused on the bison and pronghorn.

Natural or Cultural? Recalling the discussion of taphonomy in Chapter 8, you should be wondering how Hill could be certain (1) that the bison and pronghorn remains were deposited by humans and (2) that they were deposited during the same occupation of the site.

For one thing, the bones bore some stone tool cut marks (which we can distinguish from carnivore tooth marks), some were burned, and some of the larger ones had impact fractures—distinctive breaks that resulted when the Folsom people smashed the bones open to retrieve the fatty, calorie-rich marrow. Frison and Stanford also found a cluster of antelope bones, some of them burned, around a hearth.

A few of the bones did show evidence of carnivore gnawing. But tooth marks appeared on only a few bison humeri and femora, and on only three antelope specimens. So, the evidence pointed to humans as the agents responsible for the antelope and bison bones at Agate Basin.

Hill also thinks that the antelope and bison bones were deposited during the same occupation of the site. The Folsom assemblage is not large, nor is it widely dispersed; some of the remains still lie in anatomical position. This is what we would expect to see in a one-time use of the site. In addition, we might expect all the bones to be equally weathered, just as we saw at the Hudson-Meng site—an "instantaneous" herd death, where nearly all the skulls were weathered in the same way.

To reach this conclusion, Hill took bone size into account. Because antelope bones are smaller than bison bones, they are more easily broken (by carnivores and also by hunters), and more quickly covered by sediment. So, even if all the faunal remains were deposited at about the same time, the bison bones should be slightly more weathered than the antelope bones. This was the case at Agate Basin, and Hill concluded that the bison and antelope in the Folsom component were killed by the same group of people during the same occupation.

What to Count? To reconstruct human behavior at Agate Basin, Hill needed to search for meaningful patterns in the bone data, and this required that he count the bones.

Zooarchaeologists count bones in two ways, depending on their objectives. One method involves the

TABLE 9-1 NISP Counts for the Folsom Component at the Agate Basin Site

COMMON NAME	SCIENTIFIC NAME	NISP
Bison	*Bison antiquus*	1033
Pronghorn antelope	*Antilocapra americana*	297
Wolf	*Canis lupus*	7
Coyote	*Canis latrans*	3
Red fox	*Vulpes vulpes*	1
Striped skunk	*Mephitis mephitis*	1
Flat-headed peccary	*Platygonus compressus*	1
Dog	*Canis* sp. (possibly domesticated)	5
Jackrabbit	*Lepus* cf. *townsendii* or *californicus*	10
Rabbit	*Sylvilagus* cf. *nutallii* or *audubonii*	4
Grouse	*Centrocercus urophasianus*	2
Frog	*Rana pipiens*	Few
Elk	*Cervus elaphus* (antler only)	2
Camel	*Camelops* sp. (possible tool)	1

SOURCE: Hill 2001. The "sp." in some scientific names means that the genus is certain, but the species is not. The "cf." means that the specimen compares very well with one or two species within a genus, but that the researcher is not certain of the species identification. Camel became extinct about 11,200 radiocarbon years ago, and there is no good evidence that humans ever hunted them; the specimen here might be a piece that a Folsom hunter picked up someplace or evidence of an animal that died at the site long before the hunters camped there.

number of identified specimens, or **NISP.** This count is simply the total number of bone specimens that are identified to a particular taxon. Table 9-1 shows the NISP for the Folsom component at the Agate Basin site. NISP is useful for comparing large numbers of collections from different sites, but it has a severe limitation in reconstructing human behavior at a single site.

Table 9-1 suggests that bison were more important than pronghorn at Agate Basin. But what if the 1033 bison specimens came from a single highly fragmented skeleton, whereas the 297 antelope bones came from 297 different individuals? If this were the case, then antelope would be many times more important than bison at this site. Or maybe the species were butchered in different ways, with certain bones

number of identified specimens (NISP) The raw number of identified bones (specimens) per species.

becoming highly fragmented (and hence disappearing from the archaeological record altogether or turning into unidentifiable elements that are not included in the NISP counts).

Problems like this have led archaeologists to another way of comparing bone frequencies, called the **minimum number of individuals**, or **MNI**. MNI is the minimum number of individuals that are necessary to account for all the skeletal elements of a particular species found in the site. Suppose, for instance, that you excavated 100 fragments of bison bone from a site. The NISP equals 100, but what is the MNI? That is, what is the minimum number of individual bison required to account for those 100 bone fragments?

To figure this out, you must tabulate bone frequency by element (left femur, right tibia, hyoid, and so on) to determine the most *abundant* skeletal element. This process requires that you assign the specimens not only to their correct *element,* but for bones that come in pairs, to their correct *side* as well. If four right femurs show up in the 100 bone fragments, then you know that *at least* four bison account for the fragments.

MNI has some limitations as well. When bones are fragmented, it is possible that the "four right femurs" are really fragments from the same upper leg bone. To eliminate this problem, you must compare the bone fragments, one by one, to see whether two fragments could have come from the same bone. In our hypothetical example, if we found that two of the four right femur fragments could have come from the same femur, then the MNI would only be three.

Calculating MNI also depends on how you divide your site. Agate Basin was probably occupied once by Folsom hunters for a few weeks. It is what archaeologists call a *fine-grained* assemblage, meaning that it hasn't become complicated by additional, overlapping occupations. But what if the site were *coarse-grained*? What if it had been repeatedly occupied over a long period of time so that the assemblage was the result of many periods of use over decades—or even centuries? We could compute the minimum number of individuals for a coarse-grained assemblage, but this might have the unfortunate consequence of reducing hundreds of bone fragments to a very few MNI, perhaps just one or two individuals. This would obviously be

a poor choice. Sometimes investigators calculate their minimum numbers based on stratigraphic breaks observed during excavation. Once again, however, the MNI per species depends on how fine one wishes to draw the stratigraphic boundaries.

Ultimately, the decision depends on the site's specific characteristics. In general, MNI is most useful and accurate when fine stratigraphic divisions are used and when bones are not overly fragmented. The Folsom component at Agate Basin met these criteria.

Where did Hill go from here? Of the 1033 bison bones, Hill could identify 843 to element; likewise, he could identify 198 of the 297 antelope bone fragments to element. Although the antelope specimens were fragmented, Hill identified four right and one left humeri (upper arm bones). This might suggest an MNI of four (given that the single left humerus could be a match to one of the right humeri). But the single left humerus was not the same size as any of the right humeri, and so Hill concluded that *at least* five antelope were brought to the site.

Because they are larger and heavier, the bison long bones were more intact. Taking the humeri, radii, femora, and tibiae, Hill assigned each to a side and then decided, using a comparative collection, whether they were male or female (or indeterminate, because young, less developed animals don't exhibit characteristics that allow assignment to sex). He then compared their sizes to see if the rights and lefts of each sex could possibly have come from the same animal, or whether the femora and tibiae, and the humeri and radii could anatomically refit (that is, would they fit together in their usual anatomical positions; femora and tibiae, for example, articulate at the patella, the knee cap). If they did refit, then they could have come from the same animal (Figure 9-3).

From this comparison, Hill determined that *at least* four males, four females, and three immature bison were brought to the site.

So now we know the minimum number of animals that Folsom hunters killed at the Agate Basin site: 11 bison and five pronghorn antelope.

Reconstructing Human Behavior at Agate Basin By looking at which specific elements were present, Hill found that elements of the **axial skeleton** (the head, mandibles, vertebrae, ribs, sacrum, tail) for both bison and pronghorn were rare compared with bones from the **appendicular skeleton** (everything else). Bison limb bones were also more common relative to the other bison bones, and antelope lower leg bones (especially for the front legs) and toes were rare.

---

minimum number of individuals (MNI)   The smallest number of individuals necessary to account for all identified bones.

axial skeleton   The head, mandibles, vertebrae, ribs, sacrum, and tail of an animal skeleton.

appendicular skeleton   All parts of an animal excluding the axial skeleton.

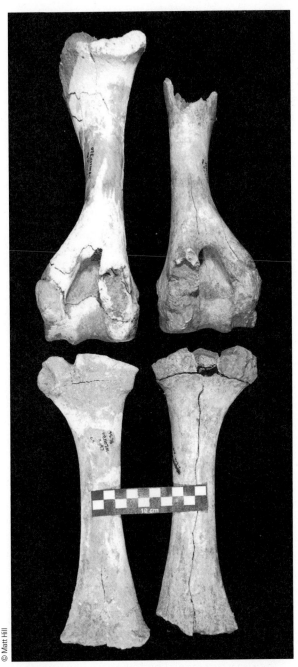

© Matt Hill

Figure 9-3 Anatomically refit calf bison humeri (top) and radii (bottom). Carnivore gnawing has removed the proximal (upper) end of the humerus on the right.

What accounts for these patterns? Viewed as food, bones function two ways—as a support for meat and as a container of marrow. Experimental research can quantify how much food value a bone represents in terms of these two entities. Bison long bones, for instance, rank high in both meat and marrow content, suggesting that hunters brought back only the high-utility portions of the bison and left the axial skeleton at the kill site.

The pronghorn skeletons at the Agate Basin site were more complete than the bison skeletons. Apparently,

the antelope were gutted and then field-dressed by removing the feet and lower limb bones, which contain little marrow and have little meat wrapped about them. The hunters then carried the rest of the antelope back to camp as more or less complete carcasses. The ribs and vertebrae may have been crushed for bone grease or consumed whole by dogs and carnivores, as suggested by taphonomic research.

Ethnoarchaeological studies suggest some other possibilities. Hunters consider several factors when deciding which parts of an animal to transport home: the distance back to camp, the number of hunters present, weather, terrain, and food needs of the household. If the animal is killed near camp, women and children might come out to help carry the entire carcass of a large animal back. If so, then the entire skeleton might end up in the camp, rather than at the kill site. If a large animal is killed far from camp, the hunters might eat some of it immediately and then butcher the animal, bringing only meat and a very few bones back to camp. In this case, most of the skeleton would remain at the kill site.

Based on such ethnoarchaeological observations, Hill suggested that hunters at Agate Basin killed most of the animals individually, relatively close to camp. The smaller antelope were carried back with minimal field butchery. However, because the bison could not be carried whole, it is likely that the Agate Basin hunters (and perhaps their wives and children) ate some of the meat attached to the vertebrae and ribs at the kill site and then transported the legs—with their large meat packages and high marrow content—to camp using the lower limbs as convenient handles.

What Do Broken Toes Mean? Although relatively rare at this site, some bison metapodials (portions of the foot) as well as bison and antelope phalanges (toe bones) were found broken open, presumably to extract the marrow. But foot bones do not contain much marrow, and they have no meat attached to them. Why did the hunters bother with toes, when they apparently had bison haunches and antelope tenderloin roasting on the fire?

Hill interprets the processing of the foot bones as evidence that, despite the 11 bison and five antelope, the Agate Basin Folsom hunters were experiencing some hard times. From paleoclimatic data, we know that the average annual temperature was some 11° centigrade colder during Folsom times; perhaps late winter or early spring storms—which can strike with a vengeance on the high plains—made that day's hunt impossible. Or perhaps the meat stored in camp was frozen, leaving the camp's inhabitants with no choice but to extract marrow from low-utility elements, such as metapodials and phalanges.

Hill also concluded that these Folsom hunters were living more hand-to-mouth than did later hunter-gatherers on the high plains. The late winter and early spring is a tough season for hunter-gatherers because game animals are lean (and lean meat is difficult to digest if that is all you are eating) and plants are not yet ripe. Many foragers survive the spring by relying on food stored from a previous fall hunt. But the data from Agate Basin suggest that these Folsom hunters lacked stored food because they were hunting on a weekly or even daily basis during the spring that they occupied the site.

This interpretation depends on knowing that the Folsom hunters camped at Agate Basin in the spring. How did Hill know this?

In What Season Was Agate Basin Occupied?

Recall from the discussion of seasonal rounds in Chapter 3 that hunter-gatherers often don't spend the entire year in a single camp or village. To understand what life was like in the past, we must pay attention to **seasonality**, the time of year that a site was used. This is important because only after we have identified the range of seasonal activities can we understand the entire seasonal round.

Hill determined the seasonality of Agate Basin by beginning with the knowledge that modern bison give birth during the last two weeks of April and the first two weeks of May. Hill assumed that bison in the past did likewise. This uniformitarian assumption seems justified because giving birth in the early spring is adaptive, allowing calves the maximum time to mature sufficiently to survive the next winter. Even considering the likelihood of climate change, it is likely that the birthing season of modern bison approximates that of their ancient cousins.

Bone development and tooth eruption in modern bison also follow quite predictable schedules (as they do for all animals, including humans). Young animals are most useful to archaeologists—indeed, once all their teeth have erupted, adults lose their value as seasonal indicators. The Agate Basin collection contained only a few young animals, but they were important in assessing the season of occupation. The teeth of the youngest bison showed that it was about 11 months old when it died. A second young bison had teeth that suggested an age of about 23 months. In other words, these two

animals were just one month shy of their first and second birthdays, respectively. Assuming that these two bison were born in late April–early May, they probably died in late March or early April. The presence of some fetal bison bones (either a late-term fetus or a newborn) supports this inference. With this information, Hill concluded that Folsom hunters occupied Agate Basin at the tail end of winter or the beginning of spring.

The Zooarchaeology of a Peruvian Civilization

Now that we know something about the basics of faunal analysis, let's jump to Peru, to see how these techniques work in a very different context.

The site of Chavín de Huántar (cha-*veen* day *whan-tar*) is one of the most celebrated ceremonial centers in the Andes. It flourished from about 2850 to 2200 BP, making it one of the earliest civilizations in South America. Located at an elevation of nearly 3150 meters (10,000 feet) above sea level, Chavín de Huántar is ringed by snow-covered mountains (with peaks rising over 5500 meters [18,000 feet]).

The initial settlement was a small ceremonial center surrounded by numerous domestic structures that made up a vigorous highland community. Its location on a key trade route midway between the Peruvian coast and the lowland tropical forest to the east made Chavín de Huántar a natural trade center.

The site has given its name to the famous Chavín art style, which some claim is the pinnacle of Andean artistry. Chavín art contains a range of fantastical and representational figures, usually combining the features of humans, snakes, jaguars, caimans (alligators), and birds with intricate geometrical and curvilinear motifs. The most elegant expression of the Chavín style is in the 150 stone carvings of the huge Chavín de Huántar temple complex (we will discuss these images in Chapter 12).

The site's ceremonial buildings are honeycombed with rooms, passageways, stairways, vents, and drains (Figure 9-4). Inside the largest structure is a knife-shaped monolith 15 feet tall, set into a narrow interior gallery. The top of the elaborately carved sculpture reached through the ceiling into a gallery above, where the priests of Chavín de Huántar, acting as the voice of an oracle, may have spoken to the worshipers below.

Chavín's art and temple architecture attract the attention of Andean archaeologists, but we also need to know something about the more mundane aspects of the Chavín lifeway.

What, for instance, did the Chavín people eat? We could look to the stone iconography expressed in their

---

seasonality An estimate of what part of the year a particular archaeological site was occupied.

© Robert Kelly

Figure 9-4 The main temple and plaza at Chavín de Huántar.

sculpture, but it is unlikely that people living at 10,000 feet in the Andes dined on alligator and jaguar. Religious iconography is not a very accurate reflection of everyday diet.

George Miller (California State University, East Bay) and Richard Burger (Yale University) took a more direct approach to the problem by looking at the trash of the center's several thousand inhabitants.

When Burger first went to Chavín de Huántar, there was no reliable chronological sequence (except for sculptural style), so he conducted basic excavations to bring temporal order to the site, creating three major temporal phases. He recovered faunal remains away from the ceremonial center, from middens associated with domestic structures that reflect the everyday diet. He recovered some 12,000 bone fragments, but the NISP was only about 2000. Although this is a small sample, the data produced some patterns that led to an interesting hypothesis about how the site's role in the regional economy changed over time.

The bones were identified, first to body part and then to taxon. Next, the investigators computed the MNI for each of the three major cultural phases. They then estimated the "usable meat values" for each phase by multiplying the MNI figures per phase by the average animal's butchered weight for each taxon.

Early Patterns at Chavín de Huántar Four kinds of camelids (animals of the family Camelidae) live today in the Andes. The llama is used mostly as a pack animal, and secondarily for its coarse hair. The alpaca is valued mostly for its fine and abundant fleece. Both of these domesticated species play important roles in religious rituals. Guanacos—wild llamas—are hunted as a source of meat. Finally, the vicuña, also a wild species, is hunted mostly for its extremely fine hair.

During the earliest or Urabarriu phase (2900–2500 BP), more than half the meat came from camelids (see Figure 9-5). Using measurements taken on the archaeological bones and comparing them to those taken on a comparative collection, Miller and Burger concluded that most of the larger camelids from the Urabarriu phase were llamas. Stable isotope analysis (a technique we will discuss in Chapter 10) of their bones suggests that these early llama herds may have consumed considerable quantities of maize and, therefore, were probably domesticated. The smaller camelids were mostly vicuña.

White-tailed deer came in second (31 percent of the available meat). Skunk, large cats (either jaguar or puma), fox (or dog), and guinea pig bones also turned up in small numbers. The bones of some of these rarer animals may have been used for tools, rather than for food (although guinea pigs are today considered a

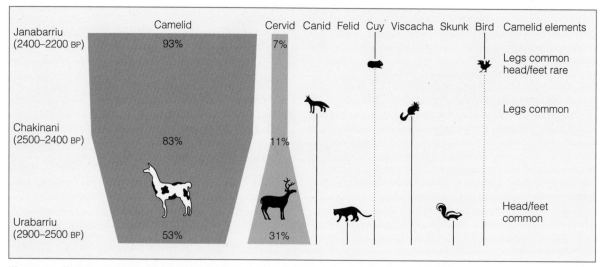

Figure 9-5 Changing relative abundance of the major animal groups in faunal remains at Chavín de Huántar. *After Miller and Burger 1995, Figure 4; courtesy of the authors and the Society for American Archaeology.*

delicacy in highland Peru). In other words, the Urabarriu phase bones strongly suggest a transitional pattern of mixed hunting and herding.

The Later Fauna at Chavín de Huántar

Things changed markedly during the subsequent Chakinani phase (2500–2400 BP). Deer frequencies drop off dramatically, and camelid frequencies jump to 83 percent, with llama bones becoming considerably more common than those of vicuña.

The faunal assemblage from the terminal Janabarriu phase (2400–2200 BP) continues this trend: Camelid bones constitute 93 percent of the assemblage. During this phase, the rapidly expanding population had virtually abandoned hunting in favor of domesticated llamas. This much seems clear.

Recall that Miller and Burger identified the bones from Chavín de Huántar to both taxon and element. The taxonomic changes through time indicated that subsistence activities changed markedly at Chavín de Huántar. But by looking at differential representation of elements (that is, body parts), Miller and Burger explored the way in which the various animal products were distributed throughout the community.

They found a curious pattern: The early Urabarriu camelid assemblage consisted mostly of head and foot bones. During the two subsequent phases, however, leg bones become considerably more frequent, with cranial and foot bones becoming rare. What does this intriguing pattern mean?

puna Native American (Quechua) term for the treeless, windswept tablelands and basins of the higher Andes.

Camelid Taphonomy As we pointed out in Chapter 8, interpretation requires middle-level theory, and one source of such theory is ethnoarchaeology. George Miller had conducted ethnoarchaeological research on contemporary South American pastoralists in the **puna,** the high grassy plateau of southern Peru. This experience helped him to analyze the remains excavated by Burger. Interestingly, Miller found that the bone refuse in modern herding communities mirrored almost exactly the early pattern from Chavín de Huántar: plenty of head and foot bones, and not many leg bones. Why?

Miller first considered the matter of bone survival. He conducted a variety of experiments on camelid bones to see which ones tend to survive and which ones disappear. Not surprisingly, he found that the extremely dense foot bones and enamel-covered teeth lasted much longer than the long, hollow leg bones and the relatively porous vertebrae.

Miller then looked at the way in which butchering patterns might create a different representation of skeletal parts. Put simply, the process of modern camelid butchering accelerates the skewing effects already suggested from the bone density studies. Because people commonly break up the leg bones to get at the marrow inside, such long bones commonly enter the archaeological record fragmented (making them more difficult to identify to element and taxon). Like other taphonomists, Miller discovered that when dogs gnaw on camelid remains, they consume spongy bones (such as vertebrae) almost entirely, but even repeated gnawing leaves dense teeth and foot bones marked, but intact. In other words, the processes involved in differential preservation—bone density, butchering patterns, and carnivore gnawing—all operated to bias the modern faunal assemblage in precisely the manner observed from the early deposits at Chavín de Huántar.

But another factor is at work here, what Miller calls the *ch'arki* effect. Today, herders of the puna preserve llama and alpaca meat by alternately drying it out in the intense Andean sun, then freezing it during the cold, high-altitude nights. (The product of this freeze-drying process—called **ch'arki** in the native Quechua language—has made its way into English as "jerky.")

But unlike the overpriced beef jerky peddled in bars and gas stations throughout the United States, Peruvian ch'arki consists of meat dried on the bone. In general, the bones of the head and feet are cut off in the ch'arki-making process and eaten at home by the local herding communities. Ch'arki is a major trade item between the highland puna herders and those living in the intermontane valleys and along the Pacific coast today.

So, what does ch'arki production look like if all you have are bones? That is, what is the archaeological evidence of ch'arki making?

The pattern depends entirely on whether you are making or receiving the ch'arki. If you're in the puna, where llama are herded and ch'arki is made, you will find lots of cranial and foot bones. These are the heavy, dense bones (without much meat attached) that nobody wants to drag around the Andes. So they are cut off and discarded, entering the archaeological record of the puna. But if you are on the receiving end of the ch'arki trade network—in the downhill intermontane valleys and along the coast—then the pattern is the opposite. The camelid bones you receive from the uplands are those still left adhering to the ch'arki chunks. So, your garbage will contain lots of leg bones and vertebrae, but not many skull parts or foot bones.

Given this simple taphonomic patterning based on the behavior of modern camelid-herding communities, we can return to the bone assemblages from Chavín de Huántar and look at the bones in a more informed manner.

The Behavior behind the Bones Remember that the faunal remains from the Chakinani (2500–2400 BP) and Janabarriu (2400–2200 BP) phases contained mostly camelid bones—mostly llama and some vicuña, with deer frequencies dropping off markedly from earlier times. The rapidly expanding population at Chavín de Huántar had forsaken hunting in favor of camelid herding. Miller and Burger also found that whereas the camelid assemblage from earlier deposits consisted mostly of head and foot bones, leg bones dominated the later archaeological record, with cranial and foot elements rare.

Middle-level studies tell us that three of the major taphonomic factors—differential bone densities, fracturing of long bones, and carnivore gnawing—all *decrease* survival of leg bones. Although these factors influenced the composition of this assemblage, the abundance of leg bones suggests that taphonomy alone cannot account for the faunal distributions.

Instead, we must look to the ch'arki effect. The ethnoarchaeological findings indicated that the observed late phase pattern at Chavín de Huántar is almost exactly the *opposite* of what we see among contemporary alpaca herders living on the puna. Obviously, there are some important differences between modern communities and that of late Chavín times. What are they?

Then and now, the valley floor surrounding Chavín de Huántar is well suited for maize agriculture but provides poor pasturage. It also lacks the cold, dry weather needed to produce ch'arki. Because llama herding is most effective in the puna, it seems likely that the ch'arki was prepared there. Thus, it appears that high-altitude herding communities traded ch'arki to the valley residents of Chavín de Huántar. In return, the valley communities may have sent agricultural products (such as maize) into the mountains, where few crops can grow.

Translated into bones, this means that discarded faunal elements (cranial and foot bones) should turn up at sites in the puna; downhill, the imported ch'arki should result in mostly upper limb bones and vertebrae entering the archaeological record of domestic dwellings along the valley floors. And this is precisely the pattern observed in the archaeological record of Chavín de Huántar and inferred for the surrounding puna sites.

From this evidence, Miller and Burger concluded that the earliest occupants of Chavín de Huántar used llamas mostly as pack animals, camelid meat being a by-product of culling the herds. Meat was also obtained by hunting vicuña and white-tailed deer. People living on the valley floor were basically self-sufficient in the Urabarriu phase, acquiring their own meat as needed.

Then, the ritual importance of Chavín de Huántar increased through time, and the local community grew in size. The associated increase in agricultural production on the valley floor made hunting of local wild species less productive, and thereafter meat was derived almost exclusively from domesticated llamas. Because the valley floor was poorly suited for llama herding, there was an increased need for long-distance trade with the high-altitude regions. Ch'arki was traded in,

ch'arki Native South American (Quechua) term for freeze-dried llama and alpaca meat.

and agricultural products (among other commodities) were traded out during the later Janabarriu phase.

The differential distribution of camelid bones thus reflects important economic and social relationships between Chavín de Huántar and surrounding communities. These exchange relationships were probably also reinforced by a shared participation in the Chavín religious cult, both at the massive valley-floor temple and at small shrines located in the various high-altitude villages. With time, the residents of Chavín de Huántar shifted from a generalized economic system with only loose ties to their upland neighbors to a more specialized subsistence pattern that depended heavily on long-distance exchange with the upland herders in the puna.

Recall that this interpretation of Chavín de Huántar's faunal assemblage is based partially on ethnographic analogy. Lidio Valdez (MacEwan University) points out that the analogy employed for ch'arki production is only one of several that could be drawn from the Andes. Ch'arki is made in other ways throughout the Andes, and each leaves a different faunal signature. Did Miller and Burger pick the right analogy? Peter Stahl (Binghamton University, New York) suggests Chavín de Huántar's local environment could have permitted ch'arki production and that further taphonomic scrutiny of the faunal assemblages suggests that they could be commensurate with on-site ch'arki production. Clearly, Miller and Burger's hypothesis is, like so many conclusions in archaeology, a "work in progress." Nonetheless, their work illustrates the utility of combining ethnoarchaeological and taphonomic research to understand patterning in archaeological faunal data.

These two examples—a Folsom camp in Wyoming and a ceremonial center in Peru—show some of the ways archaeologists pursue faunal analysis and what it can contribute to our understanding of the past. Incidentally, faunal analysis is finding new uses in studies relevant to modern conservation efforts (see "What Does It Mean to Me? Zooarchaeology and Biological Conservation," by Virginia Butler).

macrobotanical remains Nonmicroscopic plant remains recovered from an archaeological site.

paleoethnobotanist An archaeologist who analyzes and interprets plant remains from archaeological sites in order to understand past interactions between human populations and plants.

coprolite Desiccated feces, often containing macrobotanical remains, pollen, and the remains of small animals.

palynology The study of fossil pollen grains and spores to reconstruct past climates and human behavior.

STUDYING PLANT REMAINS FROM ARCHAEOLOGICAL SITES

Bones, however, are only half the story. Although plants are particularly vulnerable to decomposition, many archaeological sites contain well-preserved **macrobotanical remains** (readily recognizable plant parts): caches of corncobs, pine nuts, a hearth's charcoal, or acorn mush adhering to the inside wall of a food bowl. A counterpart to the zooarchaeologist, **paleoethnobotanists** are archaeologists who specialize in recovering and identifying plant remains, focusing on the world of plant–people interactions.

For years, much of what we knew about ancient plants came from archaeological sites in arid climates, which had a far better chance of preserving them for study. The archaeological deposits inside Danger and Hogup caves (in Utah), for instance, consisted almost entirely of plant seeds, hulls, and chaff. In places, virtually no dirt was present, even though the deposits were more than 10 feet deep. From column samples of the fill, investigators reconstructed the vegetational history near both sites. Such studies can highlight the degree to which modern plant distributions can mislead the archaeologist studying the human ecology of even the fairly recent past.

In more humid climates, plant remains generally are preserved only when they have been burned and carbonized. For this reason, the most common method of recovering plant remains is flotation (as discussed in Chapter 4). But plant remains are also sometimes preserved in waterlogged contexts (shipwrecks, mudslides, and wells), sun-dried adobe bricks, wattle-and-daub walls, and ceramics.

Archaeologists also find plant remains in curious places, such as inside ancient human stomachs (preserved through mummification) and in human **coprolites** (desiccated feces); this evidence of past diets is about as direct as one could hope for. Evidence of past plant consumption is also preserved in the chemistry of human bone (we'll discuss this in Chapter 10). And it comes in a microscopic form too, as pollen and phytoliths.

Palynology

Palynology, the analysis of ancient plant pollen and spores, has long been useful to the study of prehistoric ecological adaptations by helping to reconstruct past environments. And the basics of palynology are easy to understand.

WHAT DOES IT MEAN TO ME?

ZOOARCHAEOLOGY AND BIOLOGICAL CONSERVATION

by Virginia Butler, professor of anthropology at Portland State University

Virginia Butler.

Habitats and species around the world are being lost with increasing speed in the face of human population growth and habitat destruction. Under legislation such as the Endangered Species Act (1973), recovery plans are developed to save or re-establish species and environments. These plans often require hard decisions as to which species we save. With faunal records dating back thousands of years, zooarchaeology brings an historical perspective to these decisions.

Zooarchaeology demonstrates how past human predation and landscape alteration affected animal populations; this has important implications for wildlife management. Environments that early European explorers encountered were not free of human influence—they were occupied by Native Americans. Contemporary policy that creates preserves without considering past human actions is trying to re-create environments that never existed. For example, in the 1990s, more than 60,000 wapiti (elk) lived in the greater Yellowstone area, yet wapiti remains are rare in archaeological sites. The rarity of wapiti remains suggests that humans kept this animal's populations low through hunting. Charles Kay (Utah State University) argues that this means the "hands off" management policy in Yellowstone, which allows wapiti populations to increase unchecked, does not duplicate pre–AD 1900 conditions and has led to serious overgrazing of the park.

My research in California's Owens Valley helps us understand the effects of habitat loss and exotic (introduced) species on the loss of native fish species. The Owens Valley contains four indigenous species of fish: pupfish, chub, a minnow, and the Owens sucker, the first three of which are in severe decline. Analyzing an 8000-year zooarchaeological record, Michael Delacourt (California State University, Sacramento) and I found that both the size and abundance of the different species changed over time in response to changes in climate that affected the size of the valley's lakes. But no species was ever in danger of extinction. The only thing that changed in the last 100 years was the introduction of exotic species, predatory fish against which the indigenous species cannot compete. With this information, managers can make informed decisions about how to save the indigenous species from extinction.

Zooarchaeological research aids conservation measures in other ways. For example, when wildlife biologists re-establish a species, they try to do so with animals from a population that is closely related to the native stock. New techniques allow us to extract genetic data from skeletal remains, and these data provide the genetic signature of the locally extinct native stock. In Oregon, for example, biologists turned to archaeological remains to determine whether Alaskan or southern California sea otters are the closest genetic match to the population that formerly inhabited Oregon's waters.

In sum, zooarchaeology helps us understand long-term animal population dynamics so we can stop the loss of species diversity and conserve environments for future generations to enjoy.

Most plants shed their pollen into the atmosphere, where the wind rapidly disperses it. Pollen grains—microscopic male gametes—are present in most of the earth's atmosphere; a single pine branch can produce as many as 350 million pollen grains. Pollen grains are tenacious and under the right conditions can survive for tens of thousands of years, or even longer.

Determining what these pollen concentrations mean can be quite challenging, but the initial steps in extracting and identifying pollen are rather straightforward. Sometimes pollen is recovered by core sampling, in which a circular tube is forced downward by a mechanical drilling rig into a sediment record. Lake bottoms are often good places to prospect for pollen.

We can also take pollen samples manually from archaeological stratigraphic profiles. The surface of the excavation profile is first scraped; 0.2 to 0.3 liter of material is then extracted from the sediment with a clean trowel and placed in a sterile, sealable container. Samples are often taken at 5- or 10-centimeter intervals to provide a continuous record of the pollen rain throughout the period of deposition. The archaeologist takes the samples from the bottom of the profile to the top (rather than from the top to the bottom) so that the samples are not contaminated by falling dirt. Samples can also be taken from sealed deposits within architectural features (such as ancient floors or the fill found in pits), and they can be retrieved from artifacts such as grinding stones by washing the surfaces in distilled water.

Occasionally, we find pollen in human burials, on the inside of ceramic vessels, trapped inside the weave of ancient baskets, or even adhering to the working surface of a stone tool. The analyst must always be certain that he or she has collected the sample from a recently exposed surface so that the modern pollen rain does not contaminate it.

In the laboratory, pollen grains are isolated from the soil matrix with repeated hydrofluoric acid baths and centrifuging (pollen survives the acid baths that destroy most everything else in the sample). A sample of the solution is then placed on a microscope slide, which is scanned at magnifications between 400X and 1000X.

Palynology is possible only because different plants produce pollen that look very different under a microscope (Figure 9-6). Pine pollen, for example, has

Figure 9-6 Pollen grains at 700X. On the left is prickly pear pollen and on the right is goldenrod.

two "wings" that carry it long distances on the wind. Elm pollen, on the other hand, is a lumpy round ball. This difference means that the individual grains can be identified, sometimes to species, and tabulated until the analyst records a statistically significant number—say, about 400 to 500 grains per slide. (A skilled analyst can tabulate this number of pollen grains in 2 to 3 hours.) The palynologist then converts the counts to percentages and creates a **pollen diagram** that shows the proportional shift in pollen frequencies between stratigraphic levels within a site.

Fluctuations in pollen percentages reflect changes in plant densities, and a primary application of palynology is to reconstruct past environments. Peter Mehringer's (Washington State University) research at the Lehner Ranch Site shows how this works.

Reconstructing Past Environments at Lehner Ranch

The question of when people first arrived in North America is still hotly debated. The people who made Folsom points were among the earliest peoples in the New World, but earlier still were people who made a different kind of fluted point, known to archaeologists as **Clovis** points. The name Clovis comes from an important site near Clovis, New Mexico, where, a few years after the discoveries at the Folsom site, distinctive spear points were found lying stratigraphically beneath diagnostic Folsom artifacts. Clovis artifacts date to about 12,900 to 13,200 BP, and at about a dozen sites they are associated with the bones of extinct mammoths and mastodons.

One of those sites is the Lehner Ranch site in southern Arizona's San Pedro Valley, where C. Vance Haynes (University of Arizona) found Clovis points and stone butchering tools in association with mammoth remains. It is hard to imagine mammoths plodding among the creosote and ocotillo of the southern Arizona landscape today. Clovis hunters clearly lived

pollen diagram A chart showing the changing frequencies of different identified pollens through time from samples taken from archaeological or other sites.

Clovis The earliest well-established Native American culture, distributed throughout much of North America and dating 10,900 to 11,200 BC.

Figure 9-7 Pollen diagram from the Lehner Ranch site (Arizona).
After Mehringer and Haynes 1966, Figure 8.

in a different environment, so Haynes turned to paly-nologist Peter Mehringer to help reconstruct what that environment was like.

Figure 9-7 shows the pollen diagram from the Leh-ner Ranch site. Lehner has a complex stratigraphy, and Mehringer could not find a single locality that contained a continuous and unbroken pollen record, so this diagram is a composite, showing the results of three separate but overlapping pollen profiles.

Pollen diagrams can look daunting, but don't let them put you off. Along the left edge is the sample number and, in the next column to the right, the strati-graphic unit, accompanied by the sample's depth. In this case, samples were taken at 10 cm intervals. Be-cause this pollen diagram is a composite of three differ-ent profiles (labeled at right), some of the stratigraphic units appear more than once. For instance, Unit k

appeared at 260–270 cm in Profile I, 170–180 cm in Profile VIII, and 180–190 cm in Profile II.

Running along the top of the chart are the plant taxa: *Pinus* is pine pollen, *Juniperus* is juniper pollen, *Quercus* is oak, and so on. The horizontal scales below these are simply the percentages of the different kinds of plant pollen—for instance, *Artemisia* (sagebrush) constituted about 16 percent of the pollen found at 160 cm in Profile I. The shaded areas show the chang-ing frequencies of different pollen. For example, pollen of cheno-ams (Chenopodiaceae and Amaran-thaceae, closely related plants of the goosefoot family and amaranth) is most common at the lowest levels of the site (look at Samples 13 and 14 in stratigraphic Units g and i). We read the diagram from the bottom to the top. Doing so, we see that cheno-ams become less common through time, until stratigraphic Unit m

(Samples 23 through 28), where it begins to pick up again. The assumption is that pollen roughly mirrors the local abundance of the plant species producing it; thus, goosefoot and amaranth were common early in the sequence, then became less common and, later in time, returned.

To go further, you must recognize the difference between *local* and *regional* environments. Look around at any landscape, and you will see microenvironments that do *not* reflect the regional environment. A flowing spring in a desert, for example, might support a dense stand of spruce, aspen, and mountain mahogany. Analysis of pollen from sediments near such a spring would suggest that the environment was a dense forest, when in fact the regional environment is a vast sagebrush steppe. We need to understand what both local and regional environments looked like and, even more, we must avoid confusing the two.

Mehringer had to cope with the difference between local and regional environments at Lehner Ranch. A distinctive "black mat" marker bed in the stratigraphy at Lehner Ranch suggests that the immediate area was a wet bog during late Clovis times (Figure 9-8). Was that a local condition, or was it true for the larger regional environment? Pollen from composites (herbs such as ragweed and sagebrush) and cheno-ams (plants that prefer wetter conditions) dominate the pollen diagram, suggesting that the region was wetter. This pattern characterizes many post-Pleistocene pollen profiles from southwestern deserts, but it creates a problem because it could mask the presence of less common yet ecologically sensitive indicators. Although the dominant cheno-am and composite pollen undoubtedly

represents *locally* occurring species, it is insufficient for interpreting *regional* vegetation or climate.

To offset the high frequency of composite and cheno-am pollen, Mehringer applied a technique known as the *double fixed sum*. The dark profiles in the diagram are based on a standard summary for all pollen types identified, with the percentages based on the first 200 pollen grains encountered in each sample. A total of 25 such 200-grain sample counts are represented (for various reasons, some samples could not be run; note, for example, there is no Sample 4 in the diagram).

Mehringer then made a second, 100-grain count (represented by the lighter areas). He computed the percentages for the second count by ignoring cheno-am and composite pollen, counting only the other, rarer pollen types. By comparing the results of both counts, one can study the gross frequencies of the dominants as well as fluctuations in the densities of the rarer but more environmentally sensitive species.

The pollen from stratigraphic Units i, j, and k at the Lehner Ranch reflect the climatic conditions that prevailed during Clovis times. Look carefully at the pollen frequencies of Samples 15 and 16 in Profile I, Samples 1, 2, and 3 in Profile VII, and Samples 13 and 14 in Profile II. The environment of the time these samples represent is "read" by moving across the diagram. Notice that the normal pollen count—the dark portions of the figure—shows a significant jump in short-spine *compositae* pollen in stratigraphic Unit k. The double fixed sum count shows slightly greater abundances of pine, oak, and juniper pollen. For trees such as pine, oak, and juniper to grow on the valley floor, the regional environment must have been slightly moister and/or cooler before and during the deposition of the lower part of Unit k. Somewhat later, during the deposition of upper stratigraphic Unit k and Unit l, a sharp increase in the *compositae* categories and a decline in tree pollen signal a shift to fully modern conditions.

Overall, the vegetation represented by the pollen spectra from Lehner Ranch suggests a desert grassland, which today occupies slightly wetter sites nearby. Mehringer concluded that the climate at the Lehner site 13,000 years ago was slightly wetter and cooler than

Figure 9-8 C. Vance Haynes (right) examines the "black mat" marker bed at the Lehner Ranch site as archaeologists Nicole Waguespack and Todd Surovell look on.

© Robert Kelly

LOOKING CLOSER

PALYNOLOGY OF SHANIDAR CAVE: WHY FORMATION PROCESSES MATTER

Shanidar Cave (Iraq) has been occupied sporadically over the past 100,000 years. In the 1950s, Ralph Solecki (retired) discovered several Neanderthal skeletons (one of which was the inspiration for the shaman, Creb, in Jean Auel's novel *The Clan of the Cave Bear*) at Shanidar. Whether Neanderthals buried their dead with ritual is a hotly contested issue, and one of Shanidar's burials, Shanidar IV, an adult male, plays a key role in this debate.

Solecki took sediment samples from the cave's strata as well as from Shanidar IV. French palynologist Arlette Leroi-Gourhan (Musée de l'Homme, Paris) tested the Shanidar IV samples for pollen and found it in surprising quantities; there were especially high amounts near the feet, the shoulders, and the base of the spine. These samples contained pollen of at least seven species of wildflowers, including grape hyacinth, bachelor's button, and hollyhock.

Leroi-Gourhan suggested that the flowers had been woven into the branches of a pine-like shrub, which may have grown nearby on the Ice Age hillside. She also concluded that Shanidar IV was laid to rest between late May and early July, as that is the time when the flowers would have been in bloom. And the flowers suggested that this Neanderthal man was buried with a degree of ritual that few were willing to grant Neanderthals at the time.

But pollen is light, and it could have blown into the cave from the outside. Perhaps the pollen in the burial fill was simply what is called "background pollen rain." If so, then it should be present throughout the cave's deposits, not just in the grave.

Yet it was not; the sediments outside the grave contained far *less* flower pollen than Leroi-Gourhan found in the burial pit. In addition, pollen grains in the burial samples were clumped—some even lay in the form of the flowers' anthers—which suggests the pollen had fallen from flowers laid in the grave.

Neanderthal skull as it was being exposed at Shanidar Cave (Iraq). This person was probably killed by rooffall inside the cave.

But nothing is ever simple in archaeology. Perhaps the pollen came into the site as flowers, but does this mean the flowers were laid in the grave by the hands of a grieving Neanderthal?

Jeffrey Sommer (University of Michigan) suggests another possibility: rodents. Solecki noted that all of Shanidar's burials were riddled with rodent burrows. In fact, Solecki thought he could locate burials by tracing rodent burrows through the deposits. Many of the rodents died in the cave, and their skeletons tell us that they were *Meriones persicus*, the Persian jird.

Jirds store large numbers of entire flower heads, neatly clipped from their stems, in the side tunnels of their burrows. Sommers points out that the number of flower heads that this rodent stores is more than enough to account for the pollen that Leroi-Gourhan found.

Thus, an alternative explanation for the Shanidar burial "bouquets" is that they were placed there by the humble jird. And the search for convincing evidence of burial ritual among Neanderthals must continue.

---

today, followed by a rapid shift toward drier conditions. As many palynology studies have found, only a small shift in temperature and/or precipitation is required to produce dramatic differences in the regional environment. So, with only slight changes in rainfall and temperature, mammoths, horses, camels, and a range of other animals disappeared from the southern Arizona landscape forever.

One contribution of pollen analysis to archaeology is the reconstruction of environmental change. Pollen studies, properly applied, can also help archaeologists understand past human behavior (see "Looking Closer: Palynology of Shanidar Cave: Why Formation Processes Matter"). And pollen also can play a role in figuring out what plants were important in prehistoric diet. An example from Nevada's Stillwater Marsh shows how and introduces other sources of paleoethnobotanical information.

What Plants Did People Eat in the Stillwater Marsh?

You will recall from Chapter 3 that after Kelly's survey of the Carson Desert (Nevada), high precipitation flooded the marsh and exposed dozens of archaeological sites and human burials. We discuss the burials in Chapter 10; here we focus on the plant remains that were recovered from one site that we excavated in the wake of the flood.

Site 26CH1062 is not a particularly glamorous site (refer to Figure 3-6, page 59). It sits on a low clay dune and consists of several pits, postholes, and at least two shallow houses that were perhaps little more than windbreaks. Radiocarbon dates show that the site was occupied at least twice, once about 1400 BP and again about 1000 BP. We water-screened all the deposits and recovered a large number of stone tools, manufacturing waste flakes, shells, and faunal remains. We also floated soil samples from several of the features and retrieved many carbonized macrobotanical remains.

The macrobotanical remains were sent to paleoethnobotanist David Rhode, at Nevada's Desert Research Institute. Looking at the samples under a microscope at 15–40X, Rhode identified the various carbonized seeds and bits of burnt wood (using a comparative collection, much like those that faunal analysts use). Most of the charcoal was reed (*Phragmites australis*), greasewood (*Sarcobatus* sp.), and some willow (*Salix* sp.)—not surprising since these plants can be found today in the Carson Desert. They could have been used as firewood, in housing, or as tools.

The seeds were more interesting. Rhode found the carbonized seeds of several plants, including cattail, dock, seepweed, chenopods, pickleweed, silverscale, heliotrope, saltbush, and goosefoot. The inhabitants of

the site could have gathered any of these as food, and all occur in the area today.

One of the most abundant seeds was that of bulrush (*Scirpus* sp.). The indigenous peoples of the Carson Desert, the Paiute, used bulrush (and many other wetland plants) as food. This makes sense, because experimental data show that bulrush seeds are an efficiently gathered and nutritious resource (we'll return to these kinds of foraging experiments in Chapter 13).

But *did* people collect bulrush seeds for food? And, if so, did they collect them in the Stillwater Marsh? It is possible that the bulrush seeds came in attached to bulrush plants that were used to build windbreaks on the site or as material to make temporary basketry-like containers. Any accidental burning of these artifacts could have toasted the seeds and left them behind for us to recover. Were bulrush plants, and not just their seeds, present on the site? To answer this question, we looked at another source of plant data in archaeological sites.

Phytoliths One important method of learning about plants in ancient sites is the analysis of microscopic plant opal **phytoliths,** literally, "plant stones." As plants take in water through their roots, they also take in silica, which is then deposited in mineral form between cells, within cell walls, or sometimes in the cells themselves (Figure 9-9). Phytoliths occur in members of the grass family, as well as in rushes, sedges, palms, conifers, and deciduous trees. When dead plant material decays, the almost indestructible opal phytoliths—they can last for millions of years—are deposited in the ground.

Importantly, phytoliths take the shape of the cells in which they were deposited. Because different grasses have different cell shapes, their phytoliths also have different shapes. This means that we can identify the presence of certain kinds of plants long after those plants have decayed and disappeared.

Phytolith analysis is similar to pollen analysis, but with an important difference: Although a plant produces a single form of pollen, phytoliths can vary within a single species, and not all plants produce phytoliths. Phytoliths are most useful for identifying the abundance of different kinds of grasses, although research continues to extend this ability to other plants.

Phytolith analysis was extremely useful in the Stillwater Marsh. We sent soil samples to Linda Scott Cummings (Paleo Research Labs, Colorado) and, as expected, she found that phytoliths were well preserved. *Phragmites*, a common marsh grass, accounted for most of the phytoliths, along with several other marsh grasses. What was most intriguing, however, was the complete *lack* of sedge phytoliths, which

phytoliths Tiny silica particles contained in plants. Sometimes these fragments can be recovered from archaeological sites even after the plants themselves have decayed.

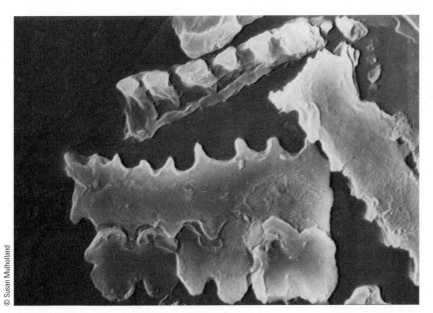

Figure 9-9 What a phytolith looks like under the microscope.

are produced by plants such as bulrush. This suggests that no bulrush plants decayed on the site. If they had, Cummings would have found their phytoliths in the soil samples.

Perhaps, then, there was no bulrush in the Stillwater Marsh 1000 years ago. Perhaps a visitor brought some bulrush seed cakes from another wetland, such as Winnemucca Lake to the west. This is a question about the regional environment. Although phytoliths can tell which plants were present on a specific site, pollen data are better for looking at regional patterns.

So, in addition to flotation and phytolith samples, we also took pollen samples from several of the features. These were sent to Peter Wigand, then at the Desert Research Institute, where he analyzed them using the protocols described previously. He found that the pollen in the samples was little different from the modern pollen rain of today; in fact, he found that sedge pollen was somewhat overrepresented in the samples: Bulrush might even have been somewhat *more* abundant in the Stillwater Marsh of the past than it is today.

So, now we know (a) that burnt bulrush seeds were present on the site, (b) that bulrush plants were not on the site, and (c) that bulrush was abundant in the wetland. Given that ethnographic data show that bulrush seeds were eaten by the Paiute, and experimental data indicate that bulrush is an efficiently gathered and nutritious food, we concluded that bulrush seeds were brought to the site to be eaten.

The macrobotanical remains were also interesting in what was *not* present. Completely missing were the seeds of upland plants such as ricegrass or piñon pine nut hulls—both important food sources to the

nineteenth-century Shoshone and Paiute in the Great Basin. This suggests that when people lived in the Carson Desert, they got their plant food exclusively from the wetland; they did not travel even a few kilometers into the low foothills to gather ricegrass, nor did they hike another 20 kilometers into the hills to gather piñon.

Site Seasonality The seasonality of the Agate Basin site was determined using faunal remains, but at 26CH1062 we used the macrobotanical remains. Recall that we found bulrush seeds, along with cattail, seepweed, dock, chenopods, pickleweed, heliotrope, silverscale, saltbush, and goosefoot seeds. We know from ethnographic and experimental data that most of these seeds ripen in mid- to late summer and into the early winter. Dock and heliotrope are gathered throughout the summer only. Late summer is therefore the only time when all of these are available, and that is probably the best estimate of when the site was occupied (although an occupation through the fall cannot be ruled out).

Wood Rat Nests

One important, if somewhat surprising, source of plant macrofossils is the ancient nests of **wood rats** (*Neotoma* sp.) that are found throughout the arid desert West (Figure 9-10). (Most people call these rodents "pack rats"; they're the same critter as wood rats.)

Wood rats are fascinating animals. They bring home extensive quantities of food and nest material, including wood, rock, bone, paper—anything they can drag into a crevice or rockshelter. Archaeologists in the western United States know that wood rat nests are good places to look for organic artifacts—arrows, atlatl pieces, and basketry fragments are all incorporated into wood rat nests (as well as small tools or

wood rats (pack rats) Rodents that build nests of organic materials and thus preserve a record, often for thousands of years, of changing plant species within the local area of the nest.

Figure 9-10 Wood rat midden in the Bighorn Mountains, Wyoming. The upper midden is a meter high.

notepaper that a forgetful archaeologist might leave out overnight!).

Field studies demonstrate that pack rats do not travel more than 100 meters from their nests to collect materials. In contrast to pollen studies, wood rat nests reflect the *immediate* environment around their nests.

After collecting material, the rats build their nests in protected locations, such as crevices in cliffs or in cave mouths or rockshelters. This certainly helps to preserve the collected twigs and branches, but the rats do something else to the nests that guarantee their preservation: They urinate all over them. And under the right conditions, their urine forms a lacquer-like covering that also helps preserves the nest material—for thousands of years. As a result, researchers throughout arid North America use wood rat assemblages to reconstruct late Pleistocene and **Holocene** vegetational change.

Holocene The post-Pleistocene geological epoch that began about 10,000 radiocarbon years ago and continues today.

Wood rat nests are often as hard as rock, so you use hammers, chisels, saws, and pry bars to excavate them. (By the way, the nests have a strong smell; some people hate it and others, oddly enough, like it.) After samples are taken from different levels in the nest, they are soaked in distilled water if they are covered with urine lacquer. After the samples dry, the analyst sorts and identifies the materials. Specimens from each sample are radiocarbon dated, and the resulting data help to reconstruct past environments.

We noted earlier that neither piñon pine nuts nor their hulls appear in sites in the Stillwater Marsh, and we suggested this meant that people did not travel to the mountains to collect them. But did people not collect piñon nuts because they did not need them, or because there was no piñon pine in the mountains 1000 or more years ago?

To answer this question, Peter Wigand and his colleague Cheryl Nowak studied a number of wood rat middens from several locations in western Nevada, including the Stillwater Range, which borders the Carson Desert. They found that evidence for piñon pine—in the form of branches, needles, and cones—did not appear in wood rat nests until about 1200 years ago in the Stillwater Mountains and considerably later in ranges farther west.

You will recall from Chapter 3 that research in the Carson Desert was aimed at understanding whether wetland food resources were preferred over those of the mountains. If we assume that past environments of the Carson Desert and Stillwater Mountains were similar to modern ones, then the data from 26CH1062 suggest that Native Americans eschewed piñon in favor of marsh plants. But the wood rat nest data suggest that piñon may not have been present in sufficient abundance to make a trip to the mountains worth the effort. This example shows that *it is essential that archaeologists make economic interpretations of subsistence data in light of paleoenvironmental reconstructions.* The former without the latter is almost useless.

Coprolites of Hidden Cave

Human coprolites are another source of information on prehistoric diet. Paleontologists first used the term "coprolite" (from the Greek *kopros* "dung" and *lithikos* "stone") about 1830 to describe fossilized dinosaur feces. Archaeologists use the term, but the feces we analyze are just desiccated, not fossilized. Coprolites are not common in the archaeological record, but they are, for obvious reasons, an excellent source of information on human diet.

Archaeologists find coprolites of many different kinds of animals, including humans, in dry archaeological sites. The archaeologist's first task is to identify which are human, and which belong to other species such as deer or mountain sheep. Believe it or not, some archaeologists have devoted time to identifying the criteria that distinguish human feces from, say, that of a bear.

David Rhode, the same paleoethnobotanist who studied the macrobotanical remains from 26CH1062, also looked at human coprolites from Hidden Cave, a site that overlooks the Stillwater Marsh (see Figure 3-3 on page 52). The cave's original opening was very small, barely large enough to crawl into; and even though the cave opens into a large chamber, it was a lousy place to live or even to spend the night. It is dark and dusty, and if you made a fire for warmth or light, the chamber would soon fill with smoke. Thus, we were not surprised when we found no hearths, stone tool waste flakes, or bones left over from meals. People did not live in Hidden Cave; instead, they used it as a place to cache various kinds of gear in pits, between 3800 and 1500 years ago.

But there were also many quids—expectorated pieces of plants (mostly cattail and bulrush) that people had chewed for their juices. And found nearby were bits of cordage, made from strips of bark rolled together. This suggests that people also used the cave as a place to escape the summer's heat, passing the afternoon by chewing succulent stalks of bulrush and cattail in the cave's cool interior while rolling bark together to make cords to tie together bundles, or to repair sagebrush bark sandals or torn baskets.

Many of the artifacts found in Hidden Cave were projectile points; these might suggest that men were the primary visitors to the cave (we'll deal with such gender assumptions in Chapter 11). Many coprolites were also found. Rhode decided to investigate the coprolites to see what the men who used the shelter were eating. He was surprised by what he found.

Rhode prepared the 19 coprolites by first soaking them in a solution of trisodium phosphate to reconstitute them (yes, really!). He then washed each specimen through fine mesh screens and dried the residue. Next, he examined and sorted this material under a microscope.

A small macrobotanical remain from each coprolite was AMS radiocarbon dated. In so doing, Rhode found that the coprolites fell into two time periods: One batch dated between 3800 and 3400 BP, the other from 1900 to 1500 BP. All of the coprolites contained abundant evidence of plants, fish, and bird remains (people may also have eaten large mammals, but obviously their bones would not appear in coprolites).

Bulrush seeds were the most common seeds, some showing evidence of burning and milling (striations left from the action of grinding stones). Cattail pollen was also common. Rhode also found small feathers of waterfowl, as well as the bones of tui chub, a species of minnow that lives in the Stillwater Marsh. In fact, fish cranial (head) and caudal (tail) bones tell us that these small fish were eaten whole. Insects showed up too, as well as snails.

Curiously, only one coprolite contained a piñon pine nut hull. This coprolite, Number 167, also contained cattail seeds and pollen. This is important because piñon nuts ripen in late September or early October, whereas cattail pollen is collected in July. Clearly, one of these resources must have been stored, and it was most likely the piñon.

All of this was intriguing, but then came the surprise. We can determine if a man or a woman voided a coprolite depending on the abundance of the sex hormones estradiol, progesterone, and testosterone. This is done using a complex technique known as high-pressure liquid chromatographic analysis. After applying this technique, Rhode found that the coprolites' levels of sex hormones clearly indicated that women had voided the coprolites. We don't know if it was also women who cached the projectile points, spit out the quids, and spun the cordage. But coprolite analysis clearly shows that it is wrong to assume that only men visited Hidden Cave.

Lipid Analysis: Squeezing Fat from Ceramics

Analyses of faunal and macrobotanical remains, phytoliths, pollen, and coprolites are fairly standard in archaeology's efforts to reconstruct the past. But archaeologists and their associates in allied fields are always developing new techniques that extract even more information from archaeological remains and increase our ability to reconstruct the past. For example, some analysts are attempting to extract ancient blood from the microcracks in stone tools and identify it to species. Another technique allows us to extract identifiable food residues from pottery.

The reconstruction of the plant component of ancient diets is more elusive than determining the role of meat. This is largely because of a substantial bias in preservation: Bone preserves better than plant remains. Macrobotanical remains are also more difficult to retrieve from archaeological sites. Flotation increases the recovery rate, but plant remains are still hard to come by: Water-screening allowed us to retrieve some

300,000 animal bones from 26CH1062 (mostly small fish bones), but through flotation we collected only a handful of macrobotanical remains. So archaeologists are always looking for new ways to retrieve information on plants from archaeological sites.

One promising way is to extract **lipids** from artifacts and even from sediments themselves. Lipids are those organic substances that resist mixing with water. This includes the fats, oils, and waxes that are found in both plant and animal tissues. Because they resist mixing with water, lipids have a tendency to remain where they were deposited (even washing in the laboratory may not remove them).

Cooking vessels are a particularly good place to look for lipids because they are released from the plant or meat when heated and are absorbed into the fabric of the pottery. Cooking vessels often have a thick carbon residue inside, the result of many simmering stews, but the best place to look for lipids is actually in the walls of the pottery itself.

How do we identify lipids? Recall from our discussion of radiocarbon dating in Chapter 6 that there are three major kinds of carbon in the atmosphere—^{14}C, ^{13}C, and ^{12}C. Recall also that plants with different photosynthetic pathways take in these carbons in different amounts. Thus different classes of plants have different ratios of ^{13}C to ^{12}C, and a plant's fatty acids register this ratio.

The archaeological sample comes from a piece of the interior of a pot. The sherd is ground up and subjected to a laboratory process that separates the fatty acids in the lipid fraction. This extract is then subjected to gas chromatography and mass spectrometry, techniques that measure the ratio of ^{13}C to ^{12}C. Different ratios distinguish the fatty acids in the lipids of plants from those of animals; ongoing research shows that different plant taxa (and, to a lesser extent, different animal species) can be identified using this technique.

One of this method's pioneers, Richard Evershed (University of Bristol, England), has identified the lipids of leafy vegetables (perhaps cabbage) from pottery in Europe. He has also identified residues of milk and of meat. Looking at medieval pots from England, he found that the amount of lipids increased from the bottom to the top of the pot. This makes sense because fats and oil rise to the top of a stew or soup as it cools, and upper portions of pots would therefore absorb more than the lower portions. In fact, on the inside

bottom of some pots he found the fatty acid signature of beeswax. This was not part of a meal, but part of the manufacture of the pot: Ethnoarchaeological research has found that many potters smear beeswax on the inside of a pot that is still warm from the kiln in order to season it.

This technique works only with cooking pots, which could record a variety of different kinds of meals. The method holds promise for reconstructing some elements of a diet that have otherwise proved elusive. There is even the possibility that lipids could be extracted from soil samples and help recover more information on plant foods, such as tubers and roots, that do not preserve well and are rarely found carbonized.

THE SYMBOLIC MEANING OF PLANTS: THE UPPER MANTARO VALLEY PROJECT

So far we have been talking about plants, animals, and people from a strictly economic perspective: What did people eat in the past, and when did they eat it? But more can be done with plant and animal remains in archaeological sites. As discussed in Chapter 2, processual archaeology emphasizes the analysis of natural resources—such as plant remains—as a key to understanding how people coped with ecological issues of the past. But postprocessual archaeology encourages us to seek other things about the past, including not only how people interacted materially with their environment, but how they interacted with it symbolically as well. The Upper Mantaro Valley Project in Peru is one example.

The Upper Mantaro Valley sits at 3300 meters (about 10,800 feet) above sea level in the central Andes of Peru. The intensively settled and cultivated valley floors are surrounded by rocky hillsides, supporting a few rocky fields, but mostly grasses, a few shrubs, and small trees (Figure 9-11). Thousands of years of intensive cultivation and herding have undoubtedly changed the character of these upland valleys, but nobody is certain just how. Although some investigators believe that the landscape was originally forested, pollen analysis suggests that this area has been relatively treeless since humans first moved in, several thousand years ago.

The Upper Mantaro Archaeological Project excavated numerous house compounds from six archaeological sites spanning the period 1500 to 500 BP

lipids Organic substances—including fats, oils, and waxes—that resist mixing with water; found in both plant and animal tissues.

Figure 9-11 Peaks in the Andes Mountains overlooking a homestead (lower right) on the puna in central Peru.

(divided into six phases: Pancán 1 through Pancán 4 and Wanka II and III). During the Wanka II phase, the population of the Upper Mantaro area aggregated into large, walled towns located on protected knolls just above the rolling upland zone. The archaeological evidence suggests that this was a time of fighting between villages, with land use probably restricted to areas close to the walled settlements. After the Inka conquest during Wanka III times, the population was relocated into small villages on the valley floor. (The Inka often relocated conquered peoples as a way to control them.)

The researchers collected 6-liter soil samples from the floors, middens, pits, and hearths encountered in each excavation unit. The more than 900 samples contained thousands of pieces of charcoal and plant fragments, recovered by both dry screening and flotation of the sediments. The recovered plant remains were classified into three simple categories: grass, stem (small-diameter twig fragments), and wood (pieces of mature wood). The wood category was further subdivided if the tree species could be identified.

Paleoethnobotanists Christine Hastorf (University of California, Berkeley) and Sissel Johannessen (U.S. Army Corps of Engineers) examined these flotation samples to analyze the changing patterns of fuel use in the central Andes of Peru. People can burn a number of different things in fires to cook food and to heat their homes. Grass, tied in tight bundles, small twigs, dung from herbivores, and, of course, mature wood can all be used. What does it mean if people use one source rather than another?

Hastorf and Johannessen found that grass, twigs, and mature wood were all used for fuel, and that mature wood was always the dominant fuel source. But it is the relative frequencies, rather than the absolute figures, that matter. Figure 9-12 graphs the ratio of wood to stems and wood to other (such as grass) fuel sources for the six phases that cover the 1000-year-long sequence of the Upper Mantaro Valley. Prior to 700 BP (during the Pancán phases), the relative proportion of mature wood fragments dropped; this means that over time, people used more grass and stems as fuel, rather than mature wood. Then, during Wanka II and Wanka III times, this trend reversed, with stem and grass remains decreasing.

Hastorf and Johannessen also noted that the species composition of the mature wood shifted through time. Up to 40 different kinds of wood are present in the Upper Mantaro Valley samples, with no particular

PROFILE OF AN ARCHAEOLOGIST

A FEDERAL ARCHAEOLOGIST

Terry Fifield is the archaeologist for the Prince of Wales Island District, Tongass National Forest, Alaska.

Terry Fifield.

Prince of Wales Island, in the southern portion of southeast Alaska's Alexander Archipelago, is an archaeological frontier. Anthropologist Fredericka DeLaguna stayed north of here when she did her southeast Alaskan fieldwork. Cultural anthropologists have studied the totem poles of Kasaan (on eastern Prince of Wales Island). Linguists have studied the Tlingit and Haida languages of the island. And today a few researchers work at select

sites. The Forest Service began to consider the island's archaeological resources in its planning efforts in the early 1970s. Through the 1980s, a Forest Service archaeologist was stationed in the city of Ketchikan, 45 miles to the east. Crews worked on Prince of Wales Island during the summer to survey planned timber harvest units and roads for historic and archaeological sites. I was one of those seasonal archaeologists in the early 1990s; I also worked for the National Park Service and Bureau of Indian Affairs in northern Alaska.

In 1994, I moved my family to the Craig/Klawock area on the west coast of Prince of Wales Island. I was the first Forest Service archaeologist to live there, and the first to have the opportunity to get to know the residents and become familiar with the land and seascape. As luck would have it, during my first summer, Dave Putnam, a quaternary geologist/archaeologist working with me, spotted a scrap of spruce root basketry eroding from a muddy riverbed in the estuary of the Thorne River. Dave and I worked closely with the state of Alaska (on whose land the discovery was located), other Forest Service resource groups, the Alaska State Museum, and local tribal people. Within a few days, having assembled a small team and having received a lot of advice, we excavated a pedestal of mud containing the

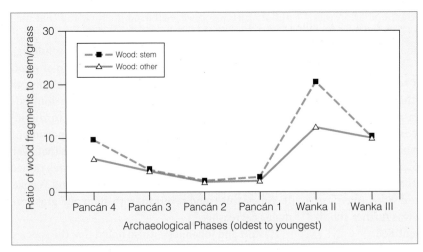

Figure 9-12 The changing ratios of wood to other fuel types through time in the Upper Mantaro area of Peru by phase. *After Hastorf and Johannessen 1991; courtesy Christine Hastorf.*

taxa being especially dominant. But the most common taxa did change in relative frequency through time. The five most popular wood types during the early Pancán phases (from yet unidentified trees) dropped out entirely by Wanka II times. And beginning around 700 BP, new wood types appeared. One notable example is *Buddleia* sp. (known as *quishuar* in Quechua), a high-elevation tree that became the most popular fuel source during Inka (Wanka III) times.

oldest example of spruce root basketry known from North America's Northwest Coast.

I made mistakes in that situation, especially in the area of consulting with Native Americans. Being new to the island, I was unfamiliar with clan and tribal boundaries and failed to locate the correct clan leaders for advice. But I did try to make the contacts, and we did one thing right. To preserve it, we immersed the basket in isopropyl alcohol–laced water for a few days and then invited local weavers to come view it. We did not know the basket's age then, but the site's stratigraphy suggested it was several thousand years old. The scene that played out in the Forest Service conference room over the next few days was a powerful one. Weavers from Klawock, Craig, and Hydaburg came by to study the 11- by 13-inch swatch of woven fabric. Haida and Tlingit alike saw the similarities between this ancient basket and the craft they had learned from their aunts and grandmothers. Before the basket was hand-carried to the Alaska State Museum in Juneau for curation, the Forest Service conference room was host to a small but moving ceremony affirming the importance of this artifact to its people and place of origin.

Study of the Thorne River Basket eventually revealed it to be a collecting basket woven of spruce root almost 6000 years ago. In 1998, the basket and its discovery were the subject of the Alaska Archaeology Week poster. The poster, featuring Margaret Davidson's technical drawing and watercolor reconstruction, was popular with Native American weavers all over southeast Alaska. People again imagined the chain of knowledge linking 300 generations of women over nearly six millennia. This important discovery provided tangible proof to today's subsistence-oriented residents that the lifeways and traditions of the island's native people extend deeply into the past.

The excitement and celebration of science and tradition surrounding the Thorne River Basket discovery has colored my approach to handling archaeological information. Here on Prince of Wales Island, where many people are of Native American ancestry, there is widespread interest in studying and understanding the past. But there is also some apprehension about where archaeological specimens go and, perhaps more important, what happens to the knowledge that scientists draw from research. I believe an essential part of what we do as archaeologists must be to communicate what we have learned to the people most affected, to the public at large, and to our professional colleagues. As with most situations involving people, it's all about communication, in this case sharing information and the excitement of learning about the past.

What Explains Wood Use?

To answer this question, let's work through the analysis step by step. First, we must consider whether the charcoal distributions on the diagram can be attributed to factors other than fuel use. Is it possible, for instance, that we are looking at changing patterns in the use of house construction materials, changing subsistence practices, or perhaps differential plant preservation through time?

Hastorf and Johannessen rejected all these possibilities. They noted that most of the charcoal comes from fire refuse accumulated over a span of several months or years. Although the possibility exists that some of the charcoal resulted from inadvertent fires (such as accidental burning of thatch roofs and roof beams), the investigators assume that the majority of the charcoal reflects intentional fuel use for heating and cooking. They also note that the composition of the house compounds (mud and stone), the general subsistence remains, and the depositional contents are basically constant throughout the 1000-year sequence. And there is little reason to believe that rates of preservation changed significantly through time.

Hastorf and Johannessen then moved to interpret the charcoal distributions strictly in terms of changing fuel use patterns. Beginning their paleoethnobotanical analysis in standard fashion, they first determined whether the archaeological patterning of fuel use revealed long-term shifts in the relationship between these highland people and their environment.

From this strictly economic perspective, the increased reliance through time on twigs and grasses during the Pancán sequence is just what one might expect in a relatively treeless landscape. Through time, the growing human population and more intensive agricultural land-use patterns made fuel wood scarce. It makes sense that as people denuded their landscape of trees, they turned to less desirable fuels, such as small shrubby plants, twigs, and grasses.

But if this is so, then why would the trend reverse during later Wanka times? Contrary to strictly ecological expectations, the archaeologically recovered plant remains show that the use of high-quality fuels actually *increased* after 700 BP.

Perhaps evidence from settlement patterns provides a clue. Beginning in Wanka II times, an elite class began social and political consolidation of the area. Maybe this elite class mandated some sort of fuel management program, perhaps in the form of tree cultivating, resulting in a greater availability of mature wood sources. This scenario is certainly possible because we know that tree cultivation was practiced during Inka times.

Fuel, of course, has an important economic role in Andean life, especially at an elevation in excess of 3300 meters where the days, to say nothing of the nights, are cold. The increased fuel management/tree cultivation explanation provides a workable, rational answer in economic terms, but it leaves several questions unanswered:

▶ Why does the change take place in Wanka II times? Why not earlier (when the population first increased) or later (when the Inka took over and restructured the location of the production system)?

▶ Why would cultivation be chosen to alleviate the fuel shortage? Why not simply go farther afield to gather fuel? Or why not just shift to lower-quality fuels?

▶ And why do certain tree taxa show up during Inka times, when they were absent before?

At this point, Hastorf and Johannessen decided to explore explanations that went beyond conventional economic and ecological factors. They delved into the ethnographic and ethnohistoric records to document the relationships among Andean people, the upland forest, and traditional fuel sources. Doing so, Hastorf and Johannessen found that wood is more than simply fuel in the Andes. It also has an important symbolic dimension.

Collecting fuel was an important aspect of Inkan life, consuming up to four hours each day for some segments of the population. We know from documentary accounts that logs, kindling, and straw were also important tribute items in the Inka state.

But trees also had important symbolic connotations in Andean cosmology. Certain sacred trees were planted at administrative sites. Others were symbolically linked with deities. In fact, the Inka burned *quishuar*, the wood that appeared during Wanka III times, in large quantities at festivals and ritually burned human figures carved of *quishuar* as sacrifices to the divine ancestor of the Inka dynasty. Trees were also symbolically associated with water, as well as with women, clouds, winter, and the moon.

From these and other ethnohistoric and ethnographic examples, Hastorf and Johannessen concluded that wood had strong symbolic as well as economic roles in Inka life, being used to cement social relations (perhaps because it was so important and so rare). Brothers-in-law, for instance, sometimes provided wood and straw to relatives at a wake (Figure 9-13).

Relating Ideology to the Past

Hastorf and Johannessen supplemented their ecological perspective with a new appreciation of the cultural relationship between ancient Andean people and their environment. But why did the change take place in Wanka II times?

Hastorf and Johannessen argue that the ideology associated with the planting of certain trees could have been a factor in establishing the local political consolidation occurring at that time. The tree symbolized family continuity on the land, with the roots symbolizing ancestors and the fruits, the children. In fact, a ritual step in contemporary marriage ceremonies is termed "to bring the branch" and involves the bringing forth of ritual offspring. The dramatic increase in the use of *quishuar* might thus be attributed to its ritual significance of bringing social groups together into

© Christine Hastorf

Figure 9-13 Ethnohistoric sketch of an Inka man linking himself to his in-laws by presenting them with wood and straw fuel at a wake. *From* Nueva Corónica y Buen Gobierno *by Guaman Poma.*

larger entities, rather than simply its mundane use as firewood.

These investigators believe that the act of planting trees—which could be interpreted as a purely economic response to a fuel shortage—was chosen from the other available alternatives because of cultural values concerning the ways in which cultivation and trees functioned as symbols of life and lineage, socially and politically.

Conclusion

This chapter has illustrated how archaeologists go about investigating the archaeological remains of plants and animals. From these remains we can determine what plants and animals people ate, what seasons of the year they were taken, and what sorts of tactics were used to hunt or gather them. They can also help reconstruct trade relations. Often, archaeologists view information from plant and animal remains as evidence of ancient peoples' purely materialistic and mundane relations with their environment. And often, that is correct. But the final example from Peru suggests that our interpretations of the past may often be layered, and that material interactions with the environment may have symbolic importance as well.

SUMMARY

1. What does a zooarchaeological study involve?

- Establish that the bones are "cultural"—left behind by people (by looking for cut marks, impact fractures, and burning).
- Identify the bones to element, taxon, sex, and age using a comparative collection.
- Count the bones using NISP (number of identifiable specimens) and MNI (minimum number of individuals). NISP is simply a count of the number of bones of a particular taxon; MNI is the minimum number of animals required to account for those bones.
- The specific elements present and their breakage patterns suggest how the animals were hunted and butchered; this also suggests whether they were hunted close or far away, whether meat was stored or traded, or if people were pressed for food.
- The links between patterns in the faunal assemblage and interpretations depend on experimental archaeology and ethnoarchaeology.

2. How do animal bones and plants help establish a site's season of occupation?

- The age of animals represented in a faunal assemblage coupled with assumptions of their season of birth help establish a site's "seasonality."

- Likewise, the modern fruiting schedules of plants represented in sites by their seeds or other edible components suggest when a site was occupied.

3. How do plants help to reconstruct ancient diets?

- The sources include macrobotanical remains (e.g., charred seeds recovered by flotation), phytoliths (silica nodules found in some plant stems), pollen, coprolites (preserved human feces), and lipids extracted from pottery.
- Each source has its strengths and weaknesses. Macrobotanical remains can be abundant, but it is not always clear if they represent food; coprolites clearly contain the remains of meals, but they are very short-term records.
- People's interaction with the environment has an economic basis, but culture may place layers of symbolic meaning on top of that interaction.

4. How can pollen help reconstruct past environments?

- Because different plant species produce differently shaped pollens, we can identify ancient vegetation by identifying pollen in archaeological sites.
- Samples are prepared and the pollen counted under a microscope.

- The varying percentages of pollen in the samples roughly track the varying percentages of the different plant species that produced them.
- Pollen is good at reconstructing the regional environment; the palynologist must take measures to ensure that the results are not biased by a local environment's pollen.
- Other sources of information, such as wood rat nests, provide evidence of local vegetation.

MEDIA RESOURCES

 Doing Fieldwork:
Archaeological Demonstrations CD-ROM 2.0
This CD, developed by the authors, shows professional archaeologists involved in various digs, many of which are referenced in the text. The presentation is organized by the main techniques used on an archaeological dig, reinforcing concepts and techniques via live examples. The CD takes you through each step automatically, or you can navigate to any point via the navigation bar. After reviewing a step in the dig process, you are taken to Check Points, which are concept questions about each step of the dig. Then you can see the answers, receive your score, and even send your scores to your instructor.

**The Companion Website for *Archaeology,*
Sixth Edition**
www.cengagebrain.com
Supplement your review of this chapter by going to the companion website to take one of the practice quizzes, use the flash cards to master key terms, and check out the many other study aids that are designed to help you succeed in your introductory archaeology course.

10 BIOARCHAEOLOGICAL APPROACHES TO THE PAST

LEARNING OBJECTIVES

AFTER READING THIS CHAPTER
YOU SHOULD BE ABLE TO ANSWER THESE QUESTIONS:

1. How do bioarchaeologists contribute to a study of the past?

2. How do bioarchaeologists determine age and sex for a skeleton?

3. How do bioarchaeologists use paleopathology and bone chemistry to reconstruct the lives of ancient peoples?

4. How are genetic data used to reconstruct population relationships and the ages of migrations?

© 2008 Duncan Stirk, Aecern Archaeology

Archaeologists excavate two women, presumably nuns, at a medieval nunnery in Yorkshire, England.

PREVIEW

THIS CHAPTER EXAMINES bioarchaeology, a specialty that straddles the fields of archaeology and biological anthropology. Bioarchaeologists study the human biological component of the archaeological record. Some bioarchaeologists study the origin and distribution of ancient diseases; others reconstruct human diets, analyze the evidence for biological stress in archaeological populations, and reconstruct past demographic patterns—all of this by exploring human bone, bone chemistry, and the DNA preserved in human tissues. Although this chapter is a bit heavy on chemistry and biology, the archaeological payoff is worth the effort.

The analysis of human remains today is a sensitive subject in many parts of the world. Handling, photographing, and sampling the physical remains of once living, breathing human beings is upsetting to many Native Americans (and to plenty of others as well). These concerns surfaced in the Kennewick case described in the Introduction to this book. Later, in Chapter 15, we discuss the laws that govern the excavation and analysis of human skeletal remains. Here, we discuss the astonishing amount of scientific information that can be gleaned from human skeletal remains (and this chapter merely scratches the surface). In the process, we will demonstrate how scientists can conduct such studies in a respectful and sensitive manner. No skeletal remains of Native Americans are portrayed in this or any other chapter.

INTRODUCTION

In Chapter 3, we described Kelly's archaeological survey project in the Carson Desert of western Nevada. We mentioned that the survey failed to find many archaeological sites in the marsh because they were obscured by sand and vegetation. However, in the mid-1980s, the greatest floods to hit the Carson Desert in a millennium exposed many sites in the marsh.

More was exposed than arrowheads and faunal remains. Kelly visited the marsh in the summer of 1986 while the Nevada State Museum was recording the new archaeological sites for the U.S. Fish and Wildlife Service (on whose lands most of the new sites were located). Many of the newly exposed sites were accessible only by airboat. Jetting up to the shore of one site, Kelly saw several human skulls rolling about in the wake. The flood had not only exposed many new sites, but dozens of human burials as well. The Nevada State Museum worked furiously to record the sites and recover the exposed human skeletal remains. They were under pressure not only because bone does not last long on the surface, but also because looters were already scouring the marsh for artifacts and skulls. This salvage work precluded the in-depth study that these remains deserved.

And so, in 1987, after the floodwaters had receded, Kelly returned to the Stillwater Marsh to excavate one of the habitation sites (Site 26CH1062, mentioned in the last chapter) and to survey the marsh for burials and human bone. By this time, Clark Spencer Larsen (Ohio State University), a noted **bioarchaeologist,** had joined the team to study the human biological component of the archaeological record. Larsen received graduate training in biological anthropology, with a focus on the human skeleton as a record of past human activity. But because he had personally excavated hundreds of human skeletons from archaeological sites, Larsen was aware of the complex nature of archaeological data.

A well-trained field archaeologist can tell the difference between human and animal bones. But few of us are trained to go beyond such simple identification. When modern archaeologists expect to encounter human remains—as did Kelly when he approached the Stillwater Marsh—they involve a bioarchaeologist from day one. And if those remains are Native American, as

bioarchaeology The study of the human biological component evident in the archaeological record.

LOOKING CLOSER

NATIVE AMERICANS AND THE STILLWATER BURIALS

The first people to find the Stillwater burials were looters, people searching for skulls to place on their fireplace mantels. Anthropologists hesitate to call any cultural practice gruesome, but that is the first word that comes to mind.

Fortunately, several dedicated amateur and professional archaeologists raised a cry, and soon the Fallon Paiute-Shoshone Tribe, located next to the Stillwater Marsh, asked that the U.S. Fish and Wildlife Service (USFWS) protect their heritage. In response, the USFWS increased patrols of the marsh, began a public education campaign, and hired the Nevada State Museum to recover exposed remains. By September 1986, more than 4000 human remains had been professionally collected and 144 burials recorded.

What was to be done with these remains? At the time, no specific legislation protected American Indian burials. But archaeologists understood this was a sensitive issue, and everyone involved at Stillwater wanted to "do the right thing."

The first right thing was to involve the local Indian community. Local solutions work better than those imposed by a distant government. And things work better if the people involved are respectful of the other side. Fortunately, the USFWS archaeologist, Anan Raymond, was the right person for this task; he consulted with the tribe shortly after the first human remains turned up and eventually drew up a Memorandum of Understanding that detailed how the remains would be treated.

At first, the tribe wished for the remains to stay put. But, knowing that looters would disturb the burials, they agreed that burials should be excavated *if* they were in danger of being disturbed; the others would be covered and their location plotted on a map so that the USFWS could periodically check them. The chair of the Fallon tribe inspected every burial located during our archaeological survey, and we excavated only those for which he gave permission.

What about analysis? Although the tribe consented to nondestructive analysis, they were hesitant to allow radiocarbon dating, stable isotope analysis, or other destructive analyses. Still, the tribe was interested in what these analyses could tell them, and they eventually permitted destructive analyses provided that (1) the tribe approve the studies, (2) destructive analysis be minimized, and (3) we use already broken bones. We stuck to this agreement, and even used CAT scans to obtain long bone cross sections rather than cut intact humeri and femora.

The tribe wanted the remains to be reburied, but Raymond wished to see the remains preserved for the future. Working in a spirit of cooperation, the parties eventually decided on a novel approach: a subterranean concrete crypt. This satisfied the tribe's desire for reinterment, yet leaves open the possibility of future analyses. Today, the Stillwater burials rest in small, individual redwood coffins in a ventilated concrete vault buried on USFWS land. The door has two locks on it: The USFWS holds the key to one, and the tribe holds the key to the other.

In the end, good scientific research resulted. Although the tribe retained the power to deny any analysis, it chose not to. We are convinced that the reason is that the tribe was consulted from the beginning and given a seat at the table—one of genuine authority, respect, and power.

---

they were at Stillwater Marsh, archaeologists likewise work with the appropriate American Indian community (or communities). So, before proceeding further, we'd like you to know that all the Stillwater evidence discussed here was approved beforehand by the local Native American community (see "Looking Closer: Native Americans and the Stillwater Burials" and "What Does It Mean to Me? Should We Excavate Human Remains?").

In 1987, we surveyed the previously flooded portions of the wetland, looking for new archaeological sites and human remains. Along with the Nevada State Museum, we recovered the remains of more than 500 individuals. This was significant because the Stillwater finds *tripled* the number of human burials known from the entire state of Nevada. These remains were studied by Larsen and a team of bioarchaeologists he assembled to handle specific analyses.

WHAT DOES IT MEAN TO ME?

SHOULD WE EXCAVATE HUMAN REMAINS?

In many places in the world, archaeologists have no qualms about excavating human skeletal remains. But in the United States, conducting research on American Indian remains is a sensitive issue. In fact, archaeologists who do field research in the United States today generally excavate human remains only if they are in the way of a construction project that cannot be rerouted. And no archaeologist would excavate a burial without consulting at least the nearest tribe (in fact, such consultation is often mandated by federal law). Sometimes this consultation works out well, as it did in Stillwater. But tribal attitudes change, and if the Stillwater remains were exposed today instead of nearly 20 years ago, it's possible that their excavation and analysis would be blocked. It has become increasingly difficult for bioarchaeologists to work with extant collections; those involved with the Kennewick case had to file a lawsuit to get access to that skeleton.

All of this raises major ethical questions. Some modern archaeologists believe that we should simply stop analyzing human skeletons, understanding this is the price to be paid for showing respect and sensitivity to modern Native Americans who find the excavation and analysis of ancestral remains disrespectful. Many other Americans would agree with them.

Although many museums curate both Indian and non-Indian skeletal remains, the proportion of Native American skeletons outweighs the non-Indian remains—reflecting, in large measure, the historical interest of American archaeology in excavating American Indian burial sites. And reburying non–Native American remains often seems to be the obvious, and respectful, thing to do. Those Civil War dead who are discovered today are sometimes studied, but always reburied. From the outset, archaeologists agreed to rebury the remains of those who died in the *Hunley*, the Confederate submarine that sank on its first mission (see "Looking Closer: Preserving the *Hunley*," page 150).

Archaeologists have long curated Native American remains in museum collections, in case new techniques enable us to learn more about the past. And such breakthroughs do occur: Who, in 1965, would have thought that within two decades we would be extracting genetic material from 7000-year-old human skeletons? We've only given you a glimpse of what we can learn from human skeletons; and each year there are new techniques. There is so much more to learn.

The scientists wish to learn more about the past in order to increase our understanding of the history of humanity. This is a good thing. But Native Americans want only for themselves and their ancestors to be treated with respect. This is also a good thing. A number of Native Americans also wish to become archaeologists and bioarchaeologists, to become involved in generating new understandings of their own past. This, too, is a good thing.

Which should we choose? Does science trump every other concern? Answer yes, and you appear ethnocentric. Do some people have the right to shut the door on an area of knowledge? Answer yes, and you would seem to condone book burning.

What is knowledge worth? What is knowledge *for*? Every archaeologist, especially those who study human skeletal remains, must carefully consider these questions today.

SKELETAL ANALYSIS: THE BASICS

Larsen first had to confirm that all the bones collected by the survey team were in fact human. After all, the flood had washed out plenty of archaeological midden, scattering ancient and recent animal bone among the human remains. Although human bone is distinctive, archaeological skeletal remains are often fragmented and weathered, making them difficult to identify. We have seen surgeons who were unable to identify a bone scrap as a piece of a human femur. But archaeologists are accustomed to seeing things in their broken, dirty, smashed forms. Larsen learned how to identify bone

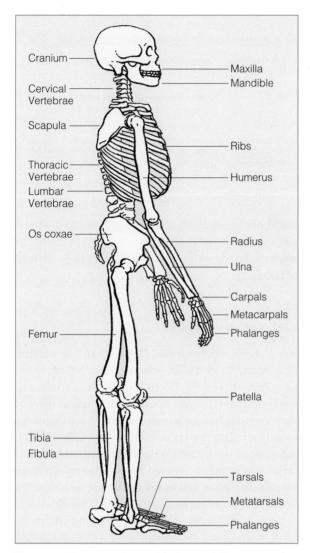

Figure 10-1 Some major bones of the human skeleton.

Cranium
Cervical Vertebrae
Scapula
Thoracic Vertebrae
Lumbar Vertebrae
Os coxae
Femur
Tibia
Fibula

Maxilla
Mandible
Ribs
Humerus
Radius
Ulna
Carpals
Metacarpals
Phalanges
Patella
Tarsals
Metatarsals
Phalanges

through classes in human anatomy and **osteology,** but his real skill was acquired simply by handling thousands of human bone fragments. Figure 10-1 shows some of the major bones of the human skeleton, including ones mentioned in this chapter.

Bioarchaeologists working with bones from grave sites are accustomed to working with well-defined sets of remains, each from a single individual; this is why, unlike zooarchaeologists, bioarchaeologists are rarely concerned with issues of MNI or NISP.

Instead, bioarchaeologists are concerned with whether the human remains constitute a **burial population,** individuals who came from a specific area and who died over a relatively short period of time (as might be found in a historic-period cemetery). The Stillwater burials came from a 16-square-kilometer area of marsh, so obviously this was not a single, well-defined cemetery. Few burials contained any grave goods (meaning that we could not use temporal types

to place the burials within archaeological phases). And only a few burials could be dated by AMS radiocarbon determinations. Most of the projectile points found in the nearby sites could be assigned to temporal types, but these time spans were quite large (600 years for the Underdown phase and 1500 years for the Reveille phase). Although hardly ideal, these temporal types provided at least some rough parameters for the living population that this skeletal sample represented.

Good preservation conditions will provide the bioarchaeologist with a nearly complete human skeleton. But sometimes, only the hardest bones survive—parts of the skull, the central portions of the limb bones, and—the hardest portion of the human skeleton—the teeth.

Ancient cultural practices can also mix human skeletal remains together and make it difficult to group skeletal remains by individual. Many eastern Native American tribes, for example, laid bodies out in a **charnel house,** where the body was allowed to decompose in the open. Eventually, the bones were cleaned of remaining flesh, bundled together, and ritually placed into a communal grave (these are known as **bundle burials**). Over time, the bones of various individuals would commingle. Careful excavation may be able to regroup bones by individual, but sometimes this is impossible. In other cases, as at the Stillwater Marsh, postdepositional processes scatter the once intact burials. In fact, of the 500 individuals recovered, only 54 were encountered as intact primary burials.

Determining Sex

After removing any nonhuman bones from the collection, Larsen assigned sex and age to the intact burials. How can we determine sex from bones (Table 10-1)? One obvious place where men and women differ is the pelvic area. Evolution designed women's hips (the hips are technically composed of two halves, the right and left os coxae or innominates) to birth children;

osteology The study of bone.

burial population A set of human burials that come from a limited region and a limited time period. The more limited the region and the time period, the more accurate will be inferences drawn from analysis of the burials.

charnel house A structure used by eastern North Americans to lay out the dead where the body would decompose. The bones would later be gathered and buried or cremated.

bundle burial Burial of a person's bones, bundled together, after the flesh has been removed or allowed to decay off the bones.

TABLE 10-1 Sex: Key Skeletal Elements

	MALE	FEMALE
Pelvis (sciatic notch)	Narrow	Wide
Pelves (subpubic angle)	Acute	Obtuse
Mandible, eye orbits	Square	Round
Supraorbital (brow) ridges	Pronounced	Slight
Skull muscle attachments	Robust	Slight

TABLE 10-2 Age: Key Skeletal Elements

Pelves (pubic symphysis)	Degenerative changes with age
Skull	Tooth eruption pattern (for subadults; e.g., first permanent molar erupts at age of 6 years)
	Degree of suture closure (more closed with age)
Long bones and pelves	Epiphyseal closure (e.g., distal femur 60% fused at 18 years, 100% at 22 years)

as a result, the **sciatic** (sy-*a*-tik) **notch,** a U-shaped indentation in each os coxa's posterior (rear) portion, is wider in women than in men. There is variation among the world's population in *how much* wider, but within a burial population, one can usually see a clear difference between those os coxae with wide and those with narrow sciatic notches. Likewise, and for the same reason, the subpubic angle, formed where the two halves of the pelves come together in front of a person's body, is wider in women than in men.

Os coxae are quite porous, making them some of the first bones to decompose. So if preservation is a problem, the bioarchaeologist must look elsewhere.

That usually means turning to the skull. Adult male skulls tend to be more robust than female skulls, with heavier brow ridges over and between the eyes, larger mastoid processes (two protrusions of bone on the bottom of the skull, one beneath each ear), and more rugged muscle attachments. Male skulls also tend to have squarer chins and eye orbits. A skilled bioarchaeologist can often "sex" a skull simply by its feel. Again, the world's populations vary in how robust or gracile male and female skulls are; but within a burial population, bioarchaeologists can usually detect discernible differences between *adult* male and female skulls. The sex of a child is difficult to determine because the sexually distinctive characteristics of bone do not develop until young adulthood.

Larsen found that the Stillwater collection contained almost twice as many males as females, but sex

could not be assigned to a large number of the burials (some of the adult burials were poorly preserved or were missing key elements; others were the skeletons of children).

Determining Age

Age at death is the next goal (Table 10-2). Like a zooarchaeologist, Larsen used osteological standards based on comparative collections. Because the pattern and timing of crown formation and tooth eruption are consistent among human populations, teeth are extremely useful for telling the age of younger individuals. Larsen determined age by recording which teeth had formed their crowns and/or erupted through the mandible or maxilla (the lower and upper jaw bones, respectively).

Patterns of bone fusion are also useful for determining age in skeletons of youths and young adults. At birth, many bones are actually several different pieces. The long bones, such as the femora and humeri, are made up of a central shaft and two **epiphyses**—the ends that articulate with other bones. The epiphyses fuse to the shaft at known rates. For example, the proximal epiphysis of the radius ("proximal" refers to the end of a long bone that is closest to the body's center—in this case, the end of the radius closest to the elbow; "distal" refers to the end of the long bone farthest from the body) completely fuses by about age 19, whereas portions of the scapula do not fuse until age 23. Noting to what extent various bones are fused can provide an estimate of an individual's age at the time of death.

By age 25, most bones are fully fused and most teeth have erupted. Aging the skeletons of mature adults, therefore, requires other methods, and these are more difficult to implement. The first is bone wear. After age 30, bones begin to wear down. Much of the wear is related to a person's activity level (as well as diet). But some bones tend to wear no matter what. One particularly sensitive area is the **pubic symphysis,** the place where the right and left os coxae meet in a person's groin area.

sciatic notch The angled edge of both halves of the posterior (rear) side of the pelvis; measurement of this angle is used to determine sex in human skeletons. Although its width varies among populations, narrow notches indicate a male and wider notches indicate a female.

epiphyses The ends of bones that fuse to the main shaft or portion of bone at various ages; most bones are fused by age 25. This fact can be used to age skeletons of younger individuals.

pubic symphysis Where the two halves of the pelvis meet in the groin area; the appearance of its articulating surface can be used to age skeletons.

As the cartilage between the two halves erodes with age, the symphysis undergoes distinct changes. At age 20, for example, the symphysis has a distinct set of surface ridges that look like ocean waves. By age 35, these ridges have disappeared, and a rim has formed along the edge of the symphysis. By age 50, the rim has disappeared, and the symphysis looks like a shriveled prune. But because the os coxae are among the first bones to decay, this useful method of determining skeletal age is not applicable to many archaeological skeletons.

Degree of tooth wear and loss also help in estimating a skeleton's age. Because teeth wear down continually with age, bioarchaeologists have generated standardized tables (from nonindustrial populations) to estimate age from the extent of tooth wear. But caution is required here too because the rate of tooth wear and loss is strongly related to diet. People dependent on food processed on grinding stones will have higher rates of wear because of the grit in their food. If that food is high in carbohydrates, people may also experience a higher rate of tooth loss from cavities (see "Cavities" later in the chapter).

Using these methods, Larsen determined that the Stillwater burials ranged in age from fetuses to individuals more than 50 years old. But because of the different indicators of age and slight error factors in the methods, skeletons are normally placed into five-year age classes (0–5 years, 6–10 years, 11–15 years, and so on). It's also difficult to pin down the age of individuals older than about 50 years.

HOW WELL DID THE STILLWATER PEOPLE LIVE?

This is how Larsen derived the basic statistics for the Stillwater population: He knew how many men, women, infants, and adolescents there were, and he knew these individuals' approximate ages. Now he could pose the questions that interested him most, such as: How well did the people of Stillwater Marsh live? Larson asked this question because he wanted to use the Stillwater population to help solve a major dilemma in anthropology.

Prior to the 1960s, many anthropologists assumed that the lives of ancient hunter-gatherers were, to use the words of seventeenth-century philosopher Thomas Hobbes (1588–1679), "nasty, brutish, and short." In this view, hunter-gatherers had to work excessively hard, lived hand-to-mouth with barely enough food, suffered from high rates of infant mortality, and lived short lives.

But research with the Ju/'hoansi (one of several groups of people collectively referred to as "Bushmen") of southern Africa's Kalahari Desert and other foragers in the 1960s suggested that hunter-gatherers actually had plenty of leisure time, adequate diets, and low levels of disease. Anthropologist Marshall Sahlins (University of Chicago) went so far as to label huntergatherers the "original affluent society." In the 1960s, this image of prehistoric peoples resonated with those seeking an alternative to the perceived excesses of modern industrial life.

Both of these conflicting characterizations were based on ethnographic data, but the observers might have been predisposed to see hunter-gatherers in one way rather than the other. Larsen thought that the skeletal data of an archaeological population could provide a more objective assessment of foraging lifeways. Larsen wanted to see whether the Stillwater foragers of 1000 years ago were closer to the "nasty, brutish, and short" or the "original affluent society" image of hunter-gatherers.

To do this, Larsen turned to **paleopathology,** the study of ancient disease, disorders, and trauma. This specialization includes the identification of specific diseases, but few specific diseases can be identified from bones (syphilis [venereal and nonvenereal], tuberculosis, and leprosy are the major ones that leave distinctive lesions and other characteristics on bone). Broken bones, even if healed, are also easy to identify; unhealed breaks are usually evidence of trauma that was the immediate cause of death.

But bioarchaeologists learn more from human skeletons when they understand the complex interrelationships among the environment, behavior, and physiology that form human bone. Larsen used this perspective to look for *nonspecific* indicators of stress, particularly those caused by nutritional deficiencies and/or nonspecific infectious disease in the Stillwater burial population. Though challenging, the study of biological stress has become an important area of bioarchaeology.

Disease and Trauma at Stillwater

Larsen found little trace of specific diseases among the skeletal remains from Stillwater Marsh—no evidence of syphilis, tuberculosis, or leprosy. He did, however, find some telltale signs of iron deficiency anemia.

paleopathology The study of ancient patterns of disease, disorders, and trauma.

Iron is essential for adequate transport of oxygen by red blood cells. But sometimes iron is limited, perhaps by a lack of red meat in the diet (a primary source of easily absorbed iron), chronic diarrhea, or parasites (such as hookworm, which can cause internal bleeding and the loss of a body's iron stores). Regardless of the specific cause, whenever iron is limited, the body tries to produce more red blood cells. Because red blood cells are produced in the marrow cavities of bone, these cavities enlarge. When this happens in the cranium, the surface of the skull takes on a spongy appearance, a characteristic known as **porotic hyperostosis**. The same phenomenon can happen to bone in the eye sockets (where it is known as **cribra orbitalia**). Larsen documented evidence of iron deficiency in only four burials from the Stillwater Marsh.

The Stillwater group showed little evidence of physical trauma. Sheilagh Brooks (1923–2008), who also studied the Stillwater materials, found only 18 individuals with bone breaks (all healed); 6 of these (5 males and 1 female) had broken noses. In general, then, the Stillwater population seemed to have been relatively healthy, suffering from few broken bones (and perhaps the occasional fistfight).

These observations were made largely on adult skeletons, but many anthropologists will tell you that, to understand overall quality of life, you must look at the children. Because they are fragile, children's skeletons are rarely well preserved, making it more difficult to find appropriate samples to study. But human bone has a "memory," and some childhood events leave a telltale record in the adolescent and adult skeleton.

Growth Arrest Features

Childhood growth may be periodically arrested because of disease, trauma, or malnutrition. Whenever this happens, the bones record it. In long bones, such as the tibia and femur, growth arrest appears as a thin line of bone perpendicular to the bone's long axis. These lines are not visible on the outside of the bone,

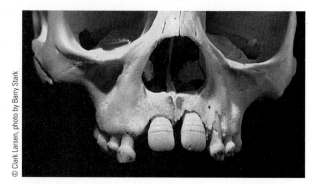

Figure 10-2 Enamel hypoplasias.

but appear in x-rays and are known as **Harris lines.** These lines form in childhood, but disappear later in life, as the bone is remodeled as it grows.

Teeth likewise register the cessation of growth. Adult teeth form, of course, in the mandible and maxilla when children are quite young. When a child becomes severely ill or is malnourished, tooth growth stops. If the child recovers, growth starts up again, but this time the episode of growth arrest is forever encoded as shallow grooves, known as **enamel hypoplasias,** across the front of the teeth (Figure 10-2). Because teeth grow at known rates, the distance from the hypoplasia to the tip of the root estimates how old a child was when the growth arrest event took place. Likewise, the width of a hypoplasia indicates the duration of the period of stress.

Since enamel hypoplasias are permanent, they are more useful measures of stress than Harris lines. For this reason, Larsen focused on enamel hypoplasias. (He could also analyze them without the cost of x-rays and with minimal disturbance to the bone.) Working with Dale Hutchinson (University of North Carolina), Larsen found that two-thirds of the individuals had hypoplasias, and that most of these occurred between the ages of 3 and 4. But the number of hypoplasias per tooth, and the average width of the grooves, was less than for other Native American populations. Larsen and Hutchinson concluded that the children of Stillwater Marsh had seen some hard times, but conditions were by no means as bad as they might have been.

The specific cause of the Stillwater hypoplasias, however, is more difficult to determine. They could have resulted from physical trauma to the face, parasitic infection, or malnutrition. We know that trauma was relatively rare (and restricted to adults), and the evidence for extensive infections was limited. Larsen and Hutchinson concluded that fluctuations in the food supply from the marsh—subject to the vagaries of local climate—most likely caused periods of malnutrition for young children.

porotic hyperostosis A symptom of iron deficiency anemia in which the skull takes on a porous appearance.

cribra orbitalia A symptom of iron deficiency anemia in which the bone of the upper eye sockets takes on a spongy appearance.

Harris lines Horizontal lines near the ends of long bones indicating episodes of physiological stress.

enamel hypoplasias Horizontal linear defects in tooth enamel indicating episodes of physiological stress.

© Clark Larsen, photo by Barry Stark

In fact, the young population might be especially hard hit by a fluctuating food supply. Among hunter-gatherers, children are often not fully weaned until they are 3, 4, or even 5 or 6 years old. This means that, if the 3- or 4-year-olds at Stillwater Marsh were in the process of being weaned during a severe winter or a lean spring, the child might very well have suffered a limited period of malnutrition. That the individual survived to adulthood, however, demonstrates that this hard time was not insurmountable.

Workload

To this point, Larsen had discovered that the people who lived in the Stillwater Marsh enjoyed a relatively healthy life. But other skeletal data show that this life came at a cost.

As we said before, bones have a memory—they are a diary that records whether you lived life as a hotshot fighting forest fires or as a couch potato. Bones can be hard to read, but they do not lie.

Bioarchaeologists use a variety of ways to determine how much physical labor a person saw in his or her lifetime. When working with the Stillwater collection, Larsen relied on patterns of osteoarthritis and the study of bone biomechanics.

Osteoarthritis **Osteoarthritis** is a joint disorder created by the loss of cartilage, often caused by mechanical stress. This condition appears as a bony growth (known as an **osteophyte**) that forms a lip around the edge of an articular surface of a long bone's epiphysis (for example, at the elbow or knee) or between vertebrae, as shown in Figure 10-3. When the cartilage disappears completely, the articular surfaces rub against one another, creating a polish known as **eburnation.** Eburnated joints are extremely painful to move.

Larsen found that *every single adult* skeleton in the Stillwater collection had osteoarthritis in at least one joint. In fact, this was the most severe osteoarthritis that Larsen had ever seen in a skeletal population. The people of Stillwater Marsh may have lived a healthy life, but they apparently had to work hard, and suffer aches and pains for it.

Males were slightly more osteoarthritic than females, but more interesting was that men and women had some significant differences in where osteoarthritis occurred. Men suffered from osteoarthritis more in the hip, ankle, and foot; women, more in their lumbar vertebrae—their lower back. Larsen suggested that the males in the Stillwater population probably did more walking—and more difficult walking—than did the

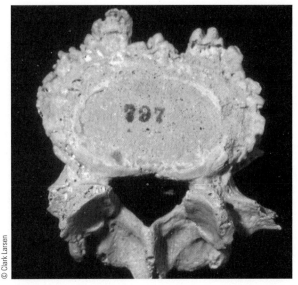

© Clark Larsen

Figure 10-3 A vertebra with osteoarthritis.

females. This makes sense because women probably foraged for plants, fish, and small game within a short distance of camps to the marsh itself, while the men probably traveled farther, into the rougher terrain of the Stillwater Mountains, in search of large game. The women were hardly taking it easy, though. They, too, had osteoarthritis that indicated they did a great deal of walking, no doubt carrying children and gear when they moved camp. But men evidently did even more walking.

Why the high incidence of osteoarthritis in the lower backs of women? Larsen pointed to two likely factors: child rearing and food processing. Because hunter-gatherer children breastfeed until they are several years old, children must stay with their mothers. And if the Stillwater women were to complete their daily foraging tasks, they had to carry the children with them. If so, then the Stillwater women probably carried children throughout most of their adult lives—with resulting strain on the lower back.

In addition, the seeds and tubers that women collected in the marsh were ground on metates. A lifetime of such seed grinding could also have given

osteoarthritis A disorder in which the cartilage between joints wears away, often because of overuse of the joint, resulting in osteophytes and eburnation.

osteophyte A sign of osteoarthritis in which bones develop a distinct "lipping" of bone at the point of articulation.

eburnation A sign of osteoarthritis in which the epiphyses of long bones are worn smooth, causing them to take on a varnish-like appearance.

women a higher incidence of osteoarthritis in their lower backs.

Biomechanics Larsen collaborated with Christopher Ruff (Johns Hopkins University) to transfer knowledge from civil engineering to the analysis of **long bone cross sections.** Civil engineers know that the type of supports used in a building is a function of how much stress the building will place on the beams (which is largely a function of the building's height). Bones are the same, except that, unlike a building's support beams, bones change their cross section over time as they respond to stress. Although the specifics are complex, the principle is simple: When femora are placed under heavy mechanical stress (for example, by routine walking over difficult terrain while carrying a heavy load), they tend to develop a more oval cross section. The cross sections of the femora of a less active person, on the other hand, are more rounded.

Larsen and Ruff obtained cross sections of the femora through CAT scans at the Veteran's Administration hospital in Reno, Nevada. Although the overall bone mass was relatively low in the Stillwater femora, bone strength was among the highest that Larsen and Ruff had ever seen. And, as was true for osteoarthritis, the femur cross sections indicated that men did more—and more strenuous—walking than did women. This could be because the Stillwater folk, especially the men, were generally robust, with large, heavy bones. But when Larsen and Ruff looked at the cross sections of the humeri (the upper arm), they found no difference between men and women, and no real difference between the Stillwater and other populations of native North Americans. This suggests that the difference in men's and women's femoral cross sections was produced by a difference in men's and women's behavior and not simply by a difference in the size of men and women.

In sum, the femur cross sections and the patterns of osteoarthritis indicated that the people living at Stillwater Marsh walked a great deal to make a successful living. And men did more walking than women.

Neither of these conclusions was particularly striking, but they were conclusive proof that the people who lived at Stillwater were nomadic, and they gave us a clearer picture of the lives of these men and women.

Paleodemography

Still another way to judge quality of life is to examine patterns of mortality. **Paleodemography** reconstructs parameters such as life expectancy at birth, the age profile of a population, and patterns in the ages of death. Bioarchaeologists do this by constructing various sorts of **mortality profiles** for a prehistoric population based on the age and sex data of burials. Mortality profiles show at what age adult males, adult females, and children died.

Paleodemography works best with well-defined cemetery populations (that is, for a skeletal sample derived from the same biological population over a few years or decades). Available radiocarbon dates showed that most of the Stillwater burials dated to the Underdown phase, but this phase covers 600 years. This means that the Stillwater population is not an ideal candidate for a paleodemographic study.

Still, bioarchaeologist Sheilagh Brooks derived some useful data from mortality profiles for the Stillwater burials. One of these profiles (Figure 10-4) shows the burial data sorted into five-year age classes by sex. Note that the 0–5 and 6–10 age categories are composed almost entirely of "unknowns" (because, as we mentioned earlier, determining the sex of very young children is almost impossible).

Why did so many children die so young? Ethnographic data show that the mortality of newborns and toddlers is very high among hunting and gathering populations—50 to 60 percent of all children born in a foraging population do not survive to 5 years of age. The Stillwater mortality profile reflects this sad fact.

There are no strong peaks in female age at death. Girls may have had a slightly higher chance than boys of dying at a young age, and men may have had a slightly greater chance than women of surviving into their 40s. The female mortality profile shows an increase in deaths beginning at age 21, the early childbearing years; this pattern is also similar to that of other foraging populations. The male profile has several peaks and no distinctive pattern. Finally, notice that few individuals are assigned to the 46–50 and 50+ age categories; this reflects a shorter overall life expectancy. Although we might regard the late 40s as the prime of life, a 45-year-old person in Stillwater was an elder.

long bone cross sections Cross sections of the body's long bones (arms and legs) used to analyze bone shape and reconstruct the mechanical stresses placed on that bone—and hence activity patterns.

paleodemography The study of ancient demographic patterns and trends.

mortality profiles Charts that depict the various ages at death of a burial population.

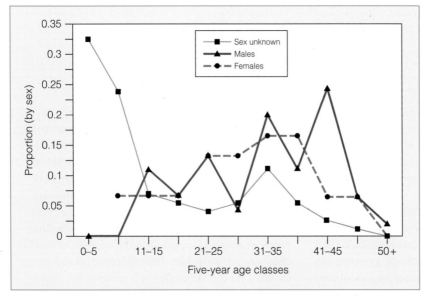

Figure 10-4 The Stillwater mortality profile, based on 144 burials. *From Brooks et al. 1988, Table 2.*

Stature

Measuring stature is yet another way to assess quality of life. Bioarchaeologists estimate stature with equations that relate the length of certain long bones to an individual's height. These equations were created, incidentally, from cadaver populations (composed of thousands of individuals who donated their bodies to science).

The femur is the best bone for computing stature (because tall people tend to have long femora and shorter people tend to have shorter femora). But because the relationship between height and femur length varies from population to population, it is important that the bioarchaeologist apply the appropriate equation. Here, for instance, is the stature formula, which has an error factor of ± 3.5 centimeters, for ancient populations in central Mexico:

$$\text{living height} = (2.26 \times \text{femur length}) + 66.38$$

This equation tells us that if a femur excavated in central Mexico measures 40 centimeters in length, it likely belonged to an individual who stood about 157 centimeters tall (5 feet 2 inches), give or take 3.5 centimeters. Different formulae are available for skeletons recovered from other parts of the world.

Height is a useful measure of overall health because it is closely related to diet. But because different populations have different genetic capacities for height, it is best to use this variable as a measure of health when looking at data for one burial population across time. Larsen did not use height estimates for the Stillwater burials because most of the burials dated to the same phase, and good comparative population data were not available.

However, Larsen did use height estimates to track health changes in another project that examined individuals who lived on St. Catherines Island and elsewhere along the coast of Georgia. Here he was interested in testing hypotheses about the effect of maize agriculture on a human population's health. He estimated the heights from skeletons of the hunting-and-gathering population (pre-950 BP) and those of the agricultural population (post-950 BP). Contrary to what you might expect, he found that the average agricultural male was 1 percent and the average female agriculturalist 3 percent *shorter* than their foraging ancestors. In this case, agriculture was a poorer diet than the previous hunting-and-gathering one, and it hit women harder than men. (If this makes you wonder why people switched from hunting and gathering to agriculture, turn to Chapter 13.)

RECONSTRUCTING DIET FROM HUMAN BONE

The people who lived at Stillwater were hunter-gatherers. But can we go beyond this general statement to talk more specifically about what people ate? Following the old adage "You are what you eat," diet can be reconstructed from human bone in several ways. We discuss how two of these methods were used on the Stillwater burial population below. The same principle can also be used to track movements of populations (see "Looking Closer: Tracing the Origins of New World African Populations").

Cavities

Dental **caries** (cavities) can help differentiate between agriculturalists and hunter-gatherer populations. You might think that cavities happen to those who do not

---

caries Cavities.

LOOKING CLOSER

TRACING THE ORIGINS OF NEW WORLD AFRICAN POPULATIONS

In 2000, during the building of a park in Campeche, on the Gulf Coast of Mexico's Yucatan peninsula, archaeologists discovered the foundation of a sixteenth-century church and a cemetery that artifacts suggested was used from the mid-sixteenth through the seventeenth centuries. This was a remarkable find because it was one of the earliest Spanish settlements in Mexico. The cemetery contained both Europeans and Native Americans, as well as ten individuals whose skeletal characteristics suggested an origin in Africa; four of these, in fact, had upper front incisors that were chipped and filed to points—a cultural modification that is virtually unknown among European and Native American populations but common among some African populations.

Were these individuals some of the first slaves brought to the New World?

We know that the slave trade was established by the early sixteenth century, when the Spanish were conquering parts of what would become Latin America. We also know from documentary sources that the Spanish at that time acquired African slaves largely from the Portuguese, through their slave port in Ghana, along Africa's so-called Gold Coast. Were the individuals buried in Campeche people who came from Africa or the local descendants of Africans who continued some of their parents' cultural practices?

To answer this question, Viera Tiesler (Universidad Autonoma de Yucatan), Douglas Price, and James Burton (University of Wisconsin, Madison) analyzed the strontium content in the teeth of ten individuals in the cemetery, including the four with dental modification. Strontium occurs naturally in bedrock and sediments, and is incorporated into human diet via plants, herbivores, and water. The strontium is incorporated into human skeletal tissue, including dental enamel. In fact, since dental enamel forms in childhood, its particular strontium content remains constant for the remainder of a person's life, and it therefore reflects where someone grew up. Two isotopes of strontium, ^{87}Sr and ^{86}Sr, vary across a landscape. This means that we should be able to trace where someone grew up by comparing the ratio of ^{87}Sr to ^{86}Sr in their dental enamel to possible places of childhood.

This is just what Price and his colleagues did. The four individuals with dental modifications had enamel $^{87}Sr/^{86}Sr$ ratios that were strikingly different from those of the other six individuals, and strikingly different from background samples taken from many places in Mexico. However, the strontium data fell comfortably within the range of water samples from the interior of Ghana, the postulated homeland of these individuals. Thus, these four individuals most likely were raised in what is now Ghana, not Mexico. Although the burials are not yet directly dated, the artifacts found with them suggest that they are the earliest documented African slaves in the New World.

---

brush their teeth regularly or properly, but this is not strictly true. Caries result when simple carbohydrates, especially refined sugar but also including starchy foods like maize or tubers, remain on your teeth. Bacteria that feed on the carbohydrates produce as a by-product an acid that dissolves tooth enamel. If you ate mostly meat, you would have few caries—regardless of whether you brushed your teeth.

The prevalence of caries, then, serves as an indicator of starchy diets (which, in ancient North America, generally means the consumption of maize). A skilled bioarchaeologist, in fact, can glance at a subject's teeth and make a good guess as to whether the person was an agriculturalist or a hunter-gatherer—just by looking for caries.

The people at Stillwater Marsh were strictly hunter-gatherers; they did not grow or eat maize. Because their diet was low in simple carbohydrates (and obviously did not include refined sugar at all), only 3 percent of the Stillwater skeletons had dental caries—a remarkably low figure.

But they were hardly free from dental problems. The Stillwater folks lost many of their teeth by middle age, generally as a result of excessive tooth wear—a product of the grit in their diet from seeds and tubers ground on metates. They also suffered from abscesses, which appear as large voids in the mandibles and maxillas. In fact, some teeth had shallow grooves worn into their sides, where a person had habitually twirled a toothpick-sized twig to overstimulate the nerves and alleviate the pain of an abscess.

Bone and Stable Isotopes

We can also reconstruct ancient diets by analyzing the carbon and nitrogen stable isotopes preserved in human bone.

We encountered the concept of isotopes when discussing radiocarbon dating (in Chapter 6). Carbon, you will remember, has both stable and unstable isotopes. One stable form, ^{12}C, makes up about 99 percent of the world's carbon; ^{13}C is also stable but accounts for only about 1 percent. The unstable isotope ^{14}C, most familiar to archaeologists because of its importance for dating, is extremely rare.

As we pointed out in Chapter 6, plants take carbon in through one of three photosynthetic pathways: C_3, C_4, and CAM. You will recall that the C_4 plants (such as maize) take in more ^{13}C and ^{14}C isotopes than do C_3 and CAM plants. Because human bones reflect the isotopic ratios of plants ingested during life, bioarchaeologists can reconstruct the dietary importance of certain classes of plants by measuring the ratio of carbon isotopes contained in **bone collagen,** the organic component of bone. A diet rich in C_4 plants (such as maize), for example, can produce bones with a significantly higher ratio of ^{13}C to ^{12}C than diets low in C_4 plants.

Nitrogen also has two stable isotopes, ^{14}N and ^{15}N. Some plants obtain their nitrogen from the air, and others absorb nitrogen from the soil. These diverse mechanisms result in different ratios of ^{15}N to ^{14}N in various plants. Using this information, bioarchaeologists can analyze a bone's stable isotope composition to determine which plants were eaten and which were not. In addition, we know that carnivores tend to lose ^{14}N through their urine, but retain ^{15}N. This means that humans who consume large amounts of meat have a higher ratio of ^{15}N to ^{14}N than those who eat mostly plants. To complicate things further, marine plants tend to have ^{15}N to ^{14}N ratios that are 4 percent higher than terrestrial plants. These differences are passed up the food chain, so marine mammals also tend to have higher ratios of ^{15}N to ^{14}N than terrestrial mammals. But you can't interpret the values blindly because of environmental differences. Hot desert soils, for instance, tend to have higher nitrogen ratios than cool forest soils—so much so, in fact, that bones of desert-dwelling individuals with purely terrestrial diets can produce nitrogen values that, in another part of the world, would suggest a marine diet. Used properly, however, differences in nitrogen values tell us whether people relied more heavily on marine than terrestrial foods or had more or less meat in their diets.

Larsen submitted samples of human bone from 39 of the individuals recovered at Stillwater Marsh to Margaret Schoeninger (University of California, San Diego), one of the world's premier analysts of bone chemistry. Along with the human bone samples, Larsen also submitted several modern plant specimens and animal bones (identified to species) to act as controls.

The actual measurement of a bone's carbon and nitrogen isotope ratios is a complex process involving a mass spectrometer and need not concern us here. But Schoeninger's findings are not difficult to understand. To make her point, Schoeninger compared the results of the analysis of the Stillwater materials to two very different populations (Figure 10-5): the skeletal remains from Pecos Pueblo in New Mexico, a maize-dependent population; and the skeletal remains of a foraging population from Ontario, Canada, which was heavily dependent on meat. In Figure 10-5, the horizontal axis plots the ratio of ^{13}C to ^{12}C—higher ratios (indicating more C_4 plants like maize in the diet) are farther to the right, and lower ratios (meaning fewer C_4 plants in the diet) to the left. Don't let the negative numbers confuse you. To make measurements comparable, Schoeninger reports the stable isotope values calibrated as deviations from an agreed-upon standard (the fossil *belemnitella*, in the Pee Dee limestone formation of South Carolina). The vertical axis plots the ratio of ^{15}N to ^{14}N, with higher ratios (more carnivorous diet) at the top and lower ratios (less carnivorous diet) at the bottom.

As Figure 10-5 shows, the Pecos population has a high ratio of ^{13}C to ^{12}C and a low ratio of ^{15}N to ^{14}N. This means that the Pecos population ate plenty of maize and very little meat. At the upper left part of the graph, the Ontario hunting population has a high ratio of ^{15}N to ^{14}N, with virtually no C_4 plants in its diet; this makes sense because the Ontario foragers lived in an environment unsuitable for horticulture and relied primarily on fish, moose, and caribou (rather than plants) for food. The Stillwater population lies between these two extremes, with very few C_4 plants in its diet, a diet that was a mixture of plant and animal foods.

Schoeninger took the results even further. Remember that she also analyzed some modern plant samples, one of which was piñon pine. It turns out that piñon

---

bone collagen The organic component of bone.

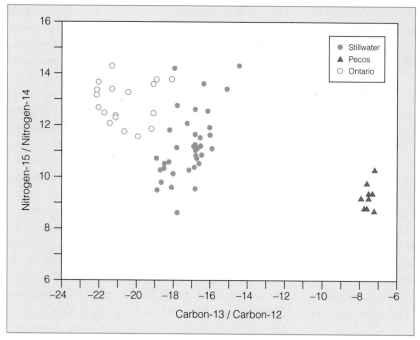

Figure 10-5 Stable carbon and nitrogen isotopes for the Stillwater burial population compared with those of Archaic Ontario hunter-gatherers and of Pecos Pueblo maize horticulturalists.

cence is particularly important because this is when bone collagen forms. If the foods available in the wetlands varied from decade to decade because of flooding, fires, climate change, or other factors, then perhaps people ate different suites of food over the years. In some years, perhaps jackrabbits were commonly roasted over the fire; in other years, bulrush seed cakes might have been the daily fare. If this dietary variability accounts for the different nitrogen ratios, then it suggests that the Pecos farmers and Ontario foragers had far more monotonous diets than did the people living at Stillwater Marsh.

has a very low ratio of ¹⁵N to ¹⁴N. Schoeninger figured that if piñon was important to the Stillwater diet, then their bones should have a much lower nitrogen ratio than the graph indicates. Because they do not, Schoeninger concluded that piñon could not have been an important component of the diet. Instead, by looking at the values for the other plant and animal control samples, Schoeninger concluded that a strictly marsh-based diet (that is, including no food plants from mountain environments) could readily account for the observed carbon and nitrogen isotope ratios in the Stillwater remains.

Note in Figure 10-5 that the Stillwater population has a greater *range* of nitrogen values than either the Ontario or Pecos populations. Schoeninger looked to see if this range was associated with an individual's age or sex. For example, if men spent time hunting large game then perhaps they ate more meat than women; or maybe children ate less meat than adults. However, there was no association between nitrogen values and age or sex.

Perhaps, then, there was a change through time, with the importance of meat increasing or decreasing through time. But, again, Schoeninger found no clear association between nitrogen values and the radiocarbon ages on the burials.

Consequently, Schoeninger suggested that the range of nitrogen values might be a product of long-term dietary variability. Although bone chemistry is a lifelong average of one's diet, the period of youth and adoles-

LIVES OF AFFLUENCE? OR NASTY, BRUTISH, AND SHORT?

Let us return to Larsen's original research question: Does the Stillwater burial population reflect human lives that were "nasty, brutish, and short" or those of an "affluent society"?

The answer, evident from these various analyses, is "Both" and "Neither." The people of Stillwater Marsh consumed a varied diet that probably went beyond their minimal nutritional needs. They were relatively healthy, generally free of serious disease, disorders, broken bones, and infections. This part seems to fit the "original affluent society" image.

But the Stillwater people worked hard, and some had aching knees and backs. Some youngsters suffered from periods of malnutrition, and few people lived much beyond 50 years. These data conform more to the "nasty, brutish, and short" model.

The point is not to pigeonhole the Stillwater burial population, per se, but to learn what life was like for people in the past. We seek to understand the various factors that influenced their diet, their rates of infection and bone breakage, their workloads, and their dental health. In some ways, the Stillwater population had a good life; in other ways, it was not so easy. Rarely can we characterize the past in simple black-and-white terms.

The people of Stillwater lived lives that were physically demanding, but not very violent. Not all people were so fortunate, though; in some places, ancient lives of violence are witnessed by the bones.

CANNIBALISM IN THE AMERICAN SOUTHWEST?

For several decades, archaeologists have been aware of human skeletal remains in the American Southwest that bear evidence of violence. But in the 1990s, several archaeologists finally put a name to this particular brand of violence: cannibalism. One of these was Christy Turner (Arizona State University). In his book *Man Corn*, he and his late wife, Jacqueline, documented nearly 300 individuals that, Turner argues, bear evidence of cannibalism. These come from 76 archaeological sites; most are Chacoan sites in the Four Corners region of the Southwest. And most of the remains concentrate in the late twelfth and early thirteenth centuries—the time of the demise of the Chacoan system, with its large pueblos and vast road network (see Chapter 3) and the construction of defensive cliff dwellings, such as those at Mesa Verde National Park (see Figure 15-1 on page 360).

The basic data can't be denied: Turner saw human bones that do indeed bear stone tool cut marks, in places that suggest flesh was stripped from them; as well as long bones and vertebrae that are smashed open, in the same way that animal bones are broken to extract the marrow. Other bones are burned, and some bear evidence of "pot polish"—abraded surfaces that are produced by stirring boiling bones in a ceramic pot.

LOOKING CLOSER

CANNIBALISM AND THE MEDIA

We can't leave the subject of cannibalism without commenting on how this archaeological story played in the press. The media seek stories that seem to dramatically overturn everything that we thought we knew; and some journalists especially like stories that make researchers look as though they are trying to hide something. In this case, allegations of cannibalism caught the attention of media all over the world, with headlines such as "American Cannibalism?" "Anasazi Cannibalism," "Researchers Divided Over Whether Anasazi Were Cannibals," and "Did Cannibalism Kill Anasazi Civilization?" PBS produced a documentary titled *Cannibals of the Canyon*. Even the television program *King of the Hill* used "Anasazi cannibalism" as a story line.

The media loved the story because it was gruesome and because it overturned cherished images of Native Americans as peaceful people living in harmony with nature and their neighbors.

Such casual treatment of cannibalism upset many Puebloan peoples. They pointed out that their oral histories contain no stories of cannibalism and, therefore, archaeologists were probably wrong (actually, there are accounts of cannibalism in Pueblo traditions). And, they asked, do 300 cases (not all of which are accepted by other researchers) spread out over a vast area and some 350 years make the Puebloan people "cannibals"? Cases of cannibalism occur in Euro-American history; most notable is that of the Donner Party, the group of 87 emigrants who, in 1846, were stranded for five months in the Sierra Nevadas and reduced to feeding off those who had already succumbed. But nobody asks whether Euro-Americans are cannibals. It seems that, despite the horrible things that some *individuals* might resort to, Euro-Americans *as a people* could not be cannibals.

Indians are understandably upset because they know that even asking the question about them implies that Indians *could be* cannibals. And that's as damaging as actually having done the deed.

The archaeologists who research this subject have done so responsibly. Their reports are written in measured tones. They make no extravagant claims. But the media will print what they think will sell (and "cannibalism" always sells). So, be careful of what you read and hear in the media. If it sounds extreme or outlandish, it probably isn't completely correct.

The bodies of these unfortunates were dismembered and boiled. In all likelihood, this means that these people were eaten. But some archaeologists take exception to this *interpretation*, pointing out that broken, cut-marked bones could be evidence of a burial ritual, a reverent form of dismemberment that is part of a number of cultures around the world today, and which is not associated with cannibalism. Others suggest that the violence could have been inflicted on "witches" only, a form of capital punishment that thoroughly destroyed any trace of a social miscreant. In either case, no one need have eaten anyone else.

There is, however, one direct case of cannibalism. In a kiva's central fireplace in a site in Cowboy Wash in southwestern Colorado, Bill Billman (University of North Carolina) found a human coprolite that contained the protein myoglobin, which exists only in human muscle tissue. The most parsimonious explanation is that one individual consumed the flesh of another and, some hours later, defecated in the center of a very sacred place.

Cannibalism is difficult to prove, but that's not really the issue here. What matters is that research by the Turners and others makes clear that the Puebloan world saw a period of intense intervillage conflict, including warfare, in the twelfth and thirteenth centuries. For most archaeologists, the more interesting and archaeologically testable subject lies not in cannibalism but in understanding cycles of violence. Why should this particular time in Southwest prehistory have seen such extreme animosity that some people would have been horribly slaughtered, and perhaps eaten? Unfortunately, this is not how this particular story played out in the press (see "Looking Closer: Cannibalism and the Media").

Most of the time, bioarchaeologists analyze human skeletons to answer questions about human behavior and quality of life. But recently developed technology now allows us to analyze the biology of ancient human populations in order to answer some old questions in new ways. The rest of this chapter explores the developing frontier of archaeology at the molecular level.

molecular archaeology The use of genetic information in ancient human remains to reconstruct the past.

nuclear DNA Genetic material found in a cell's nucleus; this material is primarily responsible for an individual's inherited traits.

gene A unit of the chromosomes that controls inheritance of particular traits.

mitochondrial DNA (mtDNA) Genetic material found in the mitochondria of cells; it is inherited only from the mother and appears to mutate at a rate of 2–4 percent per 1 million years.

ARCHAEOLOGY AND DNA

How was the world colonized? Are modern humans related to Neanderthals? When did Native Americans arrive in the New World? (see "Looking Closer: Coprolites and Colonization of the New World").

Archaeologists once relied strictly on artifacts to track ancient migrations and the historical relationships among the world's populations. But modern genetic technology provides another avenue for reconstructing the past. By using genetic material—DNA from human skeletal remains and living peoples—geneticists and archaeologists have joined forces to create a new approach to reconstructing the past known as **molecular archaeology**. As is so often true, this new approach raises as many questions as it attempts to answer.

A Little Background on DNA

Most of our genetic information exists as about 3 billion nucleotide base pairs grouped into some 50,000 genes on the 46 chromosomes inside the nucleus of each cell in our bodies. This stuff, called **nuclear DNA** (deoxyribonucleic acid), makes each human being unique, and it's inherited from both of your biological parents. Your DNA contains the recipe for your biological composition, telling your body to create blue or green eyes, to be short or tall, to have straight or curly hair. A **gene** is a segment of a chromosome, one small piece of the recipe that codes for particular biological attributes.

Nuclear DNA is important for understanding the genetics of living populations, but less so for archaeology. Nuclear DNA degrades fairly quickly, and by the time the human body decomposes, nuclear DNA is no longer intact (although sections of about 200 nucleotide base pairs can survive for thousands of years).

But another form of DNA, known as **mitochondrial DNA (mtDNA)**, is found in the cells' mitochondria (organelles responsible for the cell's energy metabolism)—outside the nucleus. mtDNA contains only about 0.0006 percent of the genetic material of nuclear DNA (a mere 16,569 nucleotide base pairs). This would seem to limit its use, but mtDNA has three interesting properties. First, although it contains only a limited segment of the total genetic recipe, each cell contains thousands of copies of it (in contrast to just the two in the nucleus). This translates to a greater probability of retrieving mtDNA than nuclear DNA. But don't think that there are gobs of mtDNA just lying around in archaeological sites. Rather, its recovery

LOOKING CLOSER

COPROLITES AND COLONIZATION OF THE NEW WORLD

Archaeologists can't afford to be picky about their sources of information; data are where you find them. At Paisley 5 Mile Point Cave in Oregon, crucial information on the colonization of the New World came from . . . coprolites.

Recall that coprolites are desiccated feces and are commonly found in the dry caves of the desert West. At Paisley 5 Mile Point Cave, Dennis Jenkins (University of Oregon) recovered more than a dozen human coprolites, three of which returned radiocarbon dates in excess of 12,000 radiocarbon years, meaning that they were some of the earliest evidence of a human presence in North America. But many creatures defecate in caves. The coprolites *looked* human, but Jenkins needed to be certain.

Jenkins tested six of the coprolites using crossover immunoelectrophoresis (CIEP), a test used in crime labs to detect human blood through the presence of human proteins; two of the three oldest coprolites tested positive. This was encouraging, but Jenkins needed to be certain. So, he turned to Danish geneticist Eske Willerslev.

Willerslev found that all six coprolites tested positive for human mtDNA. Again, encouraging, but how could Willerslev be certain that the DNA was ancient? For starters, he had the work replicated in two other labs; both returned the same results. This ruled out contamination in Willerslev's lab, but perhaps the coprolites had been contaminated during fieldwork by students' DNA—transmitted through dead skin cells, or a sneeze. To check this, Willerslev took samples from everyone who worked at or visited the site, regardless of whether they handled the coprolites or not, and compared it to the sequences found in the coprolites. None matched. So far, so good.

And yet . . . maybe humans who lived at the cave later had contaminated the coprolites with DNA from their body fluids, hair, or dead skin cells. To test this possibility, Jenkins and Willerslev came up with an ingenious solution. Wood rats also used the cave, even more than people did. If human DNA was moving through the sediments, then certainly wood rat DNA would, too. So, Willerslev tested the coprolites for wood rat DNA. But the tests were negative. So, for the time being, evidence for the earliest human presence in North America comes from the most humble of human artifacts—coprolites.

© Dennis Jenkins, Northern Great Basin Archaeological Field School Files

Excavation in progress at one of the Paisley 5 Mile Point Caves.

is made possible through the technique of *polymerase chain reaction* (PCR), which enables researchers to create billions of copies of a very small sample of mtDNA so that this genetic material can be more readily studied.

The second intriguing property of mtDNA is that you inherit yours *only* from your mother. Although mtDNA is present in the tail of sperm, after fertilization occurs the tail breaks off. This means that your mtDNA comes entirely from the ovum. If you are female, you pass along the same mtDNA to all your children. If you are male, none of the mtDNA that you inherited from your mother is passed on to your biological offspring. This makes it possible to define molecular "family trees" and to trace the movement of female lineages.

Finally, mtDNA seems to change in a particular way and at a particular rate that makes it potentially useful to archaeology. Briefly, although mtDNA is probably not completely free from the pressures of natural selection, it appears to be under less selective pressure than nuclear DNA. And because it is transferred from mother to offspring as a chunk, it does not recombine (as does nuclear DNA). Instead, mtDNA appears to change over time largely as a result of random mutations. Nuclear DNA can also change as a result of random mutation (this is, in fact, one of the main ways that new genetic material appears). But compared with nuclear DNA, mtDNA mutates rapidly, about 2.8–6.6 mutations per 10,000 years. Although this may seem slow, it is *6–16 times faster* than nuclear DNA's mutation rate. *If* one assumes that this rate of change has been constant through time, then differences in the mutations between related mtDNA samples can be used to estimate how much time has elapsed since the branches of the family tree diverged. For this reason, mtDNA is sometimes used as a "clock" to date the timing of human population movements in the remote past.

Think of it this way: Imagine a population of interbreeding humans. Women in this population are closely related and, consequently, all members of the population (not just the women) share the same mutations in their mtDNA. Now imagine that this population splits apart, and one group migrates to a region far enough away that the two groups no longer interbreed. Both will share the mutations they had prior to the migration, but chances are that future mutations in their mtDNA will not be the same. If the population

has three mutations in common and three that are different, then, assuming the clock is accurate, the population split into two about 5,000 to 10,000 years ago (at roughly 3–6 mutations every 10,000 years).

This might be a very useful tool for archaeology, if we could recover ancient DNA (or, as it is now known, **aDNA**) from organic remains recovered in archaeological sites.

Prospecting for aDNA

In 1984, Allan Wilson (1943–1991) and his student Vince Sarich (University of California, Berkeley) were the first to identify genetic materials from old tissue. When they cloned DNA from the 140-year-old skin of quagga—a recently extinct, zebra-like African beast—the Berkeley team showed that DNA could indeed survive after the death of an organism.

At about the same time, Swedish researcher Svante Pääbo (Max Planck Institute of Evolutionary Genetics, Germany) cloned DNA from a 4400-year-old Egyptian mummy. This was the first time that anyone had applied PCR techniques to ancient humans. Not long after, Pääbo pushed the barrier back another 2600 years by extracting ancient DNA from 7000-year-old human brain tissue preserved at the waterlogged Little Salt Spring site in Florida.

Initial excitement over this new frontier was tempered by the realization that it is extraordinarily difficult to prevent aDNA ancient samples from being contaminated with modern human DNA. Let's face it: DNA is *really* small and you can't just sweep a lab clean of it. This is not such a large problem when studying DNA extracted from faunal remains—the presence of human DNA would be a dead giveaway that something was amiss in the lab. But separating modern from ancient human DNA is far more difficult. As a result, labs must use some very strict protocols to prevent contamination. For example, geneticists take samples from every person who came into contact with the ancient remains to demonstrate that the sample is uncontaminated by modern DNA.

An African Eve?

Wilson's work did not stop with the quagga. Instead, he and his colleagues moved on to explore the human past as well.

Wilson and his team (including Rebecca Cann, University of Hawaii, and Mark Stoneking, Max Planck Institute of Evolutionary Genetics, Germany) collected

aDNA Ancient DNA recovered from organic materials in archaeological sites.

147 mtDNA samples from around the world (from human placentas) and compared the human data with that of a chimpanzee (as a control). The most striking fact about mtDNA is how much of it we all share. At the molecular level, all living human groups share all but about 0.6 percent of mtDNA. As you might expect, humans and chimpanzees share somewhat less, humans and horses share even less, and so forth. The 0.6 percent figure is important because it suggests a way to determine the relatedness among all living individuals and groups.

By examining the mtDNA from various modern human populations, Wilson could see what a close-knit species we really are. This was a surprise because mtDNA is supposed to evolve fairly rapidly. Components of the modern global sample turned out to be remarkably alike—both within geographical populations and between continental groups. The result was a family tree for all of (surviving) humanity. Africa provided the longest branch on the tree, suggesting this is where human mtDNA began to differentiate. Those of African descent also showed the most variability among themselves (in fact, Bushmen peoples have the most diverse DNA of any living human population) and were the most distinct from other populations of the world. Wilson argued that this pattern is precisely what one would expect *if all modern humans had descended from a single population in Africa.*

These investigators went a step further, suggesting that all the genetic composition evident in living human populations could be traced to a single ancient African ancestor. Because mtDNA is passed down strictly through the maternal line, this fictive ancestor must have been female. She was quickly nicknamed Eve, after the biblical first woman and wife of Adam.

Even more controversial than Eve's African origin was the molecular clock that Wilson and his group derived. Because geneticists assume that mtDNA changes at a constant rate, the 0.6 percent figure is important for another reason: It provides a relatively precise way to gauge the first appearance of *Homo sapiens* (modern humans). Although this so-called **molecular clock** does not keep perfect time, it does suggest some genetic limits within which human evolution may have taken place.

Wilson's molecular clock suggested that Eve must have lived about 200,000 years ago. If so, then the first descendants of Eve (early modern humans) must have fanned out of Africa to supplant other hominins about this time. This theory, which has come to be known as the "out of Africa" hypothesis, had, it turned out, also been framed independently on the basis of the fossil evidence alone.

To call the Eve hypothesis controversial is an understatement. Some biological anthropologists, such as Milford Wolpoff (University of Michigan), see strong continuity between pre- and post-200,000-year-old skulls from various parts of the Old World. To these anthropologists, the skeletal data argue for continuity in various parts of the Old World (humans had not yet colonized the New World by this date) rather than recent replacement by a migrating population from Africa. (Although Africa is still the homeland of humanity, as we saw in Chapter 5, the question here is whether *all* modern humans derive from a later African expansion.)

What Happened to the Neanderthals?

Others charged that the Eve hypothesis was based on modern genetic distributions and that it needed to be tested by using DNA extracted from ancient bone. One particularly controversial area is whether the Neanderthals of Europe and the Near East are related to modern humans or if they are an evolutionary dead end.

Neanderthals were present in Europe by at least 500,000 years ago; they also appear in the Near East and in parts of Asia. They probably co-existed with modern humans in the Near East for several tens of thousands of years, but they appear to have quickly disappeared by roughly 30,000 years ago in Europe—about the time that biologically modern humans appear there. Did modern humans drive Neanderthals to extinction, or did they interbreed with them so thoroughly that the population's distinctive appearance was genetically swamped?

Based on skeletal data, Neanderthals are strikingly different biologically from modern humans. Popularly, they are thought of as short, slump-shouldered, beetle-browed, slack-jawed brutes; calling someone a "Neanderthal" is not considered a compliment! But this says more about our cultural biases than it does about skeletal biology, for these features were probably part and parcel of an anatomy that was adapted to the cold, near-glacial environment of Europe. Neanderthals had arms and legs that were shorter relatively to the length of their torsos than modern humans, the result of selective pressure to reduce heat loss. And

molecular clock Calculations of the time since divergence of two related populations using the presumed rate of mutation in mtDNA and the genetic differences between the two populations.

Figure 10-6 A reconstruction of a Neanderthal woman.

while they had sloping chins and foreheads, and a more projecting face, their cranial capacity was probably comparable to that of modern humans. They also had especially powerful hands and arms, and were generally more robust and muscular than modern humans. One genetic study of Neanderthal remains found the genes coding for light skin and red hair (Figure 10-6).

Looking at the skeletal data, some biological anthropologists see continuity between the Neanderthals and modern Europeans, and argue that Neanderthals are part of the human line. Others see skeletal differences too large to place Neanderthals in the ancestry of modern humans. Which is it? Are Neanderthals in the human family tree, or an ancient offshoot that went extinct in the face of competition with modern humans?

Recently, several studies have extracted DNA from Neanderthal skeletal remains. An initial study looked only at mtDNA and found no overlap between Neanderthals and modern humans. But in 2010, a team of geneticists led by Svante Pääbo sequenced the nuclear DNA genome from three Neanderthals. This is nothing short of remarkable given how easy it is for nuclear DNA to degrade, and how easy it can be contaminated with DNA from bacteria and microbes, as well as with the DNA of the many people who have handled the remains over the years.

This was made possible by several new techniques that permit those who work with *a*DNA to remove contaminants. In part, this is accomplished by comparing the DNA extracted from Neanderthal remains to that of the modern human and chimpanzee genomes; other procedures help remove contamination by modern humans.

Pääbo and his colleagues could sequence about two-thirds of the Neanderthal genome. They then compared

this genome to that sequenced from living peoples in sub-Saharan Africa, Europe, and Asia. They found no trace of Neanderthal genes in the sub-Saharan African population—which makes sense because there never were any Neanderthals in sub-Saharan Africa. But the other populations carried from 1 to 4 percent of Neanderthal DNA. Neanderthals and humans interbred some 40,000 to 50,000 years ago and produced fertile offspring, most likely in the Near East where those two populations overlapped for a long period of time. They probably did not "hook up" frequently, however; otherwise, we might expect the overlap to be greater than 1–4 percent.

One suggested explanation for the lack of much interbreeding was that Neanderthals were not just physically different from modern humans, but mentally different as well. Specifically, some people have suggested that Neanderthals were unable to speak and communicate in the way that modern humans can. Geneticists know that one gene, the *FOXP2* gene, is crucial for the development of language because it controls the muscles that permit us to articulate speech. This gene, found only in humans, is absent from all other primate genomes. But Pääbo found the *FOXP2* gene in the Neanderthal sequence. This means that Neanderthals had the same physical capacity for speech as modern humans. Still unanswered, however, is whether they had modern humans' remarkable ability to use symbols, to speak using metaphors and similes, that is such a hallmark of human communication.

We are still a long way from relying on genetic evidence to reconstruct the past. But the advances that have been made in only the past 20 years are sufficiently intriguing to suggest that, whatever the answer may be, molecular archaeology provides a major new source of information on the past. If nothing else, these data will force archaeologists to reconsider whether they really do know what they think they know. And that, as we have said, is what science is all about.

CONCLUSION

Studying human skeletal remains provides an up-close way for archaeologists to understand the people of the past. Where burial populations are available, our knowledge of the past can grow by leaps and bounds. By analyzing skeletal morphology and bone chemistry, bioarchaeologists can learn a great deal about men's and women's workloads, diets, patterns of disease, trauma, and quality of life. And the field of bioarchaeology is in its infancy, each year producing new ways to analyze human bone and promising to expand our knowledge of the past considerably.

Molecular archaeology has great promise to help reconstruct human migrations, if we can figure out how to use genes as clocks. This is an area of middle-level theory that will require considerable attention in the future.

The next two chapters will move us into questions about aspects of past human lives that are even more difficult to reconstruct: understanding social and political behavior and the meaning of symbols.

SUMMARY

1. How do bioarchaeologists contribute to a study of the past?

⚙ Bioarchaeology is the study of the human biological component evident in the archaeological record; it examines the health and workload of ancient populations. This specialty requires expertise in the method and theory of both biological anthropology and field archaeology.

2. How do bioarchaeologists determine age and sex for a skeleton?

⚙ We use characteristics of several bones, notably the pelvis and skull, to determine an individual's sex.

⚙ An individual's age can be determined by tooth eruption; patterns of bone fusion, tooth wear, and bone wear are used to age individuals over the age of 25.

3. How do bioarchaeologists use paleopathology and bone chemistry to reconstruct the lives of ancient peoples?

⚙ Paleopathology is the study of those ancient diseases that leave skeletal traces. Iron deficiency, for example, leaves a distinctive spongy appearance on the skull and the interior of the eye orbits. In addition, growth arrest features, such as Harris lines and enamel hypoplasias, indicate periods of severe disease or malnutrition in childhood.

⚙ Bones respond to the routine mechanical stresses placed upon them; patterns of osteoarthritis and long bone cross sections can point to different patterns of workload between the sexes or to changes through time.

⚙ Stature estimates can track changes in the quality of diet.

⚙ Bioarchaeologists can also reconstruct diet: High frequency of dental caries indicates a diet high in simple carbohydrates and sugars. The ratios of carbon and nitrogen isotopes in bone can reconstruct the dietary importance of various kinds of plants and animals.

4. How are genetic data used to reconstruct population relationships and the ages of migrations?

⚙ Molecular archaeology uses data from living and ancient peoples to reconstruct population migrations. Especially useful is mitochondrial DNA. Although we still have much to learn about the rates at which DNA mutates, current studies show that DNA studies are important to reconstructing the past.

MEDIA RESOURCES

Doing Fieldwork:
Archaeological Demonstrations CD-ROM 2.0
This CD, developed by the authors, shows professional archaeologists involved in various digs, many of which are referenced in the text. The presentation is organized by the main techniques used on an archaeological dig, reinforcing concepts and techniques via live examples. The CD takes you through each step automatically, or you can navigate to any point via the navigation bar. After reviewing a step in the dig process, you are taken to Check Points, which are concept questions about each step of the dig. Then you can see the answers, receive your score, and even send your scores to your instructor.

The Companion Website for *Archaeology,*
Sixth Edition
www.cengagebrain.com
Supplement your review of this chapter by going to the companion website to take one of the practice quizzes, use the flash cards to master key terms, and check out the many other study aids that are designed to help you succeed in your introductory archaeology course.

11 RECONSTRUCTING SOCIAL AND POLITICAL SYSTEMS OF THE PAST

LEARNING OBJECTIVES

AFTER READING THIS CHAPTER YOU SHOULD BE ABLE TO ANSWER THESE QUESTIONS:

1. What concepts help archaeologists to reconstruct past social and political organizations?

2. What archaeological remains are important in reconstructing political organization, especially those involving inherited social inequities?

3. What archaeological remains help reconstruct social organization, especially kinship?

4. What techniques help reconstruct ancient trade networks?

© Douglas Peebles/CORBIS

A portion of Nan Madol, a ceremonial center on the island of Pohnpei in Micronesia. The walls were constructed of massive basalt columns transported from the opposite side of the island.

PREVIEW

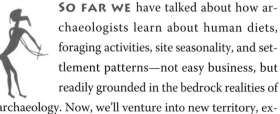

SO FAR WE have talked about how archaeologists learn about human diets, foraging activities, site seasonality, and settlement patterns—not easy business, but readily grounded in the bedrock realities of archaeology. Now, we'll venture into new territory, exploring ancient social and political organization—what these are, and how archaeologists find out about them.

This chapter looks at three key components of human society: gender, kinship, and social status. Each brings its own interpretive problems and middle-level difficulties. What men and women did in the past is essential to understanding how a society operates, yet assigning specific artifacts to men and women is difficult. Kinship is a major structuring principle of human social organization, but it leaves ambiguous traces. The archaeological record reflects social status a bit more clearly, but many ancient societies may have been organized politically in ways that have no simple ethnographic analogies today. Trade, we will see, is an important component of political and social systems, and archaeologists have various ways of tracing the movement of food and goods across a landscape. Although we are entering a more difficult realm of archaeology, we will show that reconstructing past social and political systems is not impossible.

INTRODUCTION

Recall from Chapter 2 that archaeology is firmly situated within the broader field of anthropology. Right now, we must return to archaeology's roots in anthropology to define some terms and concepts.

Social Vocabulary

Social organization refers to the rules and structures that govern relationships between individuals within a group of interacting people. These relationships are never simple because people belong to groups on many different levels; some of these crosscut one another, and others are hierarchically organized.

You, for example, simultaneously belong to one or more families (as a son or daughter, husband or wife, brother or sister) and to a town, a state, and a country. You are biologically male or female, and you may be a member of or hold office in a sports club, political party, or community organization. In other words, you play various roles in a variety of social groups. Which identity is currently operating depends upon the situation.

Some social groups are residential, consisting of domestic families or households, territorial bands, or community-level villages. Residential groups tend to be physical, face-to-face associations of people. Residential groups appear in the archaeological record as households and villages.

Other groups are nonresidential; these are groups in the abstract sense and may never actually convene. Nonresidential groups are usually manifested archaeologically through the use of symbols, ceremonies, mythologies, or insignias of membership that appear as particular styles of material culture, such as ceramics, architecture, rock art, or burials. While the residential group regulates discrete spatial matters, the nonresidential group binds these territorial units together.

A related concept is **political organization,** the formal and informal institutions that regulate a society's collective acts. Sometimes, control rests primarily at the level of the residential group; in other cases, the

social organization The rules and structures that govern relations within a group of interacting people. Societies are divided into social units (groups) within which are recognized social positions (statuses), with appropriate behavior patterns prescribed for these positions (roles).

political organization A society's formal and informal institutions that regulate a population's collective acts.

nonresidential group exerts a powerful influence. The nineteenth-century Great Basin Shoshone and Paiute, for example, lived in nuclear families, three or four of which came together in a residential group. Such groups were ephemeral, and families would come and go in an ever-changing set of associations. Clusters of families would sometimes come together for a communal jackrabbit or antelope drive. When they did, one individual, recognized for his hunting ability, would take charge, but his authority would disappear when the drive was over. Shoshone families did not "do as they pleased," but neither did they participate in a formal, permanent level of political integration above the family. This means that although behaviors such as murder and theft were considered antisocial, punishment varied depending on the particular circumstances and families involved.

Contrast this with eighteenth-century Tahitian society. At the time of European contact (in 1767), Tahiti—an island in the South Pacific with a population of some 100,000—had a horticultural economy of taro, breadfruit, yams, and coconuts. People also raised pigs and chickens, caught fish, and collected shellfish. Families lived in small villages along the coast and in the island's interior.

Unlike Shoshone bands, the membership of Tahitian villages was more or less permanent, with several strong and overarching levels of control. Tahitian villages were organized into about 20 competing **chiefdoms**. A "sacred chief" ruled each of these chiefdoms. Below the sacred chiefs were "small chiefs," and under the small chiefs were sub-chiefs. Below the sub-chiefs were the commoners. Sacred chiefs claimed to be descended directly from the gods, whereas commoners were said to exist only to provide for the needs of chiefs. A man had to marry a woman in his own class. Chiefs owned the land in their respective villages, and they had larger houses and canoes than commoners, as well as distinctive clothing. Some chiefs had craft specialists in their employ, and chiefs controlled communal fishing gear and village production.

The sacred chief also controlled the distribution of food and goods among villages. Periodically, he demanded tribute for special feasts and demonstrated his authority by redistributing food and goods to all who attended. The chief always retained some portion of the tribute for use by his household; chiefs also handed out punishments for social transgressions.

The Great Basin and Tahiti provide extreme examples of social and political organizations. To understand such differences, we will restrict the present discussion to four broad areas of human social and political behavior: gender, kinship, social status, and trade.

From Artifact to Symbol

Before doing this, we must re-emphasize the importance of middle-level theory. As you know, archaeologists use material remains to reconstruct past human activities; in Chapter 1, we talked about "thinking from things." People butcher an animal and leave behind stone tools and the bones. They make, use, and break a pot, leaving the sherds behind in a trash midden. Natural processes work on those remains and discarded artifacts are sometimes reclaimed or recycled. Archaeologists need to consider all these dimensions of artifact use and reuse when interpreting the archaeological record.

Now we add another dimension that's especially important to understanding social and political organization. While it might seem that archaeologists act as if artifacts only reflect human behavior, we know that artifacts are not just things—they are also *symbols*. Bringing flowers or a bottle of wine to dinner is a standard American way to thank a host. But such gestures would be meaningless to the Mikea (see Chapter 8), who expect their guests to show up with tobacco.

This fact—*that material culture reflects symbolic meanings as well as functional behaviors*—makes archaeological patterning even more difficult to understand because only rarely can we tell if objects are best interpreted in terms of their functional or symbolic meanings. Archaeologists are finding new ways to infer ancient social and political organization from artifacts, and this chapter provides several examples of how this works. We will return to the symbolic dimension of artifacts in Chapter 12.

ARCHAEOLOGY AND GENDER

Anthropologists distinguish between sex and gender, and between gender roles and gender ideology. Sex refers to inherited, biological differences between males and females. But gender refers to culturally constructed ideas about sex differences. Humans have only two

chiefdom A regional polity in which two or more local groups are organized under a single chief (who is the head of a ranked social hierarchy). Unlike autonomous bands and villages, chiefdoms consist of several more or less permanently aligned communities or settlements.

Figure 11-1 The site of Indian Knoll (Kentucky). In the days of WPA archaeology, a huge portion of the site was excavated, and hundreds of human burials were uncovered.

sexes, male and female—but there can be more than two genders. In some Plains Indian tribes, for example, **berdaches** (also known as "two-spirits") were men who chose to live as women, performing women's traditional roles, and even marrying men (although marriage in this case did not imply a sexual relationship).

This leads us to the difference between gender *role* and gender *ideology*. **Gender role** refers to the differential participation of males and females in the various social, economic, political, and religious institutions of a group. These roles describe culturally appropriate behavior for men and women. In some societies, women can play very public roles, for example, in politics; in others, women's public participation may be limited. **Gender ideology** refers to the culturally specific meaning and value assigned to terms such as "male," "female,"

"sex," and "reproduction." In some societies, men and women generally share equal footing. In some, men are considered of greater importance, and in some, the activities of men and women are so differently valued that adult men and women interact very little. In some traditional New Guinean societies, for example, men spend much of their leisure time in a communal men's house, rather than in their separate family homes.

These facts are important to understanding other societies, and also to understanding archaeological inference. Recognition of gender ideology led Margaret Conkey (University of California, Berkeley) and Janet Spector (retired) to accuse archaeology of a strong **androcentric** bias. Archaeologists at the time were mostly male, and they viewed the world largely in terms of men's activities and perceptions—and, in fact, in terms of white, middle-class, European male understandings of the world. Conkey and Spector found that most archaeologists failed to identify the sources of their assumptions and rarely tried to confirm or validate them. In other words, the only middle-level theory operating was the archaeologists' culturally biased view of gender roles.

As an example, consider the site of Indian Knoll in western Kentucky, a large, 2.5-meter-deep shell midden along the Green River (Figure 11-1). This midden accumulated over a long period, from about

berdaches Among Plains Indian societies, men who elected to live life as women; they were recognized by their group as a third gender.

gender role The culturally prescribed behavior associated with men and women; roles can vary from society to society.

gender ideology The culturally prescribed values assigned to the task and status of men and women; values can vary from society to society.

androcentric A perspective that focuses on what men do in a society, to the exclusion of women.

6100 to 4500 years ago. It was first excavated in 1916 by the self-trained archaeologist C. B. Moore (1852–1936) and then in the 1930s and 1940s by William Webb (1882–1964; formally trained as a physicist, Webb was almost certainly the only archaeologist to help develop the atomic bomb).

Indian Knoll is a **shell midden**—the remains of tens of thousands of shellfish meals are preserved there—but it was also a burial place. Between the two of them, Moore and Webb excavated some 1200 burials. They found that men were generally buried with axes, fishhooks, and other tools, while women were buried with beads, mortars, and pestles.

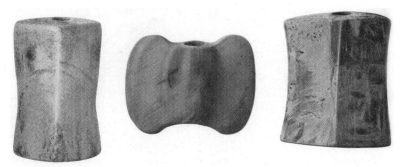

Figure 11-2 Three atlatl weights from the Indian Knoll site. *From Clarence B. Moore, 1916, "Some Aboriginal Sites on Green River, Kentucky," Journal of the Academy of Natural Sciences of Philadelphia, Vol. XVI, Plate XI.*

Some burials were accompanied by beautifully polished stones, a few inches long, somewhat triangular in cross section, with slightly convex sides (Figure 11-2). A hole was drilled neatly lengthwise down the middle of the stone. With these stones were often found pieces of whittled, slightly curved antler, a neat hook at one end.

Moore was puzzled by these enigmatic objects. He thought the stones might have served to hold cords the appropriate distance apart when weaving fishing nets; the antlers he thought might be netting needles.

But having seen well-preserved examples from dry caves in Texas and Arizona, Webb recognized these artifacts as parts of atlatls, or spear-throwers. The stones were slid onto one end of the wooden atlatl arm, perhaps 2 feet long, and the antler hook was fixed to one end, held in place by pitch or tree resin. The hook held the atlatl dart in place as the hunter took aim, and the stone weight increased the centrifugal force of the weapon as the hunter swung the atlatl overhead, launching the dart. The wooden atlatl arm and darts had decayed in the midden, but the stone and antler remained.

Webb was curious about the distribution of these atlatls. Of the 76 burials that held atlatl weights, 31 were adult males, 13 were adult females, and 18 were children (the sex of the other 14 adults could not be identified). Why, Webb wondered, did people place hunting weapons in the graves of women and children? In 1946, he wrote, "It is hardly to be supposed that infants, children, *and women* would have any practical use in life for an atlatl" (emphasis added).

Trying to explain this apparent conundrum, Webb noted that the people of Indian Knoll often buried these beautifully made atlatls intact; but they also sometimes intentionally broke the spear-throwers at the time of burial, as evidenced by the presence of all the fragments of an atlatl weight in grave fill. Knowing that atlatls were also buried with children and women, Webb argued that the artifacts reflected an intentional burial ritual, rather than grave goods for use in the afterlife. We know that in some Native American societies, people cut their hair as a symbol of mourning. Perhaps thousands of years ago at Indian Knoll, the destruction and burial of atlatls carried a similar symbolic meaning—a way for men to express their grief for a deceased child, wife, sister, or mother in a culturally appropriate way.

Notice how Webb's argument is grounded in the assumption—by no means illogical—that atlatls were interred with adult males because they were tools used by men (hence they would need them in the afterlife). This reasoning would, of course, assume that some women at Indian Knoll also hunted. But because Webb could not conceive of women as hunters, he searched for another explanation for the inclusion of atlatls in women's graves. Although Webb's final explanation could still be right, his underlying logic demonstrates the caution needed to detect our own cultural biases, especially when it comes to matters of gender roles.

Before looking at how archaeologists reconstruct what men and women did in the past, let's consider whether this difficult task is even necessary. Do we really need to know whether men or women did the hunting, or plant gathering, or other tasks? Is this concern with gender simply an imposition of the *current* American culture of political correctness? We don't think so, and the following ethnographic example demonstrates why.

shell midden The remnants of shellfish collecting; some shellfish middens can become many meters thick.

Hunting in Africa's Rain Forest

Popularly known as "Pygmies," the BaMbuti are hunter-gatherers who live in the Ituri Rain Forest of central Africa. Living in small temporary camps, they hunt a variety of animals and gather wild plants and honey in the forest. Nearly all these groups exchange meat for agricultural produce with their neighbors, Bantu horticulturalists. They also sometimes work for them in their fields.

Years ago, Colin Turnbull (1924–1994) observed that some BaMbuti hunt individually with bows and arrows whereas other groups hunt communally with nets (Figure 11-3). Among net hunters, women and children drive game (such as the duiker, a small antelope) through the forest into the nets, where men (and sometimes women) club the animals. Bow hunters shoot monkeys and other prey that seek refuge in treetops, but they, too, hunt the duiker. They sometimes hunt communally, but they also hunt alone.

These two kinds of BaMbuti societies differ in their hunting technology and they should leave different archaeological signatures—one should leave behind nets and evidence of their manufacture; the other, projectile points, bows, and arrows. Such differences in technology are precisely the sort of patterning that archaeologists seek to document and explain.

Why do the BaMbuti use different hunting methods? Turnbull attributed the difference to simple cultural preference, but other anthropologists weren't satisfied. Some argued that Bantu horticulturalists introduced net hunting to the forest and that it spread because it was more efficient than bow hunting. Those who lived close to the Bantu had already benefited from this technology, whereas those living farther away had yet to acquire it. Others suggested that net hunting was a response to the crowding created by Bantu emigration; nets were a way to extract more food from limited portions of the forest. The bow hunters, on the other hand, worked in Bantu fields, receiving produce through their labor rather than by trading meat, so they eschewed net hunting.

Others argued the reverse—that net hunting was less efficient than bow hunting and net hunters sacrificed efficiency for volume, using nets to harvest a surplus of meat for trade. Yet another explanation was that the thick undergrowth of the net hunters' environment made archery an impractical hunting technique there.

Anthropologists Robert Bailey (University of Illinois, Chicago) and Robert Aunger (University College, London) tested these competing hypotheses. Drawing upon ethnographic and environmental records, they

Figure 11-3   A young Aka girl removes a blue duiker caught in a net.

found that (1) no significant differences exist between the environments of net hunters and those of archers, (2) net hunting is no more or less efficient than bow hunting, and (3) bow hunters do not live nearer to or trade more with Bantu peoples than net hunters. In other words, the evidence contradicted every available hypothesis.

Bailey and Aunger observed that whereas women participate in net hunts, they rarely hunt in archer groups. So the question, perhaps, is not why some BaMbuti hunt with nets and others with bows and arrows, but rather *how women decide whether to participate in hunts.*

Recall that many BaMbuti trade meat with Bantu horticulturalists for produce. Some women also work as laborers for horticulturalists, and they receive some of the produce as payment. Bailey and Aunger argued that women decide to hunt or to work in fields depending on which activity gives them the greatest return for their effort. Testing this hypothesis, Bailey and Aunger found that net hunters live near Bantu with *small* gardens whereas bow hunters live near Bantu with *large* gardens.

Where gardens are small, Bantu women do not need BaMbuti women as laborers and, because they cannot work for produce, BaMbuti women help with the hunting. Presumably, net hunting is a better way to utilize this extra labor. Where gardens are large, however, Bantu women need assistance. They hire BaMbuti women, who apparently make a greater return as workers than as hunters. Without the extra labor, men hunt individually, with bows and arrows.

The key to BaMbuti hunting technology, then, may depend in large measure on women's choices. This example demonstrates that options, decisions, and activities by men and women condition the larger patterns in material culture that archaeology excels in revealing.

Reconstructing Male and Female Activities from Archaeology

Archaeology was biased for decades for a couple of reasons. For one, the field was male-dominated. And also, archaeologists were simply unaware of how much their own culture affected the way they viewed prehistory. As scientists, they thought they could be objective in their research.

These attitudes have changed significantly in recent years. Half of all professional archaeologists in the United States today are women, and few modern archaeologists would blithely make such simplistic assumptions as atlatl = male or pottery = female. We are still trying to recognize the biases inherent in archaeological research and come to grips with the reality of understanding that what men and women did in the past isn't just a matter of political correctness—it affects our understanding of prehistory.

Some feminist archaeologists believe it is unnecessary to ascribe particular tasks to men or women in order to take a gendered perspective on prehistory. But others argue that we can't answer important anthropological questions unless we know, for a particular archaeological case, whether men or women used or made this or that artifact.

Is this possible? Can we reconstruct what men and women did in the past? If so, how?

These questions raise some difficult problems of middle-level theory. In Chapter 10, we explored one approach. Skeletal analysis can tell us something about the different mechanical stresses placed on men and women, but the cause of these stresses still requires some guesswork.

Stable isotope analysis can also point to differences in men's and women's diets. Following up Christine Hastorf's and Sissel Johannessen's research in the Upper Mantaro Valley (see Chapter 9), Michael DeNiro (University of California, Santa Barbara) analyzed the carbon and nitrogen isotopes of bone samples from human skeletons dating to the different phases. He found no significant differences between men and women during the Wanka II phase, during which men and women apparently ate much the same foods. But analysis of human remains from the Wanka III phase (after the Inka had expanded into the Mantaro Valley) showed that half of the men had a considerably higher maize intake. DeNiro suggests that men participated in rituals (where maize beer was consumed) more often. If so, then not only did men participate in the public sphere of life more than women, but some men participated more than other men.

But human skeletal evidence takes us only so far. What about everything else found in archaeological sites? How would we know if a man or a woman made or used a particular stone tool, pot, or basket? Because archaeologists lack an established method for objectively deriving this sort of information from material remains, most investigators are forced to rely on ethnographic analogy or historic documents, with their inherent limitations (see Chapter 8).

Were Pots Made by Men or Women? Ceramic technology provides a case in point. There are two basic ways to make a pot. In the first method the potter constructs the vessel by hand, either by molding the clay or by rolling it into a long "snake" and then coiling it up to build the pot's base and walls; the pot's walls are then smoothed by hand.

The other technique is to work a lump of clay onto a wheel that is rotated manually by the potter (and today by a powered device). The potter then uses the spinning clay's centrifugal force to shape it by hand. The method used on a given pot is relatively easy to determine from characteristics of potsherds.

Working from this simple baseline, Prudence Rice (Southern Illinois University) surveyed ethnographic data from a variety of societies around the world and discovered that when pottery is fashioned by hand, it is usually manufactured by women. In contrast, men usually manufacture pottery made on a wheel. Archaeologists can draw on this kind of strong analogy to infer past behavior with a high (but not absolute) degree of certainty: If archaeological evidence shows that pottery was made by hand, then we infer that the pottery was *probably* made by women. By contrast, if we find evidence that pottery was made on a wheel, then we say that the potter was *probably* male.

As we cautioned in Chapter 8, this sort of analogy can be made stronger if we can actually *explain* the inferred pattern; but in this case, this explanation is not easy. There is, of course, no inherent reason why women could not have used the wheel to produce

From Corpus of Maya Hieroglyphic Inscriptions, Vol. 3 Part I, Yaxchilan, 1977. Reproduced courtesy of the President and Fellows of Harvard College. Photo by Ian Graham.

Figure 11-4 Maya carving from the site of Yaxchilan, Lintel 1. The figure at the right carrying a textile bundle is identified as a woman by the clothing she is wearing (a *huipil*).

have more to say about the Maya in Chapter 13).

The Maya developed a remarkable art style and often depicted themselves on stone stelae, on polychrome (multi-colored) pottery, in paintings and carvings on lintels inside temples and tombs, and in books called **codices,** which were long strips of paper, many meters in length when unfolded, made of pounded inner tree bark. (The Spanish considered them heretical and destroyed all they could find; only four survive today.)

The images commonly depict Maya wearing intricate, complex costumes (Figure 11-4). To the Western eye, these costumes appear flamboyant, even outlandish. But to the Maya, ways of dressing encoded immense amounts of cultural information (this is true of us, too). These figures rarely have overt sexual characteristics, in large part because of the elaborate costuming. Women are sometimes identified with a particular glyph, but not always.

Because Maya epigraphers can read Maya hieroglyphs, we know much about what these images mean. And the images themselves tell us something about Maya sex roles. For example, women are often portrayed (especially on polychrome pottery) weaving, preparing maize for meals, and serving food to others. We can identify the women because Maya iconography displays women wearing one of three distinctive dress styles: a simple wrapped garment that covers the breasts, body, and legs, but leaves the arms bare; a woven *huipil*, a housecoat-like garment that covers the entire body; and, more rarely, a jade-bead skirt, often with a fish-monster-and-shell belt. Some interpret this last style as an impersonation of the male maize god, who is also depicted with such costuming.

Despite the lack of overt sexual characteristics, Joyce could use these clothing styles to identify women on the carved stelae. Women are seen holding and offering ceramic vessels, bundles of cloth, or paper and blood-letting instruments (the Maya believed that rulers had to sacrifice their blood, often by cutting their tongues, to communicate with the gods and renew

pottery (and, indeed, many female potters do so today). The uniformitarian assumption that we discussed in Chapter 8 fails in this case.

Perhaps the reason lies in the *purpose* of pottery made on the wheel versus that made by hand. Archaeologists know that the pottery wheel is associated with craft specialization and the marketing of pottery. Thus, it appears that when pottery moves from production for the residential group to production for the nonresidential group, the task shifts from women to men. *Why* this should happen, however, is much harder to say.

An alternative approach is to use an ethnographic analogy that is historically linked to the archaeological population being studied. Rosemary Joyce (University of California, Berkeley) used this approach to create some deeper understanding of Maya men and women.

Gender in Maya Iconography In previous chapters, we have mentioned the Maya civilization of southern Mexico and Central America (and we'll

codices Maya texts, long strips of paper, many meters in length when unfolded, made of the pounded inner bark of certain trees; these texts helped analysts interpret Maya hieroglyphs on stelae.

the world). The remaining figures, the male ones, often hold weapons, shields, or scepters that represent double-headed axes—the instruments of war.

Although one might interpret the women in the images simply as servants, Joyce wondered if there was a deeper interpretation, and so she turned to ethnographic data gleaned from the codices, early Spanish observations, and modern ethnography.

The Maya participate in what anthropologists call a **cargo system,** in which a responsible, married man is selected annually to direct the ceremonial system (today this system is a combination of Catholicism and the indigenous religion). This individual is responsible for holding a number of feasts that accompany rituals; his wife, who acts as his assistant, takes on the title "Mother of" the man's named position. Other elderly women are responsible for preparing food, tending to incense for purification ceremonies, and ensuring that everyone observes appropriate manners and protocol during the feasts. In this way, men and women occupy complementary roles in the important feasts of the cargo system.

Joyce argues that women depicted in the Classic Maya stelae may have occupied similar complementary, rather than subservient, roles. She points out that Maya ethnographers discuss the complementarity of men and women, and the need for rulers to "assert claims to represent in themselves the split and complementary totality that they would like to control." Joyce suggests that the pairing of male and female figures on stelae in culturally appropriate ways could symbolize a ruler's need to combine male and female elements to acquire and maintain political power. This not only could include a claim to male/female prerogatives and powers, but might also extend to the right of male rulers to claim the products of female labor, such as weaving.

Because interpretations like these are impossible without adequate ethnographic analogy, they are subject to both the potentials and the pitfalls of all such analogies (as discussed in Chapter 8). For example, other archaeologists might point out that the cargo system is a poor analogy for interpreting Maya stelae because many of the women shown on stelae are partners in marriages between royal families—marriages that created military alliances, as they did in Europe. Thus, the purpose of women in these images may be starkly different from that entailed in the cargo system.

One way to probe the strength of an analogy is to look for additional formal similarities between the analogy and the archaeological case, and there is at least one in this instance. Joyce found that women are often paired with men on stelae—sometimes on the "backs" of stelae (that is, the stelae's side that faces away from the largest public area), whereas male figures occupy the more public side. Sometimes, the women are depicted in a spatially lower position than their male counterparts.

Joyce points out that, when viewed from prominent vantage points in a ceremonial center, women depicted on the stelae are more frequently to the left of the male images. Ethnographic data show an association between Maya women and the left hand as well as lower elevations, whereas men are associated with the right hand and upper elevations. This ethnographic pattern may hold true for Maya stelae as well and, if it does, might strengthen the analogy.

Nonetheless, modern archaeologists still find it difficult to say much with certainty about gender roles in the past, let alone move beyond such relatively mundane activities to an understanding of gender ideology. Doing so may be limited to those instances in which a close, historically linked analogy is available.

ARCHAEOLOGY AND KINSHIP

Kinship refers to the socially recognized network of relationships through which individuals are related to one another by ties of descent (real or imagined) and marriage. A kinship system blends the facts of biological descent and relatedness with cultural rules that define some people as close kin, distant kin, or not kin at all. These groups matter because they condition, and sometimes dictate, the relationships between individuals.

Kinship may not seem very significant to you—not that you don't care about your family, but most of your daily interactions with people do not involve your kin. Instead, they are with friends, teachers, government representatives, bosses, subordinates, and so on. But in the nonindustrial world, most people interact on a daily basis with people who are kin. The same was true of much of the ancient world.

So, if you fail to understand a society's kinship, you might misread people's behavior. For example, a woman from the island of Pingelap in Micronesia once

---

cargo system Part of the social organization found in many Central American communities in which a wealthy individual is named to carry out and bear the cost of important religious ceremonies throughout the year.

kinship Socially recognized network of relationships through which individuals are related to one another by ties of descent (real or imagined) and marriage.

casually listed the members of her household to Kelly: "That child there is my son, and that girl is my daughter. The young woman over there is my sister and the man next to her is her husband. Of course, my father over there [pointing to a man splitting open coconuts] is my mother's brother." If her last statement brings images of incest to mind, we assure you that you are wrong, and understanding the kinship system shows why.

Forms of Kinship

The world of kinship is incredibly complex, but we can simplify matters by concentrating on three basic forms. The first of these, **bilateral descent,** should be familiar because it is the standard kinship of many industrialized nations. In bilateral descent, an individual traces his or her relatives *equally* on the mother's and father's sides. Although you might be closer to your mother's or father's side (because of geography, divorce, or personalities), neither side of the family is *a priori* more important than the other. Evidence of this is the fact that names applied to relatives on either side of the family are the same. Father's brother and mother's brother, for example, are both "uncles" (in English).

Kinship in cultures with bilateral descent tend to lack "depth"—meaning that few individuals know who their great- or great-great-grandparents are, much less their great-great-grandparents' siblings' offspring's offspring. This is because *in bilateral descent, the nuclear family is the important economic unit.*

The next two kinds of kinship systems are strikingly different from bilateral descent because they privilege one side of the family over the other. These *unilineal* descent systems are depicted in Figure 11-5. In this figure, the triangles stand for males and the circles for females. The equal sign (=) stands for marriage, the solid horizontal lines connect siblings, and the vertical lines indicate offspring. The square (indicating either sex) places you within the kinship diagram.

In **patrilineal descent,** the nuclear family may constitute the residential unit, but the most important group is the **patrilineage,** people to whom you are related *through the male line.* The top portion of Figure 11-5 portrays this system, with the shaded individu-

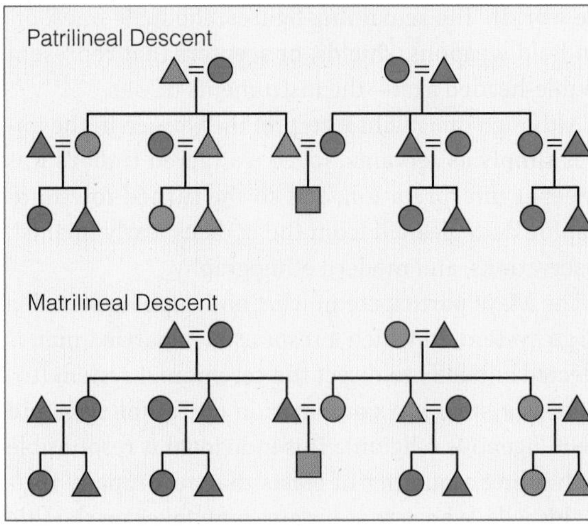

Figure 11-5 Patrilineal and matrilineal descent. The tan-colored circles (females) and triangles (males) show who belongs to one patrilineage (top) or matrilineage (bottom).

als belonging to "your" patrilineage. These are all the people who are biologically related to you through a male—your father and his siblings, your father's father and his siblings, your father's brothers' children, and your father's father's brothers' children; we could extend the same to your great-grandfather's and great-great-grandfather's generation, and so on. These individuals are members of one patrilineage.

In patrilineal descent, you acquire your patrilineage from your father. The other people in the diagram belong to other patrilineages (societies with unilineal descent commonly forbid marriage between men and women of the same lineage). So, your mother belongs to a different patrilineage than your father and, consequently, to a patrilineage other than yours.

Patrilineal societies make up about 60 percent of the world's known societies. They are associated with a wide range of conditions, including hunting-and-gathering, agricultural, and pastoral societies. They are also associated with internal warfare—that is, war with close neighbors.

Keep in mind that patrilineages contain both males and females—because anyone biologically linked to you through a male is a member of your lineage (such as your father's brother's daughters). Your father's sister is included, but not her offspring. And don't think that members of patrilineal societies are confused about matters of human reproduction. They understand the biological facts of life completely, and they do not ignore "kin" on their mother's side. But in patrilineal descent, your mother's side is simply less important. In contrast to bilateral descent, *in unilineal descent systems the lineage is the important economic unit.* The lineage, rather than the nuclear

bilateral descent A kinship system in which relatives are traced equally on both the mother's and father's side.

patrilineal descent A unilineal descent system in which ancestry is traced through the male line.

patrilineage Individuals who share a line of patrilineal descent.

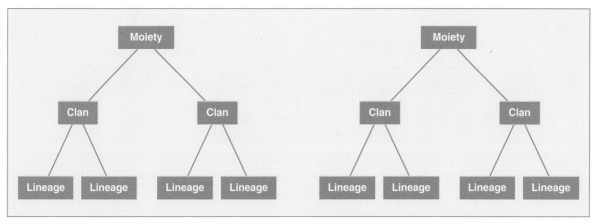

Figure 11-6 The relationships among lineages, clans, and moieties. (If moieties are present, there are two, and only two.)

family, owns or controls land and other resources. The lineage makes decisions about whether to move a village, go to war, or dig irrigation ditches. The nuclear family matters in unilineal descent systems, but it is secondary to the interests and concerns of the patrilineage.

This difference is reflected in kin terms. Men call their biological father by a term meaning "father," but they may also call their father's brother "father," and consequently, they may call their father's brother's offspring "brother" and "sister," rather than "cousins." In patrilineal descent, your mother's brother's children belong to another lineage (*their* father's lineage), so they are called by a term that we might translate as "cousin," but not "brother" or "sister." Your father's and mother's siblings are the same kind of relative in a bilateral descent system, but not in a unilineal descent system.

The bottom chart in Figure 11-5 contains the same biological facts as the top one, but they are now organized into **matrilineal descent.** Here, you trace relatives through the female line, forming **matrilineages.** In matrilineal societies, you get your lineage from your mother. Your lineage includes you, your mother, her siblings and her sisters' offspring, your mother's mother, her siblings and her sisters' offspring, and so on. As in patrilineal societies, nuclear families exist, but the primary unit is the matrilineage.

By now, you can probably guess why the Pingelapese woman said that her mother's brother was her father: In matrilineal societies, the mother's brother is a "fictive" father. The biological father, in fact, may have little to do with his biological offspring; instead, he spends his time with his sister's children. Because they are members of his lineage, it is they, not his biological offspring, who will inherit whatever resources, knowledge, or privileges he possesses.

Matrilineal societies are rare, composing only about 10 percent of the world's societies. They appear to be associated with horticulture, long-distance hunting, and warfare with distant enemies.

Finally, to complicate things even more, we must note that lineages are sometimes clustered into **clans,** a set of lineages that claim to share a distant, often mythical, ancestor (Figure 11-6). Clans, in turn, may be clustered into **moieties** (*moy*-i-tees; from the French word meaning "half"; in any society with moieties, there are only two). Moieties often perform reciprocal ceremonial obligations for each other, such as burying the dead of the other or holding feasts for one another. We come back to these terms later, but first we must consider the visibility of such abstract groupings in the archaeological record.

Do Descent Systems Appear Archaeologically?

To answer this question, let's return briefly to Madagascar's Mikea (discussed in Chapter 8), a patrilineal society that practices **patrilocal residence**—a cultural "rule," commonly associated with patrilineal descent,

matrilineal descent A unilineal descent system in which ancestry is traced through the female line.

matrilineage Individuals who share a line of matrilineal descent.

clans A group of matri- or patrilineages who see themselves as descended from a (sometimes mythical) common ancestor.

moieties Two groups of clans that perform reciprocal ceremonial obligations for one another; moieties often intermarry.

patrilocal residence A cultural practice in which a newly married couple live in the groom's village of origin; it is often associated with patrilineal descent.

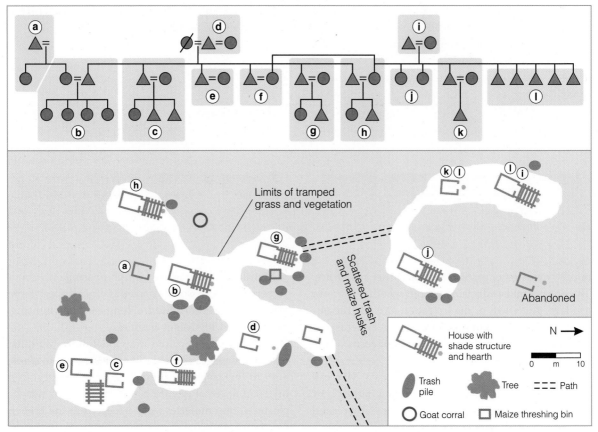

Figure 11-7 Mikea hamlet map with kinship chart. Notice how the patrilineages are linked by marriage, yet are separated on the ground.

in which a wife lives with her husband in his original village.

Recall that some Mikea live in forest hamlets of about 40 people. Figure 11-7 is a map of one Mikea hamlet, accompanied by the kinship chart of the families who lived there (a line drawn through a symbol indicates that the person is deceased). The diagram also indicates which families lived in which house. In some cases, young children (over the age of 10) and single, elderly individuals lived in small, separate houses.

This figure demonstrates several facets of Mikea hamlets. First, the houses are arranged in a linear, north-to-south scatter, their doors facing north. Second, the hamlet contains two clusters of houses, marked by trampled areas of vegetation, with an untrampled belt of vegetation and trash (mostly maize husks) between the two. A path (shown with dotted lines) connects the two clusters.

The kin diagram shows the presence of two patrilineages at this hamlet. On each side of the kin diagram is an older man and his wife, with their sons and their wives, and their unmarried children and grandchildren. Furthermore, these two patrilineages are linked

by virtue of several marriages between the sons of one of the elder couples and the daughters of the other.

This is typical of Mikea forest hamlets. Members of two patrilineages live together, somewhat united by marriage ties or a link through a woman. We say "somewhat" because there was always a palpable tension between these residential groups. For example, when Kelly gifted clothing to the hamlet depicted in the figure, one of the elder man's sons from the southern group insisted on taking charge of the distribution. And for the next two days, the northern group repeated accusations of stinginess and complained of an inappropriate distribution. Sharing (of tools and labor) occurred *within* each of these clusters, but was rarer *between* the two (see "Looking Closer: Did People Share Food at Pincevent?").

Finally, and most important, notice that the patrilineages map onto the ground: The northern cluster of houses contains men (and unmarried sisters) who belong to the same lineage, along with their wives and children. Likewise, the southern cluster contains brothers who belonged to another lineage, with their wives and offspring. The same social relationships mapped out in virtually every settlement we visited.

The difficulty, of course, is that archaeologically the Mikea hamlets appear simply as two clusters of houses. Although we might infer that each cluster represents a social grouping, we'd be hard pressed to say whether it was a patrilineage, a matrilineage, or some other grouping, such as a clan or moiety. As with gender, we might have to fall back on a strong ethnographic analogy. Let's explore how this course of action might work in archaeology.

Looking for Matrilineal Descent

Anthropologists Melvin Ember (1933–2009) and Carol Ember (Yale University, Human Relation Area Files) have devoted their careers to compiling and analyzing worldwide ethnographic data to discover underlying patterns and correlations. Some of these relate human social organization to material culture and are useful to archaeologists.

We noted previously that patrilineal societies may practice patrilocal residence. Likewise, matrilineal societies often practice **matrilocal residence,** in which the groom lives in the wife's village. The Embers found that people practicing patrilocal residence tend to live in houses less than 60 square meters in size. Mikea houses fall comfortably within this range. But the Embers found that houses in matrilocal societies are larger, generally more than 100 square meters in size. The reason for this difference appears to be that in patrilocal societies, the residential group is the nuclear family (as among the Mikea), but in matrilocal societies, clusters of sisters often inhabit one large house, dividing it into interior spaces for each nuclear family. Iroquois longhouses (in the northeastern United States) are one example. These houses were often enormous, with dividing walls separating the interior space into units, each occupied by a sister, her husband, and their unmarried children.

So, where is the uniformitarianism here? For these observations to serve as middle-level theory to reconstruct the past, we must explain *why* residential units differ between matrilocal and patrilocal societies. Anthropologists don't have a good answer to this question (yet). But recall that matrilineal societies are often associated with long-distance hunting or external warfare. Warfare with distant neighbors takes men away for long periods of time and, obviously, the men might not come back. The houses of matrilocal societies may reflect (and help create) bonds of assistance and cooperation between sisters while their husbands are away.

Can these observations help us infer kinship from archaeological remains?

Kinship at Chaco Canyon

To answer this question, we return to Chaco Canyon in northwest New Mexico. As you will recall from previous chapters, Chaco Canyon contains a number of large pueblos, or Great Houses, constructed between 1100 and 850 BP. The Great Houses were connected to one another and to a vast network of pueblos outside the canyon by the road system that we described in Chapter 3. But Chaco Canyon also contains many smaller pueblos—these first appear about 1300 BP (Figure 11-8)—and even older semi-subterranean pithouses.

Arguing from the Embers' cross-cultural patterns, Peter Peregrine (Lawrence University) suggests that Chacoan pueblo society practiced matrilocal residence. Why? The pithouses, the earliest of the Chaco dwellings, average about 15 square meters in size, placing them well below the ethnographic range of matrilocal

© Robert Kelly

Figure 11-8 A small pueblo in Chaco Canyon.

matrilocal residence A cultural practice in which a newly married couple live in the bride's village of origin; it is often associated with matrilineal descent.

LOOKING CLOSER

DID PEOPLE SHARE FOOD AT PINCEVENT?

In hunter-gatherer camps, large game is often shared, so the distribution of large animal bones in a site tells us something about social relationships. The remarkable French site of Pincevent provides an example.

Pincevent lies about 60 kilometers south of Paris, on the bank of the Seine. Here, hunter-gatherers some 12,000 years ago made their autumn camps, ambushing migrating reindeer as they crossed the river. The hunters took their kills back to camp, where they butchered, shared, and ate them.

Spring floods then gently covered each fall's midden with a thin layer of silt, preserving the spatial distribution of artifacts and faunal remains. The layers contain several hearths, each surrounded by an arc of flintknapping debris and reindeer bones, which represent different nuclear families. The distribution of reindeer bones points to how meat was shared among these families. How so?

When a butchered animal is shared, pieces of bone go along with the meat. Therefore, James Enloe (University of Iowa) and Francine David (Centre National de la Recherche Scientifique) refit broken bones from one of Pincevent's strata, IV-20, to reconstruct meat sharing. You refit bones by laying them out on a table and comparing each bone to the others to see which fragments fit back together, which joints articulate, or which are "bilateral matches" (the left and right limb bones of the same animal). If you have the patience of Job, it can be rewarding.

© James Enloe

Hearth O123 at Pincevent, with scattered flint chips and caribou bone.

The site map shows the mapped debris clusters, with each hearth numbered (for example, M89). The lines connect refits for the humeri and radiocubitus units (the radius-ulna) of several reindeer. The first thing Enloe and David learned was that at least two households shared each individual reindeer. Those hearths with no refits, such as R143 and G64, were either not occupied at the same time as the others or not included in the social network. Notice that the most refits for a hearth are with the next closest hearth; there is only one "long-distance" refit, between E74 and O123.

The upper leg is a meaty portion of a reindeer, and those elements circulate widely. Less meaty portions, such as metacarpals (bones of the forefeet) and the

houses. The early small pueblos are not isolated houses, but clusters of rooms that abut one another. Although individual rooms were small, collectively they covered from 70 to more than 300 square meters. Using the Embers' cross-cultural data, Peregrine suggests that these pueblos reflect matrilocal post marital residence. Instead of a single large house divided into interior subdivisions, Peregrine argues, the Chacoans built separate rooms, their side-by-side spatial arrangement reflecting a degree of social solidarity not seen in the earlier pithouse villages.

Not everyone agrees with Peregrine's inference, and contradictory data come from burials recovered from Pueblo Bonito in the early twentieth century. Recall that women remain in their own village under a matrilocal residential pattern, with men coming from other villages. This means that the women in such a village should be more genetically *similar* to one another than the men. Conversely, with patrilocal residence, the women should be genetically more *diverse* than the men.

In the last chapter, we discussed bioarchaeology. Bioarchaeologists can use skeletal data to track popu-

radiocubitus, remain closer to home. This makes sense: a hunter would insult a friend or relative by gifting a low-utility portion of an animal. But these facts point to some potential kinship relations. Enloe and David suggest that hearths with both meaty and not very meaty body parts were the homes of the hunters—Hearths M89, T112, and V105. These are also hearths with substantial scatters of stone tool debris, evidence of a lot of activity. But there are two smaller, less dense debris scatters, Hearths L115 and E74. Metacarpals refit between L115 and both T112 and V105, suggesting that Hearth L115 was occupied by children or an elderly relative of those living at T115 and V105.

Hearth E74 also had a small debris scatter, with few tools of poor quality. The limb bones here are mostly the radiocubitus, the less meaty portion of the forelimb. Enloe and David suggest that this hearth might be that of a grandparent of one or more of the hunters' households.

Placement of Pincevent hearths and the scatters of flint chips and bone around the hearths. The lines connect caribou humeri or radiocubitus bones that refit within and between the hearths.

lation movements. These data can include measurements (primarily of the cranium), but also some 200 nonmetric traits of the skull. Such traits include the presence or absence of foramina (holes where blood vessels pass through bone), which in certain places (for example, above the eye orbits) also provide clues to genetic affinity.

Michael Schillaci (University of Toronto) and Christopher Stojanowski (Arizona State University) analyzed the genetic traits of the Pueblo Bonito burial population specifically to determine postmarital resi-

dence patterns. Although the sample size was small, the female sample showed *greater* variation than did the male sample. Schillaci and Stojanowski suggested that, rather than matrilocal residence, the people of Pueblo Bonito practiced patrilocal or **bilocal residence** (where the married couple can choose to reside with

bilocal residence A cultural practice in which a newly married couple may live in either the village of the groom or the village of the bride.

either the husband's or the wife's family). Bilocal residence, in fact, was common at the time of European contact among the eastern Pueblos who live along the upper Rio Grande and who might be descended from the people of Chaco Canyon.

Like gender roles and ideology, kinship is an element of past social organizations that is difficult to reconstruct. But our increasing ability to use genetic data and markers coupled with strong ethnographic analogies and ethnoarchaeological studies should eventually allow us to draw some secure inferences from the archaeological record.

ARCHAEOLOGY AND SOCIAL STATUS

Status consists of the rights, duties, privileges, and powers that accrue to a recognized and named social position. In our own society, the status of "mother" is determined by both the duties she owes to her son or daughter and the responsibilities she can legitimately demand of her children. Similarly, a child owes certain obligations to a parent and can expect certain privileges in return. As you will see, gender and age play important roles in status.

Status can be assigned through *ascription* and *achievement*. An **ascribed status** is assigned to individuals at birth, without regard to innate differences or abilities. Britain's Prince Charles, for example, has high status and can expect to become king of England—not because of anything he has done, but simply because his mother is Queen Elizabeth II. His status and rights were ensured at birth.

Alternatively, many statuses are **achieved**; they require that an individual possess certain admirable qualities or have accomplished certain tasks (the importance of these qualities and tasks being culturally defined). Rather than being assigned at birth, achieved statuses are earned through individual effort. A Shoshone man who proved to be a good hunter might achieve status as a leader in hunts, but upon his death no one would automatically fill his former position.

Egalitarian Societies

The concept of status allows us to bridge from the level of the individual to that of the entire society. A society is termed **egalitarian** when there is no fixed number of positions of status; instead, the number of valued statuses is equal to the number of persons with the ability to fill them. No one individual wields complete authority over another. The important feature, then, is that *members of egalitarian societies generally have equal access to critical, life-sustaining resources.*

The social system of the nineteenth-century Great Basin Shoshone people was generally egalitarian. Anthropologists call such small-scale egalitarian societies **bands.** Authority was restricted to particular, short-term circumstances. A good hunter, for instance, might assume a temporary position of leadership when a group decided to hunt bighorn. An accomplished dancer might take charge of communal gatherings. Or the opinion of a gifted naturalist might convince others of the medicinal attributes of particular plants. But these individuals would have no authority outside their area of expertise. The key to leadership here is experience and social standing; such a social position is *not* inherited in an egalitarian society. Gender and age are the primary dimensions of status in egalitarian communities.

Ranked Societies

Ranked societies limit the positions of valued status so that not everyone of sufficient talent can actually achieve them. Such a social structure entails a hierarchy in which relatively permanent social stations are maintained, *with people having unequal access to life-sustaining resources.* Gender and age still play a role in the division of labor in ranked societies. But ranked societies tend to have economies that redistribute goods and services throughout the community, with those doing the redistributing keeping some portion for themselves. This creates one or more ranked

---

status The rights, duties, privileges, powers, liabilities, and immunities that accrue to a recognized and named social position.

ascribed status Rights, duties, and obligations that accrue to individuals by virtue of their parentage; ascribed status is inherited.

achieved status Rights, duties, and obligations that accrue to individuals by virtue of what they have accomplished in their life.

egalitarian societies Social systems that contain roughly as many valued positions as there are persons capable of filling them; in egalitarian societies, all people have nearly equal access to the critical resources needed to live.

band A residential group composed of a few nuclear families, but whose membership is neither permanent nor binding.

ranked societies Social systems in which a hierarchy of social status has been established, with a restricted number of valued positions available; in ranked societies, not everyone has the same access to the critical resources of life.

social tiers to the society. Many tribes of the American Northwest Coast (see Chapter 2) were ranked societies, as was Tahitian society (mentioned previously). Localized residential kin groups (such as a patrilineage) control resources, and economic goods flow in and out of a regional center.

Death and Social Status

The categories "egalitarian" and "ranked" define a social spectrum of statuses that can be inferred from analyses of material culture. Mortuary remains are one important source of information on extinct political systems. For the past three decades, archaeologists have used ethnographic data to show that *societies that have important social distinctions among living individuals also have material distinctions among the dead.*

Death, in a sense, is a period of separation and reintegration for both the deceased and those they leave behind. The deceased are separated from the living and must be properly integrated into the world of the dead. Social ties existed between the living and the once living, and the ceremonial connections at death reflect these social relations. Mortuary rituals reflect who people were and the relationships they had with others when they were alive. Therefore, they should reflect a person's social status.

Rank and Status at Moundville

We can examine the ranking of social status at Moundville, one of the best-known and most intensively investigated ceremonial centers in the United States. Sprawling across 300 acres, Moundville overlooks Alabama's Black Warrior River. Three thousand people once lived here, and for centuries Moundville was the largest center in the American Southeast (Figure 11-9).

This complex of about 30 earthen mounds was a bustling ritual center between about 950 and 550 BP. Like most **Mississippian** political units, this maize-based society engaged in extensive trade, and its skilled

The University of Alabama, Moundville Archaeological Park

Figure 11-9 Moundville (Alabama), looking south over Mound B; Mound A is in the center of the clearing.

artists worked in stone, ceramics, bone, and copper. Moundville contains 20 major ceremonial mounds—large flat-topped earthen structures designed to function both as artificial mountains (elevating elite residences and possibly temples above the landscape) and as mortuary areas. A stout bastioned palisade protected Moundville's large central plaza. This suggests that warfare was probably a recurring feature of life at Moundville (Figure 11-10).

Moundville was a major participant in the "Mississippian tradition," a term referring to the hundreds of societies that thrived from about 1200 to 500 BP throughout the southeastern United States. In their heyday, the Mississippian elite presided over breathtaking ceremonial centers (as at Moundville) that were invested with power by the thousands of people who lived in smaller nearby farmsteads.

C. B. Moore (who excavated at Indian Knoll) conducted archaeological investigations at Moundville in 1905 and 1906, digging into both platform mounds and village areas. The Alabama Museum of Natural History then excavated at Moundville from 1930 through 1941. More than a half-million square feet of the village areas at Moundville were uncovered during this 11-year period, in part by workers in the Civilian Conserva-

> **Mississippian** A widespread cultural tradition across much of the southeastern United States from 1200 to 500 BP. Mississippian societies engaged in intensive village-based maize horticulture and constructed large, earthen platform mounds that served as substructures for temples, residences, and council buildings.

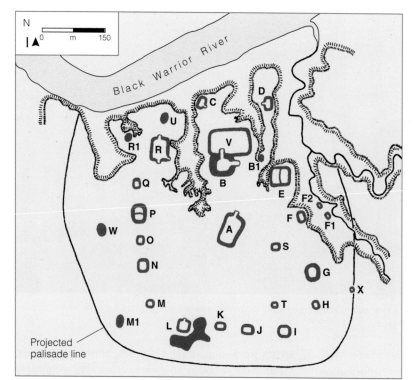

Figure 11-10 A map of the site of Moundville; the letters designate mounds mentioned in the text. *From Archaeology of the Moundville Chiefdom, edited by Vernon James Knight, Jr., and Vincas P. Steponaitis, published by the Smithsonian Institute Press, Washington, DC; copyright © 1998 by the Smithsonian Institution. Used by permission of the publisher.*

tion Corps. The more than 3000 excavated burials from Moundville provide a unique database for studying Mississippian social structure. (Sadly, many of the ceramic vessels recovered were stolen; see "Looking Closer: Help Find Moundville's Stolen Ceramics.")

The Symbolism of Grave Goods at Moundville Christopher Peebles (Indiana University) and Susan Kus (Rhodes College) took advantage of this database and analyzed Moundville's burials with an eye toward reconstructing Moundville's political organization. They began with the grave goods, many of which display the distinctive symbols characteristic of what archaeologists call the **Southeastern Ceremonial Complex.**

During the Mississippian period, artifacts that bore striking stylistic similarities appear in a number of sites and several large centers, including Moundville, across the southeastern United States from Oklahoma

Southeastern Ceremonial Complex An assortment of ceremonial objects that occurs in the graves of high-status Mississippian individuals. Ritual exchange of these artifacts crosscut the boundaries of many distinctive local cultures.

to Florida. These artifacts include conch shell gorgets and cups, copper plates, ceremonial axes and batons, effigy pipes, and flint knives—many decorated with one or more of a set of symbols, such as the "forked eye," the cross, the sun circle, the hand and eye, and the bi-lobed arrow (Figure 11-11). The distribution of these items parallels a trade network of exotic items, as well as basics such as food and salt. But the similarities in the motifs imply more than simple trade; a higher degree of social interaction was at work.

Whatever the Southeastern Ceremonial Complex really was—and archaeologists still debate it—it crosscut the boundaries of many widely separated residential groups. At each major site are artifacts that bear local symbols. At Moundville, these artifacts are specially constructed animal effigy vessels or parts of animals (such as canine teeth, claws, and shells). The local symbols probably functioned as status items within Moundville, whereas the ceremonial complex symbols designated the rank of individuals in the overall region.

Each burial mound at Moundville contained a few high-status adults, as indicated by their grave goods. These included copper axes, copper gorgets, stone disks, various paints, and assorted exotic minerals—such as galena (cubes of natural lead), mica (paper-thin sheets of translucent silicate minerals), and sheet copper. Copper and mica items often depict scalloped

© American Museum of Natural History

Figure 11-11 An image in the Southeastern Ceremonial Complex style, pounded in copper. Note particularly the forked eye motif around the eye, which probably represents a symbolic association with peregrine falcons, known for their keen vision and skill as hunters (from Spiro, Oklahoma).

LOOKING CLOSER

HELP FIND MOUNDVILLE'S STOLEN CERAMICS

Today, Moundville is a state archaeological park managed by the University of Alabama. It includes the Jones Archaeological Museum, which opened in 1939. The museum displays artifacts from the site, but not the 264 ceramic vessels and artifacts stolen from Moundville's archaeological repository in 1980. So far, the FBI has not recovered a single pot. These vessels were one-fifth of the Moundville collection—and some of the finest specimens. The thieves knew what they were looking for, and since the pots have not turned up on the art market, it's likely that the theft was carried out on behalf of a well-heeled and unscrupulous collector.

You could help recover these pieces of Native American heritage. The Moundville website (http://museums.ua.edu/oas/stolenartifacts) contains photos of all the stolen vessels. If you see any of these for sale on the web or at auctions, art houses, or flea markets, report it to the contacts listed on the website.

circles, swastikas, and the "hand-eye" motif (an open hand with an eye in the palm). Presumably, individuals buried with these artifacts had statuses and reputations recognized throughout the entire Moundville cultural system. Each mound also contained some presumably lower-status individuals who were buried with only a few ceramic vessels. Other commoners were buried in cemeteries away from the mounds with no burial goods (or, at least, none that preserved).

By correlating the presence of higher- and lower-status symbols, Peebles and Kus could infer that social status was ascribed at Moundville. Some infants and children—clearly too young to have accomplished anything noteworthy in life—were buried with lavish grave goods. These children must have been important because of who they were at birth, not because of what they had done in their short lives. This is clear evidence of a ranked society.

Two Axes of Social Patterning On the basis of ethnographic evidence, Peebles and Kus predicted that the Moundville population may have been subdivided along two major social axes, which they termed the superordinate and subordinate.

The subordinate division recognizes that certain symbols and the energy expended on mortuary ritual reflect the statuses of age and sex. With respect to age, the older the individual, the greater the opportunity for lifetime achievement, and hence the higher the deathbed rank could be. This means that at Moundville, adult burials should be more lavish than those of children, and children should be accompanied by more grave goods than infants. And because the subordinate division is also graded by gender, men and women should not be expected to have equivalent grave goods.

The superordinate division at Moundville is a partially hereditary ordering based on criteria other than age and sex. Among the elite—people whose status was assigned at birth—some individuals will be infants, some children, and the rest adults.

Peebles and Kus predicted that the statuses should form a pyramid-shaped distribution. At the base of the pyramid are the commoners, whose statuses are determined strictly by sex and age. The next step up the social ladder, the next rank, consists of those fewer individuals with ascribed status. Finally, at the top will be the paramount individuals, those who enjoy all the emblems of status and rank available in the society.

Quantitative Distribution of Moundville Grave Goods This model was tested by performing a statistical analysis of the grave goods of 2053 of the best-documented burials from Moundville. This analysis uncovered three distinct clusters and subclusters, represented by burials that contained similar kinds of grave goods (diagrammed in Figure 11-12). The seven burials of Cluster IA—the supreme division—are presumably chiefs, those individuals enjoying the highest of statuses and the ultimate political authority. All males, the elite were buried in Mounds C and

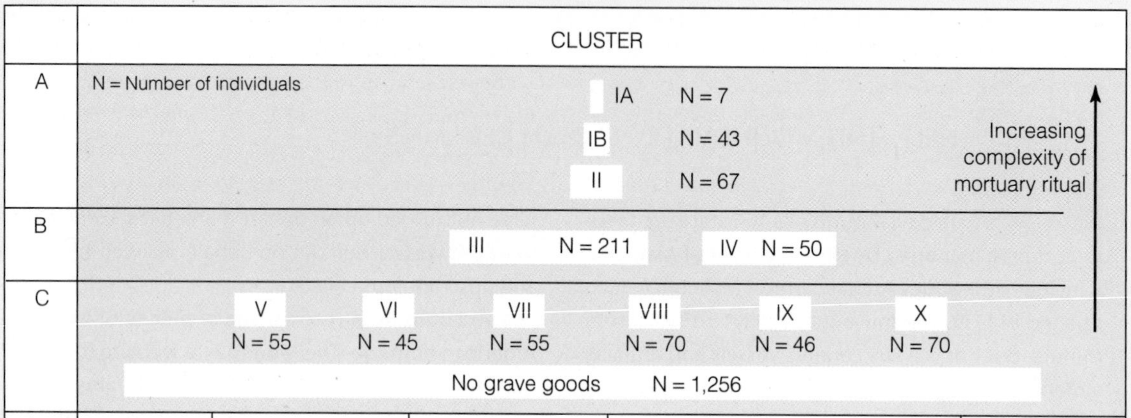

CLUSTER

Segment				
A	N = Number of individuals	IA N = 7	IB N = 43	II N = 67
				Increasing complexity of mortuary ritual
B		III N = 211	IV N = 50	
C	V N = 55	VI N = 45	VII N = 55	VIII N = 70 IX N = 46 X N = 70
	No grave goods N = 1,256			

Segment	Cluster	Characteristic	Artifacts	Burial context	Age (Infant Child % Adult)
A	IA	Copper axes		Central mound	
	IB	Copper earspools, Stone disks	Bear teeth, Red or white paint	Mounds and cemeteries near mounds	
	II	Shell beads, Oblong copper gorgets	Galena	Mounds and cemeteries near mounds	
B	III	Effigy vessels, Animal bone	Shell gorgets, Freshwater shells	Cemeteries near mounds	
	IV	Discoidals, Bone awls	Projectile points	Cemeteries near mounds	
C	V VIII	Bowls and/or jars		Cemeteries near mounds and in village areas	
	VI VII IX	Water bottles		Cemeteries near mounds and in village areas	
	X	Sherds		Village areas	
	No grave goods			"Retainers in mounds", Isolated skulls with public buildings, Cemeteries near mounds and in village areas	

Figure 11-12 The hierarchical social clusters represented in burials at Moundville. *After Peebles and Kus 1977, Figure 3.*

D, small mortuary mounds in a secluded area to the north of the plaza, and they were accompanied by a lavish array of material culture, including numerous ceremonial complex–adorned artifacts. Infants and human skulls (of individuals presumably sacrificed for the occasion) were buried as part of the Cluster IA ritual. Distinctive artifacts in these graves were large axes of copper—a metal too soft to have allowed the implements to function as chopping tools. These, then, must have served primarily as symbols, a culturally meaningful way to communicate an individual's high status and a visual reminder of the reasons for differences in people's ranks.

Cluster IB burials, both children and adult males, were interred in the mounds surrounding the plaza and in cemeteries near mounds. They also had a number of ceremonial complex artifacts plus mineral-based paints included in their grave goods. Cluster II, the final cluster of the superordinate division, included adults and children buried in cemeteries near the mounds and beneath what were charnel houses near the main plaza; their grave goods included chest beads, copper gorgets, and galena cubes.

Hierarchically below the Level A elite are those of subordinate Levels B and C (who enjoyed status largely on the basis of sex and age differences). In Cluster III, for instance, stone ceremonial axes are found only with adult males, whereas infants and children have "toy" vessels, clay "playthings," and unworked freshwater shells. Unworked bird claws and deer and turtle bones were found only with adults. The individuals in the lowest segment, Level C, were mostly buried away from the mounds and major ceremonial areas at Moundville. But some of the burials in this cluster were individuals buried as retainers and isolated skulls placed at the bases of large posts.

Burial context appears to clarify the nature of ranking in the Moundville society. The most elite were buried in a sacred area and accompanied by symbols of their exalted status. The Moundville elite also apparently lived in larger, more complex dwellings than did the commoners. Elite membership was conditioned by genealogy and, because social position was inherited within the elite, even children occupied such social positions.

Farther down the ladder, the villagers' graves also reflected their social status in life at this level, positions conditioned largely by sex and age distinctions rather than by inheritance. Their less glamorous grave goods were distributed in a different way. Graves contained pottery vessels, bone awls, flint projectile points, and stone pipes, all of which were distributed mostly to older adults. Peebles and Kus infer that these individuals were required to achieve—rather than inherit—their social status. More than half of the Moundville graves contained commoners buried with no grave goods at all.

Peebles and Kus suggested that Moundville conformed to a chiefdom model, a society similar to that of Tahiti and characterized by a status framework with few valued positions, although they saw no direct evidence for a redistributive economy.

How Well Did the Elite Eat? Similar forms of social organization have been recognized at other Mississippian sites in Tennessee, Georgia, Oklahoma, and the lower Illinois Valley. In all cases, burial populations served as the source of inference. The burial goods reflect some clear status differences between men and women and among classes. Some individuals clearly had different access to exotic goods. Did this difference also extend to some of the more basic necessities of life? For example, did the elite eat better than the commoners?

If the elite were better off than commoners, then we would expect that they had more nutritious diets, which might include eating more meat. In fact, through a faunal analysis of the trash associated with elite residences on Mounds G and Q (on opposite sides of the plaza, as shown in Figure 11-10), Ed Jackson and Susan Scott (University of Southern Mississippi) found evidence of many animals, including deer, turkey, bobcat, cougar, fox, bear, and falcon. The faunal remains indicated that those living on the top of the mounds ate the choicest cuts of meat from a wide variety of game—including imported items, such as bison and shark. The elite did indeed have access to resources that the commoners did not.

Bone chemistry, as you now know, can also tell us something about what people ate at Moundville. Margaret Schoeninger, the analyst who examined the Stillwater skeletal remains, also studied a sample of male and female remains from both low- and high-status burials. Her analysis suggested that there was little difference in the amount of maize and fish that people ate, but that men ate more meat than women, and that high-status men ate more meat than low-status men. These differences did fit the predictions, but they were not large and, although high-status men may have eaten the most meat, it does not seem that women and low-status men ate inadequate amounts.

Did these differences in diet create significant differences in the quality of life? Mary Lucas Powell (University of Kentucky) hypothesized that if the elites limited commoners' access to critical resources, then the elite should be taller, live longer, and show less evidence of caries, growth arrest features, iron deficiency (such as cribra orbitalia—see Chapter 10), infectious disease, and trauma than commoners.

In a nutshell, Powell could find no significant differences between the elite and the commoners. It appears that although differences in social status allowed the Moundville elite to live well, the commoners did not lead lives of want. However, both of these analyses are hampered by the fact that some of the highest-status burials were excavated by Moore in the early twentieth century. We have his notes and the grave goods, but Moore did not save the human skeletal remains, so the highest stratum of the Moundville hierarchy is not available for biological study.

Kinship at Moundville

Despite the differences in rank, Moundville was still an integrated society. And it may have been bonds of kinship that provided the integrating factor and that prevented extreme differences between the elite and the commoners. Indeed, although chiefdoms are internally ranked, their members commonly understand that everyone is ultimately, albeit sometimes distantly, a relative of the chief, who may even use kinship terms to refer to his followers.

To help reconstruct Moundville's social organization, James Knight (University of Alabama) employed an ethnographic analogy with the nineteenth-century Chickasaw, the Native Americans who lived in the vicinity of Moundville at the time of European contact. Knight noted that there are two major classes of mounds at Moundville. Some of the mounds contain burials; others were residential mounds, with evidence for wattle-and-daub or thatch structures on their flat tops. These mounds alternate around the square plaza so that each residential mound is paired with one and sometimes two burial mounds, forming eight burial/residential mound groups. Knight saw in this pattern a parallel to Chickasaw society.

The ethnographic data are limited, and Chickasaw society had undergone profound changes because of European contact, but Knight found that the ideal Chickasaw village had sets of houses arranged around a square plaza, just as the mounds at Moundville form a square plaza. In Chickasaw society, each set of houses belonged to a matrilocal clan that was the political and land-owning unit. In addition, the clans were grouped into moieties, which lived on opposite sides of the square village layout. The highest ranking clan of each moiety was located on opposite sides of the north end of the square plan, with lower ranking clans to the south. Thus, Chickasaw villages spatially mirrored the kinship structure (just as we saw with Mikea hamlets).

Knight wondered if this kinship pattern extended back to the inhabitants of Moundville. Perhaps, he suggested, each of the eight residential/burial mound units represents the high-ranking home of the leader of eight clans. Knight pointed out that the Moundville plaza can be neatly bifurcated by a line passing through Mound B at the north end of the plaza, through the central Mound A, and then between smaller burial mounds K and J (refer to Figure 11-10). Extrapolating from the Chickasaw analogy, the resulting halves might represent two moieties, each comprising four clans. Note also that the most elite burials were recovered in Mounds C and D; although these are not the largest mounds, they are located at either side of the north edge of the plaza.

But Moundville and Chickasaw villages exhibit crucial differences:

▶ In the Chickasaw camp layout, a large fire hearth in the center of the village structurally and symbolically united the two moieties. There was, however, no central mound or ceremonial structure.

▶ Nineteenth-century Chickasaw society was not a chiefdom and did not possess a central individual who was the uniting focus of the social and political organization. In Moundville, the large Mound B, at the north end of the site, might have been the home of the chief—the highest ranking individual—and

evidence of a tier in the social organization that was not present among the Chickasaw.

In sum, Knight's analysis of Moundville's layout, along with bioarchaeological and faunal analyses, supports a conclusion that Moundville was a chiefdom.

TRADE AND POLITICAL ORGANIZATION

In this discussion of Moundville, we mentioned the Southeastern Ceremonial Complex, a social phenomenon that included an extensive trade network. All societies—from egalitarian bands to chiefdoms to modern states—exchange goods, ideas, and services. The geographic scale of trade tells us something about the nature of the nonresidential group that a residential group was part of, and about how far-flung were their political, economic, and kinship connections.

In archaeological sites in the Great Basin, for example, archaeologists frequently find beads made of the shells of *Olivella*, *Haliotis*, and *Dentalia*—marine organisms that live along the coasts of California and Oregon. Obviously, they point to some sort of interaction between people on either side of California's Sierra Nevada.

These shell beads are not numerous in Great Basin sites. They appear as personal ornaments in some burials, but they are not exclusively associated with men or women, the old or the young. Many are found in residential sites where, because they are small, they were probably lost as they fell off clothing or a necklace. It is more difficult to say if the beads indicate exchange of goods between the peoples of the Great Basin and California or were simply the personal belongings of people (wives or husbands? emigrants?) who moved from California to the Great Basin.

Anthropologists have found that as societies change from egalitarian bands (like the Great Basin Shoshone) to ranked societies (such as those of Tahiti or Moundville), the formal trade of **exotics** becomes an integral part of the economy. Exotics are artifacts made of raw material or in a style that indicates contact with the people of a distant region. Members of the elite trade or give away exotics at competitive feasts (such as the potlatch; see Chapter 2) as a way to communicate and maintain the social order. Exotic artifacts, therefore, are symbols of status and prestige—visual reminders of a person's social, political, or religious connections to a larger world. As such, they are signs of power and, consequently, of social and political organization as well.

exotics Material culture that was not produced locally and/or whose raw material is not found locally.

LOOKING CLOSER

TRACING CHACO'S MAIZE

We've mentioned Chaco Canyon in several places in this text (e.g., Chapter 4). Recall that this canyon contains several massive pueblos—some four stories high with several hundred rooms. Obviously, many people lived in the canyon. Yet the land and climate there are poorly suited for agriculture. How did all those people get enough to eat?

Archaeologists have long suspected that food was carried to the canyon. Using strontium analyses, Linda Cordell (School of Advanced Research) has found evidence of such food transport. By comparing the $^{87}Sr/^{86}Sr$ ratio (recall that this measure was used to show the presence of African slaves in the New World; see Chapter 10) of maize samples found in Chaco Canyon's large pueblos to that of sediment samples from Chaco Canyon and several large outlying pueblos, Cordell demonstrated that some maize found in Chaco was not grown there, but was raised in fields near large pueblos located 80 to 90 kilometers away. Whether this maize was brought to Chaco as a form of taxes, tribute, or gifts is unknown, but, along with the roads (Chapter 3), it suggests that Chaco Canyon was the center of a significant social and political entity, especially about 1000 to 900 BP.

Tracing Exotics

Archaeologists have several methods to determine which objects are locally produced and which are nonlocal. In some cases, it is fairly easy to determine which objects are *not* locally produced or acquired. Recall that at Moundville, for example, some of the elite burials contained copper axes. This copper is not smelted; smelting technology did not exist in North America prior to European contact. Instead, the copper was extracted in its raw form. We know that this kind of copper deposit, called "native copper," is not found around Moundville. In fact, native copper occurs only in the southern Appalachian Mountains and near the Great Lakes. The copper artifacts at Moundville have been traced to a geological deposit in the southern Appalachian source. Likewise, the galena cubes have been traced to geological sources in Missouri and Wisconsin.

Human societies create many different kinds of trade systems, but they tend to be of two major types. The first is **direct acquisition;** as you might guess, this means that you go to the natural source of a raw material and extract the material yourself, exchange goods or services for it or for a finished artifact, or receive an artifact or raw material as a gift. Direct acquisition might entail a special trip, or it may be embedded in a foraging excursion or a visit to relatives.

The second major type is **down-the-line trade,** in which people acquire a particular raw material or an artifact fashioned from that raw material from their neighbors, who have immediate access to the raw material. These people then trade it to others who live still farther away from the source, who may in turn trade it to people living still farther away. Down-the-line trade usually results in a steady decline in the frequency of artifacts made of a particular material in sites farther and farther away from the raw material's source. Occasionally, an unexpectedly high density of the raw material at a site distant from the source may signal that the site is a secondary trading center. Down-the-line trade can move raw materials long distances. For example, archaeologists have found incised Gulf Coast shells in sites along the Missouri River in Montana.

Nobody knows how the copper axes made their way to Moundville—perhaps they were gifts sent between ranking elites—but they clearly signal that only a few people had the authority and power to acquire them or to merit receiving them. Although the copper axes had no material function—they would have made poor cutting implements—they were powerful symbols of the "connections" an elite individual had and

direct acquisition A form of trade in which a person/group goes to the source area of an item to procure the raw material directly or to trade for it or for finished products.

down-the-line trade An exchange system in which goods are traded outward from a source area from group to group, resulting in a steady decline in the item's abundance in archaeological sites farther from the source.

perhaps of his ability to draw upon social, economic, military, or religious sanctions should anyone contest his hold on power.

We mentioned that archaeologists traced the copper axes at Moundville to geological sources in the southern Appalachian Mountains. We do such tracing by "fingerprinting" an object and comparing it to similar fingerprints of known sources of the raw material. Several different methods can accomplish this (see "Looking Closer: Tracing Chaco's Maize"). We'll focus here on three such methods—one used to trace obsidian and two used to trace ceramics to their sources.

Fingerprinting Obsidian Obsidian—the volcanic glass that makes such impressively sharp implements—occurs naturally in many geologic deposits of the western United States. So, why do obsidian artifacts appear in **Hopewell** burial mounds and sites in Ohio and Illinois?

Recall from Chapter 2 that Squier and Davis mapped and studied the earthworks of the eastern United States, especially along the Ohio River Valley and its tributaries. We now know that some of the flat-topped pyramid mounds—such as those at Moundville—belong to the Mississippian period. But other mounds—including geometric earthworks and some effigy mounds—are earlier, belonging to the Hopewell culture. "Hopewell" refers to a particular archaeological culture of the American Midwest, especially the Ohio River Valley, between 2200 and 1600 BP. Hopewell peoples were predominately hunter-gatherers, although they also cultivated indigenous plants and small amounts of maize. They lived in small, sedentary villages.

Hopewell culture is known for its elaborate mortuary rituals, which suggest the beginnings of a ranked society. Many goods appear in elite Hopewell graves, including copper ornaments, incised pottery, carved mica, ceramics, and obsidian. The fact that obsidian is found almost exclusively in burials of Ohio Hopewell sites, rather than in middens, suggests that obsidian played something other than a purely functional role in Hopewell society.

Hopewell A cultural tradition found primarily in the Ohio River Valley and its tributaries, dating from 2200 to 1600 BP. Hopewell societies engaged in hunting and gathering and in some horticulture of indigenous plants. They are known for their mortuary rituals, which included charnel houses and burial mounds; some central tombs contained exotics. They also constructed geometric earthworks as ceremonial enclosures and effigy mounds.

energy dispersive x-ray fluorescence (XRF) An analytical technique that uses obsidian's trace elements to "fingerprint" an artifact and trace it to its geologic source.

Squier and Davis recorded small numbers of obsidian spear points in five Hopewell mounds, and more have since turned up in Tennessee, Illinois, and elsewhere. At the time, Squier and Davis thought that the obsidian probably came from Mexico or perhaps the American Southwest. But this was simply a guess. By the mid-twentieth century, several archaeologists proposed the Rocky Mountains as the source—specifically the obsidian outcrops in Yellowstone National Park, 2400 kilometers away. Richard Hughes (Geochemical Research Laboratory, California)—one of the world's leading authorities on obsidian sourcing—tested this hypothesis using **energy dispersive x-ray fluorescence (XRF)**.

How can XRF trace obsidian artifacts to their geologic source? Many geological deposits form slowly—over years, decades, thousands, or even tens of thousands of years. But obsidian deposits are produced during a single lava flow, and hence they are created in a geologic instant. A volcano could produce multiple flows, but because each flow forms quickly, it usually has a unique chemical "fingerprint." This fingerprint appears as particular quantities of trace elements, such as zinc, rubidium, strontium, and barium. Different flows contain different amounts of these elements. If we can fingerprint samples from all geologic sources of obsidian—a formidable but not impossible task—and then fingerprint obsidian artifacts, we should be able to match up an artifact with its source.

XRF accomplishes this goal. The analyst shoots an x-ray beam onto a piece of obsidian, causing the electrons to become excited and emit fluorescent x-ray energies. Because different trace elements emit different levels of energy, the analyst can measure the spectra of energy emitted from the piece of obsidian and determine the proportion of each trace element present—defining the sample's distinctive trace element fingerprint. Comparing the sample's trace element composition statistically with all known sources allows the analyst to find the best match and, presumably, the geologic source of an artifact. XRF is a very useful technique because it is nondestructive, works well on very small samples (down to 1 millimeter in diameter), takes only minutes to complete, and is relatively inexpensive.

Hughes's analysis confirmed that most Hopewell obsidian came from Obsidian Cliff in Yellowstone National Park. But he also discovered that some obsidian, especially that found in Illinois and Indiana Hopewell sites, came from Bear Gulch, in southeast Idaho.

We now know that obsidian from the Yellowstone region appears in small quantities at other Hopewell-age sites in Wisconsin, Iowa, Illinois, and Indiana. Instead of direct acquisition, high-ranking Hopewell individuals probably acquired obsidian through down-the-line trade—the stones' shiny black surfaces serving to remind people not of vacations to Yellowstone, but of the social ties some individuals had to high-ranking persons in other Hopewell communities.

Fingerprinting Ceramics To understand how archaeologists can fingerprint ceramics and trace them to their point of origin, we must first expand upon our earlier discussion of pottery manufacture.

© Robert Kelly

Figure 11-13 A Micronesian atoll.

The first step in making a pot, of course, is to acquire the clay. Clays occur as geologic deposits, usually water-laid, and different sources have different grain sizes and mineral composition. The mineral composition of the clay determines to some extent the kind of pottery that you can make from it. Potters use clay that is nearly pure kaolinite, for example, to manufacture fine porcelains.

After it is acquired, the clay is dried and pounded to remove any impurities. The potter then mixes in water and kneads the mixture to remove air bubbles. Clay's most important characteristic is that it is plastic; it can be modeled into shape. But as clay dries, it shrinks and then, when fired, it expands. Both processes can potentially crack the vessel.

Thousands of years ago, potters found that these problems could be alleviated by adding **temper** to the clay. Temper can be one of many kinds of materials: plant fiber, seed chaff, ash, ground-up shell or rock, sand, or even ground-up bits of old broken pots (sometimes called *grog*). The temper acts to hold the clay in place, gives the vessel strength, and prevents excessive shrinkage or expansion. After the temper is added, the potter shapes the pot and then fires it in an oven or an open-air fire, at temperatures in excess of 1000° centigrade if possible.

If we could characterize the mineral composition of clays and tempers (if sand or crushed rock was used) for both pots and likely geologic sources—as XRF does for obsidian artifacts and geologic sources—then we could fingerprint a pot and trace its geologic origins. Archaeologists do this with several techniques, including **instrumental neutron activation analysis**

(INAA). Minerals in the clay and in the pot's temper can also be identified through **petrographic analysis** (explained in the following).

Archaeologists have used these techniques to determine the sources of pottery in many different places in the world. We draw upon a case from the islands in Micronesia to show how this is done.

Tracing Pottery in Micronesia Micronesia comprises some 2500 islands in the western Pacific. Some of these are "high" islands—the tops of extinct, partially subsided volcanoes. These islands can reach elevations of several hundred feet and are primarily made of basalt and related volcanic stone. The others are "low" islands—atolls that form as coral grows up around the rim of an extinct, submerged volcano (Figure 11-13). As the coral breaks the surface of the sea, it catches sand, which eventually allows plant life to take hold. The habitable portions of some atolls are only a quarter-mile long and 200 yards wide. People first inhabited Micronesia's high islands and atolls at least 2000 years ago.

temper Material added to clay to give a ceramic item strength.

instrumental neutron activation analysis (INAA) An analytical technique that determines the trace element composition of the clay used to make a pot to identify the clay's geologic source.

petrographic analysis An analytical technique that identifies the mineral composition of a pot's temper and clay through microscopic observation of thin sections.

None of these islands is very large. Although Micronesia's islands are spread over an oceanscape the size of the continental United States, the total landmass of the islands is about the size of the state of Rhode Island. But Micronesians were expert mariners who used detailed knowledge of the wind, sun, currents, waves, swells, birds, and fish to sail across hundreds of miles of open ocean in outrigger canoes. Consequently, a lively trade existed between many of the islands, especially between high islands and atolls. On some of the high islands, such as Pohnpei, Kosrae, Guam, and Yap, were ceremonial centers and residences of the elite (see this chapter's opening photo)—the centers of chiefdoms that included not only the high island itself, but outlying atolls as well. These centers controlled the exchange of various goods, including pottery.

The high islands have sources of clay suitable for pottery; atolls, being only coral and sand, do not. Because pottery is found in archaeological sites on the atolls, it must have been imported from one of the high islands. If we knew which ones, then we could reconstruct Micronesia's trade networks.

Micronesians fashioned their pottery by hand, and they used shell, sand, and (more rarely) grog temper. Because the high islands formed through separate geologic events, the bedrock geology of each is unique. Given that the clays and some of the sands are derived from the bedrock, their mineral compositions should also be unique to each high island. This can be tested through petrographic analysis of the temper and neutron activation analysis of the clays.

The first step is to show that each high island's sands and clays are indeed unique. If they are, then a fingerprint of the clay and temper of an atoll's pottery should indicate on which high island that atoll's pottery was made. If the clays of two or more islands are the same, however, then it won't be possible to assign an atoll's pottery to one particular high island.

To conduct petrographic analysis, you cut a thin section of the pottery and grind it to about 30 microns in thickness so that the minerals are translucent. This section is mounted on a slide, and the various minerals identified beneath a polarizing microscope at 25–400×. To make source identifications, the analyst must also take samples of the temper and identify its mineral composition. Sometimes a temper is distinguished by the presence or absence of key minerals, but normally the fingerprint consists of a particular combination of a standard range of minerals (feldspars, hornblendes, and so on) and different kinds of sand (for example, calcareous beach or volcanic sands).

William Dickinson (University of Arizona) studied the sand tempers of several of the high islands as well as the temper found in pottery on several atolls, including Ulithi and Fais, located near the high island of Yap. Dickinson discovered that the sand tempers of different high islands have different mineral compositions. Comparing the tempers of ceramics on various high islands with those recovered from potsherds of Ulithi, Fais, and other atolls, Dickinson found that the ceramics on the atolls were all made using temper from the high island of Yap. Although it's possible that the temper was imported, the lack of clays on atolls suggests that people on Yap most likely made the pottery and traded it to those folks living on the atolls.

Christophe Descantes (University of California, Berkeley), Hector Neff (California State University, Long Beach), and Michael Glascock (University of Missouri) followed up on Dickinson's analysis by using INAA to study sherds from several high islands and atolls. Neutron activation analysis identifies a sherd's trace elements, those in the temper and the clay combined, by bombarding a potsherd with neutrons generated by a nuclear reactor. This produces radioactive isotopes of the elements. These isotopes immediately begin to decay (some have *very* short half-lives) and emit gamma radiation of different energy levels. By measuring the spectrum of gamma radiation, an analyst can identify the concentrations of 30 or more isotopes. This provides the trace element fingerprint of a sherd. (This technique is destructive, and it leaves the tested sherd radioactive. But where people made ceramics, potsherds are usually abundant and the archaeologist can afford to sacrifice some.)

Although the high islands have different geologic histories, it is possible that two widely separate islands could produce similar clays and tempers. But a statistical analysis of the trace element compositions of the various islands' sherds showed that most of the high islands—Yap, Palau, Chuuk, Kosrae, and Pohnpei—can be distinguished from one another.

The archaeologists then used INAA to analyze sherds from the atolls of Fais, Satawal, and Ulithi. What did they find out? In a nutshell, the trace element compositions of sherds from the atolls were all similar to pottery from Yap; none was similar to pottery of Palau, Chuuk, Kosrae, or Pohnpei. In other words, they reached the same conclusion that Dickinson had reached based on analysis of the sherds' tempers alone.

What do these analyses tell us about the relationship between the high island of Yap and the surrounding atolls?

Around 600 BP, Yap had extended its influence and political control to many outer atolls, as well as to Palau. A system of ranking on Yap was mediated in part by *rai*, large perforated limestone disks. Many of these are less than a meter in diameter but, during the early nineteenth century, some *rai* were quite large, up to 2 meters in diameter (Figure 11-14). These were transferred as part of competitive feasts similar to those held on the American Northwest Coast (see Chapter 2; *rai* are sometimes referred to as "stone money," but they are not directly comparable to currency). Interestingly, these stone disks were not produced on Yap, but were imported from Palau, some 245 kilometers to the southwest.

Yap also obtained exotic goods through a trade network, called *sawei*, between Yap and its outlying atolls (Ulithi is fairly close to Yap, but Satawal lies hundreds of miles to the east). This exchange system helped maintain a political organization that included Yap, Palau, and several atolls. The smaller atolls sent woven fiber mats, *sennit* (coconut fiber rope), and shell valu-

ables to Ulithi, which then sent the goods to Yap. In return, Yap sent taro, yams, sweet potatoes, and bananas to Ulithi, where they were distributed to the smaller atolls. Yap also sent timber for building the ocean-going canoes necessary for this trade to continue.

Some describe this exchange network as a tribute system, but specialists disagree over the inequality of the trade. Indeed, if an atoll expressed reservations about sending goods to Yap, Yapese sorcerers would threaten to bring typhoons down upon it (a considerable threat to an island whose highest point is only a few feet above sea level). But such threats were probably not necessary because the atolls seem to have received more material support from Yap than vice versa. And they could seek refuge on Yap should a storm or drought strike their atoll. The petrographic and INAA analyses of the ceramics confirm that the *sawei* system is ancient, and it both reflects and helped construct a political system that linked Yap to outlying atolls. These methods are used in many places in the world to reconstruct the spatial extent of political alliances and how they changed over time.

Figure 11-14 *Rai* displayed before a ceremonial structure on the island of Yap in Micronesia.

Conclusion

In reconstructing social and political organizations, archaeologists remember that artifacts were not just utilitarian items, but also carried symbolic meanings—meanings that could be manipulated and that played a role in how those artifacts eventually ended up in an archaeological context. Sometimes these symbolic meanings reflect elements of social and political organization—such as gender roles, kinship systems, trade networks, and political connections. However, it's hard to construct middle-level theory that allows us to infer social and political organization from archaeological remains, and it may forever require well-supported ethnographic analogy. However, new techniques—analysis of physical and chemical properties of artifacts and the use of genetic markers in human skeletal remains—give archaeology ways to test various hypotheses and continue to improve its reconstruction of the past.

In the next chapter, we go into an even more difficult area of archaeology: the analysis of symbols, concepts, and abstract thought. As you will see, reconstructing social and political organization is a walk in the park compared with trying to draw inferences from prehistoric expressions of symbolic thought.

SUMMARY

1. **What concepts help archaeologists to reconstruct past social and political organizations?**

- Archaeologists think in terms of both residential and nonresidential groups.

- How these groups operate is a matter of gender (culturally based interpretations of biology), the division of labor, kinship, and status.

- Bioarchaeological analyses provide clues as to the division of labor, but strong empirical generalizations or historically linked ethnographic analogies are often needed.

- Kinship is the socially recognized network of relationships through which individuals are related to one another by ties of descent (real or imagined) and marriage.

- Status refers to the rights, duties, and privileges that define the nature of interpersonal relations. *Ascribed status* is parceled out at birth without regard to personal characteristics; *achieved* status comes from what one accomplishes in life.

- A society is *egalitarian* if achieved status is the means whereby an individual acquires a high position. In a *ranked* society, ascribed status places people into a ranked order of privilege; ranked societies exhibit a hierarchy, and its members have unequal access to basic resources.

2. **What archaeological remains are important in reconstructing political organization, especially those involving inherited social inequities?**

- Egalitarian and ranked societies are often studied through patterning in mortuary remains, on the assumption that treatment in death reflects status in life, as well as through public and household architecture.

3. **What archaeological remains help reconstruct social organization, especially kinship?**

- Social groupings are reflected "on the ground" in terms of house spacing and placement. Genetic distance studies of human skeletal remains provide clues to postmarital residence.

4. **What techniques help reconstruct ancient trade networks?**

- Trade networks reflect the geographic scale of non-residential groups, economic patterns, and political authority. Trade is established by determining whether artifacts were made or obtained locally and by determining the source of raw materials for artifact manufacture.

- Obsidian, clay, and temper sourcing studies demonstrate the geographic scale of an economic and/or political organization.

MEDIA RESOURCES

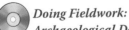

Doing Fieldwork:
Archaeological Demonstrations CD-ROM 2.0
This CD, developed by the authors, shows professional archaeologists involved in various digs, many of which are referenced in the text. The presentation is organized by the main techniques used on an archaeological dig, reinforcing concepts and techniques via live examples. The CD takes you through each step automatically, or you can navigate to any point via the navigation bar. After reviewing a step in the dig process, you are taken to Check Points, which are concept questions about each step of the dig. Then you can see the answers, receive your score, and even send your scores to your instructor.

The Companion Website for *Archaeology*, Sixth Edition
www.cengagebrain.com
Supplement your review of this chapter by going to the companion website to take one of the practice quizzes, use the flash cards to master key terms, and check out the many other study aids that are designed to help you succeed in your introductory archaeology course.

12 THE ARCHAEOLOGY OF THE MIND

LEARNING OBJECTIVES

**AFTER READING THIS CHAPTER
YOU SHOULD BE ABLE TO ANSWER THESE QUESTIONS:**

1. What is the central challenge of "cognitive archaeology"?

2. How do archaeologists study ancient religion?

3. Can archaeologists learn anything from very ancient cases that have no close cultural descendants?

© Bettmann/CORBIS

This horse was painted on the ceiling of the cave of Lascaux, in France, some 17,000 years ago.

PREVIEW

AS CULTURAL BEINGS, we all construct the world in which we live. By "construct" we mean that while we physically alter the world—through farming, architecture, trash disposal, logging, mining, and so forth—we also interpret our world symbolically, which can lead to different approaches to the physical world. In this chapter, we will concentrate on these symbolic meanings.

Some archaeologists attempt to infer the symbolic meanings of specific artifact forms, and others try to reconstruct concepts and perceptions about how the ancients viewed the world and the place of humans in it. As you might guess, symbolic approaches in archaeology raise some difficult issues. Although a huge range of human behavior falls under the category of "symbolic," we will concentrate on investigations of ritual and religion, iconography, and the interpretation of prehistoric rock art.

INTRODUCTION

When processual archaeology gained prominence in the 1960s, it generated numerous studies of prehistoric demography, settlement patterns, subsistence, technology, and the human use of landscapes, plants, and animals. These approaches relied heavily on rigorous scientific methods. The focus was heavily materialistic because processual archaeologists believed that subsistence behavior provided the infrastructure for the rest of the cultural system (see Chapter 2).

Early on, processual archaeologists were optimistic about studying all aspects of the human condition from archaeological data. But through the 1970s and 1980s, most processual archaeologists remained decidedly lukewarm toward **cognitive archaeology.** The archaeological record relating to "ideas" seemed too shaky and ambiguous—and not to be approached in an explicitly scientific, objective manner. Processual archaeologists assumed that the cognitive aspects of culture—including religion—were "epiphenomena," features of human societies that were merely derivative from the more critical technological and economic basics; as such, they were unimportant to understanding the past.

The appeal of processual archaeology is easy to understand. This research paradigm places priority on just those things that archaeologists are most confident in recovering from their sites—evidence about past environments, technologies, and economies.

But other archaeologists felt that such heavy-handed materialism dehumanized the past. They argued instead for an "archaeology of the mind"—one that emphasizes the values, ideas, and beliefs that make us all human. To be sure, any archaeology of the mind will have a more postprocessual than processual flavor because such an approach will necessarily address recovering *meanings* (rather than law-like statements or generalizations about human behavior). Today, cognitive archaeology remains largely interpretive, but we will demonstrate that such symbolic perspectives can indeed lend themselves to scientific testing as well—if appropriate linkages can be made between the interpretations of ancient symbols and those human behaviors most directly inferred from the archaeological record.

All humans interact with their world through their cultural perception of it, and modern archaeologists can ill afford to overlook the power of symbols. Take food, for example. Economic decisions might appear to be rather straightforward: Eat this food because it is nutritious and efficiently harvested, and avoid that food because it is not. Although such decisions do

cognitive archaeology The study of all those aspects of ancient culture that are the product of the human mind: the perception, description, and classification of the universe; the nature of the supernatural; the principles, philosophies, ethics, and values by which human societies are governed; and the ways in which aspects of the world, the supernatural, or human values are conveyed in art.

LOOKING CLOSER

FOOD TABOOS IN THE NEAR EAST

Traditional Jewish and Islamic faiths prohibit eating pork. This prohibition is ancient, dating back to the Near Eastern roots of both religions. Pork is a perfectly nutritious food, and pigs can be raised quite efficiently. Why, then, did this prohibition arise in these Near Eastern religions? Here we contrast two different explanations for this food taboo—the first materialist, the second symbolic.

Marvin Harris (1927–2001) argued that pigs were prohibited in the ancient Near East because they are poorly suited for life in the desert. Pigs are forest dwellers, and they do well in wet environments. Harris suggested that any food, even a formerly useful food, will be tabooed when the cost of producing it outweighs its nutritional value. In the desert, the cost of trying to keep pigs alive would indeed be high.

But why would a taboo with supernatural sanctions be necessary if the food was clearly inefficient to produce or procure? Certainly, people are rational enough to see when raising or harvesting a particular food is not worth the effort. And the prohibition against pork is only one of a lengthy list of tabooed foods. This list appears in Leviticus in the Old Testament, and later in Deuteronomy. In those passages, God prohibited the followers of Moses from eating pigs, but also shellfish, rabbits, camels, insects, and a variety of birds. Many of these, such as camels, are perfectly suited for life in the desert.

Mary Douglas (1921–2007), a symbolic anthropologist, argues that you cannot explain one of these tabooed foods without explaining all of them. She proposes a different explanation based on Near Eastern cultural ideas about animals. The prohibited animals in Leviticus were said to be "unclean," and Douglas focused on the meaning of that term. She pointed out that unclean often means "disorderly." You might say that your house is "not clean" when in fact what you mean is that clothing is lying on the floor and you haven't put the furniture back from last week's party. You might say that dishes sitting beside the sink are "dirty" when in fact you were just eating off of them moments earlier. They're not dirty; they're simply not "in their place" (washed, dried, and in the cupboard).

Taking this approach to the complete list of food prohibitions, Douglas found that virtually all the prohibited animals are ones that ancient Near Easterners saw as violating cultural ideas about the order of creation. Animals were supposed to be those that move on all four feet. Thus, insects that "swarm upon the land" are unclean because they are outside the cultural order of life. Likewise, edible animals were supposed to be those with cloven hooves and that chew the cud—such as cattle, sheep, and goats. Pigs have cloven hooves, but do not chew the cud. Consequently, they are unclean because they are an anomaly in the "natural" order of animals. Avoiding certain animals, then, had little to do with food, but with a continual affirmation of what constitutes God's order in the world.

Which explanation is right? Douglas's argument is appealing because it provides an explanation for all the forbidden animals. But it raises a new question: If pork was prohibited because it fell outside the natural order, what gave rise to that view of the world?

heavily condition subsistence practices, we also face an ever-changing background of cultural information about what is or is not edible. As we pointed out in Chapter 2, some societies consider dogs to be food, even prestigious feast foods, yet people in other cultures are repulsed by the idea of eating their "pets" (see "Looking Closer: Food Taboos in the Near East"). Certain animals may be highly valued in particular cultures, not because of their nutritional content but because of their symbolic meaning. Native peoples of New Guinea hunted cassowary birds not for food, but because their feathers were prestigious gifts that were given away at feasts.

Symbolism goes beyond food to permeate all arenas of human life. We saw in Chapter 9 that even firewood, something apparently mundane and utilitarian, was symbolically loaded for the Inka. And Chapter 11 explained how kinship involves the differential imposition of symbolic ideas about kin onto biological relationships. Male and female tasks also differ among societies, depending on what symbolic value a culture assigns to different tasks. In industrial societies, advertising tells us that clothing, houses, cars, hairstyles, tattoos, beer—virtually everything, in fact—carries symbolic meaning.

Humans live in a material world, and nobody can avoid the realities of survival. But people also live in a culturally constructed world, and material decisions are always made against a backdrop of symbolic meanings. This is why a number of archaeologists have turned to an ideational emphasis in their research, examining the active role of symbols in shaping the economic, social, and even technological structure of societies. We discussed the symbolic element of human culture in Chapter 2; now we consider symbols in more detail.

WHAT'S A SYMBOL?

The ability to use symbols goes to the essence of what it means to be human. Language is made possible by symbols; so are stories, art, and poetry. Symbols shape the way that people see, understand, and feel about the world.

To most anthropologists, a **symbol** is an object or act (verbal or nonverbal) that by cultural convention stands for something else *with which it has no necessary connection.* Consider a symbol that is familiar to most Americans: the red circle with a red line running diagonally through it. With a capital "P" in the center of the circle, the symbol tells us "no parking"; with a cigarette in the middle, it means "no smoking." (The "P" and the cigarette, by the way, are not symbols but signs because they have a connection to what they signify—the word "parking" and an actual cigarette). Virtually all Americans understand that a red circle with a diagonal line through it forbids whatever is in the circle.

Is there any *necessary* connection between a red circle with a line through it and prohibition of a certain behavior? No. In fact, this symbol might just as easily mean the opposite: Parking *is* allowed here, smoking *is* permitted here. If you were not enculturated into the meaning of the symbol, you would have no way of deducing the symbol's meaning merely from the sym-

bol itself—*because there is no necessary connection between a symbol and the thing it stands for.* Some anthropologists suggest that a few basic symbols might have an inherent meaning genetically programmed into our consciousness; red, for example, the color of blood, might carry the meaning of "danger." But most symbols we use have no such "natural" meaning. (And if you think they do, rent a car in Paris and figure out the "natural" meaning of French road signs.)

This is why symbols are so powerful. A simple symbolic act can be made to carry enormous amounts of information. In fact, the same symbol can carry different meanings under different situations. Consider a simple wink of the eye. In one situation, it can signal a playful conspiracy between two people against a third; in another, the same gesture is flirting (or harassment). But in another culture, a wink might mean nothing more than that a person has something irritating his or her eye.

Because symbols have no necessary connection to their culturally assigned meaning, they can be used in different ways. Much of the humor, pathos, and poignancy in literature and the arts comes from the playful or artful use of symbols (such as the use of the red prohibition circle in the film *Ghostbusters*). This is another way in which symbols are powerful.

But these very qualities make symbols difficult to study archaeologically. If there is no necessary connection between a symbol and what it stands for, then how does an outsider know what a particular symbol "means"? How would you know that a red circle with a line through it *prohibits* rather than *permits* a behavior? Deciphering these messages is difficult enough today, when we have access to language, informants, and observable behavior. But it is manifestly more difficult—some would say impossible—to understand symbolic behavior in an archaeological context, where the physical symbol survives, but its meaning does not.

Consider, for example, the rock art shown in Figure 12-1—one of the thousands of images found at La María, a complex of rockshelters in Patagonia (a region of southern Argentina). The central figure is a guanaco, a wild camelid once hunted by native peoples of the region. Along the guanaco's back and haunches is a series of white dots, and other white dots are on the body. In the upper right is a hand silhouette, created when the artisan placed his or her right hand on the wall and then blew paint over it. Between the hand and the guanaco runs a red, white, and black line, immediately below which is a line of red dots.

What do these images mean? Was the hand painted as part of ritual? Or is it more like graffiti "tagging"? What do the lines and dots represent? A hunting fence

symbol An object or act (verbal or nonverbal) that, by cultural convention, stands for something else *with which it has no necessary connection.*

or drive line? Or maybe a map? Does the guanaco "mean" guanaco? Or is it a symbol that stands for something else, like a lineage? What about the dots on the guanaco? Is this hunting or fertility magic, or an appeal to a supernatural being represented by the figure? There are no easy answers to these questions.

Anthropologists might interpret symbols by looking at the various ways a particular symbol is used and its (possibly varied) contexts. They might see which symbols are consciously manipulated and which are not; which can be used for humor (and who finds them funny). They might see if some symbols are exclusively used by or associated with women or men. By viewing a symbol's use in a variety of circumstances, we can construct an understanding of what the symbol means. But understanding this requires the living context of the symbol, something archaeologists do not have. And this means that ancient symbolic systems may remain forever silent as to their specific, detailed meanings.

But many contemporary archaeologists disagree, believing it's still worthwhile to explore human behavior as a system of meanings, rather than merely a series of acts that meet material needs. For some, this means relying heavily on ethnographic analogy or oral traditions (see "What Does It Mean to Me? What Role Do Oral Traditions Play in Archaeology?"). Recall how African societies treated pig bones in different ways (Chapter 8); we'll give you two more examples that explore both the potential and the limitations inherent in an archaeology of the mind.

Figure 12-1 A panel of art from a rockshelter at La María, in southern Patagonia. The central figure is a guanaco, a wild camelid.

© Robert Kelly

THE PEACE PIPE AS RITUAL WEAPON

Writing in the late 1970s, archaeologist Robert L. Hall (University of Illinois, Chicago) used the calumet—the peace pipe—to demonstrate how a cognitive approach could broaden the horizons of archaeological investigations.

Hall focused on the Hopewell culture (mentioned in Chapter 11). Hopewell "culture" probably included many different peoples speaking different languages and living in various ways, ranging from the lower Mississippi to Minnesota and from Nebraska to Virginia. But during Hopewell times (between 2200 and 1600 BP), these diverse people apparently shared a unifying set of symbols that may indicate a common set of religious beliefs. Archaeologists refer to this common set of symbols found over a wide area as the **Hopewell Interaction Sphere.**

To understand what was going on, let's first consider whether the Hopewell people shared a common religion. Broadly speaking, anthropologists consider **religion** to be a specific set of beliefs about the supernatural. Religion is a society's mechanism for relating supernatural phenomena to the everyday world. All living cultures have some form of religion, and we suppose that was true of past societies as well.

Religious beliefs are manifested in everyday life as **ritual,** a succession of discrete behaviors that must be performed in a particular order under particular circumstances—such as saying prayers at certain times of the day accompanied by particular acts or gestures. Rituals are fundamentally religious acts because they are the mechanisms by which individuals attempt to

Hopewell Interaction Sphere The common set of symbols found in the midwestern United States between 2200 and 1600 BP.

religion A social institution containing a set of beliefs about supernatural beings and forces and one's relation to them.

ritual A succession of discrete behaviors that must be performed in a particular order under particular circumstances.

WHAT DOES IT MEAN TO ME?

WHAT ROLE DO ORAL TRADITIONS PLAY IN ARCHAEOLOGY?

We point out in this chapter that ethnographic information can be crucial to an "archaeology of the mind." Some of this information might come as *oral traditions*—accounts of ancient times passed down by word of mouth from generation to generation. What do archaeologists do if oral traditions—a culture's stories about its past—conflict with archaeological data?

On the one hand, we could say that no one knows a culture's past better than its descendants. But we could point out that oral traditions are often selective in what they remember, or that they alter the nature or sequence of events to suit particular political needs. This is not a matter of lying. Oral traditions are a product of current events and sensibilities, and though they may contain accounts of past events, they are not always straightforward accounts of what "really happened" in the past.

For example, many European Americans imagine the mid-nineteenth-century settlement of the West as consisting of small, lonely caravans of Conestoga wagons nightly forming a circle to repel the Plains Indians' "wheel of death" attacks. We get this image from Western "oral" tradition—movies and novels. However, John Unruh (1937–1976), a historian who carefully read all surviving emigrant diaries of the years 1840–1860, found virtually no mention of such encounters. Most wagon trains were large, and far more people died of cholera and accidents than from Indian attacks (in fact, more Indians died at the hands of the emigrants than vice versa). There was only one account of "circling the wagons," and most attacks occurred along the Snake and Humboldt rivers in Idaho and Nevada, not on the Plains. The popular image was created by the media

(as early as 1850) to justify the taking of Native American land; in so doing, they created America's own "origin myth." Oral histories are a product of the time and culture in which they are produced; they are not purely factual accounts of the past.

Oral histories can change with time, and the older the events described, the greater the likelihood that some elements have been dropped and others added. Lakota oral traditions, for example, contain many references to horses, but the Lakota did not have horses (which were brought to the New World by the Spanish) until after AD 1740. They are a fairly recent addition to Lakota oral history.

Many archaeologists believe that oral traditions must be corroborated by archaeological data. But to many people this is insulting because testing oral traditions is in fact questioning them. Many Christian fundamentalists feel the same way. If biblical archaeology corroborates the Bible, fine. But if it does not, some would argue, it is because archaeology, not the Bible, is imperfect.

Archaeology has standards of evidence, evaluation, and self-criticism (we've discussed many in this text), but so does the study of oral traditions. Peter Whiteley (American Museum of Natural History), for example, points out that oral histories can be evaluated in terms of their *consistency*—do different people give the same account, and does the same person give the same account over time? Or are some elements of a tradition validated by independent sources (for instance, historical documents or archaeology)? By keeping these standards in mind, oral history can provide some additional data to the interpretations produced by archaeology.

---

intercede with the supernatural. Rituals often enlist supernatural powers for the purpose of achieving or preventing transformations of state in humans and nature—in other words, to make sure that good things happen and bad things do not. In some religions, individuals use rituals to influence the course of events;

in others, they help novices find their path in a world that they see as beyond their control.

This particular definition of religion is especially relevant to archaeology because of archaeology's emphasis on ritual. Rituals are behavioral acts that often entail material culture and therefore can be represented in the archaeological record. The analysis of past ritual behavior is thus archaeology's major contribution to the study of religion.

Some of the highly standardized Hopewell artifacts are perhaps indicative of rituals. One particularly intriguing artifact is the stone platform pipe, some examples of which are shown in Figure 12-2. Hopewell artists fashioned these from pipestone, often ornamenting them with carved mammals, birds, or reptiles that rest on a straight or curved base. The pipes were probably used to smoke tobacco, which is indigenous to the New World; the earliest evidence of tobacco in the eastern United States dates to about 1900 BP.

The effort taken to carve these pipes suggests that whatever rituals the pipes were involved in were a critical aspect of Hopewell ceremonial life. Hundreds of pipes were found in the so-called Mound of the Pipes at Mound City, near Chillicothe, Ohio. Some think that this mound was a monument to a master carver of sacred pipes.

What were the pipes used for? What did they signal to their users?

To try to explain these pipes, Hall looked to historical and ethnographic data. He was especially intrigued by the fact that the "peace pipe" used historically to establish friendly contact almost always took the form of a weapon. He then reasoned that all cultures engage in certain culturally dictated customs whose exact meaning and origin may be lost in time. For example, the rite of toasting with drinks in Western culture originally was the sloshing and spilling together of two persons' drinks to reduce the possibility that one planned to poison the other. But how many of us who have toasted friends realize the origin of the custom? Hall suggested that although the original functions of such gestures have lost their practical significance, the acts survive as elements of etiquette or protocol.

Hall applied similar reasoning to the Hopewell platform pipes by calling upon ethnographic data. Throughout historic times in the eastern United States, Indian tribes observed the custom of smoking a sacred tribal pipe. When the pipe was present, violence was ruled out. Moreover, the peace pipe usually was made in the shape of a weapon. The Pawnee peace pipe, for instance, looked like an arrow, and the Osage word for calumet translated as "arrowshaft." Hall suggested that the weaponlike appearance resulted from

© American Museum of Natural History

Figure 12-2 Hopewell effigy pipes. The bowl for tobacco is on the animal's back. These would have been placed on the end of a wooden stem and may represent the hook on the end of an atlatl.

a specific ceremonial custom. Could it be that, at least during the period of European contact, the peace pipe symbolized a ritual weapon?

Hall then projected his idea back into ancient Hopewell times. Suppose that the distinctive Hopewell platform pipes were also ritual weapons—but made before these people knew of the bow and arrow. At the time, the most common Hopewell weapon was the atlatl, or spear-thrower, like those that appear in Figure 12-3 (see also Chapter 11).

Hall suggested that the distinctive Hopewell platform pipe symbolically represented a flat atlatl decorated with an effigy spur. He also observed that the animal on the bowl was almost always carved precisely where an atlatl spur would be. And the curvature of the platform seemed to correspond to the curvature of the atlatl. These correspondences led Hall to conclude: "I see the Hopewell platform pipe as the archaeologically visible part of a transformed ritual atlatl, a symbolic weapon which in Middle Woodland times probably had some of the same functions as the calumet of historic times, itself a ritual arrow."

Hall then proposed that the importance of the Hopewell pipe might well extend beyond symbolism—that the platform pipe was not merely one of many items exchanged between groups, but that "it may have been part of the very mechanism of exchange." Materialist research on eastern United States prehistory has conventionally defined the Hopewell Interaction Sphere primarily in economic and environmental terms. Perhaps, by maintaining relationships between large-scale networks of ritual trading partners, far-flung

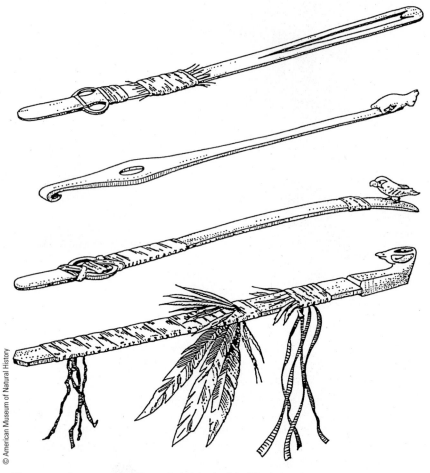

© American Museum of Natural History

Figure 12-3 Some representations of atlatls in aboriginal North American art.

we could test the *implications* of Hall's conclusions by assessing whether the archaeology of the Hopewell Interaction Sphere supports the social and political ramifications of Hall's interpretation of the stone pipes. Is there evidence of conflict in Hopewell sites? If so, how does it relate to the distribution of stone pipes and their source areas? How does the distribution of pipes across the Hopewell Interaction Sphere relate to evidence for subsistence stress (from faunal, macrobotanical, and human skeletal remains)? In other words, if we treat symbolic interpretations as hypotheses, it is possible to test them by linking them to phenomena that are more archaeologically accessible. To see how this might work, let's return to an example that we have used before, the Chavín culture of Peru.

Hopewell communities joined economic forces, looking to one another for support in lean years.

Hall suggested that a shift away from strictly materialistic thinking—toward a more cognitive approach—could generate a broader understanding of the Hopewell lifeway. Reasoning from Native American ethnographic analogies, Hall contended that peace pipe rituals served to mediate interaction over a vast area of eastern North America. By promoting a common set of symbols—perhaps linked to some common religious ideas—the Hopewell Interaction Sphere tended to reduce regional differences and promote contact and communication between discrete groups.

We pointed out that interpretations of the symbolic meanings of artifacts are difficult to test directly. But

cosmology The study of the origin, large-scale structure, and future of the universe. A cosmological explanation demonstrates how the universe developed—both the totality and its constituent parts—and also describes what principles keep it together.

EXPLORING ANCIENT CHAVÍN COSMOLOGY

In Chapter 9, we discussed the Chavín culture of the central Andes. Specifically, we looked at the faunal remains recovered from Chavín de Huántar and learned what these finds could tell us about subsistence and trade.

But the term "Chavín" conjures up to most archaeologists much more than llama bones. Archaeologists commonly consider Chavín to be Peru's first highland civilization because of its stratified social and political organization and its achievements in metallurgy, weaving, monumental architecture, irrigation systems, and stone sculpture. Chavín was the first Andean civilization.

Chavín also left a lasting legacy in Andean **cosmology.** By cosmology we mean a culture's understanding of how the world works, how it originated and developed, how the various parts fit together, what laws they obey, and, especially, the place of humans in the natural and supernatural worlds. A glimpse of a culture's cosmology can often be found in its **iconography**—its art forms or writing systems (such as Egyptian or Maya hieroglyphs) that symbolically represent ideas about religion or cosmology.

The iconography at Chavín de Huántar established the tone of subsequent central Andean cosmology. All deities of the succeeding generations in the central Andes looked more or less like the gods in the temple at Chavín de Huántar. Archaeologists Richard Burger and George Miller (whose faunal analysis of Chavín de Huántar we discussed in Chapter 9) have explored the nature of Chavín cosmology, looking in particular at the distinctive Chavín iconography that appeared over a wide area of the central Andes nearly 2500 years ago.

Figure 12-4 One of the carved stone heads on the temple at Chavín de Huántar, representing a shaman's transition from human to jaguar.

Figure 12-5 A stone carving of a jaguar outside the temple at Chavín de Huántar.

Animal Symbolism in Chavín Iconography

Chavín de Huántar has given its name to one of the Americas' most famous art styles. Chavín iconography is derived from stone sculptures at Chavín de Huántar, some examples of which appear in Figures 12-4 and 12-5. This art style was reproduced in many villages in the central Andes on locally made ceramics, textiles, goldwork, and stone.

Remember that the community of Chavín de Huántar depended on a range of animals for food, including wild deer, vicuña, llama, and guinea pigs. These were local beasts, probably encountered by local residents on a daily basis.

But the local highland animals of Chavín de Huántar are conspicuously absent from the thousands of known temple sculptures, ceramics, and textiles that display the widespread Chavín style. Instead, the Chavín style drew inspiration for its stylized fangs and talons, feathers and scales from the jaguar, crested eagle, monkey, serpent, and caiman (alligator). These creatures are native to the cloud forests and rain forests of the *eastern* Andean slope, if not the floodplains of Amazonia itself—located several hundred miles to

iconography Art forms or writing systems (such as Egyptian or Maya hieroglyphics) that symbolically represent ideas about religion or cosmology.

the east, on the other side of the Andes. These same animals play a prominent role in the mythology and religious symbolism of modern people of Amazonia, but they were utterly foreign to the inhabitants of Chavín de Huántar.

Why did the major animals in Chavín religion come from places outside the local highland environment?

Where Did Chavín Cosmology Come From?

Archaeologists have proposed several hypotheses to explain this puzzling aspect of Chavín cosmology. One holds that the climate was radically warmer and more humid during Chavín times. If so, then maybe the lowland complex of animals—the jaguar, the caiman, the crested eagle, and so forth—could have once lived in the highlands around Chavín de Huántar.

But this hypothesis is not correct. Several lines of evidence demonstrate that the climate was similar to the modern pattern during the Chavín time period (2900–2200 BP), and remember from Chapter 9 that the animal bones recovered from Chavín de Huántar belong to the same species as modern highland animals—camelids, deer, and so forth. Paleoenvironmental change cannot explain the nature of Chavín iconography.

Another hypothesis was championed by Peruvian archaeologist Julio Tello (1880–1947), discoverer of Chavín civilization and first excavator at Chavín de Huántar (in the 1930s), and later by American archaeologist Donald Lathrap (1927–1990). Plants indigenous to Amazonia—including manioc, bottle gourd, hot peppers, and possibly peanuts—all appear at Chavín de Huántar. Tello suggested that immigrants from the tropical forest introduced the lowland plants and animals to Chavín de Huántar. Lathrap attributed the migration to population pressure in the lowland Amazonian or Orinoco basin that forced the early Chavín folk into the Andean highlands. According to Lathrap, the heavy Amazonian component of Chavín religious art displayed homage and deference to the ancient homeland and subsistence regime that was responsible for the initial success of the Chavín elite.

But this hypothesis also seems to be incorrect. Lowland crops are impossible to grow in the Andean environment, and they could not have been brought with and grown by an immigrant population. Instead, their presence suggests trade or some other kind of contact between Chavín de Huántar and Amazonia. Burger also hypothesizes that if a tropical forest people had moved wholesale into the Andes, their ceramic traditions should show a direct relationship to those of the Amazonian homeland. But the earliest ceramics at Chavín de Huántar show a conspicuous lack of Amazonian characteristics; the pottery looks local rather than imported. It also is clear that the basic high-altitude mixed agricultural subsistence pattern practiced by the pioneer population at Chavín de Huántar was not Amazonian at all; it had developed in place—in the highlands—at least a thousand years earlier. The ceramic and subsistence evidence makes it unlikely that a tropical forest group was responsible for the lowland iconography evident on the earliest buildings at Chavín de Huántar.

This is why Burger advocates a third hypothesis to explain the Amazonian elements of Chavín cosmology. Chavín de Huántar occupies a strategic gateway position, in a corridor that extends from the Pacific coast to the highland Andes and down to the lowland rain forest to the east. Burger argues that Chavín's religious leaders deliberately imported Amazonian symbolism, perhaps in the belief that the exotic lowland people had especially powerful esoteric knowledge. This interpretation, supported by ethnographic and ethnohistoric documentation, suggests that shamans and healers may have made pilgrimages to the distant lowlands—viewed as the powerful source of sacred knowledge, medicinal plants, and other ritual necessities. In fact, in many parts of the world anthropologists have found that people who live outside dense forests often ascribe magical powers or sacred knowledge to their neighbors who live in the forests. Burger argues that the Chavín people imported religious knowledge from the remote, exotic tropics to the Andean highlands.

Analysis of Chavín iconography provides some details that explain the cult's remarkable success. Early sculptural evidence suggests that Chavín ideology held that priests had the ability to turn themselves into mythical beasts in order to intervene with supernatural forces. Temple sculptures clearly demonstrate that, employing hallucinogenic snuff and beverages, Chavín shamans could transform themselves into jaguars or crested eagles. Specially designed drug paraphernalia—stone mortars, bone trays, spatulas, miniature spoons, and tubes—seem to be part of the Chavín ritual toolkit. Use of similar artifacts can be documented among modern South American people. Burger believes that this analogy—based on sixteenth-century ethnohistoric sources—may explain the singular success of the Chavín cult in uniting previously unrelated cultures throughout the Andean highlands and along the Peruvian coast.

Historical documents also suggest how this religious network might have operated 2000 years earlier. The religious center was a large ritual complex featuring an **oracle,** accessible only to certain cult specialists. Based on the oracle's secret projections, cult members could provide "insider information," offering favorable intervention with the natural elements, protection against disease, and specialized knowledge concerning auspicious times for planting and harvesting.

Under this regional religious system, local communities could establish "branch shrines" by pledging support for the religion. If the pledge was accepted, a local priest was assigned; in return, local communities allotted agricultural lands to produce tribute and promised public labor for farming and herding. In effect, these local branches supported the religion's headquarters with large quantities of cotton, corn, dried fish, llamas, guinea pigs, raw materials (such as gold and obsidian), and manufactured goods (such as fine cloth).

Burger suggests that this ethnohistoric cult provides an analogy for the distinctive regional organization that characterized Chavín civilization. He hypothesizes that the oracle cult center was located at the archaeological site of Karwa, unfortunately looted during the 1970s. Iconographic elements—particularly stylized felines and raptorial birds—woven into textile fragments recovered from tombs at Karwa show unmistakable ties to the sculptures at Chavín de Huántar. Despite the nearly 400 miles separating the two sites, the complex elements of Chavín cosmology seem to have been transported intact, without simplification or misrepresentation.

The Role of Cosmology in Andean Civilization

This model suggests that Chavín iconography was a widespread religion subdivided into a number of localized branches, each sharing in the major elements of Chavín iconography—probably reflecting major deities—but complemented by distinctive localized elements. According to this view, the Chavín religion maintained its characteristic regional flavor, but also demonstrated a willingness to incorporate motifs and symbols significant to local constituencies.

Burger emphasizes that the long-standing interest of archaeologists in Chavín iconography has led to a deep understanding of how this distinctive civilization came to be. Had this research taken place within a strictly materialistic framework, Burger suggests, the direction would have been much different and consid-

erably more restricted. He stresses that regional exchange and tribute in the form of gifts to the religious center, rather than local agricultural production, contributed to the development of Chavín civilization.

The spread of Chavín elements (2500–2250 BP) across the central Andes happened at a turbulent time, following the collapse of many early coastal political systems that did not succeed at political integration. An unprecedented amount of contact occurred between distant and unrelated groups, producing a previously unknown degree of sharing of ideology and technology, reinforced by the movement of goods and people. For Burger, Chavín culture was a forerunner of the many later attempts in Andean history to create single social entities out of a diversity of local cultures.

So, why did Chavín succeed where earlier attempts failed?

Relying on historical evidence from the sixteenth-century regional ceremonial complex, Burger argues that Chavín was a large-scale religion, transcending political and ethnic boundaries. Chavín ideology and rituals were sufficiently powerful to support a hierarchical organization, with officials overseeing local cult activities and monitoring deviation among local congregations. Although diversity was evident throughout the reach of the Chavín cult, a central authority exerted its power and extracted tribute from smaller communities. Thus, Chavín religion spread not because of political expansion, but because of the extension of a powerful shared cosmology, rendered visible in ritual objects and manifested through the growth of complex regional exchange networks.

Civilization (a term we discuss in the next chapter) had appeared in the central Andes by about 2400 BP. According to Burger, the centers of Chavín culture rivaled the classic Greek cities in size and beauty, with massive public structures of finely cut and polished masonry, and the settlements were home to a complex society, differentiated by both social status and economic activities.

Burger argues that this power came from the original priests of Chavín de Huántar, who developed a growing Chavín mythology emphasizing mystique over the mundane. It was the iconography of the mysterious lowland animals that would ultimately determine the long-term success of Chavín society and economy.

oracle A shrine in which a deity reveals hidden knowledge or divine purpose.

One message of Chavín art may have been that the prosperity and well-being of the community depended on maintaining the favor of forces alien to the local habitat and daily experience—forces redolent of the powers of the distant and mysterious tropical forest. The mediation of this relationship required the services of ritual specialists. This explanation suggests that Chavín ideology—heavily emphasizing the exotic tropical forest fauna—ritually reinforced the wealth and power of Chavín de Huántar society.

Current evidence suggests that social stratification may have first appeared in the highlands in association with long-distance exchange—offering local leaders an unparalleled opportunity to control and manipulate the existing socioeconomic system. Burger argues that tribute supplied to regional ceremonial centers by travelers and pilgrims could have been a major source of wealth and power for newly emerging elites.

Religious ideology seems to have played a central role in promoting and legitimizing these profound sociopolitical transformations, suggesting that many of the key ingredients for social complexity existed in the central Andes prior to the Chavín period. Although still a hypothesis to be tested, perhaps it was the power of Chavín's symbols—rather than a change in food resources, climate, or population density—that played a key role in the development of the Andes' first civilization.

BLUEPRINTS FOR AN ARCHAEOLOGY OF THE MIND

These two examples, Hopewell and Chavín, share a couple of things. Note that in neither case do archaeologists try to interpret the exact meaning of the various symbols involved. Hall doesn't say what the raptors or other animals carved in stone on Hopewell pipes "mean." Burger and Miller don't attempt to explain what the jaguars, caimans, or crested eagles symbolized to those participating in the religion and iconography of the central Andes some 2500 years ago. Archaeologists simply cannot make the inferential leap from an ancient symbol to its past meaning based strictly on the symbol itself. We can only speak in general terms about what the symbols imply about a level of human interaction that differs considerably from a purely material interaction with the environment.

Both examples also rely on solid ethnographic and ethnohistoric data. Hall's idea that Hopewell pipes were part of a peace pipe ritual was based on copious ethnographic data on such rituals among many eastern North American peoples. Likewise, Burger and Miller would have been hard pressed to generate a viable hypothesis to account for Chavín iconography without access to a rich historical and ethnographic record of the Andes Mountains.

Good researchers will always draw upon imagination and personal feelings to think up testable hypotheses. But thinking about ancient symbolic systems can easily run amok. Without some solid way of checking ideas against facts, archaeologists run the risk of what Kent Flannery and Joyce Marcus (University of Michigan) call "a bungee jump into the Land of Fantasy." At best, archaeology can capture only certain limited aspects of ancient ideas.

Marcus and Flannery suggest that cognitive archaeology can (and should) follow relatively rigorous methods, *provided ample historical and ethnographic documentation is available.* Should such data be lacking, they warn that "far less success should be anticipated."

So, what about those truly ancient symbolic systems that lack historically linked ethnographic insights? Do we simply shrug our shoulders and turn to some other problem? To answer this question, let's examine how archaeologists have studied one of the earliest symbolic systems, Upper Paleolithic cave art of western Europe.

UPPER PALEOLITHIC CAVE ART

Remember from Chapter 10 that the lineage that would eventually become *Homo sapiens* split from the rest of the primate lineage more than 5 million years ago. But evidence for artistic expression appears only in the last 90,000 years and does not become widespread until the last 40,000 years.

The **Upper Paleolithic** (40,000–12,000 BP) in Europe is distinguished by the appearance of a complex technology of stone, bone, and antler as well as wall art, portable art objects, and decorated tools—an example of which appears in Figure 12-6. Archaeologists sometimes call this an artistic "explosion," and the metaphor is appropriate. Only a handful of objects from the preceding 5 million years can be called art (and many of these may not be artifacts at all). But many, many Upper Paleolithic sites contain engraved,

Upper Paleolithic The last major division of the Old World Paleolithic, beginning about 40,000 years ago and lasting until the end of the Pleistocene (ca. 10,000 years ago).

© American Museum of Natural History

Figure 12-6 Carved from reindeer antler, this bison probably served as the end of an atlatl and is an example of the artistic work that typifies the European Upper Paleolithic.

carved, or sculpted objects, and caves occupied by Upper Paleolithic peoples often contain wall paintings.

Cave paintings occur in 200 French caves; still more are found in Spain. Much of the painting dates to the **Magdalenian** phase (18,000–12,000 BP). However, a new site, Grotte Chauvet, was discovered in France in 1994, and AMS radiocarbon dates on the paintings (the black paint is charcoal, with fat or blood sometimes used as a binder) and some torch marks on the walls date to 26,000–32,000 BP. (Incidentally, Chavet Cave is the subject of a recent 3-D feature film, *Cave of Forgotten Dreams*, directed by Werner Herzog.)

Upper Paleolithic wall paintings have intrigued archaeologists for more than a century. More than simple line drawings, these are masterworks created by talented artisans who knew animal anatomy and behavior well. Careful shading shows the contours of animals' shoulders and haunches. Rutting stags lower their heads to bugle. Some animals may be pregnant. Many of the images were painted with brushes, and hand silhouettes by the hundreds cover some cave walls.

The paintings are deliberately dramatic. The artists understood the principles of perspective, and they sometimes employed the natural topography of cave walls to bring the animals to life. As you walk down one dark, narrow passage in the French cave of Lascaux, for example, two bulls appear to be running toward and to either side of you—a trick made possible by clever use of the cave's contours.

Upper Paleolithic paintings sometimes turn up in the most obscure places, difficult to locate even with modern equipment. The art is often found in the deepest recesses of caves, some at the very ends of passages, showing that a cave's entire passable extent was explored. Imagine entering one of these caves with only a reed torch or stone lamp burning tallow as your source of light. There are pits, pools, and rivers to avoid, narrow passageways to crawl through, and jutting rocks to duck under; and, remember, you have to find your way out again. At Lascaux, cave art even appears at the base of a deep pit. Not only does the descent into the darkness require a rope, but carbon dioxide accumulates at the pit's base, making breathing difficult.

Upper Paleolithic artisans clearly intended to place their art in places that were difficult to access. This remoteness strongly suggests a connection between the art and religious ritual, a suggestion supported by the occasional finds of bear teeth or ocher-covered flint blades stuffed into cracks in the cave walls, perhaps as offerings of some sort.

The content of the art is also intriguing. Human beings rarely appear, and when they do, they are poorly executed in comparison with the marvelous animal figures. Also, Upper Paleolithic art contains no actual "scenes." Although images often overlap, no one has identified a "story" or landscape. And whereas the cave art provides vivid evidence documenting the range of animals living in Ice Age Europe, certain animals are emphasized, especially horses, aurochs (wild cattle), bison, ibex, stags, and reindeer, with occasional mammoths, bears, rhinoceros, and large cats. The ancient artists sometimes painted some images on top of (or partially overlapping) previous paintings, suggesting that the act of making the art was more important than the final product.

What accounts for the particular forms that the art takes and the locations where these forms were painted?

Magdalenian The last major culture of the European Upper Paleolithic period (ca. 18,000–12,000 BP); named after the rockshelter La Madeleine, in southwestern France. Magdalenian artisans crafted intricately carved tools of reindeer bone and antler; this was also the period during which Upper Paleolithic cave art in France and Spain reached its zenith.

Art or Magic?

Various nineteenth-century scholars viewed Upper Paleolithic cave art romantically, as an early expression of a growing human sense of beauty and perfection. This art-for-art's-sake perspective stressed what humans could accomplish in the leisure time that technology brings. So viewed, the animals had no particular meaning; they were simply artistic expressions of the things that people saw around them. The lack of scenes or stories in the art was taken as evidence that the artistic sense was in a rudimentary stage of development.

David Lewis-Williams (University of Witwatersrand, South Africa) points out the circularity in this approach: An innate aesthetic sense is inferred from beautiful art, and the presence of beautiful art is evidence of this innate sense. The art-for-art's-sake approach likewise fails to explain why the artists chose such remote locations. If art was something done in leisure time for public enjoyment, why decorate remote, dangerous reaches of caves?

Other anthropologists suggested that the cave art involves **sympathetic magic,** grounded in the principle that "like controls like." In the late nineteenth century, Salomon Reinach (1858–1932) proposed that the images were intended to promote the fertility of game animals, thus ensuring an abundant food supply for Upper Paleolithic hunters: If you draw pregnant animals, then the real animals will become pregnant and the food supply will be ensured. Abbé Henri Breuil (1877–1961) subsequently developed a similar line of thought, suggesting that the images were a form of sympathetic magic designed to guarantee the success of a hunt: If you kill the stylized animal on the wall, you will also kill the real animal out in the valley.

It is true that the artists drew some animals with spears thrust into them (although only a few may represent pregnant animals). But whereas bison and horse are the most frequently depicted animals, most of the food bones recovered from Upper Paleolithic caves in Europe are red deer and reindeer. If this art represents sympathetic magic, then it was not very successful.

The sympathetic magic interpretation assumes that the animals are literal and that they have no symbolic meaning. But other scholars view the Upper Paleolithic cave paintings as a structured code, drawing upon a theoretical paradigm known as **structuralism.** Briefly, structuralism argues that humans understand reality as paired oppositions. The concept of "life," for example, is meaningless without the opposite concept of "death." Likewise, the concept of "male" means nothing without the opposing concept of "female." From a structuralist perspective, culture—and its material expressions, such as art—is played out in terms of such paired oppositions. So viewed, the task of the archaeologist becomes discerning and interpreting these pairs of oppositions.

Following this paradigm, French archaeologists André Leroi-Gourhan (1911–1986) and Annette Laming-Emperaire (1917–1978) argued that Upper Paleolithic cave imagery contained binary oppositions that "stand for" male and female (although Laming-Emperaire backed away from this interpretation later in her life). Criticizing what she saw as simplistic, off-the-cuff interpretations, Laming-Emperaire advocated a more systematic approach to cave art. She sought to identify not merely the animals represented in the images, but also where in a cave particular images were found (the entrance, middle chambers, the rear), their positions (such as ceiling or wall), signs of use, archaeological remains, and associations among images. In other words, Laming-Emperaire did what a good archaeologist should do: She systematically analyzed both the contents and the contexts of the images.

It remained for Leroi-Gourhan to complete the work begun by Laming-Emperaire. Rejecting previous ethnographic analogies and earlier models of cognitive evolution, Leroi-Gourhan instead assumed that the minds of Upper Paleolithic people were every bit as complex as those of modern people. Based on systematic, quantitative data collected from 66 French caves, Leroi-Gourhan's maps suggested that the various cave elements clustered into four major sets of images:

▶ Small herbivores (horse, ibex, stag, reindeer, and hind)
▶ Large herbivores (bison, auroch)
▶ Rare species (mammoth, deer, ibex)
▶ Dangerous animals (cat, bear, rhinoceros)

Working in the structuralist paradigm, Leroi-Gourhan associated the small herbivores with "maleness" and the large herbivores with "femaleness." He also defined two major groupings of abstract signs—a set of "narrow" symbols (such as rows of dots, arrow-like representations, and straight lines) that he believed were "male," and a second set of "wide" symbols

sympathetic magic Rituals in which doing something to an image of an object produces the desired effect in the real object.

structuralism A paradigm holding that human culture is the expression of unconscious modes of thought and reasoning, notably binary oppositions. Structuralism is most closely associated with the work of the French anthropologist Claude Lévi-Strauss.

(rectangles, upside-down Vs, and some curvilinear marks) that he associated with "female." In this way, the abstract symbols and the animal portrayals were viewed as complementary.

Leroi-Gourhan then looked for patterning in the placement of images within cave settings. Dividing the caves into entrances, central areas, peripheral areas, and back areas, he discovered that stags (a male sign) tended to appear in cave entrances. Male signs and images (stags, horses, and ibex) were also in the peripheral areas, whereas dangerous animals and carnivores appeared mostly in the backs of the caves. The central areas contained both male and female signs (along with horses, bison, and aurochs).

To some, the presence of a male sign at the entrance might suggest that the caves were regarded as "male" places, a stag being the equivalent of an ancient "No women allowed" sign. But keep in mind that structuralism arrays the world into oppositions. If there is a male, there must be a female. Leroi-Gourhan pointed out that central areas contain male elements placed around female elements (with male elements also found in peripheral areas and at the entrance). Where is the female to balance the male? Leroi-Gourhan said it must be the cave itself.

Armed with these inferences, Leroi-Gourhan could now interpret the "meaning" of the caves: This is where Upper Paleolithic people dealt with the oppositions and contradictions that, according to structuralist theory, are the inevitable consequence of human thought. Inside the caves, they used symbols drawn from the world of nature to create and communicate a cosmology that explained life's fundamental oppositions: male and female, nature and culture, human and supernatural, life and death.

But some empirical problems plague Leroi-Gourhan's analysis. Sometimes he used an image to determine whether a portion of a cave was "central" or "peripheral," and in others he reversed the process, assigning an indistinct painting to a particular species depending on where it was located. Both are instances of circular reasoning. And the associations that formed the baseline of his analysis have not held up as more caves are investigated. Eventually, his ideas collapsed under the very empirical standards that he had constructed; that's often how science progresses.

Of greater interest (at least today) are the ways in which Leroi-Gourhan interpreted the symbols. To pursue his structuralist paradigm, Leroi-Gourhan needed to define binary oppositions, the most prominent of which were male and female symbols. In so doing, he was required to jump from the symbol to its meaning. Because symbols take on meaning only from

culture, there is always the danger that archaeologists will draw upon their own culture, rather than that of the ancient people who created the symbols. This was clearly a problem with Leroi-Gourhan's interpretation of abstract symbols of the Upper Paleolithic. Living in a world where Freudian psychology was popular, Leroi-Gourhan interpreted "narrow" and "wide" symbols as representing male and female genitalia. We see here how a paradigm affects the way that we understand the world. It is unlikely that in a pre-Freudian world Leroi-Gourhan would have proposed that lines = penises and rectangles = vaginas.

How did Leroi-Gourhan attribute different animal species to men and women? Like most symbolic anthropologists, he looked for associations in the symbols, focusing on bison and horses. In a limited number of cave paintings and engravings, he found women depicted next to bison and men painted next to horses (although the interpretation of some figures as men or women is dubious, as is the contemporaneity of the juxtaposed images). There were also opposite associations—men with bison and women with horses—or ambiguous ones, such as men *and* women with bison *and* horses.

Recall that the same symbol can be employed in many different ways even in the same culture. Do the opposite or ambiguous associations suggest that Leroi-Gourhan is simply wrong—that bison do not really "stand for" female and horses do not "stand for" male—or are they plays on the symbolic meanings of bison and horses? Maybe the men with bison are berdaches (see Chapter 11), and the women with horses are what the Lakota called "manly-hearted women."

Or maybe this is all wrong. Maybe the bison and horses and other animals had different meanings in different caves at different times in the past. Maybe the images are **totems,** symbols of different clans (as Laming-Emperaire eventually concluded).

That Leroi-Gourhan was influenced by Freud and structuralism does not automatically mean that his interpretation of the symbols in the paintings is wrong. The problem is that *we cannot assess whether he was right.*

The most secure way to go from symbols to their meanings is by using some historical or ethnographic information, as Burger and Miller did with Chavín art and Hall did with Hopewell platform pipes. But given that we lack any associated ethnographic data for the Upper

totem A natural object, often an animal, from which a lineage or clan believes itself to be descended and/or with which lineage or clan members have special relations.

PROFILE OF AN ARCHAEOLOGIST

A NATIVE AMERICAN ARCHAEOLOGIST

Dorothy Lippert is an archaeologist with the Smithsonian Institution.

Dorothy Lippert.

Deciding to become an archaeologist was the easy part. I had no fixed ideas about what such a career would consist of other than that I would be participating in the scientific process of understanding our human past. I was unaware of the extent to which my own Native American heritage would play a role; in the beginning, I didn't realize that this part of my identity would so closely focus both my

career and my beliefs about what we are meant to do as archaeologists. My reasons for choosing this discipline initially centered on a love of history and science, although I had little patience for understanding history as a simple series of dates and even less for reducing science to sterile sets of data. Archaeology, for me, has always been a humanistic endeavor, one in which we come to know and respect people of the past in the same way we should people of the present day.

I find that archaeologists who are also Native American seem to have similar views of the discipline, particularly when talking about prehistoric archaeological work in North America. This is most likely because we know these people as our ancestors and in the course of practicing archaeology it becomes our privilege and our responsibility to care for them and to speak about their lives. A common thread within indigenous cultures is a respect for our elders, and this permeates archaeology as it is practiced by Native Americans.

In 2003, there were 11 Native Americans with doctorates in archaeology. It is my suspicion that this number reflects both the small numbers of Native Americans who hold doctorates in any subject and the emotional and scholarly hazards that archaeology holds for us. The impression that many tribal people have had up to now of archaeology is that it is something that is done to Native peoples by out-

---

Paleolithic, we must ask if there is anything we can do with this art other than admire its beauty and mystery.

Shamanism?

David Lewis-Williams offers an alternative explanation of Upper Paleolithic cave art that, although still speculative, is more firmly grounded in middle-level

theory. In brief, Lewis-Williams argues that Upper Paleolithic cave art is evidence of shamanic trances. His explanation does not rely on an interpretation of the images' symbols, and he tries to explain multiple aspects of the art, including the particular abstract elements, as well as the locations of images in caves and their association with animal images.

Lewis-Williams begins by pointing out that virtually all hunting-and-gathering societies known to anthropology practice a form of religion that involves shamanism. **Shamans** are individuals (often men, but including women in some societies) who claim to be able to access supernatural powers, spirits, or deceased individuals and tap into the power and influence that they offer to the world of the living. They do

shaman One who has the power to contact the spirit world through trance, possession, or visions. On the basis of this ability, the shaman invokes, manipulates, or coerces the power of the spirits for socially recognized ends—both good and ill.

siders. Those of us who try to practice archaeology from a Native perspective are still caught by this impression, and in some people's eyes have become outsiders ourselves. Tribal people have insinuated to me that I must not be truly Native if I can bring myself to practice archaeology. I also have the added burden of having studied human osteology. Frequently, when I meet other Native people, I don't mention that I'm an archaeologist until late in the conversation, in hopes of forestalling a negative response.

Other Natives are more supportive, saying that it's about time that we (indigenous people) started doing this work. Many understand just how difficult a career this can be and encourage me to continue. In their minds, as in my own, archaeology is a way to work for Native Americans, both the ancestors and present-day communities.

I think that many non-Native archaeologists are unaware of these kinds of reactions. Some seem convinced that archaeology done with a Native perspective will somehow be less scientific, as if their cultural heritage plays no role in their own studies. While I am a firm believer in maintaining scientific rigor in our analyses, I see no reason not to illuminate these studies with the cultural legacy that was maintained, sometimes at horrendous cost, by our ancestors. As Natives begin to participate fully in archaeology, I think the discipline will become broader in its approach and more open to combinations of different knowledge bases in order to understand a more human past.

When I speak with other Native Americans about the practice of archaeology, I find that we all tend to use this discipline to answer questions that are influenced by our cultural background. For instance, in my own studies of health and medical theory, I was interested in the ways that these were experienced by a small community whose inhabitants lived and died some 400 years ago. I could never quite see my research as the simple practice of collecting data; rather I felt myself to be engaged in communication with these ancient ones. Their cold, white bones used my breath and mind to tell this world their long forgotten story. Through the practice of this science, I became their voice.

Even when reading archaeological reports and looking through pages of dry, scholarly text, I find that I am searching for the humanity of the people whose remains or material objects are being studied. I have also realized that this perspective is not limited only to indigenous archaeologists. There are a number of non-Natives who seem to intuitively approach our science with a very humanistic flair. I believe that in the years to come, more and more archaeologists will begin to appreciate just how much more fun it is if we see our discipline as dealing with fellow beings. Shakespeare summed it up well: "You are not stones, nor bones, but men." While archaeology frequently encounters both stones and bones, it is best if we keep in mind that what we are really meeting up with are human beings.

this through trances, brought on by the use of psychotropic drugs or by fasting, dehydration, and sensory deprivation. Shamans culturally interpret the visions seen while in an altered state of consciousness as communication with the supernatural world.

The Lakota, for example, performed **vision quests** in which men would lie for days on a mountaintop until starvation, dehydration, and exposure brought about visions. These visions were a way for men to communicate with the supernatural world and locate their source of power. Africa's Ju/'hoansi used trances, sometimes brought on by hours of physically and emotionally draining dancing, as a way to contact the ghosts of deceased individuals and perform healing rituals on gravely ill members of the band.

After several decades of study, Lewis-Williams argues that much (though by no means all) of the world's hunting-and-gathering rock art is the result of shamanism. The art is a record of what a shaman saw while in a trance, a way to understand and interpret the meaning of the vision. How can Lewis-Williams say this? If anything is archaeologically inaccessible, it would seem to be what somebody saw in a trance thousands of years ago!

vision quest A ritual in which an individual seeks visions through starvation, dehydration, and exposure; considered in some cultures to be a way to communicate with the supernatural world.

Lewis-Williams relies on cross-cultural psychological and neurological research to bolster his argument. According to this research, when individuals go into a trance, they go through three levels of consciousness, each with distinctive "visual" aspects. In the first stage, a person sees dots, grids, zigzags, nested curves (like rainbows), and meandering lines. These may flicker, vibrate, merge, and break apart. Known as entoptic (from the Greek word meaning "within vision") phenomena, these images appear even with your eyes closed because they are a product of the optical nervous system. Because they are a function of the brain's hard-wiring, and given that all people everywhere (and we assume in the past, too) have the same neurology, all people should see the same entoptic images. Lewis-Williams thus injects the important element of uniformitarianism, which you will recall is essential to middle-level theory.

In the second, deeper stage of trance, a person's mind tries to make sense of the entoptic images by converting them into forms that are culturally meaningful (meaning that the particular images become culturally biased). Just as a nineteenth-century Lakota might see horses with riders on them, teepees, mountains, and bison, the mind of an Upper Paleolithic shaman would convert abstract images into things familiar to that culture, including animals such as aurochs and reindeer.

Those slipping into the third and final stage of trance will sense that they are moving through a tunnel or a vortex, with entoptic images swirling around them and merging into culturally intelligible ones. Again, this experience seems to be universal, generated by human neurology.

Shamans in many hunting-and-gathering cultures talk about reaching the "other side" by moving through a hole or cave, an experience sometimes described as "dying." Upon reaching the third stage, a person is often unable to recognize any stimulus outside the visions. The images become more vivid, and although they may merge with one another and with abstract images, a person senses that they are nonetheless real. At this point, the person has entered an altered state of consciousness and no longer understands that he or she is viewing images, but instead feels as though he or she has become part of the image.

But does an understanding of the neurological basis of trance (and dreams) help us understand Upper Paleolithic rock art? Let's look at one especially well-known site that Lewis-Williams studied: the French cave of Lascaux.

The Cave of Lascaux

Found by schoolboys in 1940, Lascaux is perhaps the most famous of all the European caves (see "Looking Closer: The Discovery of Lascaux"). The Paleolithic artists who painted the images inside Lascaux some 17,000 years ago would not recognize the outside of the cave today. The schoolboys entered the cave through a sinkhole, then crawled down a long rubble-filled tunnel. Today, however, those lucky few who can enter Lascaux (it is closed to regular public visitations) walk through two airlock doors, then step into an antibacterial footbath (to remove any microbes brought from the outside), all the time listening to the hum of an expensive ventilation system designed to maintain the cave's humidity and preserve the paintings inside.

But the inside of the cave remains much as the Paleolithic artists left it. You first enter the Hall of the Bulls, whose ceiling sparkles with calcite (see the chapter's opening photo and Figure 12-7). You are struck immediately by the immense aurochs and horses, painted in red and black, that circle the roof; at 5 meters long, the bulls are the largest in all of European cave art. Also present are smaller stags, some with many-tined antlers, as well as a bear. Many of the paintings take advantage of the cave's natural topography to accentuate a raised head or shoulders. One peculiar animal has two horns sprouting, unicorn-like, from its head. This painting is well executed, and Lewis-Williams suggests that the artist intended to create an ambivalent species.

A narrow natural ledge 5 to 6 feet above the floor seems to form a ground line for the animals (something rarely seen in Paleolithic art). But because the ledge is too narrow to stand on, the ancient artisans must have constructed platforms to reach the ceiling. Beneath these paintings is room for groups of people to have participated in rituals; whether they did so, however, is unknown.

Moving straight ahead, you enter the narrow Axial Gallery, which slopes more deeply into the earth. Many horses are on the walls here, with some aurochs and stags. Two of the horses have what appear to be spears or darts shooting toward them. A long line of black dots appear beneath a large stag in a bellowing posture; a horse faces the stag. Lewis-Williams sees these dots as evidence of the merging of abstract and representational images that occurs in trance.

Near the end of the Axial Gallery is one of the most intriguing images in Lascaux. Painted on a jutting piece of rock is a life-size image of a horse, upside-down and apparently falling through the air. This image is not

LOOKING CLOSER

THE DISCOVERY OF LASCAUX

Like so many major archaeological discoveries, Lascaux was found by accident—in this case, by a dog. Lascaux is located in the beautiful Dordogne region of southern France, a landscape rich in caves and rockshelters. In the 1940s, this was also a land of refugees, people fleeing the advancing German army. Life was hard and dangerous, but boys still found time to explore and look for buried treasure.

In September of 1940, several boys were doing just that. The eldest was 18-year-old Marcel Ravidat (nicknamed "Jailbird" after a character in the novel *Les Misérables*). His dog, Robot, became lost, and the boys eventually found him in a shallow pit. Bending down to scoop up his dog, Ravidat felt cold air rising from a small hole in the pit's bottom.

The boys had heard rumors of a tunnel that connected a sixteenth-century manor house to a local Montignac castle, a tunnel that locals said contained treasure (of course). Ravidat decided that the hole was an entrance to the tunnel, so he returned with three other boys—Simon Coencas, Georges Agniel, and Jacques Marsal—to explore it. Using improvised tools, they dug down, eventually breaking into a cavern. As their homemade paraffin lanterns lit the way, the boys crawled down a long pile of rubble. At the bottom, they found a pool of water surrounded by low gleaming white walls. They explored farther.

The boys, who thought they were in a tunnel, were stunned when they saw a vividly painted horse in the flickering lights. Holding their lights higher, they could see that the entire ceiling was painted. Reindeer, horses, a bear, and abstract markings covered the walls; bulls circled the ceiling. The boys just stood and stared. It was better than treasure.

They explored the cave over the next few days, finding more passages and images. Ravidat undertook the dangerous climb down into "the Well," where he found the now famous bird-man image. The boys guessed that the images were old, but they had no idea they were looking at some of the world's oldest art.

The boys informed their schoolteacher, who sent a message to Abbé Henri Breuil. Breuil was a priest and a scholar of Upper Paleolithic cave art. In fact, professionals acknowledged his expertise, calling him the "Pope of Prehistory."

However, with a war on there was little that could be done immediately. Breuil advised the boys to pitch camp near the cave's mouth and protect it. To their credit, the boys did exactly that. They faithfully guarded the cave, leading visitors through to prevent destruction and living in a conical log hut (after their tent burned down) heated by a woodstove through the winter of 1940–41.

But the war intensified. In the summer of 1942, Ravidat joined a resistance group, and Marsal was captured by the German army and sent to a labor camp. Coencas lost his parents, though he himself was saved by the French Red Cross. Agniel returned home to help support his parents.

And so Lascaux sat until 1947, when work finally began again at the site. In 1948, it was opened to visitors, and Marsal became a guide. The government installed a ventilation system in 1958, but by 1963, the stream of visitors had brought in more humidity and microorganisms than the system could handle, and a green fungus began to cover the paintings. The cave was closed to the public and cleaned, but remains closed to this day. Only a few people are allowed to visit the site each week, and the waiting list is several years long.

Fortunately, the French government constructed an astonishingly precise replica of the Hall of the Bulls only 200 meters from the real cave. Lascaux II opened to the public in 1983, and a reunion there in 1986 brought the four friends together at the cave again.

Lascaux continues to figure prominently in analyses of Upper Paleolithic cave art, and its magnificence is enjoyed by the thousands who visit Lascaux II each year. And it all began with a lost dog.

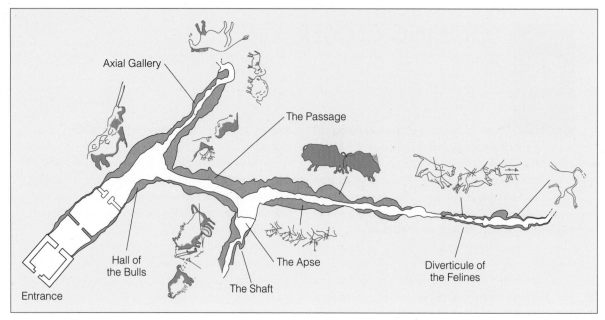

Figure 12-7 Map of Lascaux.

entirely visible until you walk around the bulge in the wall, single file. Several flint blades, covered in ochre and jammed into a crack, were found near this horse image. Walking around the "falling" horse, you encounter another horse, this one upright, and then the end of the passage.

Retracing your steps, you move back through the Hall of the Bulls and to the left. Passing through a low opening, you enter the Passage—this one longer than the Axial Gallery. The original opening was even smaller than it is today, and Upper Paleolithic artisans had to crawl through it.

In the Passage, the walls bear no calcite and the stone is softer. More horses and bulls are painted and engraved on the walls, although they are not as well preserved as in other parts of the cave. Images are piled up on top of one another, and the art here seems to be less "composed" than in the Axial Gallery and the Hall of the Bulls.

About 15 meters down the Passage, you encounter the Apse on your right, a small domed chamber with walls covered in engravings and a few paintings. Many different species are present—horses, bison, aurochs, ibex, deer, and perhaps even a wolf and lion. These images also overlay one another, producing a confusing jumble. Many engraved lines cut through the images.

Behind the Apse is the "Shaft" or "Well," a 5-meter-deep pit. Stone lamps were found at the bottom—turned upside down, as if the users meant to extinguish them. At the bottom of the pit is one of the oddest images of Upper Paleolithic art, which

we show in Figure 12-8: A bison, its head lowered in defensive posture, appears to have a spear through the body. Some interpret the lines emanating from its belly to be entrails. In front of the bison is a stick figure of a man, his penis apparently erect, who appears to be falling backward from the bison's blow. The figure only has four fingers, however, and his head looks more like that of a bird. Beneath the man is a long vertical line, with what appears to be a bird perched on its top. The meaning of this image is the source of endless speculation.

Climbing out of the Shaft, you return to the Passage and continue moving down its length. The walls contain more images for the next 15 meters or so, and then the images cease as the passage narrows and the ceiling drops. You encounter the two charging bison that we mentioned previously—the ones that appear to be running toward and around you. After dropping to your knees and crawling along the cave floor, you encounter the Diverticule of the Felines, with its soft clay walls. If you are a small person, you are crouching; a larger person might be lying on his stomach.

Here there are aurochs and horses and bison, but also large cats—panthers or cave lions. Spears pierce some, others are cut by lines or geometric markings, or they have lines emanating from their mouths and anuses. The images are well composed but seem to have been more hastily engraved than others in the cave. This section of the cave was perhaps rarely visited because otherwise its soft clay walls would not have survived so well.

What Does All This Mean?

Leaving Lascaux, you might turn to look at the Hall of the Bulls one last time, trying to imagine how the scene would appear in the flickering light of a stone lamp. Something significant obviously transpired in these dark places. The aurochs, bison, and horses painted on Lascaux's walls and ceilings were not the fleeting whimsy of a Paleolithic artist. The same images appear in many caves and were used over thousands of years.

© Charles & Josette Lenars/CORBIS

Figure 12-8 Bison and "falling man" in Lascaux. It is not known if these images were painted at the same time (as a "scene") or at different times.

We do not know the specific meanings of these world-famous images (and, in truth, we probably never will). Lewis-Williams thinks that this art is somehow related to altered states of consciousness, but the images themselves could not, of course, have been produced while the artist was in a trance state because one would need to be fully conscious to mix the paints, negotiate the cave's twists and turns with a stone lamp, and build scaffolding where needed. But Lewis-Williams thinks that the paintings at Lascaux and elsewhere provide firm evidence of Upper Paleolithic people trying to come to terms with understanding the meaning of altered states of consciousness—dreams and trances.

He sees the larger chambers, like the Hall of the Bulls, as places where communal rituals may have taken place, with people seeking assistance from a spirit world that existed below ground. Although the floor of Lascaux was damaged before it was investigated, the floors at Grotte Chauvet contain many human footprints, some 25,000 or more years old. Some of the prints are big and some are small, telling us that people of all ages visited even remote portions of this cave.

Lewis-Williams also suggests that the distribution of art within a cave may parallel the stages of trances. In the front chamber are animals that figured in the lives of Upper Paleolithic people. Here, too, we find some abstract signs—the rectangles, wavy lines, and rows of dots that appear in the early stages of trance. Deeper inside the cave, the narrowing passageway mimics the movement into the deeper states of trance. Lewis-Williams suggests that the falling horse at the end of

the Axial Gallery is not falling at all, but is instead an artist's representation of the vortex that one senses in the deeper stages of trance.

Farther into the cave, we see "confused" images, such as those in the Apse and the Diverticule of the Felines. These, Lewis-Williams suggests, may represent the merging of abstract and natural images in the deepest stage of trance or efforts by one shaman to bond with the power of another by drawing an image over that drawn by another shaman. Although rare in Upper Paleolithic art (and absent at Lascaux), occasional animal images take on human characteristics. They walk on two feet, sometimes hold their front legs in a human way, or turn to stare at the observer with an eerily human gaze. These might record instances where observers entered the deepest stage of trance and were unable to see the difference between themselves and animals.

Lewis-Williams suggests that vision quests may have been held in the deepest cave recesses. Without food or water, the total darkness and silence of a cave is a perfect medium for the production of visions. Perhaps people of the Upper Paleolithic saw caves as one place to access the spirit world.

Recall that some images make use of the bumps and contours of a cave's wall; Lewis-Williams believes this is more than a clever artistic trick. Shamans in hunting-and-gathering cultures often speak of a strong yet permeable membrane between themselves and the spirit world. Lewis-Williams suggests that the nature of trance would have suggested that portions of the spirit world lie belowground. By mimicking the vortex of trance, caves are the closest a person could come to the spirit world; the rest of the journey had to be made through trance. If the cave wall is the membrane between this world and the spirit world, then paintings and engravings were perhaps ways to access that spirit world. By using the cave's contours, the artist makes the painting more a part of the cave wall itself and, in so doing, increases its power. The flints, teeth, and bones left shoved into cracks may also have been similar efforts to break through the membrane and contact the spirit world.

In sum, Lewis-Williams argues that Upper Paleolithic art is not art for art's sake; nor is it fertility or hunting magic. Instead, he argues that the art reflects humanity's effort to come to grips with the perception that one's quotidian existence is not all that there is, to answer the question "What is the meaning of life?" And that idea gives us, denizens of the twenty-first century, a strong link to the artisans who painted bulls on the ceiling of a cave by torchlight thousands of years ago.

CONCLUSION

An archaeology of the mind attempts to move beyond the more easily accessible matters of diet and settlement patterns to religion, ritual, and cosmology. People respond to their world through culture, an integrated set of symbolic meanings that are communicated through material culture. But given that there is no necessary link between symbols and their meanings, the development of reliable middle-level theory is almost impossible, so this crucial area of human behavior often eludes archaeologists. Successful efforts rely upon historically linked ethnographic analogies, but these are limited to the more recent prehistory of regions with good ethnographic data. More ancient symbolic systems must be studied in ways that make use of uniformitarian elements of human neurology or perhaps a few symbolic universals (though these remain to be demonstrated).

SUMMARY

1. What is the central challenge of "cognitive archaeology"?

⊛ Cognitive archaeology aims to study the perception, description, and classification of the universe; the nature of the supernatural; the principles, philosophies, and values by which human societies are governed; and the ways in which aspects of the world, the supernatural, or human values are conveyed in art.

⊛ Studying these ancient modes of thought requires the interpretation of symbols, objects, or acts (verbal and nonverbal) that by cultural convention stand for something else *with which they have no necessary connection.* This means that, without some ethnographic context, there is no obvious way to connect a symbol to its meaning.

2. How do archaeologists study ancient religion?

⊛ Archaeologists attempt to understand past religions—specific sets of beliefs based on people's ultimate relation to the supernatural. Such religious beliefs are manifested in everyday life through rituals—behaviors such as prayer, music, feasting, sacrifice, and taboos. As such, ritual is a material manifestation of the abstract idea of religion and archaeology's easiest portal to the study of ancient religions.

⊛ Archaeologists also attempt to understand cosmology. This encompasses how past cultures explain their universe—how it originated and developed, how the various parts fit together, and what laws it obeys—and express their concern with what the future of the universe holds.

⊛ Where archaeologists have available some ethnographic data that are closely related to the archaeological case, they may be able to extrapolate backward from the present to the past. Even these cases, however, harbor the chance that a symbol meant something different in the past than it does in the present.

⊛ Iconography, a culture's expression of abstract ideas in art and writing systems, can also be used to reconstruct the religious and other ideas that stand behind the art.

3. Can archaeologists learn anything from very ancient cases that have no close cultural descendants?

☻ The study of ancient symbols runs the risk of becoming a free-for-all, with any interpretation being as valid as another. It is perhaps especially important, then, that the study of ancient iconography and other manifestations of a culture's cosmology and religion adhere to the canons of scientific analysis.

☻ In instances where ethnographic data are not available, archaeologists must be more restrained in their interpretations, not focusing on the specific meaning of particular symbols but looking to the more general character of thought itself.

MEDIA RESOURCES

Doing Fieldwork:
Archaeological Demonstrations CD-ROM 2.0
This CD, developed by the authors, shows professional archaeologists involved in various digs, many of which are referenced in the text. The presentation is organized by the main techniques used on an archaeological dig, reinforcing concepts and techniques via live examples. The CD takes you through each step automatically, or you can navigate to any point via the navigation bar. After reviewing a step in the dig process, you are taken to Check Points, which are concept questions about each step of the dig. Then you can see the answers, receive your score, and even send your scores to your instructor.

The Companion Website for *Archaeology*, Sixth Edition
www.cengagebrain.com
Supplement your review of this chapter by going to the companion website to take one of the practice quizzes, use the flash cards to master key terms, and check out the many other study aids that are designed to help you succeed in your introductory archaeology course.

13 UNDERSTANDING KEY TRANSITIONS IN WORLD PREHISTORY

LEARNING OBJECTIVES

**AFTER READING THIS CHAPTER
YOU SHOULD BE ABLE TO ANSWER THESE QUESTIONS:**

1. What is unilineal evolution and why did anthropology discard it?

2. What theories have been proposed to explain the origin of agriculture?

3. What theories have been proposed to explain the origin of the archaic state?

4. What is the difference between sufficient and necessary conditions in an explanation?

© Craig Lovell/Corbis

Pyramids at the Maya site of Tikal. How do societies develop from egalitarian hunting-and-gathering bands into stratified societies with elite leadership?

PREVIEW

THIS CHAPTER WILL INTRODUCE two milestones in the long-term evolution of human culture and, simultaneously, examine the role that paradigms play in interpreting the past.

Before considering these milestones, we will look at unilineal evolution, a now defunct paradigm through which nineteenth-century social scientists explained human diversity. We then concentrate on how archaeologists have explained the origins of agriculture and the origins of civilization (what we will call the "archaic state"), each a major transition in human history. As we examine the paradigms and explanatory theories used by archaeologists to understand these transitions, we emphasize two points. First, although each paradigm or theory contributes something to our understanding of these transitions, no single paradigm appears to give a complete accounting. Second, we emphasize the importance of differentiating between the *specific processes* at work, which can vary tremendously from case to case, and the *general conditions* that engender cultural change, which may be more universal.

INTRODUCTION

Archaeologists consider many kinds of questions, from small ones such as "Is this a potsherd?" to big ones, such as "What is human nature?" Answering the broader questions of cultural evolution is one of archaeology's most significant contributions to anthropology. In this chapter, we illustrate the different ways that archaeologists approach two of archaeology's perennial "big" questions: the origins of agriculture and the origins of a form of political organization that anthropologists call the "state."

The historical sciences, such as geology, paleontology, and archaeology, approach their subject matter differently than lab scientists. Laboratory scientists can repeat their experiments, changing one variable while holding others constant, to determine what effect a particular variable has on the outcome. But the historical sciences cannot do this. The Chavín civilization of the high Andes Mountains, for instance, existed only once and will never happen again. We can't rewind history and replay it with one different variable—say, by changing the mountains to a desert—to see what happens.

Among the historical sciences, archaeology has the added difficulty of human culture. We cannot ignore the "when," "how," and "what" questions of a region's prehistory; we need to know the *particular processes* and events at work in a given case, such as the rise of the Chavín state, in order to understand cultural change more generally. To answer "why" questions, archaeologists benefit from a comparative approach, one that looks for patterns among specific historical sequences that point to the *general conditions* of cultural change. To understand, for example, why civilizations and states evolved (terms we will define in the following), we compare what happened in Egypt, China, Mexico, and other places where such forms of human organization first appeared. These comparisons help define how sequences of development were similar or different, leading us to suggest hypotheses that might explain general patterns in human cultural evolution. This is the closest we can come to laboratory conditions.

Throughout this chapter, you should keep in mind a distinction between "necessary" and "sufficient" conditions of change. "Necessary conditions" *must* exist for a particular change to occur; "sufficient conditions" are the *minimal* ones needed for a change to occur. A basic knowledge of plant reproduction, for instance, is *necessary* for an agriculturalist (because you can't farm unless you know that plants come from seeds). But, as we demonstrate in the following, such knowledge is not *sufficient* to inspire all foragers to become agriculturalists. Some other condition(s) must be in place for this economic change to occur.

EVOLUTIONARY STUDIES

Why did agriculture begin when and where it did? Why did farming not appear in other places? Why did "civilizations"—with their magnificent architecture, artwork, writing, and calendars—appear in some places and not in others?

A century ago, Western scholars answered these questions with a paradigm known today as **unilineal cultural evolution.** Before going any further, you must understand that *anthropology long ago discarded unilineal cultural evolution.* So, why bring it up at all? Evolutionary frameworks have been around since before the days of Charles Darwin, some with strong racist overtones. So, at the outset, we want to be clear about which evolutionary paradigms we are endorsing, and which we believe must be avoided.

Unilineal Cultural Evolution

The nineteenth century was an exciting time for European intellectuals. Recall from Chapter 1 that Boucher de Perthes was retrieving stone artifacts from France's river gravels and claiming a great antiquity for them. By the second half of the century, it was clear that Europe, as well as the New World, had an ancient history. What, European scholars asked themselves, had the past been like?

At the same time, several European countries had established themselves as major colonial powers. In their colonies in Africa, Asia, and the Americas, Europeans encountered people who were strikingly different from themselves. Why, Europeans asked, were the peoples of the world so diverse?

They found answers to both questions in the paradigm of unilineal cultural evolution. Nineteenth-century scholarship in the West depended on Enlightenment philosophy—especially the notion of progress. Enlightenment thinking held that progress resulted from increasingly "rational" thought, which allowed people to acquire the wealth and leisure time necessary to control nature and improve themselves morally. To nineteenth-century thinkers, "progress" meant moving not only toward material perfection, but toward moral and spiritual perfection as well.

Consequently, these thinkers viewed the human past as a record of the march toward perfection. By the mid-nineteenth century, archaeology had demonstrated that Europeans had passed through several stages in their progress to modernity (enshrined in the now famous Stone, Bronze, and Iron Ages). But archaeology was a fledgling science, lacking adequate methods to reconstruct the details of the past. Stratified sites showed technological change, but without the necessary middle-level theory, the archaeological record remained silent on matters such as kinship, politics, or social organization.

But this hardly stopped Western scholars, who attempted to reconstruct the past using an Enlightenment-era version of the **comparative method.** Today, this term refers to the testing of hypotheses against a range of human societies, but in the nineteenth century, the "comparative method" translated cultural diversity into a neat, evolutionary sequence, in which different living peoples represented different stages in humanity's march of progress. The comparative method argued that people were different because some had made more progress than others, and that consequently the world's different peoples provided living snapshots of the past.

Although Enlightenment philosophy held that all people shared the same capacity for progress, it seemed that some had done better than others. Why?

Darwin and the Origin of Species With the Bible to guide them, many nineteenth-century scholars believed that the diversity of animal life arose in the biblical act of Creation. But just as the archaeological record showed that human societies had changed through time, the paleontological record likewise reflected multiple significant changes in animal life through the ages. Initially, scholars attributed this diversity to the biblical flood, but growing evidence suggested that many changes were gradual, not catastrophic. Was species diversity really a product of a one-time act of creation, or was something else involved?

With the publication of *On the Origin of Species* in 1859, Charles Darwin (1809–1882) provided a new way to understand biological diversity. Darwin's revolutionary volume suggested that because the world's food supply is inherently inadequate, the young of any species must struggle to survive. Most don't make it. The survivors who live to foster the next generation do so because of fortuitously favored characteristics. Consequently,

---

unilineal cultural evolution The belief that human societies have evolved culturally along a single developmental trajectory. Typically, such schemes depict Western civilization as the most advanced evolutionary stage; anthropology rejects this idea.

comparative method In Enlightenment philosophy, the idea that the world's existing peoples reflect different stages of human cultural evolution.

through the process of **natural selection,** some physical characteristics are passed along to the next generation, and others are not. (Exactly how this happened was mysterious because genetics was all but unknown at the time.) The evolutionary process, being gradual and continuous, eventually gives rise to new species as individuals appear with characteristics that permit them to inhabit a new environment or a new niche. Darwin's ingenious argument thus introduced the notion that diverse organisms descend from a common ancestor, and it provided evidence that the earth and its various life forms are dynamic and ever-changing.

Although the word "evolution" will always be associated with Darwin, he used the word "evolved" only once in the first edition of *Origin*. But the far-reaching implications of his work were not lost on scholars of ancient human history.

Lubbock's Pre-historic Times and Social Darwinism

Darwin's neighbor in Kent, England, was the banker and statesman John Lubbock (1834–1913). He was also an armchair anthropologist, and in 1865 he published the nineteenth century's most influential archaeology textbook, *Pre-historic Times, as Illustrated by Ancient Remains, and the Manners and Customs of Modern Savages*. In it, Lubbock married the Enlightenment's comparative approach with a rudimentary (and not entirely correct) understanding of natural selection.

Lubbock used the Enlightenment's comparative method to illustrate the lives of "paleolithic" (Old Stone Age) and "neolithic" (New Stone Age) people by reference to contemporary "primitives"—meaning the native peoples of Africa, Asia, and Australia. Lubbock argued that modern primitives were to archaeology as modern pachyderms were to paleontology. Although Lubbock made no specific analogies between particular living peoples and archaeological cultures, the implication was clear: Contemporary "primitives" were living approximations of what Europeans used to be.

natural selection The process through which some individuals survive and reproduce at higher rates than others because of their genetic heritage; leads to the perpetuation of certain genetic qualities at the expense of others.

social Darwinism The extension of the principles of Darwinian evolution to social phenomena; it implies that conflict between societies and between classes of the same society benefits humanity in the long run by removing "unfit" individuals and social forms. Social Darwinism assumed that unfettered economic competition and warfare were primary ways to determine which societies were "fittest."

Although not the only (or even the first) scholar to suggest this, Lubbock was highly influential. In fact, others soon expanded his argument, suggesting that living "primitives" were not merely "like" the past—they were, in fact, living relics of prehistory. Australian Aborigines were said to be lineal descendants of Neanderthals, and Eskimos were the descendants of the Magdalenians (the people who produced the Upper Paleolithic rock art of Europe). Using the comparative approach, these scholars barely needed archaeology. If you wanted to know what the past was, you could just find a living people who approximated the archaeological culture and describe them. There was no need to infer anything from archaeology because the past still existed!

So, why did these scholars think that some people were "back in the past" while others had apparently made so much progress?

Remember that scientific paradigms exist within a social context; for the nineteenth century, this meant colonialism. European scholars were unable to escape the belief in racial inequality that colonialism fostered. In nineteenth-century **social Darwinism,** cultural evolution became an extension of biological evolution by suggesting that social forms also compete for survival, with the richest and most powerful being the "fittest." Lower socioeconomic classes were seen as "the least fit" of industrial European society, and "primitive" peoples were the "least fit" people of the nineteenth-century world. But even top-rung Western civilization was not the evolutionary peak. Recall that Enlightenment thought was grounded in progress—technological, cultural, moral, and spiritual. Above the elite classes of Europe on the evolutionary scale stood the angels, and above the angels was God. The British aristocracy saw themselves as closer to God than, say, the Australian Aborigines. By today's standards, the hubris of colonialism is simply shocking.

Social Darwinists argued that human societies varied in their "evolutionary" status from highly evolved groups (the Europeans) to those who differed only slightly from the advanced apes. Cultural differences, they believed, were grounded in biological differences. Today, of course, we know that culture has nothing to do with biology because any person can be encultured into any culture.

Lubbock, however, argued that through the process of natural selection, humanity was improving biologically, culturally, intellectually, and spiritually. Left alone, capitalist societies would prosper and improve. In fact, Lubbock concluded on an upbeat note: "The future happiness of our race, which poets hardly ventured to hope for, science boldly predicts."

The downside, of course, was that the world's "primitives" were doomed. In Lubbock's view, these people had not evolved sufficiently, and no degree of remedial education could repair the damage done by millennia of natural selection. Although neither Darwin nor Lubbock advocated exploitation of these populations, both believed that "primitive" peoples were condemned to extinction. Thus, the paradigm of unilineal evolution provided "scientific" justification for British colonization of the world.

How "Evolution" Became a Dirty Word

In the early twentieth century, the nascent field of anthropology turned against this **ethnocentric** notion of progress. Franz Boas (1858–1942), often called the "father of American anthropology," and his students rejected unilineal evolution as a valid way of studying the human condition. In large measure, this was because of the paradigm's racist overtones and the colonial excesses that it supported. A Jewish immigrant from Germany, Boas was all too familiar with exclusion and ethnocentrism.

Boas argued that each culture is unique and should be valued as such. He believed that cultures change in ways unique to themselves and that current evidence did not warrant sweeping generalizations. Instead, Boas advocated the idea of **historical particularism.** He pointed out that because cultural evolution was so complex and had taken so many diverse paths, there was no single line of progressive evolution and, consequently, cultures could not be placed into a unilineal evolutionary scheme. Human institutions such as matrilineal descent, slavery, private property, or formal courts are associated with an array of other sociocultural features. Complex forms of kinship and elaborate cosmologies, for example, can accompany the simplest kinds of technology (as among Australian Aborigines).

Although Boas admitted to some degree of regularity in history, he believed that earlier researchers had exaggerated the patterns. And even if patterns did exist, Boas believed that the patient accumulation of ethnographic detail and historical facts must precede the construction of any generalities concerning human cultural evolution.

The Return of Evolution

Unilineal cultural evolution collapsed under the assault from Boas and his students. But research conducted under the paradigm of historical particularism eventually amassed sufficient data from ethnography and archaeology to show strong regularities in cultural evolution.

Within a decade after Boas's death—he died at lunch after presenting an antiracism lecture at Columbia University—evolution paid another visit to the halls of anthropology. Although evolutionary thinking does not dominate anthropological explanation, it does play a significant role in archaeology.

Evolutionary thought has changed markedly over time, and several current paradigms compete for Darwin's mantle. A complete description of those paradigms is beyond our scope, but before we consider explanations of world prehistory, we wish to point out three key differences between unilineal and modern evolutionism.

First, modern evolutionism contains none of the racist or moral overtones of nineteenth-century unilineal evolutionism. Contemporary evolutionism does not believe that differences between cultures are a product of differences in intellect or morality. Instead, as part of a larger materialist paradigm, modern evolutionism accentuates the role of ecological, demographic, and technological factors in conditioning how cultures change.

Second, contemporary evolutionary thinking recognizes that if natural selection is at work on cultural phenomena, it operates in a far subtler manner than it does among animals. Natural selection depends on differential reproductive success for particular traits to become more prevalent. This means that plants or animals with a favored trait survive and reproduce at a higher rate than those who lack the trait—among animals, for example, by attracting more mates or by providing more resources to their young. But whereas animals pass most behavioral traits on genetically, humans pass critical behaviors on through *culture*. Individual humans can adapt to change, alter their behavior, and adopt new technologies. Their genetic composition does not determine what "tools" they have to be successful in life. Although anthropologists debate the role of natural selection in cultural behavior, we agree that (1) cultural behavior is not genetic and therefore (2) the transmission of cultural information from generation to generation does not

> **ethnocentrism** The attitude or belief that one's own cultural ways are superior to any other.
>
> **historical particularism** The view that each culture is the product of a unique sequence of developments in which chance plays a major role in bringing about change.

depend directly on biological reproduction (although one may affect the other).

Third, although unilineal evolutionists argued over the details of the evolutionary sequence, they united in believing in a single, immutable sequence. Modern evolutionism is not concerned with the evolutionary sequence of particular cultural behaviors, such as matrilineal kinship or monotheistic religions. Today we know that the human past is vastly more complex than nineteenth-century scholars imagined it to be.

More than a century of archaeological research has amply demonstrated the intricate details that make up a particular historical sequence; this is the *specific* evolution of particular cultures. But modern evolutionary theory looks at prehistory to extract the "big picture," the *general* evolutionary pattern that characterized the deep human past. It is this long-term patterning that concerns us here.

An Evolutionary Sequence Before we can examine the origins of agriculture and the origins of the state, we must first situate these transitions within a generalized historical sequence that illustrates some patterns in human cultural evolution (Table 13-1).

Before roughly 12,000 years ago, all our ancestors lived in hunting-and-gathering bands. Although few hunter-gatherer bands survive today, they were common in many parts of the world during the nineteenth century, surviving on wild plants and animals and often changing their camps several times throughout the year. Most settlements housed fewer than three dozen people, although larger aggregations occurred when resources were particularly abundant.

Hunting-and-gathering bands are *usually* egalitarian (refer to Chapter 11). They lack hereditary differences in social rank and are integrated on the basis of age and gender. Leadership is informal and temporary, based mostly on age, competence, and personal magnetism. The Great Basin Shoshone of the nineteenth century are a frequently cited example of bands, as are the Inuit (Eskimo), South African Bushmen, and Australian Aborigines.

Were it not for the domestication of plants and animals, the entire world would still be living a hunting-and-gathering lifestyle. But we know that agriculture came into being at several places over the past 10,000 years. Archaeologists often refer to agricultural crops as "domesticated" plants because the plants are genetically manipulated versions of wild species that came to require human intervention for their continued survival. Modern maize, for example, would have a hard time propagating itself if humans stopped planting it.

TABLE 13-1 Summary of Differences among Bands, Tribes, Chiefdoms, and States

CHARACTERISTIC	BAND	TRIBE	CHIEFDOM	STATE
Subsistence	Foraging	Foraging, horticulture, pastoralism (herding)	Agriculture; pastoralists often incorporated within society	Agriculture, industrial, pastoral separated as specialists
Economic organization	Equal access to strategic resources through sharing and reciprocity	Reciprocity; limited redistribution of goods by charismatic leaders	Chief redistributes goods collected from lower-ranking people; society includes some non–food producers	Elites control access to strategic resources such as land and labor; includes many non–food producers such as craft specialists
Political organization	Egalitarian; no permanent positions of authority	Egalitarian; temporary and limited roles of authority; competitive feasting to establish rank	Differences in status based on genealogical closeness to chief, who holds a permanent, inherited office	State controlled by elites and run by administrative specialists; includes military and fiscal specialists
Social organization	Based on actual and fictive kinship; major units are nuclear family and bands of flexible membership	Kinship-based, egalitarian descent groups; less flexibility	Kinship important in determining rank; lineages ranked in clans	Class membership (elite or commoner) most important; kinship and descent important within class
Settlement pattern	Temporary camps; some seasonal settlements reoccupied	Sedentary villages (temporary camps among pastoralists)	Sedentary villages of different sizes; ranked (chief's village has highest rank)	Hierarchy of settlements reflects administrative functions; may be cities
Population density	Low	Low to medium	Medium to high	High

It was largely with the advent of domesticated plants that **tribal societies** appeared. Characterized by larger and more sedentary settlements, tribal societies occur throughout the world and vary considerably in appearance. Although community size is generally larger than that of hunters and gatherers, autonomous village societies still lack hereditary differences in rank, and larger villages maintain no authority over smaller neighboring communities. Although everyone in tribal society is equal at birth, considerable disparities in prestige can accrue during one's lifetime, and ritual privileges are often differentially distributed along gender lines. Early twentieth-century examples include the Pueblo Indians of the American Southwest, communities in highland New Guinea, and many peoples of the Amazon Basin. Some hunting-and-gathering societies—ones that lived in environments that supported high population densities without recourse to agriculture—are classified as "tribal" as well (such as those along the Northwest Coast of North America, or the Hopewell culture of the midwestern United States; see Chapters 2, 11, and 12).

A third social form, ranked society (discussed in Chapter 11), sometimes evolved when the egalitarian ethic (which downplays success and prestige) gave way to the belief that individuals are inherently unequal at birth. Commonly, certain family groups are considered to have descended from esteemed ancestors, supernatural beings, or gods; the closer this relationship, the greater one's hereditary rank and power.

In some societies, such as the Natchez (who lived along the lower Mississippi River at the time of European contact) and many African societies, smaller villages were subject to the powerful, hereditary leadership of larger, stronger neighboring communities. These societies—large-scale ranked societies with loss of village autonomy—are called chiefdoms. An example includes the prehistoric society of Moundville, which we discussed in Chapter 11.

Under certain conditions, **archaic states** evolved from competing chiefdoms. We use the term "archaic" to distinguish this ancient social form from modern industrial states, which are commonly governed by elected presidents or prime ministers. (The term "state" here refers to a form of political organization—not to be confused with its modern meaning.)

Most archaic states operated as kingdoms, characterized by a strong and centralized government with a professional bureaucratic ruling class. The appearance of archaic states marks a major shift in human social organization because these societies devalued the kinship bonds evident in chiefdoms, tribes, and bands. Archaic states maintained their authority through an established legal system and the power to wage war, levy taxes, and draft soldiers. Generally, archaic states had populations numbering (at least) in the tens of thousands, and urban centers exhibited a high level of artistic and architectural achievement. A state religion was usually practiced, even in areas of linguistic and ethnic diversity. The Classic Maya, Aztec, Inka, and ancient Egyptian societies are examples of archaic states.

One final term needs some attention: **civilization.** In common usage, "civilization" refers to behaviors that are ethnocentrically associated with proper behavior and some definition of high culture. But in anthropological terms, no such value judgments are implied. Instead, "civilization" simply refers to a constellation of elements associated with the archaic state, such as writing and bureaucratic records, calendrical systems, and the construction of monumental architecture.

Patterns in the Evolutionary Sequence This sequence tells us several things. First, we know that agriculture is a relatively recent phenomenon, developing only after the end of the Pleistocene period (about 10,000 years ago). But once it appeared, agriculture spread rapidly throughout much of the world. The domestication of plants and animals was hardly a single event; instead, the process happened several times, in several different areas of the world. Figure 13-1 shows the major hearths of plant domestication. These regions are all independent centers of domestication, unconnected to one another, although in many cases the plants they produced eventually spread over much of the globe.

Note also that the shift from egalitarian to ranked society is quite often associated with agriculture. Egalitarian societies are associated with hunting and gathering and **horticulture.** Chiefdoms and states tend to be associated with **intensive agriculture** (but there are exceptions).

Finally, we have learned that chiefdoms and archaic states appear even later in prehistory than agriculture,

---

tribal societies A wide range of social formations that lie between egalitarian foragers and ranked societies (such as chiefdoms). Tribal societies are normally horticultural and sedentary, with a higher level of competition than seen among nomadic hunter-gatherers.

archaic state A centralized political system found in complex societies, characterized by having a virtual monopoly on the power to coerce.

civilization A complex urban society with a high level of cultural achievement in the arts and sciences, craft specialization, a surplus of food and/or labor, and a hierarchically stratified social organization.

horticulture Cultivation, using hand tools only, in which plots of land are used for a few years and then allowed to lie fallow.

intensive agriculture Cultivation using draft animals, machinery, or hand tools in which plots are used annually; often entails irrigation, land reclamation, and fertilizers.

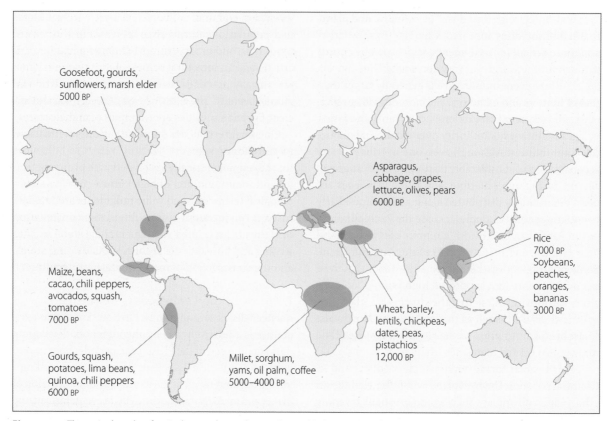

Figure 13-1 The major hearths of agriculture—places where various wild plants were independently domesticated—and the approximate dates that domestication occurred.

only in the past 5000 years or so, and they are always associated with high population densities. No hunter-gatherers live or lived in archaic states; no states are dependent on hunting and gathering for food.

In sum, a century of global archaeological research discerned some links among economy, social and political organization, and population density—links that will be well demonstrated as we explore the origins of agriculture and the origins of the archaic state.

WHY WERE PLANTS DOMESTICATED?

Scholars of the eighteenth and nineteenth centuries were largely unconcerned with explaining the *process* of plant and animal domestication. They focused instead on historical questions, such as when did plant domestication begin, and did it come before or after the domestication of animals? This was, of course, a necessary step because one cannot ask *why* something happened until you know roughly *when* and *how* it happened. But once archaeological data began to accumulate, archaeologists shifted their attention from the "what" and the "when" of plant and animal domestication to the "why."

The Unilineal Paradigm: Childe and Braidwood

The **oasis theory** was made popular in the 1940s by Australian archaeologist V. Gordon Childe (1892–1957). A prolific author, Childe was one of the first modern archaeologists to synthesize the archaeology of Europe and the Near East.

Childe knew that as the Ice Age ended, the world's climate became warmer and drier. In desert areas, Childe argued, people and animals flocked to oases, such as the Nile River, in search of water and food. This association eventually produced a symbiotic relationship between animals and people. People drove away predators and fed animals their surplus grain.

oasis theory Proposed by V. Gordon Childe, it argues that animal domestication arose as people, plants, and animals congregated around water sources during the arid years that followed the Pleistocene. In this scenario, agriculture arose because of "some genius" and preceded animal domestication.

Animals became accustomed to humans and were gradually domesticated.

Childe thus assumed that people grew crops before they domesticated animals, but he was unclear about why they became agriculturalists. He simply suggested that people became familiar with the "nobler grasses"—ancient ancestors of modern wheat and barley—that grew on the banks of the Nile, where they thrived on alluvial soil enriched by annual flooding. In his view, it remained only for "some genius" to produce similar artificial conditions elsewhere through irrigation and begin to grow wheat and barley.

Although Childe's explanation seemed plausible, the chronology for the Near East was sketchy, and no solid archaeological evidence for early food production was available. Shortly after World War II, Robert Braidwood (1907–2003) set out to search for that evidence. The hilly flanks of the mountains of southwestern Asia seemed a logical place to search because wild wheat, barley, and legumes, as well as wild cattle, sheep, and goats were to be found there.

Braidwood concentrated on the foothills of Iraq and Turkey. From his excavations, he obtained some of the first radiocarbon dates on early agriculture, and after learning that climate had been essentially stable during the period of animal and plant domestication, Braidwood rejected Childe's oasis theory.

In its place, Braidwood proposed the **hilly flanks theory,** which saw the development of agriculture as a "logical outcome" of the evolutionary tendency to specialize. As foragers "settled in" after the Pleistocene, they became familiar with their plant and animal neighbors; eventually, this accumulated knowledge permitted them to cultivate rather than simply gather plants.

Although Childe and Braidwood disagreed about the "where" and "how" of plant domestication, both assumed that humanity continually seeks to improve its technology and subsistence. And because they thought that plant domestication provided a more abundant and reliable economic base than foraging, they assumed that all it took for agriculture to appear was the *idea* and the *capacity* (the necessary plants). Anyone, they thought, with the idea and capacity would switch from foraging to agriculture. In this regard, Childe and Braidwood still subscribed to a portion of the paradigm of unilineal evolution.

But their explanations ran afoul of both archaeological and ethnographic data. If the *idea* of agriculture is a *sufficient* condition, then the transition from foraging to agriculture should be quick (at least in archaeological time). Yet, nearly everywhere, that transition was slow. In the eastern woodlands of the United States, for example, native peoples grew squash, sunflower, marsh elder, and chenopods some 4000 years ago. Maize, an import from Mexico, appeared in the woodlands about 2000 years ago. But it was only 1100 years ago that a full-fledged agricultural economy based on maize appeared. Because they obviously had the idea of agriculture 4000 years ago and maize 2000 years ago, why didn't these people become full-time agriculturalists sooner?

Ethnographic research also turned up hunter-gatherers who knew about and understood agriculture, but who continued to hunt animals and gather. Ethnographer Richard Lee (University of Toronto) once asked /Xashe, a Ju/'hoan man of Africa's Kalahari Desert, why he did not plant food. /Xashe's memorable response was, "Why should we plant when there are so many mongongos [edible nuts] in the world?"

The Materialist Paradigm: Population Pressure

Childe and Braidwood assumed that the idea for agriculture would be picked up by anyone who had it, but /Xashe reminds us that agriculture is hard work. The forager who wants seeds simply picks and processes them; but the farmer must till the soil, plant the seeds, and later harvest, process, and probably store the seeds. Why would anybody take on the additional labor of agriculture?

In the 1960s, several archaeologists argued that agriculture was related to **population pressure** brought about by slow population growth. Lewis Binford (see Chapter 1) argued that people adopt domesticated plants *only when forced to do so.* In his **density-equilibrium model,** Binford rejected Braidwood's notion that agriculture developed simply because of the accumulation of knowledge. Rather than viewing agriculture as a chance to "move up the evolutionary scale," Binford proposed that agriculture happens when population

---

hilly flanks theory Proposed by Robert Braidwood, it claims that agriculture arose in the areas where wild ancestors of domesticated wheat and barley grow. It attributes agriculture's appearance to people's efforts to continue to increase the productivity and stability of their food base, coupled with a culture that was "ready" to accept an agricultural lifeway.

population pressure The result of a population's reaching carrying capacity.

density-equilibrium model Proposed by Binford, it attributes the origins of agriculture to population pressure in favorable environments that resulted in emigration to marginal lands, where agriculture was needed to increase productivity.

LOOKING CLOSER

HUNTER-GATHERERS AS OPTIMAL FORAGERS

Optimal foraging theory belongs to the paradigm of human behavioral ecology, a framework that studies human behavior by applying the principles of natural selection within an ecological context.

Foragers do not take any food that they encounter because time spent harvesting and processing one resource is time *not* spent searching for another. Large game, for example, generally takes a long time to find, but it has a high return rate. Plant foods are easier to find, but they generally have low return rates because of high processing times. Optimal foraging models ask what foods foragers should harvest to maximize their *rate* of food intake. To develop foraging models, we need to know the return rates of the potential food resources. And we obtain these values through ethnoarchaeological and experimental research.

Steven Simms (Utah State University), for instance, was interested in return rates of the Great Basin's plant foods, such as Indian ricegrass (*Oryzopsis hymenoides*). No one collects these resources today, so he did it himself the way Shoshone women did it a century before: He walked

© Kim Hill

An Aché man hunting.

through a field, hitting the tops of the plants with a woven "seed beater" paddle and knocked the seeds into a basket held in his other hand. Simms then ground the seeds into flour using a stone mano and metate. Timing these activities, he found that after 41 minutes he had 98 grams worth of ricegrass seed flour. Knowing that ricegrass con-

---

growth outstrips an environment's **carrying capacity.** Population growth requires that some people move to more marginal environments. It is *these* people, Binford argued, who turn to agriculture to make up for the lack of high-ranked resources.

In framing this argument, Binford turned unilineal evolutionism on its head. Instead of agriculture being a step up in progress, it became the strategy implemented by the "losers"—people who had to make marginal land productive and who, in the end, needed to work harder. The unilineal evolutionists saw hunting and gathering as an onerous lifeway, with agriculture providing a breakthrough. Binford's hypothesis suggested just the opposite. Who is right?

carrying capacity The number of people that a unit of land can support under a particular technology.

teosinte A plant native to southern Mexico; believed to be the wild ancestor of maize.

Is It Better to Farm or Forage? Binford assumed that some resources were collected more efficiently than others, but he lacked the data to back up this assumption. Bear in mind that the plants we know as the major agricultural plants—such as maize, wheat, millet, and rice—*did not exist* at the end of the Pleistocene. What did exist were their wild forerunners, but these were often substantially different from the domesticated plants of today.

The wild form of maize, for example, is southern Mexico's **teosinte,** a tall tropical grass with a head of grain no bigger than your pinky. It looks nothing like the sweet corn you buy at the supermarket. Of all the wild plants that foragers in southern Mexico harvested, why did teosinte become a domesticated one?

The reason is that maize, like other plants that were eventually domesticated, has the latent genetic capacity to be modified. Human use of these plants over many generations—which included the intentional sowing of seeds with favorable characteristics (such as

tains 2.74 calories per gram, he calculated the return rate as follows:

$$(2.74 \text{ calories/gram} \times 98 \text{ grams}) / 41 \text{ minutes}$$
$$= 6.55 \text{ calories/minute}$$
$$= 393 \text{ calories/hour}$$

Using such data, a foraging model predicts which resources foragers should take upon encountering them, and which they should ignore. Simply put, it predicts whether the diet should be broad or narrow. It predicts that if high-return-rate resources become rare, diet should expand; and that if technology enhances the hunting of large animals, then small game will drop from the diet.

Kim Hill (Arizona State University) and Kristen Hawkes (University of Utah) tested this model among the Aché, seasonal hunter-gatherers in tropical Paraguay. Aché men took many animals while hunting with bows and arrows, including peccaries (65,000 calories/hour), deer (27,300 calories/hour), birds (4700 calories/hour), and

monkeys (1200 calories/hour). When the Aché used shotguns, however, their diet changed. Because shotguns don't require the line of sight necessary for bow hunting, Aché hunters could forgo lengthy stalking and shoot animals more quickly after sighting them, raising the return rate of large game. The foraging model predicted the effect: When shotguns were used, the Aché ignored birds and monkeys, and the diet breadth contracted. When the Aché returned to using bows and arrows, the diet expanded to include small game.

Foraging models cannot account for foods that are harvested or ignored because of their symbolic meaning; the model predicts which foods should be taken *if maximizing the return rate is the only foraging goal*. But with such predictions as a backdrop, foraging models can help determine which foods were or were not eaten for purely cultural reasons. For example, if the model predicts that a food should be eaten, but archaeological or ethnographic data show that it was not, this suggests that the particular food was tabooed.

size)—triggers natural selection. You can see results of this process in the vast maize fields of Iowa, the extensive rice terraces of Asia, the millet fields of Africa, and elsewhere around the world.

But in the beginning, these domesticated plants were far more modest, and one wonders: Why would hunter-gatherers have bothered with them at all? To answer this question, we must consider a resource's **return rate:** the amount of energy the resource provides measured against the amount of time it takes to procure and process it (see "Looking Closer: Hunter-Gatherers as Optimal Foragers").

Return rates can be complicated by many factors, but experimental data show that large game generally have high return rates, whereas seeds (including those of wild wheat, barley, and teosinte) have much lower rates. **Optimal foraging theory** predicts that as high-return-rate resources (such as large game animals) become scarce, foragers add lower-return-rate resources (such as seeds) to their diet. Higher-return-rate

resources can become scarce because of environmental change or because of overexploitation. Ethnographic and experimental data suggest that people may have turned to the seeds of those plants that eventually became agricultural plants when high-ranked resources, such as large game, became scarce.

But many hunter-gatherers around the world expanded their diets to include a variety of plant resources—including native peoples of California and the Great Basin—yet they did not become agriculturalists (even though California is today one of the world's major agricultural regions). And when Steve Simms (Utah State University) and Ken Russell (1950–1992) conducted ethnoarchaeological research with Bedouins in Jordan, they

return rate The amount of energy acquired by a forager per unit of harvesting/processing time.

optimal foraging theory The idea that foragers select foods that maximize the overall return rate.

found the return rate from cultivated wheat (which includes the cost of tilling the soil and sowing the seeds) was little different from the return rate of gathering wild wheat. So, what's the advantage of agriculture?

A Selectionist Perspective The answer to this question may come from a third paradigm, one that focuses on the underlying process of natural selection.

David Rindos (1949–1996) argued that plant domestication is an example of **coevolution,** the result of natural selection operating simultaneously on both plants and the people using them. He argued that because of some plants' genetic composition and because of how they must be harvested, the very act of harvesting them results in unintentional selection in such a way that the plants become dependent on humans for survival. It's this side of the coevolutionary process that makes a plant species more productive, so that humans, in turn, become more dependent on it: The humans and plants *coevolve.* This may happen, for example, when people plant seeds outside a plant's normal range. Eventually, the people and plants become mutually dependent: The people need the plants for food, and the plants need the people to survive outside their normal range. So, whether humans become agriculturalists depends a lot on the genetic capacity of the plants at hand. Eventually, those agricultural plants may provide better return rates than the available wild plants. When that happens, people eschew the gathering of wild plants for the cultivation of domesticated ones.

Rindos ignored the impact of population growth or climate change. He also ignored human intent, arguing that humans "intended" to become agriculturalists as much as certain ant species "intended" to develop symbiotic relationships with fungi. As a Darwinian paradigm, the coevolutionary approach holds that if a particular behavior, such as agriculture, increased the rate of survival of the young, then that behavior would become more prevalent.

Another Look at the Environment But humans foraged for hundreds of thousands of years before agriculture appeared in the early Holocene period. If Rindos is right, why didn't agriculture appear sooner?

Braidwood would have said that human culture was "not ready for it," but Peter Richerson (University of California, Davis), Robert Boyd (University of California, Los Angeles), and Robert Bettinger (University of

coevolution An evolutionary theory that argues that changes in social systems are best understood as mutual natural selection among components rather than as a linear cause-and-effect sequence.

California, Davis) argue that it was the environment that was not ready for it.

These scholars point out that the Pleistocene (the 2 million years preceding the Holocene) was an odd time in earth's climatic history. Thick glaciers covered vast parts of the globe and tied up a lot of the world's water supply. This means that the Pleistocene was not only colder than today; in many places, it was also drier.

Additionally, the Pleistocene atmosphere contained less carbon dioxide (this is why, you will recall from Chapter 6, late Pleistocene radiocarbon dates are so far off from their calibrated calendar ages). Plants take in carbon dioxide through photosynthesis and release oxygen. Less carbon dioxide means that plants were "asphyxiating" in the Pleistocene; consequently, plant productivity was lower. And, to make matters worse, climate was more variable during the Pleistocene than during the Holocene, making plants a less reliable source of food than animals before 10,000 years ago.

For these reasons, Richerson and his colleagues argue that agriculture *could not* have appeared before the Holocene. Rindos's process of coevolution could not have arisen until the Holocene, when plant exploitation could provide a sufficiently abundant and reliable food source. But Richerson adds that, by providing a reliable food source, agriculture caused human population to grow, and the ensuing population pressure forced neighbors to adopt agriculture as a way to increase food productivity (as Binford argued). As a result, agriculture quickly spread during the Holocene to most parts of the globe that could support it and where foraging did not provide higher return rates.

A Social Perspective

So far, each of the paradigms offered to explain the origins of agriculture has privileged the power of human intent and the conditions of environment, demography, and selection. But looking at what we know about agriculture around the world, there is another possibility. In some places, agriculture is indeed *preceded* by population growth. But in other places, such as southern Mexico (where maize was domesticated), sedentary villages appear a thousand or more years *after* plant domestication. And some regions that are suitable for agriculture, such as California, were occupied by hunting-and-gathering peoples until European contact, even though they were densely populated. Population and environment may not be the only relevant variables here.

Some archaeologists, such as Brian Hayden (Simon Fraser University), suggest that agriculture arose as a way to increase productivity so that certain individuals could garner prestige and power through competitive feasts and ostentatious displays of wealth in the form of exotic items obtained through trade (such as the potlatch we described in Chapter 2). This increase in productivity, Hayden argues, was possible because new technologies such as nets, baskets, and grinding stones allowed hunter-gatherers to harvest resources such as fish and seeds efficiently, allowing people to create the food surpluses needed for competitive feasts. Hayden argues that efforts to increase productivity for these feasts led people to agriculture.

© F. Valla

Figure 13-2 A portion of a large house at the Natufian site of Ain Mallaha, Israel (in Hebrew, "Eynan"). Note the substantial postholes that suggest the house was covered by a large, heavy roof.

To support this explanation, Hayden points to another post-Pleistocene trend: the trade of exotic goods, such as carved shells, rare stones, and beads. These trade goods (along with exotic domesticated foods) may have figured in competitive feasts or other social displays of power. Hayden suggests that this "food fight" theory explains why some of the earliest domesticates—such as chili peppers, bottle gourds, and avocados—were not essential to subsistence.

The Origins of Agriculture in the Near East

Different paradigms clearly offer different explanations for the origins of agriculture, and each one makes some sense. To evaluate these alternatives, let's turn to the archaeology of the Near East, one of the world's major hearths of plant domestication.

In the Near East, agriculture originated in a broad arc of mountains in Israel, Jordan, Syria, Iraq, and Iran—sometimes called the **Fertile Crescent**—where wild wheat and barley still grow today. Although Braidwood saw no evidence for it, significant climate change occurred at the end of the Pleistocene. Based on data from palynology and other studies, we know that around 18,000 years ago, the Near East was cooler and drier than it is today. Annual precipitation and temperature increased until about 13,500 BP but, between 13,000 and 11,600 BP, the world saw a rapid return to cooler and drier but highly variable conditions during a climatic interval known as the **Younger Dryas.** After

this time, the climate returned to wetter and warmer conditions. Then, after 9000 BP, the Near East became considerably more arid.

We can't tell exactly when intentional agriculture began because it's difficult for paleoethnobotanists to distinguish wild wheat and barley from their early domesticated forms. The best evidence suggests that a full-time agricultural economy began about 10,000 to 9000 BP. Less intensive, but nonetheless intentional, cultivation may have begun much earlier. Here is what current evidence tells us about this process.

Prior to 15,500 BP, nomadic foragers occupied the southwest Fertile Crescent, an area known as the Levant (in Israel, Jordan, and Syria). They lived primarily along major waterways and the Mediterranean coast, hunting gazelle and taking a variety of plant foods. Soon, however, these nomadic folks became sedentary. The **Natufian** culture (ca. 14,500–11,600 BP) built round, semi-subterranean structures, 3 to 6 meters in diameter, with stone foundations and probably wood-and-brush upper walls and roof; an excavated example appears in Figure 13-2. Abundant remains of house

Fertile Crescent A broad arc of mountains in Israel, Jordan, Syria, Iraq, and Iran where wild wheat, barley, and other domesticated plants are found today.

Younger Dryas A climatic interval, 13,000 to 11,600 BP, characterized by a rapid return to cooler and drier, but highly variable, climatic conditions.

Natufian A cultural manifestation in the Levant (the southwest Fertile Crescent) dating from 14,500 to 11,600 BP and consisting of the first appearance of settled villages, trade goods, and possibly early cultivation of domesticated wheat, but lacking pottery.

mice suggest a continual source of fresh garbage at these sites, which in turn suggests that people were there year-round (this conclusion is supported by seasonality studies of gazelle teeth).

Natufian settlements were located in places where natural stands of wheat and barley were readily available. People harvested these wild cereals, as demonstrated by the plant macrofossils, grinding and pounding stones, and sickle sheen on flint blades. But the plant foods appear to be wild, not domesticated, forms.

The Younger Dryas climatic interval interrupted the Natufian lifeway about 13,000 BP. Some villages were abandoned, and people returned to a more nomadic lifeway as plant foods became less abundant. Ofer Bar-Yosef (Harvard University) suggests that the Younger Dryas may have encouraged the now large Natufian population to make land more productive by husbanding and later intentionally planting "wild" cereals. The extreme climatic variability of the Younger Dryas interval, however, probably made reliance on agriculture a risky venture.

After the Younger Dryas (ca. 11,600 BP), the climate returned to the wetter, warmer, and more stable conditions that are conducive to the growth of cereals. Foragers returned to village life; but this time the villages were considerably larger, signaling a growth in local residential groups. We find these **Neolithic** sites in the mountains, within the natural range of wild wheat and barley. Away from the mountains, in the deserts, were nomadic hunter-gatherers living in small, temporary settlements.

Neolithic sites contain many large, oval dwellings, some containing two rooms. There were storage structures in each site as well, including large stone silos and bins. Flotation has recovered copious amounts of carbonized seeds of barley, wheat, and other plants. We cannot be certain if these plants were cultivated, but they were an important part of Neolithic subsistence. Neolithic peoples still hunted gazelle, and they gathered various fruits and wild seeds.

With the return of a more benevolent climate about 11,600 years ago, habitats opened up that were conducive to agriculture. Bar-Yosef estimates that human population exploded at this time by more than 1000 percent. During the Younger Dryas, people developed techniques that gave agriculture at least the return rate

of gathering wild plants. By 9000 years ago, a growing population now required that the full productivity of agriculture be harnessed, and agricultural communities appeared.

Comparing the Paradigms

So, which explanation is right?

As we pointed out in Chapter 2, paradigms reflect particular perspectives on the world—elevating some variables and downplaying others. The paradigm channels researchers toward certain explanations and guides them away from others. But because human behavior is complex, it is unlikely that any single paradigm will adequately capture the entire picture; each sees one portion of the puzzle. A complete explanation for the origins of agriculture, or any aspect of human evolutionary history, probably requires input from several different paradigms. We can see how this works in the various explanations for the origins of agriculture.

Agriculture clearly requires a working knowledge of plant foods. But the plants that would eventually be domesticated were being used at least 18,000 years ago; surely, foragers did not require *thousands* of years to understand that seeds produce plants. Unilineal evolutionists might have argued that these ancient hunters lacked the intelligence to understand plants sufficiently to be agriculturalists. But these same people were capable of fine artistry and tool manufacture, and their hunting strategies required detailed understanding of animal behavior. Certainly, these late Pleistocene foragers were every bit as intelligent as people today. Knowledge is necessary *but not sufficient* to explain the origins of agriculture.

As Childe suggested, climatic change also clearly has something to do with agriculture, although not in the way he thought. Foragers could not become agriculturalists until the environment was capable of supporting agriculture, and this may not have happened until the early Holocene. And the Younger Dryas clearly altered the Natufian lifeway, requiring that a formerly sedentary foraging population make the land more productive through the cultivation of wild wheat and barley.

Did population pressure play a role? The earliest evidence for agriculture does not come from marginal areas (contrary to Binford's expectations), but from the homeland of wild wheat and barley. Evidence from Natufian settlements also suggests that population growth caused some groups to become sedentary

Neolithic The ancient period during which people began using ground stone tools, manufacturing ceramics, and relying on domesticated plants and animals—literally, the "New Stone Age"—coined by Sir John Lubbock (in 1865).

on choice localities that included stands of wild wheat and barley. By the beginning of the Neolithic, this expanded population may have congregated around these localities and created local population pressure on resources, requiring people to expand their diets and rely more heavily on plants. Because wheat and barley respond genetically (through selection) to human harvesting by becoming more abundant, their domestication was perhaps inevitable in the face of large local populations.

What about social processes? Did competitive feasting have anything to do with agriculture? Natufian settlements do provide archaeological evidence for trade—seashells, some from as far away as the Atlantic Ocean, beads made of rare stone, and figurines carved in bone and stone. Many burials contain elaborate personal ornaments, including necklaces, belts, bracelets, and headdresses. It is possible that these ornaments indicate trade relations that, in turn, reflect social alliances. But Natufian sites lack storage structures (which appear only in Neolithic sites). And wheat and barley were important to the diets of both, not peripheral "luxury" items. Natufian and Neolithic communities were probably self-sufficient, and the need for alliances probably arose much later. However, it is likely that feasting and trade created alliances that were critical to survival when crops failed or animals migrated in the climatically uncertain world of the Younger Dryas. Agriculture may have helped make possible the feasts that, in turn, helped to form those social alliances.

Finally, what about human intentionality? Rindos claimed that human intentionality had nothing to do with agriculture, and at one level this is true: It's unlikely that a forager in the Levant woke up one morning 10,000 years ago and decided to become a farmer. But human intention must have played *some* role. The changes that occurred in the wild cereals suggest that humans *intended* to increase harvest productivity and efficiency—for example, by saving the largest seeds for the next planting, by transporting plants to favored localities, or by irrigating natural stands. They *intended* to forage as well as possible, and this intention led them to agriculture.

Processes and conditions similar to those we've described for the Near East were also at work in Asia, Africa, and the Americas. In this brief overview, we have tried to provide a feel for the paradigms archaeologists use to understand this research problem, how archaeological data can be used to evaluate hypotheses, and how most paradigms contribute some pieces to a research puzzle.

WHY DID THE ARCHAIC STATE ARISE?

We now turn to a second major transition in human cultural evolution, the origins of the archaic state. Some instances where archaic states arose are shown in Figure 13-3. Nearly every student of anthropology today lives in a state society, and some probably consider the state to be the "natural" form of human social and political organization. But not so long ago (in archaeological time), nobody lived in a state society. In evolutionary terms, states are simply the latest form of human organization (and probably not the last). How did they arise?

We first need to define what we mean by the archaic state. There are many definitions; we follow one proposed by Kent Flannery: The state is a type of very strong, usually highly centralized government, with a professional ruling class, largely divorced from the bonds of kinship that characterize simpler societies. It is highly stratified and diversified internally, with residential patterns often based on occupational specialization rather than blood or **affinal** relationships. The state attempts to maintain a monopoly of force and is characterized by true law. Not all archaic states fit this definition exactly, but it points out the salient aspects of most such political formations.

The archaic state is a complex form of sociopolitical organization. States generally have powerful economic structures and often a market system. An elite class controls the state economy and maintains authority by laws and by privileged access to key goods, services, and ideology. Archaic states generally have populations numbering at least in the hundreds of thousands, and this population is often concentrated in large cities. Some people were specialists—potters, weavers, stone masons, and so on—who depended on the labor of others for subsistence (that is, they did not grow their own food). Archaic states are also known for a high level of artistic achievement, monumental architecture, and an "official" state religion.

Theories about the origin of the archaic state date from the nineteenth-century evolutionists. As with agriculture, unilineal evolutionists argued that "civilization" appeared when people were intellectually and morally prepared to enter into a social contract and to give up some of their liberties in exchange for benefits, such as protection in time of war. As with agriculture,

affinal Relatives by marriage rather than by blood.

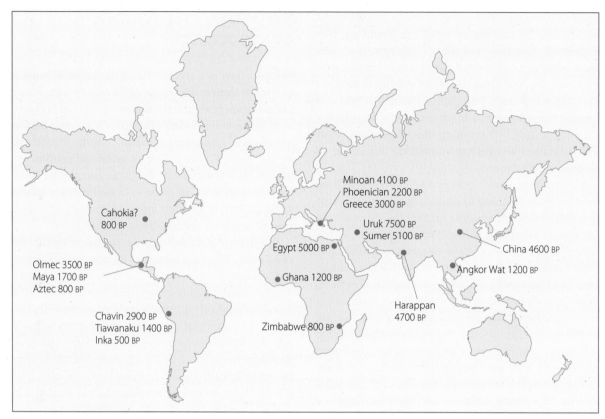

Figure 13-3 Major primary archaic states; these are places where state forms of political organization developed independently.

this approach fails to explain why states originated where and when they did.

We know that the formation of archaic states did not depend on domesticated animals, metal tools, or wheeled transportation because states appeared in places such as Central America where none of these existed prior to European contact. The first explanations we'll present—privileging irrigation, warfare, population growth, and environment—fall within the materialist paradigm. A final explanation focuses on the role of ideology and falls more within the postprocessual paradigm. As with the origins of agriculture, we believe that it's possible to reconcile these different views.

The Irrigation Hypothesis

In his influential book *Oriental Despotism* (1957), Karl Wittfogel (1896–1988) asserted that the mechanisms of large-scale irrigation were directly responsible for creating the archaic state. His **irrigation hypothesis** argued that irrigation systems require an extraordinary degree of coordination above the level of the individual farmer. How this works is shown in Figure 13-4. First, someone must construct the system, dig the channels, build the dams and headgates. This requires organization above the household because portions of the system benefit everyone, but not all portions benefit each individual household (for instance, the ones downstream from your home). Irrigation systems are inherently problematic because people living upstream could take all the water, leaving nothing for those downstream. Wittfogel pointed out that this means that irrigation systems inherently require a level of continuing control above that of the individual farmers who benefit from them.

Wittfogel argued that the great Asian societies of China, India, and Mesopotamia followed a radically different evolutionary course from societies in western Europe and elsewhere. The particular forms of archaic states in the Orient evolved because of the conditions required by large-scale irrigation: the imposition of inordinately strong political controls to maintain the hydraulic works, the tendency for the ruling class to merge with the ruling bureaucracy,

irrigation hypothesis Proposed by Karl Wittfogel, it attributes the origin of the state to the administrative demands of irrigation.

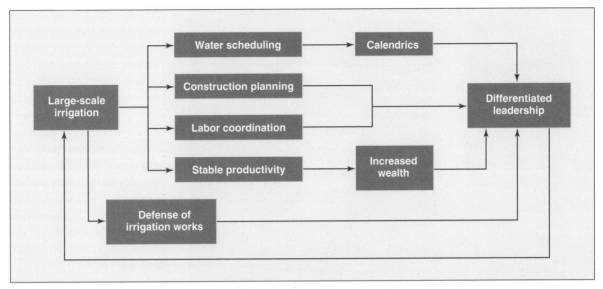

Figure 13-4 Schematic diagram of Wittfogel's irrigation hypothesis for the origin of the state.

the close identification of the dominant religion with governmental offices, and the diminution of private property and economic initiative.

Wittfogel contended that, after a creative period in which the bureaucracy began, stagnation set in, corrupting power and creating a despotic and feudal system. He also saw the hydraulic society as an initial step toward totalitarianism (a German intellectual who spent time in a concentration camp for speaking out against the Nazis, Wittfogel was vehemently antifascist).

According to Wittfogel's theory, the state evolved in direct response to the demands of large-scale irrigation. The need for coordinated labor, massive construction, and so forth led to increased wealth and military strength and eventually to the powerful ruling bureaucracy that characterized state development.

The Warfare and Circumscription Hypothesis

Ethnologist Robert Carneiro (American Museum of Natural History) terms Wittfogel's irrigation hypothesis a "voluntaristic" theory, one requiring that "at some point in their history, certain peoples spontaneously, rationally, and voluntarily gave up their individual sovereignties and united with other communities to form a larger political unit deserving to be called a state." In this respect, Wittfogel's explanation is more in line with unilineal evolutionism—that is, people give up individual freedoms when they are ready to take the next "step" in cultural development. But by studying modern tribal societies and chiefdoms, Carneiro knew that autonomous political units today never willingly surrender their sovereignty, and he saw no reason why they should have done so in the past.

Carneiro argued instead that egalitarian settlements transform into chiefdoms, and chiefdoms into states, only when coercive force is involved; warfare thus plays an especially pertinent role in the early stages of state development, as illustrated in Figure 13-5. Of course, some tribes might agree to cooperate in times of stress, but such federations are temporary and voluntarily dissolve once the crisis has passed. Carneiro's initial premise stipulates that political change of lasting significance arises only from coercive pressure. And warfare, he suggested, is the only mechanism powerful enough to impose bureaucratic authority on a large scale.

It is clear from the archaeological record, however, that warfare is considerably older and more widespread than the state. Because warfare does not invariably lead to archaic state formation, Carneiro adds that, though *necessary*, warfare is not *sufficient* in itself to account for the state. According to Carneiro, only in areas where agricultural land is at a premium—areas that are environmentally "circumscribed"—will warfare lead to state formation. Competition over land arose first where natural barriers—such as mountains, deserts, or seas—restricted the availability of arable land. The vanquished peoples had no place to flee and thus were required to submit to the expanding political authority of the victors. A centralized political authority was needed to maintain a standing army as well as to control conquered populations.

Figure 13-5 A carving of a decapitated head from the 3500-year-old site of Cerro Sechín in Peru. The carving is one of 400 decorating a stone facade that forms the base of a platform mound. The facade is covered by images of warriors and the jumbled body parts of their victims. Some archaeologists believe this frieze commemorates a mythical or historical battle.

In Carneiro's **warfare and circumscription hypothesis,** shown in Figure 13-6, the combination of population growth and circumscribed agricultural resources leads to increased warfare, which in turn fosters the centralized political organization characteristic of state-level complexity. He musters support for his hypothesis from the archaeology of archaic states near the Nile, the Tigris-Euphrates (Mesopotamia), the Indus Valley, and the valleys of Mexico and Peru—all of which evolved in areas of circumscribed agricultural land. Conversely, in areas where agricultural land was plentiful and not tightly bounded—such as in northern Europe, central Africa, and the eastern woodlands of North America—states developed quite late, if at all.

A Multicausal Theory

Scientists often propose ideas before the data to evaluate them are available. This was certainly the case with Wittfogel's and Carneiro's explanations for the rise of the state. But over the past few decades, archaeologists have studied the origins of the state all over the world, in places such as Mesopotamia, the Indus Valley,

Mesoamerica, China, and the Andes. From these studies we can see that neither irrigation nor circumscription and warfare *alone* account for all the archaeological data. In some places, irrigation exists without states; in others, states exist without irrigation agriculture. In some, warfare precedes state formation, but in others, it follows. As with agriculture, it is impossible to specify a single "prime mover" for states. No *single* condition is both *necessary* and *sufficient* to create an archaic state.

As pointed out earlier, in studying the origins of any social institution, it is important to differentiate between the *conditions* that generate cultural change and the specific *process* that creates the change in a given case. Drawing on three case studies—France, Japan (both during the Middle Ages), and the Inka—ethnologist Allen Johnson (UCLA) and archaeologist Timothy Earle (Northwestern University) searched for more general conditions rather than specific processes. They concluded that three general *conditions* are necessary and sufficient for archaic states to form:

1. High population density that strains the food production system
2. A need for a system of integration (such as trade, irrigation, or an external threat)
3. The possibility that the economy could be controlled to permit the financing of regional institutions (such as a state religion) and to support a ruling class

Given these *conditions*, any number of specific *processes* can result in a state.

Figure 13-7 shows how these conditions might result in social change as population grows after agriculture. A growing population demands that land become more productive. Horticulturalists such as Madagascar's Mikea (see Chapter 8) may use slash-and-burn farming, in which a plot of land supports one to three harvests and is then allowed to lie fallow for some time. As population grows, however, a family cannot afford a fallow period because all available land is occupied. If there are no new fields, people must

warfare and circumscription hypothesis Proposed by Robert Carneiro, it attributes the origin of the state to the administrative burden of warfare conducted for conquest as a response to geographic limits on arable land in the face of a rising population.

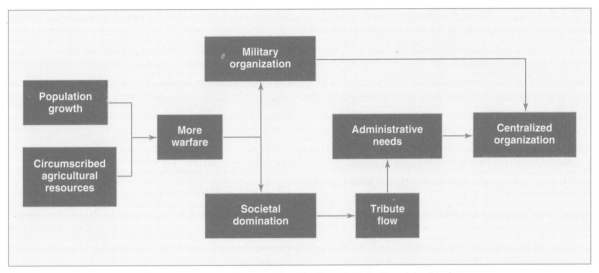

Figure 13-6 Schematic diagram of Carneiro's circumscription and warfare hypothesis for the origin of the state.

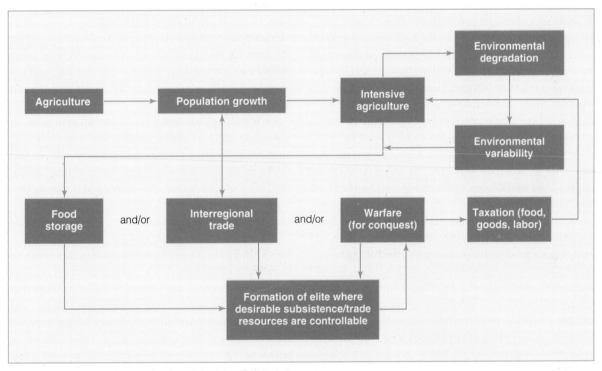

Figure 13-7 Schematic diagram of multicausal origins of the archaic state.

artificially fertilize land. The native peoples of northeastern North America did this with fish remains. In the Near East, people used manure from domesticated animals. Lacking domesticated animals, the Aztec collected the "night soil" from residents of large villages for use as fertilizer.

As the best arable land is claimed, some people are pushed to marginal lands (as Binford argued). Here they must develop intensive agriculture, using labor-intensive ways to make land more productive. In some

places, this may entail building and maintaining canals (as they fill with silt and debris). In mountainous regions, people build terraces along hillsides (as they did in the Andes Mountains), creating flat, arable land where there had been only a steep hillside. The Aztec created *chinampas*—long, low islands in shallow lakes—by dredging soil from the lake bottom and piling it up. All of these require labor, and at some point the system simply cannot produce more at a given level of technology.

So, what happens during an environmental calamity, when a severe drought, flood, or insect plague strikes?

Today, farmers in developed nations have insurance to buffer against disasters. In the past, horticulturalists also tried to buffer environmental fluctuations. The Hopi and Zuni Indians in the American Southwest, for example, plant fields of maize in different locations. They plant some on south-facing hillsides, others on hilltops, and still others on the valley floor. They know that by putting their fields in different microenvironments, they increase the probability that at least one of those fields will survive. If one field is lost to drought, another might prosper; if insects attack one field, the others might be spared.

As population grows, the need for such buffering strategies increases. These strategies include family-level decisions, such as field placement and long-term household food storage, but they also include group-level responses, such as interregional trade, conquest, or some sort of cooperative system of exchange. These group responses require a system of social integration. This is a point at which the specific *processes* of state development can differ. States have different histories and take on different characters depending on whether trade, irrigation, or warfare creates the primary need for a "system of integration" (the theory's second condition).

At some point, the individuals who negotiate the relations between groups take on a special importance. These middlemen could manipulate and exploit social ties—marriages and trade relations, primarily—between villages and centers in times of stress. They are individuals who, for whatever specific reason, hold sway over a productive resource by controlling territory and/or labor. A system of social integration therefore might create Johnson and Earle's third condition: the possibility that an individual or group could control the economy to permit the financing of regional institutions and to support a ruling class.

In times of stress, people living under high population densities compete for land and resources. Some unfortunates may petition those who control productive land for some of their stores, land, or protection. If those who control productive land do not share, they could be attacked. By allowing others to migrate to their territory or share in their stores, those on productive land could buy security. And it appears that they did this by exacting tribute or taxation from the petitioners, which they then used to support an army as well as their entourage or court. By controlling key resources, some individuals became the "elite."

Such social systems, however, require an "explanation" that provides an account of why some people are elite and some are peasants. What role does ideology play in the origin of archaic states?

The Role of Ideology in State Formation

To this point, we have explored the *material conditions* that create archaic states. Processual research provided an understanding of how significant cultural change takes place when technology and the economic base change. Subsistence-level change produces population growth that eventually requires new mechanisms to buffer fluctuations in the food base. This, in turn, causes shifts in social organization.

Ideological changes develop as a means to validate the new social organization—to explain why some people live in luxurious houses with servants and the best food while others toil in the fields and inhabit more humble abodes.

By **ideology,** we mean the cultural, religious, or cosmological ideas that provide group members with a rationale for their existence. *Ideology masks the fact that one group is exploiting another.* Unilineal evolutionism, for example, was an ideology in the sense that it provided a justification for the domination of colonized lands by Western nations.

In archaic states, ideologies are often linked to religion, and here we see how the kinship links that tie the elite in chiefdoms to the population often become severed in states. In early states, the elite claimed that they were different from everyone else and that they deserved their lofty position because they were descended from the gods. If they considered themselves kin to the peasants, then this would mean that the peasants, too, were kin to the gods. This belief could undermine the elite's control of a region's resources. That archaic states often suffered internal warfare is evidence that people can sometimes see through the ideology.

Ideologies have a tendency to take on a life of their own, and here is where they can play a causal role in the development of states. As we pointed out in the last chapter, humans see the world through their own cultural logic, a logic that is expressed as a particular symbolic system. This "cultural" world can provide its own engine of change. If kings are descended from the gods, then they should be all-powerful. If they are all-powerful, then shouldn't the entire world be under

---

ideology A set of beliefs—often political, religious, or cosmological in nature—that rationalizes exploitive relations between classes or social groups.

their rule? Possibly for this reason, states tend to be expansionist, eventually collapsing when they reach beyond their physical limits of control. Sometimes this expansion is military, and sometimes it is based on religion (we saw a possible example of this in Chapter 12's discussion of the expansion of the Chavín culture in central Peru).

The Maya: A Case Study of State Formation

As we did with agriculture, let's take these abstract ideas and see how they help us understand a particular case, the lowland Maya of Central America. Figure 13-8 shows the location of some of the sites we will mention.

We have visited the Maya in previous chapters. Here we focus on the lowland Maya, who lived (and still live) in Mexico's Yucatan Peninsula, Belize, and portions of Guatemala and Honduras. Some occupied the Petén rain forest, and others lived on the more arid Yucatan Peninsula.

By 5000 BP, agriculture had begun in the highlands to the west of the lowland Maya region. Here the Maya grew maize, beans, squashes, pumpkins, chili peppers, amaranth, and cotton. As expected, population grew after a shift to full-time agriculture, and some people apparently moved into the lowland regions.

Evidence for pre-agricultural human settlement of the lowland Maya region is limited. This is due partly to the difficulty of finding small, ephemeral sites in a forest that is dense enough to hide large stone temples, and partly to the fact that Maya settlements destroyed earlier occupations. But current evidence suggests that few people lived in the area until maize horticulturalists moved there about 4000 years ago. Settlements from this time period lack any large public buildings, elaborate burials, or exotic trade items, suggesting that the early farmers were egalitarian.

The Middle Preclassic Period: Population Growth During the Middle Preclassic Period (2900–2300 BP), population grew, emigrants arrived from other areas, and a lively trade developed in colorful feathers of tropical birds and animal skins. Archaeological surveys show that all major regions of the lowlands were occupied by sedentary, slash-and-burn horticulturalists by 2500 BP. This growth apparently approached the region's carrying capacity, for farmers were finding ways to make the land produce more food. In the swamps of Belize, for example, farmers built raised fields, much like the Aztec *chinampas* described earlier. They also grew a greater variety of crops, including not only maize but also beans, squash, tomatoes, chilies, ramon and cashew nuts, avocado, papaya, guava, and cacao (chocolate). Still, analysis of skeletal isotope data suggests that maize sometimes constituted only about 30 percent of the diet, and faunal data show that white-tailed deer, turtles, fish, and dogs were eaten.

The increase in population precipitated a change from more or less egalitarian communities to small chiefdoms. Some of these late Middle Preclassic Period centers were quite large; Nakbé, for example, covered some 50 hectares (125 acres). These centers contained large buildings and stone platforms, built with public labor. Previously, people were interred beneath the floors of houses, but during the Middle Preclassic, some individuals were buried within the stone platforms or even the large buildings. Patricia McAnany (University of North Carolina) suggests that these burials signal a shift to **ancestor worship,** a religion in which one's deceased ancestors serve as important intermediaries between the natural and supernatural worlds. From ethnographic data, anthropologists know that ancestor worship tends to occur with restrictive claims on land, and the burials within the public structures may have

Figure 13-8 A map of the lowland Maya region showing the location of some major Maya sites.

---

ancestor worship A religion in which one's deceased ancestors serve as important intermediaries between the natural and supernatural.

© San Diego Museum of Man, photo by Peter D. Harrison, ca. 1993

Figure 13-9 A painting by Carlos Vierra (1915) of Tikal based on his imagining the site's appearance soon after its abandonment.

served to justify a kin group's claim to territory. Thus, by the end of the Middle Preclassic Period, groups exerted control over land just, as we might expect, at the time when all land was occupied.

The Late Preclassic Period: Formation of Chiefdoms By the beginning of the Late Preclassic Period (2300–1750 BP), a few sites, such as Altar de Sacrificios and Seibal, developed into towns of several thousand people, but no single center emerged. The Maya built public buildings in these centers, some including the corbelled arch. (Arches with a keystone did not exist in the pre-contact New World; corbelled arches were made by piling up stone blocks, moving each layer in a little closer until the walls could be bridged with a lintel stone.) They also erected stelae using local hieroglyphic styles, and they participated in a lively trade in exotic goods, including polychrome pottery, jade, and obsidian.

Survey data suggest that the regional population grew again by some 350 percent during the Late Preclassic Period, and people aggregated into a few large settlements. El Mirador, for example, covered some 15 square kilometers and contained more than 200 stone structures. One was a pyramid some 55 meters high; another was built atop a hill, with multiple tiers cut into the hillside. Others were large public buildings decorated with plaster and stone masks of deities. And at Nakbé and El Mirador, extensive stone causeways traversed the swamps. These rose 4 meters high in places and were filled with crushed white stone.

Nonetheless, during most of the Late Preclassic, Maya political organization had no single center. Instead, many small centers controlled the territory around them.

The Classic Period: State Formation But this changed near the end of the Preclassic Period and during the Classic Period (1750–1300 BP), when the lowland Maya took on the characteristics of the archaic state. There is evidence for warfare in earlier times, but now it seems that Maya leaders wrestled for control over centers, as attested to by burned buildings, fortifications such as palisades and moats, and mass burials of males with fractured bones—all of which first appear in the Late Preclassic. The causeways connected sites, suggesting alliances between the centers. Such evidence of supra-village control and coordination is a hallmark of the state.

During the Classic Period, these centers became solidified, albeit temporarily, as states. The sites of Tikal (tee-*call*) and Uaxactún (wah-shock-*toon*) became major centers, and others soon followed. Tikal, shown in Figure 13-9, would grow to cover 16 square kilometers and house some 80,000 people (larger than sixteenth-century London). It contained numerous stone public buildings, causeways, and pyramids with remarkably steep stairways leading to ceremonial chambers and astronomical observatories on their tops (see this chapter's opening photo). Hieroglyphs became standardized across the southern Maya lowlands, suggesting the development of a common political culture and some kind of political interaction and coordination.

Survey data indicate that population continued to grow throughout the Classic Period. As many as 10 million people lived in the lowland Maya area—more than live there today. Moreover, this population was more concentrated. Many Preclassic centers were abandoned during the early Classic Period, and their inhabitants moved into the large centers such as Tikal. So, not only did the overall population increase, but there was also an *aggregation* of population in large centers during the Classic Period.

Population growth and aggregation created new problems for the Maya, exacerbating the local effects of drought and conquest. Stable isotope, macrobotanical, and faunal data suggest that the commoners had an increasingly monotonous diet of maize, while the elite continued to enjoy a more varied diet. And skeletal data show that males decreased in average height during the Classic Period.

Producing enough food to feed the growing and aggregated population may have been difficult. Many of the centers were located next to *bajos*—low-lying areas that today are little more than swampy ground. Research by Vernon Scarborough and Nicholas Dunning (University of Cincinnati) suggests that in the past, the *bajos* were shallow lakes that could have provided the Maya with freshwater. By 2100 BP, these *bajos* had filled with silt that washed in as slash-and-burn horticulture denuded the surrounding land of forest. As the *bajos* filled up, Late Preclassic centers relocated. Some researchers, in fact, argue that archaic states met their eventual demise because of such "ecocide" (see "What Does It Mean to Me? Rapa Nui and Global Ecocide").

In Classic centers, and even in some Preclassic sites, Scarborough and Dunning found extensive water collection and control devices. The Maya modified natural gullies, runnels, and basins to channel runoff into small artificial reservoirs. Causeways and plazas were not just a way to keep one's feet out of the mud; they were also part of a system of water catchment and dams. At Tikal, the paved areas could capture some 900,000 cubic meters of water in a single season. Some of the catchment basins are positioned to provide water for fields surrounding the *bajos*, although direct evidence for irrigation is still lacking.

The large centers contained rectangular ballcourts, sunken stone-walled courtyards, sometimes with stone rings mounted high on the two long side walls; one is shown in Figure 13-10. The ballgame first appears in Preclassic sites, and although nobody knows exactly how the game was played, it likely involved driving a rubber ball through the stone rings without using hands or feet. This was more than just entertainment because ballgame images depicted on polychrome pots and stone carvings clearly depict human sacrifice as part of the ritual "game." By the time of the Spanish conquest, the game was played throughout Mesoamerica with a new twist: The winning team and their supporters pursued the losers and their boosters to take their clothing and jewelry.

Commoners lived in compounds of stone-walled, thatch-roofed houses with above- and belowground storage structures. In the arid north, the belowground storage structures, called *chultuns*, probably were used to store water. Status differences are reflected in house compounds of different sizes and the presence of exotic goods such as jade and obsidian. Elite burials became more elaborate and contained exotics and labor-intensive items such as polychrome pottery.

The Maya also had an elaborate calendar (in fact, they had three; see "Looking Closer: How the Maya Reckoned Time"), and they marked the dates of events on the stelae that we have discussed in previous chapters. After years of hard work, Tatiana Proskouriakoff (1909–1985) and Yuri Knorosov (1922–1999) figured out how to read the glyphs. Using the stelae and other archaeological sources of information, we can piece together the shifting rivalries of Maya political life.

During much of the late Classic Period, the lowlands were divided into numerous centers that alternately competed and allied with one another to control stretches of land and to garner prestige. The glyphs carved on stelae and painted on pottery tell us the names of the *K'uhul Ajaw*, or "divine lord," who ruled over a Maya capital. For instance, the royal name of a seventh-century ruler of Palenque was K'inich Kan B'alam ("Great Sun-Snake Jaguar"); a fourth-century ruler of Tikal was Yax Nuun Ayiin ("First Crocodile"). Maya kings had some of the coolest names in prehistory.

But the Maya were not trying to be cool. The names were intended to reflect a king's divine status. Maya kings claimed to be descended from the gods; the stelae portrayed their lives and succession to the throne as repeating mythical events of the past. To reinforce Maya ideology, the kings conducted rituals at auspicious times according to the ritual calendar to propitiate the gods. Without these rituals, the Maya believed, chaos would reign and the universe would collapse. Kings and their power were essential to the world's continuity. Power flowed from father to son or from brother to brother, and royal families were ranked in terms of their kinship distance from the king.

Seeing themselves as descended from the gods, these kings competed with one another to determine

Figure 13-10 A ballcourt at the Maya site of Copán, Honduras. One of the two stone rings is visible above the sloping wall on the left.

© Andrea Di Martino/Alamy

WHAT DOES IT MEAN TO ME?

RAPA NUI AND GLOBAL ECOCIDE

Rapa Nui is a lonely place, a 170-square-kilometer pinpoint of land some 2300 kilometers from the next inhabitable island. Known as "Easter Island" to English-speakers, it's a mysterious place, too, with some 200 massive stone statues, or moai, standing guard over the island's grassy slopes that speak of a former complex social order—one that did not exist when Europeans first visited the island.

But it's those grassy slopes that are interesting. Studies of pollen cores show that the island, which today supports virtually no substantial native trees, was covered by palms 800 years ago. And archaeological study of faunal assemblages of the island's sites shows that the number of bird species that flitted among those palms has been reduced by more than two-thirds. In other words, the island's biota has been devastated over the past millennium. Did humans have a hand in this? Did Rapa Nui destroy itself?

Many authors present Rapa Nui as a case study in ecocide, a warning of what is to come globally if we do not change our selfish ways. In his recent bestseller, *Collapse*, Jared Diamond repeats a question that many visitors to Rapa Nui have asked: What was the person who cut down the last palm tree thinking? In this morality tale, Diamond wonders why people couldn't see the environmental catastrophe that their greed and selfishness were creating.

Polynesian people arrived on Rapa Nui about 800 years ago. They were horticulturalists, and they brought with them various crops, such as taro and bananas. They cut down trees to build homes and canoes, from which they fished for porpoises. The human population grew rapidly. From a few canoe loads of people, the population grew in only 200 years to perhaps 10,000 people—about 60 people per square kilometer.

In addition to being small, Rapa Nui is not terribly productive—it's dry and sustains a heavy salt spray from high winds. Unlike many other Pacific islands, its surrounding waters lack reefs that support fish for food. Thus, the human population quickly reached carrying capacity, and competition ensued. Carrying a Polynesian cultural custom to an extreme, they carved stone from quarries into statues, and moved them to hillsides and stone platforms. These statues were probably erected at competitive feasts, as local chiefs competed for power and prestige in ceremonies perhaps similar to the potlatch discussed in Chapter 2. Trees were needed to roll the statues along, and to lever them into place.

But when people arrived on the island, so too did another species—rats, as stowaways on canoes. Their population grew even more quickly. With no predators on the island and an ample supply of food in palm nuts and

who was the greatest among them. In fact, David Webster (Pennsylvania State University) suggests that the Maya may have seen war as a way for their kings not only to subdue unruly neighbors but also to demonstrate their ability to quell the potential for chaos in the world. Warfare, the need to control subdued centers, and the need to reward those who supported the king in these endeavors produced the political hierarchy of the Maya in the Classic Period. The stelae and other evidence on monumental architecture record the exploits of the elites. It is this hierarchy of power that qualifies Maya Classic centers as archaic states.

We know that Maya courts were places of intrigue and backroom deals, just like those of Medieval and Renaissance Europe, with lords and sublords plotting coups and competing for power. Iconography between 1750 and 1300 BP is replete with images of warfare; and some sites show evidence of violent destruction, such as the toppling of stelae, and subsequent rebuilding.

This hieroglyphic evidence also tells us that by 1300 BP, the internecine competition among the many small centers had reduced itself to a single rivalry between Tikal and Calakmul (kah-lock-*mool*). Each of these centers was allied with several smaller centers.

shoots, the rat population exploded, probably growing to some 3 million in less than four years. Terry Hunt (University of Hawaii) argues that while people took a toll on the forests, the rats alone were capable of decimating them. And as the palm nuts and shoots disappeared, the rats turned to birds' eggs. People may have cut down the last tree, but rats probably prevented a new one from taking its place.

Is Rapa Nui a parable for the twenty-first century? A microcosm of global change and what it will bring? Yes and no. People can be selfish and foolish. But wholesale environmental change does not stem from these character flaws. It comes from people going about their day-to-day business in the only ways that are available to them, and from the unforeseen long-term side effects of those ways. Prehistory is replete with such examples. In some places, irrigation led to soil salinization; in others, slash-and-burn horticulture caused deforestation and soil erosion. Even hunter-gatherers altered their environments through seasonal burning of grasslands and forests. If there is a lesson in all this, it is that we need realistic day-to-day choices that are commensurate with the long-term environmental consequences we desire.

© George Gill, photo by Chad Harris

A stone statue on Easter Island.

These alliances were the result of centuries of warfare, with one center eclipsing another only to be conquered by a former rival. Tikal and Caracol, for example, fought for 250 years. Caracol eventually eclipsed Tikal in 1446 BP, only to become an ally of Calakmul later (along with the centers of Naranjo and Dos Pilas). Tikal returned to power, allying itself with Palenque and other centers. Eventually, around 1313 BP, Tikal defeated Calakmul, captured its war effigy (a large jaguar carving), and may have killed its ruler, Jaguar Paw.

Conquered populations sent annual tribute to the royal court of the victor in the form of cotton, feathers, shells, jade, cacao, and possibly maize and labor. Much of the warfare was status-related. By dominating powerful neighbors, a king communicated his authority to his people. And by assisting that king, lesser nobles could earn privileges and acquire control over conquered resources that might permit them to move up in status.

No single Maya center was ever able to maintain control over the entire lowlands; nor did any center maintain control for many generations. Still, it appears that some tried. And in the act of trying, the Maya meet the definition of an archaic state.

LOOKING CLOSER

HOW THE MAYA RECKONED TIME

The Maya were keen observers of astronomical events, and their rituals were governed by three precise calendars.

The first of these calendars was the Long Count. One of the accompanying figures shows two sides of a jade plaque that commemorates the ascent to the throne of one of Tikal's rulers, Zero-Moon-Bird (his name appears as one of the glyphs). On one side, Zero-Moon-Bird wears a jaguar headdress and tramples a captive underfoot. On the other is a series of glyphs. Look at them closely, and you will see that five of them have bars and/or dots to their left. These are calendar glyphs, and they date Zero-Moon-Bird's coronation.

The Maya used bars to symbolize five and dots to symbolize one (a stylized shell stood for zero). The Long Count dates an event by counting the number of days that have passed since "the beginning of time." The date is given in a series of units: *Baktun* are units of 144,000 days; *katun*, units of 7200 days; *tun*, 360 days; *uinal*, 20 days; and *kin*, 1 day. The number of each unit is denoted by the bars and dots. Looking at the figure, we see that the second glyph from the top—the *baktun* glyph—has one bar (indicating 5) and three dots (3) next to it, for a total of 1,152,000 days (144,000 × 8). The next glyph down (the *katun* glyph) has 2 bars (10) and 4 dots (4), for a total of 100,800 days (7200 × 14); likewise there are 3 *tun* (1080 days), 1 *uinal* (20 days), and 12 *kin* (12 days). Archaeologists write Long Count dates

as the series of units—in this case, 8.14.3.1.12. The total number of days is their sum: The event depicted occurred 1,253,912 days after the beginning of the calendar.

Although epigraphers still debate, many place the beginning of the Maya calendar at August 13, 3114 BC. So,

© Peabody Museum, Harvard University

The front and back of the Leiden Plaque. On the back are glyphs that indicate the age of the event depicted on the front.

What Explains the Origin of the Maya State?

Archaeologists trying to explain the origins of a *particular* state find it nearly impossible to identify *the* single factor without which the state would not have formed. Instead, each explanation points to one or more important conditions. Carneiro's explanation focused on competition over land generated initially by population pressure, and some evidence supports this idea in the Maya case. Raised-field agriculture, occupation of virtually all land, the control of water, high population estimates, and

human skeletal analyses all suggest that the Maya had reached the land's carrying capacity in the Late Preclassic period. And, in a sense, Maya land was circumscribed—by the ocean to the east, the dry Yucatan Peninsula to the north, and the highlands to the west and south (which witnessed their own population growth).

But the archaeological evidence also shows that the control of water played a role in determining where the centers were erected. Although it is unclear whether the water was used to irrigate fields, this is less important than the level of organization and authority needed to construct the reservoirs and to apportion

since 1,253,912 / 365 = 3435.37, the date in the Gregorian calendar is approximately 3435.37 − 3114 = AD 321.37. We then subtract a year because the Gregorian calendar implies a "0" year BC. Count the days from the calendar's start date, and the glyph gives the date for Zero-Moon-Bird's coronation as September 17, AD 320.

The second calendar is called the *tzolk'in*, or Sacred Almanac (shown in the figure). It is best envisioned as two cogged wheels, one with the numbers 1 through 13 on it, the other with 20 named days (such as "flint knife," "monkey," and "lizard"). This defines a sacred year of 260 days (13 × 20) with each day having a unique number-name combination.

The third calendar was the *haab*, or Vague Year, which consisted of 18 months of 20 days each, with 5 extra days added at the end. (The Maya were aware that the year was 365.25 days in length, but they did not use a leap year.) The Vague Year and the Sacred Almanac worked together to produce a cycle of 18,980

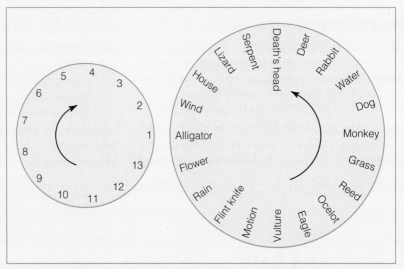

The Sacred Almanac. Each day has a name and a number. Envision the two wheels turning opposite to one another, and you can see that the current day is "1 alligator," tomorrow will be "2 wind," the day after tomorrow "3 house," and so on.

days. The exact same day—with the same number-name combination and Vague Year day—occurs only once every 52 years. The days when the 52-year cycle began over were critical to the Maya and required world renewal ceremonies.

The Maya recognized cycles of time, and a return to the beginning of time (or the end of time, some say), according to the Maya calendar, will occur on December 23, 2012.

the water. So, in one sense, Wittfogel's "irrigation hypothesis" also plays a role here.

Both explanations can be subsumed under the more general scenario of Johnson and Earle. Recall that their explanation required three conditions: (1) stress on food resources created by high population density, (2) the need for an overarching system of integration, and (3) opportunities for economic control. Each characteristic is found among the Maya of the Late Preclassic and Classic periods. The high population density placed pressure on the agricultural economy; in dry years, this pressure could be so severe that it led to outright conflict. Warfare, as well as efforts to prevent it,

required a system of social integration, as did efforts to ensure the flow of trade goods, information, and rituals between allied centers. The large centers, however, had the ability to control labor and, hence, agricultural productivity and warfare. It is possible that as one large center gained the edge in authority, families moved there and smaller centers gave their allegiance (and their labor) in return for protection. To maintain their positions of power, leaders of the large centers controlled the religion and calendrical rituals that provided a powerful integrating ideology for the Maya.

When we examine the material and ideological fundamentals of Maya culture, we see that they satisfy each of Johnson and Earle's three conditions. As with agriculture, there is no single "prime mover" to account for the development of a particular archaic state. Various paradigms each contribute something to a final explanation.

CONCLUSION

We have only briefly discussed the origins of agriculture and the archaic state. The specific developmental sequences for each differ widely throughout the world, but the variables of population, environment, warfare, trade, and ideology all seem to play key roles in one or both of these cultural changes. The specific *processes* that gave rise to the transition differ from case to case, but the general *conditions* appear to be similar. And explanations that seek to attribute these major changes in human cultural evolution to single variables—such as knowledge, environment, irrigation, or warfare—seem to be less useful than ones that incorporate a number of variables and perspectives.

Human cultural behavior and large-scale change in social and political organization are products of multiple variables that work in different combinations in different parts of the world. One of archaeology's tasks is to reconstruct these different, specific historical sequences. Another is to use these sequences to discover conditions that are both necessary *and* sufficient to account for major transitions in cultural evolution. In this chapter, we have recounted two instances in which archaeologists have tried to do precisely this.

SUMMARY

1. **What is unilineal evolution and why did anthropology discard it?**

- The nineteenth-century idea of unilineal evolution claimed that the differences among modern peoples resulted from differential progress various peoples had made toward "modernity"—which was defined as an upper-class, western European lifestyle.
- Living "primitives" were seen as providing evidence of the stages of human cultural evolution; for some scholars, "primitive" peoples were still "back in the Stone Age."
- Social Darwinism suggested that human progress depends on competition; in the nineteenth century, this theory was used to justify global imperialism, racism, and the excesses of capitalism.
- American anthropology rejected unilineal cultural evolution, replacing it with historical particularism that sought to understand each culture within itself, not as a stage in human evolution.

2. **What theories have been proposed to explain the origin of agriculture?**

- The origins of agriculture appear to have resulted from (1) climate changes at the end of the Pleistocene that were favorable for plant domestication, (2) population growth that caused foragers to take less efficient resources, including small seeds, and (3) the existence in some places of plants that responded to human foraging by becoming more productive.

3. **What theories have been proposed to explain the origin of the archaic state?**

- Archaic states appear to be a response to (1) population growth and the resultant need to intensify agriculture, (2) the need for an overarching system of social integration, and (3) the potential to control productive resources. The specific character and history of an archaic state, however, depends on the particular environmental situation, the importance of warfare versus trade, and the kind of ideology that supports the elite rulers.

4. **What is the difference between sufficient and necessary conditions in an explanation?**

- *Sufficient* conditions are those that a theory proposes are the minimal ones needed for a change (such as the appearance of agriculture or archaic states) to occur; *necessary* conditions are those that must exist for a change to happen.
- Archaeology constructs specific historical sequences, then compares them and looks for patterns to determine what conditions are necessary and sufficient to explain major cultural evolutionary transitions.

MEDIA RESOURCES

Doing Fieldwork:
Archaeological Demonstrations CD-ROM 2.0
This CD, developed by the authors, shows professional archaeologists involved in various digs, many of which are referenced in the text. The presentation is organized by the main techniques used on an archaeological dig, reinforcing concepts and techniques via live examples. The CD takes you through each step automatically, or you can navigate to any point via the navigation bar. After reviewing a step in the dig process, you are taken to Check Points, which are concept questions about each step of the dig. Then you can see the answers, receive your score, and even send your scores to your instructor.

The Companion Website for *Archaeology,*
Sixth Edition
www.cengagebrain.com
Supplement your review of this chapter by going to the companion website to take one of the practice quizzes, use the flash cards to master key terms, and check out the many other study aids that are designed to help you succeed in your introductory archaeology course.

14 HISTORICAL ARCHAEOLOGY: INSIGHTS ON AMERICAN HISTORY

LEARNING OBJECTIVES

AFTER READING THIS CHAPTER YOU SHOULD BE ABLE TO ANSWER THESE QUESTIONS:

1. Why do historical archaeology if we already have the historical records?

2. What are the three major areas of historical archaeological research today?

3. How is historical archaeology more amenable to the postprocessual paradigm than prehistoric archaeology?

© Buffalo Bill Historical Center, Cody, Wyoming; 19.69

Custer's Last Stand (1899) by Edgar Samuel Paxson (1852–1919). Historical archaeology asks: Is this how it happened?

PREVIEW

 HISTORICAL ARCHAEOLOGY IS currently one of the most important directions in American archaeology, but so far we've only glimpsed what historical archaeologists actually do (for example, in discussing Thomas's excavations at Mission Santa Catalina in Georgia). In this chapter, we look at historical archaeology in more depth.

Historical archaeology is fundamentally similar to the prehistoric archaeology you've already experienced. Both fields maintain high standards of excavation, dating, and interpretation, but because of its close relationship with the discipline of history, historical archaeology has its own distinctive flavor. Commonly less concerned with grand explanation, historical archaeologists can often shed light on lesser-known aspects of the historical past (such as the daily life of slaves), correct mistaken assumptions about history, and use the archaeological record to derive views of the past that sometimes contrast with the picture derived from documentary evidence alone. Although historical archaeology is an international field, this chapter will focus on its manifestation in the United States.

INTRODUCTION

Archaeologists have been investigating historic period sites for a very long time. In fact, the first bona fide historical archaeology in America took place more than 150 years ago. James Hall, a trained civil engineer and a direct descendant of Miles Standish, who arrived with the Pilgrims aboard the *Mayflower* in 1620 and eventually became a leader in Plymouth Colony, wanted to learn more about his celebrated ancestor. Hall located the foundations of the Standish homestead in Duxbury, Massachusetts, and in 1853 he conducted detailed excavations there.

For more than a century, Hall's field notes and artifact collection from the Standish house remained unknown to anybody but immediate family members. But when they surfaced in Mexico, in the 1960s, this important find was brought to the attention of James Deetz (1930–2000), a historical archaeologist working at Plymouth Plantation. Looking over the surviving notes, Deetz was impressed at the high quality of Hall's 1853 excavation.

After carefully gridding the site and establishing datum points to maintain vertical control, Hall made a meticulous site map. He tried to recover artifacts *in situ*, plotting their locations onto this master site map. He even recorded stratigraphic relationships within the house ruin. After the excavation, Hall cataloged each artifact, carefully numbering each find. In short, Hall's 1853 excavation technique comports nicely with today's standards of acceptable archaeological practice.

Almost simultaneously, a second pioneering exploration in historical archaeology took place in Canada, under very different circumstances.

In 1855, the Canadian government commissioned Father Félix Martin, a Jesuit priest from Montreal, to explore and excavate the site of Sainte Marie, Georgian Bay (near Midland, Ontario). Sainte Marie was a tiny mission outpost founded in 1639 to bring Christianity to the local Huron Indians. Although 800 miles west of their supply base in Quebec, the missionaries enjoyed some success, and several left the mission proper to work with surrounding Huron communities. During the winter of 1648–49, the Huron villages in this area came under attack from raiding Iroquois war parties. The resident Jesuit priests refused to flee, and several died martyrs' deaths. In March, the surviving priests abandoned Mission Sainte Marie. Although it had lasted only a decade, Sainte Marie became a sacred place in Christian history, what archaeologist Kenneth Kidd would later describe as "the pulsating heart of French missionary effort in America."

Father Martin had this heritage in mind when he went to Sainte Marie in 1855. Seeking to establish a personal link to his own Jesuit past, Martin identified the site's location, mapped and described the ruins, painted several watercolors, and conducted limited excavations. Years later, the Jesuit Order purchased the site to encourage its preservation and make it available for religious pilgrimages. Today, the Martyrs Shrine Church stands nearby, honoring both the Jesuit missionaries and the Christian Huron people who once lived there.

These two mid-nineteenth-century digs illustrate the twin themes that eventually came to distinguish the field of historical archaeology. For one thing, both excavators were motivated by a dynamic and personal connection to their own past—Hall to his Pilgrim heritage and Father Martin to the legacy of his martyred Jesuit brothers. For both men, the past had a special relevance to the present.

Both excavators also were familiar with the documentary sources relating to their excavations. This meant that before looking to the archaeology of their respective sites, they had some knowledge of what to expect: where to dig, what to look for, and generally what kind of material record they should encounter— expectations derived from basic historical sources. By themselves, however, the historical sources were incomplete and not entirely satisfying. Encountering the archaeological record—the physical remains of the past—induced Martin and Hall to undertake their own excavations.

So, what constitutes modern **historical archaeology?** Kathleen Deagan, the historical archaeologist profiled in Chapter 1, defines the field as "the study of human behavior through material remains, for which written history in some way affects its interpretation." Although this simple definition certainly captures the field, others point out that because historical archaeology encompasses the last 500 years, historical archaeology must also address the history of colonialism and capitalism. We will show you how historical archaeology takes on different flavors, depending on which of these definitions you choose.

Why Do Historical Archaeology?

At this point, you might be asking yourself why archaeologists bother with historical sites if they are already described in documentary sources. Won't archaeology, with its problems of context, preservation, and interpretation, always prove inferior to the written sources?

Documentary sources can indeed be superior to archaeology. But they can also be quite selective and biased. Slave owners wrote little about the day-to-day life of slaves because they did not think it important, and slaves only rarely wrote letters or diaries because most were illiterate (and often forbidden from learning). Most authors of documentary sources were biased toward the interests of their particular cultural, political, or ethnic group, and sometimes the documentary sources are simply wrong. Today, archaeologists look at archaeological and documentary records *as equally valid yet independent* lines of evidence. Rather than discard differences between the two as "exceptions" or "noise," we sometimes look for "ambiguities" between the historical and archaeological evidence, recognizing that *differences between the two are as important as each piece of information alone.* This is why historical archaeology is an essential component in our understanding of the relatively recent past.

Historical Archaeology: Just a "Handmaiden to History"?

In the early days, excavations in historic period sites merely supplemented the "known," documentary view of the past. In the words of Ivor Noël Hume (former director of the archaeological program at Colonial Williamsburg, Virginia), the proper role of historical archaeology was to serve as a "handmaiden to history"; the historical archaeologist was effectively "a historian with a pen in one hand and a trowel in the other."

This perspective was particularly evident in projects closely linked to historical reconstruction and restoration. Archaeologists, for instance, recovered most of the architectural detail necessary to restore and interpret public sites such as Plimoth Plantation (Massachusetts), Jamestown and Colonial Williamsburg (Virginia), and Fort Michilimackinac (Michigan). Such projects in historical archaeology began in America in the 1940s and 1950s, concentrating on a very few selected sites—particularly houses of the rich and famous, forts, and other military sites.

historical archaeology The study of human behavior through material remains, in which written history in some way affects its interpretation.

© Lin Poyer

Figure 14-1 A World War II plane in the Marshall Islands. Today, historical archaeologists study everything from the colonial past to World War II–related sites.

Colonial Williamsburg served as a model for this early-stage historical archaeology. Architectural historians concentrated most of their early excavations at Williamsburg, their goal being little more than exposing historic period building foundations. They did not dig very carefully and showed little interest in the trash middens and smaller structures that would eventually captivate archaeological interest. Only later did historical archaeologists follow the example of their colleagues in prehistoric archaeology and develop independent, artifact-based methods for dating sites and components.

Historical Archaeology Comes of Age

Things changed markedly in the 1960s, partly because of the growing impact of cultural resource management. Federal legislation from the 1960s requires that archaeology be done in advance of construction projects (we will discuss this further in the next chapter). This "applied" version of archaeology proved to be a boon for both prehistoric and historical archaeology. In the beginning, most historical archaeologists received their training on prehistoric

sites. But today, the field of historical archaeology is highly specialized, with its own journals and professional societies—not just in the United States, but around the globe. Historical archaeologists today study everything from the earliest colonial settlements to nineteenth-century mining camps to World War II battlefields (Figure 14-1).

Characteristics of Historical Archaeology

Contemporary historical archaeology is every bit as diverse as the rest of archaeology, but three key factors provide historical archaeology with a slightly different flavor from its prehistoric counterpart.

For one thing, modern historical archaeology often has a postprocessual slant to it. Because historical archaeologists typically have access to texts, ethnohistoric data, and/or oral traditions, they can often learn something about the meanings of symbols, ethnic affiliation, income, religion, occupation, family composition, economic network, and political restrictions—even before putting a trowel into the ground. It is not surprising, then, that a preeminent historian of archaeology, Bruce Trigger (1937–2006), argued that the most successful symbolic studies lie in the field of historical rather than prehistoric archaeology. Such analyses are considerably less convincing for, say, the archaeology of Paleoindian people living 12,000 years ago, for whom we lack ethnohistoric documentation or oral traditions. Historical archaeologists are hardly wed to a postprocessual agenda, but the field is certainly amenable to it.

In addition, historical archaeology, especially as practiced in the United States, deals with time periods that are considerably shorter than those of prehistoric archaeology. Documentary sources can often provide the precise years that a site was used, along with detailed information on how its use changed over time. Most prehistoric archaeologists consider themselves extremely lucky if they can date an assemblage to a span of a few centuries. Historical archaeology tends not to study large-scale processes, such as those discussed in the last chapter. Instead, the high degree of temporal resolution leads historical archaeologists to focus on the specific individuals and events that were part of those larger processes—for example, how a nineteenth-century frontier fort's trash reflects the development of the world trade system.

Finally, we must recognize that historical archaeology is often very close to us—not just temporally (the last 500 years in the United States), but also emotionally—whether one is of European, Hispanic, African, Native American, or Asian descent. The archaeology of the last five centuries records the time that all these different peoples came together and created the modern world. And discussion of this recent history is embedded in the continuing discussion of the modern world, with all its cultural, political, and ethical challenges. Because relatively few members of minority groups are professional archaeologists today, such discussions of the recent past can sometimes become emotionally charged (see "In Her Own Words: Why Are There So Few African-Americans Doing Archaeology?" by Anna Agbe-Davies).

Remember from Chapter 2 that many postprocessual archaeologists argue that archaeology should be more politically aware and proactive. For historical archaeologists, this can mean using archaeological evidence to expose the ideologies that mask the social contradictions within society and to "emancipate" people by allowing them to evaluate history for themselves.

Themes in Historical Archaeology

These characteristics suggest three major themes of historical archaeology today. Although these directions hardly capture all of historical archaeology—and each theme exists within prehistoric archaeology as well—they seem to define the dominant research domains within historical archaeology.

First, modern historical archaeology has shied away from a focus on the "oldest," "largest," and "most historically significant" sites, favoring instead the study of historically disenfranchised groups. Many historical archaeologists are working to uncover the history of African-American and Asian-American cultures, Native Americans during the historic period, and Hispanic-Americans—peoples whose histories are still sometimes ignored, only partially recorded, or related in a biased manner.

Second, historical archaeology commonly tackles questions about the recent past that history books answer unsatisfactorily. In this regard, some historical archaeologists are more like forensic archaeologists (which we will discuss in Chapter 16), collecting data like crime scene detectives to resolve disputes over the nature of key historical events.

Third, we see many historical archaeologists researching the nature of European colonialism (the developing capitalism of that time) and its effects on indigenous peoples. The postprocessual emphasis on power, for instance, meshes easily with historical archaeology's ample record of developing capitalist society of the last several centuries. Some scholars use this research to challenge standard public presentations of mainstream history, calling into question, for example, the melting pot interpretation of America's past. This approach challenges citizens to think more critically about their history.

Following are examples of each of these themes in historical archaeology.

HIDDEN HISTORY: THE ARCHAEOLOGY OF AFRICAN-AMERICANS

African-American history is inextricably linked to slavery, especially slavery on plantations. Plantation archaeology began in 1931 at Mount Vernon (Virginia), George Washington's home. In his role as director of research and restoration at Mount Vernon, Morley Jeffers Williams—a landscape architect—wanted to locate the various structural remains on the property,

IN HER OWN WORDS

WHY ARE THERE SO FEW AFRICAN-AMERICANS DOING ARCHAEOLOGY?

by Anna S. Agbe-Davies, Assistant Professor of Anthropology, University of North Carolina

African diaspora archaeology is indeed a "growth industry" within the field. How do we reconcile that fact with the fact that we still find so few black archaeologists in contract firms, university departments, and museums?

For a social science that thrives on quantitative data, we have very little statistical information to answer this question. Surveys of professional organizations based in the United States suggest that between 0.2% and 0.1% of archaeologists identify as black or African-American—though many respondents refuse to answer. Recent figures on PhDs awarded in anthropology from U.S. universities indicate that fewer than 5% of recipients identify as black or African-American—and anecdotal evidence suggests that many of these people are specialists in subfields other than archaeology.

Like members of many academic and professional fields, archaeologists want to increase the diversity of our discipline. We convene committees and task forces. Our organizations support scholarships for student members of many underrepresented groups—not just African-Americans. Formal and informal networks of mentors and peers nurture those already in the profession.

Archaeologists sometimes use functionalist arguments to explain our slow progress in becoming a discipline that reflects the diversity of our nation and our world—specifically, that people from marginalized groups who pursue advanced degrees are more likely to select fields with more obvious or predictable potential for financial success. I have only circumstantial evidence, but I disagree.

If we again look to data on PhDs, black participation is high in fields like education, law, and social service professions, but low in business and engineering, supporting my hunch that, far from emphasizing financial success, members of marginalized groups want to do work that is *meaningful* and serves the communities from which they come. Many—though by no means all—of the black archaeologists at work

Courtesy Anna Agbe-Davies

Anna Agbe-Davies.

in the United States today emphasize topics associated with the African diaspora in their research. I believe that to the extent that African diaspora archaeology makes significant contributions to the lives of black people in the present day, we will see increased black participation in this subfield.

A more important factor shaping the participation of African-Americans in archaeology generally is the lack of opportunities to study archaeology at historically black colleges and universities (HBCUs) and other minority-serving institutions. This is why the loss of a five-field anthropology department at one of the premiere HBCUs (Howard University) is potentially so devastating. I never would have discovered archaeology as the fascinating and rewarding career it has proved to be if it had not been offered at the college I attended.

As an exception that "proves the rule," I am probably the last person who should be explaining why more black people don't become archaeologists. But I, and many of my colleagues—black and not—care about the answer, so we'll keep asking.

so he conducted extensive and systematic archaeological testing. Although hardly up to contemporary standards, these excavations did permit the reconstruction of the first president's garden and out-buildings and kicked off the study of plantation archaeology as we now know it.

Most early plantation archaeology was aimed at architectural reconstruction, and prior to the 1980s, few restored plantations addressed the issue of slavery explicitly. Instead, the restorations usually emphasized the "big house" and the grandeur of the elite who lived there;

© Monticello/Thomas Jefferson Foundation, Inc., photograph by Leonard Phillips

Figure 14-2 Low-level aerial photograph showing Monticello (on the left) and Mulberry Row (the line of trees running diagonally through the middle of the photo).

guides commonly referred to slaves as "servants." This often melancholy, *Gone with the Wind* perspective focused on the passing of an antebellum way of life (one that many white people saw as genteel, although descendants of slaves hold a different opinion).

Slave archaeology began in earnest in the late 1960s—doubtless connected to, or inspired by, the social upheavals of the time—when Charles Fairbanks (1913–1984) began exploring coastal plantations in Georgia and Florida. Fairbanks was the first to study the institution of slavery from the archaeological record, and when he emphasized the richness and diversity of the Southern heritage, he clearly departed from the traditional "melting pot" theme in America. Fairbanks and his students set out to dispel myths concerning the biological and cultural inferiority of African-Americans—myths that were being used to legitimize continued segregation and discrimination (an example of the political use of archaeology).

Today, the field of African-American archaeology is a growth industry, helping to uncover information about aspects of slave life on which the documentary sources are often silent. We can demonstrate this by looking at the slave archaeology of Monticello, the home of Thomas Jefferson.

Slave Archaeology at Monticello

Visitors motoring up the serpentine driveway to Thomas Jefferson's Monticello, shown in Figure 14-2, are first struck by the world-famous architecture, the vast gardens, and glimpses of mountains in the sprawl-

ing Virginia countryside. As visitors walk through Monticello, polite guides provide them with ample details about the life of Thomas Jefferson, the third president, architect, inventor, scholar, diplomat—and archaeologist.

But only recently have we heard much about Thomas Jefferson the slave owner. In the days when Jefferson lived at Monticello, the approach to the main house, called Mulberry Row, was lined by 19 buildings—the houses and workshops of Jefferson's slaves, hired laborers, artisans, and indentured servants. The mansion at Monticello still stands, attracting tourists by the thousands, yet today aboveground traces of all but four of the structures along Mulberry Row have vanished.

Historical archaeologists working at Monticello have brought Mulberry Row back to life. Work here was begun by William Kelso (currently director of archaeology for the Association for the Preservation of Virginia Antiquities "Jamestown Rediscovery" project), and it continues under Monticello's archaeology program, directed by Fraser Neiman.

Jefferson had mixed feelings about slavery. He enslaved about 200 people at a time and knew that without enforced labor, the agrarian economy of the day would collapse. Yet he regarded the institution of slavery as preeminently brutal and immoral—and he personally favored its abolition. Recognizing this dilemma, Jefferson once said that slavery is like holding a wolf by the ears: "We can neither hold him nor safely let him go. Justice is in one scale, self-preservation in the other."

Jefferson reportedly did not mistreat the enslaved population, but he doubted whether Caucasians and

Africans could successfully create a biracial society (despite the fact that he probably fathered six children with Sally Hemings [1773–1835], one of his house slaves). Instead, he favored a plan to transport free blacks back to Africa or elsewhere.

How Well Did Jefferson's Slaves Live? Research at Mulberry Row is aimed at learning more about the living and working conditions of Jefferson's slaves. Although few ruins were visible, Kelso soon found by exploratory excavation that the subsurface record of Mulberry Row was relatively undisturbed (Figure 14-3). The residents of Mulberry Row were probably the house servants and artisans, who may have enjoyed a better standard of living than the field hands, who lived in settlements farther down the mountain.

Homes along Mulberry Row contained pig, cow, and deer bones; some of these bones were ground up, suggesting the use of meat in stews. Houses also contained ceramic assemblages, dating to AD 1770–1800, that were probably the remnants of table settings from Jefferson's home. No longer usable in the mansion (perhaps having lost a few key pieces), they were given to enslaved families. These hand-me-downs reflect the growing consumer revolution of the late eighteenth century and the availability of houseware replacements.

Social Life in Slave Houses Neiman points out that the archaeology of Mulberry Row helps to answer a question posed by the historical documents. About 1776, Jefferson mapped his plan for buildings along Mulberry Row and included a building, some 17×34 feet, which he labeled the "Negro Quarter." By 1790, this building had burned, and in 1792–1793, Jefferson built several smaller homes on the site, labeled structures r, s, and t on his 1796 map. He intended these structures to be homes for the enslaved; they were only 12×14 feet and were made of split logs, with dirt floors and chimneys of wood and mud.

In 1793, Jefferson served as President Washington's secretary of state, but he still minded the details of his plantation. Jefferson wrote to his overseer, instructing him to move Critta Hemings (the sister of Sally Hemings) and her family to the new House r. Hemings had been living in Building e—a stone house still standing today along Mulberry Row—and she was part of the house staff. According to Jefferson's description, Building e had two rooms, each about 290 square feet in size. It had a brick floor, a stone fireplace, and a single entry door decorated with a pedimented portico supported by columns.

Taken at face value, Hemings appears to have been demoted—she had moved to a smaller house with dirt floors and no architectural embellishments. Yet she continued as a house servant—normally a favored status. In fact, Jefferson instructed the overseer to place her and her family in House r because "she is wanted around the house." How do we explain this apparent paradox?

The answer comes from the archaeology. The excavations at Monticello retrieved data on nine of the slave houses located on Mulberry Row (Figure 14-4). Three of the houses date to the 1770s (based on documentary evidence and ceramic dates; see Chapter 6). According to Jefferson's maps, the "Negro Quarter" house contained

© Monticello/Thomas Jefferson Foundation, Inc.

Figure 14-3 Excavating slave dwellings built during Jefferson's lifetime at Monticello. Evident in this picture are the remains of Building l, the storehouse (foreground); Building m, the smokehouse-dairy (center); and the rebuilt walls of an 1809 stone slave house (background).

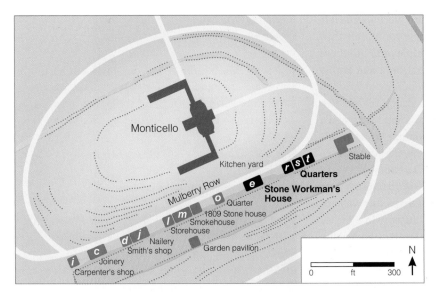

Figure 14-4 Map of Monticello showing the locations of buildings excavated along Mulberry Row. *Used by permission of the Monticello Department of Archaeology.*

two large rooms, but only a single entryway. The two rooms had separate fireplaces that shared a single flue. A second building originally had a plan similar to that of the "Negro Quarter." A third structure was a single large room, some 250 square feet in size, with a single entryway and a wood and clay fireplace.

These houses contained what historical archaeologists call "sub-floor pits," or cellars. These are rectangular holes, some 3½ × 4 feet, and 1 to 3 feet deep. The early houses at Monticello contain up to four of these pits.

These early houses at Monticello are fairly typical of slave dwellings throughout the Chesapeake Bay area in the eighteenth century (although at other plantations, early slave houses usually contain four to ten sub-floor pits). The function of the sub-floor pits is not clear, but they probably served as places for families to store important belongings. If so, then they suggest that multiple families occupied the early slave dwellings. Neiman points out that theft is a real concern in situations where you have little choice over your housemates. The sub-floor pits may have helped maintain a semblance of privacy and security in an otherwise open structure because it would have been difficult to steal something if first it had to be exhumed from a pit.

Beginning about 1790, however, a transition in housing occurred at Monticello and at other plantations in the region (Figure 14-5). Houses became smaller—about 140 square feet (although they later became larger in

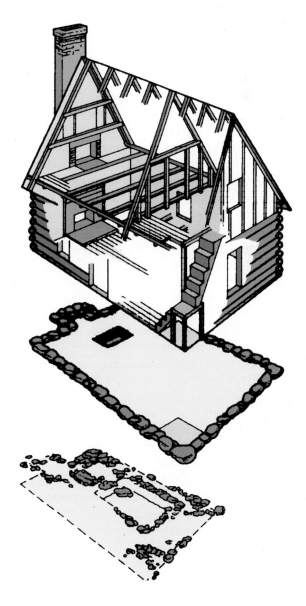

Figure 14-5 Artist's reconstruction of post-1790 slave housing at Monticello. This figure shows a view of a typical slave cabin and its foundation (with a single sub-floor pit in front of the fireplace) superimposed over the archaeological plan (servant's House o) at Monticello.

the early nineteenth century)—and were extremely modest, consisting usually of a single room. But they had only one sub-floor pit, not multiple pits, and these pits were smaller. This suggests that only one family lived there, so they did not have much need to stash possessions out of sight. Even when structures had two rooms, the rooms were separated by a solid wall, and a separate door opened into each room, permitting privacy. In fact, no sub-floor pits have been found in slave houses at Monticello that date after AD 1800.

So, when Jefferson asked that Critta Hemings and her family be moved to House r, perhaps this was not a demotion. Instead, Hemings could now live in her own house, with her immediate family, where she could control her own household. A home of her own must have seemed quite a step up in her world.

But it must have been a small consolation. After all, she and her family remained enslaved.

Beyond Plantation Archaeology: New York City's African Burial Ground

When most people think of slavery, they think of the Old South and a cotton-based economy. How many people know that slavery was deeply ingrained in the economy north of the Mason-Dixon Line as well?

But we were all reminded of this forgotten past when, in 1991, the bones of 427 enslaved Africans, interred by their own community and forgotten for centuries, were discovered beneath a parking lot in downtown New York City at a place now known as the African Burial Ground.

Slavery in Old New York? The story begins in 1626, when the Dutch West India Company unloaded its first shipment of enslaved Africans in New Amsterdam (today's New York City): 11 young men from what today is the Congo-Angola region of southwestern Africa (Figure 14-6). Two years later, the Dutch imported three African women "for the comfort of the company's Negro men." The Dutch at the time were experiencing a labor shortage in their colonies, and they found enforced labor to be the answer to building and maintaining the colony.

Some scholars argue that the Dutch treated enslaved Africans well. They point out that some had more rights than New Amsterdam's Jews, who were forbidden to own land or serve in the militia. Under the Dutch, Africans were permitted to intermarry with whites, attend white churches, own property, and enjoy the same status as whites in court.

The Granger Collection, New York

Figure 14-6
Nineteenth-century painting depicting an African being auctioned into slavery in Dutch New Amsterdam.

According to this view, the Dutch practiced half-freedom; true slavery was introduced in 1664, when the Dutch ceded Manhattan to the British. At that time, enslaved Africans made up about *40 percent* of New Amsterdam's total population. Everywhere one looked in colonial New York, there were enslaved people at work—loading and unloading ships on the waterfront, building the streets, and erecting the buildings to house the people and businesses of this bustling port city crowded onto the southern tip of Manhattan Island. And the British continued to import enslaved Africans throughout the first half of the eighteenth century.

On the eve of the American Revolution, New York City had the largest number of enslaved Africans of any English colonial city except Charleston, South Carolina. In fact, New York City had the highest proportion of enslaved people to Europeans of any northern settlement. Despite what is found in most American history books, it is clear that the African population had a significant hand in the building of colonial New York.

Eighteenth-century New York law prohibited the burial of Africans in Manhattan's churchyards. Left without a place to bury their dead, New York's African population eventually established a cemetery on a deserted tract of land lying just outside the city's protective wooden palisade (a wall that eventually gave its name to Wall Street). There, from roughly 1712 to 1790, the community buried somewhere between 10,000 and 20,000 people (mostly black, but also a few lower-class whites). A 1755 map of downtown New York clearly shows the "Negro Burial Ground" covering perhaps five city blocks.

was sufficiently worthwhile as to amount to something more than desecration of the cemetery.

Through public meetings, researchers described their methods for restoring the lost history of the enslaved Africans who were buried there. The community introduced their own research questions and thoughts about how the site should be interpreted. This community feedback was incorporated in the research design, so long as the integrity of the scientific method remained intact. The result was a better and more meaningful research project that was not only acceptable to the descendant community, but which they had become part of.

There were now two types of client: an ethical client (descendant or culturally affiliated communities) and a business client (the federal government, responsible for funding the project's research). While responsible for satisfying the legal requirements of its business client, the research team took on responsibility for seeing that agreements made with its ethical client were carried out. One such agreement was the return of skeletons for reburial and memorialization once the important data had been gathered. Thus, scientific, cultural, spiritual, and religious treatments of the cemetery would complement its significance rather than compete.

Although few artifacts remain, one woman was found wearing a string of glass and cowrie shell beads around her waist. In what is today Ghana and Benin, such beads would have been given as a wedding present. The coffin lid of one man's burial had an elaborate heart-shaped design made of brass tacks. One likely possibility being explored is the Asanti adinkra symbol "Sankofa," which means "Look to the past to inform decisions about the future."

The New York African Burial Ground tells us that archaeology, physical anthropology, and history are often important in the minds of everyday people. Whether as a basis for defining national and group identity, the elucidation of processes leading to current social conditions, or as a guide to the future, disciplines that construct the past do so within the context of broader cultural and political meanings.

It is important for a community to be empowered to evaluate its own past, for better or worse, and to honor that past in ways that are meaningful for it. African-Americans are certainly not singular in these respects. Indigenous people in many parts of the world are advocating control of their cultural patrimony, including sacred archaeological sites and skeletal remains curated by museums. National legislation has begun to protect those rights for Native Americans.

Working with the remains of the dead also means having an impact on living communities that are affiliated with the dead. Archaeologists and skeletal biologists who work with archaeological populations are well served when they have had "holistic" training in the history, ethnography, ethics, and even the political issues of living communities. These issues mark the terrain often entered when digging for the past.

citizens of New York. For example, Blakey found that English settlers were eight times more likely to live past the age of 55 than were enslaved Africans.

The African Burial Ground Today Visitors flock to the African Burial Ground center from around the world, and it has become a point of connection for Africans and Americans, white or black. Guided tours and videotapes of the African Burial Ground project are available through the Office of Public Education and Interpretation of the African Burial Ground, which is actively engaged in bringing the findings to a broader public through newsletters, workshops, and lectures. Finally, all the human remains were reburied in October 2003.

The African Burial Ground is a prime example of how archaeology can recover "lost" history. But the African Burial Ground is also a story about how a descendant community can be empowered through archaeology—though this idea also raises some important issues (see "What Does It Mean to Me? Archaeology and the Values of Descendant Communities").

A final note: The artifacts and excavation documents from the African Burial Ground were stored in the basement of one of the buildings at the World Trade Center, along with those from the Five Points Project, another large historical archaeology dig in downtown New York. Most of the African Burial Ground material was recovered after the building's collapse on September 11, 2001; fortunately, the human remains were still stored in laboratories at Howard University. But virtually everything from the Five Points Project (the neighborhood that was the setting for Martin Scorsese's film *Gangs of New York*) was lost.

Beyond Slavery

We have focused on slavery—on and off plantations—because it was a dramatic and key element of African-American history whose full impact is often not communicated in standard documentary sources. But African-American history is much more than a history of enslavement, and a number of historical archaeologists have turned their attention to the archaeology of early free black communities (see "Looking Closer: Fort Mose: Colonial America's Black Fortress of Freedom") in the South and African-American settlements in the West. Still other American historical archaeologists work to recover the history of other peoples by excavating the immigrant communities of early nineteenth-century mining towns, Chinese railroad labor camps, and early Mormon communities.

CORRECTING INACCURACIES

Historical archaeologists also attempt to correct inaccuracies in the public view of history. These inaccuracies are sometimes simple mistakes or unintentional omissions and are often innocuous. For example, recall the *Hunley*, the Confederate submarine mentioned in Chapter 7. Historians believed that the sub's explosive charge was mounted on a 22-foot yellow pine boom that projected forward from the top of the hull. But physical inspection of the *Hunley* shows that the boom was a 17-foot hollow iron pipe that jutted forward from the bottom of the hull. This is a relatively trivial detail—but other historical inaccuracies are vastly more significant.

What Happened at the Battle of the Little Bighorn?

In the 1850s, American settlers were moving west through land that was the traditional territory of several tribes, including, on the northern high plains, the Lakota. When the settlers were simply moving through, relations were not so violent, but once settlers opted to remain and forts were constructed, hostilities ensued. By the late 1860s, the Lakota had gained the upper hand and were prepared to discuss terms of peace.

By signing the Laramie Treaty of 1868, Red Cloud and other Lakota leaders agreed to cease hostilities, and the United States created the Great Sioux Reservation, which included the Black Hills in eastern South Dakota; the treaty agreed that whites would make no settlements or unauthorized incursions into this territory. Still, some Indian leaders refused to sign (among them Gall, Sitting Bull, and Crazy Horse), and they were granted permanent hunting rights in the Powder River region of Wyoming and Montana.

But the legal details of the treaty were difficult to understand (and some are still in dispute). Apparently, the treaty allowed for railroad surveys in the Black Hills, which were conducted in 1872 and 1873. But an 1874 expedition to the Black Hills to locate a military post may have been a violation. Regardless, what matters is that this expedition discovered gold, and the federal government only halfheartedly tried to stop the ensuing rush of miners. By 1875, the government was trying to reduce the size of the Sioux reservation and also ordered that the non-treaty bands relocate to the reservation. In 1876, the government sent General George Armstrong Custer to find these Lakota and move them.

On June 25, with the aid of Crow and Arikara scouts, Custer tracked a large band of Lakota, Northern Cheyenne, and Arapaho to the Little Bighorn River in Montana. Despite his scouts' warnings, he decided to attack. He broke his men into three battalions. One, headed by Captain Frederick Benteen, went to the south to cut off an escape route. Major Marcus Reno led another into the valley to attack the village from the southeast. Custer himself led the third over the river bluffs, eventually reaching a position north of the village. Reno encountered heavy resistance that brought him to a standstill, but his efforts did succeed in creating an exodus from the village. Custer apparently then moved through the low hills northeast of the river, pursuing the women, children, and elderly as they fled down the valley.

WHAT DOES IT MEAN TO ME?

ARCHAEOLOGY AND THE VALUES OF DESCENDANT COMMUNITIES

The African Burial Ground is one of many cases in which archaeologists have tried to take into account the opinions, values, and perspectives of descendant communities. Although admirable, such a stance does raise some ethical questions.

When word of the burials reached African-American leaders in Harlem, they expressed concern over the lack of community involvement in the project. As one citizen put it, "If it was an African find, we wanted to make sure that it was interpreted from an African point of view." The Government Services Administration (GSA) countered that it had made appropriate notification as mandated by law: "We didn't include the Harlem community board because the project isn't in Harlem, it's in lower Manhattan."

The situation reached a flashpoint when a backhoe operator accidentally destroyed several of the burials. Large-scale protests ensued, culminating in a one-day blockade that shut down construction. To some, the debate surrounding the African Burial Ground became a "microcosm of the issues of racism and economic exploitation confronting New York City." Archaeology never proceeds in a social vacuum.

The GSA eventually commissioned an advisory committee—comprising historians, anthropologists, museum professionals, architects, attorneys, clergy, government officials, and concerned community members—to represent the interests of the African descendant community at large.

Supported by then-Mayor David N. Dinkins (New York City's first African-American mayor), the African descendant community became actively involved in the preservation, dedication, and management of the cemetery site. Blakey's active participation became an overt symbol that the city was considering the African descendant community's wishes. But there were differences of opinion about how the remains should be treated. Some in the descendant community felt that archaeological investigations were disrespectful, adding the insult of grave robbing to the injury of slavery. Others believed that a thorough scientific study was not only a way of honoring the dead, but also a way of restoring them to their rightful place in American history.

Eventually, the government scrubbed all plans to erect the four-story pavilion. Instead, this piece of prime New York real estate was set aside as a permanent memorial. On February 25, 1993, the New York City Landmarks Commission designated the site the African Burial Ground and the Commons Historical District. Later that year, the African Burial Ground achieved National Historic Landmark status. Sherrill D. Wilson, an African-American anthropologist, noted that the sudden involvement of black scholars was "very revolutionary. . . . [Such scholarship] is going to set a precedent for what happens to African burial grounds in the future and how African heritage will be viewed by the public."

The African Burial Ground appears to have worked out to the satisfaction of most people. But it raises some questions. First, what defines a descendant community? To our knowledge, no living person demonstrated a lineal relationship to anyone in the African Burial Ground. Who decides who belongs to the descendant community?

And, once that decision is made, what is the appropriate role of descendant communities? Can anyone, with appropriate training, work on any type of site, or is the only valid work on a site done by a member of a descendant community? Can only Native Americans work on Native American sites; African-Americans on African-American sites, Euro-Americans on European sites? Do we want a world in which there is "my" history and "your" history? Is there a line between empowerment of a descendent community and balkanization of the world of knowledge about the past?

LOOKING CLOSER

FORT MOSE: COLONIAL AMERICA'S BLACK FORTRESS OF FREEDOM

African-American archaeology is not exclusively focused on slavery. Yet another perspective on African-American history was achieved through the discovery of Fort Mose, 50 miles south of the Georgia-Florida border. Here, archaeologist Kathleen Deagan and her colleagues at the University of Florida found concrete evidence of the first legally sanctioned, free African-American community in the country.

Beginning with the founding of Charles Towne (South Carolina) by the British in 1670, Spain employed free Africans to further its colonial objectives by having them populate and hold territories vulnerable to foreign encroachment. Both free and slave Africans were also used in military operations, a black militia having been established in St. Augustine. By 1673, the Spanish crown declared that all escaped fugitives from British plantations were to be granted sanctuary and, eventually, freedom in Spanish Florida "so that by their example and by my liberality, others will do the same." Like so many episodes in African-American history, the story of Fort Mose is incompletely known, a forgotten footnote to mainstream American history.

Deagan found the lost site of Fort Mose in 1986, and her excavations have provided an opportunity to re-examine the role of African-Americans in colonial

Kathleen Deagan (center) and then Florida State Representative Bill Clark (left) work with the excavation team to recover archaeological evidence at Fort Mose, Florida.

history. She is particularly interested in the effect of freedom on the blacks of Fort Mose. How much did they adapt to Spanish ways? Did they attempt to revive their African heritage?

Recognizing the relevance of the Fort Mose research, the state of Florida was quick to help out. State Representative Bill Clark, who sponsored the bill helping to finance the archaeology, has called Deagan's discovery of Fort Mose "a major historical find for black people." To Clark, himself an African-American, the excavations demonstrate that "blacks were never content to be slaves. . . . These are America's first freedom fighters."

No U.S. soldier survived to describe the battle or what Custer's final moments were like, so except for the final result, what happened was murky. Nonetheless, sensationalist newspaper accounts quickly formed an image of the battle and Custer's gallant "last stand." Years later, that vivid image was immortalized in several paintings. In 1895, Adolphus Busch (the brewery magnate) commissioned Otto Becker to paint *Custer's Last Fight*. The image shows Custer, his men bravely circled around him, almost calmly fighting a huge band of Lakota and Cheyenne. Busch then sent lithographs of the image to 150,000 saloons around the country. In 1900, Frederic Remington also painted

an image of the battle's final moments in which, again, a cool and collected Custer commands the men clustered around him.

Perhaps the most famous image is that by Edgar Samuel Paxson (the chapter's opening photo), completed in 1899, which includes 200 individuals (some of them recognizable, as Paxson studied all the available photographs of Custer's men as well as those of Cheyenne and Lakota warriors). Here we see Custer calmly standing in a whirlwind of activity, revolvers at the ready, his chest thrust out defiantly. The men of the Seventh Cavalry are gathered around him, disciplined to the end.

Images like these helped to create a fatalistic attitude toward the country's push to the west: Some would have to die in expanding the country westward, but they would die proud, knowing that what they were doing—bringing civilization to the wilderness (or massacring Indians and dispossessing them of their land, depending on your perspective)—was their God-given destiny. And Indians who stood in the way of this destiny should be punished.

But there were other images of the battle. Although none of Custer's battalion survived, many of the 1200 or so Indian warriors did, including such notables as Sitting Bull, Gall, Crazy Horse, and Black Elk (then 3 years old). Many of the Indian survivors were interviewed in the following years, and some of them drew their own images of the battle.

The Indian images tell a different story, as shown in Figure 14-8. In the first place, they are far bloodier than the paintings by Paxson and others, who sanitized the gruesome hand-to-hand combat. The Indians' images are filled with blood and entrails, decapitation and dismemberment. More important, they show groups of men spread over the battlefield—some firing, others running for their lives. Unlike the images created by white artists, the Indians' images show no grand last stand. In fact, there is nothing glorious in their pictures at all; there is only confusion and carnage. Which image is accurate?

An Archaeological Perspective on the Battle

Today, the battlefield is a national monument, but it remains a lonely and windswept place. In 1983, a brushfire burned the area, which led Douglas Scott (National Park Service) and Richard Fox (University of South Dakota) to conduct a survey of the entire battlefield. They checked a sample of the grave markers (individual gravestones marked where bodies were found some time after the battle) and systematically surveyed the battlefield using metal detectors for battle-related artifacts. They found plenty: gun parts, belt buckles, buttons, bridle pieces, human remains, and lots of spent cartridges and bullets. Each item was recorded and its location carefully mapped.

The cartridges and bullets were especially important because they are amenable to forensic analysis. Scott and Fox knew that the cavalry was armed only with .45-caliber single-shot Springfield carbines and .45-caliber Colt pistols. The Indians had these, too, but forensic studies showed they were also equipped with some 40 other types of weapons, from obsolete muzzle-loaders to repeating rifles (acquired through the illegal arms trade of the day). Careful mapping allowed Scott and Fox to ascertain combatant positions (Indian and soldier alike) using cartridge case locations and bullet orientations (which revealed the direction from which the

Southwest Museum of the American Indian Collection, Autry National Center; 1026.G.1

Figure 14-8 *Battle of the Little Bighorn* (circa 1898) by Kicking Bear (1846?–1904). Kicking Bear made this painting at the request of Frederic Remington; Custer appears in yellow buckskins at the left.

bullet was fired). Most important, in many instances they could use discharged cartridges to trace individual combatants' movements by matching the distinctive "fingerprint" that a gun's firing pin makes on the cartridge. What did they learn?

Where Was Custer? Custer's body was found on the hilltop that bears his name, surrounded by most of his headquarters staff. But where was he during the battle? We know that Custer's battalion had broken into two wings. Previous scholars argued that Custer was with the right wing because brass cartridges had been found along the path taken by the right wing, and Custer's .50-caliber Remington rifle was thought to be the only weapon on the battlefield that used brass cartridges. But Scott and Fox found many brass cartridges at the site, with firing pin fingerprints indicating that brass cartridges were fired from several different .50-caliber guns (by both soldiers and Indians). The brass cartridges, therefore, can't be used to pinpoint Custer's personal movements. We don't know where Custer himself fought; we only know where his body eventually came to rest.

Where Were the Indians and the Soldiers? Scott and Fox also found cavalry cartridge cases on Custer Hill, on the low ridges running to the east and south, and on Calhoun Hill (to the south of Custer Hill). Many more *Indian* cartridges are found in these same places (as well as on the rise coming up from the river—the direction from which the Indians would have attacked). In addition, in some places, expended government bullets were found next to government-issue cartridges. A cartridge drops to the ground as a rifle is reloaded, but obviously the corresponding bullet should appear at the target. Some of the bullets may have resulted from men shooting their horses to use them as shields. But others were probably fired by Indians, using guns they had claimed from Reno's unsuccessful attack or weapons taken from the bodies of Custer's men.

Also telling is the lack of evidence for formal skirmish lines. Army tactics at the time called for companies to form skirmish lines as a defensive measure. To do this, a company's men stood about 5 yards apart, with about 15 yards between companies. Such a tactical maneuver leaves a distinctive trace: piles of government-issue cartridges spaced about 5 yards apart. Scott and Fox found only tentative evidence for one skirmish line, on Calhoun Hill. Otherwise, the archaeological evidence fit the Indian accounts of chaos and hand-to-hand fighting.

Eventually, about 100 soldiers made it to Custer Hill, where order was apparently restored, albeit briefly. More Indians slowly arrived. Eventually, about 45 men, 5 of them mounted, made a break down a ridge to the east of Custer Hill. But Scott and Fox found no evidence of a skirmish line there. Instead, the men were perhaps trying to distract the Indians from the mounted soldiers, who were probably trying to reach Benteen. But these men, even the riders, were quickly pursued.

Eventually, Custer Hill was overrun, and more men ran down the hill to the ravine. Indians recalled that some fired into the air, but others failed even to draw their revolvers. And many did what soldiers before (and after) have done when confronted with death: They froze, with little choice but to accept the inevitable.

The battle lasted less than 90 minutes, and the final part took place not on Custer Hill, as the paintings suggest, but in the ravine, where terrified soldiers who "shot like drunken men," according to Iron Hawk, were hunted down and killed in a terrifying game of hide-and-seek.

Fox argues that Custer was moving confidently in an offensive tactical maneuver when he was caught completely off-guard, forcing a rapid transition from an offensive to a defensive posture. But Custer and his men were so rapidly surrounded that they had no time to regroup and carry out formal tactical maneuvers. The coordination of Custer's offensive attack rapidly gave way to confusion, chaos, and death. Near the top of Custer Hill, in fact, there is no sign of formal tactics. Instead, the distribution of Springfield cases suggests that men clustered together tightly in a nontactical maneuver—something that Indian eyewitnesses recalled years later—firing against the Indians who surrounded them.

To the Last Bullet? The romantic image of the battle has the soldiers holding off the Indians until their last bullet was fired. In fact, less than a month after the battle, the Helena *Herald* reported the tragedy with the headline "Not Until Their Ammunition Was Gone Were Our Troops Butchered."

But there were almost no Colt .45 cartridge cases found on the battlefield—none, in fact, on Custer Hill. A soldier could fire a revolver six times before he had to reload (unlike the single-shot carbines, from which a soldier had to remove the empty cartridge before reloading). But with their limited accuracy, handguns were good only for close combat. Close combat came so quickly and with such overwhelming force that soldiers either had no time to use their revolvers or no time to reload them (and the Indians collected the revolvers, still filled with empty or usable cartridges, after the battle). The distribution of .45-caliber Colt cartridges confirms this account.

Romantic images of the battle suggest that Custer and his men were in calm control until the very end. But the archaeology agrees with the Indians' accounts: Custer was caught off-guard. Perhaps he didn't expect the warriors to be so motivated to protect their women and children. Perhaps he expected Reno and Benteen to cut through and assist them. We don't know. We do know, however, that the popular images of the battle are inaccurate. The Battle of the Little Bighorn did not end in a "glorious" last stand. Instead, it ended like most battles: in chaos, panic, horror, and carnage.

The Monument Today A pillar was erected on Custer's Hill in 1881 as a tribute to the Seventh Cavalry. One hundred and ten years later, Congress recognized the more complex nature of the site's history and changed the name from Custer Battlefield to Little Bighorn Battlefield National Monument. At the same time, it authorized a memorial to honor the fallen Cheyenne, Lakota, and Arapaho warriors. The new memorial, dedicated in June 2003, consists of a low, circular, granite-lined earthwork and contains bronze silhouettes of mounted warriors. Its name: Peace Through Unity.

RE-EXAMINING AMERICA'S HISTORY

We now come to perhaps the most divisive aspect of historical archaeology—re-examining history. A national narrative can be contentious because a nation's history defines who its citizens are and, in no small way, creates their identity. No one wishes to identify with a history of dishonorable acts. This is why slavery was long ignored at reconstructed plantation sites and why revisionist histories of western settlement remain controversial. Going back in time, it seems, is like going deep into a people's identity. Many Euro-Americans, for example, do not welcome reinterpretations of Custer's Last Stand because the myth has become "their" history, right or wrong. Everyone wants their history to be uplifting; scholars also want it to be honest. Here's one example from Annapolis, Maryland.

Historical Archaeology in Annapolis

Working with the Historic Annapolis Foundation, Mark Leone (University of Maryland) has conducted "backyard archaeology" for decades, excavating in basements and backyards, beneath parking lots and pavements throughout Annapolis. By looking at floor plans, dishes, facades, architecture, silverware, furniture, and gardens, Leone is trying to demonstrate the degree to which our history is "constructed"—that is, written and presented for contemporary purposes. And in doing that, Leone has established the relevance of eighteenth-century Annapolis to ourselves and the way we understand not only our past, but also the present and the future.

Because of the explicit political agenda behind Leone's work, it is important to understand his theoretical perspective. Leone works within a postprocessual paradigm called **critical theory.** As applied to archaeology, critical theory stresses the importance of archaeologists' understanding of the specific contexts within which they work; it emphasizes that knowledge is situated within a cultural framework (as we pointed out in Chapter 2) and that, consequently, it can serve special interests. Critical theory assumes that domination in some form is a central element of modern capitalist society.

"Critical" in this sense means that the relationship between the assumptions and discoveries of a scholarly discipline, on the one hand, and its ties to modern life, on the other, are a central concern and subject to examination. Such an approach relates the questions, methods, and discoveries of a science like anthropology to those of the anthropologist's own culture. Critical theorists seek simultaneously to explain the social world, to criticize it, and to empower their audience to deal with it more productively by advocating change.

Pre-1760 Colonial America: The Georgian Order Before continuing, we must situate Leone's work in a larger context. Folklorist Henry Glassie (Indiana University) and archaeologist James Deetz (1930–2000) both explored the way in which changing cultural ideas were reflected in the material record of the American colonies. In so doing, they took a decidedly ideational (rather than materialist) approach to the past. Glassie examined early colonial houses in Virginia, while Deetz looked at the overall pattern of material culture in New England. Deetz argued that

critical theory A critique of the modern social order that emphasizes exploitative class interests; it aims to change and not simply to understand society.

early British colonists in New England had a **medieval mind-set** that encouraged a group-oriented, corporate, and relatively undifferentiated lifestyle. He found that by 1660, however, the culture of American colonies had changed.

Material remains of the late seventeenth century, Glassie and Deetz found, reflect a culture of increasing individualism and control sometimes known as the **Georgian order.** In this regard, American colonial culture reflected elements of the Enlightenment. You will recall from Chapter 13 that the Enlightenment focused on progress and on the ability of rational thought to control nature and improve human morality and spirituality. During the late seventeenth century, Deetz argued, Georgian attitudes created material culture patterns that emphasized control, often by partitioning space, and reflected a focus on the individual. These patterns in material culture were strikingly different from the previous "medieval" culture of the colonies. Here is how Deetz saw the differences:

▶ *Architecture.* Medieval houses had only one or two rooms, with asymmetrical floor plans. All domestic activity took place in these rooms, from sleeping and eating to working and socializing. But with the Georgian worldview, houses became functionally structured and compartmentalized, with more balanced floor plans.

▶ *Ceramics.* The medieval mind-set was characterized by plain, utilitarian earthenware. Food was served directly from the cooking pot and consumed from "trenchers," wooden trays that were shared with one or more "trencher mates." During this period, ceramics played a small role in food consumption. But in Georgian culture, ceramics were purchased as matched sets of plates and teacups. Serving vessels appeared, and one plate was allotted to each individual around the family table. And whereas medieval ceramics were natural-colored earthenwares, Georgian ceramics became progressively whiter as technology improved.

▶ *Mortuary art.* Gravestones also became white, replacing earlier green, black, blue, and red markers, and the backs were sculpted smooth, "denying their origin in the native stone." The messages engraved on the medieval tombstones reminded the living of their mortality with engraved death's heads and simple epitaphs such as "Here lies buried ...". But in Georgian culture, the typical inscription changed to "In memory of . . . ," and the urn and willow motif was used as a "symbol of commemoration." Georgian epitaphs praised the worldly achievements of individuals.

▶ *Food preparation.* Medieval diners usually attacked a portion of meat still articulated in joints, "showing in part at least the vestiges of the anatomy of the beast from which they came." But Georgian food was dominated by segmented cuts of meat that were more difficult to identify to anatomical part. Archaeologically, this change is seen as a shift from chopping bones to sawing them.

▶ *Refuse disposal.* During early medieval days, trash was simply tossed out of doors and windows, creating a sheet of refuse that domestic animals scavenged. By the mid-eighteenth century, however, trash was deposited in an orderly manner, in square pits up to 7 feet deep. Chamber pots also came into use, reflecting a desire for increased privacy.

These changes in material culture signal a shift to a culture that focused on the individual, rather than the group, and on the control of nature. Glassie and Deetz believe these patterns point to a simple cultural idea: Culture was to nature as order was to chaos. This reflects a general Enlightenment theme: For nature to be controlled, it had to be ordered, and for it to be ordered, it had to be brought into the world of culture.

Capitalism and Power in Historic Annapolis

Leone was interested not just in the operation of the Georgian worldview, but also in how and why it came to exist. He chose to examine these questions in the community of Annapolis.

Annapolis has been a small community since it was founded about 1650. It became the capital of Maryland in 1695, later experiencing a "golden age" of wealth and fame that peaked between about 1760 and the end of the American Revolution. In a move designed to symbolically subordinate the military to civil authority, George Washington came to Annapolis to resign his command of the Continental Army. The Treaty of Paris, which officially ended the American Revolution, was also signed there. During the early days of the United States, even though Annapolis remained

medieval mind-set The culture of the early (pre–AD 1660) British colonies that emphasized the group rather than the individual and in which the line between culture and nature was blurred; people were seen as conforming to nature.

Georgian order A worldview (ca. 1660/1680–1820) arising in the European Age of Reason that assumes the world has a single, basic, immutable order. Using the power of reason, people can discover what that order is and can thereby control the environment as they wish. The Georgian order is informed by the rise of scientific thought and by the balance and order in Renaissance architecture and art.

the state capital, the international, commercial, and industrial potential of nearby Baltimore attracted many of the area's wealthiest residents. Although the U.S. Naval Academy moved to Annapolis in 1845, the nineteenth century signaled an era of "gentle eclipse" for Annapolis. The 1950s saw the beginning of a commercial revival based on yachting, tourism, and new highways that defined Annapolis as a suburb of Washington, DC, and Baltimore, less than 30 miles away.

Leone and his team consciously deconstructed the ideology behind the historical development of Annapolis and its environs: Why did some people become rich? Why were some poor? What was the relationship between the two? How did the American Revolution affect these inequalities?

Eventually, Leone developed a "theory of power" to explain the growth of Chesapeake society under the European and American systems. By 1720, a class structure had developed in which a few families of the gentry controlled most of the wealth. The social position of the rest of the population—poorer whites, Native and African-Americans—remained the same before and after the American Revolution.

The Power Garden: Landscape Archaeology as Ideology Leone paid special attention to the formal landscapes of Annapolis. Recognizing that formal gardens were a new addition to wealthy households, Leone wanted to understand what this piece of material culture had to say about the formation of the Georgian order.

Shown in Figure 14-9, the best known of Annapolis's formal gardens in the late eighteenth century was that of William Paca—a signer of the Declaration of Independence. If we could ask him, Paca would probably say that he built his garden in the style that he did because he "enjoyed" it or because it was fashionable. But this only raises the question of *why* this particular garden style was fashionable.

Paca's garden, once described as "the most elegant in Annapolis," was originally built in the 1760s, behind a large, five-part Georgian mansion—which sported a facade and a floor plan exhibiting bilateral symmetry.

The garden is likewise Georgian, with a central axis, and a straight, broad path that descends through several sets of steps as one leaves the house, dividing the space into two parts. These steps lead down over a series of small terraces, creating the same visual effect of bilateral symmetry as that of Georgian architecture.

The garden survived into the early twentieth century, when it was destroyed to make room for a 200-room hotel. When the hotel was torn down in 1968, Stanley South excavated in and around the standing

© Kevin Fleming/Corbis

Figure 14-9 The William Paca garden (Annapolis).

house. Historical archaeologists then moved into the garden area, first testing and then excavating large areas. Original wall footings, documenting the terraces (which could be seen in stratigraphic profile), were found; thus, the garden's basic topography was reconstructed. Trenching and examination of the profiles showed a canal and pond at the bottom of the garden, surrounded by a natural garden (in the terminology of the time, a "wilderness") in the lowest third of the garden. Foundations of a central pavilion and springhouse and of footings for a bridge over the ponds were discovered; 125 paleobotanical samples were recovered from the wet fill. These archaeological data were combined with a few period descriptions and with a contemporary portrait of William Paca that showed the garden as background. The pavilion, bathhouse, springhouse, and Chinese Chippendale bridge have all been restored. Today, the Paca garden is open to the public as both an archaeologically based reconstruction and a horticultural experiment.

Leone first visited the restored garden in the early 1980s, and his impressions remained the touchstone for his subsequent archaeological analyses. He later wrote, "As I began to walk through the garden from the top, which is 16 feet higher than the bottom, which is 270 feet away, I found it difficult to tell distances; I felt I was being controlled, as paths, precise borders, openings, stairs, and objects that had to be stepped over operated everywhere to control me. This sensation was especially true regarding sight."

This effect is not simply the impact of fastidious design. Paca's sensibilities were affected by larger cultural ideas, and his garden expresses the Enlightenment idea of the power of Reason over Nature. By putting trees and shrubs into their "proper" places, Paca's landscape architect was demonstrating that nature controlled by culture was more lovely and desirable than wilderness—that is, than nature uncontrolled by culture.

After studying two other large gardens in Annapolis, Leone synthesized what he believed to be the rules behind the design. The Paca garden was constructed following the laws of perspective and used Baroque rules for creating optical illusions. Convergent or divergent lines of sight (to make distances appear shorter or longer, depending on the specific need in each garden) were created, and rows of beds or shrubs were formed into trapezoids and focal points (rather than strictly parallel lines) to manipulate the view. "The gardens are three-dimensional spaces," he wrote, "built consciously using rules which were well understood to create illusions for those who walked through them."

But why the illusion? Leone asked. And why would such Anglo-American gardens proliferate just before the American Revolution and then slowly disappear—like the rest of Georgian material culture—in the decades leading up to the Civil War?

For answers, Leone turned to the general body of materialist theory and formulated a hypothesis to explain governance through ostentatious displays. When money forms the only power base, Leone argued, those governing have little need to demonstrate their right or power to govern; they are in control and intend to stay that way. But ostentatious displays become important when factors other than simple wealth come into play, when it is necessary to convince the governed that those in power deserve to stay there. *Show* becomes important when those in authority do not necessarily control the purse strings or when the wealthy do not control the power structure.

The William Paca garden was built by a wealthy man who lived in a time of contradictions. Although not born to particular affluence, he married into plenty of it. Although a slave owner, he argued for the Bill of Rights. Although descended from planters and tied to merchants, he grew up and lived in economic circumstances in which he and everyone around him faced serious economic and political change.

Paca could have built his garden anytime during his lifetime, but he chose to do so when his power to protect his wealth was being diminished by Britain. Parliamentary restrictions on trade and local office-holding compromised profits and power in the 1760s. Paca was isolated socially and economically by a large and difficult-to-control slave population as well as by poor white farmers and day laborers who were anxious to learn who their future allies would be in the coming war with Britain.

Leone argues that the formal Anglo-American gardens were built deliberately to demonstrate a knowledge of—and control over—the laws of nature. Paca was trying to create the illusion that either (1) he still retained power over his own wealth or (2) he should be granted the political clout to do so. In this perspective, the garden was not a statement of what existed. Paca's garden both reflected and helped create an ideology (see Chapter 15), at a time when the wealth and prestige of his class were being undermined and diminished.

Leone points out that the Paca garden illustrates the principles that defined the layout of Annapolis as a whole. The early street patterns and building placements still dominate life in the city. This archaeological study of Paca's garden reveals that perspective and its power to invite attention are still actively used to manage relations of power in the city today. The relations among the prominence of the state capitol, the isolation of the Naval Academy, and the invisibility of the African-American community are all managed using the same spatial principles exhibited in Paca's garden. Together, Leone argues, historical archaeological and critical theory illustrate the origins of modern—and exploitative—social relations that continue to the present.

Taking Critical Theory Public

As discussed in Chapter 2, archaeology's postprocessual critique calls attention to the important role played by local politics in archaeological interpretation—and particularly to interpretation within the field of historical archaeology.

Critical theorists argue that the proper role of the historian is to unearth the beginnings of contemporary class-based ideologies—distortions that rationalize forms of exploitation, such as slavery, sexism, and racism. Applied to historical archaeology, critical theory suggests that once a repressed people can be shown a past in which things were different, they can use this knowledge to challenge and attempt to change the inequities of the present. From this position, the responsible historian (and historical archaeologist) should form alliances with members of oppressed classes and work toward social change to better the workers' condition. To the critical theorist, capitalism has negative social elements that should be confronted.

Leone grounded his research at Annapolis in the belief that archaeologists and historians should "stand up" against the oppressive excesses of capitalism. In other words, it was not enough for archaeologists simply to learn about abuse of power in the past; it was essential that this knowledge be brought forward into the present.

Photo by Archaeology in Annapolis

Figure 14-10 Cindy Chance, Department of Anthropology, University of Maryland, explains excavations in downtown Annapolis to visiting tourists, April 2008. Archaeology in Annapolis features public education using open excavations as a part of the 300th anniversary of the city's charter granted by Queen Anne in 1708. The use of archaeology to celebrate the tercentenary was organized by Ellen Moyer, the former Mayor of Annapolis.

The call for historical archaeology to become more political comes from two directions. As archaeology becomes more public, individual archaeologists are increasingly called upon to interpret their findings for the public. Such interpretation takes many forms—traditional museum exhibits, outdoor history museums, site-specific tourist facilities, and television and other media interpretations of "the past." But the problem immediately surfaces—which and whose past?

Consider the case of Annapolis, where historical preservation has played a major role in the commercial renaissance of the city. Annually, more than 1 million people visit Annapolis, a city of only about 32,000 people. As in many other small, historical towns, local residents work hard to protect those things that attract visitors.

The encapsulated history of Annapolis has been peddled to generations of tourists who buy guidebooks, listen to tour guides, and saunter through the historic-house museums (Figure 14-10). Prominent are references to the ultimate first tourist, none other than George Washington himself. Discussing his many visits, conventional Annapolis history plays up the social and domestic aspects of Washington's jaunts into the city—going to the racetrack, attending social events and plays, and visiting a host of friends and family members. In effect, the image of Washington-in-Annapolis mirrored the profile of just the sort of visitor

that Annapolis wanted to attract—the high-end tourist with some money to spend, but without an attitude.

Through the lens of critical theory, however, Leone and his colleagues noticed something interesting about the tourism process. As the tourists poured through, they were presented the history of Annapolis as a collection of disconnected units from different time periods and institutions. History-for-the-tourist was left in the hands of diverse groups and institutions, some overlapping, some in competition. Annapolis had no unified history to connect the different parts of the city. Black and white populations were presented as unconnected, as were the histories of the city of Annapolis and the Naval Academy.

As written and presented by whites, black history (viewed from the nineteenth-century perspective) was separated from white history (presented from the eighteenth-century perspective). Slavery was not seen as an antecedent to relationships between contemporary groups.

Leone and his associates—notably an archaeologist-cum-lawyer, Parker Potter—designed an on-site program for the 5000 to 10,000 visitors who stopped by each year. Tourists visiting Historic Annapolis often have a chance to walk through the ongoing archaeological excavations. Well-prepared guides explain what the archaeologists are doing and why they are doing it.

The site excursions were enormously popular with tourists and residents in Annapolis, and they seemed to rally the city's support to protect the archaeological sites of Annapolis. But in regard to social change, Leone and Potter were frustrated with the results. Potter believed that the Archaeology in Annapolis tour program failed to effect any significant change in Annapolis. "As far as I can tell," Leone has written, "[the tours] changed consciousness not at all. . . . We were speaking to the wrong audience."

For a historical archaeology of capitalism to be fruitful, Leone realized, "there would have to be a dialogue with those who see knowledge about themselves as a way of dealing with their own oppression or victimization." This was disappointing in a sense because it suggested that critical theory as a strategy for effecting social change (its avowed goal) might not work as intended (at least not by itself).

On reflection, Leone still believed that the Archaeology in Annapolis program had successfully explored the histories of the white residents who lived there (even if the white tourists to Annapolis did not seem to pick up on the message to "stand up against capitalism"). But he also realized that, in its early stages, the archaeology program had overlooked a major portion of the city by not explicitly addressing the African-American experience through archaeology.

This realization led Leone and the public programming effort at Annapolis in another direction—into the contemporary African-American community of Annapolis. The dialogue between Annapolis archaeologists and the African-American community immediately raised three related questions:

▶ Was there, indeed, any way to tell whether archaeological material was associated with African-Americans?
▶ Does the African-American community care about that record? (Some important questions: Can you tell us about freedom, not just about slavery? Is there anything left from Africa?)
▶ What would an African-American historical archaeology look like?

Faced with this entirely new direction, Leone realized, "We ourselves had to admit we did not know the answers."

So began a new interchange at Annapolis, between white archaeologists and African-Americans. No longer was the archaeologist the "teacher," with the community serving only as "listener." In this dialogue, all participants defined themselves as professionals, informants, scholars, students, and fund-raisers. Everyone involved, according to Leone, admitted ignorance on some topics, but also expressed a willingness to learn. This experiment in historical archaeology is still ongoing.

Conclusion

Historical archaeology is the growth industry of archaeology in the twenty-first century. In part, cultural resource management and the large number of historical sites that are uncovered by the construction activities of a growing population drive this growth. But it is also driven by a desire to understand the colonial and postcolonial history of the United States and the roles played by all the peoples who have found a home in America. For this reason, historical archaeology will continue to occupy a prominent place in archaeology for years to come. We expect that the processual paradigm will continue to be important, but that postprocessual approaches will play a large and significant role as issues such as power, domination, class, and resistance figure prominently in the world's recent (colonial) history.

For this reason also, historical archaeology will continue to be the source of some heated disputes. Some of these disputes will focus on who has the right to study and interpret the material remains that document the history of those other groups—Native, Hispanic-, African-, Asian-, and Euro-Americans. We predict that these debates will be less contentious and more productive if archaeologists maintain a dialogue with the public and descendant communities and yet do not withdraw from their scientific standards of excavation and interpretation.

Other disputes will focus on the proper place of politically motivated interpretations of the past. Leone, for example, suggests that capitalism creates its own view of the past, which masks the formation of inequities that are essential to the operation of capitalism today—a bourgeois class of consumers and an economically and politically repressed group of workers. But some might legitimately argue that any archaeology pursuing a political position is biased from the start, and hence all its interpretations of the past are suspect. Those in historical archaeology who pursue the paradigm of critical theory will have to meet this challenge in the future by combining a passionate desire to use archaeology to effect social change with a dispassionate and thorough scientific analysis of archaeology's data.

SUMMARY

1. Why do historical archaeology if we already have the historical records?

◉ Historical archaeology looks at material remains from past societies that also left behind some form of written documentation ("history") about themselves.

◉ Historical sources can be significantly biased—sometimes intentionally, sometimes not; archaeologists look at archaeological and documentary records *as equally valid yet independent* lines of evidence.

2. What are the three major areas of historical archaeological research today?

◉ Historical archaeology eschews the "oldest," "largest," and "most historically significant" sites, favoring instead the study of historically disenfranchised groups, including African-Americans, Asian-American cultures, Native Americans during the historic period, and Hispanic-Americans.

◉ Historical archaeology tackles questions about the recent past that history books answer unsatisfactorily. In this regard, some historical archaeologists are like crime scene detectives, collecting data to resolve disputes over the nature of key historical events.

◉ Many historical archaeologists research the nature of European colonialism (the developing capitalism of that time) and its effects on indigenous peoples.

3. How is historical archaeology more amenable to the postprocessual paradigm than prehistoric archaeology?

◉ Historical archaeology has been fertile ground for postprocessual interests because texts can provide data with which to place archaeological remains in context.

◉ The study of the symbolic meaning of material remains proceeds more comfortably in historical archaeology, where documents can provide interpretations of material culture.

MEDIA RESOURCES

Doing Fieldwork:
Archaeological Demonstrations CD-ROM 2.0
This CD, developed by the authors, shows professional archaeologists involved in various digs, many of which are referenced in the text. The presentation is organized by the main techniques used on an archaeological dig, reinforcing concepts and techniques via live examples. The CD takes you through each step automatically, or you can navigate to any point via the navigation bar. After reviewing a step in the dig process, you are taken to Check Points, which are concept questions about each step of the dig. Then you can see the answers, receive your score, and even send your scores to your instructor.

**The Companion Website for *Archaeology,*
Sixth Edition**
www.cengagebrain.com
Supplement your review of this chapter by going to the companion website to take one of the practice quizzes, use the flash cards to master key terms, and check out the many other study aids that are designed to help you succeed in your introductory archaeology course.

15 CARING FOR AMERICA'S CULTURAL HERITAGE

LEARNING OBJECTIVES

AFTER READING THIS CHAPTER YOU SHOULD BE ABLE TO ANSWER THESE QUESTIONS:

1. What federal policies help protect cultural resources, including archaeological sites?

2. What are the important elements of the 1906 Antiquities Act, the 1966 National Historic Preservation Act, and the 1979 Archaeological Resources Protection Act?

3. Is there an international black market in antiquities? If so, what can be done about it?

4. Why is the Native American Graves Protection and Repatriation Act of 1990 important to archaeologists? How does it differ from other archaeological legislation?

© AP Images/Matt Rourke

Colonial buildings, including George Washington's presidential home, in an excavation in front of the Liberty Bell Center, Philadelphia, 2007. Archaeologists unearthed a hidden passageway used by slaves beneath Washington's house.

PREVIEW

THIS CHAPTER DESCRIBES how archaeology helps conserve America's cultural heritage. Threats to this heritage come from those who loot archaeological sites for personal gain and from relentless development across the country. Over the years, the federal government has passed various laws to protect the nation's cultural heritage in archaeological sites, historic buildings, and landscapes.

These laws created an important new direction for archaeology, generally known as cultural resource management. Linked with construction, development, and federal agency activities, cultural resource management requires new ways of thinking about archae-

ological standards, principles, ethics, and training. The cultural resource management framework today dominates the practice of archaeology in America.

Another body of law safeguards the rights of indigenous peoples and regulates the repatriation of human skeletal remains and certain cultural objects to Indian tribes and Native Hawaiian organizations. Still more laws attempt to stop the flow of illegally acquired antiquities. Although this chapter focuses on the United States, many other countries have similar laws that try to preserve their cultural heritage, stop looting, and protect the rights of indigenous peoples.

INTRODUCTION

Commercial development goes on all around us. Nearly everywhere you look, you see bridges, dams, roads, pipelines, power lines, and buildings under construction. Such development destroys as much as it constructs. Roads pave over the American past. As new houses spring up, artifacts are carted away in dump trucks. As power lines go up, archaeological sites are bulldozed into rubble. Most people benefit from improved transportation, better hospitals, and more efficient communication services, but at the same time, these projects destroy America's cultural heritage. So this leaves us with a critical question: What part of our past must we save, and what part can we do without?

This problem is not unique to the United States. Most modern nations try to balance economic development and heritage preservation through laws and regulations. In this country, **cultural resource man-**

agement (CRM) is the field that conducts activities related to compliance with legislation that protects cultural resources.

It is difficult to overemphasize the importance of CRM to contemporary archaeology. Prior to the 1960s, nearly all American archaeologists worked for universities and museums. Today, the number of archaeologists in the United States not only vastly exceeds those working in the 1960s, but well over half of them earn a living by working in the framework of cultural resource management. In fact, CRM projects account for about 90 percent of the field archaeology conducted in the United States today. How did this change come about?

THE DEVELOPMENT OF CULTURAL RESOURCE MANAGEMENT

The threat to America's cultural heritage did not begin with strip malls and interstate highways. In fact, a concern with historic preservation extends to the earliest days of the United States. In 1789, for example, wealthy

---

cultural resource management (CRM) A professional field that conducts activities, including archaeology, related to compliance with legislation aimed at conserving cultural resources.

Bostonians formed the Massachusetts Historical Society in response to the destruction of John Hancock's house. The society became a watchdog to ensure that other historically significant properties were not lost. And in 1813, the federal government ordered the preservation of Independence Hall in Philadelphia. However, a systematic concern for preserving America's cultural heritage developed rather slowly, as part of a broader environmental preservation movement.

America's environmental movement can be traced to such late-nineteenth-century writers as Henry David Thoreau, John Muir, and Ernest Thompson Seton, each of whom inspired generations to take notice of the natural world and the human impact on that landscape. Some people, appalled at the needless slaughter of the Great Plains bison in the late nineteenth century, worked to save the continent's indigenous wildlife. Others, called to action by George Perkins Marsh's widely read *Man and Nature* (1864), worked to stave off the wholesale environmental degradation evident around the world.

President Theodore Roosevelt was particularly sensitive to Marsh's plea that disturbed environments should be allowed to heal naturally or be restored by specific conservation management plans. Roosevelt insisted that large areas of forest and grazing land be set aside in the United States, to protect timber supplies *for future use and development*. About the same time, John Muir (founder of the Sierra Club) argued for leaving large tracts of western lands untouched *for their aesthetic values*. These two often-conflicting philosophies remain with us today and have profound effects on modern historic preservation.

Early Efforts to Preserve America's Heritage

Archaeology and the preservation of cultural and historic properties were swept along with the conservation movement nearly from its beginning. In 1880, the Archaeological Institute of America (formed in 1879 and a major international archaeological organization today) sent Adolph Bandelier (1840–1914) to New Mexico to explore pueblo ruins there. Bandelier discovered that a local rancher had dismantled the roof of the Spanish church at Pecos Pueblo in 1858, recovering adobe and timber to construct outhouses. "Treasure hunters" had ripped out the mission's carved lintel beams and made boxes of them; they also looted graves inside the mission compound. The destruction

of America's national heritage was well underway by the mid-nineteenth century.

Reports of this destruction aroused concern among wealthy patrons of the Archaeological Institute. In 1882, several influential members tried to pass legislation in Congress that would allow the government to withdraw some lands containing important sites from public sale. But the bill went nowhere.

Where Congress refused to act, however, private citizens stepped in. One of the first sites to be protected was Ohio's Serpent Mound (see Figure 2-4 on page 27). By the 1870s, treasure hunters had heavily damaged the site; it was probably not pristine even when Squier and Davis (the Moundbuilder investigators whom you met in Chapter 2) mapped it some 40 years earlier. Frederic Putnam (1839–1915), of Harvard University's Peabody Museum, realized that the nation would soon lose this unique site. So, with the help of wealthy Bostonians, he saved it the old-fashioned way: He bought it. Harvard University owned the site until 1900, when it transferred title to the Ohio Historical Society, which owns and maintains the site today. (This "old-fashioned" approach still saves sites today through the Archaeological Conservancy, which has preserved more than 400 sites in 41 states.)

Private efforts continued to lead the way for preservation in the late nineteenth century. In 1889, several Boston Brahmins petitioned the federal government to save Casa Grande, an important pueblo site that contains a massive four-story adobe structure in southern Arizona. Their efforts paid off—first when Congress appropriated $2000 for the site's repair in 1889, and three years later when President Benjamin Harrison withdrew the site's 480 acres from future sale, thus creating the nation's first archaeological "reservation."

The Antiquities Act of 1906

Although the concern for preserving the past was sincere, the late-nineteenth-century approach was piecemeal, and the looting and destruction of archaeological sites proceeded at an alarming pace. The cliff dwellings in the Mesa Verde area of southwestern Colorado were especially hard hit. Tucked beneath massive arches in sandstone cliffs, the large pueblos of the Mesa Verde region—and the tens of thousands of well-preserved artifacts they contained—had been protected from the elements since the dwellings were abandoned in the late thirteenth century.

Figure 15-1 The site known as Cliff Palace, in Mesa Verde National Park, was occupied in the late 1200s; it was among the first archaeological sites in the United States to receive federal protection.

This fact did not escape the notice of skilled looters working the area. They tore the roofs off structures and blasted holes through the stone and adobe walls to let sunlight in. Six-hundred-year-old roof beams disappeared in the looters' campfires, hundreds of purloined pots appeared on an expanding curios market, and long-sacred kivas were damaged beyond repair.

One digger aroused special concern, even though his excavations were more careful than most—and directed at acquiring knowledge rather than curiosities for sale. Swedish scientist Gustaf Erik Adolf Nordenskiöld (1868–1895) traveled to Mesa Verde in 1891, and worked with Richard and Alfred Wetherill, local ranchers and archaeological "guides" (who had excavated innumerable sites and supervised excavations at Pueblo Bonito in Chaco Canyon; Southwestern archaeologists still debate their legacy). Nordenskiöld dug extensively at Cliff Palace (Figure 15-1), the largest of Mesa Verde's pueblos, excavating a huge artifact collection that he exported to Sweden (which eventually landed in Finland's National Museum, where it remains today).

Although archaeologists admired Nordenskiöld's lavishly illustrated publication, *The Cliff Dwellers*

of the Mesa Verde (1893), many were angry that lax American laws could not stop such an important collection from leaving the country. Again, private citizens stepped in. In 1902, the Colorado Cliff-Dwellings Association, a women's organization based in Denver, raised funds to rent portions of the Ute reservation that contained pueblo ruins. Such action by citizens, especially wealthy ones who had clout with their congressional representatives, encouraged Congress to provide formal protection of archaeological sites.

Although a number of sites, such as Mesa Verde, were legally protected between 1902 and 1906, a systematic, nationwide program eluded legislators. Then came Edgar Lee Hewett (1865–1946), a fair archaeologist but a brilliant administrator and lobbyist.

Born in Illinois, Hewett moved west as a young man to become superintendent of schools in Colorado. Pueblo ruins fascinated him, and he began excavating in 1896. Eventually, he earned a doctoral degree from the University of Geneva in Switzerland and became president of the School of American Archaeology (now the School of Advanced Research) in Santa Fe, New Mexico. In 1905, the American Anthropological Association made him secretary of a committee charged with working toward antiquities legislation.

Hewett helped hammer out the first draft of the **Antiquities Act,** which, after considerable lobbying and rewriting, was signed into law by Theodore Roosevelt in 1906. The Antiquities Act contained three important provisions:

▶ The act made it illegal to excavate or collect remains from archaeological sites on public lands without a permit from the relevant government agency.

▶ The act stipulated that permits would be granted only to museums, universities, and other scientific or educational institutions "with a view to increasing knowledge" and that objects gathered would only be "for permanent preservation in public museums."

▶ The act invested the president with the authority to create national monuments on federal lands containing "historic landmarks, historic and prehistoric structures, and other objects of historic or scientific interest" and to "reserve as a part thereof parcels of land, the limits of which in all cases shall be confined to the smallest area compatible with the proper care and management of the objects to be protected."

Roosevelt used the act immediately to designate Devil's Tower in Wyoming and Montezuma's Castle in Arizona (a pueblo cliff dwelling inaccurately named after the famed Aztec leader) as national monuments in 1906. (That same year, Mesa Verde became a national park, the first park created for its archaeological significance.)

The Antiquities Act became the foundation of all future archaeological legislation. But note that the act is not limited to archaeological sites, but includes "objects of historic or scientific interest." In fact, the first monument, Devil's Tower, falls into this category. Why? Legislation is always a compromise. Key congressional sponsors of the Antiquities Act were eager to create legislation that would allow protection of "natural wonders," such as Arizona's petrified forest (which became the fourth national monument)—hence the expansion of the Antiquities Act to include more than archaeological sites.

The River Basin Surveys

The Antiquities Act was a compromise in another way as well. Hewett knew that Congress preferred not to proclaim policies (no matter how well intentioned). Instead, legislators like to begin by "solving" problems

and, if the solutions appeal to the electorate, to then affirm the policies behind the solutions. Knowing this, Hewett shrewdly refrained from suggesting that the federal government was *responsible* for the protection of archaeological sites. Hewett instead highlighted the problems of looting and crafted the Antiquities Act to address this problem by (1) creating a permit process and (2) establishing a mechanism for protecting land. The resulting Antiquities Act thus *implied* that the government had a responsibility toward sites on federal land. Although this was progress, without solid affirmation of that policy, archaeological sites remained vulnerable to development.

Beginning in the 1930s, archaeologists became increasingly involved with site preservation as the federal government began constructing dams around the country to generate electricity, irrigate land, and control floods. Many sites were excavated during the Depression as part of the Civil Works Administration and Works Progress Administration. These government-sponsored work programs were disbanded when the United States entered World War II in 1941. But dam construction continued to threaten sites. Largely due to the unrelenting efforts of a small group of archaeologists called the Committee for the Recovery of Archaeological Remains, the National Park Service worked with the Smithsonian Institution to create the River Basin Survey program. Although archaeologists often had to cobble together funding, river basins were surveyed prior to inundation, and many archaeological sites that would have disappeared beneath the waters were recorded and excavated.

HISTORIC PRESERVATION COMES OF AGE

The River Basin Survey program amounted to admission that the federal government was responsible for the effects of its projects on archaeological sites. This statement of policy became codified during the turbulent years of the 1960s and 1970s, when concern for resource conservation reached a critical point.

In the 1960s, a large portion of the American public—many aroused by Rachel Carson's *Silent*

Antiquities Act Passed in 1906, this act (1) required federal permits before excavating or collecting artifacts on federal land, (2) established a permitting process, and (3) gave the president the authority to create national monuments.

Spring (1962)—recognized that wilderness and wildlife refuges alone could not stem the effects of pollution. By the early 1970s, an environmental movement was in full swing. The voter appeal of these popular movements was not lost on legislators, and many of them became "conservationists" as well. In fact, sufficient power came down on the side of the ecologists for laws to be drafted protecting the *nonrenewable resources* of the nation.

When most people think of nonrenewable resources, they think of redwoods, whooping cranes, and baby seals. Others relate more to energy-related assets, such as oil, coal, and uranium. But most legislators have a legal background, and in the course of legally defining national resources, they realized that properties of historic value must be included. After all, they reasoned, how many Monticellos do we have? Aren't archaeological sites nonrenewable resources too?

The concern with historic preservation was largely about the destruction of historic buildings through urban renewal and the construction of national highways in the 1950s and 1960s. Nonetheless, archaeological sites were included in historic preservation legislation and are now considered **cultural resources,** to be legally protected just like redwoods, whooping cranes, and shale oil fields. This legal protection came through various laws that established the framework within which archaeology in the United States operates today. The most important of these is the National Historic Preservation Act of 1966.

THE NATIONAL HISTORIC PRESERVATION ACT

The Antiquities Act is a short, one-page piece of legislation, intelligible to just about anyone. The **National Historic Preservation Act (NHPA),** on the other hand, is lengthy, tedious, and shot through with bureaucratic jargon. But every archaeologist working in the United States must be intimately familiar with its details.

The NHPA formally stated the policy that lay behind the 1906 Antiquities Act: "It shall be the policy of the Federal Government . . . to foster conditions under which our modern society and our prehistoric and historic resources can exist in productive harmony." Three years later, Congress made this policy even more explicit in the National Environmental Policy Act (NEPA): "it is the continuing policy of the Federal Government" to "preserve important historic, cultural, and natural aspects of our national heritage."

Whereas previous legislation approached historic preservation in a piecemeal fashion and was largely reactive, the National Historic Preservation Act created a systematic, nationwide program of historic preservation. It has therefore had far-reaching effects on American archaeology. The act created State Historic Preservation Offices, headed by State Historic Preservation Officers (SHPO, or "shippo" in archaeological slang), and the national Advisory Council on Historic Preservation. Subsequent amendments created Tribal Historic Preservation Offices on Indian reservations as well; many tribes, such as the Cherokee, Hopi, Zuni, and Navajo, now have large and successful historic preservation programs.

Historic preservation offices are tasked with creating state (or reservation) inventories of archaeological and historic properties, assisting federal agencies in complying with the State Historic Preservation Act, evaluating national register nominations (we'll discuss these in the following), and maintaining databases, such as state site files.

The NHPA requires that the government inventory federal lands for archaeological and historic sites. As a result, many archaeologists now work for federal agencies—in Bureau of Land Management field offices, for instance, or the National Park Service. No agency has been able to enumerate all of its holdings because inventories require a 100 percent pedestrian survey (of the kind that we described in Chapter 3), and the federal government manages millions of acres of land. By the late 1990s, less than 10 percent of all federal lands had been surveyed. But because NHPA mandates an inventory, federal agencies continue to whittle away at it, often by working jointly with local college and university research programs.

Anyone who becomes an archaeologist in the United States will almost immediately hear talk of "Section 106." This is an important part of the NHPA, one that governs much of the field research done today, so we need to devote some attention to it here.

---

cultural resources Physical features, both natural and artificial, associated with human activity, including sites, structures, and objects possessing significance in history, architecture, or human development. Cultural properties are unique and nonrenewable resources.

National Historic Preservation Act (NHPA) Passed in 1966, this act created (1) the National Register of Historic Places, (2) the Advisory Council on Historic Preservation, and (3) State Historic Preservation Offices, as well as (4) a process to mitigate the impact of development; it also requires that government agencies provide good stewardship of their cultural resources.

Section 106: The Government Must Consider the Effects of Its Actions on Historic Properties

Section 106 is very short, but it has had far-reaching effects. Here is what it says in its entirety:

The head of any Federal agency having direct or indirect jurisdiction over a proposed Federal or Federally assisted undertaking in any State and the head of any Federal department or independent agency having authority to license any undertaking shall, prior to the approval of the expenditure of any Federal funds on the undertaking or prior to the issuance of any license, as the case may be, take into account the effect of the undertaking on any district, site, building, structure, or object that is included in or eligible for inclusion in the National Register. The head of any such Federal agency shall afford the Advisory Council on Historic Preservation established under Title II of this Act a reasonable opportunity to comment with regard to such undertaking.

In other words: If you want to build something on federal property or modify that landscape, or if you want to construct something that requires federal funding, licenses, or permits, regardless of whose property you will build it on (all of these are what is meant by the term "undertaking"), then you must determine whether the project will adversely affect any sites "included in or eligible for" the National Register (we'll get to this later). If it will, you must *mitigate* the impact of the project. What does all this mean?

In the worst case, a project's "effect" might mean "destroy"—but it might also mean altering a site in a way that detracts from what made it significant in the first place. For example, constructing an addition to a historic building that is not compatible with the building's style could be an adverse effect, even if the original building remains intact. But note that Section 106 does not say we must protect sites at any cost; it just means that the government must understand and consider the value of prehistoric and historic sites in agency planning and activities.

If a site is deemed significant, then the contractor is obligated to mitigate the project's impact on it. Mitigating the impact of a highway, for example, might mean scientifically excavating the sites along the right-of-way. Or it might mean moving the road a little to one side. The choice made depends largely on the costs of the options.

The National Register and Archaeological Significance

Section 106 applies to sites that are "included in or eligible for inclusion in the National Register," which is a list of significant sites and places that are historically important. If an archaeological site is not "significant," the law says it does not get studied, sampled, excavated, or protected. In other words, when the bulldozers come through, the site is history. Thus, the concept of significance is crucial to the protection of sites. What does it mean?

Archaeologists use the term "significant" in two very different ways. Usually, they follow common English usage: "Blackwater Draw might be the most significant Paleoindian site in North America." "Significant" in this case is equivalent to "important," "intriguing," or "consequential." But many contemporary archaeologists use the term in a special, legalistic way that requires some explanation.

The National Historic Preservation Act authorized creation of the **National Register of Historic Places,** a listing of districts, sites, buildings, structures, and objects that are *significant* in American history, architecture, archaeology, engineering, and culture. More than 70,000 properties are listed on the National Register. Just because a site is on the register or eligible for it does not mean that it can't be altered or destroyed (although it makes it more difficult). It does mean, however, that the federal government must *consider the impact* of undertakings on sites that are on or eligible for the register.

According to NHPA's regulations, an archaeological site is significant if it meets one or more of the following four criteria:

- ▶ Association with events that made important contributions to broad patterns of history, prehistory, or culture
- ▶ Association with important people in the past
- ▶ Possession of distinctive characteristics of a school of architecture, construction method, or characteristics of high artistic value
- ▶ Known to contain or likely to contain data important in history or prehistory

Legal significance is based strictly on these four criteria. Consequently, it's difficult to get a site listed on the National Register. It's not just the archaeologist

> **National Register of Historic Places** A list of significant historic and prehistoric properties, including districts, sites, buildings, structures, and objects.

who decides, but also the responsible federal agency, the SHPO, the state review board, and the Keeper of the National Register. But note that Section 106 of NHPA does not say that a site must be on the register to be protected, only that it must be *eligible* for inclusion.

Archaeologists involved with CRM are responsible for helping to determine which sites are eligible and which are not. Exactly what standards archaeologists follow in determining significance is often a matter of heated debate. Some tribes argue that many sites are significant under the first criterion, but in the past most archaeologists sought eligibility under the fourth. In this case, the archaeologist must clearly define which research questions a site will help answer. And the nature of those questions will determine which sites are eligible and which are not—therefore, which sites are studied and which are destroyed.

Archaeologists often feel conflicted in making these judgments. Many of us think that a small scatter of waste flakes from stone tool manufacture is "significant"—in fact, Kelly's research in the Carson Desert (Chapter 3) was based almost entirely on such sites. But it would be hard to argue that those sites *individually* were significant under the NHPA's definitions.

Compliance Archaeology

Before a site's significance can be determined, you first have to find it. We learned about finding sites through sample survey in Chapter 3. CRM surveys are a little bit different.

In general, compliance with Section 106 begins with a review of the available literature and SHPO site files to see what is already known about the proposed project area. This is followed by a systematic survey, conducted according to state standards. In the parlance of CRM, the area surveyed is called the **area of potential effect (APE).** This includes the area directly affected by the construction project but also areas that are *anticipated* to be affected by the project after its completion. For example, the APE for a reservoir project might include not only the inundation zone and dam construction site, but also areas that will be developed

for recreation, such as campgrounds, boat launches, or associated hiking trails.

In research survey projects, the research question determines what the survey area will be. But in CRM, the construction project is in the driver's seat. This gives CRM surveys a different character from the kind of surveys we discussed in Chapter 3. First, since the survey area is defined by the construction project, the APE can take on an odd shape. The APE of a fiber optic cable or gas pipeline, for example, might be 100 feet wide and hundreds of miles long. In other cases, the areas that can be seen from a significant site—known as *viewsheds*—are considered part of the APE. The preservation of historic trails, such as the Oregon and California Trails, might require that an energy company place oil-drilling rigs far enough away or tuck them behind hills so that a hiker's enjoyment of a historic trail is not compromised. It is challenging, but archaeologists must devise research questions that can be addressed with such samples.

Second, the APE is often surveyed in its entirety, 100 percent. The objective is not to sample, but to make sure that no significant site will be destroyed. Significant sites may be very rare and because sample surveys sometimes miss the rarest of sites, full-coverage surveys can be necessary.

If sites are located during the survey, then the archaeologists might conduct test excavations of those sites to assess their significance. Those that are determined eligible for the register and that cannot be avoided by the project might be slated for "data recovery"—extensive excavations and associated analyses of the artifacts, ecofacts, and sediments. The construction project will receive the necessary clearance and permits only when the SHPO and agency have decided how to resolve a project's adverse effects on significant sites.

Private CRM firms carry out most of these compliance projects. If you are wondering who pays for these projects, it's the highway construction company, the mining company, the fiber optic cable company, or the government—whoever is doing the construction. Ultimately, of course, we all pay when we use the new facility—through tolls, Internet costs, telephone charges, and taxes. But put this into perspective: Although millions of dollars are spent each year on compliance archaeology, the sum is a fraction of total construction costs. The archaeology for the average pipeline, for example, is less than 1 percent of the total construction cost. In return, you are assured that irreplaceable cultural resources will be there for your grandchildren and that those

area of potential effect (APE)   The area that will be directly and indirectly affected by a construction project; in some cases it might encompass not only areas that are affected by construction but also areas seen from it.

LOOKING CLOSER

WHAT COURSES PREPARE YOU FOR A CAREER IN ARCHAEOLOGY?

The modern archaeologist is the last of the Renaissance scholars: a jack-of-all-trades and master of one. As you near the end of this text, you might be thinking about what courses would best prepare you for a career in archaeology. First, we suggest you major in anthropology and take courses in biological, linguistic, and cultural anthropology. Thereafter, consider the following:

▶ Introductory courses in geology, biology, and chemistry
▶ Geomorphology and pedology (soils)
▶ Advanced chemistry (if stable isotope analysis interests you)
▶ Vertebrate anatomy (if zooarchaeology appeals to you)
▶ Ecology and paleoecology (for instance, palynology)

▶ An introductory business course (this will come in handy if you go into CRM)
▶ Math and statistics—all you can handle
▶ Geographic information systems and computer modeling
▶ Technical writing
▶ Humanities (philosophy of science, historiography, ethnohistory, history)
▶ At least three semesters of a foreign language, especially if you wish to work overseas

Other useful skills include database manipulation, computer graphics, word processing, website construction, digital photography, use of total stations, and basic map reading. Spend summers working on archaeological projects (starting with a field school); seek internships with local CRM outfits and federal agencies.

---

significant sites that have to be destroyed to permit development will first be studied as intensively as current methods allow.

Within the last four decades, cultural resource management has radically transformed the practice of archaeology, particularly with respect to career opportunities, funding sources, and guiding philosophy. CRM provides archaeologists with several hundred million dollars a year in funding, and several thousand people make their living doing CRM archaeology. Many archaeologists employed in colleges, universities, and museums who wish to pursue "pure" research projects now find that they have to fit themselves into the CRM mold and speak the language of compliance archaeology.

Statistics suggest that any student considering archaeology as a profession will probably pursue that career in CRM. It can be extremely rewarding, if you are adequately prepared for it. Any student considering archaeology as a career should think about acquiring skills relevant to CRM in his or her program of study (see "Looking Closer: What Courses Prepare You for a Career in Archaeology?")

THE ARCHAEOLOGICAL RESOURCES PROTECTION ACT

The Antiquities Act made it illegal to collect and/or excavate a site on federal property without a permit, and the penalties for violators were pretty stiff for 1906: "a sum of not more than five hundred dollars" and/or imprisonment "for a period of not more than ninety days." But these sanctions mean little in today's world, where a single Mimbres painted bowl or Mississippian vessel can fetch thousands or even tens of thousands of dollars on the illegal antiquities market. Under the Antiquities Act alone, modern looters saw the penalties as nothing more than a small cost of "doing business." In fact, prior to 1979 there were only 18 convictions under the Antiquities Act.

So, despite the Antiquities Act's intentions, looting and site vandalism continue to destroy America's cultural heritage. The federal government estimates that of the 2 million archaeological sites presently recorded in the American Southwest, between 50 and 90 percent have already been looted to some degree. And as

Figure 15-2 A Mimbres pueblo site in the process of being looted by bulldozer; the operator plows away the pueblo walls to expose burial pits beneath the rooms. These burials often contain Mimbres bowls that fetch a high price on the antiquities black market.

off-road sports become more popular and open up access to remote regions of federal land, looting is accelerating. As shown in Figure 15-2, large-scale looting of archaeological sites is a major threat to the preservation of America's cultural heritage.

The **Archaeological Resources Protection Act (ARPA)** of 1979 tried to change this, making it a felony "to excavate, remove, damage, or otherwise alter or deface or attempt to excavate, remove, damage or otherwise alter or deface any archaeological resources located on public lands or Indian lands" without a permit. ARPA also made it illegal to sell, receive, or transport artifacts illegally removed from federal lands. The penalty for violating ARPA is a fine of up to $250,000 and/or up to 5 years in prison. (Collecting arrowheads from the surface, however, was specifically exempted and is not a punishable activity in the act.) The government can also confiscate any equipment used to loot the sites, including vehicles.

ARPA also allows judges to assess civil penalties that can take into account what it would have cost to professionally excavate a damaged site. This can result in large penalties. Looters can move more dirt in a weekend than an archaeologist would excavate in an entire season, or two or three. Add to that the cost of dates and of faunal, macrobotanical, and geoarchaeological analyses and the "archaeological value" can be high.

These penalties may seem stiff to some people. But looted sites are lost forever—they cannot be replaced—and it is difficult to put a value on such a loss. Consider also that many looters are involved in other illegal activities as well—fencing stolen goods, drugs, burglary, and so on. Some have been videotaped looting sites with automatic rifles slung over a shoulder. ARPA, in fact, has proven to be a way to track down some serious criminals (see "Looking Closer: ARPA and Elephant Mountain Cave").

Even with the added protection of ARPA, policing millions of acres of federal land is difficult and looting continues to destroy the nation's cultural heritage. Numerous federal and private agencies have taken aggressive anti-looting measures, such as site monitoring (using motion-sensitive cameras in some cases), fencing, and more diligent law enforcement. The successful "Adopt a Site" program pairs motivated avocational archaeologists with particularly vulnerable sites that benefit from continued monitoring. Still, vandalism and looting are probably the major threats to American archaeology today.

WHAT ABOUT STATE AND PRIVATE LAND?

ARPA applies to federal land. And some states have laws that cover cultural resources on state land. But these laws do not apply to private land. Many private landowners are wary of archaeologists because they believe that if they find something significant on their

Archaeological Resources Protection Act (ARPA) Passed in 1979, this act (1) prohibits the excavation or removal of artifacts from federal property without a permit, (2) prohibits the sale, exchange, or transport of artifacts acquired illegally from federal property, and (3) increased the penalties for violations of the act over those of the Antiquities Act.

LOOKING CLOSER

ARPA AND ELEPHANT MOUNTAIN CAVE

The police didn't know what to make of the mummified remains of two decapitated Indian children. But there they were, buried in Jack Lee Harelson's backyard.

In the 1980s, Harelson was an insurance agent, but his passion was looting archaeological sites. For years, he looted a cave on Elephant Mountain, on federal land in an isolated region of Nevada's Black Rock Desert. There he devastated a 10,000-year record of human occupation, stealing things such as 10,000-year-old sandals (among the oldest dated footwear in the world). Harelson also unearthed two large baskets, later radiocarbon-dated to 2000 years old, that contained the bodies of two young children, mummified in the dry desert cave. He looted the burials of rabbit nets, coiled baskets, ceremonial obsidian blades, and deer-hoof rattles. Harelson then decapitated the two children, saved the skulls, and buried the remains in plastic bags in his backyard.

Harelson's ex-business partner and his ex-wife tipped the police off to the grisly scene. In 1996, an Oregon court found Harelson guilty under ARPA and assessed a civil penalty against him. In that assessment, the BLM argued that "of the 36,000 archaeological sites recorded in Nevada, only four contain 10,000-year-old stratified records; Elephant Mountain Cave would have been the fifth and the only one in western Nevada. Harelson destroyed all of this potential and should be liable for the full civil penalty." In 2002, a federal administrative law judge agreed and used the archaeological value of the resources—that is, the cost to professionally excavate and analyze what Harelson had ripped from the cave's fragile sediments—as the basis for the assessment. His decision: $2.5 million.

But the story doesn't end here. After his conviction, Harelson turned to illegal gun sales and continued to loot sites. More important, undercover agents learned that Harelson was planning to kill five people: his ex-wife, two former business partners, an Oregon police sergeant, and the judge. In 2002, an Oregon trooper posed as a hitman, and Harelson offered him $10,000 to kill his ex-business partners. When the "hitman" brought Harelson proof—a doctored photo of one of the partners—Harelson paid him $10,000, and the SWAT team moved in.

Looters can be dangerous. If you see someone looting a site, notify the authorities; do not try to stop the looter yourself.

---

property, the government can confiscate the artifacts or even their land. In some countries, this is true. In England or Mexico, for example, so-called "treasure laws" give the government ownership of all subsurface historical resources. But this is not true in the United States. No matter how significant or remarkable a site may be, if it is on private property, it belongs to the landowner. The government cannot take it away. The only exception concerns human burials. In some states, the *intentional* destruction of a burial, regardless of its age, is a violation of state law—even if that burial is on your property.

The sanctity of private land in the United States can be frustrating because it means that the commercial mining of terrestrial (and underwater) sites for artifacts is often completely legal or subject to only a minor penalty. As a result, important archaeo-logical sites on private land can be rapidly destroyed. Archaeologists in Kentucky learned this lesson the hard way.

The Slack Farm Incident

Slack Farm sits on a pleasant stretch of rich bottomland along the Ohio River in northern Kentucky. In the fifteenth century, the Ohio River Valley was the center of a thriving chiefdom society, supported by maize agriculture. Several large sites, complete with flat-topped temple mounds such as those we described at Moundville (see Chapter 11), were the centers of large populations. Some of these Mississippian communities may have been even larger than the small towns that lie along the river today.

© David Pollack/Kentucky Heritage Council

Figure 15-3 Several hundred burials at the Slack Farm site, a fifteenth-century Mississippian burial ground, were looted and destroyed in the 1980s.

Prior to 1987, the Slack family knew of and protected a large fifteenth-century Mississippian site on their property. But when they sold the farm, the new owner was uninterested in protecting the site; in fact, he leased the property for 6 months to two men for $10,000. These two individuals, in turn, subleased portions of the land to eight others. The leasers' intent was not to grow tobacco or maize, but to mine artifacts.

Using everything from shovels to bulldozers, the ten men mined their shares and paraded the skulls and pots they recovered from the 500-year-old cemetery around town. Within a few weeks, the field looked like a war zone—pockmarked with craters (Figure 15-3). Human skeletal remains were strewn about alongside beer cans as the looters made a mad rush for valuable artifacts.

Someone in town finally alerted the police, but they could only charge the men with "desecration of a venerated object," which at the time carried a penalty of $500 and a maximum of 6 months in prison. Some of the pots they had found were probably sold on the black market for thousands of dollars, so the fine was a mere annoyance. Archaeologists later determined that although only about 10 to 15 percent of the cemetery had been disturbed, more than 600 graves had been disinterred.

Rosetta Stone A black basalt stone tablet found in Egypt in 1799 that bears an inscription in two forms of ancient Egyptian and Greek. By working from the Greek text, scholars were able to decipher the ancient Egyptian hieroglyphs.

Outrage in the Native American community and the public at large brought a halt to the looting, and archaeologists tried to assess the damage and retrieve some information (all the skeletal remains were reburied in 1988). But because the crime was only a misdemeanor, no one would prosecute, and all ten men walked away. As a result, Kentucky revised its burial laws, upgrading the penalty for intentionally desecrating a grave (including those on private property) from a misdemeanor to a felony.

Sadly, the looting of archaeological sites on private land will continue unabated until the market for artifacts disappears. Given that this is unlikely, the alternative is that an educated public must simply refuse to accept it, as at Slack Farm.

INTERNATIONAL EFFORTS TO PROTECT CULTURAL RESOURCES

Here's the grim truth: Looting of archaeological sites in the United States has reached epidemic proportions, and the international problem is even worse. In fact, illegal trafficking in antiquities *may be second only to the drug trade* in international crime.

The looting of other countries' archaeology has been going on for some time. One well-known example is the **Rosetta Stone,** a large basalt tablet inscribed in three scripts that allowed French linguist Jean-François Champollion to decipher Egyptian hieroglyphs. It was found by a French soldier in 1799 during Napoleon's conquest of Egypt. Fortunes change quickly in war, however, and by 1801 the Rosetta Stone was in the British Museum, where it is today. Many countries today demand the return of their artifacts; Yale University, for example, under threat of a lawsuit by Peru, has agreed to return artifacts excavated in the early twentieth century from the Peruvian site of Machu Picchu (see "What Does It Mean to Me? Should Antiquities Be Returned to the Country of Origin?").

WHAT DOES IT MEAN TO ME?

SHOULD ANTIQUITIES BE RETURNED TO THE COUNTRY OF ORIGIN?

The world's major museums contain artifacts that come from many different countries. The majority of these were acquired through legal channels. But some pieces have more checkered pasts. Among these are the Parthenon marbles.

The Acropolis is a limestone plateau that overlooks modern Athens. Temples and shrines adorn the plateau, among them the Parthenon, built between 447 and 438 BC and dedicated to the goddess Athena. It has been a sacred place in Greek culture for 2500 years and has served as a Catholic church, a mosque, and even a weapons depot.

The current problem began about 1800, when Thomas Bruce (better known as Lord Elgin) was British Ambassador to Turkey (at the time, Turkey ruled Greece as part of the Ottoman Empire). Elgin removed statues and portions of the 75-meter marble frieze from the Parthenon, sending them to England.

Elgin was later captured by the French and spent two years in prison, during which time the marbles were kept at his English estate, sometimes in the coal shed. Elgin spent most of his fortune removing the marbles and other Greek art treasures. Divorced, ill, and in debt, he sold the marbles to the British Museum in 1816 for a fraction of what they cost him. He died penniless in 1841.

Greece has demanded the return of the marbles ever since. The late Greek minister of culture, Melina Mercouri, argued that they symbolize Greece itself, and many Greeks feel that the sculptures belong in Greece.

The British Museum has countered that the museum acquired the marbles legally, has done nothing wrong, and that *any* return of antiquities smacks of "cultural fascism." It is true that the museum purchased the sculptures legally, and Lord Elgin always claimed he had permission from the Turkish government to remove them.

But Greece points out that the Turks, as occupiers of Greece, did not have the right to give Greek patrimony away. And, in fact, the surviving paperwork suggests that Elgin had permission only to draw, make casts, and do some small excavations; other evidence suggests that Elgin abused his political position and used bribes to remove the marbles. The British Museum counters that Elgin saved these priceless treasures from the

© Vega/Taxi/Getty Images

The Parthenon.

(continued on the next page)

(continued from page 369)

decay that political violence and pollution have visited upon the statues that remain on the Acropolis.

Britain argues that the marbles are now part of global, not just Greek, patrimony and that they deserve to be in the British Museum, where people from around the world can enjoy them. If it returned the marbles to Greece, the British Museum argues, the floodgates would open, myriad countries would demand the return of art objects, major museums would be empty, and the world would have far less access to these cultural treasures.

Greece points out that pollution is now under control in Athens and that conservation measures protect the sculptures (and that, in fact, the British Museum itself damaged them decades ago by using harsh cleaning solutions and chisels on them). The marbles themselves would be housed in a museum at the base of the Acropolis, as open to the world as the British Museum.

Should treasures like the Parthenon's marbles be removed from "your" museum and returned to their country of origin? Should we take into account the (often nefarious) ways in which artifacts were acquired in the past, or are we generating a tidal wave of litigation that will ultimately serve no one well? Do we consider whether the country of origin is capable of caring for artifacts by itself? Do we consider current national borders or those that existed at the time of the taking? Returning treasures to the country of origin seems to encourage a balkanization of the ancient world that will not serve archaeology or humanity well. And consider this: Seeking to defend the British Museum's claim to the marbles, the Parliamentary Assembly of the Council of Europe passed a resolution stressing "the unity of the European cultural heritage." Does keeping the marbles in Britain achieve this goal better than keeping them in Greece?

Because the conservation of archaeology has been linked to the environmental movement, you might think a public sensitive to issues such as global warming, forest conservation, and biodiversity would be similarly aware of international trading in looted artifacts. But this is not the case. While the sound of chain saws killing distant rain forests has been successfully linked to the personal lives of millions of Americans, the looting of foreign archaeological sites has not. There is no mistaking the scale of this problem. Thousands of graves are looted in China each year (despite the fact that the Chinese government has stiff penalties against grave robbing). Maya stelae are cut apart with rock saws and the glyphs sold individually. Thieves cut or chip rock art off caves and cliffs in North and South America, Australia, and Africa and hustle them away to waiting buyers. Armed looters ransack Peruvian tombs for gold; Spanish shipwrecks are plundered for silver; graves of World War I's dead are robbed of medals and military paraphernalia. There is literally no place in the world safe from looting. At the present rate, there will be precious little left by the end of this century.

Responsible museums today refuse to accept artifacts illegally imported from the country of origin or to display illegitimate artifacts already in their collections. Many, in fact, have returned artifacts in their collections that the museum discovered had been acquired illegally. The American Museum of Natural History forbids curators from authenticating or appraising artifacts, its Museum Shop does not sell antiquities, and the museum's *Natural History* magazine will not accept advertising for antiquities.

Like the drug trade, the illegal trade in antiquities is hard to stop as long as there is a market. We've learned this lesson many times, most recently in Iraq.

The Thieves of Baghdad

The power of the illegal international antiquities market was driven home on April 11, 2003, a few days after the U.S. military entered Baghdad. Although the Pentagon had promised to protect Iraqi cultural institutions, they left the Baghdad Museum unguarded. The looters smashed some artifacts, and destroyed much of the documentation. Although museum personnel had moved many of the more precious artifacts—most of the gold, for example—to secure bank vaults, many irreplaceable artifacts were stolen (Figure 15-4).

An investigation headed by Colonel Matthew Bogdanos, USMC (whose book on the looting gives us the title to this section), concluded that 40 items were stolen from the main galleries, and more than 13,000 items from storage rooms. As of March 2008, many artifacts had been recovered, most through an amnesty program (and Syria just returned more than 700 pieces), but others were found through raids or customs inspections in Iraq, Jordan, Italy, Great Britain, and the United States. Many of these items were outside of Iraq within days of their theft. And some 4000 to 7000 artifacts are still missing (the precise number is unknown since many records were destroyed). Incidentally, fearing similar looting, Egyptian citizens linked arms to form a human barrier around the famed Egyptian Museum in Cairo during the 2011 anti-government protests.

Figure 15-4 The aftermath of looting in the Baghdad Museum.

Although the museum was ransacked by local people looking for anything they might sell, Bogdanos's investigation found evidence of professional thieves with intimate knowledge of the museum—and keys. It was an inside job, and the thieves were selective in what they took. In the basement, for example, the only storage room entered was that containing a huge collection of ancient coins. Fortunately, the thieves dropped the keys to the cabinets and lost them in the unlit room (the electricity was off by this time; Bogdanos later found the keys). The looters lit a fire for light and, before the smoke drove them out, snatched 103 boxes that contained some 10,000 cylinder seals, pins, beads, pendants, and necklaces.

Other Iraqi museums were also hit, and archaeological sites were attacked by armed looters; many now look like bomb-scarred battlefields. One can hardly blame a poverty-stricken Iraqi farmer for exploiting an opportunity to make ten years' worth of wages in a night of digging. Instead, the blame rests with wealthy buyers in developed nations. They are the ones who drive this destruction, who encourage a country to rob itself of its cultural patrimony and to destroy irreplaceable records of human history.

What Can Be Done?

To stop the global traffic in illegally acquired antiquities, many nations (including the United States) have signed the **UNESCO Convention of 1970** with the unwieldy but accurate name of "Means of Prohibiting and Preventing the Illicit Import, Export, and Transfer of Ownership of Cultural Property." The 100 countries that have signed this convention agree, among other things, to put into place the legislation and administration to:

▶ Regulate the import and export of cultural objects
▶ Forbid their nations' museums from acquiring illegally exported cultural objects
▶ Establish ways to inform other nations when illegally exported objects are found within a country's borders
▶ Return or otherwise provide restitution of cultural objects stolen from public institutions
▶ Establish a register of art dealers and require them to register

In keeping with the convention, the United States has passed laws such as the 1983 Cultural Property Implementation Act and signed treaties with several countries that specifically prohibit the importing of artifacts without established "pedigrees" into the country. Some of these treaties "grandfather in" artifacts

UNESCO Convention of 1970 Requires that signers create legislation and the administrative structure to (1) regulate the import and export of cultural objects, (2) forbid their nations' museums from acquiring illegally exported cultural objects, (3) establish ways to inform other nations when illegally exported objects are found within a country's borders, (4) return or otherwise provide restitution of cultural objects stolen from public institutions, and (5) establish a register of art dealers and require them to register.

excavated before the treaty's date; this means that an importer must now prove that artifacts were excavated prior to a treaty's date or were otherwise obtained in ways not prohibited by the treaty. As more countries establish such treaties, it will become increasingly difficult for someone to import illegally acquired antiquities. And these treaties do work. In 2003, an appeals court upheld the conviction of Frederick Schultz, an art dealer who had been convicted under the National Stolen Property Act of conspiring to sell artifacts acquired illegally from Egypt, including the head of a statue of Amenhotep III, which he had sold for $1.2 million.

Figure 15-5 The site of Machu Picchu, in Peru.

War presents special difficulties for the protection of cultural resources, but even here, the world has worked out some agreements—most notably the 1954 **Hague Convention for the Protection of Cultural Property in the Event of Armed Conflict.** Developed after the massive destruction of antiquities during World War II, this treaty lays out wartime behaviors toward heritage resources such as museums and sites. In plain language, the Hague Convention states that an occupying force should do everything it can to prevent the looting and destruction of sites that often occurs in the chaos of war and its aftermath. Although Congress never ratified this treaty, the U.S. military has abided by it. And with good reason: During the first Gulf War, Saddam Hussein used museums and archaeological sites as military installations. As a result, some sites were bombed; for example, 400 artillery shells hit the 4000-year-old Ziggurat at Ur, in southern Iraq. After the war, sites were looted and artifacts sold on the black market. In early 2003, when war with Iraq appeared inevitable, archaeologists feared that bombing would again damage Iraq's archaeological sites, museums, and cultural institutions. Several organizations, including the Society for American Archaeology and the Archaeological Institute of America, lobbied the Pentagon for the protection of sites and museums. In response, the Pentagon drew up a "no-strike" list

that contained more than 4000 archaeological sites and cultural institutions.

Still, war is messy, and, as anyone familiar with the drug trade knows, as long as somebody is willing to pay high prices for merchandise—whether it's heroin or Iraqi antiquities—someone will smuggle it across borders. The only way to stop the trade is to stop the desire for the objects. And that task, sadly, seems almost insurmountable. Archaeologists hope that by continuing to educate the public and by strengthening laws, we will eventually reduce the population of buyers to the point where the market will collapse.

Archaeology and International Development

The illegal antiquities market is just one aspect of archaeology and national borders. Machu Picchu is perhaps the most dramatic example (Figure 15-5). Perched on a knife-like ridge at an elevation of 2300 meters (7546 feet), Machu Picchu overlooks the Urubamba River more than 300 meters below. Beside it rises a sugarloaf mountain that is daily shrouded in fog. Many people claim the site has special spiritual qualities; one woman claims she encountered an alien spaceship there.

Such gibberish masks the truth about Machu Picchu—"old mountain" in Quechua, one of the native languages of Peru. Built in the fifteenth century, it was a retreat for Inka rulers who otherwise lived in the capital of Cuzco, 100 kilometers away. Massive stone structures, plazas, terraces, and canals cover every inch of the ridge's 13 square kilometers and are made

Hague Convention for the Protection of Cultural Property in the Event of Armed Conflict An international agreement that provides rules for the protection of antiquities in wartime.

with typical Inka precision and a lack of mortar. The ridge's sides are covered with stone terraces where maize and other crops were grown.

An innkeeper in the nearby town of Aguas Calientes led explorer Hiram Bingham (1875–1956) to the site in 1911. Since that time, the site has become a tourist mecca, drawing more than 300,000 visitors each year. You can get there by walking several days from Cuzco along the old Inka road or by taking a four-hour train ride from Cuzco. From the valley floor, you ride a bus up the winding switchbacks to the site. Though well worth the effort, the trip to Machu Picchu is not easy. And Peru would like to make it easier.

Peru is a poor nation. Two-thirds of its population lives in poverty. Tourism will help the local economy, and the Cuzco–Machu Picchu area is the country's best attraction. Peru wants to build new hotels near Machu Picchu, and a high-speed railroad to bring day-tourists from Cuzco.

Peru also wants to build two cable cars to haul tourists up the mountain. Geologists have determined that the site's dramatic location places it at risk of landslides; in fact, several slides have temporarily closed the road up to the site. The proposed cable car towers will be in particularly sensitive areas and could create vibrations that could destabilize Machu Picchu's stone walls. The towers would also mar the vista that is one of the site's most attractive qualities. UNESCO, which made Machu Picchu a World Heritage Site in 1983, opposes the cable cars. Although Peru has dropped the proposal, it has suggested that it might revive it.

Peru's government is obliged to help the nation. If tourist dollars are a source of income, why should Peru suffer just so the rest of the world knows that Machu Picchu will remain pristine for their viewing pleasure? On the other hand, if tourism destroys the site, Peru loses what should have been a sustainable tourist resource. Archaeologists want people to know about the past, but we obviously don't want to see sites destroyed or their value and beauty compromised. How do we balance the need for development with the need to protect precious archaeological resources?

Many nations face this question. In some cases, sites have simply been placed off-limits. Today, you must view Stonehenge in England from a distance. Likewise, France's famous Paleolithic cave site of Lascaux (see Chapter 12) is off-limits to the public to protect its 17,000-year-old paintings from the damaging effects of humidity caused by tourists' breath.

Solutions to these problems are not cheap. France spent millions to clean Lascaux (and renewed growth of fungus will require still more cleaning) and to build a remarkably accurate scale model for visitors. And Britain has proposed building tunnels over the highways that run near Stonehenge.

But many important sites exist in poor countries that cannot afford such luxuries. If their sites are indeed "world" heritage resources, then should the international community pony up and make tourism viable in a way that maintains a site's integrity and scientific value? But if the international community has a financial and cultural interest in archaeological sites, can it also assert a proprietary interest? In early 2001, the Afghani Taliban used cannons and explosives to destroy the 175-foot-tall, 1500-year-old Bamiyan Buddhas, huge statues carved into a mountainside, because the Taliban's brand of Islam prohibits idols (Figure 15-6). The world reacted with shock and disgust, and many countries condemned the act (and some are now trying to rebuild the statues). At what point does the world's interest in its global heritage

Figure 15-6 One of Afghanistan's Bamiyan Buddhas before and after destruction by the Taliban.

override national sovereignty? Should the "world" have the authority to tell Peru what it can or cannot do at Machu Picchu, what the British can do with Stonehenge, or what the Taliban can do to statues in (what was) their country? Questions of this sort will become more common as development around the world continues unabated, and as developing nations capitalize on the economic potential of their archaeological resources.

THE NATIVE AMERICAN GRAVES PROTECTION AND REPATRIATION ACT OF 1990

So far, we have discussed government responses to the need to conserve cultural resources. But in 1990, a piece of U.S. legislation was passed whose purpose was to *rebury* some of the very cultural resources that other legislation protects and preserves. The **Native American Graves Protection and Repatriation Act (NAGPRA)** moves cultural resource law away from the area of preservation into the field of human rights legislation.

In 1988, the American Association of Museums told the Senate Select Committee on Indian Affairs that 43,306 individual Native American skeletons were held in 163 museums in the United States. Some of these were skulls removed from battlefields—including heads taken from the 1864 Sand Creek Massacre in Colorado, where soldiers and militiamen massacred some 150 Cheyenne and Arapaho, mostly women and children. Native Americans pointed out that although Indian people represent less than 1 percent of the U.S. population, their bones constitute more than 50 percent of the skeletal collection in the Smithsonian Institution.

Many senators were shocked—as they should have been. Although archaeologists had nothing to do with decapitating fallen Indian warriors, they had been aware for 20 years that many Native Americans were upset by the excavation, analysis, and display of their ancestors' skeletal remains. Walter Echo-Hawk

(Pawnee) said, "We don't expect everyone to share our beliefs; but it doesn't take the wisdom of Solomon to understand that our dead deserve to rest in peace.... All we're asking for is a little common decency.... We're not asking for anything but to bury our dead." Such statements spurred the Senate into action and brought an end to decades of wrangling that pitted museums, universities, and federal agencies against Native American tribes. In 1990, NAGPRA was signed into law.

NAGPRA provides for the protection of Indian graves on federal and tribal lands and prohibits the commercial sale or interstate transport of Native American bodies or body parts. It developed some very specific rules about who owns Native American remains excavated after 1990. It also required that all institutions that receive federal funds inventory all human skeletal remains held in their collections. Those inventories showed that American institutions held more than 117,000 sets of human remains, most from Native American burials. This inventory covered not only skeletal remains but also *funerary objects* (objects placed with a body as part of funerary ceremony), *sacred objects* (ceremonial objects necessary for current practice of traditional Native American religions), and *objects of cultural patrimony* (objects that have ongoing cultural importance to a tribe and that were "inalienable" at the time they left the tribe's possession—that is, no one had the right to give them away).

Once the inventories were completed, NAGPRA then required institutions to consult with appropriate Native American tribes determined to be "culturally affiliated" with the remains and objects regarding their repatriation. According to the national NAGPRA office, as of November 2010, the *Federal Register* has published 1400 Notices of Inventory Completion, representing "a little over 40,000 individuals and over one million associated funerary objects." Further, 520 "Notices of Intent to Repatriate" have been published, representing between 100,000 and 150,000 unassociated funerary objects and "a little over 4,000" sacred objects. Critical to the disposition of these remains and those found in the future is the definition of "Native American" and the concept of "cultural affiliation" in the law.

Native American Graves Protection and Repatriation Act (NAGPRA) Passed in 1990, this act (1) protects Indian graves on federal and tribal lands, (2) recognizes tribal authority over the treatment of unmarked graves, (3) prohibits the commercial selling of native dead bodies, (4) requires an inventory and repatriation of human remains held by the federal government and institutions that receive federal funding, (5) requires these same institutions to return inappropriately acquired sacred objects and other important communally owned property to native owners, and (6) sets up a process to determine ownership of human remains found on federal and tribal property after November 16, 1990.

Native Americans and Cultural Affiliation

NAGPRA recognizes the possibility, however slim, that European peoples visited North America before AD 1500, when Columbus's voyages opened the New World to European colonization. We know, for example, that the Vikings had a short-lived settlement in Newfoundland around the year AD 1000 (archaeologists have found and excavated the site of L'anse aux Meadows, which is mentioned in Viking sagas). Neither tribes nor archaeologists wanted non-Indian remains repatriated to Indian tribes, so NAGPRA explicitly defined "Native American" for the purposes of the law: "Native American means of, or relating to, a tribe, people, or culture that is indigenous to the United States."

Once an institution determines that remains and covered objects are Native American, they then have to decide if they are to be repatriated. But to which tribe? Many tribes expressed a desire to have only *their* specific tribal ancestors returned to them. The Eastern Shoshone on the Wind River Reservation in Wyoming do not wish their ancestral remains repatriated because they question the accuracy of museum records. The Blackfeet do not want remains returned unless the museum is *absolutely positive* the remains are Blackfeet because they don't want responsibility for the remains of a traditional enemy.

And tribes have different ideas about what should be done with the remains. The Zuni asked that skeletons identified as Zuni remain under museum curation. California's Chumash, after having reclaimed their ancestral remains through repatriation, elected to preserve them in their own repository. Many other tribes rebury or cremate repatriated remains. These differences of opinion meant that the government needed a procedure to decide which tribes have control over which remains.

That decision rests on the concept of **cultural affiliation.** Tribes that are culturally affiliated with particular burials, funerary and sacred objects, and objects of cultural patrimony are entitled to have those burials and objects repatriated to them.

How do we determine cultural affiliation? NAGPRA was quite explicit: Cultural affiliation means that there is "a relationship of shared group identity which can be reasonably traced historically or prehistorically between a present day Indian tribe or Native Hawaiian organization and an identifiable earlier group." It is determined by a "preponderance of the evidence based upon geographical, kinship, biological, archaeological, anthropological, linguistic, folklore, oral traditional, historical, or other relevant information or expert opinion." If remains or objects cannot be culturally affiliated under the law, then they are classed as "unaffiliated." Regulations passed in 2010 provide a process for repatriating those remains to the closest culturally affiliated tribe. Determining cultural affiliation is not impossible, and it has been done in many instances. But it

is often very hard to reasonably trace identity from an identifiable earlier group to an extant tribe.

There are several reasons why this is so. The archaeological and historical record shows that many Native American tribes have migrated, often from distant places. The Navajo and Apache, for example, are the only speakers of Athapaskan in the American Southwest. Given that most speakers of Athapaskan live in northwestern Canada and central Alaska, archaeologists are confident that the Navajo and Apache migrated into the Southwest (although no one is sure exactly when, it was probably not before 1000 BP). So, are human skeletal remains from Chaco Canyon culturally affiliated with the Navajo, on whose traditional lands the site sits, or with Puebloan peoples? And if the latter, which? Zuni? Hopi? Taos? San Lorenzo? Acoma? All of these peoples have moved around the landscape and developed over time into the people they are today.

We also know that some tribes formed as a result of colonialism. The Spanish introduction of horses to the Great Plains after AD 1530, for example, helped create the complex mosaic of horse-mounted bison-hunting tribes like the Lakota, Crow, Cheyenne, Comanche, and Arapaho. In the face of such radical changes in lifestyle, archaeologists often find it difficult to "reasonably trace a shared group identity" from an identifiable earlier group to an extant tribe for remains that are more than a few hundred years old.

The vast majority of archaeologists recognize that NAGPRA has forced a long overdue dialogue. But this does not mean that answers come easily. We introduced this text with a description of the discovery of "Kennewick Man," a 9400-year-old human skeleton in Washington. In that case, a judge eventually decided that the individual was *not* Native American as defined in the law, and that even if he were, he could *not* be culturally affiliated with the tribes who claimed him. This ruling points out how difficult it is to implement NAGPRA, and the importance of the intersection of scientific data and legal arguments. So, let's look more closely at how the judge arrived at his decision.

Is Kennewick Native American?

Most people would probably assume that a 9400-year-old skeleton was Native American. In fact, the

cultural affiliation In NAGPRA, "a relationship of shared group identity which can be reasonably traced historically or prehistorically between a present day Indian tribe or Native Hawaiian organization and an identifiable earlier group."

PROFILE OF AN ARCHAEOLOGIST

A CULTURAL RESOURCE MANAGEMENT ARCHAEOLOGIST

William Doelle is the president of Desert Archaeology, Inc., a cultural resource management firm in Tucson, Arizona, and the Center for Desert Archaeology, a nonprofit corporation that promotes the study and preservation of archaeological sites in the American Southwest.

William Doelle.

"Holy cow!" It was the only appropriate response to the cream-colored stone tool that had just caught my eye.

I was walking the centerline of a half-built road. It had been under construction, but representatives from the Tohono O'odham Nation in southern Arizona had protested when they observed road machinery cutting through a buried Hohokam village ("Hohokam" means "those who have gone" in the O'odham language and refers to village

sites dating after AD 700). Work was halted, and the slow legal process of compliance begun.

A competitive bid process awarded an archaeological contract to my young firm. We were in our second week of fieldwork when the cream-colored tool—a Clovis point—was found. Unable to identify any intact Clovis-age deposits, however, we concluded that Hohokam farmers who lived at what we called the Valencia site had encountered this spearpoint in their fields and brought it back to their village.

This first work on the Valencia Site on Tucson's south side took place in 1983. Despite the construction, our excavations yielded some 25 intact Hohokam pithouses. In the last 20 years, I have conducted six additional projects at this site, each one expanding our knowledge of the Valencia community between AD 400 and 1200. An overview of that work provides a cross section of the diversity in modern cultural resource management, or CRM—the professional area where I have made a living since 1974.

Our 1983 fieldwork was constrained to a narrow strip less than 20 meters wide and some 500 meters long. While we were in the field, we focused on that limited space because we had a great deal to accomplish in a very brief time—the bulldozers were waiting for us to finish. After the fieldwork, three of us volunteered to complete a map that put the site in a fuller context. I had been aware that

Department of Interior concluded that Kennewick Man is Native American simply because he predates European colonization of the New World.

But recall NAGPRA's definition of Native American: "of, or relating to, a tribe, people, or culture that is indigenous to the United States." This definition, the judge said, means that age is not *sufficient* evidence to determine that a burial is Native American under NAGPRA. Consequently, the judge ruled that the Department of the Interior was wrong to use age alone to establish that Kennewick was Native American.

For the judge, the key word in the definition, believe it or not, is the word "is" in the phrase "that *is* indigenous."

Although acknowledging that "the requirements for establishing 'Native American' status under NAGPRA are not onerous," the judge also argued that the phrase requires showing a "general relationship to a *present-day* tribe, people, or culture" (emphasis added). Kennewick, he pointed out, had no artifacts associated with it; and because it had eroded from a riverbank, the nature of any burial ritual, which is a cultural act, is gone. Thus, the judge concluded that the culture of Kennewick Man "is unknown and apparently unknowable."

This leaves Kennewick's skeletal remains. As we pointed out in the Introduction, Kennewick's cranial morphology—the shape of his skull—is different from

there was a prehistoric ballcourt just 50 meters from our excavation, but only with the complete map did the full settlement plan make sense. There was an open, central plaza, surrounded by low trash mounds that were the surface indications of residential areas.

It wasn't long before we conducted an intensive surface collection of the entire site, refined our initial map, and did further excavations to define the site's southern boundary. Archaeologists had improved the ceramic typology, and we used it to plot distributions of ceramics by time periods as short as 50 years. It was clear that initial settlement had clustered around the ballcourt and plaza, but around AD 1000 the community became more dispersed, with houses scattered along a mile of the Santa Cruz River. Two decades later, there is still debate about the reasons for this change. Were ballcourts abandoned around AD 1000, or did they last for another century? Regardless, the pattern at the Valencia Site has since been shown to hold at all other ballcourt villages in Tucson.

The next big research opportunity came along in 1991. The local community college planned a new campus in an area that we thought was outside the Valencia Site, but reexamination showed that to be wrong. So, we carried out a surface collection and testing program to provide information for the college. As it turned out, this area held an earlier, more subtle pithouse site, almost certainly the ancestral village for Valencia. Our work in 1991 helped planners to place high-impact features like new two-story buildings off the main occupation area. In the winter of 1997–98, when we conducted preconstruction excavations, we documented more than 100 early pithouses and projected a total of around 400. The arrangement of houses around a large central plaza provided the excavators with information to develop a refined model of early Hohokam villages.

My company had grown from one full-time employee in 1983 to 35 in 1997. Thus, I was largely an observer in the research process. I work on management issues like an open house for the community college, tours by the cultural committees from the Tohono O'odham Nation, and writing grant proposals so that things like storm sewers do not destroy archaeological sites. I keep watch over the rapid development of Tucson and work with various groups—such as the community college, the city, the Tohono O'odham, the archaeological community, park planners, and landscape architects—to develop plans to preserve archaeological sites.

I have found that the opportunities to be creative are tremendous in CRM, and I plan to pursue at least another decade as head of my CRM firm before retiring. These opportunities are further enhanced through the nonprofit Center for Desert Archaeology. Through grants, endowment building, and a membership program, this institution pursues a mission of preservation archaeology. We balance research, public outreach, and stewardship in our programs in the American Southwest and Mexican Northwest. Archaeology in the private sector presents unique challenges, but I have found it to offer great rewards.

that of later Native Americans. No matter how you measure it, the Kennewick skull looks more like that of southeast Asians, Polynesians, or Japan's Ainu, not other Native Americans. For this reason, the judge declared that Kennewick was not Native American and the Ninth Circuit Court of Appeals upheld this ruling.

Some archaeologists disagree with these rulings. Although the authors of NAGPRA used the present tense in the definition of NAGPRA, they certainly did not intend to exclude Native American groups that, for reasons of tragedies or warfare, left no descendants (cultural or biological). The judge even acknowledged this fact. Perhaps the key term in the definition, then, should not be the word "is," but the word "indigenous." And by any standard definition of that term, Kennewick is indigenous because he clearly lived in the United States before another colonizing population arrived.

Others point out that the cranial attributes that jointly set Kennewick apart—a steep nasal bone, projecting cheekbones, a long and narrow skull—are found individually among later Native Americans, suggesting some gene flow between Kennewick's population and later Native Americans. And this means that Kennewick meets NAGPRA's definition of Native American: "of, or relating to, a tribe, *people*, or culture that is indigenous to the United States."

Can Kennewick Be Culturally Affiliated with Modern Tribes?

Assuming that Kennewick is Native American, the next question is whether he can be culturally affiliated with the tribes who claim such affiliation. Recall NAGPRA's definition of cultural affiliation: "a relationship of shared group identity which can be reasonably traced historically or prehistorically between a present day tribe or Native Hawaiian organization and an identifiable earlier group." This is a far more rigorous definition than that of "Native American."

Cultural affiliation requires that we establish an identifiable earlier group. But with only one burial and no grave goods, it is impossible for archaeologists to identify Kennewick's social group. That alone means that Kennewick cannot meet the requirement of cultural affiliation under the law.

In addition, the law stipulates that we must show shared group identity and reasonably trace that identity over time. As we have said, this becomes more difficult the older a burial is because we have to trace the "shared group" relationship over a longer time span. The Secretary of the Interior originally decided that Kennewick was affiliated with the tribes who requested him—the Umatilla, Colville, Yakama, Nez Perce, and the Wanapum Band—based largely on the continuity of the archaeological record in the region where Kennewick was found and on oral traditions.

It is true that people have lived in the Columbia Plateau for the past 13,000 years. The law, however, does not state that cultural affiliation is based on evidence of continuity. It instead specifies a "shared group identity which can be reasonably traced" over the period of occupation. The archaeological record of the Columbia Plateau shows tremendous cultural changes over time—in the style of projectile points and houses that were used, in burial rituals, in economy and trade patterns. In fact, evidence of sedentary occupation of the region doesn't appear until 3000 years ago—6000 years after Kennewick Man died. In this particular case, archaeology cannot reasonably trace shared group identity over time.

But if archaeology can't, can oral history? We discussed the difficulty of using oral history as a way to reconstruct ancient events in Chapter 12. It is not possible to decide beforehand whether oral traditions are more or less reliable than archaeology. Each case must be decided on its own merits.

In the Kennewick case, the oral traditions of the Umatilla and other plateau peoples describe three periods of time. During the earliest time period, monsters roamed the world, and animals acted like humans. In the second time period, Coyote transformed the landscape and created people.

The third time period includes humans. Traditions associated with this period describe a lifeway that is similar to the ethnographic present; it includes hunting and gathering, salmon fishing, pithouses, and food storage. But archaeology tells us that lifestyle did not begin until well after 6000 years ago. The lifeways described in the oral traditions do not include what we know, from archaeology, of pre-6000 BP lifeways.

In some cases, the oral traditions describe natural events that could refer to the early Holocene—that is, to Kennewick Man's day. For example, there is a story of a battle between the "warm weathers" and the "cold weathers," set in a time when people died from the cold and the Columbia River froze. This might refer to the late Pleistocene environment. But it could also refer to the Little Ice Age, a global cold period from about AD 1500–1800. The same can be said of accounts of volcanic eruptions, floods, and other events or animals. Their presence in oral traditions does not *unambiguously* mean that the tradition encodes 9400-year-old observations.

Oral traditions can preserve eyewitness accounts through the use of metaphors that add power to stories and make them a memorable storehouse of moral laws. For example, oral traditions among Columbia Plateau tribes include tales in which bison turn to stone or mythical beings create valleys and hills by dragging huge fish across the landscape. But clearly, these tales do not relate eyewitness accounts, and thus they could be explanations of how a landscape came to be using observations made on that landscape long after the natural events that formed it actually took place.

Taking all these data into account, the judge decided that, under the requirements of NAGPRA, Kennewick cannot be culturally affiliated with the tribes who claimed affiliation.

What Does NAGPRA Mean by "Identity"?

Some archaeologists point out that NAGPRA is problematic because it employs the Western notion that "identity" is fixed at birth (and hence immutable). In Western culture, one is Irish or English, Spanish or Basque, French or German—implying an ethnicity with hard boundaries, both spatially and temporally. Assuming that such boundaries were "natural," the American government created them among Indians through the treaty and reservation process.

Such hard boundaries are now codified in NAG-PRA. It was not the judge's place to decide whether NAGPRA was right or wrong in its definition, but only to determine how that definition ought to be implemented in the Kennewick case. Given the law's definition and the available evidence, there is no "preponderance of evidence" to argue in favor of a cultural affiliation between Kennewick and the tribes who claimed identity with him.

But NAGPRA does not define what is meant by "identity," and this creates some discordance between conclusions reached under NAGPRA and Native American sensibilities.

NAGPRA assumes that human groups have a distinct point of formation; yet few actually do. Cultures change over time, even if we ignore the effect of migrations. NAGPRA further assumes that as one moves back in time, there is a point at which shared group identity is lost. It is lost not because the archaeological record is too poor to trace it (although that is often the case); it is lost because the differences between the modern tribe and the past group are so numerous or large that members of the modern and ancient groups would not share an identity—the ancient and modern peoples, if they could somehow meet one another in time, would not see each other as being the same.

But what is enough cultural change for the archaeologist to cut the tie of cultural affiliation between the past and the present may not be enough for Indians. Many Native Americans feel affiliated with *any* burial in their traditional territory, no matter the burial's age. In these cases, Indians feel betrayed—given that the purpose of NAGPRA was to allow tribes to bury "their" dead. In a legal sense, feelings of betrayal don't matter; the law is what it is. But such feelings do matter if we see NAGPRA as a way to do the right thing ethically. For this reason alone, Kennewick, and other cases like it, will continue to challenge archaeology and Native Americans alike.

Conclusion

Archaeology is a nonrenewable resource. Once we excavate a site, we can't dig it again. Once a site is looted, we can never get it back. Therefore, archaeologists today excavate only what they must in order to answer a research question and work to protect archaeological sites from development and theft. Archaeologists are willing to make some concessions to development; they will make no concessions to looting, within or outside the United States. From these twin concerns has grown the large field of cultural resource management and the many legislative acts designed to protect archaeological sites.

But these efforts are not enough. Without strong public support for archaeology, we will fight a losing battle against development and looting. We hope that through this textbook you have seen how much archaeology can learn from mere scraps of rock, bone, charcoal, pottery, and dirt. Archaeology needs *your* support if it is to succeed in saving the past for the future. Report site looting to local authorities. Raise a cry if someone is looting burials. Speak out against the sale of artifacts on the web and in flea markets. Stand up and be counted if a developer plans to destroy a site to put in a mall. If it seems like a daunting task, just remember the words of anthropologist Margaret Mead (1901–1978): Never underestimate the power of a small group of committed people to change the world. Indeed, it's the only thing that ever has.

SUMMARY

1. **What federal policies help protect cultural resources, including archaeological sites?**
- Although the United States has been concerned with preserving its cultural heritage for a long time, protection of cultural resources did not become policy until the National Environmental Policy Act.

2. **What are the important elements of the 1906 Antiquities Act, the 1966 National Historic Preservation Act, and the 1979 Archaeological Resources Protection Act?**
- The 1906 Antiquities Act required that individuals acquire a permit from the government before excavating archaeological sites, and gave the president the authority to create national monuments.
- The 1966 National Historic Preservation Act required that the government inventory cultural resources on its properties and ensure that develop-

ment projects consider their effects on significant archaeological sites. The act established the National Register of Historic Places and State Historic Preservation Offices.

⊙ The 1979 Archaeological Resources Protection Act provided further safeguards against the destruction of archaeological sites on federal and tribal land by increasing the penalties for excavating without a permit.

3. Is there an international black market in antiquities? If so, what can be done about it?

⊙ Yes, in fact this problem may be second only to drug trafficking. The United States and many nations around the world are working to stop the flow of illegally acquired antiquities. Although many measures have been put into place, most countries still find it difficult to stop antiquities from entering a country where buyers are willing to pay high prices for them.

4. Why is the Native American Graves Protection and Repatriation Act of 1990 important to archaeologists? How does it differ from other archaeological legislation?

⊙ The 1990 Native American Graves Protection and Repatriation Act, often seen as human rights rather than archaeological legislation, ensures that human remains, funerary objects, sacred objects, and objects of cultural patrimony are offered for repatriation to culturally affiliated tribes and Native Hawaiian organizations. This process is still underway for most of the nation's museums and universities.

⊙ This act differs from others in that it returns materials for reburial, rather than preserving them for the future.

MEDIA RESOURCES

Doing Fieldwork: Archaeological Demonstrations CD-ROM 2.0

This CD, developed by the authors, shows professional archaeologists involved in various digs, many of which are referenced in the text. The presentation is organized by the main techniques used on an archaeological dig, reinforcing concepts and techniques via live examples. The CD takes you through each step automatically, or you can navigate to any point via the navigation bar. After reviewing a step in the dig process, you are taken to Check Points, which are concept questions about each step of the dig. Then you can see the answers, receive your score, and even send your scores to your instructor.

The Companion Website for *Archaeology*, Sixth Edition

www.cengagebrain.com

Supplement your review of this chapter by going to the companion website to take one of the practice quizzes, use the flash cards to master key terms, and check out the many other study aids that are designed to help you succeed in your introductory archaeology course.

16 ARCHAEOLOGY'S FUTURE

LEARNING OBJECTIVES

AFTER READING THIS CHAPTER
YOU SHOULD BE ABLE TO ANSWER THESE QUESTIONS:

1. Does archaeology have practical value in the world today?

2. What is the attitude of archaeology toward public education?

3. As archaeologists become increasingly involved with descendant and stakeholder communities, what associated ethical problems and positive potentials arise?

© AP Images/Kirsty Wigglesworth

Archaeology students sieve through earth among the stones at Stonehenge, England, 2008. Though known for hundreds of years, this site continues to provide new knowledge about the past.

PREVIEW

THROUGHOUT THIS BOOK, we have tried to paint a realistic picture of what archaeology is all about. We have often reached into the past to demonstrate how today's archaeology has evolved the last 150 years. Now we will look forward to address two of the key challenges facing archaeology in the twenty-first century:

▶ How is archaeology relevant to the modern world?
▶ How should archaeologists share control over knowledge of the past?

As we explore these related issues, you will probably see more questions than answers.

DOING FIELDWORK CD-ROM:
ARCHAEOLOGICAL DEMONSTRATIONS 2.0

See the "Conclusion" section of the CD-ROM to learn more about topics covered in this chapter.

INTRODUCTION

We began this book talking about Kennewick Man, an important archaeological find that fostered an equally important legal case. The legalities of the Kennewick case highlight even larger issues surrounding the role of archaeology in modern society. But before we consider those issues, let's first recap some key concepts from earlier chapters.

Throughout this text, we have emphasized the "big picture" of archaeology: the role of archaeological objects in the modern world. We discussed archaeology's contribution to the larger field of anthropology and the different ways that archaeologists "think from things"—the different paradigms that we use to reconstruct and explain the past.

We then addressed the particulars of archaeological fieldwork and analysis: how we find and excavate sites; how we date and analyze artifacts and dirt; and how we interpret the remains of plants, animals, and people. You have seen how archaeologists can extract an enormous amount of information from broken, dirty bits of ancient objects to reconstruct ancient cultural behavior—and archaeology is still a relatively young science, making progress each year. We've only touched on the highlights in this text. The future promises even greater knowledge and understanding—achieved by methods that will be even more remarkable than those we've described here.

We examined two major transitions in the human past: the beginnings of agricultural economies and the origins of the archaic state. Both transitions triggered major changes in world history, each with lasting repercussions—and both processes can be known only through archaeology. These examples served to show what archaeology can learn about the past and the contribution that archaeology makes to an understanding of world history. These two examples likewise demonstrated that the different paradigms of archaeology need not compete, but can provide complementary tools for reconstructing the past.

We looked at historical archaeology and the methods for understanding the more recent past. Here we saw archaeology's special power to correct historical inaccuracies, to recover portions of history unrecorded in documents, and to bring new meaning to the present by re-evaluating the past.

Finally, we explored the "business" of archaeology—cultural resource management—and its link to laws that govern the preservation of cultural resources, which accounts for most of modern archaeology. We revisited the Kennewick case and discussed NAGPRA, a law that, instead of protecting the *objects* of the past, is intended to protect the various *interests* in the past. This law explicitly recognizes that archaeologists are not the only ones interested in antiquity and that the past holds different meanings for different people.

Throughout, "What Does It Mean to Me?" boxes highlighted issues that reinforce the point first made in the Introduction: Archaeology is as much about the living as about the dead. We will devote part of this final chapter to exploring the implications of that statement.

Virtually everyone cares about the past, to one degree or another. But people care about history for different reasons. We will always face important issues regarding (1) what is done with our knowledge of the past, (2) who gets to "tell the story," and (3) who controls access to data. We believe that archaeology plays several roles in the modern world, and although each of these functions can be beneficial, some soul-searching is required for professional archaeologists to understand and fulfill their responsibilities.

ARCHAEOLOGICAL SCIENCE: PURE OR APPLIED?

Anthropology is conventionally perceived as a **pure (or basic) science,** as the systematic pursuit of knowledge for its own sake. And it is true that anthropologists, like many other scientists, are commonly motivated more by intellectual curiosity than by the practical applications of what they learn. Anthropologists have traditionally looked for answers to the larger, holistic questions regarding the human condition: How, where, and when did humanity arise? What is the relative importance of nature versus nurture? How (and why) did major social institutions evolve? These are large-scale questions about the basic nature of the human condition, issues without immediate practical application or "relevance."

But anthropologists have long attempted to apply their findings to practical ends—that is, to do **applied science.** During World War II, for instance, some American anthropologists volunteered their services in the war effort. Several collaborated on "national character" studies—detailed memoranda on European and Asian countries that tried to characterize peoples who were either allies or enemies, or who lived in enemy-occupied territory. Anthropologist Ruth Benedict (1887–1948), for example, temporarily left her professorship at Columbia University to join the Bureau of Overseas Intelligence of the U.S. War Department during World War II. Here she spearheaded a study of Japanese national character, providing information that would ultimately prove critical for the Allied forces occupying Japan during the postwar period. Today, the Human Terrain Team in Iraq and Afghanistan includes anthropologists that help the military see situations from an indigenous perspective, to help build better relations, ease poverty, and provide protection. (Such projects are controversial;

many anthropologists oppose the practice, fearing that anthropological knowledge will be used for military purposes.)

Applied anthropology is a huge field. Applied anthropologists evaluate domestic social programs, improve corporate working conditions, develop culturally appropriate methods of delivering health care or agricultural assistance programs, and devise and implement international development programs, to mention only a few areas. Some CRM archaeologists also see themselves as applied anthropologists.

Modern archaeology likewise attempts to apply its knowledge and insights to the modern world. In this chapter, we will present multiple examples of how applied archaeology (1) brings the techniques of archaeology to nontraditional venues and (2) applies our knowledge of the human past to concrete economic or social problems.

THE GARBAGE PROJECT

Emil Haury (1904–1992) was the senior archaeologist at the University of Arizona for decades. A specialist in Southwestern prehistory, Haury continually taught his students that "if you want to know what is really going on in a community, look at its garbage."

Haury's earthy advice was not lost on his students and colleagues. In 1971, the University of Arizona launched a long-term, in-depth study of a community's garbage. But it must have surprised Haury when the Garbage Project decided to focus on the trash of contemporary Tucson.

The Garbage Project was begun by William Rathje (Stanford University), a Harvard-trained archaeologist who had previously specialized in Maya archaeology. Through the Garbage Project, Rathje applied archaeological methods to the analysis of modern American society.

Rathje was dissatisfied with available research techniques for dealing with contemporary society, particularly the dependence on questionnaires because, like many anthropologists, Rathje realized they can be problematic: Respondents may lie or give answers that they think are truthful, but actually are not.

---

pure (basic) science Systematic research directed toward acquisition of knowledge for its own sake.

applied science Research to acquire the knowledge necessary to solve a specific, recognized problem.

Archaeologists, of course, have methods designed to reconstruct human behavior from trash. Rathje reasoned, "Why can't we use these methods to study modern human behavior?"

How Do Archaeologists Collect Trash?

Although it would eventually investigate community trash and landfills around the country (Figure 16-1), Rathje's Garbage Project began in Tucson, Arizona, in 1973. Garbage was picked up from randomly selected households, and a sampling design ensured that different socioeconomic neighborhoods were included. Student volunteers from the University of Arizona sorted the garbage on special tables provided by Tucson's sanitation department. Student workers had appropriate inoculations and wore laboratory coats, surgical masks, and gloves. Students sorted garbage items into about 150 categories—under the larger headings of food, drugs, sanitation products, amusement and educational items, communication, and pet-related products—and recorded the data on forms for computer processing. The principles of archaeological classification provided objective, repeatable categories of data retrieval. The Garbage Project has involved hundreds of students and 60 participating organizations, recording more than 2 million items from 15,000 household refuse samples representing some 125 tons of garbage.

In case you're wondering, courts have ruled that garbage is "abandoned property," meaning that rummaging through someone's trash is not a crime. Nonetheless, the protocols adopted by Garbage Project ensure the anonymity of individuals and households. Volunteers do not record information such as names or addresses, and nothing is saved (although aluminum is recycled); ultimately, the garbage goes to the landfill it was originally headed for.

The Archaeology of Us

The Garbage Project has studied a number of contemporary social issues, including alcohol consumption. Years ago, the Pima County Health Department conducted interviews with a sample of Tucson households to discover how much beer people drank in a week. The sample was carefully chosen using conventional sociological procedures, and informant anonymity was ensured. Many took the health department's information as accurate measures of the rate of alcohol consumption in Tucson.

How did the questionnaires stack up against the material evidence—the beer bottles and cans that Rathje's volunteers recorded? In fact, there's a large discrepancy between front-door answers given to interviewers and back-door behavior reflected in the trash. Garbage cans don't lie, and the Garbage Project found significantly heavier beer consumption—in the form of more drinkers and higher rates of drinking—than was reported to the interviewers.

This should astound nobody. Many people drink more beer than they own up to, but the degree of distortion is noteworthy. The skewing, it turns out, correlates with socioeconomic factors. Low-income households typically distorted their interviews by reporting no beer consumption at all (low-income respondents may receive food stamps and, fearing the loss of support, might lie on surveys). Middle-income respondents did admit to drinking beer but significantly underreported the amount they actually consumed. These individuals probably gave an honest, though inaccurate, estimate because they don't perceive themselves to be "beer drinkers." These findings actually provided

Courtesy Bill Rathje, photo by Jim Sugar

Figure 16-1 At California's Sunnyvale landfill, garbage project coordinators Bill Rathje (center) and Wilson Hughes (to Rathje's left) search for newspapers to date a landfill sample.

future studies with a way to correct for this inevitable skewing in the data from health questionnaires.

In the mid-1980s, Rathje found that after the National Academy of Sciences published a report linking cancer and heart disease to a diet high in red meat, people in Tucson ate less red meat. They also discarded twice as much fat from the red meat they did buy. Consumers were obviously trying to cut down on their fat intake. But at the same time, Rathje found an increase in consumers' use of processed meats, such as lunch meats, that contain nonseparable fat. Even with a decline in red meat consumption, people's intake of fat actually *increased* because of the use of processed meat products—the exact opposite of the report's intended effect.

Myths about America's Landfills

Everyone knows that we produce a lot of trash. In fact, studies suggest that we create between 2 and 8 pounds of trash per person per day. Surprisingly, although the kinds of trash have changed—no one throws out bucketloads of ash and clinkers from coal-burning furnaces anymore—the amount generated per person has remained about the same over the last 120 years. The overall volume has increased, of course, because there are more people today (four times as many as in 1890).

Prior to the 1940s, many rural households disposed of trash in their own dumps—in a gully or along a river. In cities, garbage was used to create new land. The southern tip of Manhattan, for example, has been growing since the seventeenth century. Speculators would purchase the rights to a stretch of the East River, build piers, and then dump garbage between them. One enterprising builder acquired a ship, filled it with garbage, and then sank it between the piers (CRM archaeologists found it later). Eventually, the speculators created land that they then sold.

Formal landfills, however, did not appear on the landscape until the early twentieth century. In fact, it was not until after 1945, when the country's rural population shifted to the industrial cities, that landfills became a significant feature on the American landscape. As in previous centuries, cities used these landfills to create usable space for development; New York's La Guardia airport, for example, sits on one.

Six decades later, more than 70 percent of our garbage—180 million tons annually—goes into some 5500 active landfills across the country. Landfills are the largest human-made structures in the world; some are many times the size of such massive prehistoric structures as Khufu's Pyramid near Cairo or the Temple of the Sun at Teotihuacan outside Mexico City. The twentieth century's lasting monuments for posterity will be places like Staten Island's Fresh Kills landfill. Even before rubble from the World Trade Center was deposited there, the landfill covered 3000 acres and rose more than 150 feet in places—3 billion cubic feet of trash.

But space for landfills around large cities is rapidly dwindling; New York City, for example, trucks some of its garbage as far away as New Mexico. One reason is that old landfills were simply holes in the ground, whereas new landfills are complex places governed by a host of regulations and technologies designed to control toxic substances and methane gas. As a result, the national cost of garbage disposal is skyrocketing—$15 billion a year and rising. This means that we need to know as much about landfills as possible.

But surprisingly, prior to Rathje's studies, little was known about what is actually in landfills and what actually happens there. Rathje argues that "if we are making such a large contribution to future generations, we should know exactly what we are bequeathing them. The only way to unlock these entombed secrets is to excavate." So Rathje dug, and his research exposed a number of myths about landfills.

The Garbage Project used systematic archaeological methods to explore nine landfills across the United States, recovering about 12 metric tons of debris deposited between 1952 and 1989.

Landfills are generally covered with layers of earth on a set schedule, so they are conveniently stratified. And these strata can be chronologically ordered using newspapers and magazines. But the size of modern landfills did not allow Rathje to sample them with a trowel and dustpan. Instead, he used backhoe trenches and a 3-foot-diameter auger equipped with steel teeth that can cut through anything, including a car chassis. Each auger load was hand-sorted, allowing the Garbage Project personnel to calculate what's in America's landfills.

Let's first consider what Americans *think* is in their landfills. The Garbage Project conducted several surveys, with startling results. Many people think disposable diapers, plastic bottles, and large appliances take up most space in landfills. But Rathje's excavations show that these three items *together* take up *less than 5 percent* of a landfill's volume. All kinds of plastics take up less than 15 percent of landfills. And the percent volume of plastic is going down as manufacturers continue "lightweight" packaging—making milk jugs, for example, out of less and less plastic. The volume of plastic is going up because the population is rising, but as a percentage of our trash, the much-maligned plastic container appears to be decreasing.

So, something else must be taking up the space. A survey conducted at an Audubon Society meeting concluded that fast-food containers, polystyrene foam cups and packaging, and disposable diapers constituted 70 to (an impossible) 115 percent of landfills, but Rathje shows that these products together take up *less than 3 percent* of a landfill's volume.

So, what's in landfills? What covers the 3000 acres at Fresh Kills?

The largest component, it turns out, is *paper*—packaging, newspapers, telephone books, magazines, and mail order catalogs. Paper takes up *40 to 50 percent* of the volume in American landfills. Despite the growing commitment to local recycling programs, the amount of paper is steadily rising—up from 35 percent in 1970. The rest of a landfill consists of, in descending order of volume, construction/demolition debris, metals, plastics, other materials, food and yard waste, and glass.

And here's the really bad news: Contrary to popular opinion, paper doesn't biodegrade in landfills. The Garbage Project recovered 40-year-old newspapers, still fully readable (and some with 40-year-old hot dogs wrapped in them). Our landfills are constructed on the belief that the nasty stuff inside will decompose on its own, like some kind of monumental compost heap.

But very little in our landfills actually biodegrades. Compost heaps work only when we chop up the organics, add fluids, and regularly churn the whole batch. This doesn't happen in landfills: Nothing is chopped up, fluids are often prohibited, and debris is compacted, not churned. Methane production, a by-product of decomposition, ceases 15 to 20 years after a landfill is closed, indicating that decomposition has stopped. But Rathje's excavations show that after 20 years, from one-third to one-half of all organic materials are still recognizable. These remaining organics may eventually break down, but only after many decades, if not longer.

Most of our knowledge about solid waste disposal and landfill design comes from laboratory experiments, but the inside workings of landfills—what actually happens—have remained almost entirely unknown. Plenty of federal policies regulate landfills, but usually government planners assume what landfills contain.

Rathje doesn't assume; he digs. If we are interested in finding sensible ways to dispose of our trash, we need to know *exactly* what is being thrown away and what happens to it after it enters a landfill. By applying some archaeological approaches, Rathje learned that many of the long-held assumptions about America's garbage are just that—rubbish.

FORENSIC ARCHAEOLOGY

When Thomas was a first-year curator at the American Museum of Natural History (in the early 1970s), he received a telephone call from a Sergeant McTigue of the New York City bomb squad. At the time, McTigue was working a series of New York City subway bombings. Nearly a dozen such attacks had occurred, killing one person and injuring several others. McTigue suspected that a political protest group was behind the bombings, and he had even identified a prime suspect ("I know the creep who's doin' it.").

Before he could make an arrest, however, McTigue had to establish that, in fact, a crime had been committed. Otherwise, "the perp's lawyer will claim that it was a natural gas explosion, and we can't prove otherwise." To clinch his case, McTigue needed to produce parts of the actual detonating device that had triggered the explosion. Knowing this, McTigue kept sorting through the debris left by each underground explosion. But he never could find what he was looking for. So "the perps" remained free to bomb again, which they did with alarming regularity.

As he was investigating yet another ruined subway station, McTigue finally admitted to himself that he was a cop—trained in standard law enforcement techniques—not an expert in sorting through trash and debris. But if he wasn't, who was? That's what archaeologists do, right?

That insight brought McTigue to Thomas's office where he framed the problem in simple terms: Suppose that he were to treat each crime scene as if it were an ancient archaeological site. What are the systematic, standardized techniques that archaeologists use to recover their data?

So McTigue and Thomas spent three hours working through Archaeology 101: how to establish a three-dimensional grid system and datum point, map surface finds, remove archaeological strata, and use sifters and flotation devices. They went over note taking, photography, and cataloging. Armed with this new investigative strategy, McTigue said "Thanks" and took off.

A few days later, there was the sergeant with his bomb squad on the 6 o'clock news. They were quickly yet efficiently digging and measuring, photographing and sifting the ruins of the latest subway bombing. Except for being a little older (and also heavily armed), the police looked no different from other novices on their first "dig class." After a week or two, Thomas got another call from Sergeant McTigue, and sure enough, they'd found the detonating device they were looking for. An arrest was quickly made, and New York's subway bombings came to an end.

This is an example of **forensic archaeology**—using established archaeological techniques to assist law enforcement agencies. This has become increasingly common in the past 20 years—although, as you will see, for some tragic reasons.

Archaeologists as Crime Busters

For decades, archaeological organizations have regularly conducted seminars and workshops for law enforcement personnel; today, classes in "forensic archaeology" are taught in dozens of universities and colleges. Here, police trainees learn how to read a soil profile, probe the ground to find subsurface pits, and read topographic maps and soil reports, as well as how to find and map surface evidence. Through the use of mock crime scenes, trainees acquire basic identification skills, such as distinguishing human from animal bones, and they learn basic mapping and evidence-collecting skills.

Archaeologists also work directly with investigative teams on crime scenes. In Louisville, Kentucky, for example, Phil DiBlasi (University of Louisville) has worked on several cases involving violations of cemetery laws.

Louisville's Eastern Cemetery was established in 1843, although it was probably used for burials before then. The wealthy of Louisville were buried there along with slaves and the indigent. In the 1980s, the cemetery's backhoe operator routinely encountered bones when digging a grave, and he was just as routinely told to "get rid of them" when he brought them to the cemetery owners.

But the reuse of graves, even ones that are more than a century old, is illegal in Kentucky, where your grave is yours forever. The backhoe operator's conscience began to bother him, and he finally blew the whistle.

Kentucky's attorney general at the time was Fred Cowan, whose brother was an archaeologist. Cowan quickly saw that archaeological documentation was needed to produce the evidence needed for prosecution, and he called upon the University of Louisville's Archaeology Program, run by DiBlasi, for assistance.

Grave plots in the cemetery were roughly 40 square feet in size. By taking the total cemetery area, subtracting the square footage allotted to roads and buildings, and dividing by 40, DiBlasi calculated the maximum

Figure 16-2 University of Louisville archaeologist Phil DiBlasi (in trench) uses a backhoe trench to expose unmarked grave pits at a paupers' cemetery.

number of burials the cemetery could hold. Comparing that figure with the cemetery's records, he found that the cemetery had exceeded its capacity many years ago.

To confirm this, DiBlasi used shallow backhoe trenches, such as those shown in Figure 16-2, to show that virtually all areas of the cemetery, even those lacking headstones, contained rectangular east-west oriented pits that were most likely graves. Grave plots that still-living people had purchased were opened to see if someone was already occupying the gravesite. In every single case, DiBlasi found at least one person (and sometimes as many as three people) already in a grave. Using coffin hardware as time-markers, DiBlasi showed that grave reuse had begun by at least 1858. His standard archaeological information—plan views, stratigraphies, photographs, and artifact dating—was important in the effort to prosecute the cemetery's operators.

forensic archaeology The application of archaeological and bioarchaeological knowledge for legal purposes.

DiBlasi has since worked on a number of other historic cemeteries, collecting crime scene evidence and showing that graves allegedly removed during previous construction projects were never actually moved. In one case, DiBlasi found unmarked grave pits in the African-American section of a cemetery and, at their bottoms, coffin nails and fragments of delicate burial cloths lying in situ, but no sign of a body. This, DiBlasi argued, corroborated local oral histories that describe how this section of the cemetery was routinely robbed of cadavers in the nineteenth and early twentieth centuries—most likely by local medical students.

The Archaeology of Mass Disasters

As archaeologists become increasingly involved with criminal investigations domestically, they are also increasingly involved with international investigations. These are sad cases as they involve people who were lost in war, massacres, and assassinations. Professional archaeologists have joined investigatory teams to recover MIAs in Vietnam, excavate mass graves of missing persons in South and Central America, and work with United Nations investigatory teams to collect data for tribunals and courts from massacre sites in Croatia, El Salvador, and Rwanda. We'll just look at the last of these.

The violence in Rwanda began in April 1994, shortly after Rwandan president Juvenal Habyarimana was killed in an airline crash (allegedly caused by a missile). An ethnic war broke out between the Hutus and Tutsis and, within months, more than 500,000 people were slaughtered. Many were rumored to be civilians, including women and children who were mercilessly clubbed, burned, or hacked to death with machetes. Seeking to determine whether the deaths resulted from civil war or genocide, United Nations investigators authorized archaeological investigations at key sites in central Rwanda.

One such excavation took place at Home St. Jean, where an estimated 4000 to 6000 people were killed. The Midwest Archeological Center, a branch of the National Park Service, assisted in the investigations at the massacre site. Working with forensic specialists, the archaeological team first mapped and photographed the site. They mapped the locations of surface skeletal materials, numbering each item and collecting it for analysis. Through this process, the team discovered six potential mass graves and began working on the largest.

Once the stratigraphy was determined through hand excavation of several test trenches, the overburden was removed with a backhoe. The archaeologists then exposed human remains by standard archaeological procedures and photographed, mapped, and removed them from the grave.

The archaeologists recovered several hundred sets of remains using these procedures, making this one of the largest exhumations ever conducted in the investigation of human rights violations. Autopsies were conducted to determine sex, age, kind of trauma, and cause of death. Decomposition is rapid in tropical environments, and many of the identifications were made using the techniques discussed in Chapter 12.

Cut marks on bones showed that many individuals were killed by machetes from behind, as if they were fleeing their attackers; cut marks on the bones of hands and forearms showed that some people were mercilessly attacked with machetes, their arms raised in a desperate effort to ward off the blows. These were clearly unarmed civilians, murdered as part of a program of genocide. The meticulous archaeological documentation provided critical evidence for the United Nations tribunal, which quickly handed down numerous indictments.

Archaeologists are playing an increasingly important role in the investigation and documentation of human rights abuses (see "In Her Own Words: The Journey of a Young Forensic Anthropologist" by Clea Koff). In fact, as we write this, teams are at work uncovering mass graves in Iraq that could contain more than 300,000 bodies of people whose deaths were allegedly ordered by Saddam Hussein.

Archaeology and the World Trade Center

The story is all too well known: On September 11, 2001, two hijacked airplanes piloted by al-Qaeda terrorists slammed into the 110-story World Trade Center towers. Within hours, the towers and neighboring buildings collapsed into a massive pile of concrete and twisted steel. Rescue efforts, which had begun even before the towers collapsed, continued for days afterward.

Emotionally taxing as the attack was, cleanup efforts had to begin immediately, and they continued, around the clock, for the next 7 months. The steel girders were recycled, but the rest of the debris—more than 1.7 million tons—was hauled off in a continuous stream of trucks to the Hudson River. Here the debris was loaded onto barges and taken to the Fresh Kills landfill on Staten Island (the same landfill that Rathje had sampled years before).

IN HER OWN WORDS

THE JOURNEY OF A FORENSIC ANTHROPOLOGIST

Clea Koff earned her MA in anthropology from the University of Nebraska–Lincoln in 1999; she is the author of The Bone Woman: A Forensic Anthropologist's Search for Truth in the Mass Graves of Rwanda, Bosnia, Croatia, and Kosovo.

My first experience with archaeology was at the age of 10, digging around in my backyard to find the dead bird I had buried the previous winter. I found the bird and an old hairpin. Years later, on a college-level archaeological dig in the Greek countryside, we found Athenian coins, stone foundations, and one human skeleton. This was my first exposure to human bones and it was a profound experience. I became curious about what the bones could tell us about people, about how they lived and died.

About this time, I read a book describing how forensic anthropologists were helping investigate human rights abuses in Latin America, not only helping to return the remains of missing persons to their families, but also providing evidence to prosecute criminals. I desperately wanted to become a part of this effort and so took more classes in anthropology, archaeology, and human osteology at the University of Arizona. As part of my training, I helped the county medical examiner identify human remains and completed the Armed Forces Institute of Pathology/National Museum of Health and Medicine course in Forensic Anthropology.

In 1996, I joined a team of forensic experts brought together by Physicians for Human Rights to work on behalf of the United Nations International Criminal Tribunals for Rwanda and the former Yugoslavia, the international bodies prosecuting war criminals for genocide and crimes against humanity in those two countries. Our job was to locate, exhume, and analyze human remains from mass graves to provide evidence of the decedents' age, sex, and cause of death. For 6 months, I helped analyze five mass graves, each holding from 30 to over 400 remains. We worked long hours under the protection of military guards, and often lived in military compounds.

However, working at mass grave sites has a legacy that goes beyond the mandate of the tribunals to hold accountable those responsible for these crimes. For example, after the exhumation and analysis at

© Clea Koff/Physicians for Human Rights

Clea Koff excavating a mass grave in Yugoslavia.

the first site in Rwanda, Kibuye, was completed, a "Clothing Day" was convened. It was publicized on the radio that our team would be displaying clothing from the grave, and we asked survivors to view the clothing in the hopes of providing leads to probable identifications. This day was important as it was our first opportunity to interact with survivors of this particular massacre.

I shall never forget one woman. She looked as though she was in her fifties, wearing a traditional kanga (a large, printed piece of cloth worn wrapped around the body) over a knit shirt. She was a dignified woman who held her head high, as though not wanting to be involved in this sordid business, but having no choice.

She recognized one of the jackets on display and assented to an interview about the clothing. I asked her for her name and to whom she thought the jacket belonged. She gave a man's name, adding that he could still be alive, having removed his jacket at some point and lent it to someone who was subsequently killed at Kibuye.

(continued on the next page)

(continued from page 389)

I then asked her if she knew if this man had any surviving relatives. Yes, she replied, he'd had a sister. I asked for the sister's name and she gave one, pointedly not looking at me. The name sounded familiar, so I flipped back to the first page of the witness statement and there was that name. It was her name. She was talking about her brother.

As this dawned on me, my eyes shifted to that dirty, empty jacket baking in the sun. I thought of her brother and of my brother, and what I would feel if that thing that had come out of a mass grave looked like my brother's jacket. I couldn't look her in the eye at first, so I looked at her hands—one hand on her purse and one hand grasping her other arm, holding herself together.

I finally looked at her face, unable to talk. Her eyes brimmed ever-so-slightly with tears as she looked out into the distance. I looked where she was looking and saw nothing. I wanted to apologize, to hug her, but I had no protocol. So I just capped my pen, and put my hand on her forearm. She said nothing, I said nothing, but she held her head high. As I held that woman's arm I had a true sensation of being on the continuum of history for the Rwandans affected by the genocide.

We are irretrievably part of their process of healing. I continue to try to understand and articulate this phenomenon.

This was no ordinary cleanup operation. Besides the sheer enormity of the task, the massive rubble pile was the world's largest crime scene. The debris had to be manually searched for the remains of victims, as well as for personal effects that could help identify people whose bodily remains might have simply vanished. The debris was run through sorters to remove large objects, then it was spread out on the ground and manually searched with rakes. Later, a conveyor belt operation sped up the search.

Within days of the disaster, Brooklyn College archaeologist Sophia Perdikaris put out an informal call to archaeologists for assistance. She recognized that although archaeologists usually deal with ancient artifacts, they are also skilled at finding small things in a vast matrix of dirt and rock, at recognizing and identifying fragments of human bone, and at recognizing broken fragments of objects for what they used to be.

Overwhelmed by the response, Perdikaris asked the Society for American Archaeology for help. The society set up an online registrar and within a week had more than 300 individuals and organizations prepared to volunteer at the landfill. The FBI declined to take advantage of this resource because they were already overwhelmed with police and fire personnel who had the appropriate clearance and hazardous materials training.

Nonetheless, this effort, and his personal experience with the World Trade Center disaster, inspired archaeologist Richard Gould (Brown University) to develop a volunteer archaeological unit designed to assist at

disaster scenes. Most archaeological excavations are pretty happy affairs, with plenty of banter and good-natured ribbing. Gould shows us that the archaeology of disasters is quite different (see "In His Own Words: Disaster Archaeology" by Richard Gould).

REDISCOVERING ANCIENT TECHNOLOGY

There are also more cheerful applications of archaeology. So far, we've been looking at the utility of archaeological methods in dealing with modern problems. But the more traditional goal of archaeology—knowledge about the past—can also be applied to current problems.

Archaeologists, for example, have found ways to harness ancient technologies to benefit modern populations. Ancient techniques for growing and storing foodstuffs have often fallen into disuse and been forgotten. Yet some of these techniques were developed in places ill-suited for agriculture and might be of value to modern populations coping with strained agricultural systems.

Throughout the world, peasant populations use increasingly marginal land as populations expand and as wealthier farmers and corporations claim exclusive use of prime farmland. In addition, intensive agricultural practices sometimes lead to severe degradation of soil and water, making even highly desirable farmland less productive.

Throughout Peru and Bolivia we find ample evidence of vast expanses of former croplands during pre-Hispanic times that are all but abandoned today. Between 50 and 75 percent of the ancient Inka agricultural terraces are no longer in use. Some archaeologists suggest that along the Peruvian coastline, up to 40 percent more farmland was irrigated in preconquest times than today.

Some pre-Hispanic technologies have been completely forgotten; in other places, practices such as sunken gardens in dry coastal areas of high groundwater and systems of raised fields in waterlogged areas in the Amazon Basin (similar to the *chinampas* we discussed in Chapter 15) are used today only on a limited basis.

© Clark Erikson

Figure 16-3 Quechua farmers from the Andean community of Huatta reconstructing raised-field patterns in the seasonally flooded plain around Lake Titicaca (Peru). This reconstructed agricultural system is based on both indigenous knowledge systems and intensive archaeological research on ancient field patterns. The retaining wall and platform (at left) are made of sod blocks, and the archaeologically excavated canal appears on the right.

Several teams of archaeologists have been studying these ancient Andean agricultural systems with an eye toward reintroducing selected aspects of these technologies, as shown in Figure 16-3. Working from aerial photographs of the Lake Titicaca area along the Peru–Bolivia border, Clark Erickson (University of Pennsylvania) identified a series of ancient raised fields along the lake's margin.

Subsequent archaeological excavations revealed that, starting about 3000 years ago, farmers dug a series of parallel canals and piled the earth between them to form long, low mounds roughly 3 feet high, 15 to 30 feet wide, and up to 300 feet long. These artificial canals provided moisture during drought periods, and the organic-rich muck periodically dredged from the canals fertilized the fields (reducing the need for fallow periods between plantings). Pollen analysis showed that ancient farmers grew potatoes and quinoa (a high-altitude, protein-rich grain) on these fields. We now know that these farmers created more than 200,000 acres of raised agricultural platforms on the low-lying land near Lake Titicaca.

Experiments based on the archaeological findings show that the water in the canals running between the raised surfaces also served as heat sinks. Collecting warmth during the day and slowly releasing it at night, the canals kept temperatures around the crops about 2° higher than in the surrounding area, both

reducing frost damage and extending the length of the growing season—an important attribute at Titicaca's elevation of 3800 meters (12,500 feet).

Modern agricultural technology has damaged the delicate highland environment. Although Erickson does not advocate a naïve "turning back of the clock," he does believe that ancient methods of agriculture provide viable alternatives for rural development. For instance, experimental raised-field farming provides twice the potato yield compared to plots using conventional (modern) techniques.

The ancient technology also appears to be cost effective. Several agribusiness experiments in this area, often directed at producing cash rather than subsistence crops, required huge investments in capital. In contrast, projects involving ancient technologies used human labor to produce subsistence products and eliminated the need to import seed, chemicals, and machinery.

Erickson is cautiously optimistic when evaluating the results of these experiments. Some communities participate freely; others do not. Some began the experiment but then abandoned it. The reintroduced technology seems to work best for family-based agricultural fields, with more resistance turning up in community-owned fields. And, of course, the modern sociopolitical situation is different from that of the past, when agricultural technology and productivity were controlled by the Andean state. Today, the

IN HIS OWN WORDS

DISASTER ARCHAEOLOGY

Richard A. Gould is professor of anthropology at Brown University.

Archaeologists use their skills only to study past human cultures, or so it seemed to me until October 6, 2001. That was the day I first saw the World Trade Center disaster scene. What I found there that day and on subsequent visits to the site and its surroundings changed my outlook toward archaeology and many other things.

As I walked the streets and alleys east of Ground Zero, I encountered fragmented human remains scattered in the gritty, gray matrix of ash and pulverized building materials that covered the fire escapes, sidewalks, and dumpster tops of lower Manhattan. This initial encounter was followed by repeated visits to the area, reports to the authorities, and a rooftop survey with Brooklyn College archaeologist Sophia Perdikaris. The aftermath of this appalling disaster was initially marked by feelings of inadequacy, followed by a realization that archaeological skills could help the healing process for the victims' families and friends. By locating, recording, and recovering human remains and personal effects using archaeological methods and entering this evidence in a chain of custody, we could help victims' families and friends cope with their terrible loss.

Following a workshop at Brown University that brought together archaeologists and police, fire, and emergency services professionals, we began recruiting and training volunteers. Our team was eventually invited by the New York City Office of the Chief Medical

Richard Gould.

Examiner to perform forensic recoveries at a location next to Ground Zero, in March of 2002. By then, few remains were left undisturbed by the city's cleanup efforts, so our results were disappointing. But later, the NYC Fire Department's "Phoenix Unit" found human remains across lower Manhattan—including the specific localities I had reported earlier and at the location where we performed our trial excavations.

The lessons from this experience guided further training. Eventually, we created a volunteer unit that included safety, medical, and public affairs experts,

---

failure to adopt or continue raised-field agriculture may be due not to problems in technology, but rather to sociopolitical constraints.

Some people argue that if we do not make archaeology relevant to the modern world, then the modern world will find itself able to get along without archaeology. In this chapter, we have discussed some examples of how archaeological techniques and knowledge can shed light on modern problems and improve the lives of living peoples.

PUBLIC EDUCATION

Another use of archaeology is perhaps less directly, but no less significantly, pragmatic. Increasingly, archaeologists are incorporating the public into research programs through the active participation of interested members and through public education programs. In 1979 and 1980, for example, when we excavated Hidden Cave in western Nevada, we explicitly

which we dubbed Forensic Archaeology Recovery (FAR). We trained and prepared in a variety of ways based on advice from different agencies in Rhode Island. But we never expected what happened next.

Shortly after 11 PM on February 20, 2003, a fast-moving fire devastated The Station Nightclub in West Warwick, Rhode Island, killing 100 people and leaving others horribly burned. Almost exactly one year after our deployment to the WTC, our volunteer team was activated by the Rhode Island State Fire Marshall's Office and was at the disaster scene by February 26.

Although it was a much smaller scale than the WTC disaster, the West Warwick nightclub fire presented FAR with technical and emotional challenges that went beyond anything we experienced in New York. Twenty-two FAR volunteers responded.

The medical examiner's staff had already recovered and identified the fire's victims. Our initial task was to recover, record, and enter as evidence hundreds of personal items for the R. I. State Medical Examiner's Office to repatriate to the victims' families. The winter conditions required that we dry-sieve the frozen remains. At the request of the fire marshal, we also watched for specific items related to the investigation. While maintaining its primary humanitarian activities, FAR also came to play an increasingly investigative role.

The work took place within a limited area surrounded by a chain-link fence covered with flowers, photographs, and messages. Hundreds of mourners, survivors, and the media viewed our activities through the fence. It was like working in a fish bowl, but the FAR team remained focused on the archaeological tasks. This in itself did much to comfort and reassure those watching, as I learned by speaking with my own friends, several of whom lost relatives or close friends in the fire. It was trying at times, for myself and other members of the team, but it taught us that victims' families and friends find it reassuring to know that there are people willing to engage in this kind of recovery effort on their behalf.

Disaster scenes are always complex and chaotic. Archaeology can bring a degree of order out of chaos to comfort the people affected and to help understand the circumstances of the disaster.

FAR is continuing to train and to recruit new team members—hoping, of course, that nothing like these disasters happens again. This sort of work is not for everyone. We have found, however, that with people who combine their skills and dedication in the way that FAR has done, it is possible. As I watched the FAR volunteers at work, I experienced pride and elation at their efforts while sharing the sense of loss that comes with these kinds of disasters. Perhaps we, as archaeologists and as members of our respective communities, need closure, too. Now I think we know how to find it.

combined the scientific research project with a public education campaign.

Located outside Fallon, Nevada, away from public view, Hidden Cave had been ransacked by vandals for decades. The Bureau of Land Management put a locked gate across the cave's small opening, but looters simply cut or blasted their way through it. Some dragged tires in and burned them just to watch the black smoke pour out of the cave's mouth. BLM archaeologist Brian Hatoff figured that the only way to save the site was to stabilize the remains through judicious excavation. And, instead of doing the work quietly, he suggested that the excavation be turned into a public education campaign in the hopes that it would encourage the local community to "take possession" of the site and protect it themselves.

So, twice daily on every weekend of the excavation, dozens of people made the trek up the hot, dusty, barren hillside. On each tour, the guide introduced visitors to the region's paleoecology and archaeology,

© David H. Thomas

Figure 16-4 Archaeologists Brian Hatoff (left) and Evelyn Seelinger (right) explain Hidden Cave's stratigraphy to a tour group.

pointing out old lake shorelines and rock art along the path. Inside the cave, as Figure 16-4 shows, tourists welcomed the cave's cool relief from the summer sun as they watched the excavation in process and learned about excavation strategy and recent findings. We also actively solicited coverage of the excavation by the media.

After the fieldwork was over, Thomas published a standard scientific monograph on the site. He also created a permanent display at the Churchill County Museum in the nearby town of Fallon, and interpretive displays were erected inside Hidden Cave and along the trail (the museum also now maintains a website for the cave). Tours to the site are still run twice a month. Over the past 20 years, tens of thousands of visitors and schoolchildren have visited the site, learning to appreciate archaeology.

Several graduate programs in the United States, Canada, and Great Britain focus on the public education component of archaeology. The Society for American Archaeology maintains an online *Archaeology for the Public* website and produces educational materials for primary and secondary schools. Most state governments

sponsor an "Archaeology Month," with public lectures, tours, workshops, and educational displays. Bureau of Land Management archaeologist Jeanne Moe runs Project Archaeology, a national education program that sponsors workshops to train teachers how to teach students about the importance of stewardship of the nation's archaeological sites. And an ever-increasing number of federal, state, and local archaeological parks are a focus of educational opportunities.

It is entirely proper for archaeologists to devote some attention to public education because, after all, it is ultimately the public that financially supports their research. In addition, archaeologists know that members of an educated public are far less likely to vandalize or loot archaeological sites—and more likely to report such activities and publicly denounce them (as they did in the Slack Farm case we discussed in Chapter 15).

But taking archaeology public is not always easy. There are many different "publics," and some are less anxious than others to hear what archaeologists have to say (and a few are downright hostile). This is especially true when dealing with sites that figure prominently in American history, places such as the Little Bighorn battlefield (Chapter 14) or the Alamo.

Refighting the Battle of the Alamo

In 1836, a Mexican force of perhaps 4000 soldiers commanded by General Antonio López de Santa Anna reached the outskirts of San Antonio, Texas. The Anglo-American garrison, numbering 187 men under the command of Colonel William Travis, withdrew to the Alamo (Figure 16-5). For 13 days, the Texans withstood siege until Mexican troops breached the walls and killed the Alamo defenders.

Today's textbooks commonly pay homage to this heroic episode in the Texan war of independence against Mexico. As one historian put it, the courageous trio—Travis, Bowie, and Crockett—shed their blood upon "a holy altar." Their martyrs' deaths are commemorated in the battle cry "Remember the Alamo!" and commonly praised as a strategic move that successfully delayed Mexican forces and ultimately set up a victory for Texas at the subsequent Battle of San Jacinto, where Santa Anna was roundly defeated.

Enshrined in folklore, the Alamo remains one of America's most cherished cultural icons. According to frontier ideology, Americans arrived in Texas to transform the wilderness into a productive part of the United States. And the birth of Texas, it is written, was made possible by the death of the Alamo defenders. Many a Texan ranks the Alamo alongside Lexington and Concord in terms of historical significance.

But for many Texans of Hispanic descent, the Alamo is a recurring bad dream, excluding them from an honorable role in Texas history. More than half of San Antonio's current population is Hispanic, and many challenge the traditional heroic image of the Alamo.

The Alamo, they point out, began as a small-scale Spanish mission long before it became an Anglo-Texan shrine. Known as Mission San Antonio de Valero, it was established by a handful of brave and unarmed friars who were trying to bring Christianity to the untamed Texas wilderness. They were men of peace whose goal was saving souls.

What does this have to do with archaeology? Some members of San Antonio's Hispanic community believe that additional research should be conducted at the Alamo— archaeological research that emphasizes *not* the short-lived 1836 battle, but rather the eighteenth-century mission period. Archaeologist Anne Fox (University of Texas, San Antonio) agrees, and she believes that further excavations at the Alamo would shed new light on this little-known chapter of San Antonio history.

But there is a problem. The Daughters of the Republic of Texas (DRT) are the state-appointed custodians of the Alamo, its archaeological record, and its extensive archives on Texas history. For years, the DRT discouraged research into the Alamo-as-mission because they believed that mission period research detracted from the "true" historical significance of the Alamo as the cradle of Texas liberty.

That attitude has softened in recent years, but in the eyes

Figure 16-5 The Alamo.

© David H. Thomas

of the DRT, it is still those "13 days to glory" that constitute the Alamo's primary significance. Anthropologist Holly Breachley Brear has analyzed the social and political situation of the modern Alamo. She argues that if the DRT were to recognize the earlier mission period or to honor the Mexican soldiers who fought in the Battle of the Alamo, they would be empowering an ethnic group directly descended from the "enemy"; in so doing, they would threaten the sociopolitical power balance in modern San Antonio. But many politically active Hispanics encourage broader archaeological research and public interpretation of the Alamo-as-mission to highlight peaceful Hispanic origins within the state of Texas.

Fox finds the apprehensiveness of the DRT toward mission research troublesome because it seems to perpetuate the animosity between the current Texan and Mexican populations. Fox believes that archaeologists should just provide the historical facts and maintain a reputation of not taking sides.

But such "historical facts" can threaten prevailing ideology and place archaeologists on one side even if they don't intend to be there. During one field season, an Austin newspaper reporter complained that the archaeologists working on mission period remains outside the Alamo "seemed to be drawing as much reverent attention from the tourists as the indoor exhibits on David Crockett, William Travis, and the other heroes of 1836." The problem is clear: Archaeologists allowed to dig at the Alamo are supposed to find the concrete evidence of the "relevant" past—the 1836 past.

Fortunately, a new generation of DRT members shows an increasing interest in telling a more complete story of the Alamo. Although they still emphasize the 1836 battle, today they present a more evenhanded view. For example, they highlight the local Hispanic populace, some of whom stayed at the Alamo, and others who refused to choose sides. As time passes, the various extreme positions are moderating, downplaying fractious dichotomies such as "heroes" and "enemies."

Such are the tensions surrounding America's sacred sites. When archaeologists excavate and interpret their findings, they are increasingly faced with pressure and conflict from the various public constituencies. The world of archaeology is only beginning to appreciate the ramifications and conflicts involved when we take multiple versions of reality to the American public.

WHO OWNS THE PAST?

These examples imply that archaeology has unfettered access to the past. But the authority of archaeology is increasingly being questioned. Who has the right to acquire the data of the past? Who gets to analyze it? Who gets to use the remains of the past? We have already considered how these challenges to archaeology arise over the analysis of human skeletal remains; they are also seen in the study of Native American spiritual sites.

A Spiritual Site: The Bighorn Medicine Wheel

Look at Figure 16-6 and you will see the Bighorn Medicine Wheel, an ancient stone arrangement perched atop a 9640-foot windswept peak in Wyoming's Bighorn Mountains. There are actually quite a few medicine wheels in the mountains of the high plains, but the Bighorn Mountains site is by far the largest. Today, you reach it by driving up a gravel road to a parking lot and then walking 1½ miles up the ridge. If you arrive in July or August, you might avoid trudging through snowdrifts.

The modern visitor is first struck by the simplicity of the structure: A stone circle, or "wheel," nearly 90 feet in diameter; in the background stretches the vast Bighorn Basin.

Figure 16-6 An aerial view of the Bighorn Medicine Wheel in northern Wyoming.

Courtesy U.S. Forest Service

Inside the stone circle, 28 stone "spokes" radiate out from a central "hub," which is marked by a stone **cairn** about 4½ meters across. Five smaller cairns lie along the Wheel's periphery.

The Western world first took notice of the Medicine Wheel in 1903, when an article in *Forest and Stream* magazine pointed out similarities between the Wheel and the celebrated Aztec calendar stone. Many archaeologists trekked to the site in the following decades; most concluded that the Wheel was constructed in several stages over a long period. Cultural materials recovered in association with the Wheel date to the Late Prehistoric and early historic periods. And there is no evidence that the Wheel has anything to do with the Aztecs. On these matters, archaeologists agree.

But who built it (and why) is more controversial. Some suggest that the rock cairns were graves, each marking where a powerful person was buried. The lines of rocks (the spokes) show the different directions in which the departed ranged "on the warpath," recording the deeds of each dead chief. The rock piles at the ends of the lines may represent enemies killed in battle.

Drawing upon the ethnohistoric record, others suggested the site was for vision quests (see Chapter 12), the Plains Indian ritual in which an individual sought communication with the spirit world. For example, the Crow gave an account of the Bighorn Medicine Wheel based on the experience of Red Plume (also known as Long Hair), a famous Crow chief who visited the Wheel in the late 1700s:

> Red Plume . . . obtained his inspiration and received his medicine and the token which resulted in the application of that name by him at the Medicine Wheel. As a young man, Red Plume visited the wheel in the hope of receiving a strong medicine which would make of him a great warrior and chief. Without food, water, or clothing, he remained for four days and nights awaiting recognition from the spirits. On the fourth night he was approached by the three little men and one woman who inhabited the underground passage to the wheel and was conducted by them to the underground chamber. He remained there for three days and three nights and was instructed in the arts of warfare and in leading his people. He was told that the Red Eagle would be his powerful medicine and would guide him and be his protector through life. He was told to wear always upon his person as an emblem of his medicine, the soft little feather which grows upon the back above the tail of the eagle. This little red plume gave him his name. Upon his death, after many years of successful warfare and leadership, he instructed his people that his spirit would occupy the shrine at the medicine wheel which is not connected with the rim, except by an extended spoke, and that they might at all times communicate with him there.

Several contemporary Native American people say they have used it this way. Upslope winds whistle through countless crevices, creating a babel of moaning and shrieking voices. Some archaeological evidence suggests the rock cairns were protected by small enclosures during the early historic period, perhaps providing a modicum of shelter for those fasting, waiting, and seeking supernatural advice.

But there are other explanations. Astronomer John Eddy suggested that Native Americans constructed the Medicine Wheel as an astronomical observatory. Noting that selected stone cairns might once have held wooden poles, Eddy argued that these posts could have served as foresight and backsight, defining the azimuth of the rising or setting of some important celestial object (probably the sun).

By predicting significant celestial events such as the summer and winter solstices, the Medicine Wheel could have imparted powerful knowledge, useful for calendrical or ritual purposes. Because of its elevation—the site is buried beneath deep snowdrifts throughout the winter—Eddy focused on the summer solstice. And in a dramatic, televised re-creation, Eddy showed that two of the cairns pointed directly at the rising sun on the summer solstice of 1972. He suggested that the other cairns mark rising spots of the brightest stars in the summer dawn (stars that appear a few days before the solstice).

But there are problems with this argument. For one thing, the Medicine Wheel lacks convincing evidence for such sighting poles. In addition, the cairns are so large that precise sighting (even with a pole) would not be possible. And even allowing for poles and precision, Eddy's astronomical argument still leaves one cairn unaccounted for. Finally, the numerous collective seasonal movements of the sun, moon, and stars provide so many celestial sightings that we might expect the cairns to point to *something* significant in the heavens simply by pure chance.

> **cairn** An artificial mound of stones; often constructed as an aid to navigation, as a memorial, or to mark the location of a grave.

Other investigators suggest that the Medicine Wheel was built to aid travel, the rock piles left as directional aids to newcomers. Still others believe that the floor plan of the Medicine Wheel was a two-dimensional imitation of the 28-raftered lodge built as part of the Sun Dance ceremony. Other hypotheses hold that the Medicine Wheel may have been a boundary marker, a depiction of a mythical turtle, or an enduring stone marker demonstrating geometrical expertise.

In brief, we don't know what the Medicine Wheel was in the past. But we do know what it is today.

After taking in the simple majesty of the stone structure and the breathtaking view, the modern visitor is soon struck by the number of offerings left at the site, a scene reminiscent of the Vietnam memorial in Washington, DC. Scattered among the cairns and stone spokes are medicine bundles, antlers, coins, beadwork, photographs, bundles of sage or sweetgrass, and strips of cloth tied to the heavy wooden fence that now surrounds the site. The prehistoric use of the Medicine Wheel may forever remain an enigma, but to many contemporary Indian people the Medicine Wheel remains a holy place, one of many sacred sites where ceremonies are performed to this day.

Yet many of the most important sacred sites—places like the Bighorn Medicine Wheel—are being overrun each year by thousands of non-Indians: well-meaning tourists, scientific teams, and New Agers seeking a spiritual experience. Indians are greatly concerned that the plants, paths, shrines, rocks, and other aspects of their sacred sites are being destroyed by the curious, and their power diffused by the insensitive.

North American archaeologists agree that the Bighorn Medicine Wheel is one of America's more intriguing ancient sites—and with its stunning setting and puzzling past, the Medicine Wheel is a natural for the heritage tourist. Or is it? Should tourists be encouraged to visit the Bighorn Medicine Wheel?

How do archaeologists balance the dual concerns of bringing American archaeology to the interested public while respecting the wishes of the descendant populations still involved with many of those sites? Some Native Americans claim that all prehistoric sites are sacred. Should they be closed to the public? Should only Indians get to visit these places? Should only Indians study and interpret them?

In the case of the Medicine Wheel, a coalition representing varied interests—tribal, scientific, ecological, and governmental—is trying to protect, preserve, and respect the site. One mutual decision was to close the last mile and a half of the road to the site (allowance is made for the disabled). This solution minimizes the negative impact of tourism, respects the religious freedom of native people, and yet keeps this place accessible to those who wish to see firsthand the structure that has drawn people here for centuries.

William Tallbull (1921–1996), a Northern Cheyenne elder who had a deep and long-lasting personal relationship to the Medicine Wheel, felt it important to keep the site accessible. He believed it inappropriate to exclude anybody (see "In His Own Words: Archaeological Sites or Sacred Places? A Native American Perspective" by William Tallbull). In his perspective, if the educational and contemplative potential of sacred sites can be maintained, then they can offer an important opportunity for teaching tolerance and respect.

Whether we consider the Medicine Wheel, the Alamo, Hidden Cave, or any other site, it is impossible for archaeologists to escape a central issue: Who owns the past? This is not a question of who owns a site—that's a simple matter of property law—but who has the authority to uncover, interpret, and present knowledge gained from the past?

The past can be a powerful place to visit, and for many, archaeological sites like the Medicine Wheel are strong symbolic reminders of identity and continuity. But is it appropriate that only "descendants" should be "owners" of their past? Is the descendants' perspective the only admissible one?

Leave aside the sticky issue of defining who is a "descendant," and just consider the extreme case—giving complete power to one group of people, be they white, black, Hispanic, or Indian; rich or poor; urban or rural. Our point is a familiar one: Power corrupts, and absolute power corrupts absolutely. It's true in politics, and it's true in archaeology. The Nazis provide a vivid example of this.

Nazi Archaeology: The Danger of Owning the Past

Gustav Kossinna (1858–1931) did not live to see Hitler's ascension to power in 1933, but his work was inspirational to the Nazi elite. A linguist turned prehistorian, Kossinna sought to link Germanic culture to particular types of artifacts. Bettina Arnold (University of Wisconsin, Milwaukee) notes that Kossinna's work was intended to help the Germans rebuild their country after the First World War. In fact, his book on German prehistory was dedicated "To the German people, as a building block in the reconstruction of the externally as well as internally disintegrated fatherland."

Kossinna wrote that the presence of allegedly "Germanic" artifacts was archaeological proof dem-

IN HIS OWN WORDS

ARCHAEOLOGICAL SITES OR SACRED PLACES? A NATIVE AMERICAN PERSPECTIVE

The late William Tallbull was an elder of the Northern Cheyenne tribe.

To the Indigenous Peoples of North America, the archaeological sites found on North American soil are not "archaeological" sites. They are sites where our relatives lived and carried out their lives.

Sacred Sites such as the Medicine Wheel and Medicine Mountain are no different. To Native Americans they are living cultural sites from which help comes when "The People" needed or need help. They were/ are places where tribal peoples went in times of famine and sickness, in periods of long drought when animals would leave, or in more current times when tribes are being torn apart by politics, alcohol, or other abuses.

The men make a pledge to go and vision quest at these places, seeking help. As we leave to go to these sites, our every breath is a prayer. We follow the path to the sites, observing a protocol that has been in place for thousands of years. The Native American approaching these sites must stop four times from the beginning of his or her journey to arrival at the site. A trip to a Sacred Site was/is not done just for curiosity, but only after much preparation and seeking.

Many blessings have come to "The Peoples" in this way. Many tribes have received covenants (bundles) from these sites. Some tribes still carry the bundles that were received from a certain mountain or site. These are considered no different than the covenants given Moses or the traditional law that went with it.

When Native Peoples have been blessed by a site or area, they go back to give thanks and leave offerings whenever they get a chance. These should be left undisturbed and not handled or tampered with.

Today many of our people are reconnecting with these sites after many years of being denied the privilege of practicing our own religion at these very sacred areas. In the past, trips were made in secret and hidden from curious eyes.

If you go to see a Sacred Site, remember you are walking on "holy ground," and we ask that you respect our culture and traditions. If you come to a site that is being used for a religious purpose, we hope you will understand.

---

onstrating Germany's prior claim to vast stretches of territory, including large parts of Poland. Kossinna and his acolytes argued that waves of Germanic people had emanated from a northern European core area, carrying with them major cultural achievements such as agriculture, pottery, and metallurgy (none of which fit with the archaeological evidence as we know it). In one of his dinnertime monologues, Arnold notes, Hitler even claimed that the ancient Greeks were Germans who had migrated south.

Prehistory was largely ignored in Germany prior to Hitler's rise to power, and Arnold suggests that it was therefore easy for the Nazis to appropriate the past for their own purposes. From the time Hitler rose to power in 1933 through the end of World War II, eight new chairs of archaeology were established at German universities, and considerable funding became available for excavation. Of course, these new archaeologists were appointed and funded only if they were enthusiastic Nazi party members.

The interest in prehistory went to the highest levels of Nazi political power. Heinrich Himmler—the leader of the SS, Hitler's terrifying personal army—formed a wing of the SS called the *Ahnenerbe* ("Ancestor Heritage"). He looked to prehistory to establish an identity for the SS, using a Germanic-like rune as the source of the unit's double lightning-strike insignia. His archaeologists ventured as far as Tibet and Iceland searching for Atlantis, the Holy Grail, and Aryan kings (providing the inspiration for Steven Spielberg's and George Lucas's *Raiders of the Lost Ark*).

During the war, archaeologists were part of the *Sonderkommando Jankuhn*, a military organization led by SS archaeologist Herbert Jankuhn, which looted museums and libraries in conquered lands in the search for artifacts that would demonstrate Germany's ancestral claim on virtually all of Europe. Posters exhorted Germans to preserve and report all archaeological finds to authorities because every potsherd was "a document of our ancestors." (This attitude was not motivated by a love of prehistory, for although allegedly Germanic artifacts were preserved, unrelated archaeological sites in places such as Poland and Czechoslovakia were destroyed.)

Archaeological excavations in Germany were wildly misinterpreted to support claims for Aryan superiority, and contrary evidence was suppressed. Open-air theaters, known as *Thingstätten*, where Nazi propaganda plays were performed, were built only in places where the community could demonstrate prehistoric Germanic occupation. For many of these, Arnold points out, the archaeological data were grossly misinterpreted, if not outright fabricated.

Not all German scholars, however, were complacent; even Hitler thought Himmler sometimes went too far with his archaeological fantasizing. Opposition was nonetheless squashed, books outside the party line were banned, and scientists who would not toe the line were ostracized. There were no open debates, and the Nazi party controlled all discussion of the past.

Nazi archaeology is, to be sure, an extreme case. No form of modern archaeology is in the same pigeonhole. But extreme cases have value because they warn what can happen when a single group appropriates complete control over the past. It is precisely the issue of power and control that creates conflicts such as that over Kennewick Man. In the Introduction, we used the Kennewick case to raise some tough questions: *What gives archaeologists the right to poke into the past, to study the dead? Who owns the past, anyway? And who gets to decide?* We can now return to those questions and consider them in a broader context.

Martin's Cove: Who Should Control Sacred Sites?

Many places around the United States, as well as in other countries, are considered sacred. The Wailing Wall in Jerusalem is sacred to members of the Jewish faith; the Kaaba in Mecca, Saudi Arabia, is sacred to Moslems; and Devil's Tower in Wyoming is sacred to about 30 tribes (Figure 16-7).

Sacred sites are sensitive because they embody religious ideas and history. And they are usually ancient places and therefore contain archaeological remains. Who should own and control these places?

This issue arose when the Church of Jesus Christ of Latter-Day Saints sought to purchase about 900 acres of land in Wyoming that belonged to the federal Bureau of Land Management (BLM).

The LDS church originated in upstate New York in 1830, but followers were persecuted in town after town, and they eventually migrated to a new home in the open land of the West. They founded Salt Lake City, the religion's world center today, and many of the faithful moved there in the nineteenth century. Some moved in wagons; others put their belongings in handcarts that they bravely pushed across the prairies. In 1856, an early winter blizzard trapped one of these handcart parties along Wyoming's Sweetwater River, in a place now known as Martin's Cove. Before rescuers could reach them, 150 members of the party perished.

The LDS church considers Martin's Cove to be sacred, so it leased the land from the BLM and built an interpretive trail there. In 2001, however, the church sought to obtain the land permanently. Unable to find suitable land to swap for Martin's Cove (the usual way that the government de-accessions land), the church sought legislative action. Representative James Hansen (R-Utah) introduced a bill that would require the BLM to sell the land to the LDS church.

But many organizations opposed the sale. Some pointed out that the church was not the only group

Figure 16-7 The Wailing Wall in Jerusalem, the Kaaba in Mecca, Saudi Arabia, and Devil's Tower in Wyoming—all sacred sites to certain groups of people.

with a stake in this land. Although this is the alleged site of the handcart party's suffering (some historians place Martin's Cove at another place on the river), it also contains Native American archaeological sites and portions of the California trail, which many non–church members traveled. Should these groups surrender their interests in the land?

Another concern was that Hansen's bill would set a dangerous precedent. If the church was allowed to buy Martin's Cove, then shouldn't any organization be allowed to buy any piece of federal land that the organization considered sacred?

Devil's Tower, for example, the nation's first monument created under the Antiquities Act, is considered a sacred place by many Native American tribes. If the LDS church could purchase Martin's Cove, couldn't the tribes join forces and buy Devil's Tower? Should sacred sites on public land be sold or transferred to the organization or group that considers them sacred? Although one might assume that those who consider a site sacred will take good care of it, how can we guarantee that the owners will consider the views and opinions of other stakeholders?

And if we sell public lands that one group considers sacred, are we only furthering the balkanization of culture within the United States? At present, sacred lands that are public property are the subject of ongoing discussions about the relations between people. Devil's Tower is a good example. This nearly 1300-foot-tall basalt tower (made famous in Steven Spielberg's movie *Close Encounters of the Third Kind*) is climbed by some 5000 people each year. Some tribes wish the climbing to cease because climbing Bear's Lodge (as Devil's Tower is known to some tribes) is akin to scaling a cathedral or mosque for recreation. The monument currently has only a voluntary ban in effect for June, when Sun Dances are held nearby. Many climbers obey the ban out of respect for the tribes, although some professional guides disregard it. Should Devil's Tower be owned and controlled by the tribes? What's the right thing to do?

On the one hand, it might seem appropriate for those who consider land sacred to control it. But if we balkanize the landscape into "your" sacred land and "my" sacred land, don't we lose the continuing conversation between the peoples of different religions and cultures that is so vital to a democracy? Does this run the risk of creating "your history" and "my history"?

Apparently, the Senate thought so, and it did not support Hansen's bill. In 2003, the LDS church accepted a 25-year extension to its current lease and, for the time being, has dropped efforts to purchase the property.

Kennewick Man and Repatriation

In Chapter 15, we discussed how NAGPRA (the Native American Graves Protection and Repatriation Act of 1990) provides control over Native American burials in the United States.

This is, to put it mildly, a divisive issue. Many archaeologists in the past, and some today, are incensed that human burials and grave goods are being reburied. To these archaeologists, the Kennewick case demonstrates what happens when communities that claim descent from an ancient person are provided exclusive control over ancient remains and objects: How does this differ, some ask, from Nazi book-burnings?

A long-standing social policy in the United States emphasizes the common heritage of the citizenry. Thus, the scientific community is responsible for understanding the human condition of all, including Indian people, ancient and living. Removing cultural materials from museums and reburying skeletal remains means that selected elements of the common heritage are removed from the public domain. A vocal minority views NAGPRA (and other repatriation efforts) as blatant destruction of archaeological collections and the common American heritage. They urge archaeologists to stand up for their duties as scientists. Repatriation and reburial efforts, in this sense, are viewed as censorship, undermining the ability of scientists to inspect the work of others for errors and misinterpretations (a procedure basic to all modern, ethical science). How is it, some archaeologists ask, that we argue for laws to protect cultural heritage, yet simultaneously condone repatriation? If the objects of the past are so important that the government must protect them, then why do we willingly lose some of the most important ones, forever?

Some archaeologists warn that, decades downstream, we will look back at NAGPRA and condemn the archaeological and museum communities for shortsightedness, for caving in to political demands and allowing the destruction of irreplaceable scientific materials.

These archaeologists make some valid points. Given the far-reaching concern over the Kennewick case—in tribal, scientific, and mainstream venues—it seems clear that Americans are indeed interested in what ancient human remains have to say. And it is true that, once a skeleton is reburied, it is probably gone forever. Down the road of reburial, scientists claim, lies a balkanization of knowledge, a "tyranny of the minority" that ultimately will serve nobody.

Many American Indians and many archaeologists take a different view. The human body is a powerful symbol, especially the human skeleton—the last vestige of what was once a living, breathing person. When federal troops forced Cherokee and Choctaw people to move from their homes in the southeastern United States to Oklahoma in 1838, some families dug up the bones of their relatives and took them along on the bitter Trail of Tears, burying them after their arrival in Oklahoma.

For other Native Americans, skeletons are powerful symbols of colonialism. My God, some Indians say, they killed us, they took away our land, they tried to take away our language and traditions (and succeeded in many cases)—and now they've come for our dead! Some see science as yet another act of colonialism, another way to deny Indians their basic humanity and rights.

These are all valid points. How do we decide who is right? Should science trump all other concerns? In the specific case of human remains, the question has to be solved legally, through the balance that NAGPRA sought to establish. Ethical questions are irrelevant to the implementation of NAGPRA, which cares only about the proper legal course of action.

But these ethical concerns led to the passage of NAGPRA, and the question of who controls the dead is more than a simple question of law: It clearly involves ethical and moral standards as well. Although we can provide no simple answers, we can offer some observations.

Why *We Do Archaeology Affects* How *We Do Archaeology*

Henry Ford once said that "history is bunk," but as practicing archaeologists, we disagree. History tells us how we became the people we are today. History contains important lessons about the nature of humans and cultural change—lessons that have practical applications, lessons that help us frame and understand the challenges facing the world today. If we didn't believe strongly that we can learn from, and not just about, the past, then we would not be archaeologists.

Hardcore scientists tend to think that people should be united by a passionate belief in pure science, a passionate curiosity about the world around us. This is a laudable desire, and perhaps the day will come when we can seek new worlds of knowledge just for the sheer thrill of it.

But that day is not today. We live in a world partitioned by walls of our own social construction—barriers of race, nationality, ethnicity, wealth, and culture.

Listen to the news on any day, and you'll see that this is the greatest challenge facing the world.

And in that world, archaeology can ill afford to stick its head in the sand, claim the high moral ground of pure science, and ignore the ways that other people understand or give meaning to the past. Archaeologists often claim that we do archaeology because understanding the past will help us construct a better tomorrow. But if in doing so we tell a group of people that their interests and concerns do not matter, that scientists will tell them what is best, haven't we contributed to the major problem facing the world today—and substantially undermined any reason for doing archaeology in the first place?

For this reason, archaeologists will continue to debate and discuss the past with various groups outside archaeology, and the discussion will not be easy. Passing judgment on anybody's values or beliefs is tricky business. Should we take seriously the Asatru Folk Assembly, a group of Euro-Americans who claim to maintain an ancient Celtic religion, when they argue that Kennewick Man is their ancestor? And what about actress Shirley MacLaine, who claimed (quite sincerely from all accounts) that she's a reincarnated Inka princess? Should we negotiate with Ms. MacLaine if she were to launch a repatriation claim for Inka gold held by museums? Should we give equal time in textbooks to Erich von Däniken (see Chapter 8) and others who claims that the pyramids and other architectural wonders of the prehistoric world were built by travelers from other planets?

We don't champion any of these causes. But just because some *individuals* make frivolous claims does not justify setting aside the voices of other *groups*. Shirley MacLaine may have no rights to Inka gold, but the Peruvian government or the Quechua (the indigenous people of the highland Andes) might have very valid claims indeed. Obviously we need a dialogue, and it is important to remember that a "dialogue" implies at least two partners, participating as equals. It does *not* mean that archaeologists should abdicate their responsibility as trained observers and interpreters of the data of archaeology. In fact, it is essential that archaeologists and other interested communities work jointly because when control rests in the hands of one exclusive group—be it scientists or descendants—we run the risk of a Nazi-style archaeology. Professional archaeologists should continue to do archaeology because, if we quit, someone else will surely step in to fill the void and make their own claims about the past. We worry that the vacuum would be filled by groups like the Asatru

Folk Assembly or followers of von Däniken—people who do not criticize their own ideas, who fail to adhere to high standards of evidence, and who don't make their data and arguments explicit and public.

Archaeologists can sometimes get lost in the myriad details of archaeological investigations—the intricacies of radiocarbon dating, ceramic petrography, faunal analyses, and the like. A considered dialogue is beneficial because it continually reminds us about why we do archaeology. Many archaeologists, in fact, have already found that there are enormous advantages, both political *and* scientific, to bringing in rather than shutting out other groups.

SEEKING COMMON GROUND

A growing number of American archaeologists have developed research programs that incorporate the perspectives of Indian and other descendant communities. Each year, we see more examples of archaeologists using archaeology to help communities reconnect to their past, to establish ties broken by sociopolitical forces. Many archaeologists have worked hard to make participation in field projects financially possible for members of descendant communities. The Society for American Archaeology, for example, annually awards field school scholarships to Native American students.

More archaeologists are tackling projects in close consultation with tribal councils and descendant communities at the beginning, rather than the end, of a project, devising research in such a way that it is useful to the tribe or community. These projects often incorporate public education programs specifically designed for the descendant community. Here's an example from Alaska that demonstrates both the advantages of seeking community involvement and the pitfalls when this is not done.

Digging Kodiak: Native American Archaeologists at Work

Kodiak Island lies along the southern coast of Alaska, a land of windswept mountains and craggy shorelines. In the winter, violent storms hit once a week; even in the summer, it is cool and wet. Originally, it was the home of voles and ermines, red foxes, otters, and the fearsome Kodiak brown bear. Kodiak Island

is also the aboriginal home of the Alutiiq, an Eskimo people, who today run their own archaeological programs through the Alutiiq Museum and Archaeological Repository.

Archaeology began on Kodiak Island in the 1930s, when a famed Smithsonian Institution anthropologist—Alés Hrdlička (1869–1943; his last name is pronounced hair-*lich*-ka—although some Alutiiqs called him "hard liquor")—dug up an ancient burial ground that had been used for about 3000 years, until about 500 BP. Hrdlička excavated several hundred graves and removed thousands of associated artifacts. This collection constituted more than 5 percent of the Smithsonian's entire holdings in physical anthropology. From Hrdlička's strictly scientific perspective, the Kodiak Island bones and artifacts were an important cultural resource from which anthropologists could reconstruct millennia of the cultural and biological history of Alaska's Native peoples.

But the descendants of those buried in the cemetery remember Hrdlička as a man who did not respect the living of Kodiak Island. It was a different time, and Hrdlička saw no need to consult with the Alutiiq people. Had he done so, he might have discovered that Alutiiqs did not share Hrdlička's commitment to science, and they deeply resented it when he dug up hundreds of their ancestors and shipped them to a museum more than 7000 miles away.

Returning the Dead This resentment simmered for decades until, in the late 1980s (prior to the passage of NAGPRA or the special law that governs Smithsonian repatriations), the people of Larsen Bay, one of Kodiak's native communities, requested that the bones and funerary objects be returned to the community for reburial.

This simple request for repatriation forced curators and archaeologists to confront the knotty ethical and moral problems inherent in their treatment of Native American burial grounds.

The Smithsonian Institution immediately refused the request, pointing to the scientific importance of the collection and questioning the relationship between the modern people of Kodiak Island and those buried in the ancient cemetery. The Larsen Bay Tribal Council took offense at this knee-jerk response and continued to press for return of the collection.

After several years of controversy, the Smithsonian Institution eventually agreed to return several hundred human skeletons and funerary objects to the Kodiak Island peoples. In the fall of 1991, priests from the Russian Orthodox Church officiated at the reburial ceremony. Village elders sang hymns in the Alutiiq, Russian, and English languages. Leaders from the tribal council and Smithsonian Institution spoke as the remains were returned to Kodiak's soil.

As it turns out, this was a curious situation. For although the native community had argued for the return of archaeological and skeletal materials, at the same time it was encouraging and supporting archaeological research.

A New, New Archaeology in Kodiak Archaeology went through an important transition in the 1960s, when processual archaeology, the *new* archaeology, came on the scene. Today, another new archaeology is underway, one that recognizes multiple interests in the past.

While the Kodiak repatriation struggle was going on, Amy Steffian (then a graduate student at the University of Michigan) requested permission to dig further at Hrdlička's site. She and her colleagues argued that archaeological research could provide important clues about modern Alutiiq identity. Native community leaders not only granted her permission to excavate, but they also helped with a research grant from the Kodiak Area Native Association's bingo fund and provided student interns for the project. It's not that the Alutiiq hated archaeology; they just hated an archaeology that implied that they could not be full partners, that said their participation was not needed.

Today, Steffian serves as deputy director of the Alutiiq Museum, an outgrowth of the Kodiak Area Native Association's Culture and Heritage division. Recognizing that they were losing a record of their heritage to winter storms, vandalism, and time, the Alutiiq founded the Culture and Heritage program in 1987 to create an island-wide strategy of archaeological research and to promote educational programs on Alutiiq culture, language, and arts. Eight native corporations today fund and govern the Alutiiq Museum; they also oversee their own archaeological research projects, employing professional archaeologists to work with crews of native people and community volunteers. The Alutiiq Museum curates the resulting collections and displays artifacts in a native-governed repository. In fact, the artifacts repatriated from Hrdlička's excavation are today stored and available for study in the Alutiiq Museum.

The museum also provides professional and technical support to the "Dig Afognak" archaeological program, which is organized and staffed through the Afognak Native Corporation (see Figure 16-8). Dig Afognak offers the opportunity to live and work with native people in the remote wilderness of the Kodiak archipelago, a 20-minute floatplane ride from the city of Kodiak. Participants live in heated platform tents, dine in a large field kitchen, and bathe in a native-style sauna. Dig Afognak's purpose is "to regain, restore, and carry forward the light of our culture" and "to make the circle complete" by inviting the interested public to join the effort.

The founding of the museum and the growth of archaeological programs produced new career opportunities for native people. Alutiiq people have long participated in local excavations and are employed in various capacities in the museum. Many of the Alutiiq students involved in the archaeology program are now pursuing college degrees in history and anthropology. One of these, Sven Haakanson, Jr., became director of the museum after completing a PhD in anthropology at Harvard. Several Alutiiq women who were once interns on field projects now form one-third of the museum's staff.

Other archaeologists who conduct research on Kodiak today follow this example. Ben Fitzhugh (University of Washington), for example, excavated a 135-year-old Alutiiq-Russian site on the south shore of Kodiak with local junior high and high school students. The project discovered a 5000-year-old site beneath the Russian colonial-era site, providing an opportunity to explore changes in Alutiiq heritage unknown without the aid of archaeology. The students later presented the project's findings to the community in a series of conference-style papers. The students left the project not only with knowledge of archaeological methods and strategies, but also with bragging rights: They knew more about Kodiak's deep past than most of their parents.

Later, Fitzhugh and local high school students combined archaeological data on floor plans with the accounts of elders who had grown up in traditional earthen structures to build a replica *ciqlluaq*, or sod house, that today is an educational resource. Through projects such as these, communities take ownership of their heritage and work to promote its protection.

The beginning of this new brand of archaeology on Kodiak Island was NAGPRA. This legislation forced archaeologists to consult with local communities over their research and to do some soul-searching. Although NAGPRA calls for the repatriation of many archaeological collections, in some cases the result has been increased protection of the unexcavated archaeological record. And, ironically, NAGPRA may have engendered changes within archaeology and the Native American community whose end result will be the acquisition of more, not less, information about the past.

Courtesy Alutiiq Museum, photo by Patrick Saltonstall

Figure 16-8 Alutiiq intern April Laktonen excavates at the Outlet Site on Kodiak Island, Alaska during the Alutiiq Museum's Community Archaeology Program.

CONCLUSION

In this chapter, we have looked at the role of archaeology in the future. We examined some ways in which archaeology can be of pragmatic value—by using archaeological techniques to understand modern garbage and to gather the data needed to bring criminals to justice.

Perhaps even more important, however, will be archaeology's role in knocking down the walls that so often divide people of the world. Archaeology can do this in part through the information that it gathers. Archaeology can show, for example, how different environmental and historical circumstances work together to create the diversity of human societies. In so doing, archaeology proves that unilineal evolution and the racist assumptions that stand behind it are wrong. But archaeology also contributes not only by *what* it learns about the past, but also by *how* it goes about learning it—the way in which it incorporates different perspectives, attitudes, and concerns of descendant communities and other stakeholders in the past.

Archaeology, as we have said, is not just about the dead; it's also about the living. And, it turns out, archaeology is not just about the past; it's also about the future.

SUMMARY

1. Does archaeology have practical value in the world today?

- Although archaeology is conventionally perceived as a "pure" science, many archaeologists are finding ways to apply the techniques of archaeology to new problems, such as the analysis of contemporary garbage and landfills to help solve the nation's trash problem.
- Others are involved in forensic archaeology, working with law enforcement officials, providing training in the recovery and analysis of material remains, and generating firsthand evidence to be presented in courts of law; still others use archaeology to recover ancient technologies that benefit developing nations.

2. What is the attitude of archaeology toward public education?

- One way or another, virtually all archaeological research depends on public support. Particularly within the last two decades, responsible archaeologists have recognized the importance of returning to the public some of the benefits.
- Consequently, many archaeologists are involved in public education, adding educational components to "pure" research projects.

3. As archaeologists become increasingly involved with descendant and stakeholder communities, what associated ethical problems and positive potentials arise?

- In the past 20 years, archaeologists have become increasingly concerned with incorporating multiple voices into their research and educational efforts. In some cases, this has created problems, as the various stakeholders in archaeology contest who "owns" the past; this issue is especially prominent for sites that some communities perceive as sacred.

✹ In a growing number of cases, archaeologists have created vibrant research and educational programs that create a better understanding of the past with the input of descendant communities' perspectives.

In addition, such archaeological programs bring people of different backgrounds together and further break down social, ethnic, racial, and cultural walls that divide the world.

MEDIA RESOURCES

Doing Fieldwork:
Archaeological Demonstrations CD-ROM 2.0
This CD, developed by the authors, shows professional archaeologists involved in various digs, many of which are referenced in the text. The presentation is organized by the main techniques used on an archaeological dig, reinforcing concepts and techniques via live examples. The CD takes you through each step automatically, or you can navigate to any point via the navigation bar. After reviewing a step in the dig process, you are taken to Check Points, which are concept questions about each step of the dig. Then you can see the answers, receive your score, and even send your scores to your instructor.

The Companion Website for *Archaeology*, Sixth Edition
www.cengagebrain.com
Supplement your review of this chapter by going to the companion website to take one of the practice quizzes, use the flash cards to master key terms, and check out the many other study aids that are designed to help you succeed in your introductory archaeology course.

GLOSSARY

A horizon The upper part of a soil, where active organic and mechanical decomposition of geological and organic material occurs.

absolute date A date expressed in specific units of scientific measurement, such as days, years, centuries, or millennia; absolute determinations attempting to pinpoint a discrete, known interval in time.

accelerator mass spectrometry (AMS) A method of radiocarbon dating that counts the proportion of carbon isotopes directly (rather than using the indirect Geiger counter method), thereby dramatically reducing the quantity of datable material required.

achieved status Rights, duties, and obligations that accrue to individuals by virtue of what they have accomplished in their life.

adaptive perspective A research perspective that emphasizes technology, ecology, demography, and economics as the key factors in defining human behavior.

aDNA Ancient DNA recovered from organic materials in archaeological sites.

affinal Relatives by marriage rather than by blood.

alluvial sediments Sediments transported by flowing water.

analogy Noting similarities between two entities and inferring from that similarity that an *additional* attribute of one (the ethnographic case) is also true of the other (the archaeological case).

ancestor worship A religion in which one's deceased ancestors serve as important intermediaries between the natural and supernatural.

androcentric A perspective that focuses on what men do in a society, to the exclusion of women.

anthropology The study of all aspects of humankind—biological, cultural, and linguistic; extant and extinct—employing a holistic, comparative approach and the concept of culture.

antiquarian Originally, someone who studied antiquities (that is, ancient objects) largely for the sake of the objects themselves, not to understand the people or culture that produced them.

Antiquities Act Passed in 1906, this act (1) required federal permits before excavating or collecting artifacts on federal land, (2) established a permitting process, and (3) gave the president the authority to create national monuments.

appendicular skeleton All parts of an animal excluding the axial skeleton.

applied science Research to acquire the knowledge necessary to solve a specific, recognized problem.

arbitrary level The basic vertical subdivision of an excavation square; used only when easily recognizable "natural" strata are lacking or when natural strata are more than 10 centimeters thick.

archaeological context Once artifacts enter the ground, they become part of the archaeological context, where they can continue to be affected by human action but are also affected by natural processes.

archaeological culture A regional manifestation within a culture area marked by a particular set of material culture traits.

Archaeological Resources Protection Act (ARPA) Passed in 1979, this act (1) prohibits the excavation or removal of artifacts from federal property without a permit, (2) prohibits the sale, exchange, or transport of artifacts acquired illegally from federal property, and (3) increased the penalties for violations of the act over those of the Antiquities Act.

archaeological site Any place where material evidence exists about the human past. Usually, "site" refers to a concentration of such evidence.

archaeology The study of the past through the systematic recovery and analysis of material remains.

archaic state A centralized political system found in complex societies, characterized by having a virtual monopoly on the power to coerce.

area of potential effect (APE) The area that will be directly and indirectly affected by a construction project; in some cases it might encompass not only areas that are affected by construction but also areas seen from it.

argilliturbation A natural formation process in which wet/dry cycles in clay-rich soils push artifacts upward as the sediment swells and then moves them down as cracks form during dry cycles.

argon-argon dating A high-precision method for estimating the relative quantities of argon-39 and argon-40 gas; used to date volcanic ashes that are between 500,000 and several million years old.

artifact Any movable object that has been used, modified, or manufactured by humans; artifacts include stone, bone, and metal tools; beads and other ornaments; pottery; artwork; religious and sacred items.

ascribed status Rights, duties, and obligations that accrue to individuals by virtue of their parentage; ascribed status is inherited.

assemblage A collection of artifacts of one or several classes of materials (stone tools, ceramics, bones) that comes from a defined context, such as a site, feature, or stratum.

attribute An individual characteristic that distinguishes one artifact from another on the basis of its size, surface texture, form, material, method of manufacture, or design pattern.

axial skeleton The head, mandibles, vertebrae, ribs, sacrum, and tail of an animal skeleton.

B horizon A layer found below the A horizon, where clays accumulate that are transported downward by water.

band A residential group composed of a few nuclear families, but whose membership is neither permanent nor binding.

berdaches Among Plains Indian societies, men who elected to live life as women; they were recognized by their group as a third gender.

bilateral descent A kinship system in which relatives are traced equally on both the mother's and father's side.

bilocal residence A cultural practice in which a newly married couple may live in either the village of the groom or the village of the bride.

bioarchaeology The study of the human biological component evident in the archaeological record.

biological anthropology A subdiscipline of anthropology that views humans as biological organisms; also known as physical anthropology.

bone collagen The organic component of bone.

bonebed Archaeological and paleontological sites consisting of the remains of a large number of animals, often of the same species, and often representing a single moment in time—a mass kill or mass death.

bundle burial Burial of a person's bones, bundled together, after the flesh has been removed or allowed to decay off the bones.

burial population A set of human burials that come from a limited region and a limited time period. The more limited the region and the time period, the more accurate will be inferences drawn from analysis of the burials.

C horizon A layer found below the B horizon that consists of the unaltered or slightly altered parent material; below the C horizon is bedrock.

cairn An artificial mound of stones; often constructed as an aid to navigation, as a memorial, or to mark the location of a grave.

cargo system Part of the social organization found in many Central American communities in which a wealthy individual is named to carry out and bear the cost of important religious ceremonies throughout the year.

caries Cavities.

carrying capacity The number of people that a unit of land can support under a particular technology.

ch'arki Native South American (Quechua) term for freeze-dried llama and alpaca meat.

channel flake The longitudinal flake removed from the faces of Folsom and Clovis projectile points to create the flute.

charnel house A structure used by eastern North Americans to lay out the dead where the body would decompose. The bones would later be gathered and buried or cremated.

chiefdom A regional polity in which two or more local groups are organized under a single chief (who is the head of a ranked social hierarchy). Unlike autonomous bands and villages, chiefdoms consist of several more or less permanently aligned communities or settlements.

civilization A complex urban society with a high level of cultural achievement in the arts and sciences, craft specialization, a surplus of food and/or labor, and a hierarchically stratified social organization.

clans A group of matri- or patrilineages who see themselves as descended from a (sometimes mythical) common ancestor.

classical archaeology The branch of archaeology that studies the "classical" civilizations of the Mediterranean, such as Greece and Rome, and the Near East.

Clovis The earliest well-established Native American culture, distributed throughout much of North America and dating 10,900 to 11,200 BC.

codices Maya texts, long strips of paper, many meters in length when unfolded, made of the pounded inner bark of certain trees; these texts helped analysts interpret Maya hieroglyphics on stelae.

coevolution An evolutionary theory that argues that changes in social systems are best understood as mutual natural selection among components rather than as a linear cause-and-effect sequence.

cognitive archaeology The study of all those aspects of ancient culture that are the product of the human mind: the perception, description, and classification of the universe; the nature of the supernatural; the principles, philosophies, ethics, and values by which human societies are governed; and the ways in which aspects of the world, the supernatural, or human values are conveyed in art.

colluvial sediments Sediments deposited primarily through the action of gravity on geological material lying on hillsides.

comparative collection A skeletal collection of modern fauna of both sexes and different ages used to make identifications of archaeofaunas.

comparative method In Enlightenment philosophy, the idea that the world's existing peoples reflect different stages of human cultural evolution.

component An archaeological construct consisting of a stratum or set of strata that are presumed to be culturally homogeneous. A set of components from various sites in a region will make up a phase.

context The relationship of an artifact, ecofact, or feature to other artifacts, ecofacts, features, and geologic strata in a site.

coprolite Desiccated feces, often containing macrobotanical remains, pollen, and the remains of small animals.

core A piece of stone that is worked ("knapped"). Cores sometimes serve merely as sources for raw materials; they also can serve as functional tools.

cosmology The study of the origin, large-scale structure, and future of the universe. A cosmological explanation demonstrates how the universe developed—both the totality and its constituent parts—and also describes what principles keep it together.

cribra orbitalia A symptom of iron deficiency anemia in which the bone of the upper eye sockets takes on a spongy appearance.

critical theory A critique of the modern social order that emphasizes exploitative class interests; it aims to change and not simply to understand society.

cryoturbation A natural formation process in which freeze/thaw activity in a soil selectively pushes larger artifacts to the surface of a site.

cultural affiliation In NAGPRA, "a relationship of shared group identity which can be reasonably traced historically or prehistorically between a present day Indian tribe or Native Hawaiian organization and an identifiable earlier group."

cultural anthropology A subdiscipline of anthropology that emphasizes nonbiological aspects: the learned social, linguistic, technological, and familial behaviors of humans.

cultural depositional processes Human behaviors by which artifacts enter the archaeological record, including discard, loss, caching, and ritual interment.

cultural disturbance processes Human behaviors that modify artifacts in their archaeological context, as in the digging of pits, hearths, canals, and houses.

cultural resource management (CRM) A professional field that conducts activities, including archaeology, related to compliance with legislation aimed at conserving cultural resources.

cultural resources Physical features, both natural and artificial, associated with human activity, including sites, structures, and objects possessing significance in history, architecture, or human development. Cultural properties are unique and nonrenewable resources.

culture An integrated system of beliefs, traditions, and customs that govern or influence a person's behavior. Culture is learned, shared by members of a group, and based on the ability to think in terms of symbols.

culture history The kind of archaeology practiced mainly in the early to mid-twentieth century; it "explains" differences or changes over time in artifact frequencies by positing the diffusion of ideas between neighboring cultures or the migration of a people who had different mental templates for artifact styles.

data Relevant observations made on objects that then serve as the basis for study and discussion.

datum point The zero point, a fixed reference used to keep control over the locations of artifacts, features, etc., on a dig; usually controls both the vertical and horizontal dimensions of provenience.

de Vries effects Fluctuations in the calibration curve produced by variations in the atmosphere's carbon-14 content; these can cause radiocarbon dates to calibrate to more than one calendar age.

deconstruction Efforts to expose the assumptions behind the alleged objective and systematic search for knowledge. A primary tool of postmodernism.

deductive reasoning Reasoning from theory to predict specific observational or experimental results.

deflation A geologic process whereby fine sediment is blown away by the wind and larger items—including artifacts—are lowered onto a common surface and thus become recognizable as a site.

density-equilibrium model Proposed by Binford, it attributes the origins of agriculture to population pressure in favorable environments that resulted in emigration to marginal lands, where agriculture was needed to increase productivity.

direct acquisition A form of trade in which a person/group goes to the source area of an item to procure the raw material directly or to trade for it or for finished products.

dosimeter A device to measure the amount of gamma radiation emitted by sediments. Often a short length of pure copper tubing filled with calcium sulfate, it is normally buried in a stratum for a year to record the annual dose of radiation.

down-the-line trade An exchange system in which goods are traded outward from a source area from group to group, resulting in a steady decline in the item's abundance in archaeological sites farther from the source.

eburnation A sign of osteoarthritis in which the epiphyses of long bones are worn smooth, causing them to take on a varnish-like appearance.

ecofact Plant or animal remains found at an archaeological site.

egalitarian societies Social systems that contain roughly as many valued positions as there are persons capable of filling them; in egalitarian societies, all people have nearly equal access to the critical resources needed to live.

electron spin resonance A trapped charge technique used to date tooth enamel and burned stone tools; it can date teeth that are beyond the range of radiocarbon dating.

element In faunal analysis, a specific skeletal part of the body—for example, humerus or sternum.

enamel hypoplasias Horizontal linear defects in tooth enamel indicating episodes of physiological stress.

energy dispersive x-ray fluorescence (XRF) An analytical technique that uses obsidian's trace elements to "fingerprint" an artifact and trace it to its geologic source.

eolian sediments Materials transported and accumulated by wind (for example, dunes).

epiphyses The ends of bones that fuse to the main shaft or portion of bone at various ages; most bones are fused by age 25. This fact can be used to age skeletons of younger individuals.

ethnoarchaeology The study of contemporary peoples to determine how human behavior is translated into the archaeological record.

ethnocentrism The attitude or belief that one's own cultural ways are superior to any other.

exotics Material culture that was not produced locally and/or whose raw material is not found locally.

experimental archaeology Experiments designed to determine the archaeological correlates of ancient behavior; may overlap with both ethnoarchaeology and taphonomy.

faunal In archaeology, animal bones in archaeological sites.

faunal analysis Identification and interpretation of animal remains from an archaeological site.

faunal assemblage The animal remains recovered from an archaeological site.

faunalturbation A natural formation process in which animals, from large game to earthworms, affect the distribution of material within an archaeological site.

feature Nonportable archaeological evidence such as fire hearths, architectural elements, artifact clusters, garbage pits, and soil stains.

Fertile Crescent A broad arc of mountains in Israel, Jordan, Syria, Iraq, and Iran where wild wheat, barley, and other domesticated plants are found today.

flake A thin, sharp sliver of stone removed from a core during the knapping process.

floralturbation A natural formation process in which trees and other plants affect the distribution of artifacts within an archaeological site.

flotation The use of fluid suspension to recover tiny burned plant remains and bone fragments from archaeological sites.

flute Distinctive channel on the faces of Folsom and Clovis projectile points formed by removal of one or more flakes from the point's base.

forensic archaeology The application of archaeological and bioarchaeological knowledge for legal purposes.

formal analogies Analogies justified by similarities in the formal attributes of archaeological and ethnographic objects and features.

formation processes The ways in which human behaviors and natural actions operate to produce the archaeological record.

functional type A class of artifacts that performed the same function; these may or may not be temporal and/or morphological types.

gender ideology The culturally prescribed values assigned to the task and status of men and women; values can vary from society to society.

gender role The culturally prescribed behavior associated with men and women; roles can vary from society to society.

gene A unit of the chromosomes that controls inheritance of particular traits.

general systems theory An effort to describe the properties by which all systems, including human societies, allegedly operate. Popular in processual archaeology of the late 1960s and 1970s.

geoarchaeology The field of study that applies the concepts and methods of the geosciences to archaeological research.

geographic information system (GIS) A computer program for storing, retrieving, analyzing, and displaying cartographic data.

geomorphology The geological study of landforms and landscapes, including soils, rivers, hills, sand dunes, deltas, glacial deposits, and marshes.

georeferenced Data that are input to a GIS database using a common mapping reference—for example, the UTM grid—so that all data can be spatially analyzed.

Georgian order A worldview (ca. 1660/1680–1820) arising in the European Age of Reason that assumes the world has a single, basic, immutable order. Using the power of reason, people can discover what that order is and can thereby control the environment as they wish. The Georgian order is informed by the rise of scientific thought and by the balance and order in Renaissance architecture and art.

global positioning system (GPS) Handheld devices that use triangulation from radio waves received from satellites to determine your current position in terms of either the UTM grid or latitude and longitude.

graviturbation A natural formation process in which artifacts are moved downslope by gravity, sometimes assisted by precipitation runoff.

ground-penetrating radar (GPR) A remote sensing technique in which radar pulses directed into the ground reflect back to the surface when they strike features or interfaces within the ground, showing the presence and depth of possible buried features.

Hague Convention for the Protection of Cultural Property in the Event of Armed Conflict An international agreement that provides rules for the protection of antiquities in wartime.

half-life The time required for half of the carbon-14 available in an organic sample to decay; originally set at 5568 years, it was later changed to 5730 years.

haplogroup Genetic lineages defined by similar genes at a locus on a chromosome.

Harris lines Horizontal lines near the ends of long bones indicating episodes of physiological stress.

heat treatment A process whereby the flintknapping properties of stone tool raw material are improved by subjecting the material to heat.

high-level theory Theory that seeks to answer large "why" questions.

hilly flanks theory Proposed by Robert Braidwood, it claims that agriculture arose in the areas where wild ancestors of domesticated wheat and barley grow. It attributes agriculture's appearance to people's efforts to continue to increase the productivity and stability of their food base, coupled with a culture that was "ready" to accept an agricultural lifeway.

historical archaeology The study of human behavior through material remains, in which written history in some way affects its interpretation.

historical particularism The view that each culture is the product of a unique sequence of developments in which chance plays a major role in bringing about change.

Holocene The post-Pleistocene geological epoch that began about 10,000 radiocarbon years ago and continues today.

hominins Members of the evolutionary line that contains humans and our early bipedal ancestors.

Homo erectus A hominin who lived in Africa, Asia, and Europe between 2 million and 500,000 years ago. These hominins walked upright, made simple stone tools, and may have used fire.

Hopewell A cultural tradition found primarily in the Ohio River Valley and its tributaries, dating from 2200 to 1600 BP. Hopewell societies engaged in hunting and gathering and in some horticulture of indigenous plants. They are known for their mortuary rituals, which included charnel houses and burial mounds; some central tombs contained exotics. They also constructed geometric earthworks as ceremonial enclosures and effigy mounds.

Hopewell Interaction Sphere The common set of symbols found in the midwestern United States between 2200 and 1600 BP.

horticulture Cultivation, using hand tools only, in which plots of land are used for a few years and then allowed to lie fallow.

hypothesis A proposition proposed as an explanation of some phenomenon.

iconography Art forms or writing systems (such as Egyptian or Maya hieroglyphics) that symbolically represent ideas about religion or cosmology.

ideational perspective A research perspective that focuses on ideas, symbols, and mental structures as driving forces in shaping human behavior.

ideology A set of beliefs—often political, religious, or cosmological in nature—that rationalizes exploitive relations between classes or social groups.

in situ From Latin, meaning "in position"; the place where an artifact, ecofact, or feature was found during survey or excavation.

index fossil concept The idea that strata containing similar fossil assemblages are of similar age. This concept enables archaeologists to characterize and date strata within sites using distinctive artifact forms that research shows to be diagnostic of a particular period of time.

inductive reasoning Working from specific observations to more general hypotheses.

instrumental neutron activation analysis (INAA) An analytical technique that determines the trace element composition of the clay used to make a pot to identify the clay's geologic source.

intensive agriculture Cultivation using draft animals, machinery, or hand tools in which plots are used annually; often entails irrigation, land reclamation, and fertilizers.

irrigation hypothesis Proposed by Karl Wittfogel, it attributes the origin of the state to the administrative demands of irrigation.

kill sites Places where animals were killed in the past.

kinship Socially recognized network of relationships through which individuals are related to one another by ties of descent (real or imagined) and marriage.

kiva A Pueblo ceremonial structure that is usually round (but may be square or rectangular) and semi-subterranean. They appear in early Pueblo sites and perhaps even in the earlier (pre–AD 700) pithouse villages.

krotovina A filled-in animal burrow.

landscape archaeology The study of ancient human modification of the environment.

law of superposition The geological principle that in any pile of sedimentary rocks that have not been disturbed by folding or overturning, each bed is older than the layers above and younger than the layers below; also known as Steno's law.

linguistic anthropology A subdiscipline of anthropology that focuses on human language: its diversity in grammar, syntax, and lexicon; its historical development; and its relation to a culture's perception of the world.

lipids Organic substances—including fats, oils, and waxes—that resist mixing with water; found in both plant and animal tissues.

living floor A distinct buried surface on which people lived.

long bone cross sections Cross sections of the body's long bones (arms and legs) used to analyze bone shape and reconstruct the mechanical stresses placed on that bone—and hence activity patterns.

low-level theory The observations and interpretations that emerge from hands-on archaeological field and lab work.

macrobotanical remains Nonmicroscopic plant remains recovered from an archaeological site.

Magdalenian The last major culture of the European Upper Paleolithic period (ca. 18,000–12,000 BP); named after the rockshelter La Madeleine, in southwestern France. Magdalenian artisans crafted intricately carved tools of reindeer bone and antler; this was also the period during which Upper Paleolithic cave art in France and Spain reached its zenith.

mano A fist-sized, round, flat, handheld stone used with a metate for grinding foods.

marker bed An easily identified geologic layer whose age has been independently confirmed at numerous locations and whose presence can therefore be used to date archaeological and geological sediments.

matrilineage Individuals who share a line of matrilineal descent.

matrilineal descent A unilineal descent system in which ancestry is traced through the female line.

matrilocal residence A cultural practice in which a newly married couple live in the bride's village of origin; it is often associated with matrilineal descent.

matrix-sorting The hand sorting of processed bulk soil samples for minute artifacts and ecofacts.

mean ceramic date A statistical technique for combining the median age of manufacture for temporally significant pottery types to estimate the average age of a feature or site.

medieval mind-set The culture of the early (pre–AD 1660) British colonies that emphasized the group rather than the individual and in which the line between culture and nature was blurred; people were seen as conforming to nature.

metate A large, flat stone used as a stationary surface upon which seeds, tubers, and nuts are ground with a mano.

microwear Minute, often microscopic, evidence of use damage on the surface and working edge of a flake or artifact; can include striations, pitting, microflaking, and polish.

midden Refuse deposit resulting from human activities, generally consisting of sediment; food remains such as charred seeds, animal bone, and shell; and discarded artifacts.

middle-level theory Hypothesis that links archaeological observations with the human behavior or natural processes that produced them.

minimum number of individuals (MNI) The smallest number of individuals necessary to account for all identified bones.

Mississippian A widespread cultural tradition across much of the southeastern United States from 1200 to 500 BP. Mississippian societies engaged in intensive village-based maize horticulture and constructed large, earthen platform mounds that served as substructures for temples, residences, and council buildings.

mitochondrial DNA (mtDNA) Genetic material found in the mitochondria of cells; it is inherited only from the mother and appears to mutate at a rate of 2–4 percent per 1 million years.

moieties Two groups of clans that perform reciprocal ceremonial obligations for one another; moieties often intermarry.

molecular archaeology The use of genetic information in ancient human remains to reconstruct the past.

molecular clock Calculations of the time since divergence of two related populations using the presumed rate of mutation in mtDNA and the genetic differences between the two populations.

morphological type A descriptive and abstract grouping of individual artifacts whose focus is on overall similarity rather than function or chronological significance.

mortality profiles Charts that depict the various ages at death of a burial population.

Mousterian A culture from the Middle Paleolithic ("Middle Old Stone Age") period that appeared throughout Europe after 250,000 and before 30,000 years ago. Mousterian artifacts are frequently associated with Neanderthal human remains.

National Historic Preservation Act (NHPA) Passed in 1966, this act created (1) the National Register of Historic Places, (2) the Advisory Council on Historic Preservation, and (3) State Historic Preservation Offices, as well as (4) a process to mitigate the impact of development; it also requires that government agencies provide good stewardship of their cultural resources.

National Register of Historic Places A list of significant historic and prehistoric properties, including districts, sites, buildings, structures, and objects.

Native American Graves Protection and Repatriation Act (NAGPRA) Passed in 1990, this act (1) protects Indian graves on federal and tribal lands, (2) recognizes tribal authority over the treatment of unmarked graves, (3) prohibits the commercial selling of native dead bodies, (4) requires an inventory and repatriation of human remains held by the federal government and institutions that receive federal funding, (5) requires these same institutions to return inappropriately acquired sacred objects and other important communally owned property to native owners, and (6) sets up a process to determine ownership of human remains found on federal and tribal property after November 16, 1990.

Natufian A cultural manifestation in the Levant (the southwest Fertile Crescent) dating from 14,500 to 11,600 BP and consisting of the first appearance of settled villages, trade goods, and possibly early cultivation of domesticated wheat, but lacking pottery.

natural level A vertical subdivision of an excavation square that is based on natural breaks in the sediments (in terms of color, grain size, texture, hardness, or other characteristics).

natural selection The process through which some individuals survive and reproduce at higher rates than others because of their genetic heritage; leads to the perpetuation of certain genetic qualities at the expense of others.

Neanderthals (or Neandertals) A hominin who lived in Europe and the Near East about 300,000 to 30,000 years ago; biological anthropologists debate whether Neanderthals were in the direct evolutionary line leading to *Homo sapiens*.

Neolithic The ancient period during which people began using ground stone tools, manufacturing ceramics, and relying on domesticated plants and animals—literally, the "New Stone Age"—coined by Sir John Lubbock (in 1865).

new archaeology An approach to archaeology that arose in the 1960s, emphasizing the understanding of underlying cultural processes and the use of the scientific method; today's version of the "new archaeology" is sometimes called processual archaeology.

non-site archaeology Analysis of archaeological patterns manifested on a scale of kilometers or hectares, rather than of patterns within a single site.

nuclear DNA Genetic material found in a cell's nucleus; this material is primarily responsible for an individual's inherited traits.

number of identified specimens (NISP) The raw number of identified bones (specimens) per species.

oasis theory Proposed by V. Gordon Childe, it argues that animal domestication arose as people, plants, and animals congregated around water sources during the arid years that followed the Pleistocene. In this scenario, agriculture arose because of "some genius" and preceded animal domestication.

old wood problem A potential problem with radiocarbon (or tree-ring) dating in which old wood has been scavenged and reused in a later archaeological site; the resulting date is not a true age of the associated human activity.

optically stimulated luminescence A trapped charge dating technique used to date sediments; the age is the time elapsed between the last time a few moments' exposure to sunlight reset the clock to zero and the present.

optimal foraging theory The idea that foragers select foods that maximize the overall return rate.

oracle A shrine in which a deity reveals hidden knowledge or divine purpose.

osteoarthritis A disorder in which the cartilage between joints wears away, often because of overuse of the joint, resulting in osteophytes and eburnation.

osteology The study of bone.

osteophyte A sign of osteoarthritis in which bones develop a distinct "lipping" of bone at the point of articulation.

paleodemography The study of ancient demographic patterns and trends.

paleoethnobotanist An archaeologist who analyzes and interprets plant remains from archaeological sites in order to understand past interactions between human populations and plants.

paleopathology The study of ancient patterns of disease, disorders, and trauma.

palynology The study of fossil pollen grains and spores to reconstruct past climates and human behavior.

paradigm The overarching framework, often unstated, for understanding a research problem. It is a researcher's "culture."

participant observation The primary strategy of cultural anthropology, in which data are gathered by questioning and observing people while the observer lives in their society.

patrilineage Individuals who share a line of patrilineal descent.

patrilineal descent A unilineal descent system in which ancestry is traced through the male line.

patrilocal residence A cultural practice in which a newly married couple live in the groom's village of origin; it is often associated with patrilineal descent.

period A length of time distinguished by particular items of material culture, such as house form, pottery, or subsistence.

petrographic analysis An analytical technique that identifies the mineral composition of a pot's temper and clay through microscopic observation of thin sections.

phase An archaeological construct possessing traits sufficiently characteristic to distinguish it from other units similarly conceived; spatially limited to roughly a locality or region and chronologically limited to the briefest interval of time possible.

photosynthetic pathways The specific chemical process through which plants metabolize carbon. The three major pathways discriminate against carbon-13 in different ways; therefore, similarly aged plants that use different pathways can produce different radiocarbon ages.

phytoliths Tiny silica particles contained in plants. Sometimes these fragments can be recovered from archaeological sites even after the plants themselves have decayed.

pithouse A semi-subterranean structure with a heavy log roof covered with sod.

Pleistocene A geologic period from 1.8 million to 10,000 years ago, which was characterized by multiple periods of extensive glaciation.

plow zone The upper portion of a soil profile that has been disturbed by repeated plowing or other agricultural activity.

political organization A society's formal and informal institutions that regulate a population's collective acts.

pollen diagram A chart showing the changing frequencies of different identified pollens through time from samples taken from archaeological or other sites.

population pressure The result of a population's reaching carrying capacity.

porotic hyperostosis A symptom of iron deficiency anemia in which the skull takes on a porous appearance.

postprocessual paradigm A paradigm that focuses on humanistic approaches and rejects scientific objectivity. It sees archaeology as inherently political and is more concerned with interpreting the past than with testing hypotheses. It sees change as arising largely from interactions between individuals operating within a symbolic and/or competitive system.

potlatch Among nineteenth-century Northwest Coast Native Americans, a ceremony involving the giving away or destruction of property in order to acquire prestige.

potsherd Fragment of pottery.

principle of uniformitarianism The principle asserting that the processes now operating to modify the earth's surface are the same processes that operated long ago in the geological past.

processual paradigm The paradigm that explains social, economic, and cultural change as primarily the result of adaptation to material conditions. External conditions (for example, the environment) are assumed to take causal priority over ideational factors in explaining change.

projectile points Arrowheads, dart points, or spear points.

proton precession magnetometer A remote sensing technique that measures the strength of magnetism between the earth's magnetic core and a sensor controlled by the archaeologist. Magnetic anomalies can indicate the presence of buried walls or features.

provenience An artifact's location relative to a system of spatial data collection.

pubic symphysis Where the two halves of the pelvis meet in the groin area; the appearance of its articulating surface can be used to age skeletons.

puna Native American (Quechua) term for the treeless, windswept tablelands and basins of the higher Andes.

pure (basic) science Systematic research directed toward acquisition of knowledge for its own sake.

random sample A sample drawn from a statistical population such that every member of the population has an equal chance of being included in the sample.

ranked societies Social systems in which a hierarchy of social status has been established, with a restricted number of valued positions available; in ranked societies, not everyone has the same access to the critical resources of life.

reclamation processes Human behaviors that result in moving artifacts from the archaeological context back to the systemic context, as in scavenging beams from an abandoned structure to use them in a new one.

relational analogies Analogies justified on the basis of close cultural continuity between the archaeological and ethnographic cases or similarity in general cultural form.

relative dates Dates expressed relative to one another (for instance, earlier, later, more recent) instead of in absolute terms.

religion A social institution containing a set of beliefs about supernatural beings and forces and one's relation to them.

remote sensing The use of some form of electromagnetic energy to detect and measure characteristics of an archaeological target.

reservoir effect Samples from organisms that took in carbon from a source that was depleted of or enriched in carbon-14 relative to the atmosphere may return ages that are considerably older or younger than they actually are.

return rate The amount of energy acquired by a forager per unit of harvesting/processing time.

reuse processes Human behaviors that recycle and reuse artifacts before they enter an archaeological context.

reverse stratigraphy The result when sediment is unearthed by human or natural actions and moved elsewhere in such a way that the latest material is deposited on the bottom of the new sediment and progressively earlier material is deposited higher and higher in the stratigraphy.

ritual A succession of discrete behaviors that must be performed in a particular order under particular circumstances.

rockshelter A common type of archaeological site, consisting of a rock overhang that is deep enough to provide shelter but not deep enough to be called a cave (technically speaking, a cave must have an area of perpetual darkness).

Rosetta Stone A black basalt stone tablet found in Egypt in 1799 that bears an inscription in two forms of ancient Egyptian and Greek. By working from the Greek text, scholars were able to decipher the ancient Egyptian hieroglyphs.

sample fraction The percentage of the sample universe that is surveyed. Areas with a lot of variability in archaeological remains require larger sample fractions than do areas of low variability

sample units Survey units of a standard size and shape, determined by the research question and practical considerations, used to obtain the sample.

sample universe The region that contains the statistical population and that will be sampled. Its size and shape are determined by the research question and practical considerations.

sciatic notch The angled edge of both halves of the posterior (rear) side of the pelvis; measurement of this angle is used to determine sex in human skeletons. Although its width varies among populations, narrow notches indicate a male and wider notches indicate a female.

science The search for answers through a process that is objective, systematic, logical, predictive, self-critical, and public.

scientific method Accepted principles and procedures for the systematic pursuit of secure knowledge. Established scientific procedures involve the following steps: (1) define a relevant problem; (2) establish one or more hypotheses; (3) determine the empirical implications of the hypotheses; (4) collect appropriate data through observation and/or experimentation; (5) compare these data with the expected implications; and (6) revise and/or retest hypotheses as necessary.

seasonal round Hunter-gatherers' pattern of movement between different places on the landscape, timed to the seasonal availability of food and other resources.

seasonality An estimate of what part of the year a particular archaeological site was occupied.

sedimentary rock Rock formed when the weathered products of preexisting rocks have been transported by and deposited in water and are turned once again to stone.

seriation A relative dating method that orders artifacts based on the assumption that one cultural style slowly replaces an earlier style over time; with a master seriation diagram, sites can be dated based on their frequency of several artifact (for instance, ceramic) styles.

settlement pattern The distribution of archaeological sites across a region.

settlement system The movements and activities reconstructed from a settlement pattern.

shaman One who has the power to contact the spirit world through trance, possession, or visions. On the basis of this ability, the shaman invokes, manipulates, or coerces the power of the spirits for socially recognized ends—both good and ill.

shell midden The remnants of shellfish collecting; some shellfish middens can become many meters thick.

shovel testing A sample survey method used in regions where rapid soil buildup obscures buried archaeological remains; it entails digging shallow, systematic pits across the survey unit.

sipapu A Hopi word that loosely translates as "place of emergence." The original sipapu is the place where the Hopi are said to have emerged into this world from the underworld. Sipapus are also small pits in kivas through which communication with the supernatural world takes place.

site formation The human and natural actions that work together to create an archaeological site.

size classes A categorization of faunal remains, not to taxon, but to one of five categories based on body size.

slash-and-burn A horticultural method used frequently in the tropics wherein a section of forest is cut, dried, and then burned, thus returning nutrients to the ground. This permits a plot of land to be farmed for a limited number of years.

Smithsonian number A unique catalog number given to each site; it consists of a number (the state's position alphabetically), a letter abbreviation for the county, and the site's sequential number within the county.

social Darwinism The extension of the principles of Darwinian evolution to social phenomena; it implies that conflict between societies and between classes of the same society benefits humanity in the long run by removing "unfit" individuals and social forms. Social Darwinism assumed that unfettered economic competition and warfare were primary ways to determine which societies were "fittest."

social organization The rules and structures that govern relations within a group of interacting people. Societies are divided into social units (groups) within which are recognized social positions (statuses), with appropriate behavior patterns prescribed for these positions (roles).

soil Sediments that have undergone in situ chemical and mechanical alteration.

soil resistivity survey A remote sensing technique that monitors the electrical resistance of soils in a restricted volume near the surface of an archaeological site; changes in the amount of resistance registered by the resistivity meter can indicate buried walls or features.

Southeastern Ceremonial Complex An assortment of ceremonial objects that occurs in the graves of high-status Mississippian individuals. Ritual exchange of these artifacts crosscut the boundaries of many distinctive local cultures.

space-time systematics The delineation of patterns in material culture through time and space. These patterns are what the archaeologist will eventually try to explain or account for.

statistical population A set of counts, measurements, or characteristics about which relevant inquiries are to be made. Scientists use the term "statistical population" in a specialized way (quite different from "population" in the ordinary sense).

status The rights, duties, privileges, powers, liabilities, and immunities that accrue to a recognized and named social position.

stelae Stone monuments erected by Maya rulers to record their history in rich images and hieroglyphic symbols. These symbols can be read and dated.

strata (singular **stratum**) More or less homogeneous or gradational material, visually separable from other levels by a discrete change in the character of the material—texture, compactness, color, rock, organic content—and/or by a sharp break in the nature of deposition.

stratified random sample A survey universe divided into several sub-universes that are then sampled at potentially different sample fractions.

stratigraphy A site's physical structure produced by the deposition of geological and/or cultural sediments into layers, or strata.

structuralism A paradigm holding that human culture is the expression of unconscious modes of thought and reasoning, notably binary oppositions. Structuralism is most closely associated with the work of the French anthropologist Claude Lévi-Strauss.

symbol An object or act (verbal or nonverbal) that, by cultural convention, stands for something else *with which it has no necessary connection.*

sympathetic magic Rituals in which doing something to an image of an object produces the desired effect in the real object.

systematic regional survey A set of strategies for arriving at accurate descriptions of the range of archaeological material across a landscape.

systemic context A living behavioral system in which artifacts are part of an ongoing system of manufacture, use, reuse, and discard.

taphonomy The study of how organisms become part of the fossil record; in archaeology, it primarily refers to the study of how natural processes produce patterning in archaeological data.

taxon In faunal analysis, the classification of a skeletal element to a taxonomic category—species, genus, family, or order.

temper Material added to clay to give a ceramic item strength.

temporal type A morphological type that has temporal significance; also known as a time-marker or index fossil.

teosinte A plant native to southern Mexico; believed to be the wild ancestor of maize.

terminus post quem (**TPQ**) The date after which a stratum or feature must have been deposited or created.

test excavation A small initial excavation to determine a site's potential for answering a research question.

testability The degree to which one's observations and experiments can be reproduced.

theory An explanation for observed, empirical phenomena. It seeks to explain the relationships between variables; it is an answer to a "why" question.

thermal infrared multispectral scanning (**TIMS**) A remote sensing technique that uses equipment mounted on aircraft or satellites to measure infrared thermal radiation given off by the ground. Sensitive to differences as small as 0.1° centigrade, it can locate subsurface structures by tracking how they affect surface thermal radiation.

thermoluminescence A trapped charge dating technique used on ceramics and burned stone artifacts—anything mineral that has been heated to more than 500° C.

time-markers Similar to index fossils in geology; artifact forms that research shows to be diagnostic of a particular period of time.

total station A device that uses a beam of light bounced off a prism to determine an artifact's provenience; it is accurate to millimeters.

totem A natural object, often an animal, from which a lineage or clan believes itself to be descended and/or with which lineage or clan members have special relations.

trade language A language that develops among speakers of different languages to permit economic exchanges.

trapped charge dating Forms of dating that rely on the fact that electrons become trapped in minerals' crystal lattices as a function of background radiation. The age of the specimen is the total radiation received divided by the annual dose of radiation.

tree-ring dating (**dendrochronology**) The use of annual growth rings in trees to assign calendar ages to ancient wood samples.

tribal societies A wide range of social formations that lie between egalitarian foragers and ranked societies (such as chiefdoms). Tribal societies are normally horticultural and sedentary, with a higher level of competition than seen among nomadic hunter-gatherers.

type A class of archaeological artifacts defined by a consistent clustering of attributes.

typology The systematic arrangement of material culture into types.

UNESCO Convention of 1970 Requires that signers create legislation and the administrative structure to (1) regulate the import and export of cultural objects, (2) forbid their nations' museums from acquiring illegally exported cultural objects, (3) establish ways to inform other nations when illegally exported objects are found within a country's borders, (4) return or otherwise provide restitution of cultural objects stolen from public institutions, and (5) establish a register of art dealers and require them to register.

unilineal cultural evolution The belief that human societies have evolved culturally along a single developmental trajectory. Typically, such schemes depict Western civilization as the most advanced evolutionary stage; anthropology rejects this idea.

Upper Paleolithic The last major division of the Old World Paleolithic, beginning about 40,000 years ago and lasting until the end of the Pleistocene (ca. 10,000 years ago).

UTM Universal Transverse Mercator, a grid system in which north and east coordinates provide a location anywhere in the world, precise to 1 meter.

vision quest A ritual in which an individual seeks visions through starvation, dehydration, and exposure; considered in some cultures to be a way to communicate with the supernatural world.

warfare and circumscription hypothesis Proposed by Robert Carneiro, it attributes the origin of the state to the administrative burden of warfare conducted for conquest as a response to geographic limits on arable land in the face of a rising population.

water-screening A sieving process in which deposit is placed on a screen and the matrix washed away with hoses; essential where artifacts are expected to be small and/or difficult to find without washing.

wickiup A conical structure made of poles or logs laid against one another that served as a fall or winter home among the prehistoric Shoshone and Paiute.

wood rats (pack rats) Rodents that build nests of organic materials and thus preserve a record, often for thousands of years, of changing plant species within the local area of the nest.

Younger Dryas A climatic interval, 13,000 to 11,600 BP, characterized by a rapid return to cooler and drier, but highly variable, climatic conditions.

zooarchaeologist An archaeologist who specializes in the study of the animal remains recovered from archaeological sites.

BIBLIOGRAPHY

The following chapter-by-chapter bibliography contains the references used in each chapter as well as some additional ones that can provide the student with more in-depth reading on particular subjects. We've arranged this bibliography by chapter so that the interested student can more easily locate additional readings on a particular subject. Where direct quotes have been used, their source is indicated here at the end of the appropriate entry.

Introduction

Benedict, Jeff. 2002. *No Bone Unturned: The Adventures of a Top Smithsonian Forensic Scientist and the Legal Battle for America's Oldest Skeletons.* New York: HarperCollins.

Chatters, James C. 2001. *Ancient Encounters: Kennewick Man and the First Americans.* New York: Simon and Schuster.

Chapter 1

Babcock, Barbara A., and Nancy J. Parezo. 1988. *Daughters of the Desert: Women Anthropologists and the Native American Southwest 1880–1980.* Albuquerque: University of New Mexico Press.

Binford, Lewis R. 1962. Archaeology as anthropology. *American Antiquity* 28: 217–225.

———. 1964. A consideration of archaeological research design. *American Antiquity* 29: 425–441.

———. 1965. Archaeological systematics and the study of cultural process. *American Antiquity* 31: 203–210.

———. 1968. Archeological perspectives. In Sally R. Binford and Lewis R. Binford (Eds.), *New Perspectives in Archeology* (pp. 5–32). Chicago: Aldine.

———. 1972. *An Archaeological Perspective.* New York: Seminar Press.

——— (Ed.). 1977. *For Theory Building in Archaeology.* New York: Academic Press.

———. 1983a. *In Pursuit of the Past: Decoding the Archaeological Record.* London: Thames and Hudson. ("In His Own Words" text quoted from pp. 19, 23)

——— (Ed.). 1983b. *Working at Archaeology.* New York: Academic Press.

———. 1989. *Debating Archaeology.* San Diego: Academic Press.

———. 2001. *Constructing Frames of Reference: An Analytical Method for Archaeological Theory Building Using Ethnographic and Environmental Data Sets.* Berkeley: University of California Press.

Binford, Sally R., and Lewis R. Binford (Eds.). 1968. *New Perspectives in Archeology.* Chicago: Aldine.

Caton-Thompson, Gertrude. 1983. *Mixed Memoirs.* Gateshead, England: The Paradigm Press.

Champion, Sara. 1998. Women in British archaeology: Visible and invisible. In Margarita Diaz-Andreu and Marie Louise Stig Sørensen (Eds.), *Excavating Women: A History of Women in European Archaeology* (pp. 175–197). London: Routledge.

Claassen, Cheryl (Ed.). 1994. *Women in Archaeology.* Philadelphia: University of Pennsylvania Press.

Daniel, Glyn. 1976. *A Hundred and Fifty Years of Archaeology.* Cambridge, MA: Harvard University Press.

——— (Ed.). 1981. *Towards a History of Archaeology.* New York: Thames and Hudson.

Deagan, Kathleen. 1973. Mestizaje in colonial St. Augustine. *Ethnohistory* 20: 55–65.

———. 1978a. Cultures in transition: Fusion and assimilation among the Eastern Timucua. In Jerald Milanich and Samuel Proctor (Eds.), *Tacachale: Essays on the Indians of Florida and Southeastern Georgia During the Historic Period* (pp. 89–119). Gainesville: University Press of Florida.

———. 1978b. The material assemblage of 16th century Spanish Florida. *Historical Archaeology* 12: 25–50.

———. 1980. Spanish St. Augustine: America's first "melting pot." *Archaeology* 33(5): 22–30.

———. 1981. Downtown survey: The discovery of 16th century St. Augustine in an urban area. *American Antiquity* 46: 626–634.

———. 1982. Avenues of inquiry in historical archaeology. In Michael B. Schiffer (Ed.), *Advances in Archaeological Method and Theory.* Vol. 5 (pp. 151–177). New York: Academic Press. ("In Her Own Words" text quoted from pp. 170–171)

———. 1983. *Spanish St. Augustine: The Archaeology of a Colonial Creole Community.* New York: Academic Press.

———. 1987. *Artifacts of the Spanish Colonies of Florida and the Caribbean, 1500–1800: Vol. 1. Ceramics, Glassware, and Beads.* Washington, DC: Smithsonian Institution Press.

———. 1988. Neither history nor prehistory: The questions that count in historical archaeology. *Historical Archaeology* 22: 7–12.

———. 1991. Historical archaeology's contributions to our understanding of early America. In Lisa Falk (Ed.),

Historical Archaeology in Global Perspective (pp. 97–112). Washington, DC: Smithsonian Institution Press.

—— (Ed.). 1995. *Puerto Real: The Archaeology of a Sixteenth-Century Spanish Town in Hispaniola.* Gainesville: University Press of Florida.

——. 1996. Colonial transformation: Euro-American cultural genesis in the early Spanish-American colonies. *Journal of Anthropological Research* 52: 135–160.

Deagan, Kathleen, and José Maria Cruxent. 2002a. *Archaeology at La Isabela: America's First European Town.* New Haven: Yale University Press.

——. 2002b. *Columbus's Outpost Among the Tainos.* New Haven: Yale University Press.

Drower, Margaret S. 2004. Gertrude Caton-Thomson, 1888–1985. In Getzel Cohen and Martha Joukowsky (Eds.), *Breaking Ground: Pioneering Women Archaeologists* (pp. 351–379). Ann Arbor: University of Michigan Press.

Dunnell, Robert C. 1986. Five decades of American archaeology. In David J. Meltzer, Don D. Fowler, and Jeremy A. Sabloff (Eds.), *American Archaeology Past and Future: A Celebration of the Society for American Archaeology 1935–1985* (pp. 23–49). Washington, DC: Smithsonian Institution Press.

Grayson, Donald K. 1983. *The Establishment of Human Antiquity.* New York: Academic Press.

Irwin-Williams, Cynthia. 1990. Women in the field: The role of women in archaeology before 1960. In G. Kass-Simon and Patricia Farnes (Eds.), *Women of Science: Righting the Record* (pp. 1–41). Bloomington: Indiana University Press.

Kidder, Alfred V. 1924. *An Introduction to the Study of Southwestern Archaeology.* New Haven: Yale University Press.

——. 1928. The present state of knowledge of American history and civilization prior to 1492. In *International Congress of History, Oslo, 1928, Compte Rendu* (pp. 749–753). Paris. ("In His Own Words" text quoted from p. 753)

——. 1960. Reminiscences in Southwest archaeology, I. *Kiva* 25: 1–32.

Kidder, Alfred V., and Samuel J. Guernsey. 1921. *Basket-Maker Caves of Northeastern Arizona.* Cambridge, MA: Papers of the Peabody Museum of American Archaeology and Ethnology 8(2).

Kidder, Alfred V., Jesse D. Jennings, and Edwin M. Shook. 1946. Excavations at Kaminaljuyu, Guatemala. Washington, DC: Carnegie Institution of Washington Publication no. 561.

Lamberg-Karlovsky, C. C. (Ed.). 1989. *Archaeological Thought in America.* Cambridge: Cambridge University Press.

Mayes, S. 1959. *The Great Belzoni.* London: Putnam.

Parezo, Nancy J. (Ed.). 1993. *Hidden Scholars: Women Anthropologists and the Native American Southwest.* Albuquerque: University of New Mexico Press.

Ryan, Donald. 1986. Giovanni Batista Belzoni. *Biblical Archaeologist* (Sept): 133–138.

Stanford, Dennis. 1996. Hannah Marie Wormington 1914–1994. *American Antiquity* 61: 274–278.

Trigger, Bruce G. 1980. Archaeology and the image of the American Indian. *American Antiquity* 45: 662–676.

——. 1999. *A History of Archaeological Thought.* 2d ed. Cambridge: Cambridge University Press.

Watson, Patty Jo. 1973. The future of archeology in anthropology: Cultural history and social science. In Charles L. Redman (Ed.), *Research and Theory in Current Archaeology* (pp. 113–124). New York: Wiley.

Wauchope, Robert. 1965. (Obituary of) Alfred Vincent Kidder, 1885–1963. *American Antiquity* 31(2, pt. 1): 149–171.

Willey, Gordon R. 1967. (Obituary of) Alfred Vincent Kidder. *National Academy of Sciences Biographical Memoirs.* Vol. 39 (pp. 292–322). New York: Columbia University Press.

Willey, Gordon R., and Jeremy A. Sabloff. 1993. *A History of American Archaeology.* 3d ed. New York: Freeman.

Wissler, Clark. 1917. The new archaeology. *The American Museum Journal* 17(2): 100–101.

Woodbury, Richard B. 1973. *Alfred V. Kidder.* New York: Columbia University Press.

Wormington, H. Marie, 1937. *Ancient Man in North America.* Denver: Colorado Museum of Natural History.

——. 1947. *Prehistoric Indians of the Southwest.* Denver: Colorado Museum of Natural History.

Wylie, Allison. 2002. *Thinking from Things: Essays in the Philosophy of Archaeology.* Berkeley: University of California Press.

Chapter 2

Atwater, Caleb. 1820. Description of the antiquities discovered in the state of Ohio and other western states. *Archaeologia Americana: Transactions and Collections of the American Antiquarian Society* 1: 105–267.

Baldwin, J. D. 1872. *Ancient America.* New York: Harper.

Bapty, Ian, and Tim Yates (Eds.). 1990. *Archaeology After Structuralism: Post-Structuralism and the Practice of Archaeology.* London: Routledge.

Bell, James A. 1994. *Reconstructing Prehistory: Scientific Method in Archaeology.* Philadelphia: Temple University Press.

Binford, Lewis R. 1983. *In Pursuit of the Past: Decoding the Archaeological Record.* London: Thames and Hudson.

——. 1989a. Science to seance, or processual to "postprocessual" archaeology. In *Debating Archaeology* (pp. 27–40). San Diego: Academic Press.

——. 1989b. Review of Hodder, *Reading the Past: Current Approaches to Interpretation in Archaeology.* In *Debating Archaeology* (pp. 69–71). San Diego: Academic Press.

Boas, Franz. 1940. *Race, Language and Culture.* New York: Macmillan.

Clarke, David L. 1968. *Analytical Archaeology.* London: Methuen.

Dark, K. R. 1995. *Theoretical Archaeology.* Ithaca: Cornell University Press.

de Laguna, Frederica. 1957. Some problems of objectivity in ethnology. *Man* 57: 179–182.

Esber, George S. 1987. Designing Apache homes with Apaches. In Robert W. Wulff and Shirley J. Fiske (Eds.), *Anthropological Praxis: Translating Knowledge into Action* (pp. 187–196). Boulder: Westview Press.

Feder, Kenneth L. 1995. *Frauds, Myths, and Mysteries: Science and Pseudoscience in Archaeology*. 2d ed. Mountain View, CA: Mayfield.

Flannery, Kent V. 1967. Culture history vs. cultural process: A debate in American archaeology. *Scientific American* 217(2): 119–121.

———. 1973. Archeology with a capital S. In Charles L. Redman (Ed.), *Research and Theory in Current Archeology* (pp. 47–53). New York: Wiley and Sons.

Fotiadis, M. 1994. What is archaeology's "mitigated objectivism" mitigated by? Comments on Wylie. *American Antiquity* 59: 545–555.

Fox, Richard G. (Ed.). 1991. *Recapturing Anthropology: Working in the Present*. Santa Fe: School of American Research Press.

Gibbon, Guy. 1989. *Explanation in Archaeology*. Oxford: Basil Blackwell.

Harris, Marvin. 1968. *The Rise of Anthropological Theory*. New York: Thomas Y. Crowell.

Hegmon, Michelle. 2003. Setting theoretical egos aside: Issues and theory in North American archaeology. *American Antiquity* 68: 213–244.

Henderson, Julian (Ed.). 1989. *Scientific Analysis in Archaeology and Its Interpretation*. Los Angeles: UCLA Institute of Archaeology.

Hodder, Ian. 1982a. *Symbols in Action: Ethnoarchaeological Studies of Material Culture*. Cambridge: Cambridge University Press.

——— (Ed.). 1982b. *Symbolic and Structural Archaeology*. Cambridge: Cambridge University Press.

———. 1985. Postprocessual archaeology. In Michael B. Schiffer (Ed.), *Advances in Archaeological Method and Theory*. Vol. 8 (pp. 1–26). Orlando, FL: Academic Press.

———. 1986. *Reading the Past: Current Approaches to Interpretation in Archaeology*. Cambridge: Cambridge University Press.

———. 1989a. Post-modernism, post-structuralism and postprocessual archaeology. In Ian Hodder (Ed.), *The Meaning of Things*. One World Archaeology, no. 6 (pp. 64–78). London: Unwin Hyman.

———. 1989b. Writing archaeology: Site reports in context. *Antiquity* 63: 268–274.

———. 1991a. Interpretive archaeology and its role. *American Antiquity* 56: 7–18.

———. 1991b. Postprocessual archaeology and the current debate. In Robert W. Preucel (Ed.), *Processual and Postprocessual Archaeologies: Multiple Ways of Knowing the Past* (pp. 30–41). Carbondale: Southern Illinois University, Center for Archaeological Investigations, Occasional Paper no. 10.

———. 1995. *Theory and Practice in Archaeology*. London: Routledge.

———. 1999. *The Archaeological Process: An Introduction*. Oxford: Blackwell.

———. (Ed.). 2001. *Archaeological Theory Today*. Oxford: Blackwell.

Jefferson, Thomas. 1787. *Notes on the State of Virginia*. London: John Stockdale. (Reprinted Chapel Hill: University of North Carolina Press, 1954)

Johnson, Matthew. 1999. *Archaeological Theory: An Introduction*. Oxford: Blackwell.

Kelley, Jane Holden, and Marsha P. Hanen. 1988. *Archaeology and the Methodology of Science*. Albuquerque: University of New Mexico Press.

Kemeny, John G. 1959. *A Philosopher Looks at Science*. New York: Van Nostrand Reinhold.

Knapp, A. Bernard. 1996. Archaeology without gravity: Postmodernism and the past. *Journal of Archaeological Method and Theory* 3: 127–158.

Kroeber, Alfred, and Clyde Kluckhohn. 1952. *Culture: A Critical Review of Concepts and Definitions*. Cambridge, MA: Papers of the Peabody Museum of American Archaeology and Ethnology 47(1).

Kuznar, Lawrence. 1997. *Reclaiming a Scientific Anthropology*. Walnut Creek, CA: Altamira Press.

McGee, R. Jon, and Richard L. Williams. 2004. *Anthropological Theory: An Introductory History*. 3d ed. New York: McGraw Hill.

Meltzer, David J. 1998. Introduction. In *Ancient Monuments of the Mississippi Valley* [reprint of 1848 publication] (pp. 1–95). Washington, DC: Smithsonian Institution Press.

Mithen, Steven. 1989. Evolutionary theory and post-processual archaeology. *Antiquity* 63: 483–494.

Phillips, Philip. 1955. American archaeology and general anthropological theory. *Southwestern Journal of Anthropology* 11: 246–250. (Quote from p. 246)

Rowe, John Howland. 1965. The renaissance foundations of anthropology. *American Anthropologist* 67: 1–20.

Sabloff, Jeremy A., Lewis R. Binford, and Patricia A. McAnany. 1987. Understanding the archaeological record. *Antiquity* 61: 203–209.

Salmon, Merrilee H. 1982. *Philosophy and Archaeology*. New York: Academic Press.

Salmon, Merrilee H., and Wesley C. Salmon. 1979. Alternative models of scientific explanation. *American Anthropologist* 81: 61–74.

Sherratt, Andrew. 1993. The relativity of theory. In Norman Yoffee and Andrew Sherratt (Eds.), *Archaeological Theory: Who Sets the Agenda?* (pp. 119–130). Cambridge: Cambridge University Press.

Skibo, James M., William H. Walker, and Axel E. Nielsen (Eds.). 1995. *Expanding Archaeology*. Salt Lake City: University of Utah Press.

Spaulding, Albert C. 1968. Explanation in archeology. In Sally R. Binford and Lewis R. Binford (Eds.), *New Perspectives in Archeology* (pp. 33–39). Chicago: Aldine.

———. 1985. Fifty years of theory. *American Antiquity* 50: 301–308.

Squier, Ephraim G., and Edwin H. Davis. 1998. *Ancient Monuments of the Mississippi Valley*, edited and with an introduction by David J. Meltzer. Washington, DC: Smithsonian Institution Press.

Thomas, Cyrus. 1894. *Report on the Mound Explorations of the Bureau of Ethnology*. Washington, DC: Smithsonian Institution.

Tylor, Edward Burnett. 1871. *Primitive Culture*. Vols. 1 and 2. London: Murray. (Quote from p. 1)

U'mista Culture Centre. 1983. *Box of Treasures*. Film. Directed by Dennis Wheeler, narrated by Gloria Cranmer Webster. Alert Bay, Canada: U'mista Cultural Centre.

Webster, Gloria Cranmer. 1991. The contemporary potlatch. In Aldona Jonaitis (Ed.), *Chiefly Feasts: The Enduring Kwakiutl Potlatch* (pp. 227–250). Seattle: University of Washington Press; New York: American Museum of Natural History.

Wilk, Richard. 1985. The ancient Maya and the political present. *Journal of Anthropological Research* 41: 307–326.

Willey, Gordon R., and Philip Phillips. 1958. *Method and Theory in American Archaeology*. Chicago: University of Chicago Press.

Chapter 3

Abbott, James T., and Charles D. Frederick. 1990. Proton magnetometer investigations of burned rock middens in West-Central Texas: Clues to formation processes. *Journal of Archaeological Science* 17: 535–545.

Aldenderfer, Mark, and Herbert Maschner (Eds.). 1996. *Anthropology, Space, and Geographic Information Systems*. New York: Oxford University Press.

Allen, K. M. S., S. W. Green, and E. B. W. Zubrow (Eds.). 1990. *Interpreting Space: GIS and Archaeology*. London: Taylor and Francis.

Ammerman, A. J. 1981. Surveys and archaeological research. *Annual Review of Anthropology* 10: 63–88.

Avery, T. E., and T. R. Lyons. 1981. *Remote Sensing: Aerial and Terrestrial Photography for Archaeologists*. Washington, DC: National Park Service, Supplement 7.

Binford, Lewis R. 1964. A consideration of archaeological research design. *American Antiquity* 29: 425–441.

Boyd, Mark, F., Hale G. Smith, and John W. Griffin. 1951. *Here They Once Stood: The Tragic End of the Apalachee Missions*. Gainesville: University of Florida Press.

Carr, Christopher. 1982. *Handbook on Soil Resistivity Surveying: Interpretation of Data from Earthen Archaeological Sites*. Evanston, IL: Center for American Archeology Press.

Clark, Anthony. 1990. *Seeing Beneath the Soil: Prospecting Methods in Archaeology*. London: Batsford.

Davis, Hester A. 1991. Avocational archaeology groups: A secret weapon for site protection. In George S. Smith and John E. Ehrenhard (Eds.), *Protecting the Past* (pp. 175–180). Boca Raton, FL: CRC Press. ("What Does It Mean to Me?" text quoted from this work)

Deuel, Leo. 1969. *Flights into Yesterday: The Story of Aerial Archaeology*. New York: St. Martin's Press.

Dillon, Brian D. (Ed.). 1989. *Practical Archaeology: Field and Laboratory Techniques and Archaeological Logistics*. Archaeological Research Tools 2. Los Angeles: Institute of Archaeology, UCLA.

Donoghue, D. N. M. 2001. Remote sensing. In D. Brothwell and A. Pollard (Eds.), *Handbook of Archaeological Sciences* (pp. 555–564). Chichester, England: John Wiley and Sons.

Dunnell, Robert C., and William S. Dancey. 1983. The siteless survey: A regional scale data collection strategy. In Michael B. Schiffer (Ed.), *Advances in Archeological Method and Theory*. Vol. 6 (pp. 267–287). New York: Academic Press.

Ebert, James. 1992. *Distributional Archaeology*. Albuquerque: University of New Mexico Press.

Frison, George C. 1984. Avocational archaeology: Its past, present, and future. In E. L. Green (Ed.), *Ethics and Values in Archaeology* (pp. 184–193). New York: Free Press.

Gabriel, Kathryn. 1991. *Roads to Center Place: A Cultural Atlas of Chaco Canyon and the Anasazi*. Boulder: Johnson Books.

Garrison, Ervan G., James G. Baker, and David Hurst Thomas. 1985. Magnetic prospection and the discovery of Mission Santa Catalina de Guale, Georgia. *Journal of Field Archaeology* 12: 299–313.

Kantner, John. 1997. Ancient roads, modern mapping: Evaluating prehistoric Chaco Anasazi roadways using GIS technology. *Expedition Magazine* 39(3): 49–62.

———. 2004. Geographical approaches for reconstructing past human behavior from prehistoric roadways. In M. F. Goodchild and D. G. Janelle (Eds.), *Spatially Integrated Social Sciences: Examples in Best Practice* (pp. 323–344). Oxford: Oxford University Press.

Kelly, Robert. 2001. Prehistory of the Carson Desert and Stillwater Mountains, Nevada: Environment, mobility, and subsistence. *University of Utah Anthropological Papers* 123. Salt Lake City.

Kvamme, Kenneth L. 1989. Geographic information systems in regional archaeological research and data management. In M. B. Schiffer (Ed.), *Archaeological Method and Theory*. Vol. 1 (pp. 139–204). Tucson: University of Arizona Press.

Lyons, T. R., and T. E. Avery. 1984. *Remote Sensing: A Handbook for Archaeologists and Cultural Resource Managers*. Washington, DC: National Park Service.

McManamon, Francis P. 1984. Discovering sites unseen. In Michael B. Schiffer (Ed.), *Advances in Archaeological Method and Theory*. Vol. 7 (pp. 223–292). New York: Academic Press.

Morris, Craig. 1995. Airborne archeology. *Natural History* 104(12): 70–72.

Mueller, James W. 1974. *The Use of Sampling in Archaeological Survey*. Washington, DC: Society for American Archaeology Memoir 28.

——— (Ed.). 1975. *Sampling in Archaeology*. Tucson: University of Arizona Press.

Noble, David Grant (Ed.). 1984. *New Light on Chaco Canyon*. Santa Fe: School of American Research Press.

Scollar, Irwin, A. Tabbagh, A. Hesse, and I. Herzog (Eds.). 1990. *Archaeological Prospecting and Remote Sensing*. Cambridge: Cambridge University Press.

Sebastian, Lynne. 1992. *The Chaco Anasazi: Sociopolitical Evolution in the Prehistoric Southwest*. Cambridge: Cambridge University Press.

Snead, J., and R. Preucel. 1999. The ideology of settlement: Ancestral Keres landscapes in the northern Rio Grande. In W. Ashmore and A. B. Knapp (Eds.), *Archaeologies of Landscape: Contemporary Perspectives* (pp. 169–197). Oxford: Blackwell Publishers.

Steward, Julian H. 1938. Basin-plateau aboriginal sociopolitical groups. *Bureau of American Ethnology Bulletin* 120. Washington, DC.

Thomas, David Hurst. 1972a. A computer simulation model of Great Basin Shoshonean subsistence and settlement patterns. In David L. Clarke (Ed.), *Models in Archaeology* (pp. 671–704). London: Methuen.

——. 1972b. Western Shoshone ecology: Settlement patterns and beyond. In Don D. Fowler (Ed.), *Great Basin Cultural Ecology: A Symposium* (pp. 135–153). Reno: University of Nevada, Desert Research Institute Publications in the Social Sciences 8.

——. 1973. An empirical test for Steward's model of Great Basin settlement patterns. *American Antiquity* 38(2): 155–176.

——. 1978. The awful truth about statistics in archaeology. *American Antiquity* 43(2): 231–244.

——. 1983a. *The Archaeology of Monitor Valley: 1. Epistemology.* New York: Anthropological Papers of the American Museum of Natural History 58(1).

——. 1983b. *The Archaeology of Monitor Valley: 2. Gatecliff Shelter.* New York: Anthropological Papers of the American Museum of Natural History 59(1).

——. 1987. *The Archaeology of Mission Santa Catalina de Guale: 1. Search and Discovery.* New York: Anthropological Papers of the American Museum of Natural History 63(2).

——. 1988. *The Archaeology of Monitor Valley: 3. Survey and Additional Excavation.* New York: Anthropological Papers of the American Museum of Natural History 66(2).

——. 1993. The archaeology of Mission Santa Catalina de Guale: Our first 15 years. In Bonnie G. McEwan (Ed.), *The Missions of La Florida* (pp. 1–34). Gainesville: University Press of Florida.

Thomas, David Hurst, and Robert L. Bettinger. 1976. *Prehistoric Pinyon Ecotone Settlements of the Upper Reese River Valley, Central Nevada.* New York: Anthropological Papers of the American Museum of Natural History 53(3).

Vivian, R. Gwinn. 1990. *The Chacoan Prehistory of the San Juan Basin.* San Diego: Academic Press.

Wescott, Konnie L., and R. Joe Brandon (Eds.). 1999. *Practical Applications of GIS for Archaeologists: A Predictive Modeling Kit.* London: Taylor and Francis.

Wescott, Konnie L., and James A. Kuiper. 1999. Using a GIS to model prehistoric site distributions in the Upper Chesapeake Bay. In Konnie Wescott and R. Joe Brandon (Eds.), *Practical Applications of GIS for Archaeologists: A Predictive Modeling Kit* (pp. 59–72). London: Taylor and Francis.

Wheatley, David, and Mark Gillings. 2002. *Spatial Technology and Archaeology: The Archaeological Applications of GIS.* London: Taylor and Francis.

Willey, Gordon R. 1953. Prehistoric settlement patterns in the Virú Valley, Peru. *Bureau of American Ethnology Bulletin* 155. Washington, DC.

Chapter 4

Bird, Junius. 1980. Comments on sifters, sifting, and sorting procedures. In Martha Joukowsky, *A Complete Manual of Field Archaeology* (pp. 165–170). Englewood Cliffs, NJ: Prentice Hall.

Collis, John. 2001. *Digging Up the Past: An Introduction to Archaeological Excavation.* Phoenix Mills, UK: Sutton Publishing.

Dancey, William S. 1981. *Archaeological Field Methods: An Introduction.* Minneapolis: Burgess.

Daugherty, Richard, and Ruth Kirk. 1976. Ancient Indian village where time stood still. *Smithsonian* 7(2): 68–75.

Dibble, Harold L. 1987. Measurement of artifact provenience with an electronic theodolite. *Journal of Field Archaeology* 14: 249–254.

Fladmark, Knud R. 1978. *A Guide to Basic Archaeological Field Procedures.* Burnaby, British Columbia: Simon Fraser University, Department of Archaeology.

Folsom, Franklin. 1992. *The Black Cowboy.* Niwot, CO: Roberts Rinehart.

Fowler, Brenda. 2001. *Iceman: Uncovering the Life and Times of a Prehistoric Man Found in an Alpine Glacier.* Chicago: University of Chicago Press.

Joukowsky, Martha. 1980. *A Complete Manual of Field Archaeology: Tools and Techniques of Field Work for Archaeologists.* Englewood Cliffs, NJ: Prentice Hall.

Kirk, Ruth, and Richard Daugherty. 1974. *Hunters of the Whale.* New York: William Morrow.

Lock, Gary. 2003. *Using Computers in Archaeology: Towards Virtual Pasts.* London: Routledge.

Loud, Lewellyn L., and Mark R. Harrington. 1929. Lovelock Cave. *University of California Publications in American Archaeology and Ethnology* 25: 1–183.

McMillon, Bill. 1991. *The Archaeology Handbook: A Field Manual and Resource Guide.* New York: John Wiley and Sons.

Meltzer, David. 1993. *Search for the First Americans.* Washington, DC: Smithsonian Institution Press.

Pendleton, Michael W. 1983. A comment concerning testing flotation recovery rates. *American Antiquity* 48: 615–616.

Percy, George. 1976. The use of a mechanical earth auger at the Torreya Site, Liberty County, Florida. *Florida Anthropologist* 29(1): 24–32.

Purdy, Barbara A. 1996. *How to Do Archaeology the Right Way.* Gainesville: University Press of Florida.

Rick, John W. 1996. Total stations in archaeology. *Bulletin of the Society for American Archaeology* 14(4): 24–27.

Samuels, Steven (Ed.). 1991a. *Ozette Archaeological Research Reports: Vol. 1. House Structure and Floor Midden.* Pullman: Washington State University and National Park Service, Pacific Northwest Regional Office.

——. (Ed.) 1991b. *Ozette Archaeological Research Reports: Vol. 2. Fauna.* Pullman: Washington State University and National Park Service, Pacific Northwest Regional Office.

South, Stanley. 1994. The archaeologist and the crew: From the mountains to the sea. In Stanley South (Ed.), *Pioneers in Historical Archaeology: Breaking New Ground* (pp. 165–187). New York: Plenum Press.

Struever, Stuart. 1968. Flotation techniques for the recovery of small-scale archaeological remains. *American Antiquity* 33: 353–362.

Wagner, Gail E. 1982. Testing flotation recovery rates. *American Antiquity* 47: 127–132.

Watson, Patty Jo. 1974. Flotation procedures used on Salts Cave sediments. In Patty Jo Watson (Ed.), *Archeology of the Mammoth Cave Area* (pp. 107–108). New York: Academic Press.

———. 1976. In pursuit of prehistoric subsistence: A comparative account of some contemporary flotation techniques. *Midcontinental Journal of Archaeology* 1: 77–100.

Yarnell, Richard A. 1974. Intestinal contents of the Salts Cave mummy and analysis of the initial Salts Cave flotation series. In Patty Jo Watson (Ed.), *Archaeology of the Mammoth Cave Area* (pp. 109–112). New York: Academic Press.

———. 1982. Problems of interpretation of archaeological plant remains of the Eastern Woodlands. *Southeastern Archaeology* 1(1): 1–7.

Chapter 5

Bishop, Gale A., Harold B. Rollins, and David Hurst Thomas (Eds.). 2011. *Geoarchaeology of St. Catherines Island (Georgia)*. Anthropological Papers of the American Museum of Natural History 94.

Browman, David L., and Douglas R. Givens. 1996. Stratigraphic excavation: The first "new archaeology." *American Anthropologist* 98: 1–17.

Cook, E. R., J. Esper, and R. D. D'Arrigo. 2004. Extra-tropical Northern Hemisphere land temperature variability over the past 1000 years. *Quaternary Science Reviews* 23: 2063–2074.

Davis, Jonathan O. 1978. *Quaternary Tephrochronology of the Lake Lahontan Area*. Nevada Archaeological Survey Research Paper no. 7.

———. 1983. Geology of Gatecliff Shelter: Sedimentary facies and Holocene climate. In D. H. Thomas, *The Archaeology of Monitor Valley: 2. Gatecliff Shelter* (pp. 64–87). New York: Anthropological Papers of the American Museum of Natural History 59(1).

Dibble, Harold, Philip Chase, Shannon McPherron, and Alain Tuffreau. 1992. Testing the reality of a "living floor" with archaeological data. *American Antiquity* 62: 629–651.

Ellis, Florence Hawley. 1983. Foreword. In Stephen H. Lekson (Ed.), *The Architecture and Dendrochronology of Chetro Ketl, Chaco Canyon, New Mexico*. Albuquerque: National Park Service, Division of Cultural Research, Reports of the Chaco Center no. 6. ("In Her Own Words" text quoted from this work)

Feibel, C. S., N. Agnew, B. Latimer, M. Demas, F. Marshall, S. A. C. Waane, and P. Schmid. 1996. A new look at the Laetoli hominid footprints: A preliminary report on the conservation and scientific restudy. *Evolutionary Anthropology* 4: 149–154.

Frisbie, Theodore R. 1975. A biography of Florence Hawley Ellis and bibliography of Florence Hawley Ellis. In Theodore R. Frisbie (Ed.), *Collected Papers in Honor of Florence Hawley Ellis* (pp. 1–11, 12–21). Albuquerque: Papers of the Archaeological Society of New Mexico no. 2.

———. 1991. Florence Hawley Ellis, 1906–1991. *Kiva* 57(1): 93–97.

Harris, E. 1989. *Principles of Archaeological Stratigraphy*. 2d ed. New York: Academic Press.

Hawley, Florence M. 1934. The significance of the dated prehistory of Chetro Ketl, Chaco Canyon, New Mexico. *University of New Mexico Bulletin*, Monograph Series 1(1). Albuquerque: University of New Mexico Press.

———. 1937. Reversed stratigraphy. *American Antiquity* 4: 297–299.

Hay, Richard I., and Mary D. Leakey. 1982. The fossil footprints of Laetoli. *Scientific American* 246(2): 50–57.

Herz, Norman, and Ervan Garrison. 1998. *Geological Methods for Archaeology*. Oxford: Oxford University Press.

Holliday, Vance T. (Ed.). 1992. *Soils in Archaeology: Landscape Evolution and Human Occupation*. Washington, DC: Smithsonian Institution Press.

Jones, P. D., K. R. Briffa, T. P. Barnett, and S. F. B. Tett. 1998. High-resolution palaeoclimatic records for the last millennium: Integration, interpretation and comparison with General Circulation Model control run temperatures. *Holocene* 8: 455–471.

Leakey, Mary, and J. M. Harris (Eds.). 1987. *Laetoli: A Pliocene Site in Northern Tanzania*. Oxford: Clarendon Press.

Mann, M. E., C. M. Ammann, R. S. Bradley, K. R. Briffa, T. J. Crowley, M. K. Hughes, P. D. Jones, M. Oppenheimer, T. J. Osborn, J. T. Overpeck, S. Rutherford, K. E. Trenberth, and T. M. L. Wigley. 2003. On past temperatures and anomalous late 20th century warmth. *Eos* 84: 256–258.

Mann, M. E., R. S. Bradley, and M. K. Hughes. 1998. Global-scale temperature patterns and climate forcing over the past six centuries. *Nature* 392: 779–787.

———. 1999. Northern Hemisphere temperatures during the past millennium: Inferences, uncertainties, and limitations. *Geophysical Research Letters* 26: 759–762.

Rapp, George, and John A. Gifford (Eds.). 1985. *Archaeological Geology*. New Haven: Yale University Press.

Schiffer, Michael B. 1972. Archaeological context and systemic context. *American Antiquity* 37: 156–165.

———. 1987. *Formation Processes of the Archaeological Record*. Albuquerque: University of New Mexico Press.

Steen-McIntyre, Virginia. 1985. Tephrochronology and its application to archaeology. In George Rapp, Jr., and John A. Gifford (Eds.), *Archaeological Geology* (pp. 265–302). New Haven: Yale University Press.

Stein, Julie K. 1987. Deposits for archaeologists. In Michael B. Schiffer (Ed.), *Advances in Archaeological Method and Theory*. Vol. 11 (pp. 337–395). New York: Academic Press.

——— (Ed.). 1992. *Deciphering a Shell Midden*. San Diego: Academic Press.

Straus, Lawrence G. 1990. Underground archaeology: Perspectives on caves and rockshelters. In M. B. Schiffer (Ed.), *Archaeological Method and Theory*. Vol. 2 (pp. 255–304). Tucson: University of Arizona Press.

Thomas, David Hurst. 1983. *The Archaeology of Monitor Valley: 2. Gatecliff Shelter*. New York: Anthropological Papers of the American Museum of Natural History 59(1). (Quote is from pp. 55–56)

———. 2011. *St. Catherines: An Island in Time*. 2d ed. with a new preface. Athens: University of Georgia Press.

Thomas, David Hurst, and Matthew C. Sanger (Eds.). 2010. *Trend, Tradition, and Turmoil: What Happened to the*

Southeastern Archaic? Anthropological Papers of the American Museum of Natural History 93: 1–341.

Tuttle, Russell, D. Webb, E. Weidl, and M. Baksh. 1990. Further progress on the Laeotoli trails. *Journal of Archaeological Science* 17: 347–362.

Waters, Michael R. 1992. *Principles of Geoarchaeology: A North American Perspective.* Tucson: University of Arizona Press. (Quotes from pp. 3, 7, 11)

Chapter 6

Aitken, M. J. 1989. Luminescence dating: A guide for nonspecialists. *Archaeometry* 31: 147–159.

———. 1990. *Science-Based Dating in Archaeology.* London: Longman.

Baillie, M. G. L. 1995. *A Slice Through Time: Dendrochronology and Precision Dating.* London: Batsford.

Banning, E. B., and L. A. Pavlish. 1978. Direct detection in radiocarbon dating. *Journal of Field Archaeology* 5: 480–483.

Bannister, Bryant. 1962. The interpretation of tree-ring dates. *American Antiquity* 27: 508–514.

———. 1970. Dendrochronology. In Don Brothwell and Eric Higgs (Eds.), *Science in Archaeology: A Survey of Progress and Research.* 2d ed. (pp. 191–205). New York: Praeger.

Bannister, Bryant, and William J. Robinson. 1975. Tree-ring dating in archaeology. *World Archaeology* 7: 210–225.

Bar-Yosef, O., and B. Vandermeersch. 1993. Modern humans in the Levant. *Scientific American* 268: 64–70.

Beck, Charlotte (Ed.). 1994. *Dating in Exposed and Surface Contexts.* Albuquerque: University of New Mexico Press.

Bennett, C. L., R. P. Beukens, M. R. Clover, H. E. Gove, R. B. Liebert, A. E. Litherland, K. H. Purser, and W. E. Sondheim. 1977. Radiocarbon dating using electrostatic accelerators: Negative ions provide the key. *Science* 198: 508–510.

Berger, R. 1979. Radiocarbon dating with accelerators. *Journal of Archaeological Science* 6: 101–104.

Binford, Lewis R. 1962. A new method of calculating dates from kaolin pipe stem samples. *Southeastern Archaeological Conference Newsletter* 9(2): 19–21.

———. 1972. The "Binford" pipe stem formula: A return from the grave. *The Conference on Historic Site Archaeology Papers* 6: 230–253.

Bowman, Sheridan. 1990. *Radiocarbon Dating.* Berkeley: University of California Press.

———. 1994. Using radiocarbon: An update. *Antiquity* 68: 838–843.

Braun, David P. 1985. Absolute seriation: A time-series approach. In Christopher Carr (Ed.), *For Concordance in Archaeological Analysis: Bridging Data Structure, Quantitative Technique, and Theory* (pp. 509–539). Kansas City, MO: Westport.

Browman, David L. 1981. Isotopic discrimination and correction factors in radiocarbon dating. In Michael B. Schiffer (Ed.), *Advances in Archaeological Method and Theory.* Vol. 6 (pp. 241–295). New York: Academic Press.

Chaffee, Scott D., Marian Hyman, Marvin W. Rowe, Nancy J. Coulam, Alan Schroedl, and Kathleen Hogue. 1994. Radiocarbon dates on the All American Man pictograph. *American Antiquity* 59: 769–781.

Chase, A. F., D. Z. Chase, and H. W. Topsey. 1988. Archaeology and the ethics of collecting. *Archaeology* 41(1): 56–60, 87.

Creel, Darrell, and Austin Long. 1986. Radiocarbon dating of corn. *American Antiquity* 51: 826–837.

Dale, W. S. A. 1987. The shroud of Turin: Relic or icon? *Nuclear Instruments and Methods in Physics Research* B29: 187–192.

Deagan, Kathleen. 1983. *Spanish St. Augustine: The Archaeology of a Colonial Creole Community.* New York: Academic Press.

Dean, Jeffery S. 1978. Independent dating in archaeological analysis. In Michael B. Schiffer (Ed.), *Advances in Archaeological Theory and Method.* Vol. 1 (pp. 223–255). New York: Academic Press.

de Vries, Hessel L. 1958. Variation in concentration of radiocarbon with time and location on earth. *Proceedings Koninlijke Nederlandse Akademie Wetenschappen* B, 61: 94–102.

Douglass, Andrew Ellicott. 1929. The secret of the Southwest solved by talkative tree rings. *National Geographic* 56(6): 736–770.

Drennan, Robert D. 1976. A refinement of chronological seriation using nonmetric multidimensional scaling. *American Antiquity* 41: 290–302.

Dunnell, Robert C. 1970. Seriation method and its evaluation. *American Antiquity* 35: 305–319.

Feathers, James. 2003. Use of luminescence dating in archaeology. *Measurement Science and Technology* 14: 1493–1509.

Fleming, Stuart. 1977. *Dating Techniques in Archaeology.* New York: St. Martin's Press.

———. 1979. *Thermoluminescence Techniques in Archaeology.* New York: Oxford University Press.

Fritts, H. C. 1976. *Tree Rings and Climate.* New York: Academic Press.

Fullagar, R. L. K., D. M. Price, and L. M. Head. 1996. Early human occupation of northern Australia: Archaeology and thermoluminescence dating of Jinmium rockshelter, Northern Territory. *Antiquity* 70: 751–773.

Gove, H. E. 1987. Turin workshop on radiocarbon dating the Turin shroud. *Nuclear Instruments and Methods in Physics Research* B29: 193–195.

Grün, R. 1999. Trapped charge dating (ESR, TL, OSL). In D. Brothwell and A. Pollard (Eds.), *Handbook of Archaeological Sciences* (pp. 47–62). Chichester, England: John Wiley and Sons.

Haas, Herbert, James Devine, Robert Wenke, Mark Lehner, Willy Wolfli, and George Bonani. 1987. Radiocarbon chronology and the historical calendar in Egypt. In Oliver Aurenche, Jacques Evin, and Francis Hours (Eds.), *Chronologies in the Near East: Relative Chronologies and Absolute Chronology 16,000–4,000 BP* (pp. 585–606). Oxford: British Archaeology Reports International Series 379.

Harrington, Jean C. 1954. Dating stem fragments of seventeenth and eighteenth century clay tobacco pipes. *Quarterly Bulletin: Archaeological Society of Virginia* 9(1).

Hedges, R. E. M., and J. A. J. Gowlett. 1986. Radiocarbon dating by accelerator mass spectrometry. *Scientific American* 254(1): 100–107.

Heighton, Robert F., and Kathleen A. Deagan. 1972. A new formula for dating kaolin clay pipestems. *The Conference on Historic Site Archaeology Papers* 6(2): 220–229.

Hu, Q., P. E. Smith, N. M. Evensen, and D. York. 1994. Lasing in the Holocene: Extending the ^{40}Ar-^{39}Ar laser probe method into the ^{14}C age range. *Earth and Planetary Science Letters* 123: 331–336.

Jull, A. J. T., D. J. Donahue, and P. E. Damon. 1996. Factors affecting the apparent radiocarbon age of textiles: A comment on "Effects of Fires and Biofractionation of Carbon Isotopes on Results of Radiocarbon Dating of Old Textiles: The Shroud of Turin" by D. A. Kouznetsov et al. *Journal of Archaeological Science* 23: 157–160.

Kouznetsov, Dmitri A., Andrey A. Ivanov, and Pavel R. Veletsky. 1996. Effects of fires and biofractionation of carbon isotopes on results of radiocarbon dating of old textiles: The shroud of Turin. *Journal of Archaeological Science* 23: 109–121.

Long, A., and Bruce Rippeteau. 1974. Testing contemporaneity and averaging radiocarbon dates. *American Antiquity* 39: 205–215.

Loy, Thomas H., Rhys Jones, D. E. Nelson, Betty Meehan, John Vogel, John Southon, and Richard Cosgrove. 1990. Accelerator radiocarbon dating of human blood proteins in pigments from Late Pleistocene art sites in Australia. *Antiquity* 64: 110–116.

Marquardt, William H. 1978. Advances in archaeological seriation. In Michael B. Schiffer (Ed.), *Advances in Archaeological Method and Theory*. Vol. 1 (pp. 257–314). New York: Academic Press.

Mazess, Richard B., and D. W. Zimmermann. 1966. Pottery dating from thermoluminescence. *Science* 152: 347–348.

McDougall, I. 1990. Potassium-argon dating in archaeology. *Science Progress* 74: 15–30.

McNutt, Charles H. 1973. On the methodological validity of frequency seriation. *American Antiquity* 38: 45–60.

Michels, Joseph W. 1973. *Dating Methods in Archaeology*. New York: Seminar Press.

Nelson, Nels. 1916. Chronology of the Tano Ruins, New Mexico. *American Anthropologist* 18: 159–180. (Table 6-1 is from p. 166)

Orser, Charles E., Jr., and Brian M. Fagan. 1995. *Historical Archaeology*. New York: HarperCollins.

Ralph, Elizabeth K., and Mark C. Han. 1966. Dating of pottery by thermoluminescence. *Nature* 210: 245–247.

———. 1969. Potential of thermoluminescence in supplementing radiocarbon dating. *World Archaeology* 1: 157–169.

Renfrew, Colin. 1979. *Problems in European Prehistory*. Edinburgh: Edinburgh University Press.

Roberts, R. G., M. Bird, J. Olley, R. Galbraith, E. Lawson, G. Laslett, H. Yoshida, R. Jones, R. L. K. Fullagar, G. Jacobsen, and Q. Hua. 1998. Optical and radiocarbon dating at Jinmium rock shelter in northern Australia. *Nature* 393: 358–362.

Rouse, Irving. 1967. Seriation in archaeology. In Carrol L. Riley and Walter W. Taylor (Eds.), *American Historical Anthropology: Essays in Honor of Leslie Spier* (pp. 153–195). Carbondale: Southern Illinois University Press.

South, David B. 1972. Mean ceramic dates, median occupation dates, red ant hills and bumble bees: Statistical confidence and correlation. *The Conference on Historic Site Archaeology Papers* 6: 164–174.

South, Stanley A. 1977. *Method and Theory in Historical Archeology*. New York: Academic Press. (Table 6-4 is from p. 220)

Stafford, T. W., Jr., A. J. T. Jull, T. H. Zabel, D. J. Donahue, R. C. Duhamel, K. Brendel, C. V. Haynes, Jr., J. L. Bischoff, L. A. Payen, and R. E. Taylor. 1984. Holocene age of the Yuha burial: Direct radiocarbon determinations by accelerator mass spectrometry. *Nature* 308: 446–447.

Stahle, David W., and Daniel Wolfman. 1985. The potential for archaeological tree-ring dating in eastern North America. In Michael B. Schiffer (Ed.), *Advances in Archaeological Method and Theory*. Vol. 8 (pp. 279–302). New York: Academic Press.

Staley, David P. 1993. The antiquities market. *Journal of Field Archaeology* 20: 347–355.

Stallings, W. S., Jr. 1939. *Dating Prehistoric Ruins by Tree-Rings*. Sante Fe: Laboratory of Anthropology Bulletin no. 8.

Stuckenrath, R. 1977. Radiocarbon: Some notes from Merlin's diary. *Annals of the New York Academy of Science* 288: 181–188.

Stuiver, Minze, and Paula J. Reimer. 1993. Extended 14C database and revised CALIB 3.0 14C age calibration program. *Radiocarbon* 35: 215–230.

Stuiver, Minze, and Hans E. Suess. 1966. On the relationship between radiocarbon dates and true sample ages. *Radiocarbon* 8: 534–540.

Suess, Hans E. 1955. Radiocarbon concentration in modern wood. *Science* 122: 415–417.

Swisher, C. C., III, G. H. Curtis, T. Jacob, A. G. Getty, and A. Suprijo Widasmoro. 1994. Age of the earliest known hominids in Java, Indonesia. *Science* 263: 1118–1121.

Taylor, R. E. 1985. The beginnings of radiocarbon dating in American antiquity: A historical perspective. *American Antiquity* 50: 309–325.

———. 1987a. AMS 14-C dating of critical bone samples: Proposed protocol and criteria for evaluation. *Nuclear Instruments and Methods in Physics Research* B29: 159–163.

———. 1987b. *Radiocarbon Dating: An Archaeological Perspective*. New York: Academic Press.

Taylor, R. E., and M. J. Aitken (Eds.). 1997. *Chronometric Dating in Archaeology*. New York: Plenum Press.

Taylor, R. E., Austin Long, and Renee S. Kra (Eds.). 1992. *Radiocarbon After Four Decades: An Interdisciplinary Perspective*. New York: Springer-Verlag.

Turnbaugh, William, and Sarah Peabody Turnbaugh. 1977. Alternative applications of the mean ceramic date concept for interpreting human behavior. *Historical Archaeology* 11: 90–104.

Valladas, H., H. Cachier, P. Maurice, F. Bernaldo de Quiro, J. Clottes, V. Cabrera Valdés, P. Uzquiano, and M. Arnold. 1992. Direct radiocarbon dates for prehistoric paintings at the Altamira, El Castillo and Niaux caves. *Nature* 357: 68–70.

van der Merwe, Nikolaas J. 1982. Carbon isotopes, photosynthesis, and archaeology. *American Scientist* 70: 596–606.

van der Plicht, Johannes. 1993. The Groningen radiocarbon calibration program. *Radiocarbon* 35(1): 231–237.

Wendorf, Fred, R. Schild, A. E. Close, D. J. Donahue, A. J. T. Jull, T. H. Zabel, H. Wielowska, M. Kobusiewicz, B. Issawi, N. el Hadidi, and H. Haas. 1984. New radiocarbon dates on the cereals from Wadi Kubbaniua. *Science* 225: 645–646.

Wendorf, Fred, R. Schild, N. el Hadidi, A. E. Close, M. Kobusiewicz, H. Wielowska, B. Issawi, and H. Haas. 1979. The use of barley in the Egyptian late Paleolithic. *Science* 205: 1341–1347.

Willis, E. H. 1969. Radiocarbon dating. In Don Brothwell and Eric Higgs (Eds.), *Science in Archaeology* (pp. 46–57). London: Thames and Hudson.

Wintle, Ann G. 1996. Archaeologically relevant dating techniques for the next century. *Journal of Archaeological Science* 23: 123–138.

Chapter 7

Adams, William Y. 1988. Archaeological classification: Theory versus practice. *Antiquity* 62: 40–56.

Adams, William Y., and Ernest W. Adams. 1991. *Archaeological Typology and Practical Reality: A Dialectical Approach to Artifact Classification and Sorting.* Cambridge: Cambridge University Press.

Binford, Lewis R. 1973. Interassemblage variability—the Mousterian and the "functional" argument. In Colin Renfrew (Ed.), *The Explanation of Culture Change: Models in Prehistory* (pp. 227–254). London: Duckworth.

Cordell, Linda. 1984. *Prehistory of the Southwest.* New York: Academic Press.

Cronyn, J. M. 1990. *The Elements of Archaeological Conservation.* London: Routledge.

Dunnell, Robert C. 1971. *Systematics in Prehistory.* New York: Free Press.

———. 1986. Methodological issues in Americanist artifact classification. In Michael B. Schiffer (Ed.), *Advances in Archaeological Method and Theory.* Vol. 9 (pp. 149–207). New York: Academic Press.

Ford, James. 1954. The type concept revisited. *American Anthropologist* 56: 42–54.

Griset, Suzanne (Ed.). 1986. *Pottery of the Great Basin and Adjacent Areas.* University of Utah Anthropological Papers no. 111.

Kidder, A. V. 1932. *The Artifacts of Pecos.* New Haven: Yale University Press. (Quote is from p. 118)

Klejn, L. S. 1982. *Archaeological Typology.* Translated by P. Dole. Oxford: British Archaeological Reports, International Series, no. 153.

Krieger, Alex D. 1944. The typological concept. *American Antiquity* 9: 271–288.

Lyman, R. Lee, and Michael O'Brien. 2003. *W. C. McKern and the Midwestern Taxonomic Method.* Tuscaloosa: University of Alabama Press.

Lyman, R. Lee, Michael O'Brien, and Robert C. Dunnell (Eds.). 1997. *Americanist Culture History: Fundamentals of Time, Space, and Form.* New York: Plenum Press.

Rouse, Irving. 1960. The classification of artifacts in archaeology. *American Antiquity* 25: 313–323.

Sarich, V., and A. Wilson. 1967. Immunological time scale for human evolution. *Science* 158: 1200–1203.

Scott, G., and C. Turner. 1997. *The Anthropology of Modern Human Teeth.* Cambridge: Cambridge University Press.

Spaulding, Albert C. 1953. Statistical techniques for the discovery of artifact types. *American Antiquity* 18: 305–313.

———. 1960. The dimensions of archaeology. In G. E. Dole and R. L. Carneiro (Eds.), *Essays in the Science of Culture in Honor of Leslie A. White* (pp. 437–456). New York: Thomas Y. Crowell.

———. 1977. On growth and form in archaeology: Multivariate analysis. *Journal of Anthropological Research* 33: 1–15.

Spier, Leslie. 1917. *An Outline for a Chronology of Zuñi Ruins.* New York: Anthropological Papers of the American Museum of Natural History 18(3).

———. 1931. N. C. Nelson's stratigraphic technique in the reconstruction of prehistoric sequences in southwestern America. In S. A. Rice (Ed.), *Methods in Social Science* (pp. 275–283). Chicago: University of Chicago Press.

Steward, Julian H. 1954. Types of types. *American Anthropologist* 56: 54–57.

Sutton, Mark Q., and Brooke S. Arkush. 1996. *Archaeological Laboratory Methods: An Introduction.* Dubuque, IA: Kendall/Hunt Publishing.

Thomas, David Hurst. 1981. How to classify the projectile points from Monitor Valley, Nevada. *Journal of California and Great Basin Anthropology* 3: 7–43.

Whallon, Robert E., Jr., and James A. Brown (Eds.). 1982. *Essays on Archaeological Typology.* Evanston, IL: Center for American Archaeology Press.

Willey, Gordon R., and Philip Phillips. 1958. *Method and Theory in American Archaeology.* Chicago: University of Chicago Press. (Quote is from p. 22)

Wissler, Clark. 1926. *The Relation of Nature to Man in Aboriginal America.* New York: Oxford University Press.

Chapter 8

Agenbroad, Larry. 1978. *The Hudson-Meng Site: An Alberta Bison Kill in the Nebraska High Plains.* Washington, DC: University Press of America.

Andrefsky, William. 1998. *Lithics: Macroscopic Approaches to Analysis.* Cambridge: Cambridge University Press.

Behrensmeyer, Anna K., and Susan M. Kidwell. 1985. Taphonomy's contributions to paleobiology. *Paleobiology* 1: 105–119.

Binford, Lewis R. 1967. Smudge pits and hide smoking: The use of analogy in archaeological reasoning. *American Antiquity* 32: 1–12.

——— (Ed.). 1977. *For Theory Building in Archaeology.* New York: Academic Press.

———. 1978a. Dimensional analysis of behavior and site structure: Learning from an Eskimo hunting stand. *American Antiquity* 43: 330–361.

———. 1978b. *Nunamiut Ethnoarchaeology*. New York: Academic Press.

———. 1980. Willow smoke and dogs' tails: Hunter-gatherer settlement systems and archaeological site formation. *American Antiquity* 45: 4–20.

———. 1982. The archaeology of place. *Journal of Anthropological Archaeology* 1: 5–31.

———. 1983. *In Pursuit of the Past: Decoding the Archaeological Record*. London: Thames and Hudson. ("In His Own Words" text quoted from pp. 98, 100–101)

———. 1986. An Alyawara day: Making men's knives and beyond. *American Antiquity* 51: 547–562.

Binford, Lewis R., and James F. O'Connell. 1984. An Alyawara day: The stone quarry. *Journal of Anthropological Research* 40: 406–432.

Brandt, Steve A., and Kathryn Weedman. 1997. The ethnoarchaeology of hideworking and flaked stone-tool use in southern Ethiopia. In K. Fukui, E. Kuimoto, and M. Shigeta (Eds.), *Ethiopia in Broader Perspective: Papers of the XIIth International Conference of Ethiopian Studies* (pp. 351–361). Kyoto: Shokado Book Sellers.

Buck, Bruce A. 1982. Ancient technology in contemporary surgery. *The Western Journal of Medicine* 136: 265–269.

Chaplin, R. E. 1971. *The Study of Animal Bones from Archaeological Sites*. New York: Seminar Press.

Coles, John M. 1973. *Archaeology by Experiment*. New York: Scribner's.

Cotterell, Brian, and Johan Kamminga. 1990. *Mechanics of Pre-Industrial Technology*. Cambridge: Cambridge University Press.

Crabtree, Don E. 1966. A stoneworker's approach to analyzing and replicating the Lindenmeier Folsom. *Tebiwa* 9: 3–39.

———. 1968. Mesoamerican polyhedral cores and prismatic blades. *American Antiquity* 33: 446–478.

———. 1979. Interview. *Flintknappers' Exchange* 2(1): 29–33. ("Looking Closer" text quoted from p. 30)

David, Nicholas, and Carol Kramer. 2001. *Ethnoarchaeology in Action*. Cambridge: Cambridge University Press.

Efremov, I. A. 1940. Taphonomy: A new branch of paleontology. *Pan-American Geologist* 74(2): 81–93.

Flenniken, J. Jeffrey. 1978. Reevaluation of the Lindenmeier Folsom: A replication experiment in lithic technology. *American Antiquity* 43: 473–480.

———. 1981. *Replicative Systems Analysis: A Model Applied to the Vein Quartz Artifacts from the Hoko River Site*. Pullman: Washington State University, Laboratory of Anthropology Reports of Investigations no. 59.

———. 1984. The past, present, and future of flintknapping: An anthropological perspective. *Annual Review of Anthropology* 13: 187–203.

Frison, George C. 1989. Experimental use of Clovis weaponry and tools on African elephants. *American Antiquity* 54: 766–784.

Gamble, C. S., and W. A. Boismier (Eds.). 1991. *Ethnoarchaeological Approaches to Mobile Campsites*. Ann Arbor, MI: International Monographs in Prehistory.

Gifford, Diane P. 1981. Taphonomy and paleoecology: A critical review of archaeology's sister disciplines. In Michael B. Schiffer (Ed.), *Advances in Archaeological Method and Theory*. Vol. 4 (pp. 365–438). New York: Academic Press.

Graham, Martha. 1994. *Mobile Farmers: An Ethnoarchaeological Approach to Settlement Organization Among the Rarámuri of Northwestern Mexico*. Ann Arbor, MI: International Monographs in Prehistory, Ethnoarchaeological Series 3.

Grayson, Donald K. 1986. Eoliths, archaeological ambiguity, and the generation of "middle-range" research. In David J. Meltzer, Don D. Fowler, and Jeremy A. Sabloff (Eds.), *American Archaeology Past and Future: A Celebration of the Society of American Archaeology 1935–1985* (pp. 77–133). Washington, DC: Smithsonian Institution Press.

Gryba, Eugene M. 1988. A Stone Age pressure method of Folsom fluting. *Plains Anthropologist* 33: 53–66.

Hayden, Brian. 1979. *Palaeolithic Reflections: Lithic Technology and Ethnographic Excavation Among Australian Aborigines*. Atlantic Highlands, NJ: Humanities Press.

———. 1987. *Lithic Studies Among the Contemporary Highland Maya*. Tucson: University of Arizona Press.

Hayden, Brian, and Aubrey Cannon. 1984. *The Structure of Material Systems: Ethnoarchaeology in the Maya Highlands*. Society for American Archaeology Papers no. 3.

Henry, Donald O., and George H. Odell (Eds.). 1989. *Alternative Approaches to Lithic Analysis*. Washington, DC: Archaeological Papers of the American Anthropological Association no. 1.

Hill, Andrew. 1979a. Butchery and natural disarticulation: An investigatory technique. *American Antiquity* 44: 739–744.

———. 1979b. Disarticulation and scattering of mammal skeletons. *Paleobiology* 5: 261–274.

Hill, Andrew, and Anna Kay Behrensmeyer. 1984. Disarticulation patterns of some modern East African mammals. *Paleobiology* 10: 366–376.

Hodder, Ian. 1982. *Symbols in Action*. Cambridge: Cambridge University Press.

———. 1987. The meaning of discard: Ash and domestic space in Baringo. In S. Kent (Ed.), *Method and Theory in Activity Area Research* (pp. 424–448). New York: Columbia University Press.

Holly, Gerald A., and Terry A. Del Bene. 1981. An evaluation of Keeley's microwear approach. *Journal of Archaeological Science* 8: 337–352.

Keeley, Lawrence H. 1974. Technique and methodology in microwear studies: A critical review. *World Archaeology* 5: 323–336.

———. 1980. *Experimental Determination of Stone Tool Uses: A Microwear Analysis*. Chicago: University of Chicago Press.

Keeley, Lawrence H., and M. H. Newcomer. 1977. Microwear analysis of experimental flint tools: A test case. *Journal of Archaeological Science* 4: 29–62.

Kelly, Robert, Lin Poyer, and Bram Tucker. 2006. Mobility and houses in southwestern Madagascar: Ethnoarchaeology among the Mikea and their neighbors. In F. R. Sellet, R. Greaves, and P. L. Yu (Eds.), *Archaeology and*

Ethnoarchaeology of Mobility (pp. 75–107). Gainesville: University Press of Florida.

Kelly, Robert, Jean-François Rabedimy, and Lin A. Poyer. 1999. The Mikea of southwestern Madagascar. In R. B. Lee and R. Daly (Eds.), *The Cambridge Encyclopedia of Hunter-Gatherers* (pp. 215–219). Cambridge: Cambridge University Press.

Koch, Christopher P. (Ed.). 1989. *Taphonomy: A Bibliographic Guide to the Literature*. Orono, ME: Center for the Study of the First Americans.

Kosso, P. 1991. Method in archaeology: Middle-range theory as hermeneutics. *American Antiquity* 56: 621–627.

Kramer, Carol. 1997. *Pottery in Rajasthan: Ethnoarchaeology in Two Indian Cities*. Washington, DC: Smithsonian Institution Press.

Kroeber, Theodora. 1961. *Ishi in Two Worlds: A Biography of the Last Wild Indian in North America*. Berkeley: University of California Press.

Lehner, Mark. 1997. *The Complete Pyramids: Solving the Ancient Mysteries*. London: Thames and Hudson.

Longacre, William A. (Ed.). 1991. *Ceramic Ethnoarchaeology*. Tucson: University of Arizona Press.

Longacre, William A., and James M. Skibo (Eds.). 1994. *Kalinga Ethnoarchaeology: Expanding Archaeological Method and Theory*. Washington, DC: Smithsonian Institution Press.

Moss, Emily. 1983. *The Functional Analysis of Flint Implements—Pincevent and Pont d'Ambon: Two Case Studies From the French Final Palaeolithic*. British Archaeological Reports, International Series, no. 177.

Nelson, Margaret. 1999. *Mimbres During the Twelfth Century: Abandonment, Continuity, and Reorganization*. Tucson: University of Arizona Press.

Newcomer, M. H., and L. H. Keeley. 1979. Testing a method of microwear analysis with experimental flint tools. In Brian Hayden (Ed.), *Lithic Use-Wear Analysis* (pp. 195–205). New York: Academic Press. (Data for Table 10-1 from this publication's Table 1)

O'Connell, James F. 1995. Ethnoarchaeology needs a general theory of behavior. *Journal of Archaeological Research* 3: 205–255.

Odell, George Hanley (Ed.). 1996. *Stone Tools: Theoretical Insights Into Human Prehistory*. New York: Plenum Press.

Odell, George Hanley, and F. Odell-Vereecken. 1980. Verifying the reliability of lithic use-wear assessments by "blind tests": The low power approach. *Journal of Field Archaeology* 7: 87–120.

Perkins, D., Jr., and P. Daly. 1968. A hunter's village in Neolithic Turkey. *Scientific American* 219(5): 96–106.

Pope, Saxton T. 1974. Hunting with Ishi—the last Yana Indian. *Journal of California Anthropology* 1: 152–173.

Poyer, Lin, and Robert Kelly. 2000. Mystification of the Mikea: Constructions of foraging identity in southwest Madagascar. *Journal of Anthropological Research* 56: 163–185.

Raab, L. Mark, and Albert C. Goodyear. 1984. Middle-range theory in archaeology: A critical review of origins and applications. *American Antiquity* 49: 255–268.

Saitta, Dean J. 1992. Radical archaeology and middle-range methodology. *Antiquity* 66: 886–897.

Scheper-Hughes, Nancy. 2002. Ishi's brain, Ishi's ashes: Anthropolology and genocide. *Anthropology Today* 17(1): 12–18.

———. 2003. Ishi's ashes: Anthropology and genocide. In K. Kroeber (Ed.), *Ishi in Three Centuries* (pp. 99–131). Lincoln: University of Nebraska Press.

Schick, Kathy, and Nicholas Toth. 1993. *Making Silent Stones Speak: Human Evolution and the Dawn of Technology*. New York: Touchstone.

Schiffer, Michael B., James M. Skibo, Tamara C. Boelke, Mark A. Neupert, and Meredith Aronson. 1994. New perspectives on experimental archaeology: Surface treatments and thermal response of the clay cooking pot. *American Antiquity* 59: 197–217.

Semenov, Sergei, 1964. *Prehistoric Technology*. Trans. by M. W. Thompson. London: Cory, Adams, and MacKay.

Shea, John J. 1987. On accuracy and relevance in lithic use-wear analysis. *Lithic Technology* 16(2–3): 44–50.

Sheets, Payson D. 1987. Dawn of a new Stone Age in eye surgery. In Robert J. Sharer and Wendy Ashmore (Eds.), *Archaeology: Discovering Our Past* (pp. 230–231). Mountain View, CA: Mayfield Publishing.

Stahl, Ann B. 1995. Has ethnoarchaeology come of age? *Antiquity* 69: 404–407.

Starn, Orin. 2003. *Ishi's Brain: In Search of the Last "Wild" Indian*. San Francisco: W. W. Norton and Company.

Tindale, Norman B. 1985. Australian aboriginal techniques of pressure-flaking stone implements: Some personal observations. In Mark G. Plew, James C. Woods, and Max G. Pavesic (Eds.), *Stone Tool Analysis: Essays in Honor of Don E. Crabtree* (pp. 1–33). Albuquerque: University of New Mexico Press.

Todd, Lawrence C., and David Rapson. 1999. Formational analysis of bison bonebeds and interpretation of Paleoindian subsistence. In J.-P. Brugal, F. David, J. G. Enloe, and J. Jaubert (Eds.), *Le Bison: Gibier et moyen de subsistance des hommes du Paléolithique aux Paléoindiens des Grandes Plains* (pp. 479–499). Antibes, France: Association pour la promotion et la diffusion des connaissances archéologiques.

Trigger, Bruce G. 1981. Archaeology and the ethnographic present. *Anthropologica* 23: 3–17.

———. 1995. Expanding middle-range theory. *Antiquity* 69: 449–458.

Tringham, Ruth, G. Cooper, G. Odell, R. Voiytek, and A. Whitman. 1974. Experimentation in the formation of edge damage: A new approach to lithic analysis. *Journal of Field Archaeology* 1: 171–196.

Tunnell, C. 1977. Fluted projectile point production as revealed by lithic specimens from the Adair-Steadman site in northwest Texas. In Eileen Johnson (Ed.), *Paleoindian Lifeways* (pp. 140–168). Lubbock: Texas Tech University.

Vaughan, Patrick C. 1985. *Use-Wear Analysis of Flaked Stone Tools*. Tucson: University of Arizona Press.

Weedman, Kathryn. 2002. On the spur of the moment: Effects of age and experience on hafted stone scraper morphology. *American Antiquity* 67: 731–744.

White, Theodore E. 1953. A method of calculating the dietary percentage of various food animals utilized by aboriginal peoples. *American Antiquity* 18: 396–398.

————. 1954. Observations on the butchering technique of some aboriginal peoples, nos. 3, 4, 5, and 6. *American Antiquity* 19: 254–264.

Whittaker, John C. 1994. *Flintknapping: Making and Understanding Stone Tools*. Austin: University of Texas Press.

Wilshusen, Richard H., and Glenn D. Stone. 1990. An ethnoarchaeological perspective on soils. *World Archaeology* 22: 104–114.

Wylie, Alison. 1985. The reaction against analogy. In M. B. Schiffer (Ed.), *Advances in Archaeological Method and Theory*. Vol. 8 (pp. 63–112). New York: Academic Press.

Yellen, John E. 1976. Settlement patterns of the !Kung: An archaeological perspective. In R. B. Lee and I. DeVore (Eds.), *Kalahari Hunter-Gatherers* (pp. 47–72). Cambridge, MA: Harvard University Press.

————. 1977. *Archaeological Approaches to the Present: Models for Reconstructing the Past*. New York: Academic Press.

Chapter 9

Adams, Karen R., and Robert E. Gasser. 1980. Plant microfossils from archaeological sites: Research considerations and sampling techniques and approaches. *The Kiva* 45: 293–300.

Betancourt, Julio L., Thomas R. Van Devender, and Paul S. Martin (Eds.). 1990. *Packrat Middens: The Last 40,000 Years of Biotic Change*. Tucson: University of Arizona Press.

Binford, Lewis R. 1978. *Nunamiut Ethnoarchaeology*. New York: Academic Press.

————. 1981. *Bones: Ancient Men and Modern Myths*. New York: Academic Press.

Brewer, Douglas J. 1992. Zooarchaeology: Method, theory, and goals. In M. B. Schiffer (Ed.), *Archaeological Method and Theory*. Vol. 4 (pp. 195–244). Tucson: University of Arizona Press.

Brothwell, D., and A. Pollard (Eds.). 2001. *Handbook of Archaeological Sciences*. Chichester, England: John Wiley and Sons.

Bryant, Vaughn M., Jr., and Stephen A. Hall. 1993. Archaeological palynology in the United States: A critique. *American Antiquity* 58: 277–286.

Bryant, Vaughn M., Jr., and Richard G. Holloway. 1983. The role of palynology in archaeology. In Michael B. Schiffer (Ed.), *Advances in Archaeological Method and Theory*. Vol. 6 (pp. 191–224). New York: Academic Press.

Butler, V. L., and M. G. Delacorte. 2004. Doing zooarchaeology as if it mattered: Use of faunal data to address current issues in fish conservation biology in Owens Valley, California. In R. L. Lyman and K. Cannon (Eds.), *Zooarchaeology and Conservation Biology* (pp. 25–44). Salt Lake City: University of Utah Press.

Crabtree, Pam J. 1990. Zooarchaeology and complex societies: Some uses of faunal analysis for the study of trade, social status, and ethnicity. In M. B. Schiffer (Ed.), *Archaeological Method and Theory*. Vol. 2 (pp. 155–205). Tucson: University of Arizona Press.

Cummings, Linda Scott. 2001. Phytolith analysis. In R. L. Kelly (Ed.), *Prehistory of the Carson Desert and Stillwa-

ter Mountains: Environment, Mobility, and Subsistence in a Great Basin Wetland* (pp. 251–252). Salt Lake City: University of Utah Anthropological Papers 123.

Dincauze, Dena. 2000. *Environmental Archaeology: Principles and Practice*. Cambridge: Cambridge University Press.

Evershed, R. P., S. N. Dudd, M. J. Collins, O. E. Craig, and R. J. Sokal. 2001. Lipids in archaeology. In D. Brothwell and A. Pollard (Eds.), *Handbook of Archaeological Sciences* (pp. 331–350). Chichester, England: John Wiley and Sons.

Faegri, K., P. E. Kaland, and K. Krzywinski. 1989. *Textbook of Pollen Analysis*. 4th ed. New York: Wiley.

Frison, George C., and Dennis Stanford. 1982. *The Agate Basin Site: A Record of the Paleoindian Occupation of the Northwestern High Plains*. New York: Academic Press.

Gilbert, B. Miles. 1980. *Mammalian Osteology*. Laramie, WY: Modern Printing.

Gilbert, Robert I., Jr., and James H. Mielke (Eds.). 1985. *The Analysis of Prehistoric Diets*. Orlando, FL: Academic Press.

Grayson, Donald K. 1984. *Quantitative Zooarchaeology: Topics in the Analysis of Archaeological Faunas*. Orlando, FL: Academic Press.

Harper, K. T., and G. M. Alder. 1970. Appendix I: The macroscopic plant remains of the deposits of Hogup Cave, Utah, and their paleoclimatic implications. In C. Melvin Aikens, *Hogup Cave* (pp. 215–240). Salt Lake City: University of Utah Anthropological Papers 93.

Hastorf, Christine A., and Sissel Johannessen. 1991. Understanding changing people/plant relationships in the prehispanic Andes. In Robert W. Preucel (Ed.), *Processual and Postprocessual Archaeologies: Multiple Ways of Knowing the Past* (pp. 140–155). Carbondale: Southern Illinois University, Center for Archaeological Investigations, Occasional Paper no. 10.

Hastorf, Christine A., and Virginia S. Popper (Eds.). 1988. *Current Paleoethnobotany: Analytical Methods and Cultural Interpretations of Archaeological Plant Remains*. Chicago: University of Chicago Press.

Hather, Jon G. (Ed.). 1994. *Tropical Archaeobotany: Applications and New Developments*. London: Routledge.

Haury, Emil W., E. B. Sayles, and William W. Wasley. 1959. The Lehner mammoth site, southeastern Arizona. *American Antiquity* 25: 2–30.

Hill, Matthew G. 2001. *Paleoindian Diet and Subsistence Behavior on the Northwestern Great Plains of North America*. PhD dissertation, University of Wisconsin, Madison. (Table 9-1 is from p. 55)

————. 2008. *Paleoindian Subsistence Dynamics on the Northwestern Great Plains: Zooarchaeology of the Agate Basin and Clary Ranch Sites*. Oxford: British Archaeological Reports, International Series, no. 1756.

Holden, T. G. 2001. Dietary evidence from the coprolites and the intestinal contents of ancient humans. In D. Brothwell and A. Pollard (Eds.), *Handbook of Archaeological Sciences* (pp. 403–414). Chichester, England: John Wiley and Sons.

Kay, C. E., and R. T. Simmons (Eds.). 2002. *Wilderness and Political Ecology: Aboriginal Influences and the Original State of Nature*. Salt Lake City: University of Utah Press.

Lauwerier, R. C. G. M., and I. Plug (Eds.). 2004. *The Future from the Past: Archaeozoology in Wildlife Conservation and Heritage Management*. Oxford: Oxbow Books.

Leroi-Gourhan, Arlette. 1975. The flowers found with Shanidar IV, a Neanderthal burial in Iraq. *Science* 190: 562–564.

Lyman, R. Lee. 1994. *Vertebrate Taphonomy*. Cambridge: Cambridge University Press.

Malainey, Mary E., R. Przybylski, and B. L. Sherriff. 1999a. The fatty acid composition of native food plants and animals of western Canada. *Journal of Archaeological Science* 26: 83–94.

——. 1999b. The effects of thermal and oxidative decomposition on the fatty acids composition of food plants and animals of western Canada: Implications for the identification of archaeological vessel residues. *Journal of Archaeological Science* 26: 95–103.

——. 1999c. Identifying the former contents of late precontact period pottery vessels from western Canada using gas chromatography. *Journal of Archaeological Science* 26: 425–438.

Mehringer, Peter J., and Vance Haynes. 1965. The pollen evidence for the environment of early man and extinct mammals at the Lehner mammoth site, southeastern Arizona. *American Antiquity* 31: 17–23.

Miksicek, Charles H. 1987. Formation processes of the archaeobotanical record. In Michael B. Schiffer (Ed.), *Advances in Archaeological Method and Theory*. Vol. 10 (pp. 211–247). New York: Academic Press.

Miller, George. 1979. *An Introduction to the Ethnoarchaeology of the Andean Camelids*. PhD dissertation, University of California, Berkeley.

Miller, George, and Richard Burger. 1995. Our father the cayman, our dinner the llama: Animal utilization at Chav'n de Huántar, Peru. *American Antiquity* 60: 421–458.

——. 2000. Ch'arki at Chav'n: Ethnographic models and archaeological data. *American Antiquity* 65: 573–576.

Minnis, Paul E. 1981. Seeds in archaeological sites: Sources and some interpretive problems. *American Antiquity* 46: 143–152.

Monks, Gregory G. 1981. Seasonality studies. In Michael B. Schiffer (Ed.), *Advances in Archaeological Method and Theory*. Vol. 4 (pp. 177–240). New York: Academic Press.

Moore, P. D., J. A. Webb, and M. E. Collinson. 1991. *Pollen Analysis*. Oxford: Blackwell Scientific.

Olsen, Stanley J. 1960. *Post-Cranial Skeletal Characters of Bison and Bos*. Cambridge, MA: Papers of the Peabody Museum of American Archaeology and Ethnology 35(4).

——. 1964. *Mammal Remains from Archaeological Sites, Part 1: Southeastern and Southwestern United States*. Cambridge, MA: Papers of the Peabody Museum of American Archaeology and Ethnology 61(1).

——. 1968. *Fish, Amphibian, and Reptile Remains from Archaeological Sites, Part 1: Southeastern and Southwestern United States*. Cambridge, MA: Papers of the Peabody Museum of American Archaeology and Ethnology 61(2).

——. 1973. *Mammal Remains from Archaeological Sites, Part 1: Southeastern and Southwestern United States*. Cambridge, MA: Papers of the Peabody Museum of Archaeology and Ethnology 56(1).

Pearsall, Deborah M. 2000. *Paleoethnobotany: A Handbook of Procedures*. New York: Academic Press.

Piperno, Dolores R. 1987. *Phytolith Analysis: An Archaeological and Geological Perspective*. San Diego: Academic Press.

Rapp, George, and Susan C. Mulholland (Eds.). 1992. *Phytolith Systematics: Emerging Issues*. New York: Plenum Press.

Reitz, Elizabeth J., and C. Margaret Scarry. 1985. *Reconstructing Historic Subsistence with an Example from Sixteenth-Century Spanish Florida*. Society for Historical Archaeology Special Publication Series 3.

Reitz, Elizabeth J., and Elizabeth Wing. 1999. *Zooarchaeology*. Cambridge: Cambridge University Press.

Rhode, David. 2001. Macrobotanical remains. In R. L. Kelly (Ed.), *Prehistory of the Carson Desert and Stillwater Mountains: Environment, Mobility, and Subsistence in a Great Basin Wetland* (pp. 254–262). Salt Lake City: University of Utah Anthropological Papers 123.

——. 2004. Coprolites from Hidden Cave, revisited: Evidence for occupation history, diet, and gender. *Journal of Archaeological Science* 30: 909–922.

Rovner, Irwin. 1983. Plant opal phytolith analysis: Major advances in archaeobotanical research. In Michael B. Schiffer (Ed.), *Advances in Archaeological Method and Theory*. Vol. 6 (pp. 225–266). New York: Academic Press.

Smith, P., and M. Wilson. 2001. Blood residues in archaeology. In D. Brothwell and A. Pollard (Eds.), *Handbook of Archaeological Sciences* (pp. 313–322). Chichester, England: John Wiley and Sons.

Sobolik, Kristin. 2003. *The Archaeologist's Toolkit: Vol. 5. Archaeobiology*. Walnut Creek, CA: Altamira Press.

Solecki, Ralph S. 1971. *Shanidar: The First Flower People*. New York: Knopf.

Sommer, Jeffrey. 1999. The Shanidar IV "flower burial": A reevaluation of Neanderthal burial ritual. *Cambridge Archaeological Journal* 9: 127–137.

Stahl, Peter. 1999. Structural density of domesticated South American camelid skeletal elements and the archaeological investigation of prehistoric Andean ch'arki. *Journal of Archaeological Science* 26: 1347–1368.

Sutton, Mark Q., Minnie Malik, and Andrew Ogram. 1996. Experiments on the determination of gender from coprolites by DNA analysis. *Journal of Archaeological Science* 23: 263–267.

Valdez, Lidio. 2000. Ch'arki consumption in the ancient central Andes: A cautionary note. *American Antiquity* 65: 567–572.

Wigand, Peter. 2001. Pollen. In R. L. Kelly (Ed.), *Prehistory of the Carson Desert and Stillwater Mountains: Environment, Mobility, and Subsistence in a Great Basin Wetland* (pp. 252–254). Salt Lake City: University of Utah Anthropological Papers 123.

Wigand, Peter, and Cheryl Nowak. 1992. Dynamics of northwest Nevada plant communities during the last 30,000 years. In C. A. Hall, V. Doyle-Jones, and B. Widawski (Eds.), *The History of Water: Eastern Sierra Nevada, Owens Valley, White-Inyo Mountains* (pp. 40–62). White Mountain Research Station Symposium 4.

Chapter 10

Benditt, J. 1989. Molecular archaeology: DNA from a 7,000-year-old brain opens new vistas in prehistory. *Scientific American* 261: 25–26.

Billman, B. R., P. M. Lambert, and B. L. Leonard. 2000. Cannibalism, warfare, and drought in the Mesa Verde region during the twelfth century AD. *American Antiquity* 65: 145–178.

Brooks, Sheilagh, Michele Haldeman, and Richard Brooks. 1988. *Osteological Analyses of the Stillwater Skeletal Series, Stillwater Marsh, Churchill County, Nevada.* U.S. Fish and Wildlife Service Cultural Resource Series Number 2.

Brown, Terence A., and Keri A. Brown. 1992. Ancient DNA and the archaeologist. *Antiquity* 66: 10–23.

Buikstra, Jane E., and Della C. Cook. 1980. Paleopathology: An American account. *Annual Review of Anthropology* 9: 433–470.

Buikstra, Jane E., and L. Konigsberg. 1985. Paleodemography: Critiques and controversies. *American Anthropologist* 87: 316–333.

Cann, Rebecca, Mark Stoneking, and Alan C. Wilson. 1987. Mitochrondrial DNA and human evolution. *Nature* 325: 31–36.

DeNiro, Michael J. 1987. Stable isotopy and archeology. *American Scientist* 75: 182–191.

DeNiro, Michael J., and S. Epstein. 1981. Influence of diet on the distribution of nitrogen isotopes in animals. *Geochimica de Cosmochimica Acta* 45: 341–351.

Dongoske, K. E., D. L. Martin, and T. J. Ferguson. 1999. Critique of the claim of cannibalism at Cowboy Wash. *American Antiquity* 65: 179–190.

Ezzo, Joseph A., Clark Spencer Larsen, and James H. Burton. 1995. Elemental signatures of human diets from the Georgia Bight. *American Journal of Physical Anthropology* 98: 471–481.

Gilbert, M. Thomas P., Dennis L. Jenkins, Anders Götherstrom, Nuria Naveran, Juan J. Sanchez, Michael Hofreiter, Philip Francis Thomsen, Jonas Binladen, Thomas F. G. Higham, Robert M. Yohe II, Robert Parr, Linda Scott Cummings, and Eske Willerslev. 2008. DNA from pre-Clovis human coprolites in Oregon, North America. *Science* 320: 786–789.

Goodman, Alan, and George Armelagos. 1988. Infant and childhood morbidity and mortality risks in archaeological populations. *World Archaeology* 21: 225–243.

Green, R. E., J. Krause, A. W. Briggs, T. Maricic, U. Stenzel, M. Kircher, N. Patterson, H. Li, W. Zhai, M. H.-Y. Fritz, N. F. Hansen, E. Y. Durand, A.-S. Malaspinas, J. D. Jensen, T. Marques-Bonet, C. Alkan, K. Prüfer, M. Meyer, H. A. Burbano, J. M. Good, R. Schultz, A. Aximu-Petri, A. Butthof, B. Höber, B. Höffner, M. Siegemund, A., Weihmann, C. Nusbaum, E. S. Lander, C. Russ, N. Novod, J. Affourtit, M. Egholm, C. Verna, P. Rudan, D. Brajkovic, Z. Kucan, I. Gušic, V. B. Doronichev, L. V. Golovanova, C. Lalueza-Fox, M. de la Rasilla, J. Fortea, A. Rosas, R. W. Schmitz, P. L. F. Johnson, E. E. Eichler, D. Falush, E. Birney, J. C. Mullikin, M. Slatkin, R. Nielsen, J. Kelso, M. Lachmann, D. Reich, and S. Pääbo. 2010. A draft sequence of the Neandertal genome. *Science* 328: 710–722.

Herrmann, Bernd, and Susanne Hummell (Eds.). 1994. *Ancient DNA: Recovery and Analysis of Genetic Material from Paleontological, Archaeological, Museum, Medical, and Forensic Specimens.* New York: Springer-Verlag.

Huss-Ashmore, Rebecca, Alan H. Goodman, and George J. Armelagos. 1982. Nutritional inference from paleopathology. In Michael B. Schiffer (Ed.), *Advances in Archaeological Method and Theory.* Vol. 5 (pp. 395–474). New York: Academic Press.

Hutchinson, Dale, and Clark Spencer Larsen. 1988. Determination of stress episode duration from linear enamel hypoplasias: A case study from St. Catherines Island, Georgia. *Human Biology* 60: 93–110.

———. 1995. Physiological stress in the prehistoric Stillwater Marsh: Evidence of enamel defects. In C. S. Larsen et al., *Bioarchaeology of the Stillwater Marsh: Prehistoric Human Adaptation in the Western Great Basin* (pp. 81–95). New York: Anthropological Papers of the American Museum of Natural History 77.

Jobling, M. A., M. E. Hurles, and C. Tyler-Smith. 2004. *Human Evolutionary Genetics: Origins, People and Disease.* New York: Garland.

Kantner, J. 1999a. Anasazi mutilation and cannibalism in the American southwest. In L. R. Goldman (Ed.), *The Anthropology of Cannibalism* (pp. 75–104). Westport: Bergin and Garvey.

———. 1999b. Survival cannibalism or sociopolitical intimidation? Explaining perimortem mutilation in the American southwest. *Human Nature* 10: 1–50.

Katzenberg, M. Anne, Henry P. Schwarcz, Martin Knyf, and F. Jerome Melbye. 1995. Stable isotope evidence for maize horticulture and paleodiet in southern Ontario, Canada. *American Antiquity* 60: 335–350.

Konigsberg, Lyle W., and Jane E. Buikstra. 1995. Regional approaches to the investigation of past human biocultural structure. In Lane Anderson Beck (Ed.), *Regional Approaches to Mortuary Analysis* (pp. 191–219). New York: Plenum Press.

Kuckelman, K. A., R. R. Lightfoot, and D. L. Martin. 2002. The bioarchaeology and taphonomy of violence at Castle Rock and Sand Creek Pueblos, southwestern Colorado. *American Antiquity* 67: 486–511.

Lambert, P. M., B. L. Leonard, B. R. Billman, R. A. Marlar, M. E. Newman, and K. J. Reinhard. 2000. Response to critique of the claim of cannibalism at Cowboy Wash. *American Antiquity* 65: 397–403.

Larsen, Clark Spencer. 1987. Bioarchaeological interpretations of subsistence economy and behavior from human skeletal remains. In Michael B. Schiffer (Ed.), *Advances in Archaeological Method and Theory.* Vol. 10 (pp. 339–445). Orlando, FL: Academic Press.

———. 1995. Biological changes in human populations with agriculture. *Annual Review of Anthropology* 24: 185–213.

Larsen, Clark Spencer, and Robert L. Kelly. 1995. *Bioarchaeology of the Stillwater Marsh: Prehistoric Human Adaptation in the Western Great Basin.* New York:

Anthropological Papers of the American Museum of Natural History 77.

Larsen, Clark Spencer, Christopher B. Ruff , and Robert L. Kelly. 1995. Structural analysis of the Stillwater post-cranial human remains: Behavioral implications of articular joint pathology and long bone diaphyseal morphology. In C. S. Larsen and R. L. Kelly, *Bioarchaeology of the Stillwater Marsh: Prehistoric Human Adaptation in the Western Great Basin* (pp. 107–133). New York: Anthropological Papers of the American Museum of Natural History 77.

Marlar, R. A., B. L. Leonard, B. R. Billman, P. M. Lambert, and J. E. Marlar. 2000. Biochemical evidence of cannibalism at a prehistoric site in southwestern Colorado. *Nature* 407: 74–78.

Martin, Debra L., Alan H. Goodman, and George J. Armelagos. 1985. Skeletal pathologies as indicators of quality and quantity of diet. In Robert I. Gilbert and James H. Mielke (Eds.), *The Analysis of Prehistoric Diets* (pp. 227–279). Orlando: Academic Press.

Nei, Masatoshi. 1992. Age of the common ancestor of human mitochondrial DNA. *Molecular Biology and Evolution* 9: 1176–1178.

Ortner, Donald J., and Walter G. J. Putschar. 1985. *Identification of Pathological Conditions in Human Skeletal Remains.* Washington, DC: Smithsonian Institution Press.

Pääbo, Svante. 1993, November. Ancient DNA: Genetic information that had seemed lost forever turns out to linger in the remains of long-dead plants and animals. *Scientific American*, pp. 87–92.

Powell, Mary Lucas. 1985. The analysis of dental wear and caries for dietary reconstructions. In R. I. Gilbert, Jr., and J. H. Mielke (Eds.), *The Analysis of Prehistoric Diets* (pp. 307–338). Orlando: Academic Press.

Price, T. Douglas (Ed.). 1989. *The Chemistry of Prehistoric Human Bone.* Cambridge: Cambridge University Press.

Price, T. Douglas, Vera Tiesler, and James H. Burton. 2006. Early African diaspora in colonial Campeche, Mexico: Strontium isotope evidence. *American Journal of Physical Anthropology* 130: 485–490.

Rogers, Juliet, and Tony Waldron. 1989. Infections in paleopathology: The basis of classification according to most probable cause. *Journal of Archaeological Science* 16: 611–625.

Rothschild, Bruce M., and Larry D. Martin. 1993. *Palaeopathology: Disease in the Fossil Record.* Boca Raton, FL: CRC Press.

Sahlins, Marshall. 1968. Notes on the original affluent society. In Richard Lee and Irven DeVore (Eds.), *Man the Hunter* (pp. 85–89). Chicago: Aldine.

Schoeninger, Margaret. 1995. Dietary reconstruction in the prehistoric Carson Desert: Stable carbon and nitrogen isotopic analysis. In C. S. Larsen et al., *Bioarchaeology of the Stillwater Marsh: Prehistoric Human Adaptation in the Western Great Basin* (pp. 96–106). New York: Anthropological Papers of the American Museum of Natural History 77.

Stoneking, Mark. 1994. In defense of "Eve": A response to Templeton's critique. *American Anthropologist* 96: 131–141.

Templeton, Alan R. 1993. The "Eve" hypotheses: A genetic critique and reanalysis. *American Anthropologist* 95: 51–72.

———. 1994. "Eve": Hypothesis compatibility versus hypothesis testing. *American Anthropologist* 96: 141–147.

Turner, Christy G., II, and Jacqueline A. Turner. 1999. *Man Corn: Cannibalism and Violence in the Prehistoric American Southwest.* Salt Lake City: University of Utah Press.

Verano, John W., and Douglas H. Ubelaker (Eds.). 1992. *Disease and Demography in the Americas.* Washington, DC: Smithsonian Institution Press.

Walker, Phillip L. 1986. Porotic hyperostosis in a marine-dependent California Indian population. *American Journal of Physical Anthropology* 69: 345–354.

White, T. D. 1992. *Prehistoric Cannibalism at Mancos 5MTUMR-2346.* Princeton: Princeton University Press.

Chapter 11

Alkire, William. 1977. *An Introduction to the Peoples and Cultures of Micronesia.* 2d ed. Menlo Park, CA: Cummings.

Bacus, Elisabeth A., Alex W. Barker, Jeffrey D. Bonevich, Sandra L. Dunavan, J. Benjamin Fitzhugh, Debra L. Gold, Nurit S. Goldman-Finn, William Griffin, and Karen M. Mudar (Eds.). 1993. *A Gendered Past: A Critical Bibliography of Gender in Archaeology.* Ann Arbor: University of Michigan, Museum of Anthropology, Technical Report 25.

Bailey, Robert C., and Robert Aunger. 1989. Hunters vs. archers: Variation in women's subsistence strategies in the Ituri Forest. *Human Ecology* 17: 273–297.

Beck, Lane Anderson (Ed.). 1995. *Regional Approaches to Mortuary Analysis.* New York: Plenum Press.

Benson, Larry, Linda Cordell, Kirk Vincent, Howard Taylor, John Stein, G. Lang Farmer, and Kiyoto Futa. 2003. Ancient maize from Chacoan Great Houses: Where was it grown? *Proceedings of the National Academy of Sciences* 100: 13111–13115.

Claassen, Cheryl (Ed.). 1992. *Exploring Gender Through Archaeology: Selected Papers from the 1991 Boone Conference.* Monographs in World Archaeology no. 11. Madison, WI: Prehistory Press.

Cobb, Charles R. 1993. Archaeological approaches to the political economy of nonstratified societies. In M. B. Schiffer (Ed.), *Archaeological Method and Theory.* Vol. 5 (pp. 43–100). Tucson: University of Arizona Press.

Conkey, Margaret W., and Janet Spector. 1984. Archaeology and the study of gender. In Michael B. Schiffer (Ed.), *Advances in Archaeological Method and Theory.* Vol. 7 (pp. 1–38). Orlando, FL: Academic Press.

Costin, Cathy Lynne, and Timothy Earle. 1989. Status distinction and legitimation of power as reflected in changing patterns of consumption in late prehispanic Peru. *American Antiquity* 54: 691–714.

DeNiro, Michael J., and Margaret J. Schoeniger. 1983. Stable carbon and nitrogen isotope ratios of bone collagen:

Variations within individuals, between sexes, and within populations raised on monotonous diets. *Journal of Archaeological Science* 10: 199–203.

Descantes, Christophe, Hector Neff, Michael D. Glascock, and William R. Dickinson. 2001. Chemical characterization of Micronesian ceramics through instrumental neutron activation analysis: A preliminary provenance study. *Journal of Archaeological Science* 28: 1185–1190.

Dickinson, W. R., and R. Shutler, Jr. 2000. Implications of petrographic temper analysis for Oceanic prehistory. *Journal of World Prehistory* 14: 203–266.

Ember, Melvin. 1973. An archaeological indicator of matrilocal versus patrilocal residence. *American Antiquity* 38: 177–182.

Ember, Melvin, and Carol Ember. 1995. Worldwide cross-cultural studies and their relevance for archaeology. *Journal of Archaeological Research* 30: 69–94.

Enloe, James. 2003. Food sharing past and present: Archaeological evidence for economic and social interactions. *Before Farming* 1: 1–23.

Enloe, James, and Francine David. 1992. Food sharing in the Paleolithic: Carcass refitting at Pincevent. In J. L. Hofman and J. G. Enloe (Eds.), *Piecing Together the Past: Applications of Refitting Studies in Archaeology* (pp. 296–315). Oxford: British Archaeological Reports, International Series, no. 578.

Fitzpatrick, Scott M., William R. Dickinson, and Geoffrey Clark. 2003. Ceramic petrography and cultural interaction in Palau, Micronesia. *Journal of Archaeological Science* 30: 1175–1184.

Galloway, Patricia (Ed.). 1989. *The Southeastern Ceremonial Complex: Artifacts and Analysis*. Lincoln: University of Nebraska Press.

Gargett, R., and B. Hayden. 1991. Site structure, kinship, and sharing in Aboriginal Australia: Implications for archaeology. In E. M. Kroll and T. D. Price (Eds.), *The Interpretation of Archaeological Spatial Patterning* (pp. 11–32). New York: Plenum Press.

Gero, Joan M. 1985. Sociopolitics and the woman-at-home ideology. *American Antiquity* 50: 342–350.

———. 1991. Genderlithics: Women's roles in stone tool production. In Joan M. Gero and Margaret W. Conkey (Eds.), *Engendering Archaeology: Women and Prehistory* (pp. 163–193). Oxford: Basil Blackwell.

Gero, Joan M., and Margaret W. Conkey (Eds.). 1991. *Engendering Archaeology: Women and Prehistory*. Oxford: Basil Blackwell.

Gibson, Alex M., and Ann Woods. 1990. *Prehistoric Pottery for the Archaeologist*. Leicester, England: Leicester University Press.

Goodenough, Ward H. 1965. Rethinking "status" and "role": Toward a general model of the cultural organization of social relationships. In Michael Banton (Ed.), *The Relevance of Models for Social Anthropology* (pp. 1–24). Association for Social Anthropology Monographs no. 1. New York: Praeger.

Griffin, James B., A. A. Gordus, and G. A. Wright. 1969. Identification of the sources of Hopewellian obsidian in the Middle West. *American Antiquity* 34: 1–14.

Hastorf, Christine. 1991. Gender, space and food in prehistory. In Joan Gero and Margaret Conkey (Eds.), *Engendering Archaeology: Women and Prehistory* (pp. 132–158). Oxford: Basil Blackwell.

Hatch, James W., Joseph W. Michels, Christopher M. Stevenson, Barry E. Scheeta, and Richard A. Geidel. 1988. Hopewell obsidian studies: Behavioral implications of recent sourcing and dating research. *American Antiquity* 55: 461–479.

Houston, S. D., and P. A. McAnany. 2003. Bodies and blood: Critiquing social construction in Maya archaeology. *Journal of Anthropological Archaeology* 22: 26–41.

Hughes, Richard E. 2006. The sources of Hopewell obsidian: Thirty years after Griffin. In Douglas K. Charles and Jane E. Buikstra (Eds.), *Recreating Hopewell* (pp. 361–375). Gainesville: University Press of Florida.

Jackson, Ed, and Susan Scott. 2003. Patterns of elite faunal utilization at Moundville, Alabama. *American Antiquity* 69: 552–572.

Joyce, Rosemary. 1995. The construction of gender in Classic Maya monuments. In Rita Wright (Ed.), *Gender and Archaeology* (pp. 167–195). Philadelphia: University of Pennsylvania Press.

Knight, Vernon, J., Jr. 1998. Moundville as a diagrammatic ceremonial center. In V. J. Knight, Jr., and V. Steponaitis (Eds.), *Archaeology of the Moundville Chiefdom* (pp. 44–62). Washington, DC: Smithsonian Institution Press.

Knight, Vernon, J., Jr., and Vincas Steponaitis. 1998. *Archaeology of the Moundville Chiefdom*. Washington, DC: Smithsonian Institution Press.

Mills, Barbara. 1999. Recent research on Chaco: Changing views on economy, ritual, and society. *Journal of Archaeological Research* 10: 65–117.

Nelson, Sarah M. 1995. *Gender in Archaeology: Analyzing Power and Prestige*. Walnut Creek, CA: Altamira Press.

Orton, Clive, Paul Tyers, and Alan Vince. 1993. *Pottery in Archaeology*. Cambridge: Cambridge University Press.

O'Shea, John M. 1984. *Mortuary Variability: An Archaeological Investigation*. Orlando: Academic Press.

Parker Pearson, Michael. 1982. Mortuary practices, society and ideology: An ethnoarchaeological study. In Ian Hodder (Ed.), *Symbolic and Structural Archaeology* (pp. 99–113). Cambridge: Cambridge University Press.

———. 1995. Return of the living dead: Mortuary analysis and the new archaeology revisited. *Antiquity* 69: 1046–1048.

Peebles, Christopher S. 1971. Moundville and surrounding sites: Some structural considerations of mortuary practices II. In James A. Brown (Ed.), *Approaches to the Social Dimensions of Mortuary Practices* (pp. 68–91). Washington, DC: Society for American Archaeology Memoir 25.

———. 1977. Biocultural adaptation in prehistoric America: An archeologist's perspective. In Robert L. Blakely (Ed.), *Biocultural Adaptation in Prehistoric America* (pp. 115–130). Southern Anthropological Society Proceedings no. 11. Athens: University of Georgia Press.

———. 1981. Archaeological research at Moundville: 1840–1980. *Southeastern Archaeological Conference Bulletin* 24: 77–81.

———. 1987. Moundville from 1000 to 1500 AD as seen from 1840 to 1985 AD. In Robert D. Drennan and Carlos A. Uribe (Eds.), *Chiefdoms in the Americas* (pp. 21–41). Lanham, MD: University Press of America.

Peebles, Christopher S., and Susan M. Kus. 1977. Some archaeological correlates of ranked societies. *American Antiquity* 42: 421–448.

Peregrine, Peter. 2000. Matrilocality, corporate strategy, and the organization of production in the Chacoan world. *American Antiquity* 66: 36–46.

Powell, Mary L. 1988. *Status and Health in Prehistory: A Case Study of the Moundville Chiefdom.* Washington, DC: Smithsonian Institution Press.

———. 1991. Rank, status and health in the Mississippian chiefdom at Moundville. In Mary L. Powell, Patricia S. Bridges, and Ann Marie Wagner Mires (Eds.), *What Mean These Bones? Studies in Southeastern Bioarchaeology* (pp. 22–51). Tuscaloosa: University of Alabama Press.

Price, T. Douglas, and Gary M. Feinman (Eds.). 1995. *Foundations of Social Inequality.* New York: Plenum Press.

Renfrew, Colin, and Stephen Shennan (Eds.). 1982. *Ranking, Resource and Exchange.* Cambridge: Cambridge University Press.

Rice, Prudence M. 1987. *Pottery Analysis: A Sourcebook.* Chicago: University of Chicago Press.

———. 1991. Women and prehistoric pottery production. In D. Walde and N. Willows (Eds.), *The Archaeology of Gender* (pp. 436–443). Calgary: Archaeological Association of the University of Calgary.

———. 1996a. Recent ceramic analysis: 1. Function, style, and origins. *Journal of Archaeological Research* 4: 133–163.

———. 1996b. Recent ceramic analysis: 2. Composition, production, and theory. *Journal of Archaeological Research* 4: 165–202.

Schillaci, Michael, and Christopher Stojanowski. 2000. Postmarital residence and population structure at Pueblo Bonito. *American Journal of Physical Anthropology* Supplement 30: 271.

———. 2002. A reassessment of matrilocality in Chacoan culture. *American Antiquity* 67: 343–356.

Schoeninger, Margaret J., and Christopher Peebles. 1981. Notes on the relationship between social status and diet at Moundville. *Southeastern Archaeological Conference Bulletin* 24: 96–97.

Schoeninger, Margaret J., and Mark Schurr. 1999. Human subsistence at Moundville: The stable isotope data. In V. J. Knight, Jr., and V. Steponaitis (Eds.), *Archaeology of the Moundville Chiefdom* (pp. 120–132). Washington, DC: Smithsonian Institution Press.

Sinopoli, Carla. 1991. *Approaches to Archaeological Ceramics.* New York: Plenum Press.

Smith, Bruce D. (Ed.). 1990. *The Mississippian Emergence.* Washington, DC: Smithsonian Institution Press.

Steponaitis, Vincas P. 1983. *Ceramics, Chronology, and Community Patterns: An Archaeological Study at Moundville.* New York: Academic Press.

Waring, A. J., Jr., and Preston Holder. 1945. A prehistoric ceremonial complex in the southeastern United States. *American Anthropologist* 47: 1–34.

Wason, Paul K. 1994. *The Archaeology of Rank.* Cambridge: Cambridge University Press.

Webb, William S. 1974. *Indian Knoll.* Knoxville: University of Tennesse Press. (Quote from p. 330)

Welch, Paul D., and C. Margaret Scarry. 1995. Status-related variation in foodways in the Moundville chiefdom. *American Antiquity* 60: 397–419.

Wright, Rita (Ed.). 1996. *Gender and Archaeology.* Philadelphia: University of Pennsylvania Press.

Wylie, Alison. 1992. The interplay of evidential constraints and political interests: Recent archaeological research on gender. *American Antiquity* 57: 15–35.

Chapter 12

Anyon, Roger, T. J. Ferguson, Loretta Jackson, Lillie Lane, and Philip Vicenti. 1997. Native American oral tradition and archaeology: Issues of structure, relevance, and respect. In Nina Swidler, Kurt E. Dongoske, Roger Anyon, and Alan S. Downer (Eds.), *Native Americans and Archaeologists: Stepping Stones to Common Ground* (pp. 77–87). Walnut Grove, CA: Altamira Press.

Bahn, Paul. 1998. *The Cambridge Illustrated History of Prehistoric Art.* Cambridge: Cambridge University Press.

Bender, Barbara. 1993. Cognitive archaeology and cultural materialism. *Cambridge Archaeological Journal* 3: 257–260.

Burger, Richard L. 1992. *Chavín and the Origins of Andean Civilization.* London: Thames and Hudson.

Conrad, Geoffrey W. 1981. Cultural materialism, split inheritance, and the expansion of ancient Peruvian empires. *American Antiquity* 46: 3–26.

Conrad, Geoffrey W., and Arthur A. Demarest. 1984. *Religion and Empire: The Dynamics of Aztec and Inca Expansionism.* Cambridge: Cambridge University Press.

D'Altroy, Terence N. 1992. *Provincial Power in the Inka Empire.* Washington, DC: Smithsonian Institution Press.

D'Andrade, Roy G. 1995. *The Development of Cognitive Anthropology.* Cambridge: Cambridge University Press.

Douglas, Mary. 1973. *Natural Symbols.* New York: Pelican Books.

Echo-Hawk, Roger. 2000. Ancient history in the New World: Integrating oral traditions and the archaeological record in deep time. *American Antiquity* 65: 267–290.

Flannery, Kent V., and Joyce Marcus. 1993. Cognitive archaeology. *Cambridge Archaeological Journal* 3: 260–270.

Hall, Robert L. 1977. An anthropocentric perspective for eastern United States prehistory. *American Antiquity* 42: 499–518.

———. 1997. *An Archaeology of the Soul: North American Indian Belief and Ritual.* Urbana: University of Illinois Press.

Kehoe, Alice B., and Thomas F. Kehoe. 1973. Cognitive models for archaeological interpretation. *American Antiquity* 38: 150–154.

Laming-Emperaire, Annette. 1962. *La signification de l'art rupestre paléolithique.* Paris: Picard.

Lathrap, Donald W. 1973. Gifts of the cayman: Some thoughts on the subsistence basis of Chavín. In Donald W. Lathrap and Jody Douglas (Eds.), *Variation in Anthropology* (pp. 91–105). Urbana: Illinois Archaeological Survey.

——. 1977. Our father the cayman, our mother the gourd: Spinden revisited, or a unitary model for the emergence of agriculture in the New World. In Charles A. Reed (Ed.), *Origins of Agriculture* (pp. 713–751). The Hague: Mouton.

——. 1985. Jaws: The control of power in the early nuclear American ceremonial center. In C. B. Donnan (Ed.), *Early Ceremonial Architecture in the Andes* (pp. 241–267). Washington, DC: Dumbarton Oaks Research Library and Collection.

Leroi-Gourhan, André. 1968. *The Art of Prehistoric Man in Western Europe*. London: Thames and Hudson.

——. 1980. *Treasures of Prehistoric Art*. Translated from the French by Norbert Guterman. New York: Harry H. Abrams.

——. 1982. *The Dawn of European Art: An Introduction to Palaeolithic Cave Painting*. Cambridge: Cambridge University Press.

Lewis-Williams, David. 2002. *The Mind in the Cave*. London: Thames and Hudson.

Marcus, Joyce, and Kent Flannery. 1996. *Zapotec Civilization*. London: Thames and Hudson.

Mason, Ronald. 2000. Archaeology and Native North American oral traditions. *American Antiquity* 65: 239–266.

Mithen, Steven. 1995. Palaeolithic archaeology and the evolution of mind. *Journal of Archaeological Research* 3: 305–332.

Renfrew, Colin. 1982. *Towards an Archaeology of the Mind: An Inaugural Lecture Delivered Before the University of Cambridge on 30 November 1982*. Cambridge: Cambridge University Press.

——. 1993. Cognitive archaeology: Some thoughts on the archaeology of thought. *Cambridge Archaeological Journal* 3: 248–250.

Renfrew, Colin, and Ezra B. W. Zubrow (Eds.). 1994. *The Ancient Mind: Elements of Cognitive Archaeology*. Cambridge: Cambridge University Press.

Valladas, Hélène. 2003. Direct radiocarbon dating of prehistoric cave paintings by accelerator mass spectrometry. *Measurement Science and Technology* 14: 1487–1492.

Von Hagen, Adriana, and Craig Morris. 1998. *The Cities of the Ancient Andes*. London: Thames and Hudson.

Whiteley, Peter. 2002. Archaeology and oral tradition: The scientific importance of dialogue. *American Antiquity* 67: 405–415.

Chapter 13

Bar-Yosef, Ofer. 1998. The Natufian culture in the Levant, threshold to the origins of agriculture. *Evolutionary Anthropology* 6: 159–177.

Bar-Yosef, Ofer, and R. H. Meadow. 1995. The origins of agriculture in the Near East. In T. Douglas Price and Anne B. Gebauer (Eds.), *Last Hunters, First Farmers: New Perspectives on the Prehistoric Transition to Agriculture* (pp. 39–94). Santa Fe: School of American Research Press.

Bender, Barbara. 1978. Gatherer-hunter to farmer: A social perspective. *World Archaeology* 10: 204–222.

Bettinger, Robert L. 1991. *Hunter-Gatherers: Archaeological and Evolutionary Theory*. New York: Plenum Press.

Binford, Lewis R. 1968. Post-Pleistocene adaptations. In Sally R. Binford and Lewis R. Binford (Eds.), *New Perspectives in Archeology* (pp. 313–341). Chicago: Aldine.

Blanton, Richard E., Stephen A. Kowalewski, Gary Feinman, and Jill Appel. 1981. *Ancient Mesoamerica: A Comparison of Change in Three Regions*. Cambridge: Cambridge University Press.

Boserup, Ester. 1965. *Conditions of Agricultural Growth: The Economics of Agrarian Change Under Population Pressure*. Chicago: Aldine.

Boyd, Robert, and Peter J. Richerson. 1985. *Culture and the Evolutionary Process*. Chicago: University of Chicago Press.

Braidwood, Robert J. 1959. Archeology and the evolutionary theory. In B. J. Meggers (Ed.), *Evolution and Anthropology: A Centennial Appraisal* (pp. 76–89). Washington, DC: Anthropological Society of Washington.

Carmichael, David L., Jane Hubert, Brian Reeves, and Audhild Schanche (Eds.). 1994. *Sacred Sites, Sacred Places*. One World Archaeology, Vol. 23. London: Routledge.

Carneiro, Robert L. 1970. A theory of the origin of the state. *Science* 169: 733–738. (Quote is from p. 734)

——. 1988. The circumscription theory: Challenge and response. *American Behavioral Scientist* 31: 497–511.

Childe, V. Gordon. 1951. *Man Makes Himself*. New York: New American Library.

Coe, Michael. 1996. *The Maya*. 6th ed. London: Thames and Hudson.

Cohen, Mark Nathan. 1977. *The Food Crisis in Prehistory: Overpopulation and the Origins of Agriculture*. New Haven: Yale University Press.

——. 1981. The ecological basis of new world state formation: General and local model building. In Grant D. Jones and Robert R. Kautz (Eds.), *The Transition to Statehood in the New World* (pp. 105–122). Cambridge: Cambridge University Press.

Cowan, C. Wesley, and Patty Jo Watson (Eds.). 1992. *The Origins of Agriculture: An International Perspective*. Washington, DC: Smithsonian Institution Press.

Cowgill, George L. 1975a. On the causes and consequences of ancient and modern population changes. *American Anthropologist* 77: 505–525.

——. 1975b. Population pressure as a non-explanation. In A. Swelund (Ed.), *Population Studies in Archaeology and Biological Anthropology: A Symposium* (pp. 127–131). Washington, DC: Society for American Archaeology Memoir 33.

——. 1988. Comment on "Ecological Theory and Cultural Evolution in the Valley of Oaxaca" by William T. Sanders and Deborah L. Nichols. *Current Anthropology* 29: 54–55.

Darwin, Charles. 1958 . *The Origin of Species*. New York: The New American Library.

Demarest, Arthur A. 1989. Ideology and evolutionism in American archaeology: Looking beyond the economic base. In C. C. Lamberg-Karlovsky (Ed.), *Archaeological Thought in America* (pp. 89–102). Cambridge: Cambridge University Press.

Demarest, Arthur A., and Geoffrey W. Conrad (Eds.). 1992. *Ideology and Pre-Columbian Civilizations*. Santa Fe: School of American Research Press.

Diamond, Jared. 1988. The golden age that never was. *Discover* 9(12): 70–79.

Dunnell, Robert C. 1980. Evolutionary theory and archaeology. In Michael B. Schiffer (Ed.), *Advances in Archaeological Method and Theory*. Vol. 3 (pp. 35–99). New York: Academic Press.

———. 1989. Aspects of the application of evolutionary theory in archaeology. In C. C. Lamberg-Karlovsky (Ed.), *Archaeological Thought in America* (pp. 35–49). Cambridge: Cambridge University Press.

Durham, William. 1981. Overview: Optimal foraging analysis in human ecology. In Bruce Winterhalder and Eric Alden Smith (Eds.), *Hunter-Gatherer Foraging Strategies: Ethnographic and Archaeological Analyses* (pp. 218–232). Chicago: University of Chicago Press.

———. 1990. Advances in evolutionary culture theory. *Annual Review of Anthropology* 19: 187–210.

———. 1992. Applications of evolutionary culture theory. *Annual Review of Anthropology* 21: 331–355.

Earle, Timothy K. (Ed.). 1991. *Chiefdoms: Power, Economy, and Ideology*. Cambridge: Cambridge University Press.

Earle, Timothy K., Terence D'Altroy, Cathy LeBlanc, Christine Hastorf, and Terry Levine. 1980. Changing settlement patterns in the Yanamarca Valley, Peru. *Journal of New World Archaeology* 4: 1–49.

Ehrenreich, Robert M., Carole L. Crumley, and Janet E. Levy (Eds.). 1995. *Heterarchy and the Analysis of Complex Societies*. Washington, DC: Archeological Papers of the American Anthropological Association no. 6.

Fedick, Scott L. 1995. Indigenous agriculture in the Americas. *Journal of Archaeological Research* 3: 257–303.

Flannery, Kent V. 1965. The ecology of early food production in Mesopotamia. *Science* 147: 1247–1255.

———. 1966. The postglacial "readaptation" as viewed from Mesoamerica. *American Antiquity* 31: 800–805.

———. 1969. Origins and ecological effects of early domestication in Iran and the Near East. In P. J. Ucko and G. W. Dimbleby (Eds.), *The Domestication and Exploitation of Plants and Animals* (pp. 73–100). Chicago: Aldine.

———. 1972. The cultural evolution of civilizations. *Annual Review of Ecology and Systematics* 3: 399–426. (Quote is from pp. 403–404)

———. 1973. The origins of agriculture. *Annual Review of Anthropology* 2: 271–310.

Fried, Morton H. 1967. *The Evolution of Political Society*. New York: Random House.

Fritz, Gayle J. 1990. Multiple pathways to farming in precontact eastern North America. *Journal of World Prehistory* 4: 387–435.

Harner, Michael J. 1970. Population pressure and the social evolution of agriculturalists. *Southwestern Journal of Anthropology* 26: 67–86.

Harris, David R. 1972. The origins of agriculture in the tropics. *American Scientist* 60: 180–193.

———. 1994. Agricultural origins, beginnings and transitions: The quest continues. *Antiquity* 69: 873–877.

Harris, David R., and Gordon C. Hillman (Eds.). 1989. *Foraging and Farming: The Evolution of Plant Exploitation*. London: Unwin Hyman.

Harrison, Peter D. 1981. Some aspects of preconquest settlement in southern Quintana Roo, Mexico. In Wendy Ashmore (Ed.), *Lowland Maya Settlement Patterns* (pp. 259–286). Albuquerque: University of New Mexico Press.

Hawkes, Kristen, and James F. O'Connell. 1985. Optimal foraging models and the case of the !Kung. *American Anthropologist* 87: 401–405.

Hawkes, Kristen, James F. O'Connell, and N. Blurton Jones. 1987. Hardworking Hadza grandmothers. In R. Foley and V. Standen (Eds.), *Comparative Socioecology of Mammals and Man* (pp. 341–366). London: Basil Blackwell.

Hayden, Brian. 1990. Nimrods, piscators, pluckers, and planters: The emergence of food production. *Journal of Anthropological Archaeology* 9: 31–69.

———. 1995. A new overview of domestication. In T. Douglas Price and Anne B. Gebauer (Eds.), *Last Hunters, First Farmers: New Perspectives on the Prehistoric Transition to Agriculture* (pp. 273–300). Santa Fe: School of American Research Press.

Hill, Kim, and Kristen Hawkes. 1983. Neotropical hunting among the Aché of eastern Paraguay. In R. Hames and W. Vickers (Eds.), *Adaptive Responses of Native Amazonians* (pp. 139–188). New York: Academic Press.

Houston, S. D. 2000. Into the minds of ancients: Advances in Maya glyph studies. *Journal of World Prehistory* 14: 121–201.

Houston, S. D., and Patricia McAnany. 2003. Bodies and blood: Critiquing social construction in Maya archaeology. *Journal of Anthropological Archaeology* 22: 26–41.

Hunt, Terry. 2007. Rethinking Easter Island's ecological catastrophe. *Journal of Archaeological Science* 34: 485–502.

Johnson, Allen W., and Timothy Earle. 1987. *The Evolution of Human Societies: From Foraging Group to Agrarian State*. Stanford: Stanford University Press.

Keegan, William F. 1986. The optimal foraging analysis of horticultural production. *American Anthropologist* 88: 92–107.

Kelly, Robert L. 1995. *The Foraging Spectrum*. Washington, DC: Smithsonian Institution Press.

Kirch, Patrick. 2004. Oceanic islands: Microcosms of "global change." In C. L. Redman, S. R. James, P. R. Fish, and J. D. Rogers (Eds.), *The Archaeology of Global Change: The Impact of Humans on Their Environment* (pp. 13–27). Washington, DC: Smithsonian Books.

Lee, Richard B. 1979. *The !Kung San: Men, Women and Work in a Foraging Society*. Cambridge: Cambridge University Press. (Quote is from the frontispiece)

Lee, Richard B., and Irven DeVore (Eds.). 1968. *Man the Hunter*. Chicago: Aldine.

Lees, Susan H. 1994. Irrigation and society. *Journal of Archaeological Research* 2: 361–378.

Lubbock, Sir John. 1865. *Pre-historic Times, as Illustrated by Ancient Remains, and the Manners and Customs of Modern Savages*. London: Williams and Norgate.

Manzanilla, Linda. 2001. State formation in the New World. In Gary Feinman and T. Douglas Price (Eds.), *Archaeology at the Millennium: A Sourcebook* (pp. 381–414). New York: Kluwer Academic/Plenum.

Marcus, Joyce. 1992. *Mesoamerican Writing Systems: Propaganda, Myth, and History in Four Ancient Civilizations.* Princeton: Princeton University Press.

———. 2003. Recent advances in Maya archaeology. *Journal of Archaeological Research* 11: 71–148.

McAnany, Patricia. 1995. *Living with the Ancestors: Kinship and Kingship in Ancient Maya Society.* Austin: University of Texas Press.

O'Connell, James F., and Kristen Hawkes. 1981. Alyawara plant use and optimal foraging theory. In Bruce Winterhalder and Eric Alden Smith (Eds.), *Hunter-Gatherer Foraging Strategies: Ethnographic and Archaeological Analyses* (pp. 99–125). Chicago: University of Chicago Press.

Redman, Charles. 1999. *Human Impact on Ancient Environments.* Tucson: University of Arizona Press.

Richerson, Peter J., Robert Boyd, and Robert Bettinger. 2001. Was agriculture impossible during the Pleistocene but mandatory during the Holocene? A climate change hypothesis. *American Antiquity* 66: 387–411.

Rindos, David. 1984. *The Origins of Agriculture: An Evolutionary Perspective.* Orlando, FL: Academic Press.

Sahlins, Marshall D., and Elman R. Service. 1960. *Evolution and Culture.* Ann Arbor: University of Michigan Press.

Scarborough, Vernon. 1994. Maya water management. *National Geographic Research and Exploration* 10(2): 184–199.

Service, Elman. 1971. *Primitive Social Organization: An Evolutionary Perspective.* 2d ed. New York: Random House.

———. 1975. *Origins of the State and Civilization: The Process of Cultural Evolution.* New York: Norton.

Simms, Steven, and Kenneth Russell. 1997. Bedouin hand harvesting of wheat and barley: Implications for early cultivation in southwestern Asia. *Current Anthropology* 38: 696–702.

Smith, Bruce D. 1992. *Rivers of Change: Essays on Early Agriculture in Eastern North America.* Washington, DC: Smithsonian Institution Press.

———. 2001. The transition to food production. In Gary Feinman and T. Douglas Price (Eds.), *Archaeology at the Millennium: A Sourcebook* (pp. 199–230). New York: Kluwer Academic/Plenum.

Smith, Eric Alden. 1991. *Inujjuamiut Foraging Strategies: Evolutionary Ecology of an Arctic Hunting Economy.* New York: Aldine de Gruyter.

Smith, Eric Alden, and Bruce Winterhalder (Eds.). 1992. *Evolutionary Ecology and Human Behavior.* New York: Aldine de Gruyter.

Spencer, Charles. 1990. On the tempo and mode of state formation: Neoevolutionism reconsidered. *Journal of Anthropological Archaeology* 9: 1–30.

Tallbull, William. 1994. Archaeological sites or sacred places? Native American perspective. In David Hurst Thomas, *Exploring Ancient Native America* (pp. 238–239). New York: Macmillan.

Tylor, Edward Burnett. 1889. On a method of investigating the development of institutions, applied to laws of marriage and descent. *Journal of the Royal Anthropological Institute* 18: 245–272. (Quote is from p. 269)

Upham, Steadman (Ed.). 1990. *The Evolution of Political Systems: Sociopolitics in Small-Scale Sedentary Societies.* Cambridge: Cambridge University Press.

Webster, D. 2000. The not so peaceful civilization: A review of Maya war. *Journal of World Prehistory* 14: 65–119.

Winterhalder, Bruce, and Eric Alden Smith (Eds.). 1981. *Hunter-Gatherer Foraging Strategies: Ethnographic and Archaeological Analyses.* Chicago: University of Chicago Press.

Wittfogel, Karl A. 1957. *Oriental Despotism: A Comparative Study of Total Power.* New Haven: Yale University Press.

Wright, Henry T. 1986. The evolution of civilizations. In David J. Meltzer, Don D. Fowler, and Jeremy A. Sabloff (Eds.), *American Archaeology Past and Future: A Celebration of the Society for American Archaeology 1935–1985* (pp. 323–365). Washington, DC: Smithsonian Institution Press.

Chapter 14

Ascher, Robert, and Charles H. Fairbanks. 1971. Excavation of a slave cabin: Georgia, U.S.A. *Historical Archaeology* 5: 3–17.

Beaudry, Mary C. (Ed.). 1988. *Documentary Archaeology in the New World.* Cambridge: Cambridge University Press.

Binford, Lewis R. 1968. Some comments on historical versus processual archaeology. *Southwestern Journal of Anthropology* 24: 267–275.

Blakey, Michael L. 1995. Race, nationalism, and the Afrocentric past. In P. R. Schmidt and T. Patterson (Eds.), *Making Alternative Histories: The Practice of Archaeology and History in Non-Western Settings* (pp. 213–228). Santa Fe: School of American Research Press.

Boakyewa, Ama Badu. 1995, January 1. African Burial Ground and Five Points Archaeological Projects. Press release. Office of Public Education and Information, African Burial Ground.

Brear, Holly Breachley. 1995. *Inherit the Alamo: Myth and Ritual at an American Shrine.* Austin: University of Texas Press.

Cotter, John L. 1994. Beginnings. In Stanley South (Ed.), *Pioneers in Historical Archaeology: Breaking New Ground* (pp. 15–25). New York: Plenum Press.

Crader, Diana C. 1990. Slave diet at Monticello. *American Antiquity* 55: 690–717.

Deagan, Kathleen. 1982. Avenues of inquiry in historical archaeology. In Michael B. Schiffer (Ed.), *Advances in Archaeological Method and Theory.* Vol. 5 (pp. 151–177). New York: Academic Press. (Quote is from p. 153)

Deagan, Kathleen, and Darcie MacMahon. 1995. *Fort Mose: Colonial America's Black Fortress of Freedom.* Gainesville: University Press of Florida/Florida Museum of Natural History.

Deetz, James. 1977. *In Small Things Forgotten: The Archaeology of Early American Life.* Garden City, NY: Anchor Books.

———. 1988. Material culture and worldview in colonial Anglo-America. In Mark Leone and Parker Potter (Eds.), *The Recovery of Meaning: Historical Archaeology in the Eastern United States* (pp. 219–233). Washington, DC: Smithsonian Institution Press.

———. 1991. Introduction: Archaeological evidence of sixteenth- and seventeenth-century encounters. In Lisa Falk (Ed.), *Historical Archaeology in Global Perspective* (pp. 1–9). Washington, DC: Smithsonian Institution Press.

Fairbanks, Charles H. 1984. Plantation archaeology of the southeastern coast. *Historical Archaeology* 18: 1–14.

Falk, Lisa (Ed.). 1991. *Historical Archaeology in Global Perspective*. Washington, DC: Smithsonian Institution Press.

Fehrenbach, T. R. 1968. *Lone Star: A History of Texas and the Texans*. New York: Macmillan.

Ferguson, Leland B. 1992. *Uncommon Ground: Archaeology and Early African America, 1650–1800*. Washington, DC: Smithsonian Institution Press.

Fox, Richard. 1993. *Archaeology, History, and Custer's Last Battle: The Little Big Horn Reexamined*. Norman: University of Oklahoma Press.

Glassie, Henry. 1975. *Folk Housing in Middle Virginia*. Knoxville: University of Tennessee Press.

Handler, Jerome, and Frederick Lange. 1978. *Plantation Slavery in Barbados: An Archaeological and Historical Investigation*. Cambridge, MA: Harvard University Press.

Handsman, Russell G., and Mark P. Leone. 1989. Living history and critical archaeology in the reconstruction of the past. In Valerie Pinsky and Alison Wylie (Eds.), *Critical Traditions in Contemporary Archaeology: Essays in the Philosophy, History and Socio-Politics of Archaeology* (pp. 117–135). Cambridge: Cambridge University Press.

Hume, Noël. 1964. Handmaiden to history. *North Carolina Historical Review* 41(2): 215–225. (Quote is from p. 215)

Kelso, William M. 1986. Mulberry Row: Slave life at Thomas Jefferson's Monticello. *Archaeology* 39(5): 28–35.

Kidd, Kenneth E. 1949. *The Excavation of Ste Marie I*. Toronto: University of Toronto Press.

———. 1994. The phoenix of the north. In Stanley South (Ed.), *Pioneers in Historical Archaeology: Breaking New Ground* (pp. 49–65). New York: Plenum Press. (Quote is from p. 49)

Leone, Mark P. 1984. Interpreting ideology in historical archaeology: Using the rules of perspective in the William Paca garden in Annapolis, Maryland. In Daniel Miller and Christopher Tilley (Eds.), *Ideology, Power, and Prehistory* (pp. 25–36). Cambridge: Cambridge University Press.

———. 1986. Symbolic, structural, and critical archaeology. In David J. Meltzer, Don D. Fowler, and Jeremy A. Sabloff (Eds.), *American Archaeology Past and Future: A Celebration of the Society for American Archaeology 1935–1985* (pp. 415–438). Washington, DC: Smithsonian Institution Press.

———. 1987. Rule by ostentation: The relationship between space and sight in eighteenth-century landscape architecture in the Chesapeake region of Maryland. In Susan

Kent (Ed.), *Method and Theory for Activity Area Research: An Ethnoarchaeological Approach* (pp. 604–633). New York: Columbia University Press.

———. 1988a. The Georgian order as the order of merchant capitalism in Annapolis, Maryland. In Mark P. Leone and Parker B. Potter (Eds.), *The Recovery of Meaning: Historical Archaeology in the Eastern United States* (pp. 235–261). Washington, DC: Smithsonian Institution Press.

———. 1988b. The relationship between archaeological data and the documentary record: Eighteenth century gardens in Annapolis, Maryland. *Historical Archaeology* 22(1): 29–35. (Quotes are from p. 32)

———. 1995. A historical archaeology of capitalism. *American Anthropologist* 97: 251–268. (Quotes are from pp. 261, 262)

Leone, Mark P., Paul R. Mullins, Marian C. Creveling, Laurence Hurst, Barbara Jackson-Nash, Lynn D. Jones, Hannah Jopling Kaiser, George C. Logan, and Mark S. Warner. 1995. Can an African-American historical archaeology be an alternative voice? In Ian Hodder, Michael Shanks, Alexandra Alexandri, Victor Buchli, John Carman, Jonathan Last, and Gavin Lucas (Eds.), *Interpreting Archaeology: Finding Meaning in the Past* (pp. 110–124). London: Routledge.

Leone, Mark P. , Parker B. Potter, Jr., and Paul A. Shackel. 1987. Toward a critical archaeology. *Current Anthropology* 28: 283–302.

Leone, Mark P., and Neil Asher Silberman. 1995. *Invisible America: Unearthing Our Hidden History*. New York: Henry Holt.

Little, Barbara J. (Ed.). 1992. *Text-Aided Archaeology*. Boca Raton, FL: CRC Press.

Ofori-Ansa, Kwaku. 1995. Identification and validation of the Sankofa symbol. *Update: Newsletter of the African Burial Ground and Five Points Archaeological Projects* 1(8): 3.

Orser, Charles E., Jr. 1984. The past ten years of plantation archaeology in the southeastern United States. *Southeastern Archaeology* 3: 1–12.

———. 1995. *A Historical Archaeology of the Modern World*. New York: Plenum.

Potter, Parker B., Jr. 1994. *Public Archaeology in Annapolis: A Critical Approach to History in Maryland's Ancient City*. Washington, DC: Smithsonian Institution Press.

Rothschild, Nan A. 1990. *New York City Neighborhoods: The 18th Century*. San Diego: Academic Press.

Schoelwer, Susan P. 1985. *Alamo Images: Changing Perceptions of a Texas Experience*. Dallas: DeGolyer Library and Southern Methodist University Press.

Schofield, John, William Gray Johnson, and Colleen M. Beck. 2002. *Matériel Culture: The Archaeology of Twentieth Century Conflict*. London: Routledge.

Schuyler, Robert. 1976. Images of America: The contribution of historical archaeology to national identity. *Southwestern Lore* 42(4): 27–39.

Scott, Douglas D., Richard A. Fox, Melissa A. Connor, and Dick Harmon. 1989. *Archaeological Perspectives on the Battle of the Little Big Horn*. Norman: University of Oklahoma Press.

Scott, Elizabeth M. (Ed.). 1994. *Those of Little Note: Gender, Race, and Class in Historical Archaeology.* Tucson: University of Arizona Press.

Shackel, Paul A. 1993. *Personal Discipline and Material Culture: An Archaeology of Annapolis, Maryland, 1695–1870.* Knoxville: University of Tennessee Press.

———. 1996. *Culture Change and the New Technology: An Archaeology of the Early American Industrial Era.* New York: Plenum Press.

Shackel, Paul A., Paul R. Mullins, and Mark S. Warner. 1998. *Annapolis Pasts: Historical Archaeology in Annapolis, Maryland.* Knoxville: University of Tennessee Press.

Singleton, Theresa A. (Ed.). 1985. *The Archaeology of Slavery and Plantation Life.* Orlando, FL: Academic Press.

———. 1995. The archaeology of slavery in North America. *Annual Review of Anthropology* 24: 119–140.

Sobel, Mechal. 1987. *The World They Made Together: Black and White Values in Eighteenth-Century Virginia.* Princeton: Princeton University Press.

South, Stanley. 1977a. *Method and Theory in Historical Archeology.* New York: Academic Press.

——— (Ed.). 1977b. *Research Strategies in Historical Archaeology.* New York: Academic Press.

——— (Ed.). 1994. *Pioneers in Historical Archaeology: Breaking New Ground.* New York: Plenum Press.

Thomas, David Hurst. 1988. Saints and soldiers at Santa Catalina: Hispanic designs for colonial America. In Mark P. Leone and Parker B. Potter (Eds.), *The Recovery of Meaning in Historic Archaeology* (pp. 73–140). Washington, DC: Smithsonian Institution Press.

———. 1995. Spanish missions: Ideology and space at Santa Catalina. In Mark P. Leone and Neil Asher Silberman (Eds.), *Invisible America: Unearthing Our Hidden History* (pp. 66–67). New York: Henry Holt.

Wall, Diane diZerega. 1994. *The Archaeology of Gender: Separating the Spheres in Urban America.* New York: Plenum Press.

Weber, David J. 1988. Refighting the Alamo: Mythmaking and the Texas revolution. In *Myth and the History of the Hispanic Southwest: Essays by David J. Weber* (pp. 133–151). Albuquerque: University of New Mexico Press.

Chapter 15

Adovasio, J. M., and Ronald C. Carlisle. 1988. Some thoughts on cultural resource management archaeology in the United States. *Antiquity* 62: 72–87.

Anonymous. 1989. Archeology and the Oklahoma City Police Training Academy. *Newsletter, Oklahoma Archeological Survey* 8(4): 1.

Anyon, Roger, and T. J. Ferguson. 1995. Cultural resources management at the Pueblo of Zuni, New Mexico, USA. *Antiquity* 69: 913–930.

Blanton, Dennis B. 1995. The case for CRM training in academic institutions: The many faces of CRM. *Bulletin of the Society for American Archaeology* 13(4): 40–41.

Bogdanos, M. 2005. *The Thieves of Baghdad.* New York: Bloomsbury Publishing.

Brodie, Neil, Jennifer Doole, and Colin Renfrew. 2001. *Trade in Illicit Antiquities: The Destruction of the World's Archaeological Heritage.* Cambridge: McDonald Institute of Archaeology.

Carpenter, Edmund. 1991. Repatriation policy and the Heye collection. *Museum Anthropology* 15(3): 15–18.

Cleere, Henry (Ed.). 1993. Managing the archaeological heritage. *Antiquity* 67: 400–402.

Cook, Karen. 1993. Bones of contention. *The Village Voice* 38(18): 23–27.

Domenici, Pete V. 1991. Preface B. In George S. Smith and John E. Ehrenhard (Eds.), *Protecting the Past* (pp. v–vi). Boca Raton, FL: CRC Press.

Echo-Hawk, Roger C., and Walter R. Echo-Hawk. 1994. *Battlefields and Burial Grounds: The Indian Struggle to Protect Ancestral Graves in the United States.* Minneapolis: Lerner.

Echo-Hawk, Walter R. (Ed.). 1992. Special Issue: Repatriation of American Indian remains. *American Indian Culture and Research Journal* 16(2): 1–200.

Elia, Ricardo J. 1993. U.S. cultural resource management and the ICAHM charter. *Antiquity* 67: 426–438.

Elston, Robert G. 1992. Archaeological research in the context of cultural resource management: Pushing back in the 1990s. *Journal of California and Great Basin Anthropology* 14: 37–48.

Fowler, Don D. 1982. Cultural resources management. In Michael B. Schiffer (Ed.), *Advances in Archaeological Method and Theory.* Vol. 5 (pp. 1–50). New York: Academic Press.

———. 1986. Conserving American archaeological resources. In David J. Meltzer, Don D. Fowler, and Jeremy A. Sabloff (Eds.), *American Archaeology: Past and Future: A Celebration of the Society for American Archaeology 1935–1985* (pp. 135–162). Washington, DC: Smithsonian Institution Press.

Gathercole, Peter, and David Lowenthal (Eds.). 1990. *The Politics of the Past.* London: Unwin Hyman.

Goldstein, Lynn, and Keith Kintigh. 1990. Ethics and the reburial controversy. *American Antiquity* 55: 585–591.

Harrington, Spencer P. M. 1991, May/June. The looting of Arkansas. *Archaeology* 44(3): 22–30.

———. 1993, March/April. Bones and bureaucrats. *Archaeology* 46(2): 28–38.

Hoffman, Ellen. 1993, December. Saving our world's heritage. *Omni*, pp. 52–54, 58, 60–61.

Holloway, Marguerite. 1995. The preservation of the past. *Scientific American* 272(5): 98–101.

King, Thomas F. 1991. Some dimensions of the pothunting problem. In George S. Smith and John E. Ehrenhard (Eds.), *Protecting the Past* (pp. 83–92). Boca Raton, FL: CRC Press.

Lipe, William. 2002. In defense of digging: Archaeological preservation as a means, not an end. In Mark J. Lynott and Alison Wylie (Eds.), *Ethics in American Archaeology.* 2d ed. (pp. 113–117). Washington, DC: Society for American Archaeology.

McGimsey, C. R., III, and H. A. Davis. 1977. *The Management of Archaeological Resources: The Airlie House*

Report. Washington DC: Society for American Archaeology.

McManamon, Francis P. 1991. The many publics for archaeology. *American Antiquity* 56: 121–130.

———. 1992. Managing America's archaeological resources. In LuAnn Wandsnider (Ed.), *Quandaries and Quests: Visions of Archaeology's Future* (pp. 25–40). Carbondale: Southern Illinois University, Center for Archaeological Investigations, Occasional Paper no. 20.

———. 1994. Changing relationships between Native Americans and archaeologists. *Historic Preservation Forum* 8(2): 15–20.

McManamon, Francis P., and Alf Hatton. 2000. *Cultural Resource Management in Contemporary Society*. London: Routledge.

McManamon, Francis P., Patricia C. Knoll, Ruthann Knudson, George S. Smith, and Richard C. Waldbauer (Comps.). 1993. *The Secretary of the Interior's Report to Congress: Federal Archeological Programs and Activities*. Washington, DC: Department of the Interior, National Park Service, Archeological Assistance Program.

Messenger, Phyllis (Ed.). 1989. *The Ethics of Collecting Cultural Property: Whose Culture? Whose Property?* Albuquerque: University of New Mexico Press.

Murray, Tim. 1996. Coming to terms with the living: Some aspects of repatriation for the archaeologist. *Antiquity* 70: 217–220.

National Park Service. 1995, Fall/Winter. Special Report: The Native American Graves Protection and Repatriation Act. *Federal Archeology*.

Neary, John. 1993, September/October. Project sting. *Archaeology*, pp. 52–59.

Preston, Douglas J. 1989, February. Skeletons in our museums' closets. *Harper's Magazine* 278: 66–75. (Quote by Walter Echo-Hawk is from p. 75)

Richman, Jennifer R., and Marion P. Forsyth (Eds.). 2003. *Legal Perspectives on Cultural Resources*. Walnut Creek, CA: Altamira Press.

Rose, Jerome C., Thomas J. Green, and Victoria D. Green. 1996. NAGPRA is forever: Osteology and the repatriation of skeletons. *Annual Review of Anthropology* 25: 81–103.

Russell, Steve. 1995. The legacy of ethnic cleansing: Implementation of NAGPRA in Texas. *American Indian Culture and Research Journal* 19(4): 193–211.

Shackley, Steven. 1995, March. Relics, rights and regulations. *Scientific American*, p. 115.

Smith, George S., and John E. Ehrenhard (Eds.). 1991. *Protecting the Past*. Boca Raton, FL: CRC Press.

Smith, Laurajane. 1994. Heritage management as postprocessual archaeology? *Antiquity* 68: 300–309.

Staley, David P. 1993. The antiquities market. *Journal of Field Archaeology* 20: 347–355.

Thompson, Raymond H. 2000. Edgar Lee Hewett and the political process. *Journal of the Southwest* 42: 273–318.

Wendorf, Fred, and Raymond H. Thompson. 2002. The Committee for the Recovery of Archaeological Remains: Three decades of service to the archaeological profession. *American Antiquity* 67: 317–330.

Woodbury, Nathalie F. S. 1992, March. When my grandmother is your database: Reactions to repatriation. *Anthropology Newsletter*, pp. 6, 22.

Chapter 16

Arden, H. 1989. Who owns our past? *National Geographic* 175(3): 376–392.

Arnold, Bettina. 1992, July/August. The past as propaganda. *Archaeology* 45(4): 30–37.

Bray, Tamara L., and Thomas W. Killion (Eds.). 1994. *Reckoning With the Dead: The Larsen Bay Repatriation and the Smithsonian Institution*. Washington, DC: Smithsonian Institution Press.

Brear, Holly. 1995. *Inherit the Alamo: Myth and Ritual at an American Shrine*. Austin: University of Texas Press. (Quote is from p. 146)

Carney, Heath J., Michael W. Binford, Alan L. Kolata, Ruben R. Marin, and Charles R. Goldman. 1993. Nutrient and sediment retention in Andean raised-field agriculture. *Nature* 364: 131–133.

Connor, Melissa. 1996. The archaeology of contemporary mass graves. *Bulletin of the Society for American Archaeology* 14(4): 6, 31.

Crowell, Aron L., Amy F. Steffian, and Gordon L. Pullar (Eds.). 2001. *Looking Both Ways: Heritage and Identity of the Alutiiq People*. Fairbanks: University of Alaska Press.

Deloria, Vine, Jr. 1992a. Afterword. In Alvin M. Josephy, Jr. (Ed.), *America in 1492: The World of the Indian Peoples Before the Arrival of Columbus* (pp. 429–443). New York: Knopf.

———. 1992b. Indians, archaeologists, and the future. *American Antiquity* 57: 595–598.

———. 1993. Sacred lands. *Winds of Change* 8(4): 30–37.

———. 1995. *Red Earth, White Lies: Native Americans and the Myth of Scientific Fact*. New York: Scribner's.

Eddy, John A. 1974. Astronomical alignment of the Big Horn medicine wheel. *Science* 184: 1035–1043.

———. 1977. Medicine wheels and Plains Indian astronomy. In Anthony F. Aveni (Ed.), *Native American Astronomy* (pp. 147–169). Austin: University of Texas Press.

Erickson, Clark L. 1988. Raised field agriculture in the Lake Titicaca Basin: Putting ancient agriculture back to work. *Expedition* 30(3): 8–16.

———. 1992a. Applied archaeology and rural development: Archaeology's potential contribution to the future. *Journal of the Steward Anthropological Society* 20(1, 2): 1–16.

———. 1992b. Prehistoric landscape management in the Andean highlands: Raised field agriculture and its environmental impact. *Population and Environment* 13(4): 285–300.

———. 1993. The social organization of prehispanic raised field agriculture in the Lake Titicaca Basin. In V. L. Scarborough and B. L. Isaac (Eds.), *Research in Economic Anthropology: Economic Aspects of Water Management in the Prehistoric New World*. Supplement 7 (pp. 369–426). Greenwich, CT: JAI Press.

———. 1995. Archaeological methods for the study of ancient landscapes of the Llanos de Mojos in the Bolivian Amazon. In Peter W. Stahl (Ed.), *Archaeology in the Lowland American Tropics: Current Analytical Methods and Applications* (pp. 66–95). Cambridge: Cambridge University Press.

———. 2003. Agricultural landscapes as world heritage: Raised field agriculture in Bolivia and Peru. In Jeanne-Marie Teutonico and Frank Matero (Eds.), *Managing Change: Sustainable Approaches to the Conservation of the Built Environment* (pp. 181–204). Oxford: Getty Conservation Institute and Oxford University Press.

Ferguson, T. J. 1996. Native Americans and the practice of archaeology. *Annual Review of Anthropology* 25: 63–79.

Ford, Richard I. 1973. Archeology serving humanity. In Charles L. Redman (Ed.), *Research and Theory in Current Archeology* (pp. 83–93). New York: Wiley.

Fowler, Don. 1987. Uses of the past: Archaeology in the service of the state. *American Antiquity* 52: 229–248.

Green, Ernestine L. (Ed.). 1984. *Ethics and Values in Archaeology*. New York: Free Press.

Greenbuerg, D. W. 1929. Sheridan's historic settings. *The Midwest Review* 7(10): 50–69, 71, 90. (Quote describing Red Plume's vision is from p. 66)

Greenlee, Bob. 1995. *Life Among the Ancient Ones: Two Accounts of an Anasazi Archaeological Research Project.* Boulder: Hardscrabble Press.

Grey, Don. 1963. Big Horn medicine wheel site, 48BH302. *Plains Anthropologist* 8: 27–40.

Klesert, Anthony L. 1992. A view from Navajoland on the reconciliation of anthropologists and Native Americans. *Human Organization* 51: 17–22.

Klesert, Anthony L., and Alan S. Downer (Eds.). 1990. *Preservation on the Reservation: Native Americans, Native American Lands and Archaeology.* Navajo Nation Papers in Anthropology no. 26.

Klesert, Anthony L., and Shirley Powell. 1993. A perspective on ethics and the reburial controversy. *American Antiquity* 58: 348–354.

Kolata, Alan L., and Charles Ortloff. 1989. Thermal analysis of Tiwanaku raised field systems in the Lake Titicaca Basin of Bolivia. *Journal of Archaeological Science* 16: 233–263.

Lipe, William D. 1995. The archeology of ecology. *Federal Archaeology* 8(1): 8–13.

Long, William R. 1993, August 24. Old canals carry hope to Andes. *Los Angeles Times.*

Mansfield, Victor N. 1980. The Bighorn Medicine Wheel as a site for the vision quest. *Archaeoastronomy Bulletin* 3(2): 26–29.

Meighan, Clement. 1992. Some scholars' views on reburial. *American Antiquity* 57: 704–710.

Nicholas, Lynn H. 1994. *The Rape of Europe: The Fate of Europe's Treasures in the Third Reich and the Second World War.* New York: Knopf.

Ovenden, Michael W., and David A. Rodger. 1981. Megaliths and medicine wheels. In Michael Wilson, Kathie L. Road, and Kenneth J. Hardy (Eds.), *Megaliths to medicine wheels: Boulder structures in archaeology. Proceedings of the Eleventh Annual Chacmool Conference* (pp. 371–386). Calgary: The Archaeological Association of the University of Calgary.

Powell, Shirley, Christiana Elnora Garza, and Aubrey Hendricks. 1993. Ethics and ownership of the past: The reburial and repatriation controversy. In Michael B. Schiffer (Ed.), *Archaeological Method and Theory.* Vol. 5 (pp. 1–42). Tucson: University of Arizona Press.

Rathje, William L. 1984. The garbage decade. *American Behavioral Scientist* 28(1): 9–29.

———. 1991, May. Once and future landfills. *National Geographic* 25: 116–134. (Quote is from p. 120)

Rathje, William L., W. W. Hughes, D. C. Wilson, M. K. Tani, G. H. Archer, R. G. Hunt, and T. W. Jones. 1992. The archaeology of contemporary landfills. *American Antiquity* 57: 437–447.

Rathje, William L., and Cullen Murphy. 2001. *Rubbish! The Archaeology of Garbage.* Tucson: University of Arizona Press.

Riding In, James. 1992. With ethics and morality: A historical overview of imperial archaeology and American Indians. *Arizona State Law Journal* 24(1): 11–34.

Sabloff, Jeremy. 2008. *Archaeology Matters.* Walnut Creek, CA: Left Coast Press.

Swidler, Nina, Kurt E. Dongoske, Roger Anyon, and Alan S. Downer (Eds.). 1997. *Native Americans and Archaeologists: Stepping Stones to Common Ground.* Walnut Creek, CA: Altamira Press.

INDEX